American Views
on Madeira Wine

Annotated anthology of 19th century texts

Duarte Mendonça

American Views on Madeira Wine
Annotated anthology of 19th century texts

Copyright © 2015 by Duarte Miguel Barcelos Mendonça.

ISBN 978-989-20-6116-0

All rights reserved. No part of this publication may be reproduced, stored in a retrieval system, or transmitted in any form, or by any means, electronic, mechanical, recording or otherwise, without the prior permission of the author.

The research for this book was sponsored by
Instituto do Vinho, do Bordado
e do Artesanato da Madeira, I.P. (IVBAM)
Rua Visconde de Anadia n.º 44,
9050-020 Funchal, Madeira Island - Portugal

Design by Márcio Ribeiro

Printed by CreateSpace, An Amazon.com Company

First Edition

November 2015

Cover Ilustration
The Wine Committee by Turrel

American Views
on Madeira Wine

Annotated anthology of 19th century texts

Duarte Mendonça

Contents

1. Introduction — 1
2. Madeira Wine in Colonial America — 5
   - 2.1. The Boston Madeira Party — 11
   - 2.2. The Philadelphia Case — 16
3. Madeira Wine in the American Revolutionary War — 19
4. Madeira, a Presidential Wine — 31
   - 4.1. Founding Fathers — 31
     - 4.1.1. George Washington — 31
     - 4.1.2. John Adams — 34
     - 4.1.3. Thomas Jefferson — 35
     - 4.1.4. James Madison — 36
     - 4.1.5. Benjamin Franklin — 36
   - 4.2. Other U.S. Presidents — 41
     - 4.2.1. John Quincy Adams — 41
     - 4.2.2. Andrew Jackson — 42
     - 4.2.3. Martin Van Buren — 43
     - 4.2.4. John Tyler — 45
     - 4.2.5. James Buchanan — 46
     - 4.2.6. Ulysses S. Grant — 47
   - 4.3. Madeira Wine at the White House — 47
5. Madeira Wine and the 4th of July Celebrations — 55
   - 5.1. Newspapers — 56
   - 5.2. Books — 64
   - 5.3. Fourth of July Celebrations in Madeira Island — 67
6. Madeira Wine in American Literature — 73
   - 6.1. Travel Literature — 73
     - 6.1.1. Books — 73
       - 6.1.1.1. William Francis Lynch, USN (1819) — 73
       - 6.1.1.2. Rev. Walter Colton, USN (1832) — 74
       - 6.1.1.3. Rev. Fitch Waterman Taylor, USN (1838) — 75
       - 6.1.1.4. John Henshaw Belcher, USN (1838) — 78

6.1.1.5. William Meacham Murrell, USN (1838)	81
6.1.1.6. Charles Wilkes, USN (1838)	81
6.1.1.7. George Mulasas Colvocoresses, USN (1838)	85
6.1.1.8. Joseph G. Clark, USN (1838)	86
6.1.1.9. Rev. Franklin P. Torrey, USN (1839)	86
6.1.1.10. Jacob A. Hazen, USN (1841)	87
6.1.1.11. Samuel Rhoades Franklin, USN (1842)	89
6.1.1.12. John Adams Dix (1842)	90
6.1.1.13. Horatio Bridge, USN (1844)	94
6.1.1.14. Benjamin F. Stevens, USN (1844)	96
6.1.1.15. Charles Wainwright March (1852)	96
6.1.1.16. J. Willet Spalding, USN (1852)	104
6.1.1.17. Rev. Francis Lister Hawks (1852)	106
6.1.1.18. Rev. John Overton Choules (1853)	107
6.1.1.19. Rev. Charles W. Thomas, USN (1855)	109
6.1.1.20. William Maxwell Wood, USN (1855)	111
6.1.1.21. Frederick Hubbard (1855)	116
6.1.1.22. William F. Gragg, USN (1857)	118
6.1.1.23. James D. Johnston, USN (1857)	119
6.1.1.24. Samuel Greene Wheeler Benjamin (1872)	120
6.1.1.25. Charlotte Alice Baker (1870'S/1880'S)	121
6.1.1.26. Henry Washington Hilliard (1881)	122
6.1.1.27. Joseph Hankinson Reading (1880'S)	123
6.1.1.28. Noah Brooks (1895)	125
6.1.1.29. Anthony J. Drexel Biddle (1890'S)	126
6.1.2. Magazines	133
6.1.3. Newspapers	156
6.2. American Literature at Large (Prose)	**186**
6.2.1. Benauly (Pseud.)	187
6.2.2. Edgar Allan Poe	190
6.2.3. Rev. Frederick William Shelton	192
6.2.4. George Little	194
6.2.5. Herman Melville	195
6.2.6. James Fenimore Cooper	196
6.2.7. James Kirke Paulding	204

6.2.8. John Neal	206
6.2.9. John Richter Jones	212
6.2.10. Nathaniel Hawthorne	214
6.2.11. Newton Mallory Curtis	216
6.2.12. Oliver Wendell Holmes, Sr.	216
6.2.13. Robert Hare	218
6.2.14. Silas Weir Mitchell	220
6.2.15. William Gilmore Simms	238
6.2.16. William Taylor Adams	244
6.3. American Poetry	**246**
6.3.2. Philip Freneau	247
6.3.3. Silas Weir Mitchell	251
6.3.4. Anonymous Poems and Songs	254
7. Madeira Wine in American Reference Books	**261**
7.1. Encyclopedias	261
7.2. Wine-Related Books	269
7.3. Trade-Related Publications	275
7.4. Government-Related Books	283
7.5. Other Sources	291
8. Generic Texts about Madeira Wine in American Magazines	**299**
9. Madeira Wine in the American Press	**311**
9.1. Wine Production	311
9.2. Transportation of Madeira Wine to the United States	321
9.2.1. Madeira Wine Arrivals to America	322
9.2.2. Madeira Wine Aboard U.S. Navy Ships	326
9.3. Madeira Wine Advertised in the American Press	331
9.4. General Articles about this Commodity	336
9.5. Curious Facts Related to Madeira Wine	340
9.6. Madeira Wine used for Medicinal Purposes	355
9.7. *Oïdium Tuckery* – The Madeira Vine Disease of 1852 and its consequences	356
9.7.1. United States' Relief for Madeira	364
9.7.2. Consecutive Failures of the Wine Crops	411

9.8. Gradual Recovery of the Madeira Vines	422
9.9. Phylloxera - The Second Blow to the Island's Vineyards	423
9.10. Madeira Wine Adulterated in the U.S. and abroad	425
9.11. Madeira, a Cherished Product to Wine *Connoisseurs*	**436**
9.12. Old Madeira Wines in America	442
9.13. Madeira Wine Auctions across the United States	468
9.14. Amusing episodes involving Madeira Wine	483

10. Madeira Wine in America through British Eyes — 501

10.1. John Davis	501
10.2. Henry Bradshaw Fearon	503
10.3. Isaac Candler	504
10.4. Basil Hall	505
10.5. James Boardman	506
10.6. Thomas Hamilton	507
10.7. Sir Charles Augustus Murray	509
10.8. Frederick Marryat	512
10.9. Archibald Montgomery Maxwell	515
10.10. James Silk Buckingham, Esq.	516
10.11. John Robert Godley	517
10.12. Lauchlan Bellingham Mackinnon	518
10.13. Alfred Bunn	519
10.14. Reginald Fowler, Esq.	522
10.15. Thomas Colley Grattan	523
10.16. Sir William Howard Russell	524
10.17. John Walter	526

11. Madeira Wine in American Cuisine — 529

11.1. Recipes from Cookbooks	529
11.1.1. Soups	529
11.1.2. Meats	530
11.1.3. Fowls	535
11.1.4. Sauces	536
11.1.5. Preserves	538
11.1.6. Desserts	538
11.1.7. Drinks	543

11.2. Recipes from the Press	**544**
11.2.1. Soup	544
11.2.2. Meats	544
11.2.3. Fish	546
11.2.4. Seafood	547
11.2.5. Fowls	548
11.2.6. Pasta	549
11.2.7. Desserts	549
12. Conclusion	**553**
13. Attachments	**557**
13.1. Report of the Madeira Relief Fund Committee	**557**
13.2. Madeira Wine-Related Iconography	**570**
13.2.1. Watercolors	570
13.2.2. Plates	570
13.2.3. Henry Vizetelly's Book Engravings	574
13.2.4. Late 19th / Early 20th Century Postcards	580
13.2.5. Late 19th/ Early 20th Century Photographs	584
14. Bibliography	**587**
14.1. Books	**587**
14.2. Magazines	**594**
14.3. Newspapers (Listed by State)	**596**
15. Brief notes about the Author	**603**

1. Introduction

Madeira is a fortified wine produced for centuries in the far-off Portuguese Atlantic island bearing the same name and located off the northwest coast of Africa. In the past, especially from the late 17th century to the mid 19th century, this special wine was widely consumed in America and decanters of Madeira had a special place in the sideboards of many households across the country, being liberally served to one's guests, and associated, therefore, with American hospitality.

Over the last few years Madeira Wine exports to the United States have increased considerably, being this country, at the present moment, the largest importer of this product outside the European Union. Lately the Madeira Government, through its branch, the Instituto do Vinho, Bordado e Artesanato da Madeira (Madeira Wine, Embroidery and Handicraft Institute), has been engaged in different promotional activities, in some of the main American cities, in order to promote Madeira Wine, that has been consumed in the *land of the free* for over three centuries.

In order to recall to the present generation of Americans the paramount importance Madeira Wine once had among their ancestors, we decided to compile this annotated anthology, containing data about different cultural and historical aspects of this wine in the United States, gathered from a wide variety of 19th century American primary sources. The research was long, exhausting, but rewarding for we ended up unearthing much more data than we thought existed at first.

Even though our main focus of research were the 19th century sources, this book contains data that goes back in time, to Colonial America, a period when Madeira Wine was already widely known and appreciated in the main cities along the eastern seaboard. When the winds of change started to blow against the dominion of Old England, this wine accompanied the patriots, and was at the center of a famous rebellion, the Madeira Tea Party, (that occurred several years before the more widely known Boston Tea Party), and contributed to spark the flame of rebellion against the British rule. When the Declaration of Independence was signed, in 1776, the birth of the new and free nation was celebrated with Madeira Wine, as all sources seem to indicate, and this precious wine continued to be present in some events of the long American Revolutionary War.

Madeira was also a Presidential Wine for it was the favorite beverage of some of the Founding Fathers of America, that drank it regularly and shared it with their friends on special occasions. And the taste for Madeira continued on with some of the 19th century Presidents.

1. INTRODUCTION

From its early years, Madeira Wine played a special role in the Independence Day celebrations, when several toasts, usually thirteen, one for each State, or more, were made with this precious nectar. Needless to say it reminds us that drinking Madeira back then, in America, was considered a patriotic act.

Due to its utmost importance in the 18th and 19th century United States' society, Madeira Wine is widely represented in the American Literature – travel literature and literature at large – and we tried to present some examples of that. First we start by presenting the different American authors that visited Madeira Island and registered, later on, in their travel books, their impressions about several aspects of Madeira Wine; then we introduce some American writers who inserted references to this nectar in their novels; and, last but not least, we bring forward a few poems dedicated to Madeira Wine, some of which are true anthems to this noble wine.

Madeira Wine is also widely mentioned in American reference books and magazines, and we have gathered the most important texts we came across. Another important source we have researched was the 19th century American press, that presents a wide variety of aspects related to this wine, depicting, in general terms, the importance this product once had in the American society. And when the production came to a halt in 1852 due to a severe blight of the island's vines, the philanthropic Americans heard the appeal made from Madeira and sent an impressive relief to help the destitute islanders.

It is a fact widely known that the British Army officers who were sent to America, after the proclamation of the Declaration of Independence, to fight the rebels, acquired a taste for Madeira consumed in America and took it to England upon their return home, helping to spread a new wine-drinking tradition at their native land. Having this in mind we searched different travel books, by British authors, describing their travels in the United States, in order to find out what they wrote about Madeira Wine they encountered on many tables across the country.

Throughout the times Madeira Wine had several uses in America and, having that in mind, we dedicated a special attention in researching one of them in particular, namely its presence in the American cuisine, by retrieving old 19th century recipes that used Madeira as one of its ingredients. By doing that we make an appeal to the curiosity of our readers, in order to try them again, for a good recipe, like Madeira itself, is never too old.

Let us also add that on the different text transcriptions we decided to maintain the features of the 19th century English writing, so that through it the present-day reader might have a glimpse of the past as they go through them. In the original sources some Portuguese words were misspelled. We maintained them as they were but added the right version with footnotes. We used these as well to present innumerable annotations to the texts which, we hope, will enrich them. The majority of Madeira Wine-related texts we unearthed have no images but we tried to illustrate them by resorting to other sources.

Last but not least we present two attachments, one of which is dedicated to the pictorial field of Madeira Wine. We know that a picture is worth a thousand words and since the American texts we have researched do not contain many illustrations about this topic, we were forced to complement them by presenting a few images from other sources, portraying several phases of the Madeira production.

This anthology is the result of many hours of hard toil and we hope that it reaches its goal, which identifies the historical links of Madeira Wine to the United States, from a cultural perspective, thus helping to make this product more widely known and appreciated in the country where it feels at home.

2. Madeira Wine in Colonial America

On the marriage contract of Princess Catherine of Braganza to King Charles II of England, that occurred in 1662, it was stipulated, among other clauses, that the British could have commercial freedom in Portugal, and could export directly any product from this country to the British colonies, both in the West Indies and in New England, without having to take them to England first, to be taxed there, as was customary until then. This agreement is the origin of the arrival of the first British merchants to Madeira Island, some time after, who started dealing with Madeira Wine, and exporting it to the places afore mentioned. And in the late 17th, early 18th century, this wine started to arrive at the American shores, and was consumed in several cities along the East Coast. Little by little this precious wine established its own reputation in the British colonies, due to its superior quality, and secured a special place on many tables, at a time when America produced no wines at all and had to import them.

In this first chapter will be presented a few texts related to Madeira Wine in Colonial America, a time when this product was well known and cherished by the higher classes, and present in colonial life.

SOME NEW BOOKS.[1]
Long Island – A Volume of Curious Historical Information.

A book has been published by J. W. Bouton, which contains matter of especial interest to many residents of Long Island and New York City, and is likely also to engage the attention of all persons inquisitive as to the early history of this State and the manners that prevailed among the founders of the great republic. It is entitled *Antiquities of Long Island, by Gabriel Furman. To which is added a Bibliography by Henry Onderdonk, Jr., edited by Frank Moore.*[2] ...

But expensive as was the character of the funerals on this island and in New York, they could not compare in that respect with those among the Dutch inhabitants of the city of Albany. Judge Benson,[3] in his memoir[4] read before the New York Historical Society, describes the funeral of Lucas Wyngaard, who died in that city in the year 1756, a bachelor, leaving some estate. The invitation to that funeral was very general, and those who attended it returned after the interment, as the custom then was, to the house of the deceased toward the close of the day, and a large number of them never left until dawn of the ensuing day. In the course of the night a pipe of wine, which had been stored in the cellar for some years before the occasion, was drank; dozens of papers of tobacco were consumed; grosses of pipes broken; scarce a whole decanter or glass was left; and, to crown

---

1 *The Sun*, March 27, 1875. (New York City, NY).
2 Book published in New York, in 1875.
3 Egbert Benson (1746-1833), a native of New York City, was a lawyer, jurist, politician and a Founding Father of the United States of America. He was also one of the founders of the New York Historical Society and its first President, serving from 1804 to 1816.
4 His book was entitled *Memoir read before the Historical Society of the State of New York, December 31, 1816*, whose second edition was published in Jamaica, NY, in 1825.

2. MADEIRA WINE IN COLONIAL AMERICA

Figure 1. Egbert Benson, a Founding Father of America, had good memories of the Dutch inhabitants of New York, in Colonial Times, at whose funeral there was a lot of Madeira Wine drinking. *Engraving by H. A. Hall, 1872.*

the whole, the pall bearers made a bonfire of their scarfs upon the hearth of the room where they were carousing. This may have been a little more uproarious than most the funerals of that period, as the deceased was a bachelor, and had no widow and children in the same house to control, and, in some degree, to modify their proceedings; but yet all the funerals of that time were more than enough so under any circumstances. Even down to within the last fifty years Albany was noted for the expensive character of its funerals. That of the first wife of the late Patroon, the Hon. Stephen Van Rensselaer, it is said, cost him not less than twenty thousand dollars! All his tenants were invited, and most of them were in Albany for two or three days at his expense, and two thousand linen scarfs were given on that occasion. It was formerly the custom there for a young man immediately previous to his marriage, to send to the Island of Madeira for a pipe or two of the best wine; a portion of which being used in the rejoicings consequent upon his marriage, and the remainder stored away for his funeral and that of his wife. …

Old Dutch Funeral Customs.[5]

Lucas Wyngard died in Albany in 1726, a bachelor, leaving some estate. The invitation to his funeral was very general, and those who attended returned after the interment to the house, and a large number never left it until the dawn of the ensuing day. In the course of the night a pipe of wine, that had been stored in the cellar for some years before the occasion was drank, dozens of papers of tobacco were consumed, grosses of pipes destroyed, scarce a whole decanter or glass left, and, to crown the whole the pall-bearers made a bonfire of their scarfs upon the hearth of the room where they were carousing. Even down to within the last 50 years, Albany was noted for the expensive character of its funerals. A funeral in a respectable Dutch family at that place, and especially of the head or any principal member of it, costs from $3,000 to $4,000. That of the first wife of the patroon, Stephen Van Rensselaer, it is said, cost him not less than $20,000. All his tenants were invited, and most of them were in Albany two or three days at his expense and 2000 linen scarfs were given on that occasion. It was formerly the custom there for a young man immediately previous to his marriage to send to the island of Maderia[6] for a pipe or two of the best wine, a portion of which was used in the rejoicings consequent upon his marriage, and the remainder stowed away for his funeral and that of his wife, (An odd reversal of the order customary in Denmark in Hamlet's day.) It was also the practice in that city to send out special funeral invitations for all friends and acquaintances of the deceased being about the same

---

[5] *Springfield Republican*, April 26, 1875. (Springfield, MA); *Los Angeles Herald*, May 20, 1875. (Los Angeles, CA). Although this article repeats part of the previous one, it contains additional data that complements it, therefore we present it as well.
[6] The right spelling is Madeira. It was a common mistake, in 19th century America, to designate the island (or its famous wine) as this, or even as Madeira.

age, and likewise for all the clergy and professional men of the neighboring country and general invitations from the pulpits of the churches to the citizens at large. To the house of each person thus invited was sent a linen scarf, a pair of black silk gloves, a bottle of old Madeira wine and two funeral cakes, which were round and about the size of a dinner plate. This was done previous to the funeral and was in addition to the great quantity of spiced wine and other liquors which, with tobacco and pipes, were distributed and used at the house of the deceased immediately preceding and after the interment. When Gen. Schuyler died in that city, all the clergy, lawyers, physicians and even students in Albany and its neighborhood for many miles, were invited especially, and a scarf, gloves, a bottle of wine, with funeral cakes, given to each of them. So particular were they about the linen of which to make these scarfs, that in several instances they sent down by land to New York in the depth of winter to purchase it, and paid two dollars a yard.

The Antiquities of Long Island.[7]

The *Christian Union*, in reviewing a work of the above title, summarizes the ancient settlers of Long Island, the Dutch, in the following interesting manner:

Burials seem to have been matters to which the Dutch of Long Island devoted the most careful attention. The first money earned by a young man after coming of age was converted into coin and saved to meet his funeral expenses; it was considered a great disgrace, after the age of twenty-three, to die without saving money enough to pay his funeral expenses. It was also the custom to appropriate new clothing for each member of the family, to serve as a burial suit when occasion demanded, and such clothing was never used for any other purpose. We read that bountiful feasts were prepared for funeral parties, and that rum, brandy, gin, pipes, tobacco and cigars were passed among the attendants at funerals as a simple act of hospitality. Funeral "hospitality" reached its height in Albany, however, for there it became the custom to send out special invitations to funerals, each invitation being accompanied by a present of a linen scarf, a pair of black silk gloves, a bottle of old Madeira wine and two "funeral cakes." The age of the wine was, in the case of married people, determined by the time they had passed in wedlock, for it was the custom for a young man when about to be married to send to Madeira for a pipe or two of the best wine; part of this was used at the marriage feast and the remainder was used for funeral presents on the decease of himself or his wife. …

A VERY OLD ALMANAC.[8]

Prof. E. G. Fowler of the Newburgh *Telegraph* is unearthing the relics in that city. He has lately come across an almanac in the possession of the Rev. Rufus Emery, which was printed in 1756, in the reign of King George II. It is well preserved. The almanac contains much of interest, of which the following are extracts:

"The next Government is New York; the city of New York is their capital; and is said to contain 5,000 houses, they abound in all sorts of provisions, which they export, and

---

7 *The Ackley Enterprise*, May 21, 1875. (Ackley, IA).
8 *The Evening Gazette*, April 11, 1876. (Port Jervis, NY).

in return bring the best Madeira, which by the better sort is drank freely in the city; the number of their inhabitants is set at 100,000 and their present governor is His Excellency, SIR CHARLES HARDY, Knight."[9] ...

THE LAW-STUDENT.[10]

... Thus circumstanced, each clergyman behaved according to his disposition. A few of them, men of learning and virtue, did their duty, and eked out their slender and changing incomes by taking pupils; and it was these few who saved civilization in the colony. Others, men of rude energy and executive force, pushed the cultivation of their glebes, bought more slaves, raised more tobacco, speculated sometimes in *both*, grew rich, reduced their parish duty to the minimum, and performed that minimum with haste and formality. But the greater number lived as idle hangers-on of the wealthier houses, assisting their fellow-idlers, the planters, to kill time and run through their estates, not always dissolute, but easy-going, self-indulgent, good-natured men of the world. It was not very uncommon for the clergyman of a parish to be the president of its jockey-club, and personally assist in the details of the race-course, such as weighing the men and timing the horses. It was common for clergymen to ride after the hounds in fox-hunting; and they were as apt to nail the trophy of the day's chase to their stable-door as any other men. The names of clergymen figured among the patrons of balls, and they were rather noted for their skill at cards. All of which was just as proper for clergymen as for planters, and more necessary. But in those days the bottle was the vitiating accompaniment of every innocent delight. The race must end in a dinner, and the dinner must end under the table. The day's hunt must be followed by a night's debauch. The christening of a child must be the pretext for a day's revel. This single element of mischief converted all festal days, all honest mirth, all joyous recreation, into injury, shame, and ruin. Nothing can make any headway against the potency of wine; for it suspends the operation of that within us which enables us to resist, and finally destroys it. It vitiates the texture of the brain itself, the seat of life, and the citadel of all the superior forces. And the wine which flowed so freely at the planters' tables was Madeira, strongest of wines, so enriched by time and two long voyages, that the uncorking of one bottle filled a large house with fragrance. ...

---

9 Sir Charles Hardy (c.1714-1780), a native of Portsmouth, England, was an Admiral of the Fleet who served as colonial Governor of New York from 1755 to 1758.
10 PARTON, James, *Life of Thomas Jefferson, Third President of the United States*, Seventh Edition, Houghton, Mifflin and Company, Boston, 1883, pages 55-56. This excerpt of this biography refers to the life of the clergymen in Virginia around the 1760's, a time when Jefferson was studying Law.

NEW YORK 150 YEARS AGO.[11]
As It Appeared to a Swedish Botanist Sent to See What He Could See.

Peter Kalm,[12] the Swedish botanist, and the favorite pupil of Linnaeus,[13] was sent by the Swedish Government to the American colonies a century and a half ago to find what they were like, who inhabited the country, what grew there, how the budding cities compared with those in Sweden, and whether it would be a good place for the subjects of King Frederick to come to or to stay away from. His expenses paid by the Swedish Government, Kalm landed in Philadelphia, and from that town came by post chaise to New York, and, putting up overnight at Elizabeth, was rowed over to New York a little after sunrise on a cold morning in October.

The first thing that impressed him about New York was the frogs. These were so clamorous and created such a disturbance that he declared they drowned the singing of the birds and made it difficult for a person in old New York to make himself heard. The streets, he observed, did not run so straight as those of Philadelphia and had considerable bendings; however, they were very spacious and well built, and most of them were paved, except in high places where paving had been found useless. Most of the houses were built of brick, and were generally strong and neat; some had turned the gable ends toward the street, but the newer houses were altered in this respect. Many had a balcony on the roof, on which the people used to sit in the evenings in the summer season, and from thence they had a pleasant view. Kalm's investigation led him to the conclusion that there was no good water to be met with in the town itself, but at a little distance there was a small spring of good water, from which the inhabitants used to make tea. The wine drank in New York was brought, Kalm declared, from the Isles of Madeira, and was very strong and fiery. ...

M'ALLISTER ON CLUBS.[14] ...

... The "All Saints' Quoit Club," of Savannah, Ga., was founded before 1701. The Gibhouses, the Habeshams, the Mackays, the Hunters, the McAllisters, all convivial men, on every Saturday afternoon during the winter months played quoits "under the pine trees on Savannah's common," providing an elaborate display of old Madeira that was ever imported into this country.

The famous All Saints' Madeira of 1791 took its name from this club. This club ceased to exist after the war. ...

---

11 *The Sun*, August 12, 1892. (New York City, NY).

12 Peter Kalm (1715-1779) was among the first foreign scientists to visit the United States. Upon his return to Europe he published a book, in three volumes, between 1753 and 1761, depicting his impressions of the New World, entitled *En resa til Norra Amerika*, which was translated, later on, into Dutch, German and English. The latter version was printed in 1770, under the title *Travels in North America, containing its Natural History, and Civil, Ecclesiastical, and Commercial State*.

13 Carl Linnaeus (1707-1778), a Swedish botanist, physician and zoologist, known as the father of taxonomy and one of the fathers of modern ecology.

14 *The World*, August 28, 1892. (New York City, NY).

NEW YORK IN THE REVOLUTION.[15]

A STRAIN of melancholy mingles with the splendid progress of our great metropolis. The city spreads over the green fields where we were happy in boyhood, over streams we once knew lined with alders and murmuring amidst clustering foliage, over the meadows where we gathered berries, and the shady roads of our evening drives. It draws into its bosom the villages that shone sweetly to the setting suns of youth, secluded farm-houses where our ancestors passed their simple lives, villas once renowned as the haunts of rural fashion, and parklike scenery that bordered the tranquil Hudson with wood and grove and lawn. The fruit trees planted by our fathers, the quiet home scenes of our youth, the woods where the Indian Summer made its carnival of old, where the squirrel dropped its store of nuts at our coming, where the blackbird and the blue-jay fell before our first attempts in sportsmanship, and whose awful shadows seemed to the eye of childhood the fitting haunt of the Indian and the robber, fade like a vision before the ceaseless progress of the imperial city.

I have been led into these reflections in the endeavor to place the reader in the midst of that earlier New York, a striking passage in whose history I desire to narrate. New York, indeed, in the year 1770, was a small provincial town. The well-built portion of the city extended about a mile in length, in breadth half a mile, and formed an irregular triangle narrowing toward the Battery. Broadway was paved as far as St. Paul's, the Park was an uninclosed common, and no streets above Dey were regularly opened and graded. The churches were the finest buildings; and stately Trinity, St. George's, in the last London style, St. Paul's, and the great Middle Dutch, now the Post-office, seem even in the present day costly and remarkable structures for that early period.

Travelers, however, who visited New York, were struck by its attractions. Kalm, the Swedish naturalist, in 1740, was amazed at its opulence and beauty. To walk in Broadway, he says, was like entering a garden: the shade-trees were plentiful, the birds sang sweetly from their branches, and the frogs chanted so merrily in the elms and locusts that one could hardly hear one's self speak. The streets were narrow, and the houses a strange mingling of Dutch and English taste. But on the tops of gentlemen's houses were balconies, from whence in summer evenings opened a charming prospect of the lovely bay.

Healthful, tall, and robust, the people of New York were not so long-lived as the Europeans. They were gay, polished, and convivial, and their favorite drink was the fiery old Madeira. The ladies Dr. Burnaby thought handsome, discreet, and more "modest" than those of Philadelphia. New York society was famed for its air of easy gayety. It was more polished than that of any other city of the New World, and here the provincials came to perfect their manners and improve their taste.

But the citizens of New York, gay, social, and refined, were among the boldest of the defenders of freedom. When the Revolution came they hailed it with eager delight. Of the men of New York who created the new era something must be said. A Puritan, a Huguenot, and a Scotchman led on the general movement. …

---

15 "Harper's New Monthly Magazine," Volume XXXVII, June to November, 1868, Harper & Brothers, Publishers, New York, 1868, page 180.

CHAPTER XII[16]
LIFE IN NEW-YORK AT THE CLOSE OF THE COLONIAL PERIOD

... But this was the convivial, not the customary drink of the day. The flowing bowl was reserved for the tavern, or social gatherings. Madeira, king of wines, reigned supreme at the tables of the gentry. True, there were always to be found the wines of Sicily and the Canary Isles, the red vintages of Oporto and Bordeaux, the bright aromatic product of the Xeres and Amontillado districts, and champagne occasionally appeared. But for the staple of every-day drink, and for the more solemn occasions, – birthdays, majority-days, marriages, and funerals, the only great events of social life, – Madeira, and Madeira only, was the wine; and the skilful gentlemen who looked to his wines as his notable lady to her larder and preserve-room, knew well the process by which, with age and care, he could bring his vintages to each note in the gamut of flavor and delicacy. A gentleman's cellar was no sinecure, nor was its construction the affair of an hour or a day. As each vessel laden with the precious freight arrived (the cargo, all in casks, had no distinctive name, but thereafter took that of the year of the vintage alone), the merits of the wine would be tested. Certain vintages became famous: that of 1767 had a reputation equal to that of the later vintage of the comet year.

One cask or more were selected, duly cellared, and kept in the wood. One cask only was drawn from during the first year. The next year a second purchase was made. The partly emptied cask was filled from the new purchase; the third year the process was repeated, the new wine being used every day, and the predecessors, in the order of the importance of the occasion, according to their ages. In due time the older wines were drawn off in demi-johns, or sometimes bottled. The lees of the casks served as a base for the Jamaica rum, and gave it a wonderful aroma. But only ample cellars could afford this degenerate use. The cellars took the names of their owners when, by some luckless hap, they came to the vendue-room – a rare fate. The vintages treated by wine-merchants later took the names of the vessels by which they were received. Instances in a not remote day must be familiar, as the Essex, Jr., the Juno, and the Brahmin Madeiras were all from the same vineyard, and brought in by these vessels, while the Farquhar, the Bingham, and the Paulding Madeiras took their names from the owners of the respective cellars; the March and Benson, from the importers; the Monteiros, from the grower; the Metternich, from the origin of the grape. All these, however, are modern fashions. There is no trace of them in the colonial days. ...

2.1. The Boston Madeira Party

Five years before the Boston Tea Party took place, a major event occurred at Boston harbor, in 1768, involving a cargo of Madeira Wine just arrived at that city aboard the John Hancock's sloop *Liberty*, that passed into History as the Boston Madeira Party. The rebellious act that followed was one of the first sparks that, in the short run, would flare the American Revolution. Next will be presented a few texts about this topic.

---

16 WILSON, James Grant, *The Memorial History of the City of New-York: From its first settlement to the year 1892*, Volume II, New-York History Company, 1892, pages 454, 456.

AFFAIR OF THE SLOOP LIBERTY.[17]

Meanwhile, additional cause of offence and quarrel arose in America from the operation of the Act by which a board of customs had been established at Boston. Paxton,[18] one of the commissioners, had long been an object of general detestation to the people of Massachusetts, on account of the zeal with which he seconded all the pretensions of British prerogative; and only his absence from the province during the Stamp Act riots, had saved him from a share of the popular vengeance on that occasion. He and his colleagues now enforced the trade laws with a rigour hitherto unknown, and which contributed not a little to increase the prevailing inquietude and irritation. At New York there was printed and circulated, a manifesto or proclamation assuring the inhabitants that commissioners of customs would soon be established there as well as at Boston, and summoning every friend of liberty to hold himself in readiness to receive them with the same treatment which had been bestowed upon "a set of miscreants under the name of stamp-masters, in the year 1765." All the efforts of the governor to discover the authors of this inflammatory proclamation proved ineffectual. In this province the spirit of liberty was no way depressed, nor was even the conduct of public business obstructed by the act of parliament restraining the assembly from the exercise of legislative functions. With a plausible show of obedience to the letter of the statute, the assembly forbore to enact formal *laws*:but whenever money was needed for public purposes, they passed *resolutions* to which the people lent a prompt and cheerful obedience: and thus the act, though sufficient to exasperate, proved quite impotent to punish. It had been the practice in every quarter of British America for the officers of the customs to allow merchants and shipmasters to enter in the custom-house books only a part of their imported cargoes, and to land the remainder duty free. To this practice, which had become so inveterate that the colonists regarded the advantage accruing from it as a right rather than an indulgence, the commissioners now resolved to put a stop. A sloop called the Liberty, belonging to Hancock, having arrived at Boston laden with wine from Madeira, the captain, as usual, proposed to the tidewaiter who came to inspect the cargo, that part of it should be landed duty free; and meeting a refusal, laid violent hands upon him, and with the assistance of the crew locked him up in the cabin till the whole cargo was carried ashore. The next morning he entered a few pipes of the wine at the custom-house, as having formed all his lading: but the commissioners of the customs, declaring that the entry was false, caused the sloop to be arrested. To secure the capture, it was proposed that the vessel should be removed from the wharf and towed under the guns of the Romney man-of-war; and by the assistance of the Romney's boats this was accordingly performed in spite of the opposition of a great assemblage of the people, who, finding their remonstrances disre-

---

17 FROST, John, *The Battle Grounds of America, Illustrated by Stories of the Revolution; with Fourteen Engravings*, J. C. Derby & Co., Auburn, NY, 1846, pages 21-25; *Stories of the American Revolution; comprising a complete Anecdotic History of that Great National Event*, Grigg & Elliot, Philadelphia, 1847, pages 21-25. Another version of this episode was also told in a text bearing the same title, published in another book, entitled *Thrilling Incidents of the Wars of the United States: comprising the most Striking and Remarkable Events of The Revolution, The French War, The Tripolitan War, The Indian War, The Second War with Great Britain, and the Mexican War., with three hundred engravings.*, By the Author of "The Army and Navy of the United States", Carey & Hart, Philadelphia, 1848, pages 25-28. This latter text was transcribed in an American newspaper, namely the *Jeffersonian Democrat*, of March 19, 1857. (Published in Monroe, WI, under the title "THRILLING INCIDENTS OF THE WARS OF THE UNITED STATES – Affair of The Sloop Liberty").

18 Charles Paxton, Commissioner and Collector of Customs for Boston, at this time.

garded, assaulted the custom-house officers with a violence that had nearly proved fatal to their lives. On the following day, the populace again assembling before the houses of the collector, comptroller, and inspector-general of the customs, broke their windows, and then seizing the collector's boat, dragged it through the town, and burned it on the common. Their violence, whether satiated or not, was checked at this point by the flight of the commissioners and other officers of the customs, who, learning that renewed assemblages of the people were expected, and believing, or affecting to believe that farther outrages were meditated against themselves, hastily left the place, and took refuge first on board the ship of war, and afterwards in Castle William.[19] The city, meanwhile, resounded with complaints of the insult that had been offered to the inhabitants in removing the sloop from the wharf, and thus proclaiming apprehensions of a rescue. These complaints were sanctioned by the assembly, who declared that the criminality of the rioters was extenuated by the irritating and unprecedented circumstances of the seizure; but added, nevertheless, that as the rioters deserved severe punishment, they must beseech the governor to direct that they should be prosecuted, and proclaim a reward for their discovery. The rioters, however, had nothing to fear: nor was any one of them ever molested. A suit for penalties was afterwards instituted against Hancock in the court of admiralty: but the officers of the crown finding it beyond their power to adduce sufficient evidence of facts which though every body knew, nobody would attest, abandoned the prosecution and restored the vessel.

Figure 2. John Hancock, who refused to pay the due taxes of a cargo of Madeira Wine arrived in Boston, in 1768, a fact that set the ground for the Boston Madeira Party. Later on, he would be one of the signers of the Declaration of Independence. *Painting by John Singleton Copley c. 1770-1772.*

CHAPTER XX.[20]

... The Repeal Act reached Boston at about noon on Friday, the 13th of May. It was brought by the brig Harrison, a vessel belonging to John Hancock. Great was the general joy. The church-bells were immediately rung; the colors of all the ships were hoisted; cannons were discharged; the Sons of Liberty[21] gathered under their favorite tree, drank toasts, and fired guns; and bonfires and illuminations enlivened the evening. A general celebration was arranged by the select-men for the following Monday. The dawn, bright and rosy, was ushered in by salvos of cannon, ringing of bells, and martial music. Through the liberality of some citizens, every debtor in the jail was ransomed and set at liberty,

---

19 Designation attributed by the British to a fortification located at Castle Island, in the Boston harbor, which, in 1797 changed its name to Fort Independence.
20 LOSSING, Benson J., *The Pictorial Field-Book of The Revolution; or, Illustrations, by Pen and Pencil, of the History, Biography, Scenery, Relics, and Traditions of the War for Independence*, In Two Volumes, Vol. I., Harper & Brothers, Publishers, New York, 1855, pages 473-474, 478.
21 Designation of a group of American patriots formed to protect the rights of the colonies from the usurpations by the British government after 1766. Their main achievement was the undertaking of the Boston Tea Party. John Adams, John Hancock and Paul Revere were some of its notable members.

to unite in the general joy. "This charitable deed originated in a fair Boston nymph." The whole town was illuminated in the evening. On the Common the Sons of Liberty erected a magnificent pyramid, illuminated by two hundred and eighty lamps, the four upper stories of which were ornamented with figures of the king and queen, and "fourteen of the patriots who had distinguished themselves for their love of liberty." On the four sides of the lower apartment were appropriate poetic inscriptions. "John Hancock, Esq.," says a newspaper of the day, from which I have drawn this account, "who gave a grand and elegant entertainment to the genteel part of the town, and treated the populace to a pipe of Madeira wine, erected at the front of his house, which was magnificently illuminated, a stage for the exhibition of his fire-works." ...... "Mr. Otis, and some other gentlemen who lived near the Common, kept open house the whole evening, which was very pleasant." At eleven o'clock, on a signal being given, a horizontal fire-wheel on the top of the pyramid was set in motion, "which ended in the discharge of sixteen dozen serpents in the air, which concluded the show. To the honor of the Sons of Liberty, we can with pleasure inform the world that every thing was conducted with the utmost decency and good order." His majesty's Council, by a previous invitation of the governor, met at the Province House in the afternoon, where many loyal toasts were drunk, and in the evening they went to the Common to see the fire-works. Past animosities were forgotten, and the night of the 16th of May was a happy one for Boston. ...

A new scene in the drama now opened. The commissioners of customs had arrived in May, and were diligent in the performance of their duties. The merchants were very restive under the strictness of the revenue officers, and these functionaries were exceedingly odious in the eyes of the people generally. On the 10th of June the sloop *Liberty*, Nathaniel Bernard master, belonging to John Hancock, arrived at Boston with a cargo of Madeira wine. It was a common practice for the tide-waiter, upon the arrival of a vessel, to repair to the cabin, and there to remain, drinking punch with the master, while the sailors were landing the dutiable goods. On the arrival of the *Liberty*, Kirke, the tidesman, went on board, just at sunset, and took his seat in the cabin as usual. About nine in the evening Captain Marshall, and others in Hancock's employ, entered the cabin, confined Kirke below, and landed the wine on the dock without entering it at the custom-house, or observing any other formula. Kirke was then released and sent ashore. Captain Marshall died suddenly during the night, from the effects, it was supposed, of over-exertion in landing the wine. In the morning the commissioners of customs ordered the seizure of the sloop, and Harrison, the collector, and Hallowell, the controller, were deputed to perform that duty. Hallowell proceeded to place the broad arrow upon her (the mark designating her legal position), and then, cutting her moorings, he removed the vessel from Hancock's Wharf to a place in the harbor under the guns of the *Romney* ship of war.

This act greatly inflamed the people. Already a crowd had collected to prevent the seizure; but when the vessel was cut loose and placed under the protection of British cannon, a strong feeling of anger pervaded the multitude. The assemblage of citizens became a mob, and a large party of the lower class, headed by Malcomb, a bold smuggler, pelted Harrison and others with stones, attacked the offices of the commissioners, and, dragging a customhouse boat through the town, burned it upon the Common. The commissioners, alarmed for their own safety, applied to Governor Bernard[22] for protection, but he told

---

[22] Sir Francis Bernard (1712-1779), Governor of the Province of Massachusetts from 1759 to 1769.

them he was utterly powerless. They found means to escape on board the Romney, and thence to Castle William, a fortress upon Castle Island, in the harbor, nearly three miles southeast of the city, where a company of British artillery was stationed.

The Sons of Liberty called a meeting at Faneuil Hall on the afternoon of the 13th. A large concourse assembled, and the principal business done was preparing a petition to the governor, asking him to remove the man-of-war from the harbor. The Council passed resolutions condemnatory of the rioters, but the House of Representatives took no notice of the matter. Legal proceedings were commenced against the leading rioters, but the difficulty of procuring witnesses, and the bad feeling that was engendered, made the prosecutors drop the matter in the following spring. …

Jonathan Sewal *vs.* John Hancock.[23]

"Be it remembered, that on the 29 day of October in the Ninth Year of the Reign of his Majesty George the Third, Jonathan Sewall Esq.r Advocate General of the said Lord the King, in his proper Person comes and as well on behalf of the said Lord the King, as of the Governor of this Province, gives the said Court to understand and be informed, that on the ninth day of May last, a certain Sloop called the Liberty, arrived at the Port of Boston in said Province, from the Islands of Madeira, having on Board, one hundred and twenty seven Pipes of Wine of the Growth of the Madeira's; of which said Sloop, one Nathaniel Barnard was then Master, and that in the Night Time of the same day the said Nathaniel Barnard with Intent to defraud the said Lord the King of his lawfull Customs, did unlawfully and clandestinely unship and land on Shore in Boston aforesaid one hundred of the aforesaid Pipes of Wine of the Value of Thirty Pounds Sterling Money of Great Britain, each Pipe, the Duties thereon not having been first paid, or secured to be paid, agreeable to Law. And that John Hancock of Boston aforesaid Esqr was then and there *willfully and unlawfully aiding and assisting in unshipping & landing* the same one hundred Pipes of Wine, he the said John Hancock, at the same time *well knowing, that the Duties thereon were not paid or secured* and that the unshipping and landing the same, as aforesaid, was with Intent to defraud the said Lord the King as aforesaid, and contrary to Law; against the Peace of the said Lord the King and the Form of the Statute in such Case made and provided, whereby and by Force of the same Statute, the said John was forfeited Treble the Value of the said Goods, so unshipped and landed as aforesaid, amounting in the whole to the Sum of Nine Thousand Pounds Sterling Money of Great Britain, to be divided, paid and applied in manner following, that is to say, after deducting the Charges of Prosecution, one Third Part thereof to be paid into the Hands of the Collector of his Majesty's Customs for the said Port of Boston, for the Use of his Majesty, his Heirs and Successors, one Third Part to the Governor of said Province, and the other Third to him that informs the same.

Whereupon as this is a matter properly within the Jurisdiction of this Hon. Court, the said Advocate General prays the Advisement of the said Court in the Premises, and

---

23 QUINCY, Junior, Josiah, *Reports of Cases argued and adjudged in the Superior Court of Judicature of the Province of Massachusetts Bay, between 1761 and 1772*, Little, Brown, and Company, Boston, 1865, pages 457-458. This interesting text portrays the accusation made against John Hancock for his insubordinate attitude.

that the said John Hancock may be attached and held to answer to this Information, and may by a Decree of this honourable Court be adjudged to pay the aforesaid sum of Nine Thousand Pounds to be applied to the Uses aforesaid.
JON SEWALL, Adv.º for the King."

2.2. The Philadelphia Case

A similar case to the "Boston Madeira Party" occurred in Philadelphia, in 1769, just a year after, also involving the smuggling of Madeira wine into the United States without paying the import taxes, as an act of rebellion against the British authority.

FESTIVE FREEBOOTERS...[24]
SMUGGLERS OF THE OLDEN TIME. ...

Figure 3. " Smuggling in the olden time". *Article illustration. Author unknown.*

In the olden times when high handed pirates and low browned smugglers flourished apace Philadelphia held a place of enviable distinction in both these pretty pursuits. ...

In 1769 John Swift, the collector of customs for the port of Philadelphia, first began to make himself unpopular with the bold blades who saw the absurdity of swelling the royal coffers by paying import duties. One dark night a schooner ran up the Delaware and landed several pipes of fine old Madeira on a Philadelphia dock, whence they were snugly stowed away in a warehouse. But Collector Swift got wind of the matter and seized the cargo, placing it in a storehouse near the river. On the next night the house was broken into and the Madeira carried off in the presence of the irate Collector Swift. Warrants were issued for the smugglers and housebreakers, but they were never prosecuted.

Not long after the traitors, who had informed the collector of the landing of the pipes of wine, were found out. These law abiding scoundrels were promptly captured, ducked, set up in the pillory, then lavishly tarred. The populace appreciated the high motives and merits of the smuggler and were right "with him" all the time. During his term of office Collector Swift had many serious encounters with the smugglers which showed pretty plainly that public sympathy was not all on the side of law and order.

It must be remembered that in these days, just before the outbreak of the Revolution, the relations between the colonies and the mother country were strained almost to breaking,

---

24 *Warren Ledger*, April 2, 1895. (Warren, PA); *Hornellsville Weekly Tribune*, April 5, 1895. (Hornellsville, NY).

and the question of custom duties was chief at issue. In 1774 some hogsheads of sugar were seized by the custom officers on board the schooner Felicity, Captain Allen Moore, for being smuggled. Those goods were rescued from the king's men, who were badly beaten with clubs and staves, and this was the last overt act against his majesty's servants in the port of Philadelphia before hostilities were formally declared. ...

3. Madeira Wine in the American Revolutionary War

In this chapter a few texts will be displayed related to this war, in which Madeira Wine was present or played an important role in the course of events that led to the affirmation of the United States as a sovereign nation, independent from Great Britain. From this selection we outline the texts related to the Battle of Germantown, in which, in the heat of the battle, the blood of dead soldiers was mixed with Madeira Wine, and Mrs. Murray's heroic act in Manhattan, with her husband's Madeira.

THE BATTLE OF GERMANTOWN.[25]
III. THE REVEL OF DEATH.

– Within Chew's house this was the scene:
Every room crowded with soldiers in their glaring crimson attire, the old hall thronged by armed men, all stained with blood and begrimed with battle smoke, the stair-way trembling beneath the tread of soldiers bearing ammunition to the upper rooms, while every board of the floor, every step of the stair-case bore its ghastly burden of dying and dead. The air was pestilent with the smell of powder, the walls trembled with the shock of battle; thick volumes of smoke rolling from the lower rooms, wound through the doors, into the old hall, and up the stairway, enveloping all objects in a pall of gloom, that now shifted aside, and again came down upon the forms of the British soldiers like dark night.

Let us ascend the stairway. Tread carefully, or your foot will trample on the face of that dead soldier; ascend the staircase with a cautious step, or you will lose your way in the battle smoke.

The house trembles to its foundation, one volley of musquetry after another breaks on your ear, and all around is noise and confusion; nothing seen but armed men hurrying to and fro, nothing heard but the thunder of the fight.

We gain the top of the stairway – we have mounted over the piles of dead – we pass along the entry – we enter the room on the right, facing toward the lawn.

A scene of startling interest opens to our sight. At each window are arranged files of men, who, with faces all blood stained and begrimed, are sending their musket shots along the lawn; at each window the floor is stained with a pool of blood, and the bodies of the dead are dragged away by the strong hands of their comrades, who fill their places almost as soon as they receive their death wound. The walls are rent by cannon balls, and torn by bullets, and the very air seems ringing with the carnival shouts of old Death, rejoicing in the midst of demons.

Near a window in this room clustered a gallant band of British officers, who gave the word to the men, directed the dead to be taken from the floor, or gazed out upon the lawn in the endeavor to pierce the gloom of the contest.

Some were young and handsome officers, others were veterans who had mowed their way through many a fight, and all were begrimed with the blood and smoke of battle.

---

[25] LIPPARD, George, *Washington and his Generals: or, Legends of the Revolution.*, G. B. Zieber and Co., Philadelphia, 1847, pages 56-58. This episode was also told in the American press, namely in the *Manitouwoc County Herald*, of March 1, 1851. (Manitouwoc, WI. Published under the same titles and quoting the same book).

Their gaudy coats were rent, the epaulette was torn from one shoulder by the bullet, the plume from the helm of another, and a third fell in his comrades' arms, as he received the ball in his heart.

While they stood gazing from the window, a singular incident occurred.

A young officer, standing in the midst of his comrades, felt something drop from the ceiling, and trickle down his cheek.

The fight was fierce and bloody in the attic overhead. They could hear the cannon balls tearing shingles from the roof – they could hear the low, deep groans of the dying.

Another drop fell from the ceiling – another and another.

"It is blood!" cried his comrades, and a laugh went round the group.

Drop after drop fell from the ceiling; and in a moment a thin liquid stream came trickling down, and pattered upon the blood-stained floor.

The young officer reached forth his hand, he held it extended beneath the falling stream: he applied it to his lips.

"Not blood, but wine! he shouted. "Good old Madeira wine!"

The group gathered round the young officer in wonder. It was wine – good old wine – that was dripping from the ceiling. In a few moments the young officer, rushing through the gloom and confusion of the stairway, had ransacked the attic, and discovered under the eaves of the roof, between the rafters and the floor, some three dozen bottles of old Madeira wine, placed there for safe-keeping some score of years before the battle. These bottles were soon drawn from their resting-place, and the eyes of the group in the room below were presently astonished by the vision of the ancient bottles, all hung with cobwebs, their sealed corks covered with dust.

In a moment the necks were struck off some half-dozen bottles, and while the fire poured from the window along the lawn, while cries and shrieks, and groans, broke on the air; while the smoke came rolling in the window, now in folds of midnight blackness, and now turned to lurid red by the glare of cannon; while the terror and gloom of battle arose around them, the group of officers poured the wine in an ancient goblet, discovered in a closet of the mansion, – they filled it brimming full with wine, and drank a royal health to the good King George!

They drank and drank again, until their eyes sparkled, and their lips grew wild with loyal words, and their thirst for blood – the blood of the rebels – was excited to madness. Again and again were the soldiers shot down at the window, again were their places filled, and once more the goblet went round from lip to lip, and the old wine was poured forth like water, in healths to the good King George!

And as they drank, one by one, the soldiers were swept away from the windows, until at the last the officers stood exposed to the blaze of the American fire, flashing from the green lawn.

"Health to King George – Death to the rebels!"

The shout arose from the lips of a grey-haired veteran, and he fell to the floor, a mangled corpse. The arm that raised the goblet was shattered at the elbow by one musket ball, as another penetrated his brain.

The goblet was seized by another hand, and the revel grew loud and wild. The sparkling wine was poured forth like water, healths were drank, hurrahs were shouted, and – another officer measured his length on the floor. He had received his ball of death.

3. MADEIRA WINE IN THE AMERICAN REVOLUTIONARY WAR

Figure 4. "The Battle of Germantown", in which American forces laid siege to the Chew House, at whose attic was stored some Madeira Wine. *Drawing by Christian Schüselle, 1840.*

There was something of ludicrous horror in the scene.

Those sounds of revel and bacchanalian uproar, breaking on the air, amid the intervals – the short and terrible intervals of battle – those faces flushed by wine, and agitated by all the madness of the moment, turned from one side to another, every lip wearing a ghastly smile, every eye glaring from its socket, while every voice echoed the drunken shout and the fierce hurrah.

Another officer fell wounded, and another, and yet another. The young officer who had first discovered the wine alone remained.

Even in this moment of horror, we cannot turn our eyes away, from his young countenance, with its hazel eyes and thickly clustered hair!

He glanced round upon his wounded and dying comrades, he looked vacantly in the faces of the dead, he gazed upon the terror and confusion of the scene, and then he seized the goblet, filled it brimming-full with wine, and raised it to his lips.

His lip touched the edge of the goblet, his face was reflected in the quivering wavelets of the wine, his eyes rolled wildly to and fro, and then, a musket shot pealed through the window. The officer glared around with a maddened glance, and then the warm blood, spouting from the wound between his eyebrows, fell drop by drop into the goblet, and mingled with the wavelets of the ruby wine.

And then there was a wild shout; a heavy body toppled to the floor; and the young soldier with a curse on his lips went drunken to his God.

Let us for a moment notice the movements of the divisions of Washington's army, and then return to the principal battle ground at Chew's house.

The movements of the divisions of Smallwood and Forman are, to this day, enveloped in mystery. They came in view of the enemy, but the density of the mist, prevented them from effectually engaging with the British.

Armstrong came marching down the Manatawny road, until the quiet Wissahikon[26] dawned on the eyes of his men; but after this moment, his march is also wrapt in mystery. – Some reports state that he actually engaged with the Hessian division of the enemy, others state that the alarm of the American retreating from Chew's house reached his ear, as the vanguard of his command entered Germantown, near the market-house, and commenced firing upon the chasseurs who flanked the left wing of the British army.

However this may be, yet tradition has brought down to our times a terrible legend connected with the retreat of Armstrong's division. The theatre of this legend was the quiet Wissahikon, and this is the story of ancient tradition.

KEATING SIMONS.[27]

This gentleman was descended from one of the Huguenots. The family tradition is, that the first of them who came to Carolina was an orphan boy, received into the family of Mr. Samuel DuPre, who went from France to England, and there meeting this boy, brought him with his family to America; …

When dinner was ready, his lordship graciously invited Mr. and Mrs. Simmons to dine with him, at their own board, and of their own well provided fare. Mr. Simons said that he could not think of his wife becoming a guest, instead of presiding at her own table, and told his lordship that Mrs. Simons was otherwise engaged, but that he would accept his invitation.

Mr. Simons had cordially brought out his best wine and other liquors, but his lordship inquired of his aids if they did not bring with them some of his old Madeira, and called for a bottle or two. The wine was produced, and was certainly very fine. There was great harmony in the good opinion of its excellence expressed by the company. His lordship pretended to inquire the history of it, whether London particular, or imported direct from Madeira, and the young gentlemen had an answer ready for the occasion. A day or two after their visit, Mr. Simons was informed that the same party had passed through St. Stephen's Parish, and stayed a night at old Mr. Mazyck's plantation. None of the family being there, the servants provided every thing necessary; and when they were gone, it was found that his wine closet had been broken open, and every bottle carried off. Mr. Mazyck prized his wine, as a remedy for the gout, to which he was subject, and Mr. Simons never doubted that it was the same which his lordship enjoyed when at Lewisfield, and pretended that it was a part of his own importation. Such wine could not be imported, it could not be bought, but it might be plundered. …

---

26 Informal name attributed to the area of Roxborough, in Northern Philadelphia.

27 JOHNSON, Joseph, *Traditions and Reminiscences chiefly of the American Revolution in the South: including Biographical Sketches, Incidents and Anecdotes, few of which have been published, Particularly of Residents in the Upper Country*, South Carolina, Walker & James, Charleston, S.C., 1851, pages 294, 297-298.

[Untitled][28]

The following most interesting Revolutionary event, we cut from an Eastern journal, sometime gone by, but omitted at the time to mark the name of; and sorry are we now, that we cannot award the credit by naming the paper: –

Seventy-five years ago, there stood upon the summit of Murray Hill, a handsome country seat, the residence of Robert Murray,[29] a Quaker merchant of much eminence in New York. It was a beautiful country mansion, surrounded with gardens and fruit trees, and just far enough from the city, as it existed at that day, to be delightful, rural and undisturbed from the encroachment of unasked city visitors.

It was toward the hour of two, on a mild afternoon in September, seventy-five years gone by, that a lady in the garb of a Quakeress stood upon the portico of this dwelling, looking anxiously into the road which passed about a hundred yards in front. Her countenance was mild but then expressed great anxiety – and not without reason for ever and anon was heard the loud peal of the cannon, and the rattling fire of musketry, as if men were engaged in deadly strife, and now and then a faint cheer arose amid the clangor of arms.

Up the road in rapid retreat, passed large bodies of soldiery. Artillerymen rode along at the head of their pieces, and baggage carts and ammunition wagons mingled in the melee. It was evident the Americans were leaving the city in rapid flight to save themselves from being cut off from the entrenchments on the upper part of the island.

Three or four negro servants of both sexes stood near to her, to whom she from time to time addressed herself. Presently a black fellow came rushing towards the house, from a branch of the road, his eyes protruding from fright, and hit; mouth extended from ear to ear.

"Oh, missus! down in the meadow near de bay, is a hundred dead sojers, and de English, are driving the Mericans with guns and swords before dem! Oh, missus, sight is horrible!"

"Thee says truly, Cato – the sight is horrible. Why, oh God! will men butcher each other, defacing the image of their Creator, and for what?"

"Oh, see, missus !" exclaimed several of the servants.

Four soldiers of the buff and blue uniform of the continentals, turned from the road up the broad avenue, filled with trees, which led to the house, bearing upon a litter of reversed muskets a young man, from whose body the blood was oozing so fast, that it marked the track along the whole path. Onward they came towards the mansion.

"Cato! Maggy! bring instantly a mattrass and pillows, and place them here in this shady spot. Fly, all of thee. Poor youth! poor youth! he is dying."

---

28 "United Service Journal: Devoted to the Army, Navy and Militia of the United States", October 2, 1852, pages 122-123. (New York City, NY). This episode was also revealed in the American press, namely in the *Democratic State Register*, of December 8, 1851. (Watertown, WI. Published under the title "A Tale of the Revolution"). The episode portrayed in this article, based on true facts, inspired two Broadway shows: "Dearest Enemy", premiered in 1925, and "A Small War on Murray Hill", premiered in 1957. Prior to that, in 1903 the Daughters of the American Revolution unveiled a plaque at the corner of Park Avenue and 37th Street, in New York City, signalling Mary Murray's patriotic intervention with her Madeira wine.

29 Robert Murray (1721-1786), a native of Ireland, who emigrated with his father to Pennsylvania in 1732. There he married Mary Lindley, in 1744, the daughter of a Quaker politician, and converted from Presbyterian to a Quaker. The couple moved to New York in 1753. His business interests were mainly concerned with shipping and overseas trade, and in a few years be became a prominent merchant. The place where they used to live, in Manhattan, is still known as Murray Hill.

Figure 5. Sir William Howe, whose forces were momentarilly stopped by Mrs. Murray and her husband's excellent Madeira, allowing the American troops to safely retreat. Engraving by H. A. Hall, 1872.

The faithful negroes were absent but a moment before they returned with a mattrass, pillows, sheets, blankets, and placed them in a cool corner of the wide portico, which extended the whole length of the mansion. The soldiers came up, and the leader of the party addressed the lady: –

"Madam, our ensign is badly wounded. Our captain directed us, claiming your liberality, to leave him here. The surgeon will soon follow."

"Thee has done right. The shelter God has bestowed upon me shall be open to the unfortunate. Poor youth, poor youth," she exclaimed as they laid him upon a mattrass.

The young officer opened his eyes and gazed around him. His age was not more than twenty – fair-haired, and fair-skinned, but pale, very pale, for the signs of death were too strongly marked on his white and even brow to be mistaken. His eyes were of deep blue; as they fixed their glance upon the fine expressive features of the Quaker lady, he murmured almost audibly –

Mother.

"Poor boy, thou hast a mother living, then – one who perhaps is now lifting her voice to God to save thee from the dealings of the bloody calling into which thou hast fallen. Raise his head, soldier, a little more. He will soon be at rest. But the last sentence was murmured to herself.

The surgeon now came rapidly up the avenue, and was soon at the side of the youth. He felt of his pulse, opened his vest, and two gun shots were seen, around which the blood was fast congealing.

"Poor Dick, he has seen his last fight." said the surgeon. Either of these wounds, madam, is mortal – he cannot live at longest half an hour. Follow your companions, men, the foe is close behind. My good lady, farewell, I can be of no use here. Let me ask of you the favor to get this poor boy buried by the enemy when they inter their own dead." He bent hastily over the dying ensign, wiped away a tear, and rushed out after the soldiers.

The good Quaker lady took one hand of the youth in her own, and passed her other over his clammy brow, where the cold drops of approaching death were fast gathering. He opened his eyes for the last time, smiled upon the women whose gaze was now fixed upon him, murmured faintly, "Dear mother!" clasped her hand convulsively, and the next instant he ceased to exist.

The lady said not a word. She rose from her recumbent posture, drew a snow-white linen sheet over the bed, and with a stifled sob, looked down the avenue. In different portions of the open orchard appeared soldiers bearing the dying forms of their comrades, which they laid carefully down, and then rushed rapidly towards their regiments passing down the middle avenue. In the space of a moment, more than a dozen soldiers were placed in this way directly around the mansion.

Summoning her servants, one all, the good lady went into the orchard to aid the poor dying soldiers as far as lay in her power. Her attention had not thus long been given? before an officer, in the blue and buff uniform of Washington's staff, came riding at full speed up the road, and turning without slackening his speed toward the mansion. He reined in his steed as he reached the lady, observing her kind actions toward the soldiers.

"I have the honor of addressing Mrs. Murray?"

"If thee means the wife of Robert Murray. I am what thou callest me," replied the lady, looking up.

"My dear madam, pardon my address. The kindness I see displayed tells me I am not mistaken. The Commander-in-chief has sent me to ask the favor, if possible, of your detaining the advance of the British troops by receiving Sir William Howe[30] and his associates with your civilities, as they will probably stop to take a glass of wine, if *requested!*

"My dear madam," – and he bowed his head nearer to the lady, as if in private conference – "a portion of our troops are yet in the city, and they can only escape by the Bloomingdale Road. *You* may prevent the march of the enemy across the Island."

"Tell your General, young man, that I shall offer General Howe *all the civilities in my power.*"

Figure 6. Israel Putnam was only able to safely retreat from the war zone due to Mrs. Murray's patriotic intervention with her husband's Madeira Wine. If she had not done so, he and his men could have been captured or decimated, a fact that could have seriously compromised George Washington's final victory over the British. Engraving by Fabronius, 1864.

"Thanks, Mrs. Murray – thanks!" and the aid rode away.

Not more than five minutes had elapsed from the time the officer departed, when the sound of martial music with notes of victory filled the air, and proclaimed movements of advancing troops. Mrs. Murray went down to the road, and with two or three attendants, awaited their coming.

Indeed it was a brilliant spectacle. An advanced corps of cavalry, in scarlet uniforms, came gallantly up the hill, their trumpets and kettle drums discoursing most eloquent music – next followed a company of grenadiers, then a large number of officers in rich uniform. The foremost officer on horseback was Sir William Howe, Commander-in-chief of the British forces. In frame of body and stature, Sir William equalled Washington, both being above the ordinary height. Here the comparison stopped. The countenance of the British General, so say historians, was harsh, dark and forbidding, now and then lighting up by a smile, which seemed more disagreeable than prepossessing. Onward came the cavalcade, until they reached the gate of which Mrs. Murray was standing, upon whom all eyes were instantly turned.

"Wilt thee not stop and refresh thyselves for season at my mansion? Thee must be fatigued," she said, addressing herself to Sir William Howe and the officers immediately about him.

"Really, Clinton. I think we may as well accept this good lady's offer for a few moments – The troops have had hot work so far, and a general rest will not be amiss. Madam, we accept your offer with pleasure, the more so as it shows you to be a loyal friend of his Majesty, whom I now humbly represent as Commander-in-chief of his forces in North America."

"I am alike the friend of King George and of Congress – of William Howe and George Washington. It becomes me not, a poor, weak thing, of God's making, to dislike any of His creatures."

---

30 Sir William Howe (1729-1814), Commander-in-Chief of the British forces during the American War of Independence.

Sir William Howe bowed, he was too polite to argue political matters with the good Quakeress. He rode into the park, after commanding a general halt of ten minutes for the refreshment of the troops, followed by Sir Henry Clinton,[31] Gen. Knyphausen,[32] commander of the Hessians, Lord Percy, Generals Leslie and Grant, and his staff were dismounted, and followed Mrs. Murray to the mansion.

Refreshments of cake, wine and cold meats were ordered out upon the lawn in profusion, of which the officers partook freely – and tradition says that Sir Henry Clinton, who was a great *bon vivant*, remarked to his superior officer in an under tone, 'that if the cellars of the mansion contained any large quantities of such Madeira, he should like to be billeted there for the campaign.'

In the meantime Mrs. Murray had directed Cato, the black servant, privately to go the top of the mansion, and the instant he saw a large body of men pass a certain point on the Bloomingdale road, to give her the information by signal. I may as well remark that from the hill the road could not be perceived, but from the cupola of the dwelling it was very easily seen.

Nearer an hour then the ten minutes Sir Wm Howe gave orders for the halt of his troops had passed away, yet still before the mansion he lingered with his officers. Mrs. Murray had entertained them not only with refreshments but conversation. The younger portion of the officers had entered the orchard and amused themselves with gathering the fruit with which the trees were bending, ripened under the sun of an early autumn, and thus the time had slipped away unawares.

At length Cato made the requisite signal, and Mrs. Murray turning to the British commander, said: –

"Wilt thee and thy officers step with me to the portico of the mansion? I have a sight for thee all."

This was uttered in so quiet and grave a tone, that their merriment at their triumph over the 'rebels' instantly ceased, their glasses were put down, and Sir William Howe and their Generals followed the Quakeress as requested. Leading them to the end of the portico, she stooping down and lifting the sheet, uncovered the body of the poor continental ensign.

Handsome even in death were the features of the youth. His fair curling hair blew lightly over his marble cheek, in the soft breeze. The buff lining of his uniform was deeply streaked with his life blood, which had gathered in a clotted pool upon the mattrass. The sight was indeed one to awaken emotions in the sternest breast.

"To horse, gentlemen. Madame, such are the fortunes of war. Thanks for your courtesy; – Farewell."

This was the only response of Sir William Howe. What more could he say? In a few moments the blast of the trumpets, and the sound of the drums and fifes told that the troops were on the march to triumph and victory – *for a season*. Thank God, it was *only* for a short season.

The main facts of this sketch are true. Mrs. Murray, the patriotic Quakeress, by detaining Sir William Howe, saved a large body of American troops – near upon three thousand – under the command of Putnam,[33] who would have been penned up in the city with his

---

[31] Sir Henry Clinton (1730-1795), a General of the British forces.
[32] Wilhelm Reichsfreihen und Knyphausen (1716-1800), a German from Hesse-Cassell, who fought in the American Revolutionary War, leading the Hessian mercenaries who fought alongside the British forces.
[33] Israel Putnam (1718-1790), a native of Massachusetts, was an American army general, and the hero of the Battle

men if the British army had crossed the Island sooner. Might not the loss of three thousand troops to Washington at that time have been sufficient to change our whole destinies, as regards a Republic? It is a grave thought. At any rate, all honor to *Mrs. Murray the Quaker lady of olden times.*

[Untitled][34]

An anecdote of a different character is told of Allen's[35] sojourn in New York. Rivington,[36] the "king's printer," a forcible and venomous writer, had incurred Allen's enmity by his caustic allusions to him, and the hero of Ticonderoga swore "he would lick Rivington the very first opportunity he had!" How the printer escaped the threatened castigation shall be narrated in his own words: I was sitting, [says Rivington,] after a good dinner, alone, with my bottle of Madeira before me, when I heard an unusual noise in the street, and a huzza from the boys. I was in the second story, and, stepping to the window, saw a tall figure in tarnished regimentals, with a large cocked hat and an enormous long sword, followed by a crowd of boys, who occasionally cheered him with huzzas, of which he seemed insensible. He came up to my door and stopped. I could see no more. My heart told me it was Ethan Allen. I shut my window and retired behind my table and my bottle. I was certain the hour of reckoning had come. There was no retreat. Mr. Staples, my clerk, came in paler than ever, and, clasping his hands, said, "Master, he has come!" "I know it." "He entered the store and asked 'if James Rivington lived there?' I answered, 'Yes, sir.' 'Is he at home?' 'I will go and see, sir,' I said; and now, master, what is to be done? There he is in the store, and the boys peeping at him from the street." I had made up my mind. I looked at the Madeira – possibly took a glass. "Show him up," said I; "and if such Madeira cannot mollify him, he must be harder than adamant." There was a fearful moment of suspense. I heard him on the stairs, his long sword clanking at every step. In he stalked. "Is your name James Rivington?" "It is, sir, and no man could be more happy than I am to see Colonel Ethan Allen." "Sir, I have come – " "Not another word, my dear colonel, until you have taken a seat and a glass of old Madeira." "But, sir, I don't think it proper –" "Not another word, colonel. Taste this wine. I have had it in glass for ten years. Old wine, you know, unless it is originally sound, never improves by age." He took the glass, swallowed the wine, smacked his lips, and shook his head approvingly. "Sir, I come –" "Not another word until yon have taken another glass, and

---

of Bunker Hill, in 1775, who led the American forces in New York, in 1776, from where he was forced to retreat due to the superiority of the British forces.

34 De PUY, Henry W.[alter], *The Mountain Hero and His Associates*, Dayton & Wentworth, Boston, 1855, pages 262-263; DUYCKINCK, Evert A.[ugustus]; DUYCKINCK, George L.[ong], *Cyclopaedia of American Literature; embracing Personal and Critical Notices of Authors, and selections from their writings. From the Earliest Period to the Present Day; with Portraits, Autographs, and Other Illustrations*, In Two Volumes, Vol. I., Charles Scribner, New York, 1866, page 207. This episode was also told in the American press, namely in the following sources: *Republican Compiler*, July 26, 1847. (Gettysburg, PA. Published under the title "A REMINISCENCE"). Under the title "Singular Anecdote of Ethan Allen", it was revealed in these newspapers: *Daily Free Democrat*, September 21, 1850. (Milwaukee, WI); *Green Bay Advocate*, October 10, 1856. (Green Bay, WI); *Jeffersonian Democrat*, November 21, 1856. (Monroe, Green Co., WI).

35 Ethan Allen (1738-1789), a native of Connecticut and an American Revolutionary War patriot, famous for the capture of Fort Ticonderoga, at the beginning of the conflict, and one of the founders of the state of Vermont.

36 James Rivington (1724-1802), an English-born American journalist, publisher of an infamous Loyalist newspaper, the *Rivington's Gazette*.

then, my dear colonel, we will talk of old affairs, and I have some queer events to detail." In short, we finished two bottles of Madeira, and parted as good friends as if we had never had cause to be otherwise."

CHAPTER III.[37]

... About half way across the beach we met a group of travellers, who proved to be General McIntosh[38] and suite going to the north to join the army.

We mutually stopped to exchange civilities and learn the news. Our minds had for several days been depressed in reflecting upon the critical condition of our national affairs. Gracious God! how were we astonished and transported with joy, on hearing from the General that Burgoyne[39] and his whole army were prisoners of war. In confirmation of the intelligence, he presented us a handbill, printed at Charleston, containing the articles of capitulation. We involuntarily took off our hats and gave three hearty cheers in concert with the roaring of the surge. All considered this glorious event as deciding the question of our eventual Independence. In triumph we carried the joyous news to the hospitable seat of William Alston, Esq., one of the most respectable and affluent planters in South Carolina. We arrived at the close of the day, but were received with open arms, and entertained in the most sumptuous style. With music and his best madeira, we celebrated the great event we had announced, in high glee, to a late hour of the night. ...

JANUARY 25.[40] – A despicable pamphlet lately published in Boston, now commonly called the "*Grey Maggot*," has asserted, "That the only apology which could be made for the conduct of the Continental Congress in adopting the Suffolk resolves,[41] was that they came into this vote immediately after drinking thirty-two bumpers of Madeira, of which the next morning, when their heads were cool, they were ashamed, and then prudently determined not to do the business till after dinner for the future!" If it would not offend the characters of that truly august assembly to take so much notice of this most impudent and false assertion, as seriously to contradict it, we would say, that it appears from the minutes of Congress, that as they sat till late in the afternoon, they never did any

---

37 WATSON, Winslow C., *Men and Times of the Revolution; or, Memoirs of Elkanah Watson, including Journals of Travels in Europe and America, From 1777 to 1842, with his correspondence with public men and reminiscences and incidents of the Revolution*, edited by his son, Winslow C. Watson, Dana and Company, Publishers, New-York, 1856, page 42.

38 General Lachlan McIntosh (1725-1806), a native of Scotland who moved to America early in his life with his parents and a group of a hundred Scottish people, and founded the town of New Inverness, GA. In 1770 he became a leader in the independence movement in Georgia and, in 1776, was commissioned as a colonel of the Georgia militia, and was engaged in the defence of Savannah.

39 General John Burgoyne (1722-1792), a British Army officer who fought in the American War of Independence passing into History as the man who, during the Saratoga campaign, surrendered his army of 5000 men to the American troops, on October 17, 1777.

40 MOORE, Frank, *Diary of the American Revolution. From Newspapers and Original Documents*, Volume I, Charles Scribner, New York, Sampson Low, Son & Company, London, 1860, page 16.

41 The Suffolk Resolves were endorsed by the First Continental Congress on September 17, 1777. These resolves were originally drafted by the leaders of the Suffolk County, in Massachusetts, and contained some measures against the British rule in that state, including the boycott of British imports. Curiously enough, in the list of products not to import was listed Madeira Wine, which can be seen as a nonsense, since many Founding Fathers cherished this wine a lot, and even used to drink it during the Continental Congress in which these Resolves were passed, as can be seen in this text.

business after dinner, and that the Suffolk resolves were acted upon Saturday, in the forenoon. From this instance the public may see to what an astonishing height of unblushing falsehood and the basest calumny against the most respectable characters, the enemies of our common rights have now attained; and how ready they are to perform any dirty drudgery for the sake of procuring or preserving a titled or lucrative place.

4. Madeira, a Presidential Wine

This chapter contains a selection of texts related to the wine taste of the first American Presidents, from the Founding Fathers to the ones that followed them in leading the country. Through them it will be seen that Madeira Wine was present at the White House from the earliest days of the Nation.

4.1. Founding Fathers

4.1.1. George Washington[42]

WASHINGTON AND HIS TIMES.[43]

The New York *Evening Post*, in a notice of the last volume of Irving's Life of Washington,[44] introduces the following anecdotes of Revolutionary times: ...

CAMP LIFE OF WASHINGTON.

On the authority of the Marquis de Chastellux,[45] we have a sketch of Washington's camp life in the winter of 1780:

"There were twenty guests at table that day at head-quarters. The dinner was in the English style, large dishes of butcher's meat and poultry, with different kinds of vegetables, followed by pies and puddings, and a desert of apples and hickory nuts. Washington's fondness for the latter was noted by the Marquis, and indeed was often a subject of remark. He would sit picking them by the hour after dinner, as he sipped his wine and conversed.

"One of the General's aides-de-camp sat by him at the end of the table, according to custom, to carve the dishes and circulate the wine. Healths were drunk and toasts were given; the latter were sometimes given by the General, through his aide-de-camp.

"The conversation was tranquil and pleasant. Washington willingly entered into some details about the principal operations of the war, "but always," says the Marquis, "with a modesty and consciousness which proved sufficiently that it was out of pure complaisance he consented to talk about himself."

"It was about half-past seven when the company rose from the table, shortly after which,

---

[42] George Washington (1732-1799), a native of Colonial Virginia, was one of the main Founding Fathers of the United States. He served as the commander-in-chief of the Continental Army during the American Revolutionary War. He was unanimously elected as the 1st President of the United States of America in 1788, serving for nine years, until 1797.

[43] *Memphis Daily Appeal*, July 12, 1857. (Memphis, TN).

[44] Title of a biography of George Washington, in three volumes, by Washington Irving, published between 1855 and 1859, through Belford, Clarke & Company, in Chicago, New York and San Francisco. This text presents an excerpt from Chapter V, Volume III, page 52. Irving also inserted the following reference to Madeira Wine and George Washington in Chapter XXVI, Volume I, page 193: «Dinner was served at two o'clock. He ate heartily, but was no epicure, nor critical about his food. His beverage was small beer or cider, and two glasses of Madeira. He took tea, of which he was very fond, early in the evening, and retired for the night about nine o'clock.»

[45] François Jean de Beauvoir, Marquis de Chastellux (1734-1788), a French military officer that served during the war of American Independence as a major-general in the French expeditionary forces led by general Comte de Rochambeau. During the war he acted as the main liaison officer between the French commander-in-chief and George Washington.

4. MADEIRA, A PRESIDENTIAL WINE

those who were not of the household departed. There was a light supper of three or four dishes, with fruit and abundance of hickory nuts; the cloth was soon removed; Bordeaux and Madeira wine were placed upon the table, and the conversation went on. Colonel Hamilton was the aid-de-camp who officiated, and announced the toasts as they occurred. "It is customary," writes the Marquis, "towards the end of the supper, to call upon each one for a sentiment – that is to say, the name of some lady to whom he is attached by some sentiment, either of love, friendship, or simple preference." …

NEW PUBLICATIONS.[46]
PERSONAL TRAITS OF WASHINGTON.
RECOLLECTIONS AND PRIVATE MEMOIRS OF WASHINGTON.[47] …

… At a quarter before three precisely, the industrious farmer always returned, changed his dress, and dined at 3 o'clock. He ate heartily at his meal, with no decided taste for any particular kind of food, with the exception of fish, of which he was excessively fond. He partook sparingly of dessert, drank a home-made beverage, and four or five glasses of Madeira wine. After the removal of the cloth, he drank to the health of every person present, and then gave his only toast, "All our friends."

The afternoon was usually devoted to the library. …

[Untitled][48]

An old gentleman who was intimate with George Washington Custis, the adopted son of Washington, has recently given some of Custis' reminiscences for publication. Among other things, it is stated that when the Father of this Country was first elected to the Virginia House of Burgesses among the items of his election expenses were found a hogshead and a barrel of whisky, thirty-five barrels of wine, and forty-three gallons of beer. Washington was never known to be intoxicated, but usually drank five glasses of Madeira wine with his dessert after dinner.

TRADITIONS OF WASHINGTON.[49]
How He Looked, Talked and Lived – His Work and Recreation.
[Washington Cor. Cleveland Herald.]

I have spent much time recently in the grass-grown streets of Alexandria, Va., chatting with the old citizens about George Washington, and gathering together such traditions to

---

46 *New York Daily Tribune*, March 3, 1860. (New York City, NY).
47 Title of the New York's edition of this book, (by his adopted son, George Washington Parke Custis, with a Memoir of the Author, by his daughter, and Illustrative and Explanatory Notes, by Benson J. Lossing), published through Derby & Jackson, in 1860. On the previous year, an edition had been published in Washington, D.C., printed by William H. Moore, under the title *Recollections and Private Memoirs of Washington*, by G. W. Parke Custis, of Arlington.
48 *Springfield Globe-Republic*, January 11, 1885. (Springfield, OH).
49 *The Daily Yellowstone Journal*, January 31 and February 26, 1885. (Miles City, MT).

him as have come down to them from their fathers. Mr. William Carne, the youngest man I talked with, was perhaps 50 years old. He is a newspaper correspondent and litterateur, and he has for years been interested in gathering traditions of Washington. ...

"He was rather fastidious as to his dress, though he wore plain clothes when not on military duty. He always shaved himself, but had a servant to comb and tie his hair every morning. I have heard Mr. Custis say that he rose very early at Mount Vernon, often before daybreak, and as early as 4 a. m. He would, at sunrise, go to his stables and look at his blooded horses. When he came back he had a light breakfast of corn cakes, honey, and tea, or something of that sort, and then he ate nothing more until dinner. I am speaking of his later years. After breakfast he rode over his estate, and at 3 had returned and was dressed for dinner. Dinner was a big meal at Mount Vernon, and Washington ate nothing after it. He usually drank five glasses of Madeira wine at dessert, but I have never heard of his being drunk. He was not opposed to the moderate use of liquor, and when he was first elected to the house of burgesses of Virginia, among the items of his election expenses were a hogshead and a barrel of whisky, thirty-five gallons of wine, and forty-three gallons of beer. ...

Figure 7. George Washington, the 1st President of the United States, whose favorite drink was Madeira Wine, used to drink two glasses a day. *Portrait started by Gilbert Stuart and finished by Peale.*

The Washington Family's Wine.[50]

The Washington drank wine at their dinners, and the collection of Washington's household effects in the National museum in Washington shows that the family possessed much aesthetic taste. Their china contained many choice bits. In the collection there is an immense punch bowl and several wine services, and the chaplain of congress the time Washington was president records a presidential dinner at which he says that Gen. Washington had a silver pint cup of beer at his plate, which he drank while eating. The Washington family had much fine wine in their cellars at Mount Vernon; but though Washington drank a glass or so of Madeira at his meals, there is no record of his ever having drunk too much. That Martha Washington appreciated the value of good wine is evidenced by her will. In it she gives a pipe of wine to George Washington Parke Custis, and directs that all the wine bottles in the Mount Vernon vaults be equally divided between her granddaughters and grandson. – Frank G. Carpenter.[51]

---

[50] *The Daily Yellowstone Journal*, March 18, 1887. (Miles City, MT).
[51] Frank George Carpenter (1855-1924), a native of Ohio, was an author, photographer and lecturer on geography, and wrote a series of popular travel books.

4. MADEIRA, A PRESIDENTIAL WINE

GEORGE WASHINGTON[52]
Gossip About Him Gathered From Various Sources.
OF HIS LIFE AND CHARACTER. …
Washington as a Drinking Man.

Everyone drank in the days of Washington, and the father of this country always had wines on his table. I have nowhere seen it stated that he ever drank to excess, although he usually consumed five glasses of Madeira wine at dessert. During his youth he was a very fair politician, and among the items of his election expenses when he was a candidate for the house of burgesses of Virginia were a hogshead and a barrel of whisky, thirty-five gallons of wine and forty-three gallons of beer. …

4.1.2. John Adams[53]

Figure 8. John Adams, the 2nd President of the United States, also used to drink Madeira regularly. *Painting by Asher B. Durand.*

MY DEAR,

Sitting down to write you is a scene almost too tender for my state of nerves.

It calls up to my view the anxious, distressed state you must be in, amidst the confusion and dangers which surround you. I long to return and administer all the consolation in my power, but when I shall have accomplished all the business I have to do here, I know not, and if it should be necessary to stay here till Christmas, or longer, in order to effect our purpose, I am determined patiently to wait. …

I shall be killed with kindness in this place. We go to Congress at nine, and there we stay, most earnestly engaged in debates upon the most abstruse mysteries of state, until three in the afternoon; then we adjourn, and go to dine with some of the nobles of Pennsylvania at four o'clock, and feast upon ten thousand delicacies, and sit drinking Madeira, Claret and Burgundy till six or seven, and then go home fatigued to death with business, company, and care. Yet I hold it our surprisingly.

Yours, most affectionately,
JOHN ADAMS.

---

52 *The Kansas City Journal*, February 20, 1898. (Kansas City, MO); *The St. Paul Daily Globe*, February 20, 1898. (Saint Paul, MN. Published under different titles: "PRESIDENT WASHINGTON – SIDELIGHTS ON THE NATION'S FIRST CHIEF – Washington as a Drinker"); *The McCook Tribune*, February 17, 1899. (McCook, NE. Published under the title "Washington as a Drinking Man").

53 John Adams (1735-1826), a native of Massachusetts, was an American Founding Father, a statesman, diplomat, and a leading advocate of American independence from Great Britain. He served as the 2nd President of the United States, from 1797 to 1801, and also as Vice-President, during Thomas Jefferson's administration.

4.1.3. Thomas Jefferson[54]

JEFFERSONIAN SIMPLICITY.[55]

Extracts from an old account book kept by Thomas Jefferson while he was President, give us some idea of the remarkable "simplicity" with which his name of late has been associated. His trip to Washington from Monticello after he was elected, occupied five days and cost $21 current money. ...

The first year of his Presidency wiped out his salary of $25,000 with something to spare. From March 4, 1801 to March 4, 1802 he paid out for – Wines [$]2797.38 ...

The peculiar weakness of the great man was wine, of which he kept on hand a large stock of the choicest vintage. During the eight years which he occupied the Presidential mansion he spent for this exhilarating drink:

Figure 9. Thomas Jefferson, the 3rd President of the United States, was a true *connoisseur* of Madeira, which he often drank, both at the White House and at his mansion, in Monticello. *Portrait by Rembrandt Peale, 1800.*

$2,622.33 in 1801
1,975.72 in 1802
1,253.57 in 1803
2,668.94 in 1804
546.41 in 1805
659.38 in 1806
553.97 in 1807
75.58 in 1808
Total, $10,855.90

It will be observed that the decline in this item of expense was very rapid during the last four years. The first term had probably taught the second President that bit of Yankee economy, namely, to let every man pay for his own "treat."

Madeira was his favorite beverage, which he bought by the pipe. During his first term of four years, he emptied eight pipes of this brand alone. It is not to be presumed that he drank all the liquor for which he paid. He had, as most Presidents have, accommodating friends. ...[56]

---

54 Thomas Jefferson (1743-1809), a native of Virginia, was an American Founding Father, the principal author of the Declaration of Independence, in 1776, and the 3rd President of the United States, serving from 1801 to 1809.

55 *Biddeford Daily Journal*, February 20, 1885. (Biddeford, ME).

56 A shorter and untitled version of this text – and somewhat critical of its content – was revealed, a year later, on another source, namely in *The Marshall Statesman*, of March 19, 1886, (Marshall, MI), in these words: «We hear much democratic talk now-a-days about "Jeffersonian simplicity," – it is all humbug. Thomas Jefferson was a genial man, of urbane manners and fascinating powers of conversation. He spent $11,000 for Madeira wine used at the White House during his eight years of rule. Cleveland seems to have imitated "Jeffersonian simplicity" in eight respects, for it is reported that there were eight kinds of wine on his tables at a late state dinner.»

4.1.4. James Madison[57]

Figure 10. James Madison, the 4th President of the United States, although of temperate habits, used to drink a glass of Madeira a day, and used to serve choice Madeira to his guests at home. *Painting by John Vanderlyn.*

… Mrs. Madison was a remarkably fine woman. She was beloved by every body in Washington, white and colored. Whenever soldiers marched by, during the war, she always sent out and invited them in to take wine and refreshments, giving them liberally of the best in the house. Madeira wine was better in those days than now, and more freely drank. …

Mr. Madison, I think, was one of the best men that ever lived. I never saw him in a passion, and never knew him to strike a slave, although he had over one hundred; neither would he allow an overseer to do it. … He was temperate in his habits. I don't think he drank a quarter of brandy in his whole life. He ate light breakfasts and no suppers, but rather a hearty dinner, with which he took invariably but one glass of wine. When he had hard drinkers at his table, who had put away his choice Madeira pretty freely, in response to their numerous toasts, he would just touch the glass to his lips, or dilute it with water, as they pushed about the decanters. For the last fifteen years of his life he drank no wine at all. …[58]

4.1.5. Benjamin Franklin[59]

Although he had never been a US President, Benjamin Franklin was one of the signers of the Declaration of Independence and an influential Founding Father of America, and therefore we insert here some extracts of his autobiography, where it can be seen that Madeira Wine was present at some important moments in his early life, either when he became a printer, or when he managed to borrow some cannons from the English-appointed Governor of New York to be used in the defence of Philadelphia, in the 1740's against an eventual attack of Spanish or French military forces, and also in 1756, when a newly-appointed Governor of Philadelphia tried to become his friend by drinking Madeira together.

---

[57] James Madison (1751-1836), a native of Virginia, was an American statesman and political theorist, and the 4th President of the United States, serving from 1809 to 1817. He is hailed as the "Father of the Constitution" for being instrumental in the drafting of the United States Constitution and as the key champion and author of the United States Bill of Rights.

[58] JENNINGS, Paul, *A Colored Man's Reminiscences of James Madison*, George C. Beadle, Brooklyn, 1865, pages 16-18.

[59] Benjamin Franklin (1706-1790), a native of Boston, MA, was one of the Founding Fathers of America. He was also a leading author, printer, political theorist, politician, postmaster, scientist, musician, inventor, satirist, civic activist, statesman, and diplomat. On the scientific field, he is noted for his discoveries and theories regarding electricity. He earned the title of "The First American" due to his early and tireless campaigning for colonial unity, and was also the first United States Ambassador to France.

CHAPTER II.[60]

... Sir William Keith,[61] governor of the province, was then at Newcastle, and Captain Holmes, happening to be in company with him when my letter came to hand, spoke to him of me, and showed him the letter. The governor read it, and seemed surprised when he was told my age. He said I appeared a young man of promising parts, and therefore should be encouraged; the printers at Philadelphia were wretched ones; and, if I would set up there, he made no doubt I should succeed; for his part, he would procure me the public business, and do me every other service in his power. This my brother-in-law Holmes afterward told me in Boston, but I knew as yet nothing of it; when, one day, Keimer and I being at work together near the window, we saw the governor and another gentleman (who proved to be Colonel French, of Newcastle, in the province of Delaware), finely dressed, come directly across the street to our house, and heard them at the door.

Keimer ran down immediately, thinking it a visit to him; but the governor inquired for me, came up, and with a condescension and politeness I had been quite unused to, made me many compliments, desired to be acquainted with me, blamed me kindly for not having made myself known to him when I first came to the place, and would have me away with him to the tavern, where he was going with Colonel French to taste, as he said, some excellent Madeira. I was not a little surprised, and Keimer stared with astonishment. I went, however, with the governor and Colonel French to a tavern, at the corner of Third-street, and over the Madeira he proposed my setting up my business. He stated the probabilities of my success, and both he and Colonel French assured me I should have their interest and influence to obtain for me the public business of both governments; ...

CHAPTER VIII.[62]

... The officers of the companies composing the Philadelphia regiment, being met, chose me for their colonel; but, conceiving myself unfit, I declined that station, and recommended Mr. Lawrence, a fine person, and a man of influence, who was accordingly appointed. I then proposed a lottery to defray the expense of building a battery below the town, and furnished with cannon. If filled expeditiously, and the battery was soon erected, the merlons being framed of logs and filled with earth. We bought some old cannon from Boston; but, these not being sufficient, we wrote to London for more, soliciting, at the same time, our proprietaries for more assistance, though without much expectation of obtaining it.

Meanwhile, Colonel Lawrence, Mr. Allen, Abraham Taylor, and myself were sent to New York by the associators, commissioned to borrow some cannon of Governor Clinton.[63] He at first refused us peremptorily; but at dinner with his council, where there was great drinking of Madeira wine, as the custom of that place then was, he softened by degrees, and said he would lend us six. After a few more bumpers he advanced to ten; and at length

---

60 WELD, Rev. H. Hastings, *Benjamin Franklin: his Autobiography; with a narrative of His Public Life and Services.,* with numerous designs by *J. G. Chapman*, Harper & Brothers, Publishers, New York; Sampson Low, London, 1849, pages 48-49.
61 Sir William Keith (1669-1749), a native of Scotland, was a lieutenant-governor of colonial Pennsylvania and Delaware, who is noted for encouraging young Benjamin Franklin to set up his own printing business in Philadelphia.
62 WELD [1849], pages 174-176.
63 George Clinton, who served as Governor of New York from 1777 to 1795.

Figure 11. Benjamin Franklin, in his young days, standing guard during the defense of Philadelphia. *Book illustration. Author unknown.*

Figure 12. Benjamin Franklin drinking Madeira Wine with the newly-appointed governor of Philadelphia, Captain William Denny. *Book illustration. Author unknown.*

he very good-naturedly conceded eighteen. They were fine cannon, eighteen-pounders, with their carriages, which were soon transported and mounted on our batteries, where the associators kept a nightly guard while the war lasted, and among the rest I regularly took my turn of duty there as a common soldier. ...

CHAPTER XII.[64]

Our new governor, Captain Denny,[65] brought over for me the before-mentioned medal from the Royal Society, which he presented to me at an entertainment given him by the city. He accompanied it with every polite expressions of his esteem for me, having, as he said, been long acquainted with my character. After dinner, when the company, as was customary at that time, were engaged in drinking, he took me aside into another room, and acquainted me that he had been advised by his friends in England to cultivate a friendship with me, as one who was capable of giving him the best advice, and of contributing most effectually to the making his administration easy; that he therefore desired of all things to have a good understanding with me, and he begged me to be assured of his readiness on all occasions to render me every service that might be in his power. He said much to me, also, of the proprietor's good disposition toward the province, and of the advantage it would be to us all, and to me in particular, if the opposition that had been so long continued to his measures was dropped, and harmony restored between him and the people; if effecting which, it was thought no one could be more serviceable than myself; and I might depend on adequate acknowledgments and recompenses. The drinkers, finding we did not return immediately to the table, sent us a decanter of Madeira, which the governor made a liberal use of, and in proportion became more profuse of his solicitations and promises. ...

---

[64] WELD [1849], pages 250-251.
[65] William Denney, who served as Deputy Governor of Pennsylvania from 1756 to 1759.

LONDON, February 10.[66]

While Dr. Franklin was at Paris, last war, he happened to mention at his table, that he had but little Madeira wine, upon which an American guest sent him three dozen. A few days later, this gentleman was thrown into the Bastile, and confined there several weeks, without the least information what he was accused of, only, on his earnest enquiry, one of the officers told him he was afraid it would go hard on him, and asked him whether he was a Catholic, and would be attended by a Priest, which he, being a Protestant, refused. After some time, a bottle of wine was brought, and he was asked whether he knew what wine it was, and was ordered to drink it; he complied, and answered, that he believed it was some of his own Madeira. At length he was released, and then discovered that Dr. Franklin had been taken ill soon after he received his present, and the suspicious French emissaries imagined that this injured gentleman had been hired by the English court to poison the Doctor.

OBSERVATIONS ON THE GENERALLY PREVAILING DOCTRINES OF LIFE AND DEATH.[67]
TO THE SAME.[68]

Your observations on the causes of death, and the experiments which you propose for recalling to life those who appear to have been killed by lightning, demonstrate equally your sagacity and humanity. It appears that the doctrines of life and death, in general, are yet but little understood. …

I have seen an instance of common flies preserved in a manner somewhat similar. They had been drowned in Madeira wine, apparently about the time when it was bottled in Virginia, to be sent to London. At the opening of one of the bottles at the house of a friend where I was, three drowned flies fell into the first glass which was filled. Having heard it remarked that drowned flies were capable of being revived by the rays of the sun, I proposed making the experiment upon these. They were therefore exposed to the sun, upon a sieve which had been employed to strain them out of the wine. In less than three hours two of them began by degrees to recover life. They commenced by some convulsive motions in the thighs, and at length they raised themselves upon their legs, wiped their eyes

Figure 13. Benjamin Franklin in London, in 1767. This Founding Father of America used to drink Madeira Wine regularly. In a letter to a French disciple he describes the famous episode of two flies having survived the Atlantic crossing in a corked bottle of Madeira wine and being resurrected in London through their exposure to the sun's rays. *Painting by David Martin, displayed in the White House.*

---

66 *The Massachusetts Gazette,* May 15, 1786. (Boston, MA); *The Independent Ledger, and The American Advertiser,* May 15, 1786. (Boston, MA). Benjamin Franklin lived in Paris for several years, from December 1776 to 1785, serving as Commissioner for the United States. Around the end of his office a peculiar incident happened to him, involving Madeira Wine, as narrates this late 18th century newspaper article.

67 [FRANKLIN, Benjamin], *The Essays, Humorous, Moral and Literary, of the late Dr. Benjamin Franklin,* John West and Co., Boston, 1811, pages 62-64. This letter by Benjamin Franklin underlines the qualities of Madeira Wine to preserve life, an episode which was seen as an anecdote by the American press of the time.

68 To Jacques Barbeau-Dubourg (1709-1779), the French disciple of Benjamin Franklin, and translator of his works.

with their forefeet, beat and brushed their wings with their hind feet, and soon after began to fly, finding themselves in Old England, without knowing how they came thither. The third continued lifeless until sun-set, when, losing all hopes of him, he was thrown away.

I wish it were possible, from this instance, to invent a method of embalming drowned persons, in such a manner that they might be recalled to life at any period, however distant; for having a very ardent desire to see and observe the state of America an hundred years hence, I should prefer to an ordinary death, the being immersed in a cask of Madeira wine, with a few friends, until that time, then to be recalled to life by the solar warmth of my dear country! But, since, in all probability, we live in an age too early, and too near the infancy of science, to see such an art brought in our time to its perfection, I must, for the present, content myself with the treat, with you are so kind as to promise me, of the resurrection of a fowl or a turkey-cock.

It should also be mentioned that Benjamin Franklin passed by Madeira island, at least once, in August 1762, upon his return to America from England, where he lived for some years.[69] The sources we checked do not mention his views about Madeira Wine – in one of them he only alludes to the island's grapes, among other fruits grown there – but during his short stay at Madeira he surely must have tried, or even bought, some wine to take home with him, in a time when Madeira Wine trade with the United States was at its peak.

---

69 «Dr. Franklin sailed from England about the end of August, having resided there more than five years. In a letter, dated at Portsmouth on the 17th of that month, bidding farewell to Lord Kames, he said; "I am now waiting here only for a wind to waft me to America, but cannot leave this happy island and my friends in it without extreme regret, though I am going to a country and a people that I love. I am going from the old world to the new; and I fancy I feel like those, who are leaving this world for the next; grief at the parting; fear of the passage; hope of the future." He arrived at Philadelphia on the 1st of November. The fleet, in which he took passage, under the convoy of a man-of-war, touched at Madeira, and was detained there a few days. They were kindly received and entertained by the inhabitants, on account of the protection afforded them by the English fleet against the united invasion of France and Spain. Not longer after his return to Philadelphia, he wrote to Mr. Richard Jackson a full account of the island of Madeira, its population, soil, climate, and productions; but the letter has never been published, and it is supposed to be lost.» SPARKS, Jared, *The Life of Benjamin Franklin*, Tappan & Dennet, Boston, 1844, page 269. On another source Benjamin Franklin mentions, in a letter to a friend in London, an experiment he did aboard the ship that took him to Madeira on that year: «To Dr. Pringle, London. *Relating a curious Instance of the Effect of Oil on Water*. PHILADELPHIA, Dec. 1, 1762. During our passage to Madeira, the weather being warm, and the cabin windows constantly open, for the benefit of the air, the candles at night flared and ran very much; which was an inconvenience. At Madeira we got oil to burn, and with a common glass tumbler or breaker, slung in wire, and suspended to the ceiling of the cabin, and a little wire hoop for the wick, furnished with corks to float on the oil, I made an Italian lamp, that gave us a very good light all over the table. [...]» [FRANKLIN, Benjamin], *Memoirs of Benjamin Franklin. Written by Himself, and Continued by his Grandson and Others, with his Social Epistolary Correspondence, Philosophical, Political, and Moral Letters and Essays, and his Diplomatic Transactions as Agent at London and Minister Plenipotentiary at Versailles, Augmented by much matter not contained in any former edition with a Postliminious Preface*, In Two Volumes, Vol. II, M'Carty & Davis, Philadelphia, 1840, page 279. On another book it is also stated that after his second return to England, in December 1764, he wrote a letter to Lord Kames, describing his homeward bound trip to America two years before, where he briefly describes the island of Madeira: «"We had a pleasant passage to Madeira, where we were kindly received and entertained; our nation being then in high honor with the Portuguese, on account of the protection we were then affording them against France and Spain. It is a fertile island, and the different heights and situations among its mountains, afford such temperatures of air, that all the fruits of northern and southern countries are produced there; wheat, apples, grapes, peaches, oranges, lemons, plantains, bananas, and so forth. Here we furnished ourselves with fresh provisions of all kinds; and after a few days proceeded on our voyage, running southward until we got into the trade-winds, and then with them westward till we drew near the coast of America. [...]"» HOLLEY, O.[rville] L.[uther], *The Life of Benjamin Franklin*, George F. Cooledge & Brother, New York, [1848], pages 369-370.

4.2. Other U.S. Presidents

4.2.1. John Quincy Adams[70]

THE KENT AND HONE CLUBS.[71]
Interesting Reminiscences by Mr. Thurlow Weed.

Mr. THURLOW WEED has contributed to the Commercial Advertiser some interesting reminiscences respecting the Kent and Hone Clubs of this City, inspired more especially by the receipt of a note from Mr. ROBERT L. Hone, inclosing a brief account of the public dinner given by 250 prominent citizens to DANIEL WEBSTER[72] in 1831 – this account being copied from the manuscript journal of Mr. HONE's father, Mr. PHILIP HONE,[73] an old merchant prince and former Mayor of our City. …

Mr. ROSWELL L. Colt[74] resided in Park-place. He was a widely known, highly enterprising, and universally respected merchant and manufacturer. In 1808 or '9, he became the clerk of Mr. OLIVER, of Baltimore. Toward the close of the war of 1812, Mr. OLIVER sent young COLT to Europe to purchase depreciated American securities, and he lay in a large stock of goods for shipment by the first vessels that should leave England upon the restoration of peace. These trusts were so successfully executed that Mr. OLIVER not only took young COLT into partnership, but gave him his daughter[75] in marriage, and finally, when Mr. OLIVER died, Mr. COLT inherited the

Figure 14. John Quincy Adams, the 6th President of the United States, was a true *connoisseur* of Madeira Wine. At a public dinner given in 1831 he was able to identify eleven types of Madeiras that had been brought unannounced to the table. *Photographic copy of a daguerreotype taken in 1843.*

well-chosen varieties of old Madeiras, protected by dust and cobwebs in the wine-vault of his father-in-law. I remember, on one occasion, to have been present, along with Mr. Hone, Mr. Grinnell, Mr. Blutchford, Gen. Bowen, Gen. J. W. Webb, Edward Curtis, Charles King, Gov. Seward, &c., &c., at a dinner given by Mr. Colt to ex-President John Quincy Adams. Madeira wines had not then gone out of fashion. Indeed, except a glass of hock with the oyster or his half-shell, a glass of sherry after soup, and champagne with meats, Madeira was the staple during and after the dessert. Gentlemen who on those occasions passed the largest number of approved brands, such as "Essex, Jr.," "Donna Gama," "Bingham," "Rapid,"

---

[70] John Quincy Adams (1767-1848), a native of Massachusetts, and son of former President John Adams, was the 6th President of the United States, serving from 1825 to 1829. He was also one of the greatest diplomats in American history, Senator and Congressional representative.

[71] *The New York Times*, March 19, 1871. (New York City, NY).

[72] Daniel Webster (1782-1852), a native of Massachusetts, was a leading American statesman and senator during the period leading up to the Civil War. He was also the 14th and 19th United States Secretary of State.

[73] Philip Hone (1780-1851) was Mayor of New York City for a single term, from 1826 to 1827. He is also notable for his diary, kept from 1828 to the day he died, in 1851, which was published, in two volumes, in 1889, in New York, through Dodd, Mead and Company, in two volumes, under the title *The Diary of Philip Hone 1828-1851*. This work contains several references to Madeira Wine, of which this is one.

[74] Roswell Lyman Colt (1779-1856).

[75] Margaret Oliver (1790-1856).

"Reserve," "Farquhar," "Benefactor," "Butler," "March and Benson of 1809," "Black Cork," &c., excited the admiration, if not the envy, of their neighbors. At this dinner, Mr. COLT, after the cloth had been removed, produced fourteen different kinds of delicious old Madeiras, and the circumstance which occasioned general surprise was, that as the different wines passed quietly around the table unannounced, the peculiarly delicate taste of Mr. ADAMS enabled him to name eleven of them! ...[76]

4.2.2. Andrew Jackson[77]

Jackson's Last Night in the White House.[78]

The New York Times has a voluminous account of the past life of William Allen,[79] of Ohio. When he was elected senator, being in Washington on the 3rd of March, he went to the white house where, being well-known to the attendants, he was shown into the president's bed chamber. Chief Justice Taney[80] and Senator Forsythe, of Georgia, afterward minister to Spain and secretary of state, were already in the room, and Jackson himself active and to a certain extent restless, as usual, stood in the middle of the room smoking a short corn cob pipe. He congratulated Allen warmly upon his election to the senate, and then calling to a young trishman who acted as his body servant and waiter, turned to his visitors and said:

"Gentlemen, I think the occasion will warrant me in breaking over one of my rules. Let us drink a little Madeira."

The wine was brought. Jackson took a small glassful – it was the first liquor he had been known to touch for several months – and then, asking his friends to excuse him for a few moments, he finished writing the letter upon which he was engaged, sealed, directed it, and lighting his cob pipe again took a whiff of two, and stood silently watching the face of a great, tall, old-fashioned clock which stood in the corner. It was five minutes before midnight, five minutes before the beginning of the day upon which Andrew Jackson would cease to be president of the United States. Slowly the minute hand moved around the dial. The silence of the room became almost painful. It was

---

[76] A summary of this article was published in another source, under the title "Personal": «At a dinner given by a private gentleman of New York, at which JOHN QUINCY ADAMS was one of the guests, there were fifteen varieties of Madeira wine on the table, and such an expert and connoisseur was Mr. Adams that he was able to name nine of the varieties by the taste and bouquet without seeing the labels on the bottles.» *Lancaster Daily Intelligencer*, September 5, 1881. (Lancaster, PA); *The Saint Paul Daily Globe*, March 19, 1882. (Saint Paul, MN. Published with a slight difference, i. e., the text starts with the expression "Some fifty years ago,".

[77] Andrew Jackson (1767-1845), a native of South Carolina, was the 7th President of the United States, being in office from 1829 to 1837. He was both a politician and Army general, having defeated the Creek Indians at the Battle of Horseshoe Bend, in 1814, and the British at the Battle of New Orleans, a year after. He was nicknamed "Old Hickory" because of his toughness and aggressive personality, having fought duels, some of which were fatal to his opponents.

[78] *The Decatur Daily Review*, July 28, 1879. (Decatur, IL). This same episode was recounted under a different title, "How Jackson Went Out of Office.", in a different source, namely in *The Postville Review*, of July 17, 1886. (Postville, IA).

[79] William Allen (1803-1879), a native of North Carolina, who moved to Ohio after the death of his parents. He was a Democratic Representative, Senator, and the 31st Governor of Ohio.

[80] Roger Brooke Taney (1777-1864), a native of Maryland, was the 5th Chief Justice of the United States, holding that office from 1836, until the day he died, in 1864. One of his controversial rulings was that African Americans, having been considered inferior at the time the Constitution was drafted, were not part of the original community of citizens and therefore could not be considered citizens of the United States.

broken by the clear, sharp bell of the clock striking the last hour of a day that had gone forever. Then Jackson, starting suddenly and looking towards his friends, said, with a quick nervous laugh:

"Gentlemen, I am no longer president of the United States, but as good a citizen as any of you."

Subsequently he expressed to them a feeling of great relief at the prospect of escaping from the official cares which had begun to weigh most heavily upon him, saying to Allen, among other things of the same sort, "I am very glad to get away from all this excitement and bother."

That day Van Buren was inaugurated president of the United States, and Jackson, at the end of his second term, left the white house – left it so poor that he was obliged to borrow $5,000 with which to rebuild "Hermitage," his old family mansion, which some time before had been burned to the ground.

Figure 15. Andrew Jackson did not drink much but during his last day at the White House he drank a little Madeira to celebrate his departure from office. *Photographic copy of an 1844-45 daguerreotype.*

4.2.3. Martin Van Buren[81]

[Untitled][82]

The ship HENRY CLAY recently arrived at New York, from India, having on board a cask of wine marked "MARTIN VAN BUREN, Vice President of the United States." Upon this fact the Mercantile Advertiser remarks: "That Henry Clay,[83] or even a ship bearing his name, should have been the medium of furnishing Martin Van Buren with the first cask of Madeira wine from India, for the table of the Vice President, may be considered a pleasant little incongruity; but that its arrival in this country should have been delayed until Mr. Van Buren, so much needs it to keep up his spirits, in some degree heightens the joke, more particularly as it is no doubt thought by some that Mr. Clay has *perhaps* had a little hand in preparing the bitter home draught to Mr. Van Buren, while the ship Henry Clay has been instrumental in bringing Mr. Van Buren a cordial to revive his sinking energies."

---

[81] Martin Van Buren (1782-1862), a native of New York, was the 8th President of the United States, serving from 1837 to 1841. Before his presidency he had been the 10th Secretary of State, from 1829 to 1831, and the 8th Vice President, from 1833 to 1837, both under President Andrew Jackson. He was the first President to be born a United States citizen, having grown up in a Dutch speaking family. He was also the first self-made man to occupy such a high position, having been born into poverty and becoming wealthy through his law practice.

[82] *Alexandria Gazette*, May 30, 1834. (Alexandria, VA). The same fact was also published, in other words, in another source, namely in *The Richmond Whig & Public Advertiser*, of May 30, 1834. (Richmond, VA. Published under the title "From the New York Advocate. – HENRY CLAY AND MARTIN VAN BUREN.").

[83] Henry Clay (1779-1852), a lawyer, politician and orator who represented Kentucky in both the Senate and the House of Representatives, being also Secretary of State between 1825 and 1829.

WASHINGTON IN VAN BUREN'S TIME.[84]
An Anonymous Writer in The Atlantic.

Figure 16. Martin Van Buren, the 8th President of the United States, used to give numerous entertainments at the White House, and was also a guest in many private parties in Washington, at which the choicest Madeira Wine was served. *Engraving by John Sartain reproducing an 1839 painting by Henry Inman.*

… President Van Buren endeavored to restore the good feeling between the Administration and Washington "society," which had been ruptured during the political rule of General Jackson. He gave numerous entertainments at the White House, and used to attend those given by his Cabinet, which was regarded as an innovation, as his predecessors had never accepted social invitations. Ex-President Adams, the widow of President Madison, and the widow of Alexander Hamilton[85] each formed the centre of a pleasant coterie, and the President was open in the expression of his desire that the members of his Cabinet and their principal subordinates should each give a series of dinner-parties and evening receptions during the successive sessions of Congress.

The dinner-parties were very much alike, and those who were in succession guests at different houses often saw the same table ornaments, and were served by the same waiters, while the fare was prepared by the same cook. The guests used to assemble in the parlor, which was almost invariably connected with the dining-room by large folding doors. When the dinner was ready the folding-doors were thrown open, and the table was revealed, covered with dishes and cut-glass ware. A watery compound called vegetable soup was invariably served, followed by boiled fish, over-done roast beef or mutton, roast fowl or game in their season, and a great variety of puddings, pies, cake and ice-cream. The fish, meat and fowl were carved and helped by the host, while the lady of the house distributed the vegetables, the pickles, and the dessert. Champagne, without ice, was sparingly supplied in long, slender glasses, but there was no lack of sound claret, and with the dessert several bottles of old madeira were generally produced by the host, who succinctly gave the age and history of each. The best madeira was that labeled "the Supreme Court," as their Honors the Justices used to make a direct importation every year, and sip it as they consulted over the cases before them, every day after their dinner, when the cloth had been removed. Some rare old specimens of this Supreme Court wine can still be found in Washington wine-cellars. …

---

[84] *New York Daily Tribune*, June 27, 1880. (New York City, NY); *The Harrisburg Daily Patriot*, July 6, 1880. (Harrisburg, PA). Under the title "Washington Fifty Years Ago.", this article was published in the following sources: *The Fresno Republican*, August 7, 1880. (Fresno, Fresno County, CA); *Racine Daily Argus*, November 19, 1880. (Racine, WI); *The Athens Messenger*, March 3, 1881. (Athens, OH).

[85] Alexander Hamilton (1755/57-1804) was a Founding Father of the United States, soldier, economist, political philosopher, one of America's first constitutional lawyers and the first United States Secretary of the Treasury.

4.2.4. John Tyler[86]

PRESIDENT TYLER.[87]
THE WAY THE EARLY VIRGINIA PRESIDENTS BOUGHT THEIR WINE.
Rum From Santa Cruz and Wine From the Island of Madeira – ...

Gen. John Tyler, the son of the president, who was his father's private secretary while he was in the White House and who still lives at Washington, has given me some interesting fa ts regarding the way the early Virginia presidents bought their wines. Said he: "My father's cellars were always full of choice wines and liquors, all of which he imported himself, as was the custom of the old Virginia families of his day. His brandy he bought at London through William Taylor, of Norfolk, who was a noted wine dealer forty years ago. It cost $4 a gallon and was of a quality which you could now hardly get for $20 a bottle. His rum was imported for him in the same way from Santa Cruz; and his Madeira, which was the staple wine of the time, was brought from the Island of Madeira in the way common among the old Virginia planters. Every year my father would set aside ten or twelve acres for Madeira corn. This was a short eared, pearly grained variety noted for his hardiness. It was the only kind of corn at that day which would stand the long shipment across the ocean. Each of these acres would produce from fifty to a hundred bushels of corn. When it was harvested it would be sent to a ship which a number of the planters, such as Chief Justice Marshall[88] and others, had chartered to carry their corn to Madeira. At the island this corn would be exchanged for wine, the rate being one bushel of corn to a gallon of wine, and the wine would be brought back in the same ship to Virginia. It came to us in barrels or pipes and we bottled it at home. ...

– Frank G. Carpenter in Lippincott's Magazine.

Figure 17. In his younger years, a long time before being elected as the 10th President of the United States, John Tyler used to get his Madeira Wine directly from the island, and would pay for it through the exchange of several hundred bushels of corn from his own plantation, in Virginia. Engraving c. 1826. Author unknown.

---

86 John Tyler (1790-1862), a native of Virginia, was the 10th President of the United States, serving from 1841 to 1845. Before being elected Vice President in 1840 he had served as state legislator, governor, U.S. Representative and U.S. Senator. He reached the Presidency after the death of President William Henry Harrison (1773-1841), the first American head of state to die in office.
87 *Springfield Globe-Republic*, December 13, 1886. (Springfield, OH); *Hamilton Daily Democrat*, December 20, 1886. (Hamilton, OH); *The Critic*, December 26, 1886. (Logansport, IN); *Titusville Morning Herald*, December 29, 1886. (Titusville, PA); *Wichita Eagle*, February 3, 1887. (Wichita, KS); *Eau Claire Daily Free Press*, February 7, 1887. (Eau Claire, WI).
88 John Marshall (1755-1835), a native of Virginia, was appointed Chief Justice of the United States Supreme Court by President John Adams, in 1801, being in office until 1835. His court opinions helped to lay the basis for American constitutional law and made the Supreme Court of the United States a coequal branch of government along with the legislative and executive branches. He was the longest-serving Chief Justice and the fourth longest-serving justice in the US Supreme Court history, having dominated the court for over three decades. Previously he had served in the U. S. House of Representatives and was Secretary of State, under the same President, from 1800 to 1801.

4.2.5. James Buchanan[89]

From the Philadelphia Press.
Mr. Buchanan's Madeira.[90]

Figure 18. James Buchanan, the 15th President of the United States, loved "a good glass of nutty old Madeira" and cherished this wine so much that he even thought about renaming the state of Ohio as "island of Madeira". *Portrait by George Healy, 1859.*

Our excellent President, Mr. Buchanan, has taken it into his head that the sovereign State of Ohio should be called the "island of Madeira," that everybody worth of his favor should be called Medary; that Medary should be appointed to all the offices, and that nobody but Medary should get any place whatever. – We always knew that Mr. Buchanan was fond of a good glass of nutty old Madeira – the Wager Madeira – the Reigart Madeira – the regular Madeira of the old school. But, then, there must be an alternative; we cannot live on fish all the time. A change now and then is good for the strongest constitution; even the Turk must rest from his indulgences. Not so, however, with Mr. President Buchanan. He has fallen dead in love with Sam Medary[91] – or, as they syllable it in Ohio, Sammedary. Our worth Executive has no eyes for anybody else. He sees Sam only; he drinks Medary only. Vain to remind him that there is such a statesman as William Allen[92] at Chillicothe; that Dave Tod lives near Cleveland; and that old Pennsylvania is full of representatives in the Buckeye State[93] – the President sees Sam and longs for Madeira only. …

TOPICS OF THE DAY.[94]

Some idea of the quality of the wine which President Buchanan was accustomed to keep may be inferred from the following reminiscence which Mr. C. W. Mitchell of Saratoga Springs communicates to the New York World:[95]

---

[89] James Buchanan (1791-1868), a native of Pennsylvania, was the 15th President of the United States, being in office from 1857 to 1861. He was the only president from this state, the only president who remained a lifelong bachelor, and the last president born in the 18th century.
[90] *Cleveland Morning Leader*, November 18, 1858. (Cleveland, OH).
[91] Sam Medary (1801-1864), a native of Pennsylvania, moved to Ohio in 1825, where he served, later on, in the Ohio House of Representatives and the Ohio State Senate. He was appointed by President James Buchanan as the 3rd Territorial Governor of Minnesota, in 1857.
[92] See Note 79.
[93] Nickname of the state of Ohio, derived from the abundant buckeye trees that once covered its hills and plains.
[94] *The Washington Critic*, January 28, 1886. (Washington, DC).
[95] This newspaper published the same thing, in slightly different words, nine years after, under the title "Wine at the White House – (Correspondence of the Philadelphia Times.)": «It is a well-known fact that President Arthur gave many wine suppers in the White House to his personal friends, and that some of them were exceedingly hilarious. President Garfield was not a total abstainer, and neither was President Hayes. It has never been denied that Gen. Grant had a fondness for strong drink, and during the war President Lincoln expressed the belief that it would be a good thing to have all his Generals drink the same kind of liquor that Grant drank. I was here when Abraham Lincoln was elected, but shortly before President Buchanan left the White House I visited the Executive Mansion and went to the wine cellar with Mr. Goodchild, the steward. President Buchanan had about as fine an assortment of wines as any gentleman ever kept, and he made a liberal use of them for himself and for his friends. I recollect that there were a number of bottles

"About the time that Mr. Buchanan's term of office expired, I had occasion to visit the White House in search of the steward, Mr. Richard Goodchild, to whom I always presented my bills for game, oysters, fish, &c., furnished by Mr. John Hancock, at that time proprietor of a restaurant located on Pennsylvania avenue. I found Mr. Goodchild in the wine cellar, overseeing the packing of wines, &c., belonging to President Buchanan. Mr. Goodchild called my attention to a few in number (I won't say one was uncorked and a portion drank) of quart chunky black bottles, about the same shape as quart bottle used for bottling Congress water. The bottles contained Madeira wine and the label, written thereon, read, 'Madeira wine, bottled 1776.' If my memory serves me right, there were less than twelve bottles, but the wine was there. I can taste it to this day. It was old-time rock, sure."

4.2.6. Ulysses S. Grant[96]

More Presents Coming In.[97]

WASHINGTON, Feb. 8. – President Grant has received a cask of noble Madeira wine by the United States ship Guerriere, which lately arrived from the European squadron. It is a present from that celebrated warrior Admiral Alden,[98] commonly known as Fighting Jimmy.

The Hon. George M. Robeson,[99] Secretary of the Navy, has also received a quarter of a cask of the same wine. This shows that in Fighting Jim's opinion he is of just one-quarter as much importance as Gen. Grant. …

4.3. Madeira Wine at the White House

[Untitled][100]

Two hours is the time of a White House dinner, consisting of eleven courses of meats, followed by game, ices and fruits, with sherry, hock, sauterne, champagne and old Madeira.

---

of choice Madeira wine which the labels said had been bottled in 1776. Mr. Goodchild remarked that he would not be there much longer, nor in any position to extend a favor to a friend, and so he uncorked one of those bottles. I never tasted such good wine before or since. I remember the taste and the effect of that wine as though I had partaken of it only yesterday.» *The World*, May 13, 1895. (New York City, NY).

96 Ulisses S. Grant, born Hiram Ulysses Grant (1822-1885), was a native of Ohio, and the 18th President of the United States, serving from 1869 to 1877. Before reaching the Presidency he had been a successful general in the second half of the Civil War. Under Grant, the Union Army defeated the Confederate military, which effectively put an end to the war and secession with the surrender of Robert E. Lee's army at Appomattox. President Grant believed in the protection of African-American voting and civil rights.

97 *The Sun*, February 9, 1872. (New York City, NY).

98 James Alden, Jr. (1810- 1877), a native of Portland, ME, who was a Rear-Admiral in the U.S. Navy. At this time of his life and career he was commanding the European Fleet.

99 George Maxwell Robeson (1829-1897), a native of New Jersey, was a politician of the Republican Party, who had served in the Union Army during the American Civil War and was also Secretary of the Navy during the Grant administration.

100 *Daily State Gazette*, February 22, 1870. (Trenton, NJ. Published in the "MISCELLANEOUS AND NEWS ITEMS" section).

MR. SCHURZ[101] remarks, that the fathers of the Republic would tell us, if they could, to praise them less and imitate them more. And yet Carl keeps right on drinking lager beer, and smoking Havana cigars, though it is well known that Washington's favorite drink was Madeira wine, and that Jefferson always smoked Virginia leaf in a corn-cob pipe. – *Denver Tribune*.[102]

THE PRESIDENT'S TABLE. ...[103]

... THE PRESIDENT'S WINES, CIGARS, ETC.

Figure 19. Chester A. Arthur, the 21st President of the United States, once received an offer of some "Resurrection Madeira", a famous wine that had been buried during Sherman's march to the sea, in order to avoid being looted by the Union Army. Photo by Charles Milton Bell, 1882.

... A LETTER FROM "UNCLE SAM."

The attention of THE STAR reporter was attracted by a letter which was tacked to the shelf containing bottles of choice Madeira. Upon examining it he found that it was an autograph letter from the lamented Sam Ward[104] to the President,[105] giving the history of the neighboring Madeira, which he had sent to the President in 1881. The letter was written in the famous epicure's characteristic style. He went on to say that during Sherman's march to the sea[106] the Charleston Jockey club buried their old and choice Madeira wine, and thus saved it. Some six years previous to the date of the letter the wine was exhumed and sold to a member of the house of Baring & Co., of London, and was shipped to England. Through English ignorance of the proper treatment of such wines it never recovered from the voyage, and its owner grew sick of his purchase. Learning three years later that the whole lot was for sale Mr. Ward and Jim Keege purchased it, and by proper treatment restored the pristine glory of the wine. Mr. Ward presented several demijohns of it to the President. Owing to the loss of the original catalogue, the exact age of the wine could not be ascertained, but none of it was less than 40 years old, and most of it over half a century. Mr. Ward gave directions how it should be bottled and stored, and subscribed himself "Yours, affectionately, Uncle Sam." ...

---

101 Carl Christian Schurz (1829-1906), was a German revolutionary, American statesman, Union Army general, during the American Civil War, and also a journalist, newspaper editor, orator and Senator, being the first German-born American elected to the Senate. He also served as the 13th Secretary of the Interior, from 1877 to 1881.
102 *The Weekly Kansas Chief*, December 23, 1875. (Troy, KS).
103 *The Evening Star*, July 14, 1884. (Washington, DC).
104 Samuel Cutler Ward (1814-1884), a native of New York City, also know in his days as "Uncle Sam", was a poet, author and gourmet, who was widely known in post-Civil War America as the "King of the Lobby", for combining delicious food, fine wine and good conversation to create a new type of lobbying in Washington.
105 Chester Alan Arthur (1829-1886), a native of Vermont, was the 21st President of the United States, serving from 1881 to 1881, who is widely mentioned in this newspaper article.
106 William Tecumseh Sherman (1820-1891), a native of Ohio, was an American soldier, businessman and educator. He served as a General during the American Civil War. His famous "march to the sea", the name commonly attributed to the Savannah campaign, was marked by the capture of the cities of Atlanta and Savannah, and the destruction of everything he found on his way, in order to undermine the Confederates' capacity to wage war.

CHAPTER II.[107]
TRAVELING IN "YE OLDEN TIME."

… The expense of living at the Indian Queen was not great. The price of board was one dollar and seventy-five cents per day, ten dollars per week, or thirty-five dollars per month. Transient guests were charged fifty cents for breakfast, the same for supper, and seventy-five cents for dinner. Brandy and whisky were placed on the dinner-table in decanters, to be drunk by the guest without additional charge therefor. A bottle of real old Madeira imported into Alexandria was supplied for three dollars, sherry, brandy, and gin were one dollar and a half per bottle, and Jamaica rum one dollar. …

CHAPTER VII.[108]
THE KITCHEN CABINET.

… Assemblies were held once a week between Christmas Day and Ash Wednesday, to which all of the respectable ladies of the city who danced were invited. It was also customary for those of the Cabinet officers and other high officials who kept house to give at least one evening party during each session of Congress, invitations for which were issued. … At ten the guests were invited to the supper-table, which was often on the wide back porch which every Washington house had in those days. The table was always loaded with evidences of the culinary skill of the lady of the house. There was a roast ham at one end, a saddle of venison or mutton at the other end, and some roasted poultry or wild ducks midway, a great variety of home-baked cake was a source of pride, and there was never any lack of punch, with decanters of Madeira. …

CHAPTER XII.[109]
JACKSON[110] AND HIS ASSOCIATES.

… One evening – as the story is told – at a dinner-party, over the Madeira and walnuts, which formed the invariable course in those days, Mr. Preston launched forth in a eulogium on the extraordinary power of condensation, in both thought and expression, which characterized the ancient Greek and Latin languages, beyond anything of the kind in modern tongues. …

---

107 POORE, Ben Perley, *Perley's Reminiscences of Sixty Years in the National Metropolis*, Vol. I., A. W. Mills, Publishers, Michigan, [1886], pages 43-44.
108 POORE [1886], pages 108-109.
109 POORE [1886], page 178.
110 Andrew Jackson. See Note 77.

CHAPTER XVI.[111]
SOCIAL AND POLITICAL LIFE AT WASHINGTON

... The dinner-parties were very much alike, and those who were in succession guests at different houses often saw the same table ornaments, and were served by the same waiters, while the fare was prepared by the same cook. ... Champagne, without ice, was sparingly supplied in long, slend glasses, but there was no lack of sound claret, and with the dessert several bottles of old Madeira were generally produced by the host, who succinctly gave the age and history of each. The best Madeira was that labelled "The Supreme Court," as their Honors, the Justices, used to make a direct importation every year, and sip it as they consulted over the cases before them every day after dinner, when the cloth had been removed. Some rare specimens of this wine can still be found in Washington wine-cellars. ...

CHAPTER XIX.[112]
HARRISON'S[113] ONE MONTH OF POWER.

... The diplomatic representative of Great Britain, during the greater part of the Jackson Administration was the Right Honorable Charles Richard Vaughan,[114] who was a great favorite among Congressmen and citizens at Washington, many of whom were his guests at the Decatur Mansion, then the British Legation. He was a well-educated and well-informed gentleman with the courteous manners of the old school. When recalled after ten years' service at Washington, he was a jovial bachelor of fifty, fond of old Madeira wine and a quiet rubber of whist. ...

CHAPTER XXXIV.[115]
PIERCE[116] AT THE HELM.

... Old Madeira wine has always been very popular in Washington, especially on the tables of their Honors the Justices of the Supreme Court. For many years supplies were obtained from the old mercantile houses in Alexandria, which had made direct importations prior to the Revolution. During the Fillmore Administration[117] many Washington cellars were replenished at the sale of the private stock of wines and liquors of the late Josiah Lee, of Baltimore. Fifty demijohns of various brands of Madeira were sold at prices

---

[111] POORE [1886], pages 221-222.

[112] POORE [1886], page 262.

[113] William Henry Harrison (1773-1841), a native of Virginia, was a military officer and politician, being also the 9th President of the United States, serving only for a month, in 1841. He died on his 32nd day in office, victimized by a pneumonia. His Presidency was the shortest in the U.S. presidential history.

[114] Sir Charles Richard Vaughan (1774- 1849), a British diplomat who was appointed Envoy-extraordinary and Minister-plenipotentiary to the United States in 1825.

[115] POORE [1886], pages 429-430.

[116] Franklin Pierce (1804-1869), a native of New Hampshire, was the 14th President of the United States, being in office for a single term, from 1853 to 1857. Before reaching the Presidency he had served in the U.S. House of Representatives and the Senate. He also took part in the Mexican-American War, becoming a brigadier general in the Army.

[117] Millard Filmore (1800-1874), a native of New York, served as the 13th President of the United States, from 1850 to 1853.

ranging from twenty-four dollars to forty-nine dollars per gallon, and one lot of twenty-two bottles commanded the extreme price of fifteen dollars and fifty cents per bottle, which at five bottles to the gallon is at the rate of seventy-seven dollars and fifty cents per gallon. ...

THE TASTES OF PUBLIC MEN.[118]
Different Styles of Drinks That They Affect.
From the New York World.

... Gen. Washington invariably drank five glasses of madeira at dinner, and the item of whiskey formed a large part of his campaign expenses when he ran for the House of Burgesses of Virginia. Thomas Jefferson was a good judge of wines, and spent $11,000 for drinks while he was President. He never put wine on the table until after the cloth was removed. Webster,[119] who visited him at Monticello, says that his wines were of the rarest kinds. Madison[120] had a good wine cellar, but he drank only a single glass of madeira at dinner, and his body-servant said that he did not believe he had drunk a quart of brandy in his whole life. Andrew Jackson served barrels of orange punch to his guests the night after he was inaugurated, and his punch was brought in buckets into the East room, and the carpet ruined by the eagerness of the guests to get at it. President Tyler[121] imported his own madeira, and his brandy cost him four dollars a gallon. He brought his rum from Santa Cruz, and he raised the corn on his own estate which was exchanged for his madeira wine. Old stagers tell me that Franklin Pierce drank more than he should have done while he was in the Senate and before he was elected President, and that Buchanan's[122] wine cellars were preyed upon by his servants.

... President Arthur[123] was a connoisseur of wines. He had them at all his state dinners, and usually at his private ones as well. His choicest brand was some Madeira which Sam Ward[124] gave him, but he never drank to excess. President Cleveland[125] is said to be fond of beer, though I am told at the White House that he does not drink two dozen bottles a year. He uses wines at his state dinners, and has a fine barrel of old brandy in his cellar. ...
FRANK G. CARPENTER.

---

118 *The Anderson Intelligencer*, January 5, 1888. (Anderson, SC).
119 Daniel Webster. See Note 72.
120 James Madison. See Note 57.
121 John Tyler. See Note 86.
122 James Buchanan. See Note 89.
123 Chester A. Arthur. See Note 105.
124 See Note 104.
125 Stephen Grover Cleveland (1837-1908), a native of New Jersey, was the 22nd President of the United States, being in office in two nonconsecutive terms, from 1885 to 1889 and from 1893 to 1897, and therefore is the only American to be counted twice in the numbering of the presidents.

PRESIDENTIANA.[126]

The pictorial record of the Presidents of the United States which THE CALL published on Sunday is a history of manners and customs as well as politics. Even in the small matter of costume and personal appearance it illustrates the fluctuations of taste and fashion. …

The Presidents differed in their table habits. Washington and the Adamses[127] drank fine old Madeira, but with moderation. Jackson,[128] Johnson[129] and one or two others always kept a whisky-bottle on the shelf, and somewhere near was a glass and a pitcher of water. Buchanan[130] took his wine at dinner, but rarely indulged afterward. Lincoln[131] was as indifferent to what he drank as he was to what he ate. If he had a preference it was for sound old rye. Grant[132] and Arthur[133] were fond of champagne; the latter was compelled by his health to be careful not to indulge freely. Polk[134] and Hayes[135] were teetotalers and reveled on toast and water. Mr. Harrison[136] took a little wine at dinner, but very little, and he was particular about its quality. At a banquet in this city a special wine was ordered for him. Mr. Cleveland[137] was some time ago ordered by his doctors to be careful of his living, and now, while he is not a total abstainer, he rarely drinks anything but water. It is curious that of all the Presidents we have had there has been but one who was ever seen drunk.

---

126 *The Morning Call*, March 6, 1893. (San Francisco, CA).
127 John Adams and John Quincy Adams. See Notes 53 and 70.
128 Andrew Jackson. See Note 77.
129 Andrew Johnson (1808-1875), a native of North Carolina, was the 17th President of the United States, serving from 1865 to 1869. As Abraham Lincoln's Vice President he reached the presidency when Lincoln was assassinated, on April 14, 1865, at a time when the Civil War was coming to an end.
130 James Buchanan. See Note 89.
131 Abraham Lincoln (1809-1865), a native of Kentucky, was the 16th President of the United States, serving from 1861 until his assassination in 1865. He successfully led the country through the American Civil War, preserving the Union while ending slavery and promoting economic and financial modernization.
132 Ulysses S. Grant. See Note 96.
133 Chester A. Arthur. See Note 105.
134 James Knox Polk (1795-1849), a native of North Carolina, who was the 11th President of the United States, being in office from 1845 to 1849. Before reaching the Presidency he had served as the 17th Speaker of the House of Representatives, from 1835 to 1839, and Governor of Tennessee, from 1839 to 1841.
135 Rutherford Birchard Hayes (1822-1893), a native of Ohio, was the 19th President of the United States, serving from 1887 to 1881. As president he oversaw the end of the Reconstruction and the United States' entry into the Second Industrial Revolution but failed to reconcile the divisions that had led to the American Civil War fifteen years before.
136 William Henry Harrison. See Note 113.
137 Stephen Grover Cleveland. See Note 125.

4.3. MADEIRA WINE AT THE WHITE HOUSE

5. Madeira Wine and the 4th of July Celebrations

Contemporary wine-related books claim as a fact that Madeira Wine was used to toast the signature of the Declaration of Independence on the 4th of July, 1776. We did not find that reference in American primary sources, namely in the press of the time, neither did John Hancock, the author of the book *Oceans of Wine: Madeira and the Emergence of American Trade and Taste*. (YUP, 2009). However we do not deny that possibility since Madeira Wine was widely consumed in Colonial America, in the major cities alongside the eastern seaboard – and Philadelphia was one of them – as well as used on solemn occasions and, last but not least, was the favorite wine of the Founding Fathers of the Nation. However, adding two and two together it all points to the strong possibility that Madeira Wine was, in fact, used to toast the birth of America as a new sovereign country, thus making it what we might term the 'Independence Wine'.

After the proclamation of the Declaration of Independence by the Second Continental Congress, this document was also proclaimed with great joy and excitement in many cities and capitals throughout the newly-established country, and we found evidence of two of them, in which toasts were drunk to celebrate this festive occasion, one in Richmond, VA, and the other one in Newport, RI. In the former this event was accompanied by "patriotic toasts",[138] which, in the America of the time, was a synonym to Madeira toasts, and in the latter, thirteen toasts were drunk, in honor of the thirteen new States,[139] which we assume were also made with Madeira Wine, a cherished product among the Newport's elite. Having in mind these contemporary sources to the Declaration of Independence we might not be too far from the truth by saying that there was more than one toast to America as a free country on that day, probably thirteen, one for each new state.

---

[138] «WILLIAMSBURG, *August* 10./ [...]/On Monday last, being court day, the Declaration of Independence was publicly proclaimed in the town of Richmond, before a large concourse of respectable freeholders of Henrico county, and upwards of 200 of the militia, who assembled on that grand occasion. It was received with universal shouts of joy, and re-echoed by three vollies of small arms; The same evening the town was illuminated, and the members of the Committee held a club, when many patriotic toasts were drank. Although there were near 1000 people present, the whole was conducted with the utmost decorum, and the satisfaction visible in every countenance sufficiently evidences their determination to support it with their lives and fortunes.» *The Pennsylvania Ledger: Or the Virginia, Maryland, Pennsylvania, and New-Jersey Weekly Advertiser*, August 24, 1776. (Philadelphia, PA).

[139] «Thursday last, at 11 o'clock in the forenoon, his Honour the Governor, attended by such members of the Upper and Lower Houses of Assembly as were in town, and a number of the inhabitants, went in procession to the State-House, escorted by the Cadet and Light Infantry companies, where at twelve o'clock was read the act of Assembly concurring with the Most Honourable General Congress, in their Declaration of INDEPENDENCE; the Declaration was also read, at the conclusion of which thirteen vollies were fired by the Cadets and Light Infantry; the Artillery Company next fired 13 cannon, and a like number of new cannon (cast at Hope Furnace) were discharged at the Great Bridge; the ships Alfred and Columbus likewise fired 13 guns each, in honour of the day – At 2 o'clock his Honour the Governor, attended and escorted as above, proceeded to Hacker's-hall, where an elegant entertainment was provided on the occasion; after dinner the following toasts were drank, viz./ 1. The 13 free and Independent States of America./ 2. The Most Hon. the General Congress./ 3. The Army and Navy of the United States./ 4. The State of Rhode-Island and Providence plantations./ 5. The Commerce of the United States./ 6. Liberty to those who have spirit to assert it./ 7. The friends of the United States in every part of the earth./ 8. General Washington./ 9. The Officers of the American army and navy./ 10. May the Crowns of Tyrants be crowns of thorns./ 11. The memory of the brave officers and men who have fallen in defence of American liberty./12. May the Constitution of each separate State have for its object the preservation of the civil and religious rights of mankind./ 13. May the Union of the States be established in justice and mutual confidence, and be as permanent as the pillars of nature. [...]» *The New-York Journal; or, The General Advertiser*, August 8, 1776. (New York City, NY).

5. MADEIRA WINE AND THE 4TH OF JULY CELEBRATIONS

5.1. Newspapers

In the first decades of the United States as a free country, the Fourth of July was usually celebrated with Madeira Wine, which was liberally used to make patriotic toasts to the anniversary of the Independence, and we found some evidences of that fact in the American press of the time. According to our research, the first 19th century text that alludes to it was a poem, published in 1800, in a newspaper, by someone who hid behind the pseudonym Phylographon. Other than this interesting poetical composition we also present six more texts in which Madeira Wine can be seen being used,to make multiple toasts, during the Independence Day.

For the GEORGETOWN GAZETTE.[140]

HUZZA! for the 4th of July,
Its blest approach is nigh,
    To make us glad;
We'll caper, dance and sing,
We'll make the town to ring,
    And cheer the sad.

John Adams long ago,
Said, that it must be so,
    We must be free;
Tho' Dick'son wife and good,
His arguments withstood,
    With specious plea.

Prepare that little gun,
Which now we shoot for fun,
    Let's make a noise;
'Till rouse the sluggish louts,
When join'd with all our shouts,
    And please the boys.

This gun in times of yore,
When fir'd along our shore,
    Mow'd Britons down;
But since we've blessed peace,
The deadly *ball* shall cease,
    But not the *sound*.

Man well the trusty fort,
That guards our pleasant port,

---

[140] *The Georgetown Gazette*, July 2, 1800. (Georgetown, SC).

Figure 20. "Congress Voting Independence". After the proclamation of the Declaration of Independence several toasts to the new nation (one for each new state) were most likely made with Madeira Wine.
Painting by Edward Savage and/ or Robert Edge Pine.

> Keeps safe the fair;
> Let Sampit's muddy stream,
> With its red light'ning gleam,
> And mount in air.
>
> Huzza! for *Dinner* then,
> Good capon, duck and hen,
> And turkey too;
> In Independence's cause,
> We'll exercise our jaws,
> And waste renew.
>
> Good old Madeira wine,
> We'll string along the line,
> To fire our souls;
> Sing songs, crack merry jokes,
> And swear we're noble folks,
> Not tyrants' tools.
>
> We'll toast our president,[141]
> And those good men he's sent,[142]

---

141 John Adams. See Note 53.
142 Allusion to William Vans Murray (1760-1803), a native of Maryland, an American lawyer, politician and statesman, who was sent to France, in February 1799, by President John Adams, on a peace mission that put an end to the Quasi-War with France, with the Convention of 1800, also known as the Treaty of Mortefontaine, signed on September 30,

> To Madame France;
> We'll swear unless she do,
> Her good old ways renew,
> We'll hurl the lance.
>
> When drunk as lord and king,
> We'll real about and sing
> Equality;
> Buss ebon ladies bright,
> To cheer the blessed night,
> When *we* are free.
> PHILOGRAPHON.

[Untitled][143]

On Monday, 4th July, inst. a very respectable company of federal republicans assembled at the house of Mr. Richard Newman, in Contreville, Queen Ann's County, and after partaking of an excellent dinner, and some good Madeira, captain James Kent was chose president, and the company drank the following toasts, to wit:

1. The Day that ranked America among the independent nations of the world – May it ever be celebrated by free and independent citizens.
2. The memory of the illustrious George Washington.
3. The president of the United States.[144]
4. The virtuous minority.
5. Unison to all parties on conflictual ground.
6. The memory of those heroes that fell in the glorious revolution.
7. The commerce, agriculture and manufactures of the United States.
8. Rufus King,[145] late envoy at the court of St. James's.
9. The constitution of the United States – May it stand the test of time, and receive the United support of all true Americans.
10. The army.
11. The navy.
13. May the spirit and principles of Washington preside in our army, navy, and all the departments of government.
14. Restoration to the judiciary system of the United States.
15. The tree of rational liberty – May its sacred branches never be blasted by anarchy or tyranny.
16. The true interest of America – May that predominate over the interest of party.

1800. Also sent in this mission were Oliver Ellsworth (1745-1807) and Richardson Davie (1756-1820).
143 *Eastern Shore Herald and Intelligencer*, July 19, 1803. (Easton, MD).
144 Thomas Jefferson. See Note 54.
145 Rufus King (1755-1827), a native of Massachusetts, was an American lawyer, politician and diplomat who served as the U.S. Minister to the Court of St. James from 1796 to 1803, and later on, from 1825 to 1826.

17. The American Fair – The Spirit of '76.
The greatest good order, peace and harmony, prevailed through the whole.

Capt. JAMES KENT, *President*,
Capt. JACOB SETH, *Vice President*.
4th July, 1803.

[Untitled][146]

On the 4th inst. a number of the inhabitants of Plymouth and Thornton assembled at Colonel Baker's in Campton, where they were joined by the most respectable citizens of that town, to commemorate a DAY so justly noticeable by every real friend to America. Having walked in procession to the meeting house, where an Oration was delivered by John Rogers, Esq. of Plymouth, they returned to the festive table, elegantly spread, under the shady bower; and with hilarity, well tempered glee, and decorum, spent the social hour: in which the following toasts were drank in the pure juice of Madeira, accompanied each by the discharge of a cannon – viz.

1. *The Day we celebrate* – may it never be forgotten, till Americans shall forget themselves.
2. *The United States of America* – may political Quacks and foreign Mountebanks never again be suffered to feel their pulse or finger their *Cash!*
3. *The memory of WASHINGTON* – the great – the good.
4. JOHN ADAMS – the *Solon* of Massachusetts, and the *Belisarius* of America.
5. *The President of the Union*[147] – let him rise in the esteem of the virtuous, in exact proportion as he shall sink in the view of knaves.
6. *The State of New-Hampshire* – may she continue to emerge, till not a single digit shall remain eclipsed.
7. *Governor GILMAN*[148] – let him continue in Office till a greater crime than well doing shall appear in evidence against him.
8. *The two Houses of Congress* – may their doors always fly open to Truth and Equity, whenever they shall knock for entrance.
9. *Doctor Napoleon Bonaparte* – the meritorious inventor of a certain cure for that terrible fever called Liberty & Equality.
10. *The Navy of England* – the only check to French plunder and domination.
11. *The American Navy* – may it increase and flourish in spite of Folly and *Dry Docks*.
12. *Morris, Ross, Bayard, Griswold* – and all other veteran defenders of our Constitution and Laws.
13. *The Rev. CLERGY* – learned, virtuous and watchful – may they ever guard

---

[146] *Courier of New Hampshire*, July 14, 1803. (Concord, NH); *Dartmouth Gazette*, July 23, 1803. (Hanover, NH. Published under the title "INDEPENDENCE – From Plymouth, July 12").
[147] Thomas Jefferson. See Note 54.
[148] John Taylor Gilman (1753-1828), who served twice as Governor of New Hampshire, from 1799 to 1805, and later on, from 1813 to 1816.

their flocks from the shoals and quicksands of danger and deception, as well from the quags of barbarism and superstition.

14. *Pemigewasset*[149] - may its waters never be polluted by turbid streams from the fountains of corruption.

15. *Ohio and Mississippi* – may a freshet of just indignation ever sweep from their channels all barriers to their peace and prosperity.

16. *The Farmers of this County* – let them never, for the sake of mere novelty, yoke *asses* with their oxen.

17. May every sword become a ploughshare, and every spear a pruning hook, throughout the world.

THE CINCINNATI.[150]

The birth day of our National Independence was commemorated on the 4th inst. at Boston, by his decreasing band of war-worn veterans in their usual spirit of renewed friendship and interesting recollections. They dined together at Concert Hall, which is always reserved for their accommodation, told their old stories, sung their old songs, and fought over, in review, their old battles; and as this sort of harmless fighting precludes the shedding of blood, plentiful libations of Madeira and Claret were poured out in lieu of it.

The following historical items, in form of toasts were each recognized and attested to in full flowing bumpers: –

1st *Toast* – The day, and the memory of the immortal WASHINGTON! His valor and skill defended in the field, what wisdom and patriotism decreed in the cabinet.

2d *Toast* – The President of the United States.[151]

3d *Toast* – Independence! – boldly declared, pertinaciously denied, but fairly proved and confirmed by the 10 following arguments: –

4th *Toast* – 1st *arg.* – Lexington! – Where we taught our foes
'The true war dance of Yankee reels
'And manual exercise of heels.' – McFingal.[152]

5th *Toast* – 2d *arg.* – Bunker's Hill! – Where more execution was done by father's long gun, than by kings' arms and bayonets.

6th *Toast* – 3d *arg.* – Retreat from Ty' – . We lost our tents and baggage, but Burgoyne and his army were soon pledged to redeem them.

7th *Toast* – 4th *arg.* – Saratoga! – Thousands drink health at her springs, but there the British Lion drank death from our Brooks. – [Drank after the President had retired.]

---

149 Author's Note (AN): *A river running near the place of meeting.* [Name of a river from the state of New Hampshire].
150 *National Aegis*, July 11, 1821. (Worcester, MA).
151 James Monroe (1758-1831), a native of Virginia, was the 5th President of the United States, serving from 1817 to 1825. He was the last president who was a Founding Father of America, the third of them to die on Independence Day.
152 Quote from the poem "McFingal: a Modern Epic Poem. Or, The Town-meeting", a mock poetical composition by John Trumbull (1750-1831), an American poet from Connecticut.

8th Toast – 5th arg. – Princeton! – A coup de main! – Planned by genious without supplies, and executed by bravery without slices and stockings.
9th Toast – 6th arg. – Trenton! – A ruse de guerre – Where with a great many light before them, the enemy lost their Hessians in the dark.
10th Toast – 7th arg. – Brandywine and Germantown! – Battles won and lost. New troops always gain by fighting.
11th Toast – 8th arg. – Monmouth! – A fair trial of strength and discipline by day, and the result acknowledged by the enemy, in their retreat by night.
12th Toast – 9th arg. – Stoney Point! – A tough storm! which swept the enemy's standard from the walls, and tore up his proud defiance by the roots.
13th Toast – 10th arg. – Yorktown! – A stubborn fact! which produced a verdict in our favor, and left no cafe for the Court at Westminster.
14th Toast – The American Fair! – We fought for Liberty and Independence, but reject not the silken chains which Beauty offers.
Volunteer – Old times! Some of us are old enough to remember them – the rest will never forget their influence.

The advance of this Corps, able to take the field upon this occasion, consisted of only 21, supported by about the same number of vigorous and spirited recruits who fill their fathers' vacancies in the line, and who will ever do the honor to their memory. – *Gazette*.

From the Nantucket Inquirer.[153]
FOURTH OF JULY.

We have no disposition to undervalue an orderly and decent commemoration of the day on which took place the act of casting from our nation's neck the yoke of thraldom. We are fearful however that these celebrations are becoming rather bacchanalian; and that amidst the festivities which they call forth, there is not always that serious and patriotic remembrance of the occasion which is calculated to perpetuate its blessings. When half a dozen glasses of Madeira have comfortably been ingurgitated, a man's brain most commonly begins to be a little misty; insomuch that the year 1776 is very rarely perceptible through so foggy a medium. Of this we may judge from the usual series of *toasts*. At first it is "the day we celebrate" – anon come the "heroes of the revolution" – and the "statesman of the present age." drank up in very modest libations. But soon as the liquor has attained its level and commences flowing *up hill*, the guests, laying in its copious flood, likewise begin to grow valorous and pugnacious. Then we hear of bravery, and chivalry, and conquests, and blood, and thunder! The "army and the navy," bayonets, gunpowder and all, are gulped down together – and "our enemies," perchance, are at the next moment vomited forth in utter ignominy! Finally the more rebellious passions become prostrate, the uproar sinks beneath the table, and the last effort subsides into a sentiment in *honour* of "the fair sex."

---

153 *Salem Gazette*, July 18, 1823. (Salem, MA). Referring that this article had also been transcribed from the *Nantucket Inquirer*, it was published in these sources: *Rhode Island American, and General Advertiser*, July 22, 1823. (Providence, RI); *Vermont Journal*, August 4, 1823. (Windsor, VT); *American Sentinel*, August 13, 1823. (Middletown, CT); *Edwardsville Spectator*, September 13, 1823. (Edwardsville, IL).

The newspapers from all quarters are crowed with insignificant details of these junkettings – as though it were popular debauchery, and not national virtue, on which we must rely for the maintenance of our Independence. Some of the papers are literally crammed with odes, and prayers, and orations, and processions, and toasts. About 100 of the latter we counted in a single paper; among which our eye glanced accidentally upon this: "Republicans and Federalists: May they unite in one general cause, in support of Government, Religion, and Laws." This is probably an improvement upon the Boston Tobacconists' sign-board, whereon were delineated an Indian with a pipe, a Frenchman with a snuff-box, and a Sailor with a quid of pigtail – having this elegant motto:

These three unite in one cause,
One smokes, one snuffs, and t'other chaws.[154]

COMMUNICATED.
CUMBERLAND CELEBRATION.[155]

CUMBERLAND, 6th July, 1835.

On the 4th inst., the people of this and some of the adjacent counties, met together for the purpose of celebrating the Anniversary of the Fourth of July, '76, when our fathers proclaimed us free – and we *were free*. The day was ushered in by an Oration from the Rev. John Kirkpatrick, which was distinguished for the depth of its research into the happy consequence that have flowed from our triumphant effort to liberate ourselves from foreign tyranny. ...

... After this, the ladies and their admiring train of beaux, returned to the dancing-room, while the cloth was removed, and the coolers of ice stationed at convenient points, were filled with bottles of the finest Madeira, and the richest Claret. The officers of ceremony were called by the managers, as by previous election and arrangement, to their several stations. Randolph Harrison, President; John C. Page, 1st Vice President; Edward J. Carrington, 2d Vice President; Henry J. Irving, 3d Vice President. The President proceeded to announce the Regular Toasts, responded to by the Vice Presidents; which were drunk amidst the loud huzzas of the company, repeated according to the feeling inspired by their several characters. Patriotic songs were occasionally interspersed, at the call of the company, which gave life and animation to the scene.

> 1st. The Day we celebrate: A day, revolting to Tyranny, because it gave birth to American Independence. Let us cherish and celebrate it as Freemen should.
> 2d. The People – the legitimate source of all power.
> 3d. The Cause of Freedom: This experiment has been fully tested, and Man is demonstrated to be capable of self-government. Let Philantropists rejoice at the result.
> 4th. Thomas Jefferson: His name will live while Freedom has a votary.
> 6th. The Memory of Lafayette – the friend of our country: His name will be revered as long as Virtue and Patriotism shall be esteemed, or Liberty find an advocate.

---

154 Under the title "FOURTH OF JULY TOATS.", a part of this text, starting from "When half a dozen glasses of Madeira...", until the very end, was published in another source, namely at the *Newburyport Herald*, of July 18, 1823. (Newburyport, MA).
155 *Richmond Enquirer*, July 14, 1835. (Richmond, VA).

7th. The President of the United States:[156] Presiding over the only free Government known to the world.

8th. The Signers of the Declaration of Independence: May the hallowed fire which they kindled on the shrine of freedom, continue to burn till the dark regions of despotism shall be illumined by its flames.

9th. The States: The Pillars upon which rests the fabrick of our National Government: Accursed by thousands who desire or attempt to destroy the symmetry and harmony of the structure.

10th. James Madison: May the evening of his days be as peaceful and happy as the morning of his life has been useful to his country.

11th. The memory of John Randolph of Roanoke.

12th. The Orator of the Day.

13th. The Ladies of Virginia: The purest of the pure, and fairess of the fair.

VOLUNTEER TOASTS.

By the President. The memory of the Heroes of the Revolution: Their deeds of valour are engraven upon our hearts, and will be handed down to our latest posterity.[157]

By Edmund W. Hubbard. France and the United States: May justice and magnanimity prompt each country, neither to refuse what is clearly due from one to the other, not to exact what justice must refuse, and a sovereign power cannot submit to.

By Charles R. Woodson. My Country: May its liberty and prosperity be as durable as its existence, and its existence as lasting as time. ...

A Temperate Speech.[158]

At a Temperance[159] Dinner on the 4th of July at Boston, attended by a large number of persons, the President of the day[160] said that he was gratified to see his friend the editor of the Advocate present, and would be glad to hear from him on this occasion. ...

We have seen the decanter driven from the side-board, the demijohn from the closet, and, in a degree, even the wine glass from the dinner table, and the social evening party. But who could think of a dinner on the fourth of July, or any public, or even social occasion, where wit, and sentiment, and eloquence were to preside, without Madeira or Champagne? not to name all the other kinds of pains, in which these liquids are disguised? "It cant be done," "it cant be done"! has been the answer to all arguments for banishing wines from the festive board. ...

---

156 Andrew Jackson. See Note 77.
157 AN: The excellent toast of the 1st Vice President was not sent up to the Chair.
158 *Alexandria Gazette*, July 14, 1837. (Alexandria, VA); *The Charleston Courier*, July 26, 1837. (Charleston, SC).
159 A movement that advocated the abolition of consumption of alcoholic beverages.
160 B. F. Hallett.

5.2. Books

In five different books, published both in the United Kingdom (by British travellers in America) and in the United States, can also be found some references to Madeira Wine being used to celebrate the 4th of July. The first one is an excerpt of a text published in 1812 by John Melish (1771-1822), a Scottish writer who had moved to Philadelphia the previous year, and refers to a 4th of July celebration held in Georgia.

CHAPTER V.[161]
Louisville.

LOUISVILLE is the present capital of the state of Georgia, and is situated on the northeast bank of the Ogechee river, 70 miles from its outlet, and 100 miles west from Savannah. It consists of about 100 dwelling houses, and contains about 550 inhabitants, of whom nearly one half are slaves. …

On Friday, the 4th of July, I had quite recovered from indisposition, and walked out in the morning to see the state-house. …

This being the anniversary of American independence, the day was ushered in by the firing of great guns; and military companies had collected in Louisville, from the whole country round. On my return to the tavern, I found a considerable number of the military assembled there. I was waited on by a committee of the artillery company, and received a very polite invitation to dine with them, which I accepted with pleasure, being anxious to observe the mode of celebrating this day, so important in the annals of America.

About 3 o'clock we sat down to dinner. The captain took his place at the head of the table, the oldest lieutenant at the foot; the committee gave the different orders, and all were on an equal footing. Several of the state officers dined with them.

After dining they drank Madeira wine to a series of toasts, one for each state, which had been previously prepared. Among the number were "The day we celebrate;" "The land we live in;" "The president of the United States;"[162] "Memory of general Washington." "Memory of Benjamin Franklin." "Memory of John Pierce," &c. Each toast was followed by a discharge of artillery, and the music played an appropriate air. A number of excellent songs were sung, and the afternoon was spent with great conviviality and good humour. …

Next we present an excerpt of a book by Sir Charles Augustus Murray, an English author, published in London and New York, in 1839, in which he refers that both Madeira Wine and Champagne were used to celebrate the 4th of July in a special celebration held at Fort Leavenworth, in the Old West, which was shared with a delegation of Pawnee Indians.

---

[161] MELISH, John, *Travels in the United States of America, in the years 1806 & 1807, and 1809, 1810, & 1811; including An Account of Passages Betwixt America and Britain, and Travels through Various Parts of Great Britain, Ireland, and Upper Canada.*, Illustrated with Eight Maps., In Two Volumes, Vol. I., Thomas & George Palmer, Philadelphia, 1812, pages 39, 41-43.

[162] James Madison. See Note 57.

On the 4th of July, the usual commemoration took place, of firing twenty-four guns; after which ceremony we adjourned to an excellent dinner; and madera[163] and champagne were the order of the day. We had spent an hour or two in the festivities of the table, when news was brought in that a hundred and fifty Pawnees had arrived, under the guidance of Mr. Dogherty, one of the principal Indian agents; and, upon an invitation from the officers, twelve or fourteen of their chief warriors came into the mess-room. I had already seen many Indians, but none so wild and unsophisticated as these genuine children of the wilderness. They entered the room with considerable ease and dignity, shook hands with us all, and sat down comfortably to cigars and madera.[164] I was quite astonished at the tact and self-possession of these Indians, two-thirds of whom had never been in a settlement of white men before, nor had ever seen a fork, or table, or chair in their lives; yet, without asking questions, or appearing to observe what was passing, they caught it with intuitive readiness, and during the whole dinner were not guilty of a single absurdity or breach of decorum. ...[165]

In the novel *Jack in the Forecastle*, by the American novelist John Sherburne Sleeper (1794-1878), published in 1860, there is a brief reference to Madeira Wine being used, at sea, to celebrate the 4th of July.

CHAPTER XX.[166]
DECLARATION OF WAR.

... The captain now seemed really alarmed. He ordered me in a loud voice to come aft, and told the crew to follow him in the cabin, leaving the schooner to manage matters with the thunder storm and take care of herself. He produced a bottle of "old Madeira" from a locker, and filled several glasses; and while the short-lived storm raged fearfully above our heads, he insisted on every man drinking a toast in honor of the Fourth of July, and set the example himself by tossing off a tumbler filled to the brim. ...

On the autobiography of James Marion Sims (1813-1883), considered the "Father of American Gynecology," he recounts his first (unhappy) experience with Madeira Wine, at the age of nine, at a 4th of July celebration at his father's home.

---

[163] The right spelling is Madeira.
[164] The right spelling is Madeira.
[165] MURRAY, Charles Augustus, *Travels in North America during The Years 1834, 1835, & 1836. Including A Summer Residence With The Pawnee Tribe Of Indians, in the Remote Prairies of the Missouri, and A Visit to Cuba and the Azore Islands*, in Two Volumes, Vol. I., Richard Bentley, London, 1839, page 253.
[166] SLEEPER, John Sherburne, *Jack in the Forecastle: or, Incidents in the Early life of Hawser Martingale*, Crosby, Nichols, Lee and Company, Boston, 1860, page 224.

CHAPTER IV.[167]
I start to college and get homesick – My first experience with wine not a success.

... Soon after I arrived at college the new friends I had made there invited me to go to Mr. Isaac Lyon's oyster saloon and join them in an oyster supper. It was always the habit of the young man inviting his companions to Lyon's to stand the treat of oysters and wine for the crowd. I never had taken a glass of wine in my life before but once. That was the fourth of July, when I was about nine years old. There was a celebration at my father's house, and dinner was served under the great mulberry trees in the yard. A half-dozen boys of us were given places at the lower end of the table. While toasts were being drunk, some gentlemen passed the wine to the boys and they were all allowed to help themselves. I am sure I didn't drink more than two table-spoonfuls of Madeira wine; the other boys drank much more than I did. Everybody was having a good time and enjoying the occasion exceedingly. Unfortunately, I had to be carried to the house, in the course of half an hour, and put to bed, dead drunk. I was exceedingly mortified, and I never drank any liquor after that until I went to college. The first night that I went to supper with the young men at Mr. Lyons's I indulged in a small glass of Madeira. The others drank freely; none of them seemed to feel it. When we started to return to the college I had to go with a man on each side of me. I was so drunk that I would have fallen if left alone. I felt very unhappy about it. I said: "Boys, it is very odd that you can all drink wine and I can not. But I am determined to learn to drink wine." ...

Another celebration of the 4th of July at sea took place in the seas of China, aboard the U.S. Steam-Frigate *Powhatan*, that had previously passed by Madeira at the end of 1857, as will be seen on the next chapter. In the narrative of her cruise, James D. Johnston states that this occasion was celebrated with John Howard March's Navy Madeira.[168]

CHAPTER IV.[169]
... – Salute to the Fourth of July – ...

... English transports, and French gun-boats continued to arrive, until the number swelled to thirty vessels, anchored in our immediate vicinity; all of which, however, were soon to be dispersed to various ports on the coasts of China and Japan; but it appeared remarkable that so large an accession to the force of the Allies should have joined that already assembled here, just in time to contribute their quota of gunpowder to the celebration of our National Jubilee. The 4th of July falling on Sunday, no official notice was taken

---

[167] SIMS, J.[ames] Marion, *The Story of My Life*, Edited by his son, H. Marion-Sims, D. Appleton and Company, New York, 1884, pages 83-84.

[168] John Howard March, a native of New Hampshire, was the U.S. Consul at Funchal, Madeira, from 1816 to 1861, and also a wine merchant. On his early years at the island he was a partner of the New York's wine importing company, March & Benson, and a few years later he established his own exporting company, John Howard March Co. Among his customers were many Naval officers that stopped at Funchal, who named the wine purchased from him as "Navy Madeira".

[169] JOHNSTON, James D., *China and Japan: Being a Narrative of the Cruise of the U.S. Steam-Frigate Powhatan, in the years 1857, '58, '59, and '60. Including an Account of the Japanese Embassy to the United States. Illustrated with Life Portraits of the Embassadors and Their Principal Officials.*, Charles Desilver, Philadelphia, Cushings & Bailey, Baltimore, 1860, pages 95-96.

of the great event usually commemorated on that day, but the occasion was by no means permitted to pass unnoticed in the way of private "celebration," for the dinner which we had in the wardroom of the Powhatan, would have rejoiced the heart of an Alderman – while the amount of J. Howard March's best Navy Madeira, which went down in libations to the glorious old heroes of the Revolution, is something beyond my present powers of calculation. …

5.3. Fourth of July Celebrations in Madeira Island

So far we have seen some 4th of July celebrations in America but next we will take a look at these events held in Madeira, the land of the wine, as they were accounted for, in several sources, from 1792 to 1857.

[Untitled][170]

The last Anniversary of Independence was celebrated at Madeira by our Consul, Mr. PINTARD[171] – at whose house a number of American Captains of vessels, and other gentlemen, dined on the occasion; when a variety of sentimental and patriotic toasts were drank.

Next we present a text describing a special 4th of July celebration held in Funchal, Madeira, in 1835, organized by a few Madeirans who had been exiled for some time in the United States for political reasons. Let us add that this was the first text we found describing, in detail, the celebration of the Independence Day on the island. During the event an Oration was delivered and several toasts were made, in the American fashion, and although this source does not mention with which they were made, we clearly foresee that it was with Madeira Wine.

From the Journal of Commerce.[172]
LATEST FROM LISBON.

We have been favored with Lisbon papers to the 2^d of August inclusive. They contain an account of the celebration of American Independence at Funchal, the capital of Madeira, on the 4th of July last. The Oration delivered on the occasion, by Mr. DaCUNHA, is published

---

170 *Gazette of the United States*, September 1, 1792. (Philadelphia, PA); *The Mail; or, Claypoole's Daily Advertiser*, September 14, 1792. (Philadelphia, PA); *The Diary; or, London's Register*, September 6, 1792. (New York City, NY); *The North Carolina Journal*, September 19, 1792. (Halifax, NC).

171 John Marsden Pintard, a native of New York, and American Commercial Agent in Funchal from 1783 to 1790, the year he was appointed as the 1st U.S. Consul for Madeira, by President George Washington. Pintard remained in office until 1803.

172 *The Evening Post*, September 18, 1835. (New York City, NY); *The Mercury*, September 24, 1835. (New York City, NY. Published under the title "LATEST FROM LISBON."). A summary of this text was published in another American source, under the title "Celebration of the 4th of July at Madeira", at the *New Bedford Mercury*, September 25, 1835. (New Bedford, MA).

entire in the Lisbon Oceano of August 2d,[173] accompanied by some editorial remarks. We make the following translations.

FUNCHAL, 4th of July, 1835.[174]

Those inhabitants of Madeira who during the usurpation[175] found an asylum in the United States of America, desiring to manifest their gratitude to the citizens of that country for the hospitality they received among them, determined to celebrate the 59th anniversary of American Independence by a patriotic dinner. They accordingly invited all other citizens of Madeira who had visited the United States, to unite in the celebration. The dinner took place on the above mentioned day, at 7 o'clock in the evening. The numbered persons present was 28. Dr. Lourenzo Jose Noniz,[176] member of the Cortez,[177] was chosen President; Alexandre Luis da Cunha,[178] Vice President; and Messrs. Caetano Alberto d'Aranjo[179] and Joao Chryssostimo da Silva Barretto,[180] masters of ceremonies. The dining hall was brilliantly fitted up, and at night its windows were illuminated. On one side was a full portrait of the immortal Washington, adorned with the American flag, and in front a magnificent painting representing the surrender of Lord Cornwallis, with all the British Army, to the American Hero, – decorated with the tri-colored banner. Flags of the Free Nations adorned the sides of the hall. The ceremony closed at about 11 o'clock in the evening, and during the whole time the most perfect harmony

---

173 The original source of this text was not a Lisbon paper but rather a Madeiran one, entitled *A Flor do Oceano*, of August 2, 1835, that, in fact, published the long Oration delivered by Alexandre Luis da Cunha, which occupies three out of four pages of this edition. On the other page, the first one, was published the editorial article, which was also translated and published in *The Mercury*, which we present in one of the next footnotes. Just as a curiosity regarding the name of this Madeiran newspaper we add that the expression "A Flor do Oceano" – The Ocean Flower – was a well-known 19th century epithet used by foreigners and Madeirans alike to designate the Madeira island.

174 The original version of this text was published in the Madeiran newspaper *A Flor do Oceano*, of July 12, 1835.

175 The usurpation of the Power in Portugal by D. Miguel I, from his niece D. Maria II, in 1828, that gave rise to the Liberal Wars, that went on until 1834.

176 The right spelling is Lourenço José Moniz, who was a Deputy at the Cortes, in Lisbon. Lourenço José Moniz (1789-1857), a Medicine graduate from the University of Edinburgh, where he took his Phd in 1815, returned to the island after finishing up his studies. In Madeira he worked both as a doctor and as a teacher, having been appointed Principle of Funchal's Lyceum and Director of the Medical-Cirurgical School of Funchal. Shortly after he was appointed Deputy at the Cortes, a position that he occupied for over twenty years. He had lived for a long time in the United States and France.

177 The right spelling is Cortes, the designation of Portugal's parliament prior to 1910, during the Monarchy.

178 Alexandre Luis da Cunha (1803-1852) was the Director of a Madeiran newspaper, *O Defensor da Liberdade* (The Defender of Freedom), that was published between June 2, 1827 and April 26, 1828. Shortly before he ended the publication of his newspaper he was arrested and did a month time in jail, due to a sentence against him for abuse of freedom of the press. Due to that and to the political events of the time, the instauration of an absolutist regime, led by D. Miguel I, and his "yearning to breathe free", he was forced into exile, in the United States. During his stay in America he gathered his impressions about the New World on a 99 page book that he published, in Portuguese, at Rio de Janeiro, in 1832, under the following title: *The United States of North America in 1830-31 – or a concise description, geographical, political, commercial, &c. of the same*. *Phenix Gazette*, August 1, 1832. (Alexandria, VA). A year later he published, in New York, the English version of his work, entitled *The United States of America*. *The Evening Post*, January 15, 1833. (New York City, NY). While he was exiled in the United States he got married in New York to an English lady, Miss Charlotte E. Cox, on April 7, 1834. *New-York Spectator*, April 17, 1834. (New York City, NY). After the end of the Liberal Wars, in 1834, he returned to Madeira, where he worked as a teacher of French and English, and continued his work on the press, founding three new newspapers: *A Chronica* (The Chronicle), published between 1838 and 1840; *O Defensor* (The Defender), published between 1840 and 1847; and *Correio da Madeira* (Madeira's Mail), published between 1849 and 1851. He died on the following year, on October 14, 1852.

179 The right spelling is Araújo.

180 The right spelling is João Crisóstimo da Silva Barreto.

prevailed. Annexed are the regular toasts, given by the illustrious President, all of which were received with hearty cheers.

1. The day we celebrate; the memorable Fourth of July, 1776.
2. Her faithful Majesty, Queen Donna Maria II.
3. The prosperity and greatness of the U. States.
4. Our gratitude for hospitality received.
5. The memory of General Washington.
6. The Congress of the United States, and the present President,[181] the Hero of New Orleans.
7. The memory of the 55 Patriots who signed the Declaration of Independence.
8. The memory of Lafayette.

VOLUNTEERS.

By Mr. Aroujo.[182] The American Fair – their virtues cannot be exceeded.

By Dr. Oliveira. The American Federation – may its duration be perpetual.

By the Vice President. The brave Portuguese who in imitation of the Americans, knew how to restore to us with their blood the country we had lost.

By the President. The State of Virginia; where are lodged my dearest sympathies; the birth-place of Washington, Jefferson, and other heroes.

By the Vice President. The city of Baltimore; its inhabitants have ever been distinguished for their noble hospitality; and towards them are directed my warmest affections.

By Mr. Oliveira. The Portuguese who in 1820 gave the first impulse to Portuguese liberty.

Many other patriotic toasts were offered, embracing the objects most dear to the hearts of freemen, and were all unanimously received with the greatest enthusiasm.

After the first regular toast, the Vice President arose and delivered an address, in which he explained the reasons which moved the persons present to celebrate this great day, as well as its causes and consequences.[183]

---

181 Andrew Jackson. See Note 77.
182 The right spelling is Araújo.
183 The text continued with these paragraphs: «[The Editor of the Oceano thus comments upon these proceedings.]/ We love to see gratitude evinced, – and we know too well how much it is esteemed by Portuguese hearts, to omit the publication of so decided a testimony of respect on the part of our grateful citizens towards the United States of America, which gave them a country when the usurpation of that degenerate member of the house of Braganza had deprived them of their own. But the heart which is sensible to kindness, is not less sensible to injury. And although our fellow citizens are certainly bound to concur with these their grateful brethren in the sentiments they cherish in remembrance of the hospitality they received among that Free People, yet none of them can forget that their tyrant found a remarkable support in the American Government, and in many American citizens a partiality for the despotism which oppressed us./ America ………………………. [here a line is left blank, probably erased by the censors,] ………….. was the first to acknowledge that Usurper who determined to keep Portugal enslaved, – and in opposition to a Queen who came to fraternize the Portuguese with the citizens of the New World!! Its ships of war *shamefully* lent themselves to the service of that wretch; at one time encouraging the factious by their presence in the Tagus, at another violating in our own port the blockade established by the legitimate Queen, and protecting the entrance of American merchant vessels, and even keeping on board clothing and medicines for the rebels!! ……………. [Here again several lines are left blank] …………. all these, and other facts which are omitted, necessarily occur to the mind

5. MADEIRA WINE AND THE 4TH OF JULY CELEBRATIONS

The following text was written by an unidentified Naval officer, in 1838, and describes, in vivid terms, the celebration of the 4th of July in Madeira by the officers of the U.S. frigate *Constitution* who were guests of the American Consul, and toasted the festive day with different brands of Madeira Wine.

[Untitled][184]

An officer on board the U.S. frigate Constitution, in writing to the editor of the Boston Traveller, from Hampton Roads, says, "I have just time to say that we left Mahon for the United States on the 15th of June. After a passage of eight days we arrived at Gibraltar; on the 26th stood out of the bay, an 11 knot breeze taking us in 64 hours over 700 miles to the Island of Madeira, in fair view of its vine-clad hills and vallies teeming with fruits and flowers. Here we passed the 4th of July, and dressed ship in honor of the day; at meridian fired a salute of 26 guns, the band closing with the national air: the occasion was complimented by an elegant dinner given by the American Consul at the island;[185] numerous invited guests were present, consisting of the Commodore and officers of the Constitution, the civil and military authorities, foreign consuls, &c. The luxuries of the land were furnished forth, and the dessert was crowned with the delicious fruits and wines of the island: old Madeira, Malmsey, Tinta, and other prime brands, passed in bumpers in commemoration of the day, mutual pledges went round, and the feast was enlivened with the music of operas, waltzes, and national airs.

"In the evening the Constitution was brilliantly illuminated; lights shone from the mast heads; those planted along the batteries gave her the appearance of a line of battle ship; twenty-six rockets were let off from the quarter-deck, blue lights cast their strong gleams from the yard arms, and illumined, like a thing of enchantment, the image of the ship. So closed the day and its festivities. At midnight we bade adieu to our hospitable host and his guests, who accompanied us to the beach, where we embarked, and soon after got under way for *home*; and here we are, with bright faces and glad hearts, counting the minutes which separate us from our friends."

In 1854, the Fourth of July was properly celebrated in Madeira by the officers of the U.S. Ship *Marion*, who were guests at a dinner offered them by an American wine merchant who lived on the island. At a given moment one of the guests beg leave to make a toast to America, which was drunk in Madeira Wine of 1776.

---

when gratitude for other conduct becomes an act of pure justice; and we sincerely desire to erase them from our memory; – for the well-deserved praise due to a Free People should not suffer the least diminution in consequence of these odious exceptions./ We are aware that the policy of the American Government was not perhaps that of the American people; and we would not be so unjust as to judge the free and generous citizens of America by those of their fellow citizens who are ready to make their own interest paramount to almost everything else. – Let us be, then, both generous and grateful. Let us renounce our sense (remorsos) of their unworthy conduct, and unite with our grateful fellow countrymen in applauding the distinguished hospitality which the persecuted man finds in the United States, where the sympathy extended to the citizen suffering in the cause of Liberty, is ever conspicuous.»

184 "The Army and Navy Chronicle," Volume VI, New Series, From January 1, to June 30, 1838, B. Homans, Washington City, 1838, page 106.
185 John Howard March. See Note 168.

From Madeira.[186]

... I was here on the 4th of July, the natal day of the Americans. The United States ship *Marion* was here; and I cannot tell which was the most pleased, the Americans or the Portuguese, at the exchange of courtesy. At sunrise, the *Marion* hoisted her national standard at the mast-head, and fired 21 guns. ...

Mr. WELSH,[187] an American citizen, gave a magnificent dinner to the ware room officers of the Marion, inviting many of the Mogado[188] of the Island. The dinner passed off delightfully. When the cloth was removed, Mogado[189] BRINGAN[190] asked permission to give a toast, and gave, "The Fourth of July – the natal day of a free and independent country"; which was drank in wine, of the vintage of 1776, with three times three. ...

Finally we present an account of a merry Fourth of July celebrated in Madeira, in 1857, aboard a U.S. Navy ship, where most certainly Madeira wine was drunk by its officers to toast the Independence Day.

From the African Squadron.[191]
Correspondence of The Star.

U.S. SHIP ST. LOUIS,
FUNCHAL, MADEIRA, JULY 17, 1857.

I have nothing new to write to you. The Fourth we spent here, and had quite a joyous time on board the ship. The ship was dressed off with flags, flowers and evergreens, and looked very well, indeed. We had also an excellent band from shore, and Jack amused himself by dancing to the sweet music which it discoursed. The dinner, which was a splendid one, was prepared on shore but served on board, and when set out the tables groaned beneath the weight of good things. Of course the boys "pitched it" with knife and fork, but for the first time had to give in and own themselves "beat." However, as they could not destroy the good things set before them, they have the satisfaction of knowing that they endeavoured to do their best. After dinner enough was sent on shore to feed two hundred of the poor, whose hearts were made glad by such a supply. The whole wound up with a display of fireworks in the evening. Really, as the Dutchman said, "the Fourth of July was on board the St. Louis," and, I have no doubt, all who participated with us will long, remember the Fourth of July, 1857, on board this ship. ...

---

[186] *The New York Times*, August 14, 1854. (New York City, NY).
[187] George Day Welsh, a native of Philadelphia, who had established himself in Funchal, as a wine merchant, at the beginning of the 19th century. A Master's Thesis was written about him and his presence at Madeira by a graduate student of the University of Madeira, José Manuel de Abreu, in 2004, under the title "George Day Welsh nas Relações entre a Madeira e os Estados Unidos da América (Primeira Metade do Século XIX)" or, in English, "George Day Welsh in the Relations between Madeira and the United States (First Half of the 19th Century)".
[188] The right spelling is morgado (rich proprietor).
[189] The right spelling is morgado.
[190] Bringan is not a Madeiran surname. Maybe the author meant to say Bringão, possibly a nickname this person was known for.
[191] *Evening Star*, August 20, 1857. (Washington, DC).

6. Madeira Wine in American Literature

6.1. Travel Literature

Throughout the 19th century hundreds, if not thousands, of Americans passed by Madeira during their Atlantic journeys and some of them wrote, in a vivid way, their personal impressions about the island, depicting it in several aspects and perspectives. Later on these were gathered in their travel books or published in magazines and newspapers across the United States, upon their return home. The majority of those writers belonged to United States Navy, and that can be explained by the fact that the island of Madeira, back then, was an important port of call for the USN ships that cruised the Atlantic in different expeditions and missions, in order to get supplies, coal, livestock and other commodities, such as Madeira wine.

6.1.1. Books

In the American travel literature published in book form with references to Madeira we were able to identify twenty-nine different authors. A recurrent theme of their writings about this vine clad island is its celebrated wine, enumerating its different types and describing its production. Next will be presented excerpts of those interesting texts, arranged not by the year of publication but rather by the dates in which its authors visited Madeira (mentioned between brackets in front of each author's name) in order to provide a chronological view of the references to Madeira Wine accompanied by a brief note about each author and their literary works, and a summary of the wine-related topics they tackled.

6.1.1.1. William Francis Lynch, USN (1819)

William Francis Lynch (1801-1865), was a native of Norfolk, Virginia, where an important Navy Yard was located. He was appointed a midshipman of the U.S. Navy in February 1819. About the same time he joined the crew of the US frigate *Congress*, a ship that had been fitted out for a distant cruise to China, being the first U.S. warship to visit that country. During that voyage William Lynch wrote a journal, a portion of which was revealed to the American public, in a periodical, several decades later. Because of the positive impact it had on "lovers of light reading" he decided to publish it sometime after, as he mentions in the Preface of his book, entitled *Naval Life; or, Observations Afloat and On Shore. The Midshipman.*,[192] which was published in New York, in 1851. In Chapter II he inserts a brief description of Madeira – where he arrived after 20 days from Norfolk, presumably at the end of February or beginning of March 1819 – where one may find some references to the island's vines and the importance of its wine production.

---

[192] LYNCH, William Francis, *Naval Life; or, Observations Afloat and On Shore. The Midshipman.*, Charles Scribner, New York, 1851.

CHAPTER II.

... Madeira, for its arable ground, is perhaps one of the most productive spots in the world. Every niche among the mountains, the sides of every ravine, and the summit of every hill, wherever half an inch of soil can be found, is highly cultivated. Places, that in the United States would only be traversed by the sportsmen in quest of game, are here covered with the luxuriant vine, pendent from which the grape hangs in innumerable tempting clusters. ...

The Portuguese live in haughty seclusion, and the trade of the island is almost monopolized by the English. A few of our enterprising countrymen are settled here, and by their open-handed hospitality cheer the path of the stranger.

Besides wine, its principal export, this island produces rye, maize, wheat, some arrow root, a species of bean, and figs, bananas, pine-apples, apples, pears, peaches, and a very large, mild-flavored onion.[193] ...

6.1.1.2. Rev. Walter Colton, USN (1832)

In 1835, the Naval Chaplain Walter Colton, Officer of the United States Navy, published in New York a book entitled *Ship and Shore: or Leaves from the Journal of a Cruise to the Levant*.[194] This book describes the trip he did aboard the frigate *Constellation*, Captain Read, to Madeira, Lisbon and the Mediterranean in 1832. We could not find the exact date of his arrival at the island, but it should have been somewhere in May of that year, for he arrived at Lisbon – the second stop of his sea journey – on June 5, which we know for a fact. He dedicated six of the first chapters of his book to his impressions of Madeira, and at the beginning of the eighth we found his views about the island's wines.

CHAPTER VIII.
Sketches of Madeira – Physical Features – Wines – ...

The Island of Madeira is full of marvel and romance. It was thrown up into this breathing world by some volcanic convulsion; it was discovered by a wandering love-adventure;[195] its every aspect is one of wildness and beauty; and its wines prompt the most rich and unearthly dreams. There is nothing about it that has the smallest cast of sameness, except its climate; and that could hardly be improved by any changes wider than the slight vibrations, through which it passes, and which are full of softness and vitality. It is indeed a fairy land, – the paradise of the Atlantic, – the gem of the ocean. But I will look at some

---

193 LYNCH 1851, pages 20-21.
194 [COLTON, Rev. Walton], *Ship and Shore: or Leaves from the Journal of a Cruise to the Levant*, Leavitt, Lord & Co., New York, 1835. This first edition was published anonymously, but the following ones, published in New York in 1851 and 1860, under a slightly different title – *Ship and Shore; in Madeira, Lisbon, and the Mediterranean* –, presented the name of its author, adding that the book had been revised by Henry Theodore Cheever.
195 Allusion to the Machin's Legend, a theme exploited by many authors, including Washington Irving, who claims that Madeira Island was accidentally discovered by the British eloped lovers Robert Machin and Anna d'Arfet.

of the more marked and discriminating features of this singular island.

Its southern coast descends in easy and green declivities to the sea. These warm slopes are covered with the choicest vineyards; the vine seems to reel under its purple burthen. Where the ascent is so steep as to render it necessary, it is thrown off into parapets, which may be seen rising above each other in a lengthened series. So precious is this southern exposure, that where there is no native soil, the rock is covered with earth, brought from a distance, with great labor and expense. The wines of these vineyards for richness of body, deliciousness of flavor, and immunity from injury by time and indifferent treatment, are not equaled in the world. Who has not seen the hospitable host half in a rapture, as he bade his delighted guests fill their glasses from a little of the "old south side" left him by some worthy ancestor. But "who hath redness of eyes? – they that tarry long at the wine."

Figure 21. Rev. Walter Colton. *Engraving from the frontispiece of his book* The Sea and the Sailor: notes on France and Italy *(New York, 1856). Author unknown.*

The northern shore of the island rises from the wave in a bold, elevated range of rock; but what it gains in majesty it loses in other respects. The vine is inferior to its sister of the south, and as if to punish it for its want of sweetness, instead of being supported by fine trellis-work of cane, it is left to climb up some bramble, or reluctant tree, as it can; and then after all its best efforts, is still more deeply punished by being worked up into brandy. Sometimes indeed, it has the good fortune to be removed in its infancy to the south side; and then it never fails to secure affection and esteem.[196] ...

6.1.1.3. Rev. Fitch Waterman Taylor, USN (1838)

In 1840, Rev. Fitch Waterman Taylor, Chaplain of the East India Squadron, published in New York a book, in two volumes, entitled *The Flag Ship: or A Voyage Around the World, in the United States Frigate Columbia; attended by her consort The Sloop of War John Adams, and bearing the broad pennant of Commodore George C. Read.*[197] This Squadron had been selected by the US government to circumnavigate the globe. The *Columbia* left the Hampton Roads, in Norfolk, VA, on May 6, 1838, and arrived at Madeira on the 27th. The third section, or chapter, of his book is dedicated to Madeira, and in it there are a few paragraphs about the island's vines and process of making wine, the description of two kinds of wine and the quantity of wine produced, which he quoted from an English author.

---

[196] [COLTON] 1835, pages 88-89.
[197] TAYLOR, Rev. Fitch Waterman, *The Flag Ship: or A Voyage Around the World, in the United States Frigate Columbia; attended by her consort The Sloop of War John Adams, and bearing the broad pennant of Commodore George C. Read*, Vol. I., D. Appleton & Co., New York, 1840. This book had several other editions, under a slightly different title – *A Voyage Round the World, and visits to Various Foreign Countries, in the United States Frigate Columbia; attended by her consort The Sloop of War John Adams, and commanded by Commodore George C. Read* – which were published in New Haven and New York in 1842, 1846, 1847, 1850 and 1855.

SECTION III.
Madeira. Funchal, capital of Madeira. … Shrubbery and vines. …
Cultivation of the grape and process of making wine. Tinto. Malmsey. Quantity of wine produced. …

We have come to anchor, in full view of one of nature's most beautiful landscapes. Funchal, the capital of Madeira, is about two miles from our frigate; and the southern exposure of the island lies, in its enchantment, before us. Think of a fairy isle, raising its high peaks abruptly 8,000 feet above the bosom of the blue deep, and tracing its waved outline indistinctly among the mystic and dark clouds, which hang, like spirit-shapes, on its high and misty cones; while, everywhere else, around and farther yet above the cloud-capt peaks, the sky is blue and clear; and the soft breeze and the mimic-gale from the sea strike balmy, like an eastern atmosphere, upon the cheek. And then, think of the elevated acclivities, and deep ravine, broken into thousand crests, throwing their every shaped shadows over their own mountainous and cragged and unique landscape; and every peak, and every slope, and every ravine, covered with vineyard and garden, and ever-green-tree and shrub and flower, varying from the palest gold of harvest time to the deepest and prevailing verdure of the freshest meadow; and then the villas, or country residences of the English merchants and the wealthier Portuguese, which are here called *quintas,* of all dimensions, with red-tiled tops, and piazza and balcony and corridors for promenade and look-outs, and trellised terraces for the embowering vines; …[198]

The island of Madeira has been known to Americans principally for its wines; and in former years, on account of the quantities of bread-stuffs which were imported into the island from the United States. In later years the number of vessels arriving here from the United States has diminished; while it is still a matter of some interest in our commerce.

The principal part of the trade is in the hands of the English merchants, who have their permanent residences on the island, with their families.

The following particulars in connection with the cultivation of the vine and the manner of securing its product, may not be uninteresting, as given, in substance, in a sketch by Mr. Bowditch.[199] The best kind of grapes for making wine are the Bual, Sercial, Verdelho, Negro Molle,[200] and Malvasia. They are said not to be palatable, as eating fruit. The vines are propagated by cuttings, which are planted in trenches. The usual mode of training the vines is on trellises, made of common cane, and from two to three feet above the ground. The commencement of gathering the grapes for pressing is early in September. The grapes are first trodden by the feet, in a trough made of wood, or excavated in the rocks; and the first juice, thus expressed, is distinguished as the *vinho da flor.* The bruised grapes are then collected within the coils of a thick rope, made of the twisted shoots of the vine, and repeatedly subjected to the press for the second quality, called *must.* This is mixed, usually, with the *vinho da flor,* and transferred the same day into casks to ferment. The rapidity of the fermentation depends partly on the warmth of the weather, and also on the perfect maturity of the grape. The more violent action

---

[198] TAYLOR, 1840, pages 47-48.
[199] Reference to the Englishman Thomas Edward Bowdich, author of *Excursions in Madeira and Porto Santo, During the Autumn of 1823, While on His Third Voyage to Africa,* published in London in 1825, where he makes several remarks to Madeira wine.
[200] The right spelling is Negra Mole.

commonly ceases in about a month or six weeks; but a certain degree of fermentation continues to go on, particularly in the richer qualities of vines. The liquors are clarified by a kind of gipsum, brought chiefly from Spain. This is the last process of the operation. Near the beginning of the year the wine is racked from the lees.

In the case of the Tinto wine made of the black grapes (negro molle) the grapes undergo only one pressure from the lever, and are afterwards drained through a sieve, which allows the husks and seeds to pass, the stalks only remaining behind. The whole is put into a vat open at the top and strained three or four times during the day, until the fermentation has ceased. Then it is racked off into casks.

In making the white wines, the different kinds of grapes are commonly mixed together, except the Malvasia or Malmsey,[201] and the Sercial. The Malmsey grapes are suffered to ripen for a month later than any other, until the skin begins to shrivel. The Malmsey grape is produced only on a few spots, enjoying a peculiar warmth of exposure. The grape does not always produce a sweet wine. Indeed it only does so in one or two situations. In other cases sugar, burnt by a particular wood, is thrown in.

The Sercial also will succeed only in particular spots. The quantity produced scarcely equals fifty pipes a year.

A quantity of brandy, from two gallons a pipe and upwards, is generally thrown into the wines intended for exportation, with the exception, it is said, of the Tinto. In the war time, when, from the great demand, the merchants were unable to keep a great stock on hand, it was usual to ripen the wines by the use of stoves, raising the heat gradually from 60 to 100 degrees; and it is still the practice to subject a certain portion of the vintage to the operation of this artificial temperature. The mellowness of the wine is, no doubt, thus accelerated, but at some expense of the delicacy of its flavor.

The average quantity of the produce throughout the island is one pipe to the acre, though in some instances four pipes have been obtained.

The wine from the north of the island is generally inferior in quality. It is nearly all consumed on the island, or converted into brandy. There are about twelve distilleries. Three pipes of wine make one of brandy.

The quantity of wine produced during the five preceding years, according to a statement furnished me by the American Consul,[202] is as follows:

In 1834,   15,000 pipes.
In 1835,   15,500   "
In 1836,   29,000   "
In 1837,   29,000   "   ...[203]

---

201 AN: The Malmsey wine has been known formerly as forming a luxuriant beverage of the more opulent classes in England. It is frequently mentioned by Shakespeare, and is seen in all the accounts of ancient feasts, and in the household books of the nobility of former times. The Duke of Clarence, according to English historians, was drowned in a butt of it; and whether from any particularly inspiring property it possesses, we do not pretend to say, but a certain portion of this sweet wine is allowed, as the annual stipend of the poet laureate. It was formerly brought to England from Malvisia, a town on the east coast of the Morea, from whence it derived its name. And from the grape, originally transplanted from Malvisia to Madeira, as is supposed, the modern Malmsey is produced.
202 John Howard March. See Note 168.
203 TAYLOR, 1840, pages 106-109.

6.1.1.4. John Henshaw Belcher, USN (1838)

In 1840, another book was published, in two volumes, in New York and Boston, depicting the trip of the *Columbia*, entitled *Around the World: A Narrative of a Voyage in The East India Squadron, under Commodore George C. Read., By an officer of the U.S. Navy*.[204] As we can infer from its title it was anonymous, but we found out that this book was written by John Henshaw Belcher, a Professor of Math and a member of the crew,[205] who dedicated a little more than four chapters to his impressions of Madeira. In some of them he describes the island's vineyards and makes some references to its famous wine.

CHAPTER IV.

… As we rounded the high and majestic Point de Sol,[206] three and a half leagues westward of Funchal, and the nearer one of Cama do Lobos,[207] a beautiful amphitheatre expanded before us, extending from the open roadstead, in continuous sloping acclivities, far back among the mountains: the vine-clad knolls intervened, and the whitened city of Funchal lay embosomed in the arena beneath, smilingly lighted by the last rays of the sun.[208] …

CHAPTER V.

… Near Funchal, there are three or four streamlets that tumble from the mountains, and after passing through vineyards, which they irrigate, are conducted through the city by deep canals, called lavados;[209] toward one of these, the Santa Luzia canal, in the eastern part of the city, our guide had led us. It was bordered on either side by broad avenues ascending to the mountains, and very prettily shaded with plane-trees. The Egyptian aram myrtles and geraniums, were growing spontaneously by the way-side; and in the pools of the almost dry bed of the canal, the washerwomen were beating clothes upon the rocks. On the west side there was a singular but rich quinta, belonging to the English ex-consul,[210] beautifully adorned by a garden with various plants and urns, and statues, seen through trellis-work; but being fancifully shaped and gorgeously painted yellow, it obtained the appellation of *Potu Moutarde*, or the mustard pot.[211] …[212]

Our kind friend, having an engagement, left us at the chapel; but we had not proceeded far when another gentleman politely addressed us and said, that he perceived we were

---

204 [BELCHER, John Henshaw], *Around the World: A Narrative of a Voyage in The East India Squadron, under Commodore George C. Read., By an officer of the U.S. Navy.*, Vol. I., Charles S. Francis, New York, Joseph H. Francis, Boston, 1840.
205 Other sources indicate the name of Joshua Sidney Henshaw as being the author of this book.
206 The right spelling of the name of this village is Ponta do Sol. As a matter of curiosity we add that the paternal grandfather of the American writer John dos Passos was a native of this village, having emigrated to the U.S. in the 1820's.
207 The right name (and present-day denomination) of this village is Câmara de Lobos, although in some 19th century Portuguese books and Madeiran newspapers it is also referred as Cama de Lobos.
208 [BELCHER] 1840, page 54.
209 The right spelling is levadas, or waterways.
210 Henry Veitch.
211 This unique building still exists and is associated to the Madeira Wine Institute.
212 [BELCHER] 1840, pages 60-61.

American officers, and as he had himself been a stranger in a strange land, he would be happy to guide us in a walk. He very slyly took us around to the opposite side of the city into his own house, where we regaled on the choicest Malmsey, and Tinta, and Sercial wines, all from his own vintage, and ripened in his own cellar – that ever was quaffed by American lips; luscious in flavour as the richest grape, smooth as oil, and lingering about the sides of the glass, long after the bulk was drained, precisely like – nothing but good old wine. Reader! cross the Atlantic, if you can, to sip that precious nectar, in the pure balmy air of Madeira, for you can never taste it elsewhere: and if you are an invalid you may gain health by it, and meet others on the same errand. Humbolt[213] says of this island, in connection with Teneriffe, and he is not alone in it, that, "no country seemed to him more fitted to dissipate melancholy, and restore peace to an agitated mind, or, where the natural beauty of the situation, and the salubrity of the air so fully conspire to quiet the spirits, and invigorate the body."[214] I would not, however, be understood to recommend this place to Americans in preference to East Florida, unless the invalid be of that questionable kind, who desires a sea voyage, and can partake of the generous wine freely; for the writer has tried and proved, as an invalid, the unrivalled salubrity of the American Montpelier.[215] …

CHAPTER VI.

… From the cemetery ascending a little farther, the sight was gladdened on every side by the vine and fruit-planted terraces that wreathed the hills far and near with beauty, while over the walls and amid the trellices of nearer gardens, were blooming flowers, that made the air redolent of their thousand reviving sweets. …[216] …

CHAPTER VII.

… There are two roads to the Corrál,[217] and we had chosen the most intricate, which was but little better than a rugged foot-path. We passed along between castle-walls high and turreted, one of which bounded the domain of an English ex-consul,[218] with a private chapel attached, as is the case with all the Portuguese estates. …

Here and there a train of peasants met us, men and women, with burdened asses, in single file, from the interior parishes; the women bore faggots upon their heads, the asses had bags of corn, while the men were bent over with goat skins full of wine about their necks.

The mountain vintners have a singular skill, they tell us, in breaking up the bones within a goat or kid, and extracting every part of the corpus by the mouth, without a single incision

---

[213] Friedrich Wilhelm Heinrich von Humboldt (1769-1859), better known as Alexander Humboldt, was a German geographer, naturalist and explorer.
[214] Quote from Chapter III of the book *Travels and Researches of Baron Humboldt; being a condensed narrative of his journey in the equinoctial regions of America, and in Asiatic Russia: – together with analysis of its more important investigations*, published in New York, in 1833, by William MacGillivray.
[215] [BELCHER] 1840, pages 64-65.
[216] [BELCHER] 1840, page 67.
[217] The right spelling is Curral [das Freiras].
[218] Henry Veitch's estate, at Jardim da Serra, Estreito de Câmara de Lobos. This place still exists. In the early 2000's it was restored and transformed into a charming hotel.

of the pelt. These then serve them, as of old the like vessels did the Egyptians and Israelites, for wine and water cases: and these are the bottles into which, if new wine be put when they are old and dry, the bottles will burst. But it is right curious to see a bulging goat-skin full of wine, hanging around a man's neck, with the feet fastened in front for a handle or bridle: there is a very good picture of one so collared in the volume of the Pictorial Bible.[219] ...

CHAPTER VIII.

Malte Brun[220] says, "the quinta gardens of Madeira are not attractive;" but we Americans found them exceedingly so; and two or three of us devoted a day to visiting several of them, together with the institutions of the city. But having an engagement, we could not proceed till we had called upon our old friend Mr. B * * *,[221] where, as we tasted once more his delicious *tinta*, we were favoured with the most eloquent encomiums, like those of Will Boniface on his ale, concerning the precious juices of the island. And certainly one was not obliged to "fancy" his wine "Burgundy" to "make it worth ten shillings the quart."

"This tinta, you perceive, gentlemen," said our host, "is very different from either port or claret; it has more body than the last, is less astringent than the first, and has much of the Homolem flavour. It is known in England, and I think in your country, by the name of London particular. I wish I could give you a taste of the Bual: that is red wine also, but more like Burgundy. Our best white wine, the Sercial, from a choice grape, is pleasantly acrid you know, and yet luscious and invigorating; but I suppose you get very little of it in the United States. The wine, that we send mostly to America, is our dry Madeira. It is from a wild grape, brought originally from Cyprus. Then I suppose a little of our lady's wine, the Malmsey, reaches you. It is a wine I am fond of myself. It is mixed mostly in Machico, a favourite district, where formerly the famous Madeira sugar was cultivated, having a peculiar aromatic flavour, and a violet odour. The grape of the Malmsey, I think, was brought from Candia. Then besides these we have our white Bastardo, our Muscatel, our Verdelho, Branco, Baboso, Ferral, Dodo de Dama,[222] and many other fancy kinds."

"But, are all these from different kinds of grape?"

"Why, mostly. We count in Madeira about twenty-one species of grape; though, if we allowed for the effect of the soil and culture, as the French government did in making out 1,400 varieties in their collection, we should also have a vast variety. Our best kinds of grape are the White Muscadine, the Esperione, the July Black, and the Sweet-Water. But the different points of exposure for a vineyard, the dryness or extra moisture of the season, the manner of curing, whether by the furnace or estufa houses, or otherwise, besides age, affect the qualities of our wines."

"How much do you think is exported from Madeira annually? or, how much goes to the United States?" "Why, we don't make over thirty thousand pipes in any year. Then about

---

219 [BELCHER] 1840, pages 77-79. On the 2nd volume of the *Pictorial Bible*, published in London, in 1837, there is, on page 513, an engraving of a girl pouring wine from a leathern wine-bottle, but not of a man carrying a goatskin on his neck.

220 Author of the reference book *Universal Geography, or a Description of all the Parts of the Globe, on a New Plan, according to the Great Natural Divisions of the Globe; accompanied by Analytical, Synoptical, and Elementary Tables*, published in New York and Boston, in 1826. His views on Madeira Wine are inserted on the section 7.1. of this anthology.

221 It could have been Mr. Blandy, an English wine merchant in Funchal.

222 The right expression and wine type is "Dedo de dama", or, in English, Lady's finger.

ten thousand pipes are distilled into brandy, and not more than a third of the remainder goes to the States."

"That certainly is very strange," we remarked, "for besides what is drunk by private families in the States, there are at least twenty-five thousand pipes served out at our hotels in a year; under the name of Madeira." "Ha, ha, there is some yankee trick about that," said he; "but come, let us take another taste of the Sercial, and we will commence our round before the heat of the day."[223] ...

6.1.1.5. William Meacham Murrell, USN (1838)

In 1840, William Meacham Murrell, another member of the crew of the *Columbia*, published a book in Boston depicting this frigate's worldwide travel, under the title *Cruise of the Frigate Columbia around the world, under the command of Commodore George C. Read, in 1838, 1839 and 1840*.[224] On the first chapter he briefly describes Madeira, where he also arrived on May 27, 1838, and mentions its vines and wines.

CHAPTER I.
... – Madeira – Description thereof – ...

... This island is situated in the Atlantic ocean, in 32° 34' north latitude, and from 18° 30' to 19° 30' west longitude. It is composed of one continual hill of a considerable height, extending from east to west, the declivity of which on the south side is cultivated, and interspersed with vineyards; and in the midst of this slope the merchants have fixed their country seats, which form a very agreeable prospect. ...

... Its wine, which derives its name from the island, is in the highest estimation, especially such as has been on a voyage to the East or West Indies, as it matures best in the hottest climates.[225] ...

6.1.1.6. Charles Wilkes, USN (1838)

In 1838, the United States organized a scientific expedition with the intention of exploring the Southern Seas and the Pacific Ocean, and several Navy ships were selected to participate in this mission: the sloops of war *Vincennes* and *Peacock*, the gun brig *Porpoise*, the tenders *Sea-Gull* and *Flying-Fish* and the store-ship *Relief*. Several scientists, naturalists and draughtsmen were among the members of the scientific corps. Charles Wilkes (1798-1877), a native of New York City and member of the American Philosophical Society, was the Commander of the Expedition. Seven years later, in 1845, he published in Philadelphia the book entitled *Narrative of the*

---

223 [BELCHER] 1840, pages 85-87.
224 MURRELL, William Meacham, *Cruise of the Frigate Columbia around the world, under the command of Commodore George C. Read, in 1838, 1839 and 1840*, Benjamin B. Mussey, Boston, 1840.
225 MURRELL 1840, pages 18, 20.

6. MADEIRA WINE IN AMERICAN LITERATURE

United States Exploring Expedition. During the years 1838, 1839, 1840, 1841, 1842.,[226] where he describes, in the first chapter, his travels aboard the *Vincennes*, including his impressions of Madeira, where he arrived on September 16, 1838. In that section of his work he describes, among other things, the streets of Funchal and the mode of wine transportation, mentions the late wine exports and also mentions the winemaking process. His personal observations about the island's staple commodity are complemented with three interesting wine-related sketches.

CHAPTER I.
MADEIRA.
1838.

Figure 22. Charles Wilkes, Commander of the United States Exploring Expedition that cruised the seas from 1838 to 1842. *Engraving from the frontispiece of the 1852's London edition of his book. Author unknown.*

... The streets of the town are very narrow, without sidewalks, and to our view like alleys, but their narrowness produces no inconvenience. They are well paved, and wheel-carriages are unknown. The only vehicle, if so it may be called, is a sledge, of some six feet in length, about twenty inches wide, and only six or eight inches high, on which are transported the pipes of wine. Two strips of hard wood are fastened together for runners.

This sledge is dragged by two very small oxen, and slips easily on the pavement, which is occasionally wet with a cloth. It is no doubt the best mode of transportation in Funchal, for their wine, on account of the great steepness of their streets. Smaller burthens are transported on men's shoulders, or in hampers and baskets, on the backs of donkeys.[227] ...

Wine is the staple commodity: the produce during the year 1837 was 14,150 pipes. The export the year previous to our visit amounted to 8,435 pipes, of which about 3,800 pipes, valued at $793,000, went to the United States. The imports only amounted to $105,000, in staves, rice and oil. The 5,700 pipes that remain, include the home consumption,

---

226 WILKES, Charles, *Narrative of the United States Exploring Expedition. During the years 1838, 1839, 1840, 1841, 1842.*, In Five Volumes, and an Atlas, Vol. I., Lea & Blanchard, Philadelphia, 1845. This book had several other editions, both in England and the United States, and some of them came to light under a different title: *Narrative of the United States Exploring Expedition. During the years 1838, 1839, 1840, 1841, 1842*, In Five Volumes, and an Atlas, Wiley and Putnam, (Printed by C. Sherman, Philadelphia, U.S.A.), London, 1845; *Narrative of the United States' Exploring Expedition, during the years 1838, 1839, 1840, 1841, 1842. Condensed and Abridged.*, Whitaker and Co., London, [1845]; *Voyage Round the World embracing The Principal Events of the Narrative of the United States Exploring Expedition*, In one volume, Geo W. Gorton, Philadelphia, 1849; *Narrative of the United States Exploring Expedition. During the Years 1838, 1839, 1840, 1841, 1842, in Five Volumes, with Thirteen Maps*, Philadelphia, 1850; *Voyage Round the World, embracing The Principal Events of the Narrative of the United States Exploring Expedition.* In one volume., George P. Putnam, New York, 1851; *Narrative of the United States Exploring Expedition. During the Years 1838, 1839, 1840, 1841, 1842, in Two Volumes, with Numerous Engravings*, Ingram, Cooke, and Co., London, 1852; and *Narrative of the United States Exploring Expedition. During the Years 1838, 1839, 1840, 1841, 1842, in Five Volumes with Thirteen Maps*, G. P. Putnam, New York, 1856. The first listed English edition of this book, of 1845, contains the engravings related to Madeira wine, but the 1852 does not, whereas all the other American ones does.
227 WILKES 1845, pages 10-11.

and what is stored for refining. Wine in Madeira is generally the engrossing topic, and the inhabitants are much alive and justly jealous of their reputation for it. An amusing excitement existed during our visit. A London paper

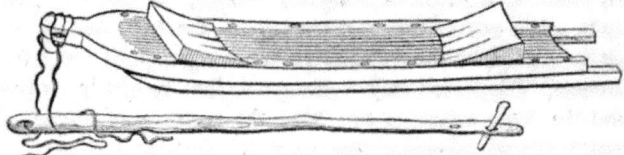

Figure 23. Madeiran sledge used to carry wine casks. *Book illustration. Sketched by J. Drayton. Engraved by F. E. Worcester.*

(The Times) had asserted that foreign wine had frequently been introduced into Madeira and afterwards exported as the genuine article, to the United States in particular, and what gave more force to the story, it was stated as a fact that seventy pipes had lately been entered at the expense of $1000, and remanufactured. Every body was up in arms. The commercial association of Funchal passed resolutions denouncing the publication in strong terms, as designed by certain interested persons to injure the reputation of the wine of Madeira. So strict are the laws to prevent frauds, that even genuine Madeira, after being once shipped, cannot be returned to the island. I heard, however, of an attempt, and but one, to smuggle in Teneriffe and Fayal wines, which was discovered. The casks were broken, the wine destroyed, the boats confiscated, and the smuggler condemned to be transported to the coast of Africa. ..."[228]

Such of the peasantry as do not gain a subsistence in the vineyards, have usually a small patch of ground which they cultivate, raising grain, corn, potatoes, and the taro (Arum esculentum), in quantities barely sufficient to eke out a scanty living. The cultivation is commonly performed by hand, although a plough of very simple construction is sometimes used. Many of the peasantry are employed as carriers, and one is much struck by their numbers when entering Funchal early in the morning, with sheepskins[229] filled with wine on their shoulders, that look at a distance more like the live animal than a filled skin. These skins are preserved as entire as possible, even the legs of the animal being retained. They are generally kept steady by a band that passes over the forehead, which supports a great part of the weight. About twenty-five gallons, weighing more than two hundred pounds, is a load. They move rapidly, and carry this load five miles for a mere trifle. To us, one of the most remarkable features in the population, was to see a female not only thus employed, but a stout mountain lass trudging up a steep path with ease, under a load that would have staggered one of our labourers even for a short distance.

The manner of expressing the juice I have nowhere seen particularly described; and although a description of it may not add a relish to the cup, yet it will show the manufacture as conducted according to the old custom, at the present day. A friend of our consul[230] was obliging enough to show us his works, and the machinery for expressing the juice from the grape. It was in a rude sort of shed. On our approach we heard a sort of song, with a continued thumping, and on entering saw six men stamping violently in a vat of six feet square by two feet deep, three on each side of a huge lever beam, their legs bare up to the thighs. On our entrance they redoubled their exertions, till the perspiration fairly poured from them; the vat had been filled with grapes, and by their exertions we were enabled to see the whole process. After the grapes had been sufficiently stamped, and the men's legs well scraped, the

---

228 WILKES 1845, pages 18-19. Part of this paragraph, from the 3rd sentence to the end, was published in another American source, namely at the *Alexandria Gazette*, of March 5 and April 5, 1845. (Alexandria, VA, divulged under the titles "Madeira a genuine wine." and "GENUINE WINE.", respectively, and quoting the book *United States Exploring Expedition*).
229 Wine was carried, back then, in Madeira, on goatskins and not sheepskins, as states this author.
230 John Howard March. See Note 168.

6. MADEIRA WINE IN AMERICAN LITERATURE

Figure 24. "Wine-Carriers". *Book illustration. Sketched by J. Drayton. Engraved by R. S. Gilbert.*

Figure 25. "Wine-Press". *Book illustration. Sketched by Charles Wilkes, USN. Engraved by F. E. Worcester.*

pulp was made into the shape of a large bee-hive, a rope made of the young twigs of the vine being wound around it. The lever was then used, which has a large stone or rock attached to it by a screw. Much time is lost in adjusting this, and much consultation and dispute had. The juice flows off, and is received in tubs. The produce of the press is on an average about fifty gallons daily. Each gallon requires about ten bushels of grapes. The taste is very much like sweet cider. The process is any thing but pleasing, and endeavours have been made by English residents to substitute machinery, but the prejudices, vexations and difficulties experienced have caused them to give up the attempt. The general average is from one to three pipes of wine per acre annually.

The south side of Madeira, as is well known, although not the most fertile, produces the finest wines. Every point which can be cultivated successfully is attended to, and earth is brought to increase the soil from other parts. The kinds of grapes are various, and the wines manufactured as numerous. The common Madeira is obtained from a mixture of Bual, Verdelho, and Negro Molle[231] grapes; the Malmsey and Sercial, from grapes of the same name. There is a great difference in the spots, and peculiar exposure, where the vine grows, and different kinds of wine are produced, according to the state of maturity to which the grape is allowed to arrive [at] before being gathered. After being expressed, it is put into casks, undergoes the process of fermentation, is clarified with gypsum or isinglass, and a small portion of brandy is added, two or three gallons to the pipe. ...[232]

---

[231] The right spelling is Negra Mole.
[232] WILKES 1845, pages 21-23. A synopsis of this text was revealed in the book *United States Exploring Expeditions: Voyage of the U.S. Exploring Squadron, commanded by Captain Charles Wilkes, of the United States Navy, In 1838, 1839, 1840, 1841, and 1842: together with Explorations and Discoveries Made by Admiral D'Urville, Captain Ross, and other navigators and travellers; and an Account of the Expedition to the Dead Sea, under Lieutenant Lynch*, written by John S. Jenkins, and printed by Alden & Beardsley in Auburn and Rochester, New York, in two editions, in 1855 and 1857, between the pages 34 to 36, as follows: «... The hauling of heavy articles is principally done by the small oxen of the island, on sledges resembling the stone boats in use among American farmers. These are employed altogether in the seaport towns, for conveying pipes of wine; but the liquor is brought from the interior, in sheep-skins, sowed together so as nearly to preserve the form of the animal, which are slung over the backs of the peasants./ ... / The difference between the imports and exports of Madeira, indicates a high state of prosperity. The former barely exceed one hundred thousand dollars annually, principally consisting of staves, rice, and oil; while more than eight thousand pipes of wine, valued at over one and a half million of dollars, are exported during the same period. Most of the cereal grains, sugar, coffee, and taro, are produced in abundance. Large quantities of fine beef, vegetables, and fruit, are furnished, also, to the vessels that stop at the island. But the great staple is the far-famed Madeira wine, the best qualities of which, the connoisseur need not be told, come from the "south-side." Great care is taken to maintain the reputation of the wine, and the laws are so strict, that even the genuine article, once shipped, cannot be introduced into the island./ The method of manufacturing the wine is certainly very primitive, and differs but little from that in vogue among the nations of the East in olden times. The grapes are deposited in an elevated vat, usually about six feet square and two feet deep, under an open shed covered with a thatch roof. Some half a dozen bare-legged and bare-footed peasants, then spring into the vat, and commence stamping furiously, accompanying their motions with a rude song. After this process has been continued for a sufficient length of time, the legs of the men are scraped, and the pomace set up in the shape of a cone, and bound about with the young cuttings of the vine. A lever, to which a large stone, or rock, is attached by a screw, is now applied, and the juice expressed into tubs, – one gallon being generally obtained from two bushels of grapes.

6.1.1.7. George Mulasas Colvocoresses, USN (1838)

Lieutenant George M. Colvocoresses, a USN officer, was also a member of the 1838 American scientific expedition who traveled the world, making its first stop at Madeira, also on September 16, 1838, during the vintage time. Fourteen years later, in 1852, he published in New York a book entitled *Four Years in a Government Exploring Expedition; To the Island of Madeira – Cape Verd Islands – Brazil – Coast of Patagonia – Chili – Peru – Paumato Group – Society Islands – Navigator group – Australia – Antarctic Continent – New Zealand – Friendly Islands – Fejee Group – Sandwich Islands – Northwest Coast of America – Oregon - California – East Indies – St. Helena, &c., &c., In one volume.*[233] In the preface he states that this book had been compiled from a Journal that he had kept in obedience to a "General Order" from the Navy Department. On the first chapter he describes Madeira and writes some lines about the culture of the grape and about the island's wine carriers.

CHAPTER I.
FROM NORFOLK TO MADEIRA.

…The chief production of Madeira is the grape,[234] and that which grows near the seashore is said to make the best wine. The quantity exported last year amounted to 8,450 pipes, of which about 4,000 pipes, valued at 793,000 dollars, went to the United States. There is a great difference in the spots where the vine grows, and some estates produced much better quality of wine than others, though the kind of grape cultivated is the same. After the juice is expressed it is put into casks, undergoes the process of fermentation, is clarified with isinglass, or gypsum, and about three gallons of brandy to a pipe of wine is added. The common Madeira is obtained from a mixture of Verdelho, Bual, and Negro Molle[235] grapes; the Malmsey and Sercial, from grapes of the same name. …[236]

In passing through the streets of Funchal, you meet with many of the country people,

---

The must is drawn off into casks, in which it ferments; it is then clarified with gypsum or isinglass, and the necessary spirit imparted to it by the addition of two or three gallons of brandy to a pipe. ….»

233 COLVOCORESSES, George Mulasas, *Four Years in a Government Exploring Expedition; To the Island of Madeira – Cape Verd Islands – Brazil – Coast of Patagonia – Chili – Peru – Paumato Group – Society Islands – Navigator group – Australia – Antarctic Continent – New Zealand – Friendly Islands – Fejee Group – Sandwich Islands – Northwest Coast of America – Oregon - California – East Indies – St. Helena, &c., &c., In one volume.*, Cornish, Lamport & Co., Publishers, New York, 1852. This book had several other editions, under the same title. The second was edited by R. T. Young, Publisher, in New York, in 1853, and the fifth one was published by J. M. Fairchild & Co., in the same city, in 1855.

234 AN: "The vine was introduced in 1425, from the island of Candia; but it was not actively cultivated till the early part of the sixteenth century. It is propagated from cuttings, planted at a depth of from three to six feet and there is generally no produce for the first three years. During the second spring they are trained along a net-work of canes (which is extensively grown in low, moist situations, for that purpose), and supported by stakes, about three or four feet from the ground. The inferior descriptions of wine, after being clarified, are subjected, in stoves, to a temperature of 140° to 160° Fahr. for six months, by which process of forcing they assume an apparent age, but, at the same time, a dry and smoky flavor, which can never be entirely eradicated. This class of wines is shipped annually, in large quantities, to Hamburgh, where it undergoes a process which changes its character to that of Hock, under which name a large portion of it finds its way into the English and American markets. The wines of Madeira, with the exception of Tinta, should be kept in cellars of a moderate and equable temperature, and should be placed, for a short period, at a moderate distance from the fire before decanted, and the decanter heated in like manner." BY ONE WHO RESIDED FIFTEEN YEARS ON THE ISLAND.

235 The right spelling is Negra Mole.

236 COLVOCORESSES 1852, pages 15-16.

who have come either to trade or to obtain employment. They are a hardy, athletic race, and to all appearance remarkably polite and kind-hearted. Whenever we meet them, they invariably saluted us. They are extensively employed about the town as carriers, and a stranger is at times apt to be struck with the novel character of their load; when at a distance, he sees them bearing on their shoulders what he supposes to be a live sheep, but on nearer approach he discovers that they are only the skins of that animal filled with wine.[237] These skins are preserved as entire as possible, even the legs being retained; they are kept steady by a band which passes over the forehead and supports a considerable part of the weight. Twenty gallons is considered an ordinary load, and they will carry it to any part of the city for a pistareen.[238] ...

6.1.1.8. Joseph G. Clark, USN (1838)

Joseph G. Clark, another member of this scientific expedition, who also traveled aboard the *Vincennes* with Charles Wilkes, published a book in Boston, in 1847, containing his impressions on Madeira, although very brief. In the work *Lights and Shadows of Sailor Life, as exemplified in fifteen year's experience, including the More Thrilling Events of the U.S. Exploring Expedition, and Reminiscences of an Eventful Life on the "Mountain Wave."*[239] there is just a minor reference to Madeira Wine.

CHAPTER I.
... – The Madeira Islands – ...

... The weather is still favorable, and the breeze propitious. At daylight the island of Madeira, just appeared in sight, was looming above the watery horizon. About three o'clock, P. M. we came up with these justly celebrated islands, and I need not attempt a description of the sublime and picturesque scenery, or the rich and highly cultivated hills. At sunset we arrived off the town of Funchal, and came to anchor in Funchal Roads near the town.

... The Madeira Islands consist of Madeira[,] Parto Santo[240] and the Desert Isles. Madeira, the principal island, is distinguished for its wines, which are exported to various parts of the world; its capital is Funchal.[241] ...

6.1.1.9. Rev. Franklin P. Torrey, USN (1839)

Franklin P. Torrey, a native of the Green Mountain State, Vermont, who we assume was a Navy chaplain, published in 1841, in Boston, a book entitled *Journal of a Cruise*

---

[237] See Note 229.
[238] COLVOCORESSES 1852, pages 19-20.
[239] CLARK, Joseph G., *Lights and Shadows of Sailor Life, as exemplified in fifteen year's experience, including the More Thrilling Events of the U.S. Exploring Expedition, and Reminiscences of an Eventful Life on the "Mountain Wave."*, John Putnam, Boston, 1847. This book had another edition, in the same city, on the following year, by another publisher, Benjamin B. Mussey & Co.
[240] The right spelling is Porto Santo, nowadays a touristic resort par excellence, with its 9-km long yellow sandy beach.
[241] CLARK 1847, page 22.

of the United States Ship Ohio, Commodore Isaac Hull, Commander, in the Mediterranean, In the Years 1839, '40, '41.[242] This ship had left the New York harbor, for her maiden voyage, on the 4th of December 1838, bound for the Mediterranean, where she spent some months prior to arriving at Madeira, on October 22, 1839. On the brief journal entry referring to this island the author inserts a few complimentary words about its wine, adding that the officers had bought some for their own use.

… Tuesday the 22^d, Wednesday and Thursday. We laid off the Island of Madeira, which is 616 miles from the Rock of Gibraltar. Fired a signal gun for a Pilot at 5 o'clock. Madeira – so long noted for its superior quality of wine, which is carried to every nation and clime, and is a source of the chief wealth of its inhabitants – her scenery is most beautiful, her soil is rich and highly cultivated, her buildings are neat and handsome, her inhabitants are industrious. The purest quality of wine is made from a small black grape, nearly resembling the small Frost grape in America. The officers purchased a quantity of wine for their private use, which we took on board.[243] …

6.1.1.10. Jacob A. Hazen, USN (1841)

In 1854, Jacob A. Hazen, a former Navy sailor, published a book in Philadelphia under the title *Five Years Before The Mast; or, Life in the Forecastle, aboard of A Whaler and Man-of-War*,[244] in which he depicts his life at sea. From this book we have selected two passages, from two chapters, one dealing with a bottle of old Madeira wine used to settle a kind of a diplomatic incident aboard a U.S. Navy ship, at Brazil, and another referring to the author's arrival at Madeira, on August 1841, aboard the U.S. Ship *Columbus*, where he remained for four days. In his impressions of the island he also mentions its wine, especially the effect it had on the members of the crew who went ashore.

Chapter Ninth.
The adventurer introduces himself on board an American man-o'-war
and becomes a member of the Uncle Sam's Mess.

… The ship Independence, under the command of Commander John B. Nicholson, sailed from Boston harbor for Cronstadt,[245] in May 1837, with Mr. George M. Dallas[246] on board, as Minister Plenipotentiary to the court of Russia. On her way thither, the vessel touched at the harbor of Portsmouth, in England. Now whether it was that the treatment

---

[242] TORREY, F.[ranklin] P., *Journal of a Cruise of the United States Ship Ohio, Commodore Isaac Hull, Commander, in the Mediterranean, In the Years 1839, '40, '41.*, Samuel N. Dickinson, Boston, 1841.
[243] TORREY 1841, page 37.
[244] HAZEN, Jacob A., *Five Years Before The Mast; or, Life in the Forecastle, aboard of A Whaler and Man-of-War*, Willis P. Hazard, Philadelphia, 1854.
[245] Also spelled Kronstadt, a municipal town of St. Petersburg, Russia.
[246] George Mifflin Dallas (1792-1864), a native of Philadelphia, was a Senator for his home state and later on served as the 11th Vice President of the United States. In 1837 President Martin Van Buren appointed him as Envoy Extraordinary and Minister Plenipotentiary to Russia, a position he held for two years.

on board was too severe, or whether it was that the crew partook of so large a sprinkling of British seamen as to cause desertion it is difficult to say, but from some cause or other, it is certain, that a large number of those men who were permitted to set their feet on English soil, suddenly took their departure for parts unknown. The ship, in consequence, became short of hands; and the commodore on reaching Copenhagen,[247] either with, or without the consent of his own government, thought proper to replace the deficiency by shipping twelve Danish sailors. These men were promised their discharge at the end of two years, within which period the commodore doubtless supposed the cruise would be terminated. But such, however, happened not to be the case. Their term of service had now expired, and what was to be done? The commodore desired them to continue service until the ship proceeded to the United States; but this they from day to day hesitated to do, and finally denied duty altogether. The commodore remonstrated with them, and endeavored to reason them into obedience, but they remained refractory and stubborn, and for a period of four days kept "backing and filling" about the decks like a drove of baulky mules. They would be cajoled by no Yankee commander, they said – they were the liege subjects of his Danish Majesty, who expected their return, and return they would. An expedient was at length resorted to, for the purpose of reconciling the misunderstanding. The commodore invited on board the Danish minister, to the court of Brazil, who, on being made acquainted with the circumstances, undertook to accommodate matters. The men were called aft on the quarter deck, when they were introduced to his Danish Majesty's representative, who at once opened to them the burden of his mission. He extolled their loyalty, praised their patriotism, flattered their vanity by frequent allusions to the ardent manner in which, he said, the American commodore had spoken in praise of their courage, obedience, promptness and bravery; and after spinning out a speech some twenty minutes in length, in which he advised them to continue faithful to the American service until the vessel returned to the United States, wound up by informing them, that he would assume the responsibility of their absence from their sovereign's dominions.

The harangue proved effective. The men returned to their duty; while the skilful diplomatist, dined with the Yankee Commodore, and cracked a bottle of old Madeira wine to the success of the negotiation. Is it not a little humiliating to an honest American mind, to witness a foreign ambassador thus called into the service, to aid the United States government in maintaining subordination in their own navy?[248] …

Chapter Sixteenth.
Voyage to Gibraltar.

… Early in August we drew into the vicinity of the Western Isles, and passed within view of Fayal and Pico. We there bent our course in a southeasterly direction, and after about a week's run, anchored in front of the castle of Funchal, at the Island of Madeira.

I am unable to say why the Commodore stopped at this place, unless it was for the purpose of letting the apprentice boys have a run on shore; and this had better not have been done, for they all got drunk before they were on shore six hours, and nine days afterwards,

---

247 Capital of Denmark.
248 HAZEN 1854, pages 171-173.

seven of the ten, were placed under the hands of the surgeon to be cured of venereal diseases. But then we had grapes and oranges of an excellent quality, and at prices so low that all hands were enabled to buy; and this more than compensated for the inconvenience we experienced from drunken and diseased boys.

Madeira is an island of considerable note in the wine trade. It belongs to the Portuguese government, and lies about six hundred miles southeast from that country. The general features of the island are of a volcanic cast. The surface of the country is broken and uneven, shooting up, in places, into irregular ridges, and abrupt peaks, and terminating along the shores in rocky ledges and precipices of frightful height. Funchal, the capital, is situated at the foot of a mountain near the sea, and contains a population of near twenty thousand inhabitants. The harbor is a very poor one, and ships anchoring in it, are never secure from being cast away during stormy weather. …

The commodore, having gratified his curiosity in respect to the Island by a short sojourn among its inhabitants, reappeared on board the ship at the end of four days, upon which we again bent our course to seaward, and bore away in the direction of Gibraltar.[249] …

6.1.1.11. Samuel Rhoades Franklin, USN (1842)

In January 1842 Samuel Rhoades Franklin left the Hampton Roads for the Pacific aboard the U.S. Frigate *United States*, which, back then, was deemed the swiftest ship in the Navy. After a journey of 18 to 20 days he arrived at Madeira, his first port of call. Later in life, in 1898, he published a book, in New York and London, entitled *Memories of A Rear-Admiral Who has Served for More than Half a Century in the Navy of the United States*,[250] where he describes his first visit to Madeira, in Chapter III. In it he mentions the name of the U.S. Consul to Madeira and wine merchant, John Howard March, and also the fact that aboard his frigate many casks of Madeira Wine – for the Commodore and his friends – were stocked in the ship's spirit room.

CHAPTER III.

The First Cruise – Madeira and Rio – …

… Our stay at Madeira was to be short – I think it was only three days – so we Midshipmen were allowed to go on shore, half of our number at a time. It was our first foreign port, and we of course enjoyed it to the fullest extent. … At this time our Consul was Mr. Howard March; he was also a wine merchant, and lived in great luxury. I dined with him once, but I do not remember whether it was at this time or upon some subsequent visit. I remember distinctly, however, that he produced some rare old Madeira that was nearly as white as water. At the time about which I am writing, Madeira wine was still much drunk in this country. We received on board many casks of if for the Commodore and his friends who had given him orders for it, and who wished their wine to have the benefit of a three

---

249 HAZEN 1854, pages 291-293.
250 FRANKLIN, Samuel Rhoades, *Memories of A Rear-Admiral Who has Served for More than Half a Century in the Navy of the United States*, Harper & Brothers Publishers, New York and London, 1898.

years' shaking up before it was delivered to them at home. I recollect distinctly some of the names of well-known people on the barrels, as they came on board to be stored away for a cruise, deep down in the spirit-room of the Frigate. After everybody had had an opportunity of a run on shore, and our stores for the next passage had been received on board, the spirit-room well stocked for its curing process, and after the delights of our three days' sojourn, we were not unwilling to proceed towards our station in the Pacific, for there was a feeling that I think we all shared, of strong desire to be there.

We sailed from Madeira in the early days of February, bound for Rio de Janeiro. …[251]

6.1.1.12. John Adams Dix (1842)

Mid 19 century Madeira was a renowned destination for consumptives, who sought its balmy airs to recover their shattered health. John Adams Dix, a native of New Hampshire and politician who lived most of his life in New York City, whose wife was sick and seeking a cure for her condition, went to Madeira with her in October 1842, aboard the ship *Mexican*, and arrived there on November 11. He spent that winter on the island, where he remained until March 17, 1843. Two years later he was elected Senator and had a brilliant career that led him to be, decades later, Governor of New York. In 1850, he published anonymously, in New York his book entitled *A Winter in Madeira. And a Summer in Spain and Florence*.[252] According to our research he was the first non-USN officer to publish a book with impressions of Madeira, in which he dedicates nine chapters to the island. In three of them he wrote extensively about different aspects of Madeira Wine. In Chapter II he describes the Oxen and Cursa [corça] and the wine bearers from the vineyards, in the next one he refers to Câmara de Lobos as a wine-producing district, and last but not least, in Chapter V he mentions the depression of the commerce of Madeira, the taxes levied on foreign grains and export duties on wine, and also the exports of wine from 1828 to 1842.

CHAPTER II.
FIRST IMPRESSIONS OF MADEIRA.
… Oxen and cursa. – … – Wine-bearers from the Vineyards. – …

… We are now out of the Praça Constitucional, and are passing through a narrow street. It is twenty-five feet wide, perhaps – not more; and yet it is fully equal in width to the other streets of the city. It is paved, like them, with small stones – a covering which would not resist for a single day the heavy-wheeled vehicles constantly passing through ours. How is it that these pavements are everywhere so even and unbroken? The cause is soon obvious. We meet no carriages or carts – no vehicles, in short, on wheels. Here

---

251 FRANKLIN 1898, pages 26-27.
252 [DIX, John Adams], *A Winter in Madeira. And a Summer in Spain and Florence*, William Holdredge, New York, 1850. This book had at least four editions in a short period of time, the second one, by the same publisher, was issued in New York in 1851, and the fifth one was edited by D. Appleton & Company in the same city, in 1853. From the second edition onwards this book presented the name of its author.

comes a sledge, or, as the Portuguese call it, a cursa.²⁵³ It is drawn by two diminutive oxen, and yet it has a pipe of wine, weighing hard upon half a ton. What a primitive vehicle it is! It certainly can not date farther forward in the advance of civilization than the deluge. It is a plank about eight feet long, some sixteen inches wide, and four or five thick, the fore end slightly pointed. On each side, underneath, it has two shoes of wood running from stem to stern; and above, on each end, there is a cross-piece of the width of the principal piece of wood, to prevent the load from slipping either way. The plank is hollowed in the centre from one end to the other, to about the rotundity of a wine-cask, which is its most usual loading, though it carries every thing else that is to be carried. The driver is walking by the side of his cattle, and shouting to them as if it were necessary to compensate for their lack of size and strength by the noise he makes. A small boy accompanies him, carrying in his hand a long mop of rope yarn, or coarse cloth, which he now and then dips in the water he meets with in the streets and throws it down in front of the sledge. The sledge passes over it, and, the bottom being thoroughly moistened, glides over the pavements with greater ease, not only lightening the labor of the cattle, but preventing the danger of fire from friction. Uncouth as this mode of transportation is, it is the only one adapted to the condition of the city. …²⁵⁴

Figure 26. John Adams Dix. *Engraving from the frontispiece of the first edition of his book.*

Here is a sight of a still more novel character than any we have seen yet – a body of countrymen from the vineyards. They come in single file, like the donkeys, whose province they seem to have usurped, for they are full as heavily laden. Each one has a goat-skin of wine on his head or shoulders, or around his neck. What a variety of modes they have of carrying their loads! and such loads, too! The skins seem to have been taken off entire. They have no openings excepting at the legs and neck, and these are tied up tightly to keep in the rosy fluid they contain. The man who leads the way is singing at the top of his voice; and the others keep time, as well as they can, with his hoarse intonations. The skins are not quite full; and as the procession moves on, and the liquid within them vibrates with the motion, you feel every moment as if some of these thin coverings would burst, and wine enough to make a hundred hearts glad would be poured out upon the unthankful pavement.

The dress these wine-bearers have on, must be characteristic of the interior of the island. It is nothing more than a cotton shirt and a pair of loose cotton or tow breeches, just long enough to cover the knee, and buttoned tight under it, leaving the leg bare to the bottom of the calf. Below this is a goat-skin boot, coming above the ankle. Some of them have blue cloth jackets, or long, gray, shapeless coats, thrown over the skins of wine, to be put on when they shall have discharged their loads; and these complete their dress.²⁵⁵ …

---

253 The right spelling is corça, although in 19th century Portuguese it was spelled as corsa.
254 [DIX] 1850, pages 40-42.
255 [DIX] 1850, pages 45-46.

CHAPTER III.
THE CITY OF FUNCHAL AND ITS ENVIRONS.
… – Camera de Lobos.[256] – Wine-producing District . – …

… Our next visit was to Camera de Lobos,[257] or, as it is now more generally but not properly called, Cama de Lobos.[258] It is a small village, about five miles, by water, and six by land, west from Funchal. The ride there is exceedingly interesting. It leads you through the finest suburb of the city, by the parish church of San Martino,[259] and near the round-topped hills we saw from Nossa Senhora do Monte. We found them, as we passed, terraced and cultivated to their very summits. The whole country, indeed, may be said to be a succession of terraces and planes. It is only by building up walls and creating artificial levels above them, that the soil can be secured from the effects of the rains, which in winter pour down from the hill-tops, accumulating as they descend, and cutting up the defenceless portions of the surface into gullies and ravines. The quantity of labor expended in creating and securing these artificial levels, is enormous. It would hardly have been sustained by any ordinary object of agriculture. But this portion of the island is devoted principally to the cultivation of the vine. It is within a circle of some twelve miles in diameter around Funchal that the best wines are produced. They have usually commanded high prices, and the proprietors have been enabled to invest largely in the improvement of their lands. …[260]

CHAPTER V.
CITY OF FUNCHAL.
… – Impost on Foreign Grains and Export Duty on Wines. – … – Exports of Wine from 1828 to 1842.

… The decline of the commerce of the island of Madeira is to be traced, in some degree, to the pecuniary embarrassments which exist in other countries, though it is also, to a great extent, to be attributed to causes of domestic origin. Its entire product for exportation consists of its wines, an article of luxury. When the countries in which they are consumed are prosperous, its annual supply is absorbed. But when commercial depression and embarrassment call for economy and retrenchment on the part of the consumers of its wines, the usual demand is diminished, and a surplus accumulates. This is the case at the present time. Such a season of inactivity in business has never before been known. Little wine is exported. Large quantities remain on hand; and the islanders, who rely on sales for the support of their families, are reduced to great embarrassment for want of money. As a temporary resource, many are selling off ornaments and jewelry which they can dispense with. Almost every day some such articles are offered to us – laces, ear-rings, breastpins, and gold chains – the former at very low prices, and the latter for the value of the gold contained in them. But for the animal influx of invalids, who come here to pass the winter months, and who expend, at the lowest calculation, $150,000 in Funchal, the suffering would be still greater. This foreign tribute is, in fact, to a large portion of the amount, a

---

[256] The right spelling is Câmara de Lobos.
[257] The right spelling is Câmara de Lobos.
[258] See Note 207.
[259] The right spelling is São Martinho, a parish of the outskirts of Funchal.
[260] [DIX] 1850, pages 104-106.

consumption of the products of the island, or the employment of its labor. It puts in requisition the services of a great number of persons in the city, and brings from the interior the articles of subsistence which are necessary for the support of the foreign visitors.

The Madeira wines were first brought into notice in the western hemisphere by the city of Charleston, in South Carolina. From that city the island received large supplies of rice, which constituted a considerable portion of the subsistence of its inhabitants. A more natural or beneficial traffic to the islanders there could not well be. They were profiting largely by it. They found a ready and advantageous vent for their staple, and they received in return a cheap and nutritious article of food. In an evil hour, Portugal, under the influence of the protective system – a system which too often turns the industry it seeks to regulate and benefit into unnatural and unprofitable channels – imposed a heavy duty on rice imported from any but its own dominions. The object was to protect the rice of Brazil. The object was accomplished: the rice of Brazil obtained a monopoly of the Madeira market. The trade with Charleston was destroyed; for the impost on rice amounted to a prohibition. But Brazil does not want the wines of Madeira; and the people of the island, at least those who can afford it, eat bad rice at prices comparatively high, without being able to pay for it directly with their own products. What a comment on the folly of governments in attempting, for the benefit of particular districts of country or classes of people, to give a direction to human industry and force it out of the channels in which it naturally circulates! …

The extent to which the commerce of Funchal has fallen off might be better understood, if its shipping-list for the last year could be compared with those of former years. This, unfortunately, is impossible, for want of authentic registers. The number of vessels which entered the port in 1842, was 366; of which 72 were Portuguese, 188 English, 29 American, 15 French, Danish 5, Sardinian 33, Spanish 7, Greek 6, and 11 from various countries. From 1807 to 1815, the number of vessels entering the port is said to have been from 400 to 500 yearly. A better criterion, perhaps, of the commercial prosperity of the island, may be found in its exports of wine, its only product for foreign consumption. The amount entered for exportation at the custom-house in Funchal, for a series of years, is as follows:

Year	Amount		Year	Amount
1828	9623 pipes.		1836	7913 pipes.
1829	8104 "		1837	8123 "
1830	5499 "		1838	9828 "
1831	5533 "		1839	9043 "
1832	7163 "		1840	7975 "
1833	8683 "		1841	7157 "
1834	9228 "		1842	6270 "
1835	7730 "			

It will be seen that the export for 1842 was the least during the eleven years of which it terminates the series, and nearly half of this amount is said to have been sent abroad on speculation to find purchasers, and not on actual sales and orders. In earlier and more prosperous years the annual export sometimes rose to 15,000 pipes. …

6.1.1.13. Horatio Bridge, USN (1844)

Horatio Bridge (1806-1893), a native of Maine, was a Commodore of the United States Navy that joined the African Squadron which had the mission of patrolling the West Coast of Africa to prevent slave ships from taking Negroes to America, where they were widely used, especially in the southern plantations. In the long time spent off the coast of Africa, some Navy ships would sometimes come to Madeira in order to get provisions and to rest their crews. He left New York for his long-term mission alongside the western African coast on June 5, 1843. Several months later, on January 18, 1844, he arrived at Madeira, aboard the U.S. ship *Saratoga*. After his return to the United States, he published an anonymous book, in 1845, in New York and London, entitled *The Journal of an African Cruiser; Comprising Sketches of the Canaries, The Cape de Verds, Madeira, Sierra Leone, and other places of interest on the West Coast of Africa*[261], adding that it had been edited by Nathaniel Hawthorne – his former college mate, who owed his literary career to Bridge. This book dedicates the Chapter XI to Madeira, in which, among several topics, its author elaborates on Madeira wine, its production and commerce.

CHAPTER XI.
… – Dissertation upon Wines – The Clerks of Funchal – Decay of the Wine-Trade – …

… A sketch of Madeira would be incomplete indeed, without some mention of its wines. Three years ago, when it was more a matter of personal interest, I visited this island, and gained considerable information on the subject. Madeira then produced about thirty thousand pipes annually, one third of which was consumed on the island, one-third distilled into brandy, and the remainder exported. About one-third of the exportation went to the United States, and the balance to other parts of the world. The best wines are principally sent to our own country – that is to say, the best exported – for very little of the first-rate wine goes out of the island. The process of adulteration is as thoroughly understood and practised here, as anywhere else. The wine sent to the United States is a kind that has been heated, to give it an artificial age. The mode of operation is simply to pour the wine into large vats, and submit it for several days to a heat of about 110º. After this ordeal, the wine is not much improved by keeping.

There are other modes of adulteration, into the mysteries of which I was not admitted. One fact, communicated to me by an eminent wine-merchant, may shake the faith of our connoisseurs as to the genuineness of their favorite beverage. It is, that, from a single pipe of "mother wine," ten pipes are manufactured by the help of inferior wine. This "mother wine" is that which has been selected for its excellence, and is seldom exported pure. The wines, when fresh from the vintage, are as various in their flavor as our cider. It is by taste and smell that the various kinds are selected, after which the poorer wines are distilled

---

[261] [BRIDGE, Horatio], *The Journal of an African Cruiser; Comprising Sketches of the Canaries, The Cape de Verds, Madeira, Sierra Leone, and other places of interest on the West Coast of Africa*, Wiley and Putnam, New York and London, 1845. This book had several other editions, both in the UK and in the USA, published namely by Wiley and Putnam, in London, in 1845, and by George Clark and Son and S. Richardson, both in Aberdeen and London, in 1848, and last but not least, by George P. Putnam & Co., in New York, in 1853. The former two editions did not present the name of its author on the cover, what only happened on the last one.

into brandy, and the better are put in cases, and placed in store to ripen. The liquor is from time to time racked off, and otherwise managed until ready for exportation. It is *invariably* "treated" with brandy. French brandy was formerly used, which being now prohibited, that of the island is substituted, although of an inferior quality.

Besides the "Madeira wine," so famous among convivialists, there are others of higher price and superior estimation. There is the "Sercial," distinguished by a kind of Poppy taste. There is the Malmsey, or "Ladies' wine," and the "Vina Tinta," or Madeira Claret, as it is sometimes called. The latter is made of the black grapes, in a peculiar manner. After being pressed, the skins of the grapes are placed in a vat, where the juice is poured upon them and suffered to stand several days, until it has taken the hue required. The taste of

Figure 27. Horatio Bridge. 19th century photograph. Author unknown.

this wine is between those of Port and Claret. There is a remarkable difference in the quality of the vintages of the north and south sides of the island; the former not being a third part so valuable as the latter. The poorer classes drink an inferior and acid wine.

The vineyards are generally owned by rich proprietors, by whom they are farmed out to the laborer, who pays half the produce when the wine has been pressed; the government first taking its tenth. The grape-vines run along frame-work, raised four or five feet from the ground, so as to allow the cultivator room to weed the stalks beneath. The finest grapes are those which grow upon the sunny side of a wall. At the season of vintage, the grapes are placed in a kind of canoe, where they are first crushed by men's feet (all wines, even the richest and purest, having this original tincture of the human foot), and then pressed by a beam.

Perhaps the very finest wines in the world are to be found collected at the suppers given by the clerks, in the large mercantile houses of Madeira. By an established custom, when one of their corps is about to leave the island, he gives an entertainment, to which every guest contributes a bottle or two of wine. It is a point of honor to produce the best; and as the clerks know, quite as well as their principals, where the best is to be found, and as the honor of their respective houses is to be sustained, it may well be imagined that all the *bon-vivants* on earth, were they to meet at one table, could hardly produce such a variety of fine old Madeira, as the clerks of Funchal then sip and descant upon. In no place do mercantile clerks hold so respectable a position in society as here; owing to the tacit understanding between their principals and themselves, that, at some future day, they are to be admitted as partners in the houses. This is so general a rule, that the clerk seems to hold a social position scarcely inferior to that of the head of the establishment. They prove their claim to this high consideration, by the zeal with which they improve their minds and cultivate their manners, in order to fill creditably the places to which they confidently aspire.

At my second visit to Madeira, I find the wine trade at a very low ebb. The demand from America, owing to temperance, the tariff, and partly to an increased taste for Spanish, French, and German wines, is extremely small. Not a cargo has been shipped thither for three years. The construction given to the tariff, by the Secretary of the Treasury, will infuse new life into the trade.

The hills around the city of Funchal are covered with vineyards, as far up as the grape will grow; then come the fields of vegetables; and the plantations of pine for the supply of the city. ...[262]

6.1.1.14. Benjamin F. Stevens, USN (1844)

Benjamin F. Stevens, a native of Boston, MA, joined the U.S. frigate *Constitution* at the end of 1843, as a clerk to her commander, Captain John Percival.[263] During the cruise bound to Japan Stevens wrote a narrative with its main events and presenting vivid descriptions of places visited, that was later published at the "United Service Magazine". From this source it was reprinted, in New York, in 1904, under the form of a book, entitled *A Cruise of the Constitution. Around the World on Old Ironsides*[264] *– 1844 to 1847*.[265] The ship departed from New York on May 29, 1844, and after a brief stop at Faial, in the Azores, the *Constitution* arrived at Madeira at the evening of June 24th. Stevens went ashore on the following day and had the chance to visit a vineyard, which he briefly describes.

... A walk through a vineyard is worth a great deal; here millions upon millions of grapes are hanging, shortly to be turned into wine, and upon the season arriving for that operation, great rejoicings are held all over the island among the laboring classes.[266] ...

6.1.1.15. Charles Wainwright March (1852)

Charles Wainwright March (1814-1864), a native of New Hampshire, was a Harvard graduate, lawyer, journalist, essayist and writer. On October 1, 1852, he started a journey from Southampton to Madeira, aboard the brig *Brilliant*, and arrived at Funchal, after a stormy passage, on the 18th but was unable to land until the next day, due to a sea storm that raged the seashore of the capital of the island. He spent that winter in Madeira and, during his sojourn gathered a lot of data, that later on was passed into his book, *Sketches and Adventures in Madeira, Portugal, and the Andalusias of Spain*,[267] published in New York, in 1856. This book was published in a semi-anonymous kind of way, for it just stated that it had been written by the author of *Daniel Webster and his Contemporaries*. He was the nephew of the U.S. Consul in Funchal, John Howard

---

[262] [BRIDGE] 1845, pages 89-91.
[263] During his short stay at Madeira Captain John Percival bought a cask of Madeira Wine, some of which still existed in America four decades later. See section 9.12. of this anthology.
[264] "Old Ironsides" was the nickname attributed to this frigate after her battle with the British ship *Guerriere*. The *Constitution* is very famous for her actions during the War of 1812 against Great Britain, when she captured numerous merchant ships and defeated five British warships, the HMS *Guerriere, Java, Pictou, Cyane* and *Levant*. As a matter of curiosity we add that the last two ships were taken in the vicinity of Madeira island. This frigate still exists and is the world's oldest commissioned naval vessel afloat.
[265] STEVENS, Benjamin F., *A Cruise of the Constitution. Around the World on Old Ironsides – 1844 to 1847*, New York, 1904.
[266] STEVENS 1904, page 10.
[267] [MARCH, Charles Wainwright], *Sketches and Adventures in Madeira, Portugal, and the Andalusias of Spain*, Harper & Brothers, New York, 1856.

March – a native of New Hampshire and also a wine merchant in Madeira, so praised for his liberality by many Americans that passed by the island and were his guests – but he omitted that fact in his entire book. In it there are ten chapters about the island and in two of them – III and VIII – there are references to Madeira Wine, the latter being totally dedicated to this theme, which makes him the first American author to dedicate a full chapter to this matter. In Chapter III he mentions the garden and establishment of the American Consul – due to his family ties with him he had privileged access to everything and described his wine-related properties in detail – and also the terrible blight that had fallen upon the grapes on the summer of that year. On the other hand, in Chapter VIII, which is illustrated with two interesting sketches related to wine transportation on the island, Charles W. March describes in vivid detail the vintage, the making of wine, the origin of the Madeira grape and also alludes to the various kinds of wine the island produced at that time.

CHAPTER III.
THE GARDEN AND ESTABLISHMENT OF THE AMERICAN CONSUL – ... – THE LANDED PROPRIETORS.

... And the evening *réunions* at the consulate were pleasant, and dwell gratefully on the memory. Whist was the general occupation, with tea and toast for the sole refreshment. I do not recollect to have seen wine introduced at all, and no stronger potations are known in polite society. The Portuguese are no wine-bibbers, though they cultivate the vine. They place their choicest vintage upon the table from courteous habit, but indulge even at dinner sparsely; after dinner, most rarely, if ever. ...[268]

But the old hospitality of the island can hardly be kept up. The blight has fallen upon the grape, and there is no longer "fruit in the vine." In former times, no persons any where lived more comfortably or sumptuously than the *noblesse de la vigne* of Madeira. They had handsome town houses and elegant country residences, many clubs, and a retinue of servants. They kept an open and a luxurious table. This must all be changed. There are many wealthy residents still; but their former hospitality and large expenditures must decrease with decreasing incomes. Thirty years since, when a house exported annually some hundreds of pipes at a romantic profit, the height of great extravagance even was hardly felt. With regal incomes, these "royal merchants" laughed at all outlays. But with change of times must come change of habits. There can be no exportation of wine, for there are no grapes, and consequently there can be no income. The proprietors, who are now drawing upon their stored wines to keep up their establishments, will soon find that resource exhausted. They must relinquish their old occupation, and devote capital and energy to other pursuits.[269]

---

268 [MARCH] 1856, page 37.
269 [MARCH] 1856, page 40.

CHAPTER VIII.[270]
THE VINTAGE – THE ORIGIN OF THE MADEIRA GRAPE – THE VARIOUS KINDS OF WINE.

One of the nicest times in Madeira is the gathering in of the vintage. It is made half-holiday – labor united with festive enjoyment, like a husking in New England, or rather as it *was* in my boyhood. New England since only indulges in *isms* – abolition-ism, temperance-ism, and rheumat-ism.

The grapes mature some time in September – early in the month in the southern part of the island – and there is scarcely a more grateful sight than these round, plump, purple pendants from the vine, which is trained along a net-work of canes, some three or four feet above the ground –

> "Sweet is the vintage, when the showering grape
> In Bacchanal profusion reels to earth,
> Purple and gushing" –[271]

holding out the word of promise to the eye, and *keeping* it to the hope.

The women and girls, with a portion of the men, go into the vineyards with their baskets and gather carefully the grapes. These they bring in on their heads, safely balanced. Would that these girls were prettier, that we might think of Hebes[272] pouring out such wine! But Providence apportions its blessings.

The grapes thus gathered are picked over, "escolhido," and the good and indifferent separated – the best reserved for the costliest wine. They then are thrown into the wine-press, a wide, clumsy trough of wood, into which men jump, barefooted, with their trousers rolled up, and trample out the juice. The advantage of expressing the juice with the feet is said to be that they give way to the stem and seeds, and do not squeeze out and mix their bitterness with the pure juice. Too much care can not be bestowed upon this delicate product of the vine. After the first expression has been drawn off, the remaining portion is collected together in some integument, and fastened by a cord, subjected to a lever pressure. The grapes all exhausted, the juice is conveyed to the store-houses in goat-skins, which are said to give it additional flavor, and there emptied into casks for the process of fermentation, which usually lasts four or five weeks. Water is thrown into the wine-press, after the juice has been carefully extracted, and this, mixing with the refuse, and undergoing the same process as the juice before, forms the "agoa pè,"[273] literally foot-water, which is retailed at the ventas[274] to the lower classes at a moderate price, which they drink often immoderately, and induce diarrhea, particularly if used after the fermentation has commenced.

---

[270] 80% of the contents of this chapter were divulged by Charles W. March in an article that he published in the edition of December 5, 1853 of the *New York Daily Tribune*, under the title of "Madeira and a voyage thither". This newspaper article, which we present on the section 6.1.3. of this anthology, has a different beginning and the remaining text has some modifications, when compared with this one, published three years later, in 1856. Therefore we consider the newspaper text as the original version. By reading both of them the curious reader may find its similarities and differences.

[271] Quote from the CXXIV stanza of Lord Biron's poem "Don Juan".

[272] Although spelled this way by the author, it all indicates that he intended to refer to Hebe, the goddess of youth in Greek mythology.

[273] The right spelling is Água-pé, in present-day Portuguese.

[274] The right spelling is Vendas, the Portuguese word that designates a small grocery store. Ventas is a pejorative Portuguese word to designate one's face.

The vintage bringing into Funchal the peasantry, with their filled goat-skins, makes a *fiesta* – a frolic; and of an evening you hear every where in the environs the simple harmony of the machête[275] – a small guitar, used to accompany the voice and dance. Every body dances here, and every body sings, if not with much grace, with great *abandon*; and as the delicious evenings tolerate these festivals out of doors, you see and hear all around you merriment and innocent revelry.

Figure 28. "Bringing Wine to Market on Goat-Skins." *Book illustration. Author unknown.*

The wine, having ceased fermenting, is drawn off the lees, and put into sweet casks, when it is clarified with eggs, ox blood, or usually with gypsum; a *soupçon* of brandy, also made of the grape, having been previously added to each pipe to prevent the acetous fermentation.

The grapes that furnish the best wines are not agreeable to the palate; there are other grapes, however, most grateful in the mouth, which, with the fresh figs, the orange and the banana, constitute the customary *avant-bouche* of breakfast.

The grape, it is generally allowed, came from Cyprus some four centuries ago, through the patronage of the royal house of Braganza. It soon improved, under the temperate climate and on the volcanic soil of this island: for the whole history of the vine has demonstrated that volcanic or calcareous soils are best adapted to its cultivation. In the neighborhood of Vesuvius, and within reach of its influence, flourish the choicest vines of Italy, the Falernian and others. Hermitage, the boast of France, affects the *débris* of decomposed hills, or mixture of calcareous and granitic soils; and, generally, the wines that most gladden the heart of man spring from the mold of the earth.

The fancy of the grape for certain soils and positions was not unknown to the ancients. They soon found that the vine throve best in slopes, basking in the sunshine, and on limy soil, and governed its cultivation accordingly. They early discovered, too, how much age develops and enhances the intrinsic value of wines. The cob-webbed bottle was as much of a boast then as now. Horace, Bacchus's poet-laureate, dwells enthusiastically on contemporaneous *amphora* which, with him, first saw the light, "Consule Plauco," while Plaucus was Consul, some forty years before, and sings its merits under an inspiration, it may be, borrowed from itself. In earlier Greece, the cultivation of the vine reached the dignity of a fine art. Her poets built lofty verse in grateful commemoration of their indebtedness:

"It made Anacreon's soul divine."

Their best and oldest wine they reserved for the greatest occasions – for the bridal-feasts, the coronation, or sacrifice to the gods. When the embassadors of Agamemnon sought Achilles's tent, with large offers of reparation, upon the acceptance of which depended the fate of Troy, before the son of Thetis would permit them to unfold their message, he directed Patroclus to bring out some of his father's own selected wine, and to serve it out in unmeasured goblets.

---

275 A small stringed guitar, typical of Madeira, also known as *braguinha*, that in the mid 1870's would be taken to the Sandwich Islands (Hawaii) by Madeiran emmigrants, and there, some time after, became known as the *ukulele*.

And though Homer, for reasons best known to himself, withholds the confession, there can be no doubt that the success of the mission is mainly to be attributed to the free circulation of the cup. Even Ulysses seemed to lay aside his craft, and Achilles to forget his wrongs; and ever since that occasion, in all elevated and polished society, the bottle has passed from right to left; as Homer tells us Achilles passed it.

The soil of Madeira resembles that of the Campagna Felice, where grew and grows the historic Falernian; nor are the flavor and aroma of the best wines of the two unlike, or their sanitary properties. It is a vulgar prejudice that Madeira naturally produces gout. It has been the fashion to decry it from the time the Prince-Regent[276] forsook it for Sherry; as every one who affected to be à la mode, thought it necessary to join with royalty. Those who have deemed it expedient to make a specific charge against the wine, accuse it of producing this "old-gentlemanly" complaint – the gout. The opinion, however, of the most eminent physicians is to the contrary. So is experience on the island. Nowhere do they drink older or better Madeira than where it is made, and nowhere do they suffer less from the gout. Indeed, the disease is unknown to the natives or residents. Doubtless, excessive indulgence in Madeira wines would injure health and shorten life; and this may be said with equal truth of other wines, particularly of Champagne, which, from the too frequent admission of deleterious substances in the manufacture, is sure to undermine the constitution.

Brandied wines of any kind intoxicate, and therefore injure. It is the peculiar felicity of Madeira wines that their own alcoholic qualities are sufficient to their own safety. "Nothing in them doth suffer a sea-change" by exportation, for the worse. They support themselves, like virtue. That they are sometimes mixed with foreign spirits, and thus become pernicious, is true, as virtue herself suffers by contact with vice; but *caveat emptor*,[277] let the buyer know the producer.

The discoveries of science have greatly facilitated the proper cultivation of the grape. The study of chemistry, particularly, has done much to improve the fruit by a careful and enlightened investigation of the properties and capacities of the soil. Nor has such been the sole accomplishment of experimental study. *The aspect which the vineyard lends to the sun* has proved an all-important consideration. The same vines upon the same soil, and under the same care have given very different results – a difference traced to variations of aspect. The vine, to produce a wine of exquisite flavor, should, like the sunflower,

> "Turn to its God when he sets,
> The same look it turned when he rose."

It should bask in its heat all the time it is above the horizon.

The judicious selection of the plants, seasonable pruning of the vine, proper irrigation and careful maturing of the fruit – such are some of the assiduities necessary to the perfect development of the qualities of the grape. By these the astringent properties, which reside in the unreclaimed vine, and which affect injuriously the stomach, are removed; while the rich saccharine matter, the aroma, and those undefined intrinsic virtues which promote cheerfulness, are brought out and developed. No plant of the earth requires more devoted attention, or more abundantly rewards it.

---

276 George Augustus Frederick (1762-1830), later King George IV who, from 1811 until his ascension to the throne, in 1820, served as Prince Regent during his father's (George III) final mental illness.
277 Latin expression meaning "Let the buyer beware".

Some of the island proprietors attach vineyards to their quintas (country seats), mingling the useful and the ornamental. The American Consul, Mr. March,[278] had most of the grounds of his quinta[279] covered with the vine. It is a pleasant little villa on the so-called "New Road,"[280] about a mile from Funchal; and faces sun and sea. The grounds are some fifty acres in extent; a greater part the two sides of a ravine, or bed of an exhausted torrent[281] – terraced with the vine from the bottom to the highest ground. The soil is composed of a certain fresh mold, the product of an annual dissolution of the rocky hillocks or mounds above, dislodged and borne down by the tempestuous storms of winter. The fertile slopes of the "Cote d'Or" of Burgundy, which furnish the Romanee and Chambertin, have a soil of the same kind. *Non inexpertus loquor.*[282] For last summer, accompanied by Monsieur Jules Lausseure, one of the largest wine-growers in the district, I went over those regions, so dear to nature and to the gourmand, and made myself as well acquainted with the properties *as the production* of the soil. I recollect to have taken to my lodgings a portion of the soil which was pointed out to me as calcareous, and the effervescence which resulted from the application of vinegar, indicated the presence of a considerable quantity of lime.

Figure 29. "Hauling Wine on a Sledge With Oxen." *Book illustration. Author unknown.*

The owner of this quinta, cognizant of the eminent merits of the soil and situation, has devoted, and is devoting, much time, labor, and expense to its proper management. Great care is bestowed upon the selection of the cuttings, great nicety in planting, and great assiduity in pruning them. The soil is always kept clean, properly irrigated, and cleared of insects and weeds; and if the grape recover from its present blight, he will reap, many times told, the cost of his outlay and labor. The vineyard, so carefully and scientifically cultivated, will doubtless afford an annual vintage of fifty pipes of Sercial and other wines, the choicest and most costly that the island produces.

The capital of these merchant-proprietors are their vineyards and their stored wines. The latter may be denominated their bank, upon which they determine the extent of their transactions. The long established houses have a large capital in their vaults – a specie capital. I counted many hundred pipes of wine in the store-houses of the Consul;[283] wines of different vintages and denominations, ranging in price according to character and age, from $2 50 the gallon, to as high a sum as the most extravagant would wish to

---

278 John Howard March, the author's uncle.
279 Quinta Magnólia, which still exists, although smaller in size. At the present day it is located at Rua Dr. Pita and John Howard March's manor house is still there, and holds the Foreign Cultures Library, which has several reading rooms dedicated to a few countries, among which there is the American Culture Corner, devoted to the United States' Culture and Literature.
280 Or "Caminho Novo", in Portuguese. Former denomination of the present-day Estrada Monumental, a 9-km road built originally in the 1850's that links Funchal to Câmara de Lobos.
281 Named Ribeiro Seco.
282 Latin expression meaning "I do not speak without knowledge".
283 Located at Rua de São Francisco, in Funchal, that still exists, under a different owner, belonging since 1913 to the renowned Madeira Wine Company, established in that year through the merger of different wine companies.

pay. Other old houses such as Newton, Gordon & Co., Blackburns, Oliveira & Davies, have also large store-houses filled.

All the wines of the island pass, with the stranger, under the general designation of Maderia[284] wines. In the mean time, there is as great a difference between the different wines of the island as between Madeira and Sherry, or Sherry and Port. Some are dry, some full-bodied, some of a fruity taste. Some are light, and others heavy. Some that would have delighted our grandfathers, men of strong heads, and others better suited to modern capacities. They are various in color, too. There are those of deeper red than Port, while others again are paler than sherries. Indeed, there is hardly a taste which could not be gratified with some of the wines of the island.

The wines of the south side of the island are the best; and, indeed, in aroma, delicacy of flavor, and cheerful properties, are unsurpassed anywhere. The finest are the Sercial, the Malmsey, the Bûal,[285] the Tinta or Burgundy Madeira, and the Tinto.

The Sercial is called a *dry* wine. Of a verity, if taken in full glasses, the victim would be *very* dry the morning after. It is potent, and to be treated accordingly. But its bouquet might "create a soul under the ribs of death,"[286] if any thing could. It sends an odor through a room sweeter than pastils. A glass after soup confirms the grace before, and predisposes the soul to the fullness of a gratitude – *the sense of favors to come.*

On my descent down "the wide and winding Rhine," I stopped at the Château of Johannisberg, the property of the celebrated Metternich.[287] With some trouble I gained admission to the cellars, and tasted their rich contents. The major-domo (whose German designation I know not how to spell) gave me much information regarding the wines – all which to hear I patiently inclined. The best wine he had, he told me with emphasis, came from a vine he had caused to be transplanted from Madeira, and which, on that island, produced a wine called Sercial. On that hint I spoke "right out in meetin';" I told him I was recently from Madeira – had often drunk the Sercial there, and dared not believe *that* wine *could* be improved. "Wait," says he, swallowing the bait like a famishing trout – and, releasing a huge key from the bundle at his girdle, bade me follow; which indeed I did. He came to a "bodega," or storehouse, better built and guarded than the rest. He entered. From a crypt, such as in churches they place the images or relics of the saints in, he drew out a bottle, "beautiful exceedingly," and carefully extracted the cork. I fear a doubt might be thrown upon my reputation for veracity if I should venture to tell the whole truth of the effect of the perfume from that uncorked bottle! The remorseless spider, "pleased with the grateful sense," left his protected covert to draw nearer, and extended his antennae to catch the aroma. If a spider could be so moved, what must have been my feelings? more easily imagined than described. The major poured out, and I drank. Unconsciously I held out my glass to be replenished – "Not for a crowned head!" was his somewhat amazed reply.

This wine sells on the estate at five dollars the bottle, and is mostly bought up, before vintage, for the royal houses of Europe. Prince Metternich, by this and other experiments,

---

[284] The right spelling is Madeira.
[285] The right spelling is Bual.
[286] Line from Act II, Scene I, of the play "Comus: A Masque", by John Milton (1608-1674), a renowned English poet.
[287] Prince Klemens Wenzel von Metternich (1773-1859), a German politician and statesman who served as Foreign Minister of the Holy Roman Empire and its successor, the Austrian Empire, from 1809 to 1848. His castle stood amidst vineyards that produced the best Rhine wine.

has done much to improve his native grape, which will induce many to palliate, if not wholly to excuse, the part he performed in the "Holy Alliance."

The Malmsey is too luscious a wine for ordinary use. It should be taken as a *liqueur,* and, as such, only by women and children. It is one of the rarest and most costly wines of the island, and is produced nowhere else. Little of it is grown, and that little only with the greatest care. The slightest fog or moisture blights it, and years often pass without a vintage. The old monks[288] cultivated this vine, cherished it, and loved its juice. Its rich flavor gladdened their cloisters and warmed their devotions. In the solitude of their cells, weary of a world that had given them so little, or wholly intent upon another that promised them so much, they were wont to pass their hours in prayer, in vigils, and recuperative potations – potations which gratified mind and soul more than bodily appetite. What wanted they of Paradise save an Eve? whom they may indeed have had. It was the introduction of this, "Heaven's last best gift," that, in a great degree, caused their expulsion from monasteries, "if ancient tales say true, nor wrong these holy men."[289]

The Bûal[290] is a delicate and a mellow wine. Its grape, like an Andalusian maiden, should be gathered at the very moment of maturity. Either wither rapidly after. Unlike Sercial, which should be kept at least one half the time Horace demands for poetry, the Bûal is pleasant in its infancy. Yet time, that softens every thing, adds additional mellowness to this. The grape grows scarcer each succeeding year, and the wine of course dearer. The best on the island is produced from the vineyards of Padre João, in the district of San Martinho[291] – a priest of the Holy Catholic Church, a worthy man, well skilled in the vine.

The Tinta, also called the Madeira Burgundy, because it has all that sun-set glow of the latter wine, boasts a flavor of peculiar excellence. It gains its rich warm color from the husks of the grape, which are allowed to remain in the cask during fermentation, and which give to the wine some of the astringent properties of port. Its peculiar excellence is ephemeral. Unlike the other island wines, it gains no value from age. Two or three years are its grand climacteric. Thence it gradually loses its tender flavor and delicate aroma, becomes morose, insipid, soured, like ladies of "a certain age," and, like them, should be sedulously avoided.

But in its prime, Claude's coloring is not warmer, nor Moore's verse more exciting. "Burning Sappho" might have taken her fill of it before the Leucadian leap,[292] or, from her history, might have been often addicted to it; for no wine, unless perhaps its immediate parent, Burgundy, would sooner beget the frenzy of love.

The Tinto is a dark red wine, from a grape larger, softer and juicier than the Tinta. It is sometimes known as "the pure juice of the grape," being naturally less potent than the others. Mixed with water, it is very palatable, and a fit accompaniment for the meats, with which it should leave the table.

Then there is also the Verdeilho,[293] a rare wine produced from the white grape. It is a strong-bodied wine, too potent for general consumption, and seldom used in its natural state.

---

288 The Jesuits.
289 Last line of the 7th stanza of Canto I of Lord Byron's romaunt (verse romance) "Childe Harolds Pilgrimage".
290 See Note 285.
291 See Note 259.
292 Reference to Sapho's leap to death from the Leucadian promontory when she discovered that her love for Phaon was in vain.
293 The right spelling is Verdelho.

Such are the best of the normal wines of the island. Others are made of their commixture, among which that exported as "Madeira Wine;" the component parts of which are principally the Verdeilho,[294] the Tinto and Bûal; and wines of various kinds, differing in color, taste and quality, are mingled together from the "mother butts," and exported.

Instead of keeping their wines in cellars, as many of us do, the Madeira proprietors store them above ground. The interior of their "bodegas" – store-houses – is kept deliciously cool, the heat and glare of the sun being watchfully excluded. It is a perfumed promenade through them, hedges of butts diffusing on either side an unrivaled fragrance – an ever-fresh bouquet of various aromas. Some visitors are accustomed to scent their handkerchiefs or fingers; others, *their breath*.

A bountiful season has given from 25,000 to 30,000 pipes; of which, however, it is safe to say, never more than one fifth was good wine. It behooves the intended purchaser, therefore, to acquaint himself with the exporter's reputation for *good taste* as well as probity.

Intoxication is rarely or never the vice of vine-producing countries. Neither in Portugal, Spain, on the Rhine, nor in France, did I see other than an exceptional case of inebriety. In Madeira, even among the peasantry, a drunkard is a less reputable person than a thief; necessity, they say, may sometimes make the one, but nothing save his own degraded inclination, the other. They drink wine always, and never to excess. "No nation is drunken," says Jefferson in his Letters, "where wine is cheap;[295] and none sober where the dearness of wine substitutes ardent spirits as the common beverage."[296] It is the discovery of the process of distillation which (like the civil feuds of Rome) "has filled the world with widows and with orphans." Prohibit distillation, and abolish the duties on wines, and no necessity would exist for the enforcement of "Maine Laws."[297]

6.1.1.16. J. Willet Spalding, USN (1852)

At the end of 1852 the United States sent an expedition to Japan in order to take Commodore Perry,[298] as an Envoy of this nation, with a mission to establish a treaty of

---

294 The right spelling is Verdelho.

295 This sentence, associated to Madeira, had been revealed in the American press two years before the publication of March's book, in these terms: «"No nation is drunken," says Jefferson in his Letters, "where wine is cheap; and none sober, where the dearness of wine substitutes ardent spirits as the common beverage." In Madeira, even with the peasantry, a drunkard is less reputable than a thief – necessity may male the one, nothing but inherent depravity the other. They drink wine always, and never to excess."» *Grand County Herald*, January 30, 1854. (Published in Lancaster, WI).

296 Quote of a Thomas Jefferson's letter to M. de Neuville, written at Monticello on December 13, 1818: «… I rejoice, as a moralist, at the prospect of a reduction of the duties on wine, by our national legislature. It is an error to view a tax on that liquor as merely a tax on the rich. It is a prohibition of its use to the middling class of our citizens, and a condemnation of them to the poison of whiskey, which is desolating their houses. No nation is drunken where wine is cheap; and none sober, where the dearness of wine substitutes ardent spirits as the common beverage. It is, in truth, the only antidote to the bane of whiskey. Fix but the duty at the rate of other merchandise, and we can drink wine here as cheap as we do grog: and who will not prefer it? Its extended use will carry health and comfort to a much enlarged circle. Every one in easy circumstances (as the bulk of our citizens are) will prefer it to the poison to which they are now driven by their government. And the treasury itself will find that a penny a piece from a dozen, is more than a groat from a single one. This reformation, however, will require time. …» RANDOLPH, Thomas Jefferson (editor), *Memoir, Correspondence, and Miscellanies, from the papers of Thomas Jefferson*, Volume IV, Letter CXLVI, Charlottesville, 1829, pages 311-312.

297 [MARCH] 1856, pages 74-86. Reference to the Maine Law, passed in 1851, in this state, which is associated with the implementation of the Temperance movement in the United States.

298 Matthew Calbraith Perry (1794-1858), a Commodore of the U.S. Navy who commanded a number of ships. He

amity between America and Japan, which would open the door of trade between the two countries. On their way a first stop was made at Funchal, where the ships of the expedition arrived on December 11. Three years later, in 1855, J. Willet Spalding, an officer of the U.S. Steam-frigate *Mississippi*,[299] the Flag ship of the expedition, published in New York a book containing minute details of the long sea journey, under the title *The Japan Expedition - Japan and around the world - An account of three visits to the Japanese Empire with sketches of Madeira, St. Helena, Cape of Good Hope, Mauritius, Ceylon, Singapore, China, and Loo-Choo*.[300] In the first chapter one can find his impressions of Funchal, some of which are related to the island's wine, namely a description of the transportation of a cask of wine through the streets of the capital of the island, and also of a visit to the residence of the American consul and wine merchant, John Howard March.

CHAPTER I.
… The Wine – A Consul – …

… The continued "Boo-ah" resounding in the streets, as the driver of the sleds with casks upon them spurs up the two poor little oxen, whom a small boy leads with a string from the horn, soon convinces you that you are in the land of the elevating "Tinta," and generous "Serchal."[301] Should the sled drag heavily over the stones, the small boy throws down in front of it a wetted cloth, passing over which, the runner is lubricated.

On reaching the residence of the American consul, we dismounted and partook of a lunch, which his hospitality invariably provides for his visiting country-men. It is unnecessary to tell with what gusto, men who eighteen days before were gathered around a stove in their own land, were now in the genial air of Madeira, windows open, and perfume coming in all around from beautiful plants, partook of the rich treat of guavas, the small banana, and the Mandarin orange just plucked from the tree that thrust itself in the casement. The snack over, we ascended to the consul's observatory; a fine glass, mounted on a tripod, swept the offing and anchorage, giving every object much nearness. Our old ship lying stately at her anchors, was just saluting with twenty-one guns the Portuguese flag floating at her fore, which was promptly returned by the fort on Loo Rock. Around and below us were patches of green-vine and trellis, amid an expanse of red tile roofs, on many of which were placed wine-casks that they might sweeten in the sun. We then descended to the wine-houses, where butt after butt of large dimensions, reached by foot ladders, of Tinta and Serchal,[302] and "Navy," told how the delightful grape of the island had swelled into fullness, and then been crushed into wine. Ah! Clarence, thou shouldst have lived till now. …[303]

---

served in several wars, namely in the American-Mexican War and the War of 1812. He played a key role in the opening of Japan to the West with the Convention of Kanagawa, in 1854.
299 The *Mississippi* was the second steam-frigate built in the United States for the Navy, and the sister ship of the *Missouri*, the first one, which was destroyed by fire, off Gibraltar, during her maiden cruise to the Mediterranean. They were the first USN side-wheeled steamers capable of ocean travel.
300 SPALDING, J. Willet, *The Japan Expedition - Japan and around the world - An account of three visits to the Japanese Empire with sketches of Madeira, St. Helena, Cape of Good Hope, Mauritius, Ceylon, Singapore, China, and Loo-Choo*, J. S. Redfield, New York, 1855.
301 The right spelling is Sercial.
302 The right spelling is Sercial.
303 SPALDING 1855, pages 19-20.

6.1.1.17. Rev. Francis Lister Hawks (1852)

The long sea journey to Japan was described in another book, published in 1856, in Washington, by order of the Congress of the United States. It was written by Francis Lister Hawks (1798-1866), a native of North Carolina, who was a priest of the Episcopal Church and also a politician. His book was entitled *Narrative of the Expedition of an American Squadron to the China Seas and Japan, performed in the years* 1852, 1853, *and* 1854, *under the command of Commodore M. C. Perry, United States Navy, by order of the Government of the United States. Compiled from the original notes and journals of Commodore Perry and his officers, at his request and under his supervision*.[304] In the second chapter of this illustrated book there are some brief references to the U.S. Consul to Madeira and wine merchant – and to Madeira Wine trade and wine transportation through the streets of Funchal. On one of the images of the book, depicting the area at the back of Funchal's cathedral, a cask of wine can be seen being carried away.

CHAPTER II.
… – EXPORTS OF THE ISLAND – NOVEL MODE OF CONVEYANCE – …

… Funchal still retains its character for hospitality, and by no one was this virtue more gracefully exercised towards the members of the expedition than by Mr. J. H. March, who for more than thirty years has filled the office of consul of the United States,[305] and in the enjoyment of his large fortune takes delight in making welcome to his houses, both in town and country, such of his countrymen as are deserving of his attentions.

The town consists of a wide street along the sea shore, containing several good buildings. From this, numerous small streets extend back at right angles, for a considerable distance

---

304 HAWKS, Francis Lister, *Narrative of the Expedition of an American Squadron to the China Seas and Japan, performed in the years 1852, 1853, and 1854, under the command of Commodore M. C. Perry, United States Navy, by order of the Government of the United States. Compiled from the original notes and journals of Commodore Perry and his officers, at his request and under his supervision.*, Beverley Tucker (Senate Printer), Washington, 1856. This book had at least one more edition, under the same title and published in the same year, through D. Appleton and Company, in New York, and by Trubner & Co., in London. In the following year (1857), a summary of this book was published by Robert Tomes, under a different title. As a matter of curiosity it should be mentioned that Robert Tomes had assisted Francis Hawks in the preparation of his book, about the same theme, by "comparing the various journals, documents &c., arranging chronologically the incidents gathered from all sources, and presenting them in a connected form," as the latter mentions in the "Prefatory Note" of his work. Having prepared all that material, we infer that he had decided to publish his own book about this subject. However, as far as what Madeira and Madeira wine is concerned, this new work adds little to what had already been said about these topics in the previous source. In Chapter I we can read the following paragraphs: «…/ As the streets of the city are paved in such a manner as to forbid the use of wheel carriage, sedan chairs and hammocks were until very lately used, not only by invalids, but by all others. A substitute is however now adopted, which consists of the ordinary sledge used for conveying casks of wine and other heavy articles, surmounted by a gaily decked carriage-body and drawn by a yoke of oxen. …/ …/ Wine is the chief product of Madeira. When the island was however first settled by the Portuguese, sugar was cultivated, but this was discontinued after the islands of the West Indies were brought under culture, and the attention of the agriculturist was concentrated upon the production of wine. The export of this has been large, and principally to England. The amount has been estimated as high as £500,000 per annum. …» TOMES, Robert, *The Americans in Japan: An Abridgment of the Government Narrative of the U.S. Expedition to Japan, under Commodore Perry*, D. Appleton & Co., New York and London, 1857, pages 4-5. There is also another English edition of this book, published two years later, under a slightly different title. TOMES, Robert, *Japan and the Japanese; A Narrative of the U.S. Government Expedition to Japan, under Commodore Perry*, Second Edition, Trübner & Co., London, 1859.

305 John Howard March had been appointed US Consul at Funchal in 1816 and by the time Francis Hawks visited Madeira he had been in office for 36 years.

up the slope of the hill. The population amounts to some twenty thousand. The commerce of the island is considerable, and most of it is with England. Its exports have been said to amount to the value of £500,000 per annum. Wine is the principal commodity. When the island was first settled by the Portuguese, sugar was cultivated to a considerable extent, but this was discontinued after the West Indies were brought under culture, and wine became the staple. ...

As the streets of the city are paved in such manner as to forbid the use of wheel carriages, sedan chairs and hammocks were, until very recently, used not only for invalids, but by all persons making visits. The inconvenience of these vehicles has led to a substitute, which consists of nothing more than the ordinary sledge used for transporting casks of wine and other heavy articles through the streets, surmounted by a gaily decorated carriage body, and drawn by a yoke of oxen. This is now the fashionable conveyance, and in such an one did the Commodore, with his flag captain and aid, make all his official visits. There are stands in the streets, as for our cabs and carriages, where these vehicles may be found with the oxen yoked, and all things prepared for immediate transportation.[306] ...

Figure 30. "Funchal Cathedral." Aspect of a busy street in the capital of Madeira where can be seen an ox sledge carrying a cask of wine. *Book illustration. Author unknown.*

6.1.1.18. Rev. John Overton Choules (1853)

In the early 1850's the American millionaire Cornelius Vanderbilt – the second richest man in the United States, second in wealth to John Jacob Astor – built a large steam yacht, the *North Star*, at the expense of half a million dollars, to take his family on a pleasure trip to Europe. He was the second wealthy American to take a grand tour of the Old World in a private yacht, the first one being George Crowninshield, a few decades earlier, in 1817, aboard the *Cleopatra's Barge*. Rev. John Overton Choules (1801-1856), although a native of Bristol, England, emigrated to the United States in 1824 with his family. At the time of this trip on the *North Star* he was the leader of the Second Baptist Church in Newport, Rhode Island, and was invited by Vanderbilt to join his family on the long sea journey. Previous to this trip,

Figure 31. The steam yacht *North Star*, which visited Madeira on September 1853 during her homeward bound voyage. *Book illustration. Author unknown.*

---

306 HAWKS 1856, pages 83-84.

Choules had already been to Europe and had published a book with his impressions, entitled *Young Americans Abroad, or Vacation in Europe*. The *North Star* left the United States on May 20, 1853, and after visiting several European ports, had its last call in Madeira, where it arrived on September 12, 1853, before returning to the United States. A year later Rev. Choules published a book in Boston and New York, containing a detailed account of the long sea voyage, entitled *The Cruise of the Steam Yacht North Star; a narrative of the Excursion of Mr. Vanderbilt's Party to England, Russia, Denmark, France, Spain, Italy, Malta, Turkey, Madeira, etc.*[307] Chapter XXIII is dedicated to Madeira and, among Choules' impressions of the island, one can find his references to the blight of the vineyards, a brief history of its vines, and a description of several types of wines.

CHAPTER XXIII.
... BLAST OF THE VINEYARDS – THE VINE – WINES OF THE ISLAND – ...

... Madeira is known to all the world by its production of wine, and as a favorite resort for consumptive persons. ...

We were all very sorry to find the island laboring under a sad calamity in the total destruction of the vineyards. Instead of producing twenty-five thousand pipes of wine, as used to be done, this year the amount will fall below two hundred! No one can form an adequate idea of the blasted appearance of the vines who has not seen them. They look as if they had been scorched by fire. We could not obtain grapes to eat. The fear is entertained that the vines are so injured that several years must elapse ere another crop can be realized. The vine was brought here in 1425, but the best varieties were introduced by the Jesuits in the close of the 16th century. I observed many of the vines trained on chestnut-trees; but the impression is entertained that the grape is better when grown near to the earth. The vintage occurs early in September. The usual rate of production is calculated in good seasons at a pipe of wine to the acre. The inferior wines are sent in large amounts to Hamburg and Cologne, where, under the hands of doctors, it is made into hock, and sent over Europe and to America.

Very many of the wines here raised are rarely seen off the island. The principal wines of Madeira are as follows:

Malmsey, a light-colored wine, made from a large oval grape, which, when ripe, is of golden hue; its bunches are thin and long. The best wine of this grade is made on estates belonging formerly to the Jesuits. It is difficult to raise the vine, as a little fog or dampness destroys the flower. This is the costliest wine of the island, and is worth about four hundred dollars a pipe on the spot.

Bûal.[308] – This is a delicate wine, produced from a round, straw-colored grape, the size of a small marble. This grape is now scarce, and the wine is very high.

Sercial is a dry, light-colored wine, produced from the round hock grape, which hangs in thick clusters. This wine must obtain considerable age to become acceptable to the palate. The grape is never eaten; its price is high.

---

307 CHOULES, Rev. John Overton, *The Cruise of the Steam Yacht North Star; a narrative of the Excursion of Mr. Vanderbilt's Party to England, Russia, Denmark, France, Spain, Italy, Malta, Turkey, Madeira, etc.*, Gould and Lincoln, Boston, Evans and Dickerson, New York, 1854.
308 The right spelling is Bual.

Tinta or *Madeira Burgundy*. – This is made from the small black Burgundy grape. It receives its rich claret color from the husks of the grape, which are left in the casks during fermentation. This wine is best when newly made, and after two years loses its aroma. Its value has been from three hundred to three hundred and fifty dollars a pipe.

Figure 32. "Madeira – Funchal from the Sea." Book illustration. Author unknown.

Tinto is a dark wine from the Negra Molle grape, which is larger than the Burgundy. It is used with others in the composition of Madeira wine.

Madeira. – This is the great wine of the island. It is made from a combination of grapes. When new, it is of a light claret, violet hue; but this subsides as it advances to maturity. This wine is usually sent on a voyage to the East or West Indies, and takes its name accordingly in the markets. It has generally commanded on the island from one hundred to two hundred and sixty dollars a pipe.

Besides these, there are Verdêlho,[309] Palhete, Surdo and Negrino[310] wines.

All the wines of Madeira require an equable temperature.[311] …

6.1.1.19. Rev. Charles W. Thomas, USN (1855)

Rev. Charles W. Thomas, a graduate of a Southern university, accepted in 1855 the chaplaincy of a squadron about to cruise off the coast of Africa, and was engaged in that mission up to 1857. During that time he was attached to the sloop-of-war *Jameston*, then the flag ship of the African Squadron, and employed his free time in writing a book, that he published in New York, in 1860, under the title *Adventures and Observations on the West Coast of Africa, and its islands. Historical and Descriptive Sketches of Madeira, Canary, Biafra and Cape Verd Islands; Their climates, inhabitants and productions. Accounts of places, peoples, customs, trade, missionary operations, etc., etc., On that part of African coast lying between Tangier, Morocco and Benguela*.[312] The last section of this book is dedicated to Madeira – where the author arrived on July 8, 1855 – and contains six chapters. In the second and fourth ones the author refers to Madeira Wine.

CHAPTER II.
MADEIRA – CONTINUED.
History – …

To the wine-dealers and wine-drinkers of the world, the name Madeira has been familiar

---

[309] The right spelling is Verdelho.
[310] The right spelling is Negrinho.
[311] CHOULES 1854, pages 338, 342-343.
[312] THOMAS, Rev. Charles W., *Adventures and Observations on the West Coast of Africa, and its islands. Historical and Descriptive Sketches of Madeira, Canary, Biafra and Cape Verd Islands; Their climates, inhabitants and productions. Accounts of places, peoples, customs, trade, missionary operations, etc., etc., On that part of African coast lying between Tangier, Morocco and Benguela*., Derby & Jackson, New York, 1860. This book also had an abridged English edition, published in London, in 1864 – during the American Civil War – whose preface was written by W. Mathew Thomas, brother of the author.

for ages. By many of our countrymen it is heard with associations the most sacred, for there many a beloved consumptive has prolonged a precious life, or closed, amidst its soft and balmy airs, a season of suffering. This is our reason for introducing a sketch of its history.[313] …

CHAPTER IV.
MADEIRA – CONTINUED.
… – The Vine and the Wine of Madeira – …

… Early in the morning of a July day, and while the dew still sparkled in diamonds on the grass and hedge-rows, Dr. C., Lieutenant A., and myself, engaged three good horses, with their attendants, and a lusty fellow to carry a basket of provisions, and took up our road through fragrant lanes, and gardens of banana and coffee-trees, for the distant mountains. Our route lay through the parish of San Antonio,[314] one of the prettiest, most populous and productive districts of the island, and which, in the wine-producing days of the Madeiras, furnished the best wine.

Tell us something of the wine, says one. Ah! reader, if you have a *penchant* toward good wine, let us offer you our sympathy, for the days of "old Madeira" are ended; the years of the sweet Malmsey, and the luscious Sercial, and the Bûal,[315] and Tinta, and Verdelho, and Palhête,[316] and Surdo, and Negrinho, natives of these hills, are numbered.

The island, which once produced, for foreign markets, fifteen thousand pipes of wine (the harvest of 1809) is now known no more among wine-producing countries.

This is the fifth year (1857) in which no wine has been produced. For three years the vine-dresser waited in anxious hope, but the blight confirmed to grow worse, and at length the much loved and long cherished vine was cut down to make room for the more homely growths of corn and sugar-cane. This disease manifests itself in the spring, in the crumpled appearance of the leaf, and the withering of the young fruit. Scientific men suppose that the vine, having been so long the only crop cultivated in the wine districts, has at length exhausted those properties of soil which gave it fruitfulness, and that these properties can only be restored by a process which may require ages for its development. Those chemical agents known to abound in grape-producing soils, have been applied here without perceptible effect, and now the vine which of yore produced bunches as abundant as leaves, has disappeared from the hill-sides and vales, and is found only in gardens, cherished by the sanguine owner in hopes of better days, or preserved by that sentiment which says,

"Woodman, spare that tree."[317]

The above theory of the blight may be correct; but our observation, in parts of the island where the vine is in a comparatively new soil, suggests an objection, for here we witnessed the same diseased condition of the plant, and as fully developed, as in those soils where, from being too long the unvaried crop, it is supposed to have exhausted certain essential

---

313 THOMAS 1860, page 423.
314 The right spelling is Santo António.
315 The right spelling is Bual.
316 The right spelling is Palhete.
317 Title of a famous ballad written in 1837 by the American poet George Pope Morris (1802-1864).

elements. The wine now in the island is in the hands of a few wealthy merchants, and is held at a price which is daily increasing. Is it not a little remarkable that Madeira wine is as abundant in the American market as ever, and that it can be bought at any country store in the interior at a price which is *lower* than the present first cost in Madeira! If you doubt the genuineness of the article examine the – label!

The varieties of the vine cultivated in Madeira were not indigenous; they were imported from Cyprus in the early settlement of the island, and the failure of the present gene-ration contributes, with observation of kindred effects in other plants, to confirm our belief in an opinion which is not generally entertained by naturalists, but which has, nevertheless, long existed, viz., that exotic plants will eventually "run out."[318] ...

6.1.1.20. William Maxwell Wood, USN (1855)

On October 24, 1855 the U.S. Steam-frigate *San Jacinto* left New York bound for Siam, China and Japan, and its first stop was made at Madeira island, where the vessel arrived on November 11, 1855. Aboard this ship traveled William Maxwell Wood (1809-1880), a native of Baltimore, Maryland, and Naval doctor, who had been appointed Surgeon of the Fleet. Some years after his return to the United States, he published in New York, in 1859, an interesting book entitled *Fankwei*;[319] or, *The San Jacinto in the Seas of India, China and Japan*,[320] in which he dedicates two chapters to the island – the fourth and the fifth. In the former he mentions the origin of Madeira grapes and the consumption of Madeira at home and abroad, and in the latter he presents a long and interesting text about different aspects of Madeira Wine, including his description of a tasting of '76 "Independence Wine" from the collection of an English gentleman in Funchal. In it he also mentions the blight of the vine, the famine that ensued and the relief that was sent from the United States, adding also some thoughts about the first steps of another emerging industry, the embroidery, a delicate work done by women in order to complement the household income.

IV.
Madeira.

... But Madeira, to the wide world, does not mean the island or its forests. Soon after the occupation of the island, Prince Henry, son of King John of Portugal, sent the colony seeds and the materials of agriculture. Among them were a few slips of vine from the isle of Cyprus. What a future was before those vine slips; and where have they not borne the word "Madeira," associated with the glowing liquid which had its origin in them, and upon which the fortunes of the island have flowed? In the northern palaces of the Muscovite and the castles of the German. Diffusing its blessings with that of constitutional govern-ment, it appears on the table of both cit and noble, dispelling the gloom of England's fogs.

---

318 THOMAS 1860, pages 447-449.
319 Oriental expression meaning "foreign devil".
320 WOOD, William Maxwell, *Fankwei; or, The San Jacinto in the Seas of India, China and Japan*, Harper & Brothers, New York, 1859.

Figure 33. William Maxwell Wood, USN. In his visit to the island, in 1855, he drank "Independence Wine" or, in other words, Madeira Wine from the vintage of 1776. *19th century painting. Author unknown.*

Adopted by the conquering Saxon, it has followed him in Africa and the Indies, amid the orange groves of Southern and the forests of Northern America, in the wastes of the ocean and the perils and privations of the camp. In all climes Madeira has been found, cheering social and festive communion. It has been heard in pledges of patriotic fervor, in those of love and friendship to present and absent. Entombed at the birth it appears at the bridal, and as the dusty and cobwebbed bottles come to light, they are regarded with a reverential awe due to the provident spirits of the departed ancestry who first deposited them in the vaults where they have ripened.

But whilst we are thus sentimentalizing under the shadow of Madeira upon days and usages which are falling beneath the onslaught of "Maine Laws"[321] and teetotalism,[322] our ship has run along the rocky shores until, just off a point, and standing out isolated in the sea, is the "Loo Rock," with a fortress upon its summit. …[323]

V.
Wine.

Now that the world has had its faith shaken in the generative principle of nobility, and doubts both the justice and the expediency of those institutions, which, as Pascal[324] says, "give to the infant in the cradle an influence and consideration that could not be acquired by half a century's practice of every virtue," we hear of merchant princes, and it is to be hoped that in further progress we shall hear of engine, loom, and anvil princes.

Madeira has its wine princes, and where could one be supposed to taste the juice of the grape in higher table perfection than in the house of one of these noblemen, who live in a style justifying the title?

If I take any curious, inquiring reader with me to the table of one of these princes to which I am invited, he must not fear a wine debauch. This place of epicurean refinements and of delicate bouquets is not that in which a man puts pints and bottles under his belt, overwhelming all delicate perceptions. The wine drinkers of Madeira are true epicures. A highly-flavored glass or two during dinner, a lengthened coqueting with a glass of some choice vintage after the cloth is removed, and that is all. Indeed those of the most nicely discriminating tastes rarely *drink* wine at all. Of course this commendable moderation may be in some degree departed from when they have a set of strangers desirous of taking advantage of a chance visit to go through all the choice vintage at one sitting. Well, we have dined and taken a glass of the ordinary table wine, generally known abroad as "London Particular," or else a glass of a dark port looking

---

321 See (2nd part of) Note 297.
322 Practice or promotion of complete abstinence from alcoholic beverages.
323 WOOD 1859, pages 29-30.
324 Blaise Pascal (1623-1662), a French physicist, mathematician, inventor, writer and Christian philosopher.

and astringent-tasted Vino-Tinto.[325] Both are pronounced to be extraordinarily good, of course. As we are now drinking for wine information, we inquire what these wines exactly are. But stop – we will say nothing about the matter until there is a greater variety under discussion. The dinner is over, the dessert finished, the cloth removed, and with the nuts – among which are plates of roast chestnuts – old Virgil's "castanea nuces" – enormous nuts, such as, according to Professor Owen, antediluvian megatheria may have sat upon their hind quarters and picked from the top of the tree – decanters are placed at each end of the table, and the silver necklaces suspended from their throats indicate them to be *Malmsey – Bual – Sercial* – the aristocracy of wines. In addition to these we have the *Verdeilho*[326] and the *Tinta*. These five constitute the principal wines of the island of Madeira. They are all named from the kind of grape from which they are made. There are three others, but they make only a low order of wine seldom seen. The *Verdeilho*[327] is that generally used and known as Madeira, London Particular, etc. It is deepened in color by a slight addition of Tinta, and flavored by the rich and aromatic Buol.[328] Sercial is also a highly-flavored wine. Malmsey is generally known to be a sweet, luscious and cordial-like wine. These three last are the most costly. The Tinta is made by pressing the husks and seeds with the juice. According to Dr. Christison[329] and others, the proportion of alcohol in these wines is as follows:

Madeira (Verdeilho)[330]	20.35
Sercial	18.50
Malmsey	15.60
Tinta	20.35

It may not, even with the most delicate and fastidious, detract from the flavor of the rosy fluid to know that it has washed the feet of not over cleanly Portuguese laborers, for it has all been trod out by bare feet in the winepress. Having tasted gently of these choice wines, another element of quality was brought under discussion – the element of age. Our host told us that the bottle he was then having opened, was of the vintage of 1815 – going on while Napoleon the Great was off the island on his way to St. Helena, and was, therefore, at the present drinking, forty years of age. But neither its age, nor its unhappy historic association, was the cause of its excellence; but at that period L'Este, a hot, dry wind, the Sirocco or Harmattan of Africa, was of more than usual prevalence, and the grapes ripened in superior richness. It was, to my, and I believe to the general taste, a finely-flavored wine. Next, with due ceremonies and honors, a bottle was opened which our host, an English gentleman, told us was their "Independence" wine, being of the vintage of '76. My companions all thought it very superior, but, to me, it had very much the taste of a vapid medicated ether, and I honestly pronounced it, to my taste, unmitigated trash, and I remembered to have tasted, eighteen years before, a wine at the same table which had

---

[325] The right spelling is Vinho Tinto.
[326] The right spelling is Verdelho.
[327] The right spelling is Verdelho.
[328] The right spelling is Bual.
[329] Robert Christison (1797-1882), a Scottish toxicologist and physician who, at different time periods, was president of different organizations, namely the Royal College of Surgeons of Edinburgh, the Royal College of Physicians of Edinburgh and the British Medical Association. In 1839 he published the article "Notice upon the Alcoholic Strength of Wines", where he alludes to Madeira, at "The Edinburgh New Philosophical Journal".
[330] The right spelling is Verdelho.

made the same impression upon me. My associates earnestly opposed the correctness of my judgment, and I found myself in a minority of one. I ventured to sustain myself by quoting the opinion of Dr. Christison, which seems to be founded both on reason and experience, viz., that wines do not improve by great age. Like ourselves, they have their growth to their best condition and then deteriorate; but the period of deterioration is different for different wines, or under varying circumstances for the same wine. At this stage of the discussion our host directed a bottle to be brought with great care from a specially named corner of the garret, and when brought he took it carefully in his hand, drew, and decanted it himself, and handing a glass to me, he said, "Now taste that, and tell me what you think of it, and be careful don't commit yourself." The wine was very clear, and of a pale amber color. I tasted it, mild, unspirituous, aromatic, and at once said, "It is the best on the table, and by far the best I ever tasted in my life." It was then handed to my companions, who all thought it very good, but by no means equal to the '76. Our host then said, with an earnestness and solemnity befitting the occasion, "It is a rare wine – a wonderful wine: there can be nothing superior to it, but it is one *hundred years old*;" and thereafter our host and myself took up with the centenarian; but the Seventy-sixers, with commendable consistency, and perhaps from patriotic motives, stuck to their first judgment. How much honest judgment, or that enemy to progress, pride of opinion, had to do with our pertinacity, none of us will ever know.

In even all this tasting there had been but little wine-drinking – none of that reeking debauchery unfortunately so often seen in our own country, which mars, blunts, and vitiates the palate, and makes wine really grateful only from the amount of alcohol it conveys, and brandy itself more grateful than wine. It is, however, somewhat to our credit that the best Madeira, and that the least brandied, is sent to the United States, and besides coming to us the best, our climate improves it more than that of Europe does.

I trust that honestly-observed facts in relation to the character of wines, and in reference to the social habits of an eminently wine-drinking country, will not be considered as a eulogium upon its use, but if those who use wine habitually in the United States all used it as I have seen it used in Madeira, temperance men might rejoice; but upon that "if" the propriety of its use may depend.

> "Bright are the blushes of the wine-wreathed bowl,
> Warm with the sunshine of Anacreon's soul;
> But dearer memories gild the tasteless wave
> That fainting Sidney perished as he gave.
> 'Tis the heart's current lends the cup its glow,
> What e'er the fountain whence the draught may flow."[331]

It would really seem as if the hand of Providence was directing physical influences in favor of total abstinence by the blight which has come over the grapes in wineproducing countries. Upon a former visit to this island I rode to the Great Curral or Curral das Freiras, an enormous chasm, which seems, when it first bursts upon you, to open to the earth's centre, with its six thousand feet of depth inclosed by the red, rugged pinnacled

---

[331] Excerpt of the poem "A Sentiment", by Oliver Wendell Holmes (1809-1894), an American doctor, professor and author, from Cambridge, MA. On section 6.2.12. of this anthology we present some excerpts of one of his novels, containing references to Madeira Wine.

rocks shooting away to the clear sky above you; but away down in the bottom of the depth you see miniature houses and a church, and they are two thousand feet above the sea.

It is a long up-hill ride of eighteen miles to the point which looks down into the Curral, and much of it is along the edge of frightful precipices, and much of it also, when I made the excursion, was through vineyards where vines arbored over the road, or trellis work, and hung their rich bunches just above your head and ready to your hand. But now such scenery no longer exists. The prophecy of Joel the son of Bethuel is in literal fulfilment. "Awake, ye drunkards, and weep and howl, all ye drinkers of wine, because of the new wine; for it is cut off from your mouth."[332] For four years this winepress has not been trodden, and the vine, fruit, leaf and stem, has disappeared. The annual product of the island was from fifteen to twenty thousand pipes, and this past year not two hundred were made in the whole island. The whole stock on hand is only about ten thousand pipes, not more than the half of one good year's product, and this will be exhausted in from five to ten years; even if the grape were to be recovered now, it would take several years before the new wine would be fit for exportation. The disease, a mould or fungoid growth, has so far resisted all methods of cure, and scarcely more than a lingering hope exists of the recovery of the vine; this hope would have the more encouragement if they could ascertain certainly that the disease had ever existed before and passed away, but although documents and records have been carefully searched, the only evidence of the kind is in some old leases which specify that the rent is to be paid unless a failure of the grape occur.

It is well known that in the first year of the present failure great distress and famine prevailed in the island, which was relieved by contributions from various parts of the world, and especially from the United States,[333] by the introduction of the sugar-cane, sweet potatoes and other roots and fruits, abundance of which, at low rates, are now found in the markets. The Irish potatoes are of very superior quality, equal to the best in any part of the world. Those which are of the first quality are the product of seed sent out from the United States during the famine.

I suppose it would not do to talk about Madeira and not say any thing of the extent of population, although any gazetteer would give the information. That of the island is a little over one hundred thousand, and that of Funchal about eighteen thousand. But there has been much emigration, diminishing the population. Famine drove away many. Demerara, offering a premium for laborers, drew off many; and a recent Protestant reformation has driven from their kindred and genial home, to the wilds of America, several hundred martyrs for conscience' sake.[334] And as, like our own Pilgrim fathers, they sought

"Freedom to worship God,"[335]

---

[332] A Bible versicle from Joel 1:5-15.
[333] See section 9.7.1. of this anthology, dedicated to this subject.
[334] Reference to the Madeira Exiles, a large group (of about 2000 Madeirans) that was forced into exile after suffering persecutions in the island, due to the fact that they had embraced a Protestant religion, Presbyterianism, preached by Robert Reid Kalley, a Scottish doctor and missionary. Through the help of the American Protestant Society they ended up settling in Jacksonville and Springfield, IL. Some had gone to Demarara first, but others went from Madeira directly to the United States, in the early 1850's.
[335] Last line of the last stanza of the poem "The Landing of the Pilgrim Fathers in New England", by the English poetess Felicia Hemans (1793-1835).

may their descendants be equally rewarded. Although the changed agriculture of the island has removed the apprehension of starvation, yet the destruction of trade and commerce caused by the wine blight has necessarily brought poverty to very many, and to some who have been in elevated and prosperous circumstances. The female members of such families, turning to account the exquisite skill in embroidery for which they are celebrated, devote themselves to the working of edgings, handkerchiefs, collars, sleeves, etc., which are sold by their servants to the strangers visiting the island. If the very low price at which this fine work is offered were not an inducement for those who can afford it, to buy, the reflection that one is at once gratifying his own taste and relieving a necessity, ought to be.[336] …

6.1.1.21. Frederick Hubbard (1855)

Frederick Hubbard (1817-1895), a native of Hamilton, NY, was a Hamilton College graduate and worked as Superintendent of Construction for various sections of the New York and Erie Railroad. In 1855, at the age of 38, he went on a Grand Tour of Europe and the East. During his long journey he wrote a journal, which he entitled *Notes of Travel in Europe and the East in the years* 1855-1856, *and* 1857: *A Yankee Engineer Abroad*, which was recently discovered, transcribed and published, in two volumes, by Linnaeus C. Shecut II,[337] who added some footnotes to the original text. Frederick Hubbard arrived at Madeira, from Southampton, on November 27, 1855, aboard the steamer *Conway*. In Part I of his book, entitled "Europe", can be found his impressions of Madeira, among which are his testimony about the destruction of the Madeira vineyards, in the aftermath of the blight that had ruined them three years before. Also worth underlining is his views concerning the relief sent from America to help the destitute ones, affected by the failure of the grapes, and the solutions found by the Madeirans in order to overcome this situation, by trying new crops.

VI.

MADEIRA – FUNCHAL – SUNSHINE AND FLOWERS

… The country houses about Funchal, *quintas*, as they are called, present one of its most attractive features. … The garden-walks are paved with mosaic pebble-work and covered by trellisses for grapevines, upheld by slender pillars of masonry. Stone, as the cheaper material, is universally employed in place of wood. These garden-avenues, leading to fanciful little bowers and lookouts on the corners of the walls, must have been very beautiful when the vines were in their prime, and their full loads of "gushing grapes" gave rich promise of a glorious vintage. Now, in the blight of the vine, its high place is usurped by various less dignified substitutes. Plebeian squashes and ignobile pumpkin-vines rear their homely progeny in the soft Madeiran atmosphere and fatten on the juices which should

---

[336] WOOD 1859, pages 36-43.
[337] HUBBARD, Frederick; SHECUT II, Linnaeus C., *Notes of Travel in Europe and the East in the years 1855-1856, and 1857: A Yankee Engineer Abroad*, Part I, "Europe", AuthorHouse, Indiana, 2010.

have gone to "make glad the heart of a man."[338] In the more ornamental grounds near the houses, Flora[339] has gracefully elbowed Bacchus[340] aside, and hung-out her gay and glowing treasures in the richest and wildest profusion. ...[341]

The "sunny south side" on which Funchal is situated is the richest wine-growing district of the island. Every accessible patch of land, up to a high elevation on the mountainsides, is under careful cultivation. ...

But a few years back, the whole island of Madeira was smiling with prosperity. The vine yielded its produce in "Bacchanal profusion," and the husbandman rejoiced in the fruits of his labour. The inhabitants were industrious and happy, and honest labour could insure itself a reward. But a vast change has now fallen upon it; and in a single season, a sudden and unexpected visitation has turned its beauty into mourning. The vines have been smitten like Jonah's gourd, and are now nearly all withered and dead. The empty trellises of the vineyards bear melancholy witness to their departed glory. The cause of this sudden blight has escaped detection, nor has a cure been yet discovered for the hopeless disease of the vine. It is possible that the curse may be removed in time, but many years must even then elapse before Madeira can be what it has been.

The calamity fell upon the island like a thunderbolt. The inhabitants were wholly unprepared for the sudden emergency. The vines had been their sole means of support, and they had nothing left to depend upon when their staff was taken away. The necessary consequence was utter destitution – to the extent that actual famine prevailed over the island. The sufferings of the starving peasantry excited the sympathies of the humane in distant lands. An appeal was made for their relief; and, as soon as possible, succour was sent in from various quarters. Three vessels under the star-spangled banner were the first arrived on this errand of mercy.[342] They came at a most important juncture, when general distress was at its climax, and came full-freighted with the offerings of liberal hearts. Bread and money were dealt-out freely to the needy and famishing, and many a family was saved by this timely arrival from the horrors of actual starvation. The vessels discharged their burdens and returned to their respective homes – but they did not return empty-handed. The "blessings of those who were ready to perish"[343] furnished them a richer cargo than ever they had borne before. Several years have passed since then, but have not effaced the gratitude of the inhabitants of Madeira towards the country that responded so promptly and liberally to the call of suffering humanity. It was after all but an ordinary act of charity – but it has gained for our nation a worthier fame than the bombardment of a hundred Sevastapols.[344]

Since the destruction of the vineyards, the industry of the inhabitants has been turned into other channels. The land is suitable to the cultivation of almost every plant on the surface of the globe. Fine fruits, the natives of both northern and southern climes, are now

---

338 A Bible versicle from Ecclesiastes 10:19.
339 The goddess of flowers and the season of Spring, in Roman mythology.
340 Roman god of wine.
341 HUBBARD 2010, page 41.
342 See section 9.7.1. of this anthology, dedicated to this subject.
343 Line from the poem "The Rescuers", by the English novelist Charlotte Mary Yonge (1823-1901).
344 Allusion to the Siege of Sevastopol, that lasted from September 1854 to September 1855, during the Crimean War. During this conflict, the allies (French, Ottoman and British forces) landed at Eupatoria on September 1854, intending to make a triumphal march to Sevastopol, the capital of Crimea, with 50.000 men, but this long traverse took a year of fighting against the Russians.

raised here. There is some cultivation of coffee and cotton. The sugar-cane is planted with good success, and the raising of cochineal[345] is beginning to attract attention.[346]

6.1.1.22. William F. Gragg, USN (1857)

In 1857, the United States government sent another mission to China and Japan, as it had done on former years. In fact, this is the second time the *Mississippi* visited Madeira, for it had passed by this island on December 1852, during its previous trip to Japan. In 1857, the *Mississippi* left the Brooklyn Navy Yard on August 18 and arrived at Madeira on September 4. Aboard this ship traveled William F. Gragg, which we assume was a Naval officer, who kept a journal during the long sea journey. Upon his return to the United States he published it in Boston, in 1860, under the title *A Cruise in the U.S. Steam Frigate Mississippi, Wm. C. Nicholson Captain, to China and Japan, From July,* 1857, *to February,* 1860.[347] At the beginning of the book he inserts his impressions of Funchal and mentions a visit he paid to the American Consul, and ends by stating that the *Mississippi* boarded, on its outward bound trip, a large amount of Madeira wine, thus proving that this precious nectar was highly approved by the US Naval officers.

CRUISE OF THE MISSISSIPPI.

... We anchored in Funchal Roads at eleven, A.M., on the 4th of September. In port, we found the United States Sloop-of-War "Germantown," Commander Page, on her way from Norfolk to China, by the way of Bombay; ... During our sojourn in the port, the American Consul, and others of note residing in the place, extended to Captain Nicholson and his officers every attention they could expect. ...

... We visited the residence of our most excellent consul, Mr. March, of the firm Howard & March.[348] He is, in every sense of the word, a perfect gentleman. His house is always open to his countrymen, and is as free to the destitute seaman as it is to the masters of ships. He is beloved by all in the place. He is very charitable, and gives away yearly large amounts of money, clothing, &c., to the poor. He is reported as being very rich, – may he long live to enjoy the same! The grape crop of the island is fast running out, and wine is becoming higher in price every year. ...

On the tenth of the same month, everybody being on board, and the officers having laid in a good supply of "Old Madeira," and the crew a plenty of oranges and banana, and

---

345 An insect (*cocus cacti*) imported from the Canary Islands in the mid 19th century, in order to produce the valuable red ink used in the textile industry, Although an interesting idea on the part of some Funchal merchants, in order to create another source of revenue that could replace the profits obtained until then by the wine trade, it never succeeded. Its failure can also be attributed to the Madeira peasants. Since the insect was raised on a cactus (*opuntia tuna*), the natives preferred to eat its fruit, the prickly pear (*tabaibo*, in Portuguese), instead of having it destroyed by the cochineal insects.
346 HUBBARD, pages 44-45.
347 GRAGG, William F., *A Cruise in the U.S. Steam Frigate Mississippi, Wm. C. Nicholson Captain, to China and Japan, From July, 1857, to February, 1860.*, Damrell & Moore, Printers, Boston, 1860.
348 His firm was designated otherwise, as John Howard March Co.

ten live bullocks for the use of all hands, we steamed up, hove up our mud-hooks, turned our beautiful stern towards the town, and stood off towards the south, taking in tow the "Germantown." ...[349]

6.1.1.23. James D. Johnston, USN (1857)

In 1857, the United States government sent another steam frigate to China and Japan, and upon its homeward bound trip it brought the first Japanese diplomatic embassy to America. But it all started on December 11, 1857, when the *Powhatan* left Norfolk, Virginia. Aboard this vessel's outward bound journey were two special guests: the former U.S. President Franklin Pierce and his wife, who were travelling to Madeira, to spend the Winter there, seeking a cure of the latter on the balmy airs of the island. At Madeira, where the ship arrived on December 27 of the same year, they were guests of the American Consul. Also travelling on the *Powhatan* was the Lieutenant James D. Johnston, who kept a journal written during the long sea trip. Upon his return to the United States, in 1860, he published in Philadelphia and Baltimore, a book entitled *China and Japan: being a narrative of the cruise of the U.S. Steam-Frigate Powhatan, in the years 1857, '58, '59 and 60. Including an account of the Japanese Embassy to the United States.*[350] During his short stay at Funchal, Madeira, he compiled some data for the first chapter of his work, namely some references about the U.S. Consul and the consequences of the blight of 1852 that destroyed the vines, which later on were replaced by sugar cane, that could be seen growing on the city slopes.

CHAPTER I.
... Arrival at Madeira – Hospitalities of J. Howard March, Esq. – ...

... Our brief stay at Funchal was rendered particularly pleasant by the princely hospitalities of Mr. March. The reputation of this gentleman, as a liberal and most agreeable host, is world wide; and I can add but little to what has been already said in his praise by all who have enjoyed his society, or received the freedom of his luxurious abode. He has acquired a large fortune by the sale of the best wines formerly produced here, and of which he seems to have retained a very respectable stock for the consumption of his friends – being himself one of the most abstemious of men – more from necessity than choice, however. ...

The mountain steeps of Madeira are covered with rich and luxuriant vegetation. Terraces are everywhere visible, and every available and accessible spot is made to yield its quota to man's support. The culture of the grape formerly made the chief wealth of the island, but has now been totally abandoned, and the sugar-cane waves its graceful leaves where the Bacchanalian vine so long held sway, and made one's mouth water in contemplation of the delicious fluids to be extracted from its fruit. The disease which in 1852 destroyed the vines, has proved incurable, and the cultivation of the grape has been unwillingly

---

[349] GRAGG 1860, pages 6-8.
[350] JOHNSTON, James D., *China and Japan: being a narrative of the cruise of the U.S. Steam-Frigate Powhatan, in the years 1857, '58, '59 and 60. Including an account of the Japanese Embassy to the United States*, Charles Desilver, Philadelphia, Cushings & Bailey, Baltimore, 1860. This book had a second edition in 1861 under the same title and by the same publishers.

relinquished by the owners of the soil, for the less profitable and congenial production of sugar, though as yet to no considerable extent.[351]

6.1.1.24. Samuel Greene Wheeler Benjamin (1872)

Figure 34. Samuel Greene Wheeler Benjamin. In his impressions of Madeira he inserted some references to Madeira Wine. *Portrait from his book* Persia and the Persians, *published in London, in 1887.*

Samuel G. W. Benjamin (1837-1914), an American statesman, journalist, author and painter, visited Madeira for the first time in 1872, and in the ensuing years made three more visits to the island, and in one of them he stayed there for a period of six months. He was passionate for Madeira's rugged landscapes and drew a large number of paintings depicting them, which he sold in Boston.[352] Upon one of his visits he gathered a bunch of facts about the island in order to include them in a book prepared to "meet a growing want of the travelling public". In fact, around the 1870's the American steam liner companies started organizing tours to the Mediterranean, thus implementing tourism towards the Old World. His text about Madeira was published in different American magazines and was also compiled in his book entitled *The Atlantic Islands as Resorts of Health and Pleasure*,[353] published in New York, in 1878. In Chapter V are located his impressions of the island, among which one can find a narrative of his rambles through the wine district of Câmara de Lobos, and some thoughts about the wine production of Madeira, the blight that had destroyed the vines years before and the measures taken to overpass that calamity, among other interesting facts.

CHAPTER V.
Madeira.

"MADEIRA is an island lying off the coast of Africa, in the latitude of Charleston, S. C., a resort for invalids. It is said to be exceedingly rich in natural beauty, and its wine is famous." …

---

351 JOHNSTON 1860, pages 17, 19-20.
352 At the end of his book *The Life and Adventures of a Free Lance*, published in New York, in 1914, there is a partial list the paintings he did since June 1871, which were sold at prices ranging from $60 to $600. Among them one can find his Madeira-related paintings, which he named as follows: 'Atalaya Rock – Madeira', 'Ponto Forado – Madeira', 'Atalaya Rock', 'Foul Weather off Ponto Forado', 'Bugio Island with bark', 'Porto da Cruz – Madeira', 'Penha d'Aquia – Madeira', 'Fishing boats of Madeira Scurrying home', 'Volcanic Rocks – Madeira', 'Courtado Peak', 'Brazen Head and Fort Santiago', 'Coast Scene – Madeira', 'Faial Beach – Madeira', 'Fishing Boats of Porto Santo' 'Loo Rock – Madeira' and 'Surf on Coast of Madeira'. Some of them illustrate his Madeira-related article in this book but the original paintings should be in American private collections.
353 BENJAMIN, Samuel Greene Wheeler, *The Atlantic Islands as Resorts of Health and Pleasure*, Harper & Brothers, Publishers, New York, 1878.

Soon after leaving the limits of Funchal we came in sight of the village of Cama do Lobos[354] and Cabo Giram,[355] a vertical cliff 2185 feet high,[356] bathing its feet in the sea waves. It is the loftiest sea cliff in the world.[357] Leaving this on our left, we entered the Estreito district, which is virtually the wine-growing district of Madeira, the slopes being densely covered with vines trained on trellises which often overarch the road. The little wine raised on the north side and at Porto Santo is of inferior quality, and is changed into brandy, which is mixed with the best Madeira. The vine was first introduced into the island from Cyprus in 1425, and the red volcanic soil gave it a flavor which brought it into rapid repute. The Shakespearian student will remember Poins's allusion to it when he says to Falstaff, "Jack, how agrees the devil and thee about thy soul, that thou soldest him on Good-Friday last for a cup of madeira!" Until 1852 this noble wine continued to sparkle on the board of those whose cellars contained the rarest wines. In that year the yield was about 20,000 pipes; then, without warning, a blight – a fungus on the plant and fruit, called the *oïdeum Tuckeri* – made its appearance, and in 1853 the yield fell to 100 pipes! This has continued until within twelve years. The suffering resulting from the sudden collapse of the wealth-bearing resources of the island was beyond computation. After a while the cultivation of the sugar-cane restored a portion of Madeira's lost prosperity. Still later, a way was found of counteracting the spread of the blight, and partially resuming the production of wine. This is done by blowing the powder of sulphur flowers over both vine and grapes, a very laborious process, as may be easily imagined. Madeira wine, *par excellence*, is made from the mixture of grapes dark and white, and from a light claret color gradually pales into a topaz hue of surpassing richness. Four other sorts are also produced – Malmsey, Bual, Sercial, and Tinta, all excellent. The first is too well known to require further mention; the last, from the Burgundy grape, is a mild, red wine.[358] …

Figure 35. "Church of Nostra Senhora do Monte". This sketch presents Madeira's most celebrated church, Nossa Senhora do Monte. At the bottom some people are seen busily engaged in harvesting the grapes. *Book illustration, presumably drawn by its author.*

6.1.1.25. Charlotte Alice Baker (1870'S/1880'S)

In 1882, this native of Boston published at her hometown the book entitled *A Summer in the Azores, with a glimpse of Madeira*,[359] depicting an Atlantic journey she

---

[354] The right spelling is Cama de Lobos. Note 207.
[355] The right spelling is Cabo Girão.
[356] Cabo Girão, a major touristic attraction of Madeira, is 580 meters high, which corresponds to 1902 feet.
[357] It is not. It the second highest sea cliff in the world.
[358] BENJAMIN 1878, pages 94, 116. This text from this author, including the transcribed segment about Madeira Wine, had been previously published at the "Scribner's Monthly, an illustrated magazine for the people", Volume 9, Issue 2, December 1874, pages 210-221, under the title "Rambles in Madeira."
[359] BAKER, Charlotte Alice, *A Summer in the Azores, with a glimpse of Madeira*, Lee and Shepard, Boston, 1882.

Figure 36. Charlotte Alice Baker. *19th century photograph. Author unknown.*

once undertook, starting on June 12 of an unmentioned year, which we suppose was at the end of the 1870's or at the beginning of the 1880's. After spending some months at the Western Islands she proceeded to Madeira, on an unnamed ship that had departed from New Bedford, MA, and arrived there on September 9. She dedicates a few chapters of her book to Madeira, in which there are some brief references to the island's vineyards and its staple product, wine.

MADEIRA.

Tuesday, Sept. 9

… The land seems to rise in very narrow, natural terraces from the sea, back upon the mountain-slopes, and in the intervening valleys. These terraces are of the most vivid green, being devoted to the culture of the sugar-cane. Sugar-mills are planted here and there along the shore. For twenty miles, we steam along quite near the shore. …

Every accessible shelf of rock, every available spot, is cultivated, and clad in richest verdure. This is the region of vineyards from which the famous Madeira wine is made.[360]

ON HORSEBACK.

Sunday, Sept. 14

… The men rested the hammock-poles upon a wall, and by terms went in for a smoke and a draught of Madeira wine. The gentlemen dismounted. I kept my seat. The clouds came down to our level, and it began to rain hard. We were tired and chilly, and gladly sipped a little of the soft, rich wine. Very little genuine Madeira wine ever finds its way to the United States. It is made from a mixture of black and white grapes, and when three or four years old is of a rich topaz color. Wine of this age is retailed in the shops for fifty cents a bottle, and the newer from twenty-five to thirty-six cents.[361] …

6.1.1.26. Henry Washington Hilliard (1881)

Henry Washington Hilliard (1808-1892), a native of North Carolina, was a U.S. Representative and during the Civil War served as a colonel in the Confederate States Army. Later in life he was appointed U.S. Minister to Brazil by President Hayes. When General Garfield took the Presidency Hilliard presented his resignation and requested a leave of absence to return home. During his homeward bound trip, from Rio to Europe, which started on June 15, 1881, aboard the *Iberia*, of the Pacific Steamship Line, he made a brief stop at Madeira, and noticed its verdant hills covered with

---

[360] BAKER 1882, pages 132-133.
[361] BAKER 1882, page 157.

vineyards. He mentioned this in his book *Politics and Pen Pictures at Home and Abroad*,[362] published in New York, in 1892. Being from the Carolinas, where much Madeira Wine was consumed throughout the 18th and 19th centuries, it must have been a thrill for him to see the island where this wine was made.

Figure 37. Henry Washington Hilliard. Book illustration. Author unknown.

CHAPTER XXXVII.
... – Madeira – ...

...The captain of the *Iberia* had instructions to call at Madeira for a number of English people who had passed the winter and spring in that delightful climate and wished now to return home. The morning was fine when we reached Madeira, and we stopped there several hours. The island was a place of much interest to me, and I saw its vine-clad slopes in their full summer verdure. We took on board a considerable number of passengers, who gave new animation to the ship, and resumed our voyage.[363] ...

6.1.1.27. Joseph Hankinson Reading (1880'S)

Joseph Hankinson Reading, an American missionary in Africa in the 1880's, published a book in Philadelphia, in 1890, entitled *The Ogowe Band – A Narrative of African Travel*,[364] whose third chapter is dedicated to Madeira, and is illustrated with some photographs. In the book there are no clues as to when his passage by Madeira took place – the author only mentions the month of September – but we assume that it might have been sometime in the 1880's. In the text related to Madeira he describes the aspect of Funchal from the sea, where vineyards were seen, mingled with sugar-cane plantations, and also a conversation held about the economic life of Madeira, no longer based on wine exports, like before and, last but not least, a visit made to the country seat of Mr. Reid,[365] where a visit was made to its vineyard, whose grapes had already been picked up.

CHAPTER III.
MADEIRA.

... Just before them the city of Funchal lay, built in solid squares near the waterside, and then climbed the mountain in several directions. Along the beach, boats laden with

---

[362] HILLIARD, Henry W.[ashington], *Politics and Pen Pictures at Home and Abroad*, G. P. Putnam's Sons, New York and London, 1892.
[363] HILLIARD 1892, page 405.
[364] READING, Joseph Hankinson, *The Ogowe Band – A Narrative of African Travel*, Reading & Company, Publishers, Philadelphia, 1890.
[365] This house and grounds still exists and at the present time belongs to the world famous Madeira Botanical Garden.

Figure 38. "City of Funchal, Madeira." As far as we know, this is the first B&W photo of the island inserted in a book published in the United States in the 19th century. *Book Photograph. Author unknown.*

merchandise were arriving and departing, oxen were drawing heavy loads in various directions, and numbers of people were hurrying to and fro. Above, the clouds were just rising from the mountain tops; among the peaks yawned great canyons as though the mountain had been forcibly rent asunder. The lower slopes of the mountain were terraced and planted with grapes and sugarcane, which were now being ripened by the autumn sun. Above the town were many country-seats, almost hidden from view by the orange and lemon orchards that surrounded them. Near the sea, in sheltered situations, were small fields of bananas, their broad leaves waving gently in the slight breeze. …[366]

Judge McGee and Captain Davis were content to enjoy themselves in comfortable repose on the cool veranda. While the young folks chattered away in the garden, they engaged in a quiet talk about the industrial condition of the island. The Captain informed Mr. McGee that Madeira was not as prosperous as in former years. Then wine was the principal article of export and it brought high prices; but a mysterious disease killed most of the vines and no branch of agriculture has since been found so profitable. "The island now lives," said the Captain, "almost entirely upon its trade with passing steamers. A few English tourists come out to spend the winter, but not so many as formerly. Every day there are new places of attraction opened on the continent, and besides, it is getting to be pretty well understood that Madeira is not especially healthy."

Judge McGee remarked that he had heard Madeira spoken of as a sanitarium. …[367]

When part way up, the sleds halted in an open place to rest, and there was a lively time comparing experiences. They were now up among the gardens and low stone huts of the peasant people, but they were so occupied in describing the recent situation that they did not take time to look about them. The rest of the way was toilsome work, and when they had mounted another thousand feet, they were glad enough to turn off into the pleasant grounds in the midst of which was the mountain home of Mr. Reid, a Scotch merchant. Mr. Reid gave them a hearty welcome, and so did his daughter, who was just home from school in England.

The view from the piazza was grandly beautiful. In front upon the terraced mountain-side were gardens, vineyards, and patches of sugar-cane. At their feet was the city of Funchal, its white buildings seeming wondrously near, so clear was the air. …

While the gentlemen were talking about the state of trade and the various industries of the island, Miss Reid took the girls with her into the vineyard. The main crop had already been gathered, but some bunches had been left here and there, and it was a new pleasure to the girls to be in a real, sure enough vineyard, one that was, very likely, like those they had read of in the Bible, in the land of Palestine. The grapes were good, and grateful to the taste, more especially after one has been several days at sea, but they could scarcely be called luscious. Many kinds sold in the Philadelphia markets are as good, if not better.

---

366 READING 1890, page 37.
367 READING 1890, page 43.

While they were enjoying the grapes Miss Reid entertained them with a description of the kind of life young people live in Madeira, and of her own school-days in London. ...³⁶⁸

6.1.1.28. Noah Brooks (1895)

The journalist Noah Brooks (1830-1903), a native of Maine, published in New York, in 1895, the book entitled *The Mediterranean Trip, A Short Guide to the Principal Points on the Shores of the Mediterranean and the Levant.*³⁶⁹ In its Foreword we can read that "The author of this little book has been over the route herein described and has visited the ports referred to. It has been his aim to furnish the American tourist with sufficient information to guide his steps in the countries visited ...". Madeira was the second port of call of his Mediterranean tour, the first one being at Ponta Delgada, in the Azores. In his work Noah Brooks provides some quick notes and facts to every port visited, but does not mention when he arrived at Madeira nor in which steamship he did travel.³⁷⁰ In the third chapter of his book, dedicated to Madeira, and illustrated with a photograph of Funchal's landscape, the author inserts a brief allusion to Madeira Wine, referring to the recovery of the vineyards and the increase of wine production and exports.

Figure 39. "Funchal". Aspect of the city seen from the East. *Book Photograph. Author unknown.*

MADEIRA – FUNCHAL

... The temperature of the island is equable, varying between 63º and 75º; and the fall of the thermometer during the night is usually inconsiderable. The salubrity of the climate has made Madeira one of the famous health-resorts of the world, persons afflicted with pulmonary consumption being especially benefited by residence here. During the depression caused by the failure of the grape crop, the people, who would have been otherwise reduced to penury, subsisted almost entirely on the gains from temporary visitors, chiefly from England. The wine yield, after having sunk to a nominal figure, has now increased to a considerable amount, and the quantity exported is very large. Other exports are fruits, cochineal, embroidery, and fine needlework. ...³⁷¹

---

368 READING 1890, pages 45-47.
369 BROOKS, Noah, *The Mediterranean Trip, A Short Guide to the Principal Points on the Shores of the Mediterranean and the Levant*, Charles Scribner's Sons, New York, 1895. This book had another edition, in 1906, under the same title and by the same publisher.
370 According to a chronicle that he wrote in Funchal on February 6, 1895, entitled "MADEIRA AND THE AZORES", and published in *The New York Times* on the 24th, we know that he was in Madeira at the beginning of that month, having arrived aboard the *Fuerst Bismark*.
371 BROOKS 1895, pages 24-25.

6.1.1.29. Anthony J. Drexel Biddle (1890'S)

In 1896, Anthony J. Drexel Biddle published *The Madeira Islands*,[372] in Philadelphia, in which the references to Madeira Wine are very scanty.[373] However, on the second edition of this book, edited four years later, in two volumes and under the same title,[374] he inserts a chapter about it, which consists mostly of transcriptions from other sources and is enriched with several photographs and other illustrations.

CHAPTER XXIII

THE VINE AND THE WINE

Introduction of the Wine. – Shortly after the settlement of Madeira the wine was brought from Crete, but it was not until the sixteenth century that the grape was cultivated to any great extent.

The largest shipments of wine from Madeira were made between the years 1788 and 1828. The following table will serve to illustrate the progress and history of the wine product in Madeira.

Quantity of Madeiran Wines consumed by the World, Year by Year, since 1774. – TOTAL SHIPMENTS FROM MADEIRA.

Year	Shipments in Pipes	Year	Shipments in Pipes	Year	Shipments in Pipes	Year	Shipments in Pipes
1774	7,073	1822	10,558	Financial year from July, 1850, to June,		1872	1,654
1775 to 1787	Not obtainable	1823	8,983			1873	2,154
		1824	10,980			1874	2,060
		1825	14,431			1875	2,322
1788	10,819	1826	9,338	1851	7,301	1876	2,568
1789	11,762	1827	8,424	1852	6,690	1877	2,476
1790	13,715	1828	9,624	1853	4,201	1878	2,125
1791 to 1797	Not obtainable	1829	8,104	1854	2,227	1879	2,923
		1830	5,499	1855	1,776	1880	3,691
		1831	5,533	1856	1,891	1881	3,417
1798	12,429	1832	7,164	1857	1,798	1882	4,260
1799	11,666	1833	8,683	1858	1,284	1883	3,854
1800	16,981	1834	8,875	1859	1,328	1884	4,399
1801	16,732	1835	7,730	1860	1,013	1885	4,905
1802	14,333	1836	7,913	1861	1,259	1886	5,227
1803	12,967	1837	8,123	1862	981	1887	4,247
1804	11,011	1838	9,832	1863	723	1888	5,372
1805	13,223	1839	9,041	1864	840	1889	5,195
1806	14,015	1840	7,976	1865	536	1890	5,562
1807	16,701	1841	7,157	1866	823	1891	6,346
1808	13,994	1842	6,270	1867	819	1892	6,077
1809	15,363	1843	7,386	1868	874	1893	5,168
1810	11,273	1844	7,054			1894	5,289
1811	9,575	1845	7,179	For the regular year of		1895	5,997
1812 to 1819	Not obtainable	1846	8,190			1896	5,917
		1847	5,577				
		1848	5,829	1869	987		
1820	13,754	1849	7,379	1870	1,110		
1821	9,916			1871	1,511		

---

372 BIDDLE, Anthony J. Drexel, *The Madeira Islands*, First Edition, Drexel Biddle & Bradley Publishing Company, Philadelphia, 1896.

373 Those references are the following: «Three-fourths of the wine trade are in the hands of the English, and nearly all the larger shipping firms and banking houses are owned and financiered by Englishmen. And here is where the "rub" comes: the Portuguese hate the English.» BIDDLE 1896, page 35; «As remarked upon once before in a previous paper, the English own about three-fourths of the world-famous Madeira wine trade. About the largest of the English companies handling the Madeira wine is "Scott, Gordon and Company," who have their headquarters just outside of Funchal, and who own wines here, there and everywhere about the entire island./ More prominent among the staple products exported from Madeira are wine, sugar, cayenne pepper, guava jelly and molasses.» BIDDLE 1896, page 59; «At Paul do Mar, a little village about three miles up the coast from Calheta, every inch of the soil is under cultivation. This is the chief locality for the growing of the grapes which make the world-famous Sercial wine.» BIDDLE 1896, page 83.

374 BIDDLE, Anthony J. Drexel, *The Madeira Islands*, Volume I and II, Drexel Biddle, Philadelphia, 1899. This book had an English edition, under the same title, published in 1900, in London, through Hurst & Blackett, Limited. It also had a Second American edition, under a different title: *The Land of the Wine: Being an Account of the Madeira Islands at the Beginning of the Twentieth Century, and from a New Point of View*, published by the author in Philadelphia and San Francisco, in 1901.

N.B. – It will be understood that the years from 1851 to 1868 are all financial years of from July of the one year to June of the other. In 1869 the customs went back to the old way of keeping their books, from January to December of each year.

Statistics before the year 1774 are not obtainable.

The oldest and largest wine-shipping house in Madeira is that of Messrs. Cossart, Gordon & Co., established in the year 1745 by Mr. Francis Newton.

History of Good Wine as shown in the Life Work of Francis Newton. – This young gentleman started in business for himself under the most trying and adverse circumstances, for he was unfamiliar with the language and with the laws and customs, and he had the ill will of the community for a long time because he was a Protestant, and therefore, in the eyes of the Madeiran Romanist, a heretic. But, with indomitable energy and perseverance, Mr. Newton fought every obstacle until he overcame it. His first mission was to improve the product, which, at the time of his arrival, was very large, but of inferior quality, being merely the fermented grape juice with little or no treatment. By his efforts the wine was improved, for he built warehouses, put in elaborate appliances for the manufacture of a higher grade of wine, and employed several skilled wine-makers from the grape-growing provinces of France and the German Rhine to instruct the natives in the proper handling of the product of the vine. At this time Mr. Newton was joined by several partners, – Messrs. Gordon, Cossart, Murdoch, Johnston, and Spence.

When the Wine first became Famous. – The improvement in the wine began to attract general attention, and it was not long before the price of the best product merited an advance of from twenty pounds to forty-five pounds per pipe. London became a heavy consumer, and continental cities bought largely.

When the Demand exceeded the Supply. – The following extract from a letter sent by Newton, Gordon, Murdoch & Co., to the partner, Mr. Newton, who was in London in behalf of his business during the winter of 1801, may be of interest as serving to show the extraordinary demand that there was for the wines of Madeira at the beginning of the nineteenth century.

Extract from a Letter from Newton, Gordon, Murdoch & Co., Madeira, to Francis Newton, London, 20 January, 1810.

"There are not one hundred pipes of *old wine* in the hands of the natives for sale. The exports of the year 1800 exceeded all previous exports, being upwards of seventeen thousand pipes, and, should the demand for our wine increase as much as it has done for some years, the island will not be able to supply the requisite quantity."

India also became a heavy consumer of Madeiran vintages. In the year 1800 Newton, Gordon, Murdoch & Co. received the following orders from Bombay alone, ordered by the following firms:

Dec. 6, 1799............................300 pipes, David Scott & Co.
Aug. 2, 1800............................250 pipes, Forbes, Smith & Co.
Total .... 1,050 pipes.

6. MADEIRA WINE IN AMERICAN LITERATURE

Another large order which stands in their books reads as follows:

From William Simon's Letter, dated East India House, 28 July, 1809.

"Three hundred and thirty pipes of best India Market Madeira wine. One hundred and twenty pipes best London Market Madeira. For account of the East India Company and to be shipt on board their ships of the season 1809/10."

After one hundred and fifty years, Cossart, Gordon & Co. (the present firm name of the original Newton, Gordon, Murdoch & Co.) are still, as already stated, the leading wine-merchants.

The Responsible Wine-Merchants of Madeira. – But other responsible houses that do a considerable business in wine-making and handling are the following, alphabetically listed:

Wine-Merchants.

Araujo & Henriques.	Giorgi & Co., Antonio.
Blandy Bros. & Co.	Miles, Henry P.
Correa, J. A. (Golden Gate).	Payne & Son, John.
Cunha, A. P.	Rodrigues & Co. Francisco.
Cunha & Co.	Welsh Bros.

Vines and Stores of Cossart, Gordon & Co. – Cossart, Gordon & Co. own vineyards here and there throughout the island. Their head-quarters are situated just outside the town, and comprise six distinct sets of buildings, – Estufa, Serrado, Martins, Thiago, Aula, and Pateo armazens (stores).

The Estufa Stores, where the Wines are subjected to Heat. – The estufa stores comprise a block of buildings two stories high, divided into four compartments. In the first of these common wines are subjected to a temperature of 140° F. – derived from flues heated with anthracite coal – for about twelve weeks; in the second compartment wines of an intermediate quality are heated to 130° F. for a period of some eighteen weeks; the third is for superior wines which are kept heated between 110° and 120° F. for the term of one-half a year. The "calor,"[375] or fourth compartment, is heated by the warmth derived from the surrounding compartments. It has a temperature varying from 90° to 100° F. Here are kept the high-grade wines. The reason given for thus heating the wine is that the germs of fermentation which remain in it may be destroyed, and, moreover, that the wine will have nothing to delay its maturing, so that it may be shipped in its second and third year without further addition of spirits.

The use of this estufa in Madeira dates from the commencement of the present century. The great bulk of the wine undergoes a treatment such as here described before it is shipped.

During the preparation of the following account of the wine and its manufacture the writer derived much assistance from Cossart, Gordon & Co., in Funchal, and also by recourse to Henry Vizetelly's famous book "Madeira and its Wines."[376]

---

[375] Portuguese word for heat.
[376] Vizetelly's famous book about the island's wines is entitled *Facts about Port and Madeira*, whose Madeira Wine-related illustrations we present at section 13.2.3. of this anthology.

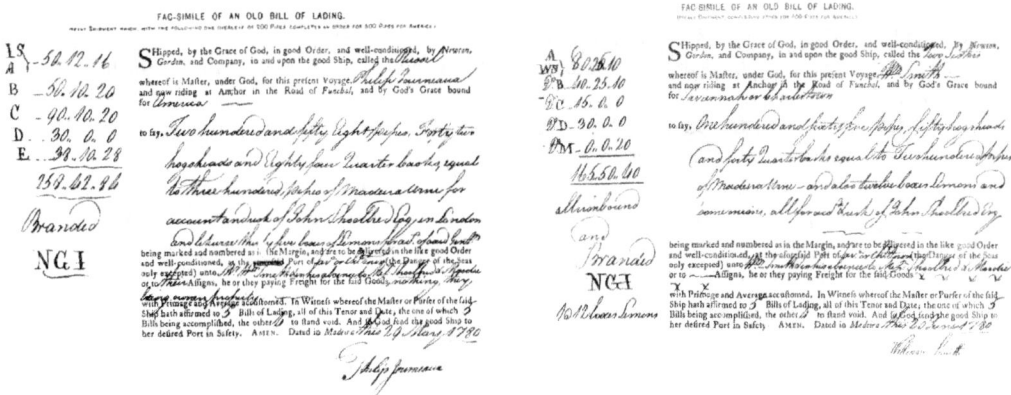

Figures 40 and 41. "Fac-Simile of two Old Bills of Landing". *Book document images.*

Wine-making Grapes described. – The following descriptions of the principal kinds of wine-making grapes in the island of Madeira are quoted from the above-named work.

Verdelho. – "A small oval grape, hardly as large as a coffee-berry, when ripe of a rich golden hue, full of flavour, and saccharine. The leaf of the Verdelho has seven lobes, the sinews of which are not strongly marked; it is of a dark green, but perfectly bald, and the two lower lobes are very indistinct."

Verdelho, at the present time, is the principal wine-making grape in the island, at least two-thirds being of this species.

Tinta. – "A small black Burgundy grape of fine flavour. The leaf of the Tinta has seven lobes, decreasing in size, and the sinews are very deep and rounded; the middle lobe is subdivided into two others, both indistinct."

The Tinta grapes in smaller vineyards are usually pressed together with the Verdelho and other white grapes. In the larger vineyards where there may be a sufficient quantity of it to make it worth while to be plucked separately, such is done, and a red wine is made which is called Tinta, from the grape. The husks of the grapes are allowed to remain in the wine during the process of fermentation, and impart to the wine its deep-red colour and peculiar astringency. This red wine is much esteemed amongst the natives, and used as a *vin ordinaire*, being drunk in its first or second year; after that time it begins to lose its colour and character, and in course of time becomes a tawny-coloured Madeira.

Malvazia, or Malmsey. – "Malvazia Candida is a medium-sized grape, of a rich gold colour when ripe, and hangs in long, thin, pendulous bunches. The leaf has four very deep and rounded sinews with two others less distinct; each dentation has a small yellow tip; the back of the leaf is as smooth as the upper surface, and is of a deep yellow-green. Its epithet, 'Candida,' is a corruption of 'Candia,' whence this Malmsey vine was imported in the fifteenth century by the Infante Dom Henrique."

Malmsey Madeira is a rich white wine, of peculiar bouquet, imparted to the wine by the husks of the grape being allowed to remain in the wine during fermentation. It is considered one of the most valuable of the wines of Madeira, and even when young commands a high price. The best grapes are grown on rocky soil, and should be allowed to remain on the vines until they become almost raisins. The produce of Malmsey on the island is but small.

Bual. – "A round, straw-coloured grape of medium size, leaf with four of the sinews very deep and sharp, the two lower indistinct, the indentations sharp and irregular, the leaf hairy on both sides." The wine made from the Bual grape is of delicate and mellow character. The Bual is not a common grape, and the wine made from it always commands a high price.

Sercial. – "A round, white grape, the same as the Reisling of the Rhine; the leaf has four rounded sinews; the nerves are very strong and by their projections give a cockled appearance to the leaf; it is a yellow-green and cottony on both sides." This vine will not succeed in all places or soils. It is mostly grown near the sea-coast at Paul do Mar and Ponta do Pargo, two places on the west coast of the island. The wine is very unpleasant to the palate when new, and requires some eight years to become matured. When old it is considered one of the finest of the wines of Madeira.

Malmsey, Sercial, and Bual may be considered as specialties of Madeira wines, as their production is but small and the wines are sought for only by connoisseurs.

Amongst other wine-producing grapes may be mentioned the "Negro Molle,"[377] a large, juicy, black grape, the Maroto, the Tarantrez,[378] the Carão de Moça, Malvazia Roxa, Malvazião, the Listrão, the Bastardo, and some others. All these, however, are usually pressed together with the Verdelho species in the making of Madeira wine.

Verdelho, the King of Wine-Producing Grapes. – All these different kinds of grapes in Madeira, with the exception of the specialties before mentioned, such as Bual, Tinta, Malmsey, and Sercial, are gradually giving way before the Verdelho, which is without doubt the king of wine-producing grapes.

Cossart, Gordon & Co.'s Book. – Cossart, Gordon & Co. publish a book descriptive of their establishment,[379] and by way of describing it they quote a chapter from Henry Vizetelly's work.

Wine-making described by Henry Vizetelly. – While the writer is familiar with the plant of Cossart, Gordon & Co., he appreciates his utter incompetency to prepare an account which would be equal to that of Mr. Vizetelly. He, therefore, requites the following from the chapter by Mr. Vizetelly as republished by Cossart, Gordon & Co.

The Serrado Stores. – The ground on which the Serrado stores stand comprises between four and five acres, with armazens of a single story occupying three of its sides, the cooperage being on the fourth. Here we observed casks being made in precisely the same fashion as is followed at Jerez, with the exception, perhaps, that the adze which the men handle so dexterously is a trifle heavier and clumsier than the one used by their Jerez brethren.

Coopers. – The Funchal coopers work by the piece, and each pipe, which is certainly a well-made article, costs something like a couple of pounds. Round about the cooperage were piles of American oak staves, already trimmed or in the rough, while in the centre of the plot of ground were sheds in which the casks are measured, branded, scalded, and steamed, together with a couple of large tanks.

The vacant space between the sheds and the stores is occupied with rows of casks of various sizes, fresh from the cooperage, and undergoing a seasoning with water. When this is completed the casks are transferred to the armazem de Avinhar, there to be filled with common wine, which remains in them for two or three months. In these stores there are always in use for this purpose from two hundred to three hundred pipes of wine, which after frequent employment is no longer suitable, and is distilled into spirit. In the rear of the cooperage is a dried-up watercourse, a steep ravine some forty feet deep, which intersects the town of Funchal, and is mostly bordered by an avenue of shady plane-trees.

The Season for a Freshet. – During winter the water rushes down here from the mountains, bringing with it huge boulders fully a ton in weight, and sweeping away whatever it encounters in its progress.

The Flood of 1803. – In the year 1803 the rushing torrent overflowed the steep banks of the ravine, carrying away a store of Cossart, Gordon & Co.'s, which had been erected at the verge, together with several hundred pipes of wine, all of which were lost. The same flood swept away the British consulate (some distance lower down) and a church, not to speak of other damage.

---

377 The right spelling is Negra Mole.
378 The right spelling is Terrantez.
379 That book was entitled *Cossart, Gordon & Co, established 1745, the oldest and by far largest shippers of Madeira wines*, Cossart, Gordon & Cie, [Funchal?], 1885.

Figure 42. "The Vintage at Blandy's". *Book photograph. Author unknown.*

Shade for the Labourers. – All the unoccupied ground at these Serrado stores is planted with vines trained on corridors, interspersed here and there with a mango, fig, or custard-apple tree. Trelissed vines, moreover, cover in all the walks in front of the various stores, enabling the men employed in them to be always under shade. The first store which we visited – a long narrow building some three hundred feet in length, with square grated openings along its front to allow of the free admission of air – is capable of holding six hundred pipes, in triple rows of two tiers each. It is used for receiving "vinho em mosto," or newly-made wine.

Scarlet Geraniums. – Scarlet geraniums about a man's height are trained all over its front, and under the broad canopy of trellised vines – stretching from the roof of the store to that of the opposite shed – empty casks waiting to be "wined" are stowed away.

When the Produce of a Vineyard is purchased. – It is a common practice with the Madeira wine-shippers to purchase the produce of a vineyard before the grapes are pressed, in which case they either send some one especially, or appoint an agent residing in the locality, to see the that the grapes are not gathered until they are ripe, and the work in the lagar[380] is properly done, and to arrange for the transport of the "mosto" to their Funchal wine-stores. There the "mosto" continues fermenting, with the bung-hole of each cask simply covered over with a leaf, generally until the middle of November. Either before or after the fermentation a small quantity of brandy is added, varying in quantity according to the quality of the "mosto," but seldom exceeding three per cent.

Racking and Lotting of Wine. – When the wine has thoroughly cleared itself, it is racked and lotted according to its quality, and afterwards forwarded to the "estufa" or heating magazine. [A specialty with regard to the wines of Madeira of which the writer has previously spoken.]

Fining for the Pateo Stores. – In face of the store where the mosto is received is a store for brandy; and thence we proceed under the vine-covered corridors to other stores containing wines a year old, just arrived from the "estufa," – wines which, after having received a further modicum of spirit (varying from one to three gallons per pipe), were undergoing racking and fining preparatory to being passed on to the Pateo stores of the firm. There they will remain in butts holding four hundred gallons each, until fully matured for shipment. It should be noted that the mosto is fermented and the wine heated, racked, and passed from one store to another in what are termed canteiro or scanting pipes, each holding one hundred and thirty gallons, old wine measure.

Where the Sun is used instead of the Estufa. – The artificially-heated estufas are used only by the larger shipping houses, who, however, heat wine in them for other shippers at a stated rate.

---

380 Wine-press.

Others accomplish the desired object by placing their wines in a kind of glass house, where they remain exposed to the full heat of the sun. In the daytime a temperature of from 120º to 130º F. is secured, which, however, becomes considerably lowered during the night, a circumstance which is regarded by many as detrimental to the development of the wine. In the country districts where estufas in no form exist, the holders of wine place the butts out in the open air in favourable positions to secure the full influence of the sun's rays.

Wine sent on a Sea Voyage to Mature. – The practice prevalent for many years past of sending Madeira on a voyage to the East or West Indies and home again is simply a variation of this method of maturing the wine by subjecting it to a high temperature, the heat which it encounters in these latitudes when shut up in the ship's hold being necessarily very great.

Precautions against Leakage under Heat. – In the estufas I am now describing – which, if packed full, are capable of heating one thousand six hundred pipes of wine at one time – the pipes are placed on end in stacks of four, with smaller casks on the top of them, a narrow gangway being left between the different stacks to admit of the passage of a man for the purpose of ascertaining that the casks do not leak, as when subjected to great heat they are naturally inclined to do. A hole about the sixth of an inch in diameter has been previously bored in the bung of each pipe to allow the hot vapour to escape, otherwise the pipe would burst. As it is, the casks not frequently leak, as we perceive by numerous dull patches in various parts of the floor, rendering it necessary for the different compartments of the estufa to be inspected once during the daytime and once during the night, in order that any mishap of this kind may at once be rectified.

The Risky Proceeding of Tapping Wine in Air-Tight Compartments. – Each compartment is provided with double folding-doors, and after it is filled with wine the inner doors are coated over with lime, so as to close up any chance apertures. When it is necessary to enter the estufa, the outer doors only are opened, and a small trap in the inner door is pushed back to allow of the entrance of the man in charge, who passes between the various stacks of casks, tapping them one after the other to satisfy himself that no leakage is going on. On coming out of the estufa, after a stay of a full hour, he instantly wraps himself in a blanket, drinks a tumblerful of wine, and then shuts himself up in a closet, into which no cool air penetrates, provided for the purpose. Messrs. Cossart, Gordon & Co. usually place their wines in the estufa during the months of January and February, which admits of their removal to other stores before the next vintage commences.

Loss of Wine through Evaporation. – During the time they are in the estufa they diminish some ten or fifteen per cent, through the evaporation of their aqueous parts.

The Counting-House. – There still remain the Pateo stores to be noticed. These are situated in the rear of the firm, where all the books and papers relating to its transactions since its first establishment are carefully preserved.

The Pateo Stores, where Certain Specialties are kept. – Passing beneath an archway and across a narrow court planted with flowers, among which are geraniums trained level with the first-floor windows, we enter a small store, forming a kind of anteroom to the stores which follow. The first of these contains wines in butts holding four pipes each, in perfect condition for shipment, and only needing to be drawn off. Here we tasted a few specialties, including some Branco secco, made exclusively from the "verdelho" species of grape, which, having been perfectly fermented, possessed all the qualities of a remarkable fine dry Madeira; also some Sercial from Ponta do Pargo, of vintage 1865, exceedingly dry and clean-tasting, and slightly pale.

Where the Choice Wines are stored. – In the store above were wines of different qualities and ages, including some Palhetinho, or straw-coloured wine, delicate in flavor and with a fine bouquet; also several still paler wines, going under the Yankee cognomen of Rainwater Madeira, on account of their remarkable softness and delicacy. Here also were stored a vintage wine of 1863, – a Vinho do Sol, as it was called, from its having been matured by exposure to the sun, and never having passed through the estufa, – and finally a pale, delicate Malmsey, of the preceding year's vintage, with a highly developed bouquet, which promised to become a wine of a singularly choice character.

The Oldest Wines. – In the armazem de Vinhos Velhissimos – the ground-floor of building on the southern side of the courtyard – were some large butts containing reserve wine of

6.1. TRAVEL LITERATURE

Figure 43. "Vine Growing in the Suburbs". In this image the vine trellices can be clearly seen. *Book photograph. Author unknown.*

great age and numerous soleras, including a Cama de Lobos,[381] the origin of which dates back to 1844 – a deep-coloured, powerful wine of fine high flavor, replenished from time to time by wine from the bastardo variety of grape. A São Martinho solera,[382] dating from the year 1842, was a soft choice wine with fine bouquet, while a Bual solera going back to the year 1832 proved remark bly delicate in flavour. There were also a couple of Malmsey soleras founded respectively in the years 1835 and 1850, the former of which had all the qualities of a choice liqueur; together with a Verdelho vintage of the year 1851 which had never been exposed to artificial heat: a sound mellow wine of the highest character.

Flavouring and Colouring Wines of Inferior Quality. – At the end of this solera store is a store containing Surdo, or sweet wine, and Vinho Concertado, or boiled mosto, thinned by the addition of some ordinary wine, and which, like the Jerez vino dulce and vino de color, are used for flavouring and colouring wines of inferior quality.

Light, Tasty, Moderate-Priced Wine. – Proceeding through the arched-passage leading into the little garden, planted with bananas, rose-trees, and geraniums, and having vines trained in corridors over the walks, we came upon another store containing wines of later vintages from the north side of the island, which are light and agreeable to drink, and are shipped at what appears to be a very moderate price.[383]

6.1.2. Magazines

The American views about the vineyards of Madeira and its famous wine, published in book form throughout the 19th century, by different U.S. citizens that passed by the island are complemented by a wide array of texts containing accounts of Madeira, published in different magazines. In our research we were able to locate at least eleven, edited from 1821 to 1879, in several American cities, which we have arranged

---

381 Wine produced at Câmara de Lobos, a village often referred to as Cama de Lobos, in 19th century sources.
382 Solera (or soleira, in Portuguese) designates a pile of casks used to age different kinds of wines, such as the Madeiras, in which the older wines are kept at the ground level, whereas the younger ones are kept on top.
383 BIDDLE 1896, pages 103-130.

chronologically, by order of publication. The first one was published anonymously in a masonic magazine, in 1821, in New York, and describes Funchal with its numerous vineyards, mentions the high demand for Madeira wine and summarizes the history of the wine, how it is made, and the different types produced on the island, among other topics.

THE ISLAND OF MADEIRA.[384]

… The city of Funchal is very delightfully situated at the foot of this lofty range of mountains, on the south side of the island; which forms a kind of amphitheatre, and has a beautiful appearance from the shipping as you approach it, the environs abounding with vineyards, generally in the most luxuriant state; and in the midst of the green foliage of the vine, orange, lemon, pomegranate, bananas, myrtle, cypress, cedar, &c, are numerous villas belonging to the native gentry, or to the British merchants, which, being quite white, add greatly to the beauty of the scene. …

The convulsed state of Europe, for so many years, occasioned such an increased demand for the wines of Madeira, that they have, in consequence, advanced to nearly treble the price at which they were sold at the commencement of the French revolution. The cause is removed, but the effect is still continued, by the impolicy of the British merchants, who out-bid each other in their purchases from the Land proprietors and wine jobbers: this rise in the price of wine has produced an increase of income to the landholders, and thus, (to use the language of one of their own writers) many now live in splendour, whose parents were content with the simple manners of their neighbours on the opposite coast of Barbary. Both sexes dress now in the highest style of English fashion; while most of the principal families have their card and music parties, routs, balls, &c. …

When the island was first colonized, prince Henry had the sugar cane transplanted hither from Sicily; and, at one time, there were forty sugar mills on the island, that article then forming the staple commodity; now there is only one mill remaining, at which little sugar is made, but that little is excellent, and has a scent like the violet.

Instead of the cane, vine is now cultivated, the produce of which is well known and esteemed all over the world: the vines run on trellises of cane work, about three feet from the ground, and the grape is usually fit for making into wine at the beginning of September, when they are obliged to tie up all the dogs, to prevent their getting at the grapes, of which they are very fond. Great quantities are destroyed by rats, lizards, and wasps.

The wine-press is a wooden trough about six feet square, and two feet deep; over which is a large clumsy lever. When the trough is nearly filled, about half a dozen peasants, bare legged, get in, and with their feet press out the precious juice; after which the husks and stalks are collected in a head, and pressed with the lever, this last pressing produces the strongest and choicest wine. The best wine is produced on the south side of the island, and when first made, is as deep coloured as port; ferments for about six weeks after it is made. It is computed that about twenty thousand pipes are made annually, of which about two thirds are exported, principally to Great Britain and British colonies, and the remainder is consumed on the island.

---

384 PRATT, Luther, "The American Masonic Register, and Ladies' and gentlemen's magazine", Benedict Bolmore, New York, 1821, Volume I, pages 60-62, 100-102. Note: this text was transcribed from an undetermined English publication.

There are many different descriptions of grapes, the largest size, and which is merely a table grape, and is not made into wine, is about the size of a muscle plumb, and the bunches are so large as sometimes to weigh twenty pounds.

The wines shipped from Madeira, are classed Tinta, or Madeira, Burgundy, Malmsey, Sersial,[385] and simple plain Madeira; the three first are thirty pounds per pipe dearer than the latter, which is 60*l*. per pipe of 110 gallons free on board. This high price is occasioned by the want of unanimity among the English merchants, or indeed a want of good faith towards each other, for they appear occasionally to rouse from their lethargy, meet at their consul's, and agree to give only certain prices for the wines at the press, but, immediately after, each outbids the other, and the wine jobber laughs in his sleeve, and profits by their folly. Were a dozen of the principal wine shippers to be unanimous, they might, with ease reduce the wines at the press one third of the present exorbitant prices, and could, of course, make a similar reduction in the shipping prices, when they would consequently have larger orders; but what can scarcely be credited is, that when they had what they term a factorial meeting, to affix the shipping-prices for 1819, all but two of the sapient assembly were for raiding the price £8 per pipe; and when these two proved to a demonstration that such conduct would only induce the wine-jobbers to make a similar rise, and merely add to their coffers, already overflowing with the effect of the merchants' past follies; the meeting still deemed it necessary to adjourn for a few days, before they would allow themselves to be convinced.

No foreign wine is allowed to be imported, not even a few dozens of Port for private use, although it is the produce of the mother country; this is being very strict indeed, yet it is justifiable, as a very few years since a discovery was made of a smuggle into the island of a number of pipes of wine from the island of Fayal and Teneriffe; and had not the most rigid methods been adopted the wine of Madeira would have lost its reputation, as no one who imported wine from thence could have been certain of having it genuine: consequently the wines were seized, and the heads of the casks were knocked out in public market-place, which overflowed with the contents: the boats that landed it were confiscated, and the smugglers condemned to transportation, or to pay to the crown, in addition to losing the wine, twice its amount. ...

The second account was also published anonymously, on the following year, in Baltimore. It presents a description of the island as seen from the sea, with its vineyards, the ancient origin of Madeira wine, its mode of cultivation, the vintage time and the mode of production of this celebrated nectar.

The Island of Madeira,
ITS WINES, VINES, GEOLOGICAL PHENOMENA, &c. &c. &c.[386]
Communicated for the American Farmer

---

385 The right spelling is Sercial.
386 SKINNER, John S., *The American Farmer, containing Original Essays and Selections on Rural Economy and Internal Improvements, with Illustrative Engravings and the Prices Current of Country Produce*, Vol. III., J. Robinson, Baltimore, 1822, pages 35-36. NOTE: article inserted in the edition of April 27, 1821, of the *American Farmer*.

The island of Madeira was not known to the ancients, and some accounts attribute its discovery to the accident of two lovers flying from persecution, having been stranded on its coast. The Lady died a short time after the shipwreck, and the faithful swain inconsolable for her loss, survived her only a few days.[387] …

… On approaching the Island from the sea it presents a variegated and beautiful appearance. – The sides of the hills are cloathed with vines, and flowering shrubs, and the Ravines, and mountains covered with forest trees; streams of water are seen bursting from between the rocks, and falling into the ocean, and the prospect is terminated by a mass of mountains, and by the lofty summit of the Ruivo rising from the clouds, which hover round its base. …

… The landing is a steep beach and the boats used to unload the ships are drawn up high and dry by means of a windlass, worked by oxen. The wine is carried off in lighters, and men are constantly employed swimming and floating the pipes through the surf, which at times runs very high. Funchal is situated in about the same latitude as Charleston, in South Carolina, but enjoys a much milder climate. …

The whole Island appears to have been of Volcanic origin. … The soil on the South of the island is of decomposed Scories, and Volcanic sand, impregnated with Sal-ammoniac, which gives the hills a reddish tint, and is one cause of the excellence of the wines, as appears from those produced at the foot of Vesuvius, called Lacrymae Christi, and the rich wines of Catania, made from the Vineyards on the sands of Mount Aetna. …

The Sugar Cane was formerly much cultivated, and the Sugar of Madeira was highly esteemed – the cultivation of the vine has now the preference, and the Sugar plantations on the South of the island are not very extensive.

The Vine was originally brought from Cyprus – it is planted from cuttings in straight rows; a southern aspect is sought for, and is necessary to making the best wine. The labourer standing with his back to the South, opens a trench about four feet deep, and with his hoe draws the earth up in ridges; the cuttings are then planted in this inclined plane at from 6 to 12 inches apart, according to the number of plants; if when they have taken they are found to be too close, they are afterwards thinned. – After they begin to sprout, the earth from the second ridge is thrown into the first trench, and so on successively, leaving the vine inclining to the S and buried nearly 6 feet. I have likewise seen cuttings planted by burying the centre, and leaving both extremities out of the earth; where the land is dry stones are thrown into the trench. Great care is taken to prune off the unhealthy sprouts. When the plant is sufficiently grown to require support, a cane lattice work is erected on posts, higher on the N. side, and inclining gradually to the S. which gives an equal exposure to the sun, and throws off the rain. – The lattice work, which is made of our swamp cane, is raised three or four feet from the ground, and the vine is drawn through and laid upon it. This method I have never seen practiced elsewhere.

In Italy and in the South of France the vines are festooned on poles, or trained from tree to tree, and in the North they cling to poles stuck perpendicularly in the earth; in Madeira they are exposed on a flat extensive surface and must ripen more equally. The planting takes place immediately after the vines are pruned in January or February, and the longest cuttings are chosen for that purpose. It is generally three years before any benefit is received from a new Vineyard, and six before it comes to perfection.

---

387 See Note 195.

Bad vintages are occasioned either by a long continuance of foggy weather in April, May, and June; E. or Sirocco winds in July and August, or untimely and heavy rains in August and September.

The lands are in possession of Morgados or large land holders, and are generally entailed. The farmer holds his tenure on condition of paying half the produce, which added to the exaction of tithes, the presents to the curates, and high price of provisions, has diminished the cultivation of the Vine, and raises South wine when first brought to the merchant at Funchal at $120 the pipe.

The vintage commences on the south of the island early in September, and lasts to the middle of October. Great care should be taken to pick the grapes clean, by cutting off the unripe, or rotten fruit. The grapes are gathered when full ripe, and after some few have become raisins. They are put into a square vat pierced with holes not large enough to let the skin of the Grape fall through, they are then stamped by men, and drained into a receiver, the refuse is afterwards pressed. After a slight fermentation the wine is drawn off into casks, or sent to town in goat skins, on men's shoulders, or in barrels on Asses and Mules. There is a great variety of Grapes, and they are all mixed to make the common wines. The Tinta, a very high flavoured red wine, is made from the Negromole[388] and Verdella,[389] the Sercial from a grape brought originally from the banks of the Rhine; and the Malmsey from the Malvasia Grapes, which are kept on the vine until two thirds of them become raisins, it is generally sweetened with sugar. The Buas [Bual] is the best Grape, and the wine made exclusively from the grape is of the highest flavour.

When the Wine dealer receives the Wine if it be in must, or perfectly new, it is put into casks and worked for several days, with a sort of paddle introduced at the bung hole. It is then left to settle, and when the fermentation has ceased, and the new wine become clear, it is drawn off into casks, containing from 4 to 800 gallons, and from five to ten gallons of Brandy added to 120 of Wine. Only the best French brandy is used, and as it costs in Madeira more than wine, it is used as sparingly as possible.

The wine is then left to ripen, each quality separate. When drawn off into pipes to be shipped, they are mixed according to the judgment of the wine taster, whose skill consists in having observed what wines mix best. It is then lined with isinglass; an ounce is put into a cask of 110 gallons, and the wine agitated with a paddle, and being left to settle, in a few days it becomes perfectly clear. In order to prepare the pipes, they are kept for some months filled with water – they are afterwards washed with boiling water, and rinsed with brandy; a large lighted match of sulphur is then put into the bung hole, and when the pipe is full of smoke, the bung is closed tight until the cask is wanted. The latter part of this process is repeated every time the cask is emptied.

The wines from the North of the Island, and such as are not of the first quality are kept for some months in Estufas, or hot houses to mellow them. They change the temperature by moving then to different floors. The heat of the Estufa is from 90° to 100° of Fahrenheit. The produce of the Island seldom exceeds 30,000 pipes – about 15,000 are annually exported, the remainder being consumed in the Island, where it constitutes the common drink of the inhabitants. …

---

388 The right spelling is Negra Mole.
389 The right spelling is Verdelho.

The third account, presumably written by an unknown Naval officer, was published in 1833, in New Haven. In this text there is a section dedicated to Madeira's soil, vines and grapes, in which the author mentions the innumerable vineyards he found on the island, the fact that the best wine was produced on its south side, the different kind of grapes cultivated, some recommended wine merchants – among which is John Howard March, the U.S. Consul – and the mode of cultivation of the vines.

Art. II – *Miscellaneous Notices, in a letter to the Editor, dated from an American National Ship, off Cape de Gatt, in Spain, August 11, 1832.*[390]

Notice of Madeira.

I mentioned that we stopped at the island of Madeira. Few things can be imagined more beautiful than this gem of the ocean, (as it is called) as it disengaged itself from the darkness, one fair morning, toward the close of last month, and its lofty, picturesque mountains, its ravines with their cascades, and its numberless vineyards, became rapidly developed. ...

Soil, Vines and Grapes.

The soil of the island is formed from these tufas, and to them, together with the uniform mildness of the climate, the peculiar character of Madeira wine is owing. The soil, as may be supposed from all this, is by no means uniform. In a ride to the Corral,[391] along a road which led us for some miles about half way between the mountainous district and the beach, we passed, one while, along vineyards whose richness and beauty could not be any where excelled; at another, among naked, red hills, with here and there a stunted pine; then, across deep ravines, with walls of naked basalt, and here and there below, a little field of yams or cane, and then we suddenly emerged again into districts, where for miles were seen only the rich clusters of the grape. The fruit was then beginning to ripen, and hung in great profusion, from the cane trellis work, usually at a height of four or five feet from the ground. The vintage, however, is not expected to be as productive this season as usual. The crop had promised to be larger than customary, until about a week before our arrival, when a hot wind from Africa, called the Leste, to which this island is exposed, had blown upon it with great violence for a few days, and a large portion of the grapes immediately withered and dropped from the vines. ...

Wines

The best wine is produced on the southern side of the island, that of the northern side called *Verdelho*, being in no respect superior to the wine from other places. It is a singular circumstance however, that in forming a vineyard, cuttings from the *Verdelho* are always preferred. The richer soil and milder temperature act so as to produce from this the most

---

[390] SILLIMAN, Benjamin, "The American Journal of Science and Arts", Vol. XXIV, July 1833, New Haven, pages 237-243.
[391] The right spelling is Curral (das Freiras).

valuable fruit, while cuttings from the southern side, are always found to give wine of an inferior quality. The grape usually met with is white with a light tinge of yellow; it is oval and of a delicious flavor; the blue grape is also frequently seen, and I could not ascertain that the color made any difference in the wine. The difference varieties of grape produced on the island, are ranged under the heads of the *Verdelho*, the *Bastardo*, the *Negro Molle*,[392] the *Bual*, and the *Tinta*. The "Madeira wine" is generally a mixture of all these, in greater or less proportions, but the flavor is chiefly owing to the *bual* and *tinta*. The *tinta* is often kept separate, and being left to ferment with the husks remaining on the cask, takes from them a deep red color like that of Burgundy, which however, leaves it as it grows older. In flavor, it has a close resemblance to good *port*, except that it is not so rough; it costs on the island about one half more than the "Madeira." Considerable quantities are exported to England, but in our country it is almost unknown, except, I believe, at Washington. It is the only red wine produced on the island. The *Malmsey*, at least the best of it, is from a vine said to have been imported from Candia about four centuries ago. Its fermentation is checked sooner than that of other wines, in order to increase its sweetness.

Much of the wine which in the United States, passes by the name of Madeira, has probably never been near the island whose name it bears, and indeed unless the consumer imports it himself, or has it imported by some trusty person, he will run great risk of being deceived. Even in importing for private consumption, particular pains are necessary, as the merchant in Madeira, I believe, in answering orders, always distinguishes between that intended for individual use, and the market. The best houses or "brands," as they are technically called, are that of Marsh, (the U.S. Consul,) Gordon, & Co. (English,) Leacock, (English,) and Olivera,[393] (Portuguese.) We purchased a pipe of eight years old wine there, for private use, for $180, which I believe may be considered a fair price. The consul had some of the same age, kept in the garret, and valued at $220 the pipe; owing to evaporation, he considered it less profitable to himself at this, than the other at $180.

An acre, under the most favorable circumstances, will produce as much as four pipes of good wine; but one pipe to the acre, is the usual average. From one to three acres are considered as much as one family can well attend to. In the richest parts of the island, the cottages are scattered so thickly as, to a vessel sailing along the coast, to appear like a endless succession of villages. Their houses are thatched, and are generally nothing more than miserable hovels of basalt, cemented with mud, and without a chimney; but I have never, any where, been treated with greater respect than among this simple, and I believe, industrious peasantry. One half of the wine goes to the landholder, as rent; the remainder is usually purchased by the wine merchants, a considerable time before the vintage, one third of the money being paid at the time of purchase, and the remainder on delivery. The price given by the latter, for the best "Madeira," is $70 a pipe. The wine is racked once a month, during the first year, and once every fourth month, during the second, the loss at each racking, being about a gallon; from one to two gallons of brandy are put into each pipe during the fermentation.

My stay was too short to enable me to gather much information on the mode of cultivating the vine, and I take the liberty of quoting from the book of Mr. Bowdich,[394] a

---

392 See Note 388.
393 The right spelling is Oliveira.
394 See Note 199. This author quoted Bowdich's work, with some minor adjustments of his own, from page 110 to 112.

work bearing in itself evidence of close observation, and which is spoken of as a production of great correctness and excellence. It is said that the vines will last sixty years, if planted wide enough apart. The ground being turned up, the trenches are dug from four to seven feet deep, according to the nature of the soil. And a quantity of loose or strong earth is placed at the bottom to prevent the roots from reaching the stiff, clayey soil beneath, which would oppose their growth. They water the ground three times, if the summer has been dry, leaving the sluices open until the ground is pretty well soaked; the less the ground is watered, the stronger the wine, but the quantity is diminished in proportion. Some cultivators lay cow-dung at the roots of the vines when they plant them, and when the wine becomes poor, mix a fresh quantity with the soil at the surface. Others believe that animal manure injures the flavor of the grape, and instead, sow the *Lupinus perennis*[395] among the vines; this they do in January of every second year, cutting it down and burying it, by turning over the surface of the soil after the small rains, which prevail for about ten days, at the end of April. On the cutting of the Verdelho, (or northern vine,) they engraft any other variety they may wish; the grapes yield no wine until the fourth year. The stalks of the *Arundo Sagitatta*[396] are used in making frames for supporting the vines in the southern parts of the island, and the *Salix rubra*,[397] for tying them to this trellis work. In the northern parts of the island, the vines are trained around the chestnut trees, this firmer support being necessary, it is said, on account of the higher winds prevailing there. The vines in Madeira, give fruit as high as 2700 feet but no wine can be made from it; the greatest height at which they are now cultivated for this purpose, is in the valley of the Corràl das Frieres,[398] which is 2080 feet above the sea. There is much dispute as to the best month for pruning the vines. Some prefer February, others the middle of March; it depends principally however, on their foresight as to the weather, when the flowing takes place, which is six weeks or two months after the pruning. As to the treatment of the vines, I have observed that the produce of a particular season, must frequently be treated one year, very differently from that of another. When the grapes are green, the fermentation must be checked; when they are wet from unseasonable rains, it must be assisted; generally speaking, the riper the fruit, the more difficult the fermentation. A very agreeable *liqueur* is made in the island, from the second pressure of the grape, (the first being made with the feet,) into which, an equal quantity of brandy is immediately thrown, to stop the fermentation and produce sweetness. Gypsum is pretty generally used to clarify and mellow the wines while working, unless they happen to be of a green vintage."

From all this, I think it must be apparent, that the attempt to produce Madeira wine in our country, from cuttings from the vines of that island, must be entirely hopeless. Even on the island of Madeira itself, it can be produced only on the southern side. Its flavor is owing chiefly to two causes, the peculiar nature of the soil, and the remarkably uniform temperature of the climate; here too, the vineyards unless supplied with cuttings from another part of the island, would be in danger of speedily deteriorating. Indeed,

---

[395] Scientific name of the plant commonly known as Indian beet or Blue Lupine.
[396] Scientific name of a wild cane grown in Madeira, with which were made the vine trellises.
[397] Scientific name of a kind of willow grown in the vicinity of the island's creeks which are used for a wide variety of purposes, such as binding things or, more importantly, to make the island's famous wickerworks, a long-time tradition of the parish of Camacha.
[398] The right spelling is Curral das Freiras.

in our cold climate, and with our soil, every effort to produce more than grapes for our table must produce disappointment, unless we can do something with our own hardier grape. And such, I believe has already been the experience both in Pennsylvania, and in the States further west.

The fourth text was also written by an unidentified Naval officer and was published in Richmond, in 1841. In it one can see a description of the island, with vineyards everywhere, the way in which the vines were trained, how Madeira Wine was made and stored, among other topics.

Extracts from the Journal of an American Naval Officer.[399]

… Madeira, for its arable ground, is perhaps one of the most productive spots in the world. Every niche, among the mountains, the sides of every ravine, and the summit of every hill, where one-half an inch of soil can be found, is highly cultivated. Places that in the United States would only be traversed by the sportsman in quest of game, are here covered with the luxuriant vine – pendant from which, the grapes hang in innumerable tempting clusters. Spots here and there rendered soft and spongy by the oozing from the superincumbent rocks, are made beautifully conspicuous by the long, rich, half melancholy foliage of the banana – its straw-colored fruit now and then discernible among the gigantic leaves. …

The vines in Madeira are trained unlike any I have ever seen, on horizontal trellises or frame-work, about two-and-a-half or three feet above the ground. The English prefer the perpendicular trellice and close pruning, which, they think, insures wine of a better quality. The vine yields but one crop annually. The grapes are gathered on the south side very early in September, on the north side from two to three weeks later. Immediately after the vintage, the grapes are thrown into large wooden vats, and pressed with weights or a lever and screw; afterwards from four to six men, according to the size of the vat, stripped to their trowsers, and those rolled up, trample the pumice with their feet. The juice is conveyed by pipes into large tubs, and immediately after, it is poured into goat-skins, and carried directly to the town, on the backs of mules, and the shoulders of men and boys. Two different modes of preparation are then pursued. By some of the merchants, the new wine is poured into hogsheads and pipes, that had been filled with water six or eight months previous: and the wine remains undisturbed from three to any number of years. The other mode, is to pour the juice into immerse cauldrons, called "etouffes," which are heated for the purpose of giving the wine a flavor, which, if it were left to itself, it could only acquire by age. Frequently the new wine is mixed with a small proportion of the vintage called "Bual," remarkable, above all others, for its body and flavor, and bearing a corresponding price. Madeira is supposed to yield about thirty-five thousand pipes per annum. The new wine, direct from the vats, varies in price according to the reputation of the vineyard – usually from 30 to 35 cents per gallon, except the very superior quality, which, it is said, sometimes commands 80 cents. …

---

399 "The Southern Literary Messenger: devoted to Every Department of Literature and the Fine Arts", Vol. VII, Richmond, 1841, page 482.

The fifth text was also published anonymously,[400] in New York, in 1843, in an agricultural publication. Although the references to Madeira Wine are short, the images they convey are most interesting: vineyards everywhere and disposed in terraces, wine as the main business of the island, and the rich perfume of the pure wine scented in the streets of Funchal as the author walked by the wine stores.

ORIGINAL CORRESPONDENCE.[401]
For the American Agriculturist.

The Island of Madeira, and its Grape Cultivation.

… The precipices and the ravines are the wonderful features of Madeira scenery. There is much cultivation on the island, for the soil is very fertile, as indeed, all volcanic soils are – everywhere you see vineyards. The vines are trained along a frame work about 3 feet from the ground, and when the leaves are out, as they are beginning to be at this time, a vineyard presents a very beautiful appearance. The island, where the vine is cultivated, being terraced, adds much to the beauty of the scenery, for each vineyard seems to be composed of several, rising one above the other. Everything here tells of the great business of the island – all the people have more or less to do with wines, no matter what may be their occupations. You see the vineyard on the mountain slope, and as you pass through the streets of Funchal, your nostrils are constantly saluted by the perfume of wine in the vaults, which, by the way, are all on a level with the streets; and a very pleasant perfume it is too. For one, I like the odor, though I cannot drink the wine. The population here are very temperate, though theirs is the wine business. I just said I liked the odor of wines in a wine vault. There certainly is a perfume which you can perceive as you pass a wine vault here, which I never noticed in America, and which I think is very pleasant. I attribute the agreeable nature of the smell, to the fact that there is nothing *but* wine in the vaults, and that the wines are not so much adulterated as with us. …

Due to its unique climate, mid 19th century Madeira was a favorite resort for consumptives from Europe and also from the United States. Therefore it is not a surprise that the next text was written in Madeira by a Boston doctor, who had gone there in search of a cure for his pulmonary condition. In an account of the island written by him and published in Philadelphia, in 1850, he also mentions the staple product of the island, wine, by referring to the different types of it, how the vines are treated, the mode of making wine, and ending by saying that the priests on the island were entitled to one-tenth of all the wine made.

---

[400] This text was preceded by the following summary, which provides some information about its author, without disclosing his name: «We have just been favored with a package of letters from a young friend of ours, addressed to a relative in this city, from the Island of Madeira. He sailed for that place last February, and arrived in March, and as the letters contain some notices of the manner of cultivating the grape in Madeira, and other topics which we thought might interest our readers, we have made a few extracts. His lungs were dangerously affected when he left home; but we add with great pleasure, that the voyage out and residence there for a few months, proved very beneficial to him, and he has now returned to this city a comparatively hearty and well man.»

[401] "The American Agriculturist; Designed to Improve the Planter, the Farmer, the Stock-breeder, and the Horticulturist", Vol. I., New York, 1843, page 337.

For Friends' Review.

Notes on the Island of Madeira, during the winter of 1849-50.
By CLARKSON T. COLLINS, M. D., formerly Editor of the New York Medical and Surgical Reporter.

By way of explanation to those who may see these hastily written notes, I will briefly remark, that a pulmonary attack compelled me to seek a change of climate. In the Fifth month, 1849, I had a slight attack of haemorrhage from the lungs, which was repeated on several subsequent occasions. In consequence of these attacks, I resolved to seek the restoration of my health by a sea voyage and a change to a milder climate for the winter. My wife and I left New York in company with five other passengers for the Island of Madeira, and five for Rio de Janeiro, on board a barque, E. Corning, master, on the morning of the 31st of the Tenth month, 1849. …

The grape vines are cultivated on the sides of the mountains, but they do not thrive so well very high up; and the best wine is made from the grapes cultivated on the south side. An acre of vines yields, on an average, about three pipes of wine. There are about half a dozen different kinds of wine on the island, but the most common is that known as "Madeira", the world over; they have a dark wine called Tinta, which is a little like Port, but it is seldom exported. The Malmsey is the only kind of sweet wine made, and is very expensive. I have seen wine that could not be bought for less than $10 a gallon, on account of its great age. A good article of Madeira, which any respectable house would ship from here, is worth two dollars a gallon before it leaves the ware house of the owner, and is then subjected to a small duty by the Portuguese government, at the time the shipment is made, before it leaves the island.

The vines are trimmed or cut about the last of the First month, at which time they dig about the roots, and in a dry season they are obliged to irrigate them by means of water conducted down the sides of the mountains. Most of the water used for culinary purposes is obtained from fountains. Men, women and children are daily seen carrying their water pots or pitchers from the fountains, on the tops of their heads. At one of the fountains in Funchal, during the time of day when there are the most people getting water, (which is from six to seven, P. M.,) police officers are stationed to see that they are all served in turn.

Mode of making Wine. – The vintage begins about the middle of the Ninth month. I will illustrate by mentioning the manner of conducting affairs on a medium sized estate, say from six to ten acres. Ten or fifteen of the native Portuguese are employed; each one is provided with appropriate shears to cut the stems, and a basket that holds about a bushel. One man will gather about half an acre in a day. They manage to gather the grapes of a vineyard in two or three I days, at most, and as they fill their baskets they carry them to the press house, and empty them into a bin, which holds about thirty bushels. When the bin is full they have a large number of baskets full, ready to throw into the bin as the others are pressed

Figure 44. Clarkson T. Collins, M.D. *19th century litograph. Author unknown.*

---

402 LEWIS, Enoch, "Friend's Review; A Religious, Literary, and Miscellaneous Journal", Volume III., Published by Josiah Tatum, Philadelphia, 1850, pages 548-551.

out. The bin has two or three apertures on one side to let the juice escape as it is pressed out, and a large tub is placed at the apertures to receive the juice. All things being ready, the men take off their boots, roll up their pantaloons, and as many as conveniently can, get into the bin, tread down the grapes, and stamp them with their feet until they are well mashed. These Portuguese are not generally noted for their *cleanliness*; they are of Moorish origin, and appear much like the North American Indians, except a few who have a slight curling of the hair. They never think of *washing their feet* before getting into the bins. One of the English ladies of the island, the wife of an extensive wine dealer, who owns a fine vineyard, told me that they considered it very healthy for children to tread out the grapes, and that sickly children were stripped and put in upon the grapes to make them more robust. All of her children had been brought up on the island, and each one had been allowed to tread the grapes when they had the men employed at that occupation. After being well trodden by the feet, the mass is subjected to pressure by means of a large beam with blocks of stone suspended at one end, the other end being fastened so as to make the pressure bear upon the mass in the bin.

When the grapes have been deprived of their juice, the mass is then given to the poor workmen, who add water to it and press it again, making a sweet liquor, which they drink when new, and often make themselves sick by it. The juice is generally permitted to stand one night in the tubs, where a sediment collects in the bottom; it is then transferred from the open tub into casks and allowed to stand about four weeks to ferment; then it is purified by means of isinglass or the whites of eggs, and again transferred to other casks; at which time a small quantity of brandy is added, I believe about two gallons to the hundred. The brandy is distilled from inferior grapes, or those raised on the north side of the island.

There is much more alcohol in pure Madeira wine than many people are aware of; for it yields twenty per cent on distillation. They do not generally export wine before it is five or six years old. There are Roman Catholic priests located in every part of the island, or in other words, the island is divided into parishes, and at the time of the vintage, the priest of each parish sends his collector round and receives one-tenth of all the wine that is made. This is the law of Portugal, under whose government this island is conducted. I was told that the English took the liberty of giving them the poorest of the wine. …

The seventh text about Madeira was also written by an American physician, from New York, in an article about the climate of the island, published in that city, in 1865. He also classifies the island as a good resort for invalids, but states that it was no longer as good as it was before the disease of the vines, that occurred in 1852, which led to its destruction and to a radical shortage of Madeira wine.

ARTICLE XLIV. – *Climate of Madeira.* By JAMES T. ALLEY, M.D., New-York.[403]

I commence my description of the different places of resort, with the island of Madeira, not because all things considered, it is superior to some others, but because it has obtained

---

[403] ADAMS, R. E. W., (*et allii*), "The North American Journal of Homeopathy", Volume XIII, William Radde, New York, 1865, pages 480-482.

a greater popular reputation, and for that reason it is important that its merits and defects should be fully known. …

… To a large number of invalids not a little of the benefit of change of climate is due to the pleasant rides and walks and all those exercises and amusements which can pleasantly occupy the mind. These are lacking at Madeira. It is even less interesting than formerly, for previous to 1852, the luxuriant and fruitful vines produced the finest and best grapes in the world for wine. It was during the year 1852 that disease first appeared in the vines, and at present, although the world continues to drink "Madeira," there is almost none produced on the island.[404] This greatly detracts from the business aspects of the place, and little as it might be missed in other localities could here be but illy spared. The soil and climate of Madeira are well adapted to the growth of fruit and vegetable productions. Three crops of potatoes are easily obtained in one year, and other vegetables in proportion. …

The eighth set of impressions about the island, published anonymously in a Boston magazine, in 1866, provides a special insight into the vines and wines of Madeira. In this precious text one may read about different topics such as the origin and history of the island's vines, the importance the Jesuits once had in the plantation of vineyards, the blight of 1852, the different types of wine produced and its main features, the revitalization of the vines after a 10-year period of decay, and last but not least, the description, in vivid terms, of the vintage feast in Madeira, a special occasion for rejoicing and general happiness.

VINES AND WINES.[405]

It will be important to many of our friends engaged in the wine trade, as well as interesting to the public generally, to learn that the Vendemmia[406] or vintage feast has been this year celebrated in Madeira with all the honors and ceremonies which belonged to its observance in the day of the island's greatest prosperity.

The grape, as is well known, is not one of the indigenous fruits of Madeira, having been introduced about three hundred years ago during the governorship of a Portuguese noble named Alver.[407]

After the departure of this man from the island, the cultivation of the vine for a long time was neglected, the people in general meeting with no encouragement.

---

[404] AN: In consequence of the failure of the wine and potato crop in 1852, a large number of the natives must have died from starvation, but for foreign assistance. It is creditable to Americans that they forwarded nearly $30,000 for their relief, being nearly two-thirds of all the assistance received.

[405] "Every Saturday: A Journal of Choice Reading selected from Foreign Current Literature", Vol. I., January to June, 1866, Ticknor and Fields, Boston, 1866, pages 460-463. This article could have been a transcription from an Irish magazine, where it was published *ipsis verbis*, namely at the "Dublin University Magazine, a Literary and Political Journal", Vol. LXVII, January to June, 1866, George Herbert, Dublin; Hurst & Blackett, London, 1866, pages 458-462.

[406] The right spelling is vindima.

[407] The right spelling would be Álvaro or Álvares. The first Governor of Madeira with this name was Pedro Álvares de Cunha, who served from 1712 to 1715. However, it is a fact universally known that the vines were introduced in Madeira shortly after its settlement, as ordered by Prince Henry.

In the beginning of the sixteenth century, however, some nine or ten Jesuits landed at Funchal. These men were not only sages and scholars, but they were men strong in resources from repeated successful trials. No sooner had they touched the brown sands[408] of Madeira with their sandalled feet, and breathed the pure atmosphere, stealing ever with refreshing fragrance from the groves and gardens, than they justly estimated the amount of wealth which slumbered amongst the everlasting hills of Madeira, like living crystal in a rock, and they resolved at once on effecting important changes in the agriculture of the country.

They found that both soil and climate were particularly suited to the cultivation of the vine, and accordingly they procured cuttings from Candia, Cyprus, and Burgundy, and once more the hills in the neighborhood of Funchal were clothed with amaranthine vineyards. Adopting the Eastern custom, they trained the vines over trellised arches, allowing the rich clusters to droop through the leafy roof, beneath which thousands of delicate flowers lifted up their heads, wooing the sunny gleams which came and went, as the soft wind stirred the broad foliage above.

The rock-ribbed spaces lying between one leaf-woven colonnade and another were left open, and of course presented wildernesses of flowers and ferns, the latter sending up their tremulous fronds from every crevice and fissure, shading and softening the gorgeous beauty of the scarlet and purple and golden flowers.

While on the subject of ferns, I may as well mention that one of those most difficult to find now in Madeira, is one which for centuries was thought to be indigenous only on the shores of the lovely lakes of Killarney,[409] – the *Trichomanes radicans*.[410] Even in the childhood days of the writer, it grew there in such profusion that tourists were in the habit of carrying it away in corn-sacks. Now, however, its beautiful filmy fronds must be carefully sought for in moist little nooks, and in the crevices of the rocks, or they will escape being discovered.

Having planted numerous vineyards on the hills, the Jesuits next turned their attention to the low grounds, and to the northern coast; but instead of watching, step by step, the progress of their judicious labors, it may be as interesting, and more profitable, to examine into the present appearance and prosperity of the island.

Comparing it with the years previous to 1852, before the sudden and fearful blight "Oidium Tuckeri" had destroyed its thousands of vines, the balance is against it; but comparing the current year with any other during the past twelve, and the scale preponderates in its favor. The vines are recovering, and in all directions men are planting new vineyards.

The vines blossom in May and June, and frequently of late years, when they appeared most fresh and healthy, then, like a plague breath, came the blight, and they died off hopelessly. The disease first attacks the leaves, which, from a beautiful green, turn brown in a few hours; a clammy, whitish substance then appears, and they, shrivel and roll up, never more to spread their fragrant surface to the skies.

This effect is attributed by some to an aphis; others say the stocks are worn out, and, like last year's nests, are fit for nothing. The chief remedy used is sulphur, and it is no uncommon circumstance to see two or three barrels of this powerful disinfectant dragged on sledges to a vineyard, to be sprinkled over the fruited plants, thus saving the grapes, but in a great degree destroying the flavor of the wine.

---

408 In Madeira Island there are no "brown sands", as stated by the author, but rather pebble beaches.
409 Irish city located in the Kerry County.
410 Scientific name of the aerial root bristle fern.

There were at one time between thirty and forty kinds of grape used in making the wines; now the island does not produce such a variety. The best grape for the wine known as "Madeira" is a small kind, of a reddish-brown color, called "Verdeilho."[411] Its flavor is rich, and the skin remarkably thick. The clusters are small, each grape being no larger than a good black currant.

The Vinta Tinta, or colored wine, sometimes called "Madeira Claret," and "Madeira Burgundy," is made of various kinds of purple grape. To heighten the color, the juice, when expressed, is poured into a vat, into which the skins have been thrown, and allowed to stand until it has acquired the desired hue. Its flavor somewhat resembles that of Claret.

"Malmsey," or "Ladies' wine," is manufactured from the *Malvazia Candida,* which grows in no other situation in the world *better* than in front of the cliffs beyond Cabo Jiraö,[412] or Cape Turn Again. Down almost to the water's edge the vine is cultivated, covering the very sands with verdure and beauty and fragrance, while from the heights come rills of limpid water, carried by means of conduits, to cool and nourish the shingly soil. There is a magnificent view of this headland from the new road,[413] which rims along the southwestern coast for about three miles. If looked upon at sunset it will never be forgotten; when its lofty summits are gleaming with golden splendor, – when the ravines, touched by the departing rays, have grown luminous to their most inaccessible depths, – when the vineyards are glowing with the rainbow-hues of the dewy hour, and the two rivers, Socorridos and Vasio Gil[414] (which, taking their rise high up in the Curral, unite near the base under the name of the "Curral River"), flow like a stream of molten silver into the sea.

The sweet dry Sercial, the delicate and delicious Bual, and many others, belong peculiarly to the neighborhood of Funchal. There is one grape, however, which I must not omit to mention, on account of its curious mercantile notoriety. It is a Hock grape, small and sour, grown chiefly in the northern parts of the island, and is so unpalatable that not only the rats and lizards, who lay all other vines under heavy contributions, leave it untouched, but even the "wild bees, humming their drowsy song," refuse to use it in making their "honey hoards." The wine made from this grape is all shipped to Hamburg, from whence it is exported to England, and being there mixed with other wines of a somewhat better quality, is sold at a considerable profit under the name of "Hock."

During the last two years there has been a steady improvement in the vines, so much so, that in every direction new vineyards are being planted. This work is usually done in November, and if a visitor desires to witness the operation, he has but to choose any soft sunny day, when the trees are trembling in the fragrant air, – when the deep blue waters of the bay are coming in with a quiet murmur, and the foam is lying at the base of the Pontingua[415] Rock like carded wool, – and wandering, without a guide, eastward from Funchal along the sea-cliffs, he can hardly fail of seeing husbandmen planting a vineyard.

Imagine a number of graceful rustics, of medium height, athletic, free in their motions, heaving the "euxada,"[416] a kind of light pickaxe, instead of digging with the spade. They work as if in sport; there is no appearance of lusty labor; they look careless and merry;

---

411 The right spelling is Verdelho.
412 The right spelling is Cabo Girão.
413 See Note 280.
414 The right spelling is Vasco Gil.
415 The right spelling is Pontinha, a nickname for Funchal's oldest pier.
416 The right spelling is enxada.

while the cheering song, and the electric joke which opens every throat at the same instant, keeps each man's heart dancing to its own music.

Having made deep parallel trenches, they next plant cuttings two and a half feet apart, and then, I am sorry I must add, they plant cabbages and batatas,[417] and other vegetables between the rows of vines; thus effectually depriving them of the necessary amount of moisture and nourishment. Returning in February, you find that the vineyard has been covered with cane trellis-work, presenting a succession of arched corridors about four feet and a half in height, over which the vines are wreathed and intertwined, so that when they are fruited, the clusters shall fall through and receive the benefit of the heat radiating from the earth, as well as that from the sun's rays, coming tempered through the mantle of soft green.

Or it may be that instead of leafy corridors, straight rows of cane have been placed behind the cuttings, which, holding them by their tendrils, encircle and garland them with living beauty. Gathering the fruit is a fatiguing work, and is always performed by the men, and it is also men's feet which press it, when it is thrown in the huge wooden troughs to be crushed. The average produce is a pipe of wine per acre, of which a tenth belongs to the government; one half of the remainder to the owner of the vineyard; and the residue to the farmer or cultivator.

During the month of September, the Vendemmia,[418] or vintage festival, usually occurs; but for ten years – from 1852 to 1862 – it was only spoken of as a thing of the past. During that period the cheerful peasantry of Madeira suffered toil and sorrow, distress and want; yet in the end the Oïdium Tuckeri, like the potato famine in Ireland, has proved a benefit, by discovering to the people fresh sources of independence within their reach, and by forcing the government to the expenditure of thousands of pounds in the improvement of their city, their villages, and their public roads.

THE VINTAGE FEAST.

The Vendemmia[419] may be said to resemble the English harvest-home, though it is far more picturesque, having all the advantages of a sunny sky, splendid scenery, and costumes bright as "blossoms flaunting in the eye of day,"[420] and fitting like dresses in a picture.

The sun has hardly streaked the "east with purpic light" on the morning of the festival, before the strains of vocal and instrumental music are heard approaching Camacha, a village situated on the Serra, or rather St. Antonio da Serra,[421] from every direction, – from the interior of the island, from the well-known northern routes, and from the sea, which is dotted with gayly-painted boats, coming in from the numerous little villages lying along the coast, between Funchal and Canical[422] on the east, and Funchal and Magdalena[423] on the west.

Groups of peasants follow each musician, and for hours the roads leading to the Serra are bright with the picturesque multitude. The dress of the men on those occasions

---

417 Portuguese word for potatoes.
418 See Note 406.
419 See Note 406.
420 Line from the 6th stanza of the poem "Flowers", by Henry Wadsworth Longfellow (1807-1882), an American poet and educator.
421 Santo António da Serra, a parish belonging to the Santa Cruz municipality.
422 The right spelling is Caniçal.
423 The right spelling of this parish is Madalena do Mar, in the district of Calheta.

generally consists of white linen "quakes,"[424] very much like our modern knickerbockers; buff goat-skin boots, white linen shirts, blue vests ornamented with several small solid gold buttons, and blue carapuças[425] with long gold tassels. The blue cloth with which these latter articles are made is imported from Portugal, generally from the well-known firm of Correa and Company, or it may be from the rival house of Lafourie and Company. The women are, as usual, dressed in bright colors, some wearing native manufactures, but the greater number clad in the gayly striped cotton sent to the Funchal market by the Lisbon Weaving Company; while their lenços[426] are of fancy shot silk from the factories of Joze Barboza, or have come from the celebrated cotton looms of La Luz. Their jewelry has only the fault of being too heavy; their chains are like ropes, their bracelets like golden cables.

Arrived at the Serra, the first object of attraction is the Church of St. Antonio. It is a small building, somewhat resembling in its outer structure an English village church, with a low square tower.[427] The walls are of a brilliant white, bordered with black. On the present occasion a tall flagstaff runs up from the tower and sustains an enormous crimson banner, on which the arms of Portugal are embroidered in silk, the huge crown only being worked in gold.

Surrounding the church is a square, answering the purposes of the adro of the Mount church, which is crowded with people who cannot obtain an entrance into the edifice, where a high mass is being performed; – the Vendemmia,[428] like every other festa celebrated in Madeira, beginning with a religious service.

While the multitude are thus engaged, let us look at the scene around us. The Serra is dotted with barracas and tables heaped with provisions, beside each of which stands a little barrel of wine; while from the branches of the oak-trees hang quarters of the best beef the island can afford. On the right, in a hollow, we see what looks like a roofless hut, but from the red light glaring up from between its walls we know that they are roasting whole the fat ox on which the vine-dressers are to feast in the afternoon. On the left, at a short distance from the church, is the cemetery, surrounded by a low wall. In the centre stands a wooden cross, and thick and close around it lie the mounds of bare red earth, beneath which the dead await the call of the last trumpet. Between this and the church there is a long, low building, having a pretty open verandah running along the front. This is known as the "Pilgrim's house,"[429] and is abundantly provided with culinary utensils, and mattresses stuffed with the soft silky hair which grows round the roots of the beautiful rare fern, *Dicksonia culcita*.[430] As lodgings are given gratis to all who bring their own provisions, this place is generally over-crowded during the Vendemmia,[431] but chiefly with elderly people, the young preferring to sleep in the tents, or under the trees in the circa or grove, at the opposite extremity of the Serra.

---

424 Attempt to phonetically transcribe the Portuguese word "cuecas", that in the 19th century Madeira referred to the male's baggy knee trousers. Nowadays this word means underwear.
425 Portuguese word to designate the funnel-like traditional hats used by the Madeirans in the 19th century.
426 Portuguese word for handkerchiefs, that the Madeiran women used to wear around their necks.
427 In mid 19th century this church was rebuilt and enlarged thanks to a generous contribution by the American Consul in Madeira, John Howard March and, when finished, was officially blessed on August 23, 1857, about five years before the occurrence of this Vintage Feast.
428 See Note 406.
429 "Casa dos Romeiros", in Portuguese. This building no longer exists at Santo da Serra. In the past many churches of Madeira's countryside used to have their own "Pilgrim's house".
430 Scientific name of a fern known in Madeira as feiteira.
431 Scientific name of a fern known in Madeira as feiteira.

At this season of the year this beautiful bower wears that rich autumn dress, of which

> "Every hue
> Is but a varying splendor."

Bright-hued flowers are jewelling the earth under the soft shade of trees, whose tall trunks, from the roots to the topmost branches, are adorned either by the graceful fronds of the *Capillus Veneris*[432] and *Davalia Canariensis*,[433] or that curious lichen familiarly known as "old man's hair," hanging in gray tresses of half a foot in length, and waving loosely about with the faintest breeze.

There are many pleasant walks in the circa, but there is one which has a peculiar though melancholy interest for English visitors: it is known as the "Hydrangea Walk." Between rows of this beautiful shrub, whose branches are drooping beneath the wealth of *innumerable* large blue flowers, you pass on till about half-way through, when a slight rising in the centre of the path attracts your attention. You inquire why it has not been levelled, and are told that it is a *grave*. He who sleeps beneath had renounced the religion which the state declares no man must forsake, nor even be suspected of leaving, lest his grave be made in the streets or highways, where his friends and neighbors cannot choose but trample on his dust.[434] About a mile from the Serra, where three ways meet, there is another such grave, and there are many others scattered through the island.[435]

While we are still admiring the singular spectacle presented by the Serra, the bell of the church rings out a merry peal; the service is over, and the multitude is swarming over the plain. It is a novel and picturesque sight, though some of its details are mean and unpleasant. The first rush is to the refreshment tables, and there, in drinking a sort of wine made from pears, oranges, lemons, and grapes, even the honest hearts of the Madeiran peasants catch an unnatural spark, and shouts, whistling, and fantastic attitudes, such as one sees in the highlands of Scotland and the west of Ireland, accompany the dances, which commence all over the Serra at one o'clock.

In feasting and amusement the day is passed, and also a greater part of the night, when, just as the brief, dim half-hour of dawn comes round, the bells clang out a summons to the young maidens to commence the preparation of the morning meal, – a last feast, for the time, of beef and wine and fine bread.

As soon as this is ended the whole multitude join in a dance, called the cachuca,[436] though differing altogether from the Spanish dance of the same name. When this is over every woman takes her partner's hat, and wreaths it with the beautiful blue flowers of the hydrangea, while the men on receiving them back make the mountains re-echo with their nearly shouts. Presently the Serra assumes a new aspect. Borequerous,[437] who had

---

[432] Scientific name of the Venus-hair fern, one of the many species of Adiantum, or Maiden hair fern.
[433] Scientific name of the Deers foot fern.
[434] Everything indicates that this could have been a grave of a Madeiran Presbyterian convert, the Protestant religion introduced in the island by Robert Reid Kalley, a Scottish doctor and minister, some decades earlier. Such converts, according to the "laws" of the time, could not be buried in Catholic cemeteries but rather in paths' crossroads.
[435] The parish of Santo António da Serra was among the places from where more Madeirans embraced this new religion, in great measure because of the fact that Robert Kalley lived there for a while, at Quinta das Ameixieiras, where he used to preach to hundreds of people from that village, hence the allusion to other similar graves in that area.
[436] The right spelling would be Cachuça, the designation of a Spanish solo dance, similar to a Bolero.
[437] The right spelling is Burroqueiros or burriqueiros (in the plural form), words that once designated horse attendants. In Madeiran slang the word burriqueiro is still used to designate someone who is always following somebody else.

been ill the morning watching for the proper moment, now appear galloping into the Serra from all directions. Madeirans of every rank are graceful and fearless as Arabs on horseback; the borequerous,[438] therefore, soon find customers, but the Lisbon ponies are in the greatest demand; they are well known to be strong, swift, and active, and though the riders will not be permitted to try their speed through the streets of Funchal, there will be many a well-contested race on the new road[439] before the sun sets.

In a gleesome picturesque procession the multitude enter Funchal, and pass through all the principal streets, loudly cheered at every step, as the harbingers of a promise of a golden future.

The ninth Madeira-related text was published, anonymously, in an 1870 Boston magazine. It starts by quoting an encyclopedia article about Madeira, that contains an allusion to the blight of 1852, and then continues with a personal description of the island, mentioning its fertile land that produced everything, including the grapes, with which was made a better wine than the French and German wines. Describing Funchal the author refers the mode of transportation of casks of wine, in sledges. As for wine proper, one can read about the different wines of Madeira and also a brief description of the gathering of the grapes, in September.

THE MADEIRA ISLES.[440]

These are an island group belonging to Portugal, situated in the Atlantic Ocean, about 440 miles from the coast of Morocco and 210 miles north of Teneriffe, of which Madeira is the largest. This island is 34 miles long and about 5000 feet high, on which is an extensive plain, called Paul de Serra.[441] The easterly portion of the island, though elevated, is less so than that of the west . From the central mass, are steep ridges extending to the coast, where they form perpendicular precipices of from 1000 to 2000 feet high. These cliffs are interrupted by a few small bays, where a richly-cultivated valley approaches the water between abrupt precipices, or surrounded by an amphitheatre of rugged hills. These narrow bays are the sites of the villages of Madeira. The most striking peculiarity in the mountain scenery of the island, is the jagged outline of the ridge, the rudely-shaped towers and sharp pyramids of rock which appear elevated on the tops and sides of the highest peaks, as well as on the lower elevations, and the deep, precipitous gorges which cut through the highest mountains almost to their very base. The most remarkable of these gorges is called the Curral or Coural.[442] The road round the island is, in many places, exceedingly picturesque, being led often between lofty cliffs, or along the front of precipices overhanging the sea. One of the most remarkable portions of this winding road is the Estroza Pass,[443]

---

[438] See previous Note.
[439] See Note 280.
[440] "Ballou's Monthly Magazine", Volume XXXI, From January to June, 1870, Office American Union, Flag of Our Union, and Novelette, Boston, [1870], pages 208-211.
[441] The right spelling is Paul da Serra.
[442] The first name is the right spelling of the designation of this place.
[443] The right spelling is Entrosa. The zigzag shaped "Vereda da Entrosa", as it is termed on Portuguese, is located on a steep slope at the rivermouth of Ribeira do Porco, at Boaventura, in the northern side of Madeira.

on the north side of the island. Although the island be rough and mountainous throughout, its steeps are clothed with rich and luxuriant verdure. Terraces are visible on every side, and every available and accessible spot is turned to advantage. On leaving Funchal, the capital of the island, fruits, flowers and vegetables crowd upon the sight; in the lower portions, groves of orange and lemon trees are mingled with the vineyards; higher up, bananas, figs, pomegranates, etc., are seen; and again, still higher, the fruits of the temperate zone – namely, apples, currants, pears and peaches. Coffee and arrow-root, both of excellent quality, are also grown. Wheat, barley, rye and Indian corn are raised, but only to the extent of about one-fifth of the quantity consumed; consequently, the almost total destruction of the vines in 1852 brought the inhabitants into the greatest distress. The people are industrious, sober and civil. They are of the old Arabian stock, and have little if any mixed blood among them. The men are very muscular, rather above the medium height, strongly built, and capable of enduring great fatigue. The women are generally very ugly. The houses of the lower order are wretched huts, the door being the only aperture for light and smoke. The language is Portuguese, spoken rapidly.

This is the dry account which the encyclopedia gives of Madeira, but visitors and sojourners are eloquent in praise of its climate and the many delightful things to be enjoyed there, saying, "What a man seeks more than Madeira affords, savoreth of evil," and as Plato, they say, placed his Atlantis somewhere west of the Columns of Hercules, it is probable that Cape de Verdes, the Canaries and Madeira compose the Isles of the Blest, where the Grecian poets were wont to send their heroes when they were done with them. "In beauty and sublimity of scenery," we quote from one,[444] "it is unsurpassed by lands more famous for both, while the matchless moderation and salubrity of climate are world-renowned. Its soil produces, spontaneously, the fruits of the tropics – the orange, the pomegranate, the banana, the guava, the citron and olive – and, with cultivation, though not in equal perfection, the pear and the apple, as well as other productions of colder latitudes. The grape that is nourished in most favored spots affords a wine of richer color and superior excellence to any of sunny France, or the boasted vineyards of Germany; while the fish of its waters, the game of its mountains, its herbage-fed and luscious beef, turkeys, and various web-footed birds, supply a rich and abundant table. What can one find more, in any country of Christendom, to gratify a well-informed taste?"[445] Besides these advantages, it is spared the enervation of tropical countries, and culture, taste, refinement, control society as in lands nearer the social centres. Man never wants here occupation or amusement who is true to his own nature.

The city of Funchal, the capital of Madeira, is built upon the base of a large range of mountains, which rise to the height of 4000 feet above the level of the sea, and protecting it, like the sides of an amphitheatre form a magnificent background to the view from the deck of a vessel when approaching it. This is the best view of Funchal; in this the tact that "distance lends enchantment" is verified. At close contact it is prosaic. The streets are for the most part narrow and irregular, with little regard to symmetry or convenience. They are paved with cobble-stones gathered from the beach, and the clatter of horses' iron-shod feet along the way is not in harmony with the peaceful beauty and grace of

---

[444] From Charles W. March, author of the book *Sketches and Adventures in Madeira, Portugal, and the Andalusias of Spain*, as we have seen on section 6.1.1.15. of this anthology.
[445] Quote from the 4th paragraph of Chapter II of March's book.

the surroundings. Carriages are seldom known, the kind of vehicle most in use being a sort of sledge for transporting pipes of wine from one place to another. Travelling is performed in sedan-chairs or on horseback. There are several churches and convents, and in the centre of the town is an open square planted with exotic trees.[446] The town is defended by four forts. The English and Portuguese merchants have elegant villas in the suburbs, upon the terraced hillsides, where all fruits and flowers abound, and where the morning is ushered in with the songs of myriads of birds and the plashing of cool water from the mountain springs. …

Madeira received its name from the fact of its abounding with wood – the name, in Portuguese, signifying wood. The south side has been devastated, but the north retains its pristine characteristics. The trees remain untouched, save by Time. But Madeira is associated in our minds with the cultivation of the grape, and wine has hitherto formed the most of its commerce, but of late years, owing to disease of the vines, the stock has greatly diminished, causing ruin to proprietors and want to the people. At present not more than half a crop is attainable, and the quality has deteriorated. The grapes that furnish the best wines are not agreeable to the palate; there are other grapes, however, most grateful to the taste, that are highly prized. The wines of Madeira need no brandy to protect them, their own alcoholic properties being sufficient. No sea-change can affect them. Though all are known as Madeira wines, there is a great difference between them – some dry, some full-bodied, some fruity, some light, some heavy. The wines of the South are the best, and comprise the Sercial, the Malmsey, the Bual, the Tinta or Burgundy Madeira, and the Tinto. These are the normal varieties, and there are many shades of quality besides. "A glass of Sercial," a writer says, "after soup confirms the grace before, and predisposes the soul to the fullness of gratitude – the sense of favors to come."[447] The Malmsey is too luscious a wine for ordinary use, and is used by women and children only. It is produced nowhere else but in Madeira.

The gathering of the vintage, in September, is made a half-holiday of. The women and girls, with a portion of the men, go into the vineyards with their baskets and gather the grapes very carefully. These they bring on their heads, nicely balanced. The grapes are then picked over, the best reserved for the costliest wine. They are then thrown into the wine-press, a wide, clumsy trough of wood, into which men jump, barefooted, with their trousers rolled up, and trample out the juice. This mode of expressing the juice with the feet is said to tread out the seeds and stems without crushing them and giving their tastes to the wine. The pulp is then squeezed under a lever, when the liquid is conveyed to the juice-houses in goat-skins, and there emptied into casks for the process of fermentation, which usually lasts four or five weeks.

The equable climate of Madeira is well suited for pulmonary complaints. It knows no extreme of heat nor cold, and no sudden atmospheric reverses.

The tenth article was published in New York, in 1877, by another doctor, A. L. Gihon, then Medical Director-General of the U.S. Navy. He chose the topic of Madeira wine to start his text about the island, alluding briefly to its history and worldwide fame

---

[446] Named Praça da Constituição. Nowadays this area is known as Avenida Arriaga.
[447] Quote from Chapter VIII of March's work.

and also stating that even though there was a shortage of supply of the product in its native land, in America it was easily found in every city, thus implying that it was adulterated in the United States, (which was not far from the truth, as will be seen in section 9.10 of this anthology). In this short excerpt can also be found a brief reference to the blight of 1852, the extreme poverty that it caused on the island, and a few words about the relief that was sent from America to help the needy. (This is another topic to be also developed ahead in this book, in section 9.7.1).

"A SUMMER CRUISE AMONG THE ATLANTIC ISLANDS"[448]
By Dr. A. L. Gihon

II. – THE MADEIRAS.

Two years after its final settlement by the Portuguese, the vine was imported into Madeira from the island of Candia or Crete, and found so congenial a soil that its wine became renowned as the most delicious beverage it has been granted man to taste. Madeira has been a household word in every language of Europe, but in 1860 there were only four hundred pipes remaining on the island; and though Madeira is still offered for sale in every city of the United States at reasonable rates, it is not difficult to imagine its source. The Madeira wine of commerce was itself a compound of the various productions of the island, known by special names as Bual, Sercial, etc., each possessing a distinctive character. At one time the production amounted to twenty-five thousand pipes a year, but in 1852 the same terrible disease which spread over the other Atlantic islands appeared among the vineyards, and destroyed its culture, taking from the island its fair name, ruining thousands of wretched people, and depriving man of a blessing; for since man will yield to the craving nature has implanted in him, and every where furnished him the means of gratifying, it is a blessing when he can drink of wine like this rather than some vile substitute. Fortunately the *oidium* appears to have been destroyed or to have disappeared, and new plants introduced from the United States and Europe are thriving, with every promise of restoring to the island its former celebrity among wine-producing countries. The mildew which attacked the vine has not impaired the fertility of the island in any other respect. ...

Since the failure of the vine the condition of the peasants has been one of extreme poverty. They are patient and industrious. Many of the men earn a scanty living by the manufacture of inlaid-work, etc., which has attained some celebrity abroad, and the women by needle-work and embroidery, which rival the French in fineness, beauty, and durability. They have been visited by famine, and cherish grateful recollections of the charitable contributions of food they received from the United States. Here, as in Fayal,[449] our country for many years had the good fortune to be represented by a gentleman, Mr. March, whose personal worth, princely charities, and eminent patriotism endeared him to the whole island.

Madeira, from having been once the favorite rendezvous of our African squadron, and the source of the delicious beverage to which it has given name, is better known to

---

[448] "Harper's New Monthly Magazine", Volume 54, Issue 323, New York, April 1877, pages 664-676.
[449] In Fayal, one of the Azores islands, the U.S. Consulate was occupied, in the 19th century by three generations of the Dabney family, from Boston.

Americans than any other island in the Atlantic. Several lines of steamers bring it prominently into European notice. ...

Last but not least, let us have a look at the eleventh article, published anonymously, in 1879, in a New York prestigious magazine. This small article, where one can find some references to the island's vineyards and wine production, is profusely illustrated with five Madeira-related engravings, three of which can be associated with Madeira Wine.

THE ISLAND OF MADEIRA.[450]

Of all the many pleasant resorts familiar to the individual in search of that necessary boon of life, health, Madeira is undoubtedly one of the most pleasant, and at the same time the most beneficial.

This beautiful island is situated on the west coast of Africa, and, owing to its agreeable climate, it has long been a favorite resort for invalids. The coast line is remarkably regular, there being not a single indentation that can be called a bay. The mountain slopes rise directly from the sea, and are furrowed by deep and fertile valleys. These valleys are watered by limpid streams, and covered with vineyards and gardens, the former being formed on the rocky declivities to the height of more than 2,000 feet. ...

The agriculture is conducted in the primitive Portuguese manner, and with rudest implements. Vines were first introduced into the island in 1421, and wine was, until the middle of the present century, the staple production of the island. Most of the wine-growers are English, and the chief commerce is with England, whose products are received into the island at one-half of the usual duties. ...

Figure 45. "Going up the Corral." The village of Curral das Freiras was (and still is) a major touristic attraction in Madeira due to its unique landscape. In this illustration a rider can be seen returning to Funchal, with his *burroqueiro* (horse attendant) holding the horse's tail. Over their heads is a vine trellice. Many foreigners who visited the island in the first half of the 19th century reported that many paths were covered with them. *Article illustration. Author unknown.*

---

[450] "Frank Leslie's Popular Monthly", January 1879, New York, 1879, pages 60-61.

Figures 46 and 47. "Costumes of Madeira - The Vine-dressers" and "Costumes of Madeira - A Woman and a Child". Engravings portraying some Madeirans standing by some trellices. *Article illustrations. Author unknown.*

6.1.3. Newspapers

The accounts of Madeira published in travel books and magazines are complemented, in a larger way, by the ones revealed in the American press. In this section will be compiled and organized, by order of publication, twenty different texts, from 1833 to 1899, written by different authors, some of them anonymous, who passed by the Ocean Flower, viz. Madeira Island, throughout the 19th century, and published in different U.S. newspapers their impressions about the island, in which are included their views on the Madeira Wine. Some of these articles were published in more than one source, for it was a common practice, in 19th century American press, to transcribe articles from other newspapers within the same State, or even from a different one.

The first text, in the form of a letter, was written by Rev. Walter Colton, a Naval officer, who passed by Madeira aboard a Navy ship, in 1832, who published it anonymously in Connecticut, the following year. This author saw a Paradise in Madeira, and its vine-clad hills contributed much to that image. He also alludes to the wines produced in the southern and northern coasts, underlying that the "south side" one was the best the island afforded.

Correspondence of the Jour. of Commerce.[451]

U.S. SHIP CONSTELLATION,
Island of Madeira, 20th May, 1832.

The island of Madeira is full of marvel and romance. It was thrown up into this breathing element by some volcanic convulsion; it was discovered by a wandering love adventure;[452] its very aspect is one of mildness and beauty; and its wines prompt the most rich and unearthly dreams. There is nothing about it that has the smallest cast of sameness except its climate, and that could not be improved by any change wider than the slight vibrations through which it passes, and which are so full of vitality. It is indeed a fairy land – the paradise of the Atlantic – the gem of the ocean. But we will look at some of the more marked and discriminating features of this singular island.

Its Southern coast descends in easy and green declivities to the sea. These warm slopes are covered with the choicest vineyards. The vine seems to reel under its burthen. – Where the land is so steep as to render it necessary, it is thrown off into terraces, which may be seen rising above each other, in a lengthened series; and so precious is this sunny position, that where there is no native soil, the rock is covered with earth brought from a distance with great labor and expense. The wines of these vineyards, for richness of body, deliciousness of flavour, and immunity from injury by time and exposure, are not equalled in the world. Who has not seen the hospitable host smack his lips and kindle as he bade his delighted guests fill their glasses from a little of the "old south side" left him by some worthy ancestor.

The Northern shore of the Island rises from the wave in a bold and lofty range of rock, but what it gains in majesty, it loses in other respects. The vine is inferior to its sister of the South, and as if to punish it for its want of sweetness, instead of being supported and encouraged by fine trellice work of cane, it is left to climb up some bramble, or reluctant tree, as it can; and then, after all its best efforts, it is still more deeply punished by being worked up into brandy. Sometimes, indeed, it has the good fortune to be removed in its infancy to the south side, and then it never fails to secure affection and esteem. ...

The following text, by an unknown author, was published in 1843, in Boston. Part of it had already been presented in the fifth text of the previous section, but in this source it has one more chapter. Its author refers to the fertility of the island's soil, and the predominance of vineyards in the landscape. He alludes also to a depression that Madeira Wine trade was experiencing by then, due, in part, to lesser exportation to the United States where other wines were being consumed and Temperance movements exhorted the banning of alcoholic beverages.

---

[451] *American Mercury*, January 21, 1833. (Hartford, CT). Although this letter was published anonymously we know that it was written by Rev. Walter Colton. This text corresponds to the first three paragraphs of Chapter VIII of his book, as we have seen on section 6.1.1.2. of this anthology.
[452] Reference to the Machin Legend. See Note 195.

FUNCHAL: ISLAND OF MADEIRA.[453] Madeira is nothing more nor less than an immense mountain, 35 miles long from east to west, and 20 broad from north to south, and is entirely volcanic. The island is seen at an immense distance at sea. ...

... There is much cultivation on the island, for the soil is very fertile, as, indeed, all volcanic soils are. Everywhere you see vineyards. The vines are trained along a frame work about three feet from the ground, and when they leaf out, which they are beginning to do at this time, give to the vineyard a very beautiful appearance. The island, where it is cultivated, being terraced, adds to the beauty of the vineyard; for each vineyard seems to be composed of several, rising the one above the other. Every thing here tells of the great business of the island. All the people have more or less to do with vines, no matter what may be their occupation. You see the vineyard on the mountain slope, and as you pass through the streets of Funchal, your nostrils are constantly saluted by the perfume of wine in the vaults; which, by the way, are all on a level with the streets; and a very pleasant perfume it is too. For one, I like the odour, though I cannot drink the wine. The population here are very temperate, though theirs is the wine business. I just said I liked the odor of wines in a wine vault. There certainly is a perfume which you can perceive as you pass a wine vault here, which I never noticed in America, and which I think is very pleasant. I attribute the agreeable nature of the smell, to the fact that there is nothing but wine in the vaults, and that the wines are not so much adulterated as with us. ...

... In former times the sugar cane was successfully cultivated, and once gave employment to more than one hundred sugar mills; but the grape has superseded the sugar cane, and I believe that there are now but one or two mills. The wine trade is said to be in a very depressed condition at present, and I learn that it is expected to improve in some time. I doubt myself if Madeira ever again sees those prosperous days which she once enjoyed, when so great was the demand, that even the wretched wines of the north side of the island were shipped as good south side Madeira wines. The use of French wines, and other light wines, and temperance societies, are diminishing the demand for the produce of this island, and will continue to do so; and I see no cause why a reflecting stranger should lament over it, though it does not injure the trade of the island – for whatever decreases the traffic in wines, as well as in ardent spirits, seems to me to lead to the increase of human happiness and human virtue. [Journal of Commerce].

The following text is an extract of the first account of Madeira, by John Adams Dix, who had spent the winter of 1842 on the island, as we have already seen in section 6.1.1.12. Eight years after he would publish a book about the island, entitled *A Winter in Madeira and a Summer in Spain and Florence*. The present text was published in 1843, in New York, and contains his impressions about Funchal, with its vineyards dominating the landscape. He also mentions the wine as being the only article of export, and provides some statistics about it.

---

453 *Daily Evening Transcript*, January 4, 1843. (Boston, MA).

MADEIRA.[454]

[From the Northern Light.]

BY JOHN A. DIX.

The island of Madeira, both in respect to the mildness and salubrity of the climate, and its romantic scenery, is one of the most interesting and beautiful regions in the world. …

Nothing can be fancied more luxuriant or rich than Madeira in spring, when the vines have put forth their leaves, and the delicate vegetation, which shrinks from the very moderate cold of its winter, has come out again. Though a perpetual verdure reigns throughout the lower parts of the island at all seasons of the year, he who would see it in full beauty, should not leave it until the first of June. Then it becomes more like a region of romance than the habitations of plodding men. For miles the whole face of the earth is buried under the broad, rich foliage of the vine, and wherever you go, flowers of exquisite beauty and plants of singular forms rise up around you, and load the air with fragrance. In winter, when looking down from the high mountains, by which the surface of the island is broken, you can see the trellis-work of cane, on which the vines are trained, covering the earth, as it were, with a vast web. But in the spring all this disappears, and the earth appears but one mass of living green; everything is covered with leaves, and the ranges of mountains are so near that the blue, which depends on distance, is scarcely perceptible.

… The only article of export is wine. When there is an active demand for it, all is prosperity and abundance. But when the demand flags or ceases, there is a corresponding depression. It is a wretched reliance for any people; and there is no doubt that the industry of the island might be turned to objects calculated to give it a steady and permanent prosperity. From 1818 to 1820 the annual export of wine was sometimes equal to 15,000 pipes. The decrease may be estimated by the following statement of the amount entered for exportation during the last fifteen years: in 1828, 9,623 pipes; in 1829, 8,104 pipes; in 1830, 5,499 pipes; in 1831, 5,533 pipes; in 1832, 7,163; in 1833, 8,683; in 1834, 9,228; in 1835, 7,730; in 1836, 7,913; in 1837, 8,123; in 1838, 9,828; in 1839, 9,043; in 1840, 7,975; in 1841, 7,157; and in 1842, 6,270 pipes. Let the wine drinkers look at our custom house returns for the years above named, and consider how much of these exports was destined to England, Russia, and the north of Germany, and they will have some idea of the liquor they have drunk under spurious names. …

The next excerpt of a letter by whom we presume to be a Naval officer, was published in 1844, in New York. Although short, it is very interesting, since the author refers that Madeira Wine presented to him by the U.S. Consul was so good that he had to suspend his temperance pledges and enjoy it to the full.

---

[454] *Albany Evening Journal*, November 24, 1843. (Albany, NY); *St. Lawrence Republican*, December 5, 1843. (Ogdensburg, NY); *Pennsylvania Inquirer and National Gazette*, December 13, 1843. (Philadelphia, PA). This is probably the first text John Adams Dix wrote about Madeira. Seven years later he would publish a book about the island, of which we present the Madeira Wine-related excerpts on section 6.1.1.12 of this anthology.

Correspondence of the Eagle.[455]

U.S. SHIP CONSTITUTION
Rio de Janeiro, Sept. 2ᵈ, 1844.

... At Madeira we had to suspend our temperance pledges. I am not sure but a taste of friend March's (our consul) 14 years' old would have tempted some of our more zealous advocates of the cause to a temporary delinquency in their duty. One fact may be interesting. The exportation of Madeira wine to the United States was formerly several thousand pipes annually. Last year it dwindled down to hundreds, and fears are entertained by the manufacturers that it will not be necessary to enumerate beyond two figures, or tens, to express the amount total for the present year. ...

The following text, published originally in Providence, RI, by an unknown author, depicts Madeira as a paradise. And in that paradise wine had a special place of honor. According to him, in the island the vineyards abounded, and could be seen for miles. He also alludes to several kinds of Madeira Wine, briefly describing them.

The Modern Paradise.[456]

A letter in the Providence Journal gives this glowing description of the Island of Madeira – which has long been called the Paradise for invalids: – ...

But I need not tell you that the pride of Madeira is the grape, nor need I tell you of the variety and perfection in which it is produced, not of the commercial importance which it gives to the island. The best portions of the land and the hill sides are covered with vineyards, and the mountains are terraced as high as the vines will grow. You can ride for miles along the steep and narrow paths with the vine making a continuous arbor over your head. The finest wine is made from the grape on the south side of the island, but an excellent quality is produced in less favoured exposures. A soldier is not more jealous of his honor than are the people of Madeira of the reputation of their wines, and stringent legal provisions are made to guard against adulteration and against passing of inferior qualities for those of higher value. The vine is not indigenous here, but was introduced at an early period from Crete or Cyprus.

Besides the Madeira and the Malmsey wine, which are generally exported, and the Sercial and the Tinto, which are occasionally sent abroad, there are many other varieties, but the vineyards in which they are cultivated are small, and from the want of concert among the cultivators, and the absence of any proper division of labor, they are seldom kept separated, but are all mixed together in the wine which is exported under the general name of Madeira. Malmsey is esteemed the finest sweet wine, and Tinto has the flavor of Burgundy. The Sercial is considered the finest dry wine. The best varieties of the grape are the Negro Mole,[457] the Verdelha,[458] and the Bual, but there are near thirty other

---

[455] *The Brooklyn Daily Eagle*, November 20, 1844. (Brooklyn, NY).
[456] *The Boston Recorder*, July 7, 1848. (Boston, MA); *Alexandria Gazette*, July 12, 1848. (Alexandria, VA).
[457] The right spelling is Negra Mole.
[458] The right spelling is Verdelho.

varieties in greater or less repute. The most assiduous care is devoted to the cultivation of the vine, and is particularly manifested in irrigation, for which purpose the mountain streams are diverted through the vineyards, and the water is most scrupulously economised. Of the produce one-tenth is taken by the government, and the balance is divided equally between the cultivator and the owner of the soil. Each part in person, or by deputation, attends at the wine press.

The following letter was written by a man who had traveled, as a guest, to Madeira aboard the *Decatur*, belonging to the African Squadron. He arrived at Madeira on the 18th of March 1848 and noticed the decline in Madeira Wine trade, although there was a good production of wine. As to the qualities of the Madeira, he states that the ones found in Charleston were better than the ones sold in the island, and explains why.

Correspondence of the Register.
PORTO PRAYA, de ST. Jago,
May 31st, 1848.

MADEIRA AND THE CANARIES.[459]
No. I.

I had been suffering severely, and was slowly recovering from the acclimating fever of this island, when I received a very kind invitation from the commander and officers of the Decatur, to accompany them on a windward cruise to Madeira and the Canaries. You may be sure that I was not long in accepting, particularly as it had been more than hinted to me, by all the physicians within reach, that a change of climate, for a time, was necessary to my life's being saved. – Accordingly, on the 6th of March, I bundled myself and "traps" on board ship, and we were soon bounding away from the land of "chills and fever," towards that gem of the ocean – Madeira.

We anchored in the bay of Funchal, after a remarkably quick run of but twelve days, and had the good luck to find late news, though but little of it, from the United States. …

The commerce of the island is greatly reduced, by the decline of the wine trade, and but few American vessels touch here now. Still, the yearly production of the immense vineyards that cover the island is very great, and altho' grain and coffee are raised in some quantities, it will be long before the attention of the natives is turned to raising any other staple than wine. – Of the well-known excellence of the wines of Madeira, it would be useless here to speak; but it is a remarkable fact that the best qualities of Madeira wine can never be obtained in Madeira. The gentry of Charleston, in South Carolina, have the reputation of possessing the finest stocks of Madeira wine in the world, and this is attributed to the great improvement given the wine by a sea voyage, and the climate of our Southern States. …

M. D. P.

---

[459] *Salem Register*, July 26, 1849. (Salem, MA).

Next we present a short excerpt of a text written by the wife of a Naval Lieutenant, from Trenton, NJ, who had gone to the island with her husband and an attendant, having arrived there on October 1849. It seems like someone of the party was going to pass the Winter in Madeira, for health reasons. As to Madeira Wine this unknown lady mentions that it was the main business of the island, and briefly describes its mode of production.

For the State Gazette.
Island of Madeira.[460]

… The manufacture of wine is the principal business of the island. The vine is cultivated as high up the mountain as 200 feet, but it mostly grows wild. The wine press is of the rudest construction, being simply some boards laid together in the shape of an oblong box with a spout to it. The grapes are laid in this box and several men and boys with their bare feet trample upon the grapes till all the juice is expressed. The peasants bring in the juice in leathern bottles on their heads, singing as they come in groups. The liquor stands for two years before it is fit for the market. …

The next two texts were written by Charles W. March, (nephew of the U.S. Consul to Madeira, John Howard March), during his visit to Madeira in 1852, and were part of a series of articles about the island that he published in the *New York Daily Tribune*, of which he was an editor. In the first text we find a first-hand description of the effect of the destruction of the vines of Madeira by the *oïdium tuckeri*, namely the shadow of famine that hung above the Madeirans due to the failure of the grapes.

MADEIRA, AND A VOYAGE THITHER.[461]
IV.

Correspondence of the N. Y. Tribune.

MADEIRA, November, 1852.

But a day of suffering hangs over this devoted peasantry, compared with which, I fear, all antecedent sufferings might well be considered easily endurable. The miseries of poverty, always so harassing here, threaten to be fearfully aggravated by the almost total failure of the vine. Upon the grape whole parishes have leaned for food; that of Funchal particularly, on the northern side of the island,[462] numbering three thousand souls, cultivates no other means of subsistence. The fruit of the vine has been their meat, their drink, their raiment, and only earthly prop. To what can they now look for subsistence? How can they, and thousands like them, hope to escape starvation? Neighbors, nor masters, nor friends, nor relatives can aid them, for none of these have themselves more than the means of mere existence. The grape has failed, and with it many comforts, and all superfluities. The

---

[460] *State Gazette*, May 13, 1850. (Trenton, NJ).
[461] *New York Daily Tribune*, June 8, 1853. (New York City, NY).
[462] Funchal, the capital of Madeira, is located on the southern side of the island.

rich can but scantily aid the poor from out of their own vastly restricted resources; while many, in comfortable circumstances before, now apprehend with too much reason the sufferings which they have alleviated in others. Contributions of the charitable wealthy have hitherto supported the Infirmaries, the Poor-houses, the Convents, and other eleemosynary establishments; but these must in a great measure be withdrawn, and a state of misery supervene, at the bare contemplation of which the mind recoils.

Already, however, succor, although to a small extent, has been received from England – enough to raise hope of more effectual relief. A committee has been appointed by the Governor,[463] composed of the English and American Consuls,[464] and other leading men of the Island, to receive and distribute charitable contributions; and no doubt is entertained of large assistance, particularly from the two great countries, England and the United States, alike distinguished for wealth and generosity.

Should such assistance be not forth-coming, God help the miserable wretches – if only to an early death! …

As we have already mentioned, on a footnote of the section 6.1.1.15 of this anthology, the following text by Charles W. March is the first version of the contents of Chapter VIII of the book he published in 1856, in New York, under the title *Sketches and Adventures in Madeira, Portugal, and the Andalusias of Spain*. In short, it is one of the best texts written by an American author about Madeira Wine.

MADEIRA AND A VOYAGE THITHER.[465]
THE CULTURE OF THE GRAPE

To write of Madeira and omit the vine would be to act the play, and leave out the character of Hamlet.

The grape came from Cyprus, some four centuries since, under the patronage of the Royal House of Braganza, and soon begun to improve in the temperate climate, and on the volcanic soil of the island. All history demonstrates that volcanic soils are best adapted to the cultivation of the vine. The neighborhood of Vesuvius affords the choicest wines of Italy, the Falerian and others. Hermitage affects the *débris* of decomposed hills; and the wines generally that make most glad the heart of man are the produce of the mouldy earth.

This fancy of the grape was not unknown to the ancients. They knew as well that the vine throve best in elevated exposures, under the rich beams of the sun, and governed its cultivation accordingly. Also, how age developed and enhanced the intrinsic goodness of wines. The cobweb-covered bottle was no less boasted in the olden time than now. Horace, the Poet Laureate of Bacchus, speaks enthusiastically of his contemporaneous amphora,

---

463 José Silvestre Ribeiro.
464 George Stoddart and John Howard March, respectively.
465 *New York Daily Tribune*, December 5, 1853. (New York City, NY); *The Daily Picayune*, December 11, 1853. (New Orleans, LA. Published accompanied by the following preliminary note: «We have been favored by its author, Charles W. March, Esq., with the following interesting letter, in advance of its publication in the New York Tribune, for which paper, as one of a series, it was written. Mr. March is one of the most brilliant writers of our country, and this letter may be taken as a favourable specimen of his style.»).

which with him first saw the light, "Consule Plauco," and sings its praises under an inspiration perhaps borrowed from its juice. In earlier times, age was no less respected for its mellowing and enriching qualities. The poets of Greece built up lofty verse, in grateful commemoration of its benefits:

> "It made Anacreon's soul divine."

When the ambassadors of Agamemnon sought Achilles' tent with offers of reparation, before he permitted them to unfold their message, he directed Patroclus to bring out some of its dearest old wine and serve it round. And to illustrate how time-honoured even trivial usages become, it is worthy of remark that his manner of passing the bottle from right to left continues to the present day.

The soil of Madeira resembles that of the Campagna Felice, where grew the historic Falernian; and the flavor and aroma of the two wines are not unlike. It is a vulgar prejudice that Madeira wine naturally induces gout. "Give a dog an ill name and hang him." It has been the fashion to decry Madeira ever since the Prince Regent[466] forsook it for Sherry. Those who have not known what else to urge against it have charged it with this old-gentlemanly complaint. The opinion, however, of the most eminent physicians is to the contrary. So is experience. Nowhere do they drink more, better, or stronger Madeira than on the Island, and nowhere do they suffer less from gout. Indeed, the complaint is unknown among the natives and residents. Doubtless excessive indulgence in Madeira wine would injure health, and shorten life - but this may be said with equal truth of other wines; with much more fatal truth of Champagne, which, from the admission of deleterious substances in the manufacture, too often undermines the constitution.

Brandied wines of any kind intoxicate and injure. It is the peculiar felicity of Madeira wines that its own alcoholic qualities are sufficient to its own safety. "Nothing in it doth suffer a sea change," by exportation, for the worse. It support itself, like virtue. That it sometimes is mixed with foreign spirits and thence become pernicious, is true; but *caveat emptor*.[467] Let the buyer know the producer.

The discoveries of science have aided greatly in the cultivation of the grape. The study of chemistry, particularly, has done much to improve the fruit by a careful and enlightened investigation of the properties and capacities of the soil. Nor has this been the sole accomplishment of experimental science. *The aspect that the vineyard lends to the sun* has proved an all-important fact. The same vines upon the same soil, and with the same care, have given very different results – a difference traced to variations of aspect. The vine, to produce a wine of exquisite flavor, must, like the sunflower,

> – "turn to its God when he sets,
> The same look it turned when he rose."

It should bask in the heat all the while the sun is above the horizon.

The judicious selection of the plants, the seasonable pruning of the vines, proper irrigation, and careful maturing of the fruit – these are some of the assiduities to the full development of the qualities of the grape. By these, the astringent properties which reside in

---

466 See Note 276.
467 See Note 277.

the uncultivated vine, and which affect unpleasantly and even injuriously the palate and the stomach, are removed; while the rich saccharine matter, the aroma, and those intrinsic virtues which promote cheerfulness, are brought out and strengthened. No plant of the earth needs refined attention so much or rewards it more copiously than the vine.

Some of the Island proprietors attach vineyards to their quintas (or country seat,) mingling the useful with the ornamental. I visited often the quinta[468] of the American Consul.[469] It is about a mile from Funchal, on the so-called New Road,[470] and faces the sea and sun. The grounds are some twenty acres in extent, overhanging a ravine, with gentle hills in the rear. They are terraced with the vine from the bed of the ravine to the highest ground. The soil is formed of a certain fresh mould, the product of an annual dissolution of the rocky banks or mounds above, washed down by the tempestuous storms of winter. The fertile slopes in the "Cote d'Or" of Burgundy, which produce the Romanee and Chambertin wines have a soil like this. *Haud inexpertus loquor.*[471] For last summer, accompanied by one of the largest growers of wine in the district, Monsieur Jules Lausseure, I went over those regions, – so dear to nature and the gourmand, – and made myself as familiar with the properties, *as with the production* of the soil.

The owner of this quinta, cognisant of the eminent merits of the soil, has devoted and is devoting much time, labor, and expense, to its proper management. Great care is taken in the selection of the vines, great nicety in planting, and great assiduity in pruning them. The soil is kept clean, properly irrigated and freed from insects and weeds, and when the grape recovers from the present blight he will reap the return of his attentive labor. The vineyard so scientifically cultivated will doubtless give an annual vintage of fifty pipes of Sercial wine, the most exquisite and costly the island produces.

The capital of these merchant-proprietors is their vineyards and their stored-houses. The latter may be considered their bank, upon which they determine all their transactions. The old established houses have a large capital in their vaults – a specie capital. I counted nearly a thousand pipes in the store-houses of the Consul,[472] wines of various vintages and denominations, and ranging in price, according to age and quality, from $2 50 the gallon to as high a sum as extravagant fancy would choose to pay. Other old houses, Newton, Gordon & Co., Blackburns, Oliveira & Davies, have also large quantities on hand.

All the wines of the Island pass with us under the general designation of Madeira wines; in the meantime, there is as great distinction between them as between Madeira and Sherry, or Sherry and Port. Some are dry, some rich, some of a fruity taste. Some are light and others heavy. Some that would have delighted our grandfathers, men of strong nerves, and others more suited to modern capacities. They are various in color, too. There are those of deeper red than Port, while others again are paler than sherries. Indeed, there is hardly a taste not be gratified by the wines of the island.

The wines produced upon the south side of the Island are the best, and in aroma, body and exquisite flavor are unsurpassed nowhere. The finest are the Sercial, the Malmsey, the Bûal,[473] the Tinta or Burgundy Madeira, and the Tinto.

---

468 See Note 279.
469 See Note 278.
470 See Note 280.
471 See Note 282.
472 See Note 283.
473 The right spelling is Bual.

The Sercial is called a dry wine. Certainly if taken in large quantities, it would make its victim very dry the morning after. It is potent, and to be treated accordingly. But its bouquet might "create a soul under the ribs of death,"[474] or, what is more practicable and therefore more useful, draw one out of a fit of "the hysteries." A glass after the soup confirms the grace before, and predisposes the mind to the fullness of gratitude – *the sense of favors to come.*

On my descent down "the wide and winding Rhine," I stopped at the Château of Johannisberg, the property of the celebrated Metternich.[475] With some trouble I gained admission to the cellars and tasted their rich contents. The major-domo (what his German designation was I can't transcribe) gave me much information regarding the character of his wines. The best, he told me, was from the vine he had caused to be transplanted from Madeira, and which produced in that Island a wine called Sercial. He had sold it as high as £ 1 2/ the bottle, (upward of $5.) At his *earnest* solicitation, and knowing it would gratify him, I tasted the wine, and pronounced it well worth that seemingly extravagant price. By this and other improvements of his native grape, Prince Metternich will be endeared to the present and future ages, when the part he took in the formation of "the Holy Alliance" will be forgotten, or remembered only to be execrated!

The Malmsey is a luscious wine – too much so for the refined taste. It can be given to children and convalescent women. Nevertheless, it is one of the rarest and most costly wines. Little of it is grown, and none without great care. The slightest fog or moisture blights it, and years often pass without a vintage. The old monks[476] cultivated this vine; cherished it, and delighted in it. Its rich flavor gladdened their cloisters, and warmed their devotions. In the solitude of their cells, weary of a world that had given them so little, or wholly devoted to another that promised them so much, they doubtless passed their hours in prayers, in vigils and recuperative potations – potations which the mind and soul rather enjoyed than the bodily appetite. What wanted they of Paradise save an Eve, with whom, however, like our first progenitor, they perhaps would have been unable to retain it? Indeed, it was their introduction of Eves into the monasteries that caused, in a great degree, the expulsion of the monks,

"If ancient tales say true, nor wrong these holy men,"[477]

The Bûal[478] is a delicate and a mellow vine. The grape, like an Andalusian maiden, should be gathered at the moment of its ripeness. They both wither rapidly on maturity. Unlike Sercial, which should be kept at least one half of the time Horace allows to poetry before it sees the light, the Bûal[479] is good when young. Time, however, that softens everything, adds additional mellowness to this. The grape is becoming scarce, and the wine consequently dearer. The best raised on the island is from the vineyards of Padre João, in the district of San Martinho[480] – an excellent priest and cultivator of the vine.

---

474 See Note 286.
475 See Note 287.
476 See Note 288.
477 See Note 289.
478 The right spelling is Bual.
479 The right spelling is Bual.
480 See Note 259.

The Tinta, sometimes called Burgundy Madeira, because it has all the sunset glow of that famous wine, boasts a flavor of peculiar excellence. It gains its rich deep color from the husks of the grape, which are allowed to remain in the cask during fermentation, and which give to the wine some of the astringent properties of Port. Its peculiar excellence is ephemeral. Unlike the other wines of the island, it gathers no additional value from time. Two or three years are its grand climacteric. Thence it gradually loses its delicate aroma and copious flavor – becomes sour, morose, insipid, like ladies of "a certain age," – only to be tolerated, when without other companionship.

But in its prime, Claude's coloring is not more warm, nor Moore's verse more suggestive. "Burning Sappho" might have taken her fill of it, before the Leucadian leap[481] – for no wine, unless perhaps its immediate parent Burgundy, is more likely to excite the phrenzy of love.

The Tinto is a dark red wine, from a grape larger, softer and juicier than the Tinta. It is known as "the pure juice of the grape," being naturally less potent than the others. Mixed with water, it is very palatable and fit accompaniment to meats, but should leave the table with the cloth.

Then there is also the Verdeilho,[482] a rare wine produced from the white grape. It is a strong-bodied wine, too potent for general consumption, and is therefore but seldom used.

Such are the best of the normal wines of the island. Others are made of their commixture, among which that exported as "Madeira Wine," whose component of which are principally the Verdeilho,[483] the Tinto and Bûal;[484] and wines of various kinds, differing in color and quality, are mingled together from the "mother butts," – off-spring of many parents – and exported, "cheap for cash or approved credit."

Instead of keeping their wines in cellars, as we mostly do, the Madeira proprietors store them above ground. The interior of their "bodegas" (store-houses) is kept deliciously cool and subdued, the heat and glare of the sun being sedulously excluded. It is a delightful walk through them, hedges of butts on either side diffusing a fragrance more grateful to the sense than wild flowers – a bouquet of countless perfumes. Some visitors have been known to scent their fingers or handkerchiefs with the delicious fragrance, others, *their breath*.

A bountiful season gives (or has given) from 25,000 to 30,000 pipes, of which, however, it is safe to say, not more than 5,000 is good wine. It behooves, therefore, those who purchase to acquaint themselves with the character for probity and *good taste* of the exporters.

Intoxication is rarely or never the vice of vine-growing countries. In Madeira, even with the peasantry, a drunkard is less reputable than a thief – necessity may make the one, nothing but inherent depravity the other. They drink wine always, and never to excess. "No nation is drunken," says Jefferson in his letters, "where wine is cheap; and none sober where the dearness of wine substitutes ardent spirits as the common beverage."[485] It is the discovery of the process of distillation that (like the civil feuds of Rome) "has filled the world with widows and with orphans." The prohibition of distillation and abolition

---

481 See Note 292.
482 The right spelling is Verdelho.
483 The right spelling is Verdelho.
484 The right spelling is Bual.
485 See Note 296.

of duties on wines would be of vast more benefit to the morals of our country than all Maine Laws,[486] even if they could be enforced.[487]

Next we present the excerpt of a text, by an anonymous author, published in New York, in 1854, reporting another failure of the grape and describing how the 4th of July was spent in the island, in which Madeira Wine of 1776 was used to toast the Independence Day. He also reproaches John Howard March, the U.S. Consul to Madeira and wine merchant, who had tried to sell him some Madeira Wine on that day, which he considered an outrage.

From Madeira.[488]

By the schooner *Sarah Maria*, 32 days from Madeira, we learn that there was another entire failure of the wine crop, owing to the blight having appeared in the vine and grape.

The following is an extract of a letter dated July 12, 1854:

I am sorry to inform you that the grape crop has again failed. I was informed by many intelligent wine-growers, that they do not think the present vine will ever produce – but where are they to get others? All countries are alike afflicted. What is the cause of this blight? Is it the prayers of the temperance people? Many growers are digging up the vine and planting grain and vegetables – the latter they will grow in great quantities, and I have no doubt that if the New-York and Marseilles Straw Company will make the island a stopping place, it will become the market garden of the United States. … I was here on the 4th of July, the natal day of the Americans. The United States ship Marion was here; and I cannot tell which was the most pleased, the Americans or the Portuguese, at the exchange of courtesy. At sunrise, the Marion hoisted her national standard at the masthead, and fired 21 guns. …

Mr. WELSH,[489] an American citizen, gave a magnificent dinner to the ware room officers of the *Marion*, inviting many of the Mogado[490] of the Island. The dinner passed off delightfully. When the cloth was removed, Mogado[491] BRINGAN[492] asked permission to give a toast, and gave, "The Fourth of July – the natal day of a free and independent country"; which was drank in wine, of the vintage of 1776, with three times three. …

I was no little astonished to see and hear that the American Consul kept his store open all day, preparing to ship some wine for the United States. I noticed that he closed his store on St. Peter's Day, (possibly he may be a Catholic), permitting the Almighty Dollar

---

486 See (2nd part of) Note 297.
487 Under the title "Wine.", and preceded by the following introduction – "A correspondent of the New York Tribune, closes a very interesting description of the island of Madeira, and the main kinds of wine produced there, with the following very sensible paragraph:" – this last paragraph of March's article was revealed in *The Texan Mercury*, of January 21, 1854. (Seguin, Guadaloupe Co., TX).
488 *The New York Daily Times*, August 14, 1854. (New York City, NY). We had already inserted a small excerpt of this text on section 5.1. of this anthology.
489 See Note 187.
490 The right spelling is morgado (rich proprietor).
491 The right spelling is morgado.
492 See Note 190.

to get the better of his Patriotism. I heard that his house received a proper rebuke from the 1st Lieutenant of the American corvette: Some wine was sent off to the corvette. The Executive sent it back, saying that it was his National Day, and could not be received. I am confident that if a servant of Old England should neglect to pay the proper respect to her National Day, he would be dismissed, and very deservedly so.

W.

An excerpt of a text, written by an unknown Naval officer, and published in Ohio, in 1856, with his impressions of Madeira, where he had arrived on the 11th of November of the previous year, is presented next. This author mentions the famine the islanders suffered years before as a direct consequence of the failure of the grape in 1852, and states that the culture of the vine has been abandoned. He implies that Madeira Wine sold in America is adulterated, mentions the Catawba imported from his country as an attempt to recover the island's vines, and informs us that he was served wine at the house of a Portuguese aristocrat.

Notes from the Engineer's Mess-Room.[493]

STEAM FRIGATE SAN JACINTO,
OFF COAST OF AFRICA, Dec. 15th, 1855.

… But, to make a long story short, we came in sight of the island of Madeira on the 11th of Nov., in the morning, and, at 3 o'clock p. m. of the same day, were safely moored off the town of Funchal. …

… It will be remembered, that, a few years since, the island suffered from famine caused by the failure of the grape crop, which had been heretofore the almost sole dependence of the people. Such a state of things will probably not occur again, as the culture of the grape has been partially abandoned and other necessaries are raised in abundance in its place. There are vast quantities of wine in the island yet, and of excellent quality. The stuff sold in the United States called "Madeira Wine," tastes about as much like the pure article which is had in the island, as lager-beer does like water. I did not see a drunken person whilst on the island. Success to Catawba and blessings on thy frosty brow, "old Nick," for thou hast aided the good cause wonderfully, and future generations will bless thee for it! …

… Upon our return we stopped at the house of a Portuguese Count, and were regaled with fruit and delicious wine. Whilst trying to talk with his lady and resting ourselves, along came some of our messmates, who also had been up to the church.[494] After doing full justice to the lady's wine, we again set out on our return and then commenced some tall horse-racing. …

The next excerpt of a text, by an unknown author, published in New York City, in 1859, states that wine is no longer produced on the island, due to consecutive failures of the grapes, and that it would take a long time for the island to be covered with vineyards again.

---

493 *Daily Commercial Register*, March 15, 1856. (Sandusky, OH).
494 Of Our Lady of the Mount, in Funchal.

"The Wooded Isle;" or, Madeira to American Eyes.[495]

… The choicest fruits of both tropical and temperate regions are to be had in the greatest abundance and cheapness at Madeira. Of luxuries in this shape there is no end. The fruit which has made the Island so noted – the grape from which the luscious wine was made – is no longer produced. The wine-press is a thing of the past! It is decreed that no portion of earth should be exempt from want, sorrow and trouble. The sudden and entire failure of the grape crop a few years since, entailed a famine upon this, the fairest spot on earth, and necessitated the production of more of the necessaries, and fewer of the luxuries of life. I believe that ere long the hills of Madeira will be vine-clad as of yore. …

Next we present an excerpt of a letter by W. L. Palmer, a Naval officer, written at Madeira, in 1870, and published in New Jersey, in the same year. The author describes the mode of cultivation of the grape and, although not being an authority on wine, he allegedly tried some Madeira and gave his opinion about it.

Maderia[496] Correspondence.[497]

U.S. S. SAVANNAH, FUNCHAL,
Maderia, Aug. 3, 1870.

I should have written you from England, but while there I was so busy sightseeing that I had neglected all my friends. – Since we came to Funchal, I have been on shore nearly all the time, and have had no time for letter writing.

… We came to anchor here last Saturday, and I have explored nearly all the island already. …

These islands were settled by the Portuguese in 1421, about which time the vine was conveyed from Crete. Wine is the chief article of export, although there is a great difference in the flavour and quality of that manufactured here. As you have been trying your hand at farming this summer, you may feel an interest in knowing how the grape is cultivated. The ground is at first trenched from three to seven and from seven to nine feet deep, according to the nature of the soil, and to prevent the roots from reaching the hard clay bottom beneath, and thus obstruct the growth, a quantity of loose and stony earth is sprinkled over the bottom. If the ground is very dry it is watered three times, the sluice being left open until it is thoroughly saturated. It is found that the less the ground is watered the stronger the wine, but the quantity is diminished in proportion. The vine will grow as high as 2,900 feet, but it will produce no wine at that altitude. …

I know you are not an adept in wine any more than myself, but if you have never tasted you have at least heard of the Madeira wine. It has a bitter sweetish taste, uniting great strength and richness of flavour with an exceedingly fragrant aroma. Of course I am

---

495 *The New York Times*, July 27, 1859. (New York City, NY).
496 The right spelling is Madeira.
497 *Watertown Daily Times*, September 6, 1870. (Watertown, NJ).

speaking of the genuine, such as, after being kept ten years in wood, is allowed to mellow twice ten years in glass. It is then truly *firmisima wine*, and for fear you will think my eulogy is inspired by its vapors, I will close by signing myself,

Most truly,
W. L. PALMER.

The following text, by Philip Prootyr, was also written in Madeira, in 1871, and published in New York the following year. He arrived in the island aboard the U.S. frigate *Wabash*, having as special passengers General Sherman and the son of President Grant. The author mentions the importance of the *levadas* (waterways) in the irrigation of the cane plantations and vineyards. About the latter, he mentions that after the blight of 1852 it was replaced by the sugar cane but, in 1871 the vineyards were abundant again, and that the Madeirans had learned, by the use of sulphur, to control the fungus. As to the cost of wines, he refers to new wines sold at reasonable values whereas older wines attained higher prices.

THE WINE AND WOMEN OF MADEIRA.[498]
Social, Sanitary and Scenic Circumstances.
&c., &c., &c., &c.

[Correspondence of the Eagle.]

FUNCHAL, Madeira, December 15, 1871.

This peaceful isle has been frighted from out its dull propriety by the advent of the frigate Wabash, bearing the pennant of Real Admiral Alden of the United States Navy, and carrying as passengers the illustrious hero of the march through Georgia,[499] and the son of the President, Lieutenant Frederick Dent Grant,[500] of the Fourth Cavalry. ...

By means of an excellent system of water courses, called by the Portugueses, Lerados,[501] the water is brought from the mountains to the cane plantations and vineyards. These water courses are national works, and more labor has been expended upon them than upon any other governmental work in the Island. They are built of stone, and follow the natural courses of the mountain torrents. The sluices are small in dimension, but great in number, and furnish an ample supply of good and clear water, not only for the use of the town but for all the cane plantations and vineyard. In former times

THE CANE AND VINE STRUGGLED FOR THE MASTERY,

and for awhile the cane had the advantage. The soil of the West Indies, however, proved a more fitting place for it, and by its abundant production there, its cultivation in Madeira has been greatly interfered with. In 1852 a blight fell upon the vines in the island, and for

---

498 *The Brooklyn Daily Eagle*, January 16, 1872. (Brooklyn, New York).
499 General William T. Sherman. See Note 106.
500 Frederick Dent Grant (1850-1912), a native of Missouri, the son of the Army General and President of the United States Ulysses S. Grant, was an American soldier and United States minister to Austria-Hungary.
501 The right spelling is Levadas.

a time the cultivation of the sugar cane superseded the grape, but when a favorable season again came, the grape asserted its supremacy, which it has ever since maintained.

The destructive fungus which once bade fair to destroy the vineyards, is now entirely under control. The people have learned to meet its ravages, and although each year it reappears in its original vigor, still it is checked almost entirely by the specifics used.

The principal reason why the vine will continue to be celebrated here in preference to the cane, is that it requires but little attention, a pre-requisite in every half or whole tropical country. When once planted a vineyard will bear four or five years without care. But little water is required, and that little is furnished by the Lerados,[502] without exertion on the part of the keeper of the vineyard, and lastly the blight is so far amenable to care, that its ravages need no longer be feared.

Notwithstanding all the drawbacks to the making of as good wine now as in former times, the price of Madeira remains good. Ordinary wine commands from $2 to $5 per gallon, while old vintages demand their weight in gold.

THE TROUBLE IS WITH NEW WINE,

that the process by which the blight is eradicated, the use of sulphur, contaminates the juice, and during the process of fermentation sulphuretted hydrogen is generated, which gives to the wine an unpleasant taste. Care, however, will prevent this, and the wines are yearly increasing in quality as well as in quantity. …

PHILIP PROOTYR.

The next text was written in Funchal by an anonymous author and published in New York, in 1882. It is very well written and depicts several aspects of Madeira Wine at the time, including an important reference to the second blight that hit the island's vineyards, in 1872, which lead to a decrease of wine production. He also describes the visits he made to some vineyards, both in Santa Cruz, Funchal, and Estreito de Câmara de Lobos, as well as the process of making wine.

SPANISH WINES.[503]
The Vineyards and Wines of Madeira.
The Voyage to the Island – The Scarcity of Madeira Wine Caused by the Phylloxera. The Vintage at Santa Cruz and Sao Joao.[504] The Lizards – Manufacture of Wine – A Lovely Country and Scenery – Doctoring Diseased Vines – The Land of Garlic.
[Correspondence of the Eagle.]

FUNCHAL, August 8.

In coming to Madeira to witness the vintage and make myself acquainted with the wines the island produces, not the least point of curiosity was as to how that so magnificent a

---

502 The right spelling is Levadas.
503 *The Brooklyn Daily Eagle*, September 3, 1882. (Brooklyn, NY). In the past (and sometimes in the present), it was (is) quite common for Americans to refer that Portugal (and Madeira) belongs to Spain, hence the mistake in the main title of this article.
504 The right spelling is São João.

wine, once famous throughout Europe, should have gone out of fashion to the extent that Madeira appears to have done. It has escaped the attacks directed against sherry and port, for no one pretends the wine to be either plastered or unduly alcoholized; neither has any medical oracle published his ignorance of the details of its vinification. At the end of the Fifteenth Century Madeira was already exported to Europe, and by the middle of the Sixteenth was in high favor at the Court of Francis I., of France. That it was well known in England no long time afterward is evidenced by the reference Shakespeare makes to it in Henry IV., where Poins twits Falstaff respecting the compact he had made with Satan for his soul, which he accuses droughty Jacky of having "sold him on Good Friday last for a cup of Madeira and a cold capon's leg." First, however, I have something to say about the present wine produce of the island, and how far it has been affected by that scourge of the vine, the phylloxera vastatrix, and other causes. I propose, also, to give a rapid *resume* of the mode in which the wine is cultivated and trained, and of the system of vinification common throughout the island.

WE MADE THE VOYAGE

out on board the Algiers, belonging to a Spanish steamship company. A more enjoyable five days' sail from Barcelona can scarcely be conceived. At daybreak, on our fifth day out, we sighted the Island of Porto Santo rising phantom like out of the sea. Here and at Madeira Columbus for some time resided, marrying the daughter of a Portuguese governor of the former place, prior to his setting out on his adventure in search of a new world. Before noon we were steaming past the group of small islands known as the Desertas and in full view of Madeira itself, the barren, rocky shores of which, as it first came into view, took us somewhat by surprise. All became changed, however, as we approached nearer the Funchal, when the fertility of the island became obvious enough. Soon after the steamer let go her anchor we were on our way to the shore, where, owing to the steepness of the beach, oxen draw the boats up. Oxen, moreover, dragged our baggage on a sledge to the Custom House, while other oxen conveyed us in a basket carriage, which slid along on runners over the paved streets, to our point of destination. Because of its steep and peculiarly paved roads vehicles on wheels are never used in Madeira. Our first excursion was to a vineyard in the occupation of Messrs. Krohn, lying just above the little seaside hamlet of Santa Cruz, a favorite Spring time place of resort, situated some dozen miles or so eastward of Funchal and in full view of the Desertas group. Four sunburned, sinewy boatmen rowed us thither in an hour and a half. A little bay, a few boats, a cluster of white houses, more or less hidden by trees, some little cottages perched half way up the mountain, with patches of vines, sugarcanes and sweet potatoes planted on terraces along the sides of a ravine – these are the main features of Santa Cruz viewed from the sea. On landing we crossed the praça, or public promenade, planted with shady trees, then passed through a grove of laurel trees some forty of fifty feet high, and were soon ascending the slope on which is situated the vineyard we had come to see. Like most of the

VINEYARDS OF MADEIRA,

its area is limited, comprising merely four acres, walled on all sides. It is on the slopes of a ravine, but the surface has been leveled by bringing soil from other parts so as to present only a gradual ascent toward the further end, where there is a pleasant country house, planted round about with rare tropical and other trees. These comprise oleanders, brilliant in flower and rich in perfume; anonas,[505] yielding the aromatic and refreshing custard apple; guavas, producing a fruit resembling the strawberry in flavor, with coffee and pepper trees, and many others. Steep heights laid out in cultivated terraces, and with fir trees crowning their summits, enclose the vineyard on both sides. The majority of the vines, which are mainly of the Verdelho variety, with an insignificant sprinkling of tintas, or black grapes, are trained on low horizontal trellises, raised about four feet from the ground, and formed *latudas*;[506] this is almost a counterpart of the Kammerbau system[507] of training prevalent in certain wine districts of Germany. The remaining vines are trained higher from the ground, in what is called corridor fashion, the trellises overhead affording a pleasant shade from the Summer heats. Those trellises are constructed of cane or pine, with chestnut poles serving as supporters. The island is overrun with lizards. They scale the loftiest walls and feed upon the grapes, while as to bees, although it is forbidden to keep them in the neighborhood of the vineyards, the interdict is disregarded, and the best branches are commonly lost through their depredations. The pickers here were all men black bearded, bare footed, and in ragged raiment, with their skins almost as brown as their mahogany colored breeches. They cut out the grapes and flung them into round, open baskets with handles, emptying these afterward into a large basket. The latter basket holds grapes about sufficient to produce a barrel of mosto,[508] equal to a trifle over nine gallons. The casa do lagar, or pressing house, was in the center of the vineyard, the lagar itself being a huge wooden trough, with a large wooden beam hanging across it, which aids in the extraction of the juice from the piled up grape skins, after these have been well trodden by several pairs of brawny feet. Before, however, the treaders mount into the lagar. The grape's own weight produces a steady flow of juice into the adjoining vat – a rivulet which becomes a torrent when the treading commences. The men distributed about the lagar commence with a slow, steady movement, then spread out their arms and grasp the huge intervening beam, rapidly advancing and retiring one from the other, occasionally turning rapidly half way round, now to the right and now left, their frantic movements presently subsiding into a slow, monotonous kind of jig. We were unable to witness the conclusion of the operation, and set off on our return to Funchal. Reaching Funchal we rode up a steep, paved road, which in parts was merely so many stone steps, to Sao Joao,[509] to witness the vintage of the place in a vineyard of about thirteen acres in extent, and very carefully cultivated by its owner, M. Leacock, whose house is one of the oldest in the Madeira wine trade, dating back as it does to the year 1749. Here the vines, planted on ridges forming a trench between the different rows, are trained along horizontal wires, supported by strong posts, which meet together at the top in the form of an inverted V. The vines, too, are more closely pruned than is usually the case, the prevalent practice being to allow them to run largely to wood. M. Leacock's vineyard

---

505 Portuguese word for custard apples.
506 The right spelling is latadas, the Portuguese word for trellis.
507 A trellising system, dating back to the Roman Empire that survived in some parts of Germany until the 18th century, namely at the wine region of the Palatinate. This system consisted on training the vines on vertical wooden structures.
508 Portuguese word for must, the juice grape fresh from the wine press.
509 The right spelling is São João.

WAS ATTACKED BY PHYLLOXERA

a few years ago, and many of the vines were seriously affected. The owner, however, by watchful care and judicious treatment, including the application to the principal roots of the vine of a kind of varnish which in this instance seems to have proved specific, has succeeded in restoring most of the diseased vines to a comparatively healthy condition. Not only is the Madeira vinegrower in dread of the phylloxera – he has to guard his vines against the oidium as well. This he accomplishes by freely sulphuring them, one disadvantage of which is the difficulty of getting rid of the sulphur from the fruit. This M. Leacock affects by the aid of bellows and brushes, which women have been taught to use with patience and skill at the season of the year when the skins of the grapes commence to shine. Although the vineyard comprises less than thirteen acres, the grapes will be picked this year at no less than eight different times, only the perfectly ripe bunches being gathered on each occasion. The vintage which commenced on the 4th, owing to this circumstance, will last for a period of fully three weeks. The pickers were barefooted women, in light gowns and white linen jackets, with red and yellow handkerchiefs tied over their heads. Their pay was equal to fifteen cents per day, while the men who collected the grapes in the larger baskets and trod them in the lagar received an equivalent to thirty-two cents.

THE PRESSING HOUSE

is a low stone building with high pitch roof, lighted by a couple of small windows and shaded by the spreading branches of a fine specimen of the nespera japonica.[510] It is provided with a couple of lagars, the larger of which is capable of pressing four to five pipes of mosto[511] at a time. We found six men at work in it, three on either side of the cumberstone dividing beam or vara. The first juice that ran off was emptied into a balceiro, or small vat, holding about eighty gallons, and provided with a tap at the lower part to enable the juice to be drawn off after the little sulphur that had remained on the grapes had settled at the bottom. The treaders went through much the same movement as I have already described, and when the expressed juice could no longer escape from the lagar, through the aperture being stopped up with the crushed grapes, the latter were all piled up in the center or at the sides and pressed and patted with the hands, the juice as it escaped being strained by passing through a basket hung on to the bica, or spout of the lagar. This piling was repeated three times, known as the first, second and third overtura,[512] or opening, and then came another operation – the piling of the mass in a central heap for the cord, which was ociled neatly round it with intervening spaces through which the juice could exude. A stout, wooden disc, strengthened with cross pieces, was placed on the top, and on this several square billets were laid transversally with a stout board over all. On this pile the beam is brought to bear by means of the perpendicular screw at one end of it, resting on a huge stone a few feet from the lagar. The juice pressed by this means is called "O vinho da corda."[513] After an hour or two of this work, the solid mass is broken up with

---

510 Scientific name of the loquat tree, very abundant in Madeira. Contrary to what the scientific name indicates, this tree is originary of China, not Japan.
511 See Note 508.
512 The right spelling is abertura.
513 "Rope wine", in English.

the hands or with hoes, if necessary, and then commences the repiza,[514] a vigorous dancing and jumping movement executed to time upon the apparently dry grape skins. This is done in order effectually to bruise those grapes that are in the condition of raisins and have become softened from soaking in the expressed juice. The repiza[515] lasts for half and hour or so, the men enlivening their labors with a variety of jokes, practical and other. Occasionally two of them on one side of the vara will suddenly seize a comrade and toss him over to the other side, where the men will receive him with open arms, but only to fling him back over the beam again, amidst the laughter of the party. The grape skins are now piled up again, and once more pressed, after which water is poured upon them and they are well stirred up and pressed for the last time, yielding what is called *agua do pe*,[516] literally foot water, a weakish liquor given to the work people to drink. After we had passed out of the Funchal district, we crossed the ravine of the

RIBEIRO SECCO,[517]

the narrow mountain road being bordered by blackberry hedges, with wild honeysuckles, roses and geraniums, and occasional prickly pears. Here and there the fazendas, or cultivated lands, which, owing to the rocky, mountainous character of the region, are often the merest plots, are enclosed by stone walls up which the young lizards may be seen scampering. We pass under trellises of vines, by patches of sugar canes and shady fig trees, with small water courses gurgling along at our side. On our right rise peaks of Sao Martinho[518] and Santo Antonio,[519] the former covered half way up its sides with vines, while the loftier peaks beyond are covered with chestnuts and pines. We continually meet brown, bony and barefooted peasant women, and we also encounter a party of toiling borracheiros[520] bringing down newly made wine in sheep and goat skins[521] slung over their backs and kept steady by straps across their burning foreheads. At length we reach the Church of Sao Martinho[522] – a grove of cypresses indicating the adjacent cemetery – and pass the village force, where all the male gossips of the neighborhood seemed to be congregated. Sao Martinho[523] is an important viticultural district, yielding a high class wine with fine bouquet; and fortunately the vines have been only slightly attacked by the phylloxera. The vintage had already commenced. It was anticipated that this year's yield would be only a very moderate one, the grapes having rotted from an excess of moisture. Our first halt was at a place called Terra dos Alhos – in other words, the land of the garlic. Shortly after starting again we descended half way down the ravine of the Ribeiro dos Socorridos,[524] the sides of which are covered with built up terraces planted principally with sugar canes

---

[514] The right spelling is repisa, which designates the act of threading again the remains of the grape clusters, after they had already suffered the pressure of the wooden lever.
[515] See previous Note.
[516] The right spelling is água-pé.
[517] The right spelling is Ribeiro Seco.
[518] The right spelling is São Martinho.
[519] The right spelling is Santo António.
[520] Portuguese word for wine carriers.
[521] Charles Wilkes, who had visited Madeira in 1838, also refers the use of sheep skins to carry wine – as we have seen on section 6.1.1.6. of this anthology – although it is known today that in the past only goat skins were used for this purpose.
[522] The right spelling is São Martinho.
[523] The right spelling is São Martinho.
[524] The right spelling is Ribeira dos Socorridos, whose valley divides the municipalities of Funchal and Câmara de Lobos.

and a few fig trees, then turning to our left we ascended a steep rugged path on the opposite side of the ravine which conducts to the peak of

CAMA DE LOBOS.[525]

From this breezy height we look down upon one side on a little fishing village with its rocky headlands and the grand Cabo Girao[526] and its miniature bay, and on the other into a fertile hollow, formerly covered with vines, which yielded one of the finest and most robust of Madeira growths. A year or two ago vines sloped down from the summit of the peak on all its sides and occupied every cultivated spot in the rear of the village, but the phylloxera has destroyed them nearly all, and the famous wine growing district of Cama de Lobos,[527] which used to produce 3,000 pipes annually, will yield this year merely 100. A rich Frenchman who has become a large land owner in this and adjacent districts, informed us that even two years ago Cama de Lobos[528] yielded upward of a couple of thousand pipes, but nearly the whole of the vines have since been rooted and up and sugar canes planted in their place wherever a fair supply of necessary water could be obtained. Higher up the mountain is the district known as the Estreito de Cama de Lobos,[529] some of the vines of which have been planted at an altitude little short of a couple of thousand feet above the sea shore, or several hundred feet higher than the vine will thrive with certainty. As yet the phylloxera has only attacked the lower vines, but the others have suffered more or less from the unusual rains of the past Spring and Summer. We set forth again and in the course of two hours we made our way to the summit of Cabo Girao.[530] From this place we obtained a view of the district known as the Quinta Grande, the vines of which, but slightly affected by phylloxera, will give a very fine yield. There we look over the perpendicular sides of what is said to be the highest cliff against which the sea dashes in the world.[531] The altitude is 2,000 feet,[532] and the vineyards formed by landslips at its base, and the produce of which is much esteemed, when viewed from above look scarcely larger than a sheet of foolscap paper. After an hour's repose we descended on foot along a villanous break neck road to the picturesque fishing village of Cama de Lobos,[533] where many of the men wear flat, green glazed hats of the circumference of a small umbrella. A boat which we had ordered took us back to Funchal, and we rode up to the mount by the light of a brilliant moon.

A.

The next text was written in 1890, in Funchal, and published in Baltimore in the same year. Its author, who hid himself behind the initials D. W. C., was presumably a Naval officer, who had arrived at the island on September 18 of that year, aboard the U.S. Flagship *Pensacola*. He dedicates a section of his article to Madeira wine, providing interesting

---

525 See Note 207.
526 The right spelling is Cabo Girão.
527 See Note 207.
528 See Note 207.
529 The right spelling is Estreito de Câmara de Lobos.
530 See Note 526.
531 See Note 357.
532 See Note 356.
533 See Note 207.

details about its production, different types, the way of preparing a *borracho*, or a she-goat skin to be used by the *borracheiros* (wine carriers) to carry the wine from the countryside to the wine stores in Funchal. He also presents some wine-related statistics and mentions the Isabella and Catawba vines brought from the United States to graft the Madeiran vines after the blight of 1852.

ON THE PENSACOLA.[534]
A Pleasant Voyage from New York to Madeira.
INTERESTING SCENES AT FUNCHAL.
... – Agricultural Methods and Grape Culture – How Some of the Famous Wines Are Made – ...
[Special Correspondence of Baltimore Sun.]

U.S. FLAGSHIP PENSACOLA,
(Making Passage from Funchal, Madeira, to Porto Grande, Cape Verde,) Sept. 28. – ...

THE INTRODUCTION OF VINES

into Madeira was in 1421, and from that time until in 1852 wine was the staple product of the island. The richest wine district was the valley of the "Cama de Lobos,"[535] which is situated on the south side of the island, and where grows the famous grape from which the "Malmsey" wine was made. All the finest grapes were first introduced from stocks brought from Candia in 1445. The grapes are almost all of them white, and are grown on trellises, where they ripen, and about one-half the crop is allowed to become half dry, or raisins, before being gathered. This is said to be very necessary in order to produce the best wine. The four principal wines are the "Malmsey," the "dry Madeira," "Sercial" and the "Tinto." When the grapes are gathered and the juice is pressed from them it is stored in casks, and finally it is sold to a wine merchant in Funchal, who stores it in casks in the store-house, where it undergoes fermentation, and from year to year older wine is added to take the place of that which has evaporated. For instance, the casks are stored in rows, commencing at one end of the store-house, the oldest first, the next vintage second, the third vintage next, and so on until the new wine, or grape juice, is in the last cask. As the grape juice evaporates the cask is filled from the cask next ahead; the cask next to the grape juice is filled from the next ahead, and so on until the evaporation from each cask has been replace by wine from that of the next oldest cask, and in that way the wine is not only improved in quality, but is increased in price also.

There are one or two dealers who claim, and in all probability very truly, that they have wine dating back to 1800 and 1816. After the wine has reached a ripe old age it is no longer allowed to remain in the wood, but is bottled and carefully stored. The fresh grape juice is brought to market in goat skins, which hold about ten gallons each, one of these filled skins being carried upon the shoulders of a man. The only skin which can be used is the skin of a she goat, and it is not difficult to imagine why the pelt of a she goat is selected instead of the larger and tougher skin of William. The preparation of the skin is simple. When the goat is slaughtered the head is cut off and then the feet; a reed stem is inserted between the skin and the flesh; air is blown in until the skin is well inflated; then it is stripped off

---

534 *The Sun*, October 30, 1890. (Published in Baltimore, MD).
535 See Note 207.

in one piece by turning it back from the neck and shoulders first. Thus the pelt is taken off in a perfectly whole piece, and there are only such orifices as those left after cutting off the feet and head. The skin is prepared by shaving the hair off and dressing it with some preparation, after which the skin is turned, flesh side out, and all the orifices are tied up, and while yet green is inflated and allowed to dry. When wanted for use the skin is filled with water, and when it has absorbed enough to make it usable the water is emptied and the skin filled with grape juice, the opening used to fill the skin being again tied up, and the grape juice is ready to be carried to market.

Often a company of twenty-five to forty men in a squad, with a leader singing as he marches at their head, may be seen coming along the road, each man with a goatskin of wine on his shoulders, going to the city. After the wine is emptied from the skins and the skins inflated the squad returns, each with a skin on a long stick, carried over the shoulder, and one would imagine them to be a squad of men carrying a lot of dressed sheep on sticks after the head and legs were cut off – the general shape of the animal being so well preserved. This mode of transportation is a very old one, and though it would be much easier to transport the grape juice by boat, and it could be done in much less time, yet the natives are proud to be on the custom of their ancestors in this, as well as in many other things.

The sale of spurious wines under the name of "Madeira" had the effect to reduce the production of the island from about twenty-two thousand pipes in 1813 to about three thousand pipes in 1844. In 1851 an insect called the "oidium" began to make its appearance and destroyed the grapes and finally almost all the vines, so that the product decreased from 16,000 pipes in 1850 to 29 pipes in 1855.

In 1857 sulphur treatment was resorted to, and by its use the disease was controlled and the vines so much improved that the vintage of 1861 was very good, and since then both the quantity and quality of the wine have improved. Catawba and Isabella vines from the United States were imported and used to graft the Madeira grape upon, it being found that the American vine was hardy and resisted the disease, so now the Portuguese government supplies the American vine, free of charge, to the vine growers of Madeira, though no wine is made from the American grape. The "Sercial" grape and vines were the only species not attacked by the "oidium," and the natives say the grape is so bitter that nothing will eat it; not even the rats and lizards, which often destroy many grapes, will touch them. The wine made from the sercial grape is very fine after it has aged, but it requires a much longer period than the other wines do before it is good for sale. …
   D. W. C.

Livingston Hunt wrote a text about Madeira island that was published in Washington, D.C., in 1895, in which he makes reference to the famous wines of Madeira. In it he also alludes to the almost inexpressive imports of Madeira Wine to the United States, mentions the vintage time in the island as one of the happiest events of the year, and provides some figures about the island's wine production.

IN QUAINT MADEIRA[536]
Picturesque Sights in This Island, Where the Grape Flourishes. ...
Written Exclusively for The Evening Star. ...

The Famous Wines.

A land where the people are pleasant, where the temperature is always that of our spring – (the thermometer rarely going below 60 degrees or above 76 degrees Fahrenheit, except on the mountains) – and where nature is always beautiful, is surely well worth a visit; but even with the mention of all these attractions, Madeira is not yet done justice to. We must add to the list the famous and delicious wines that she produces. These are not the favorites that they were in former times, though the reason for this is hard to find. England for a long time used to smack her lips and sing songs to old Malmsey, but about fifty years ago believed that she had discovered the superiority of sherry to Malmsey, and the people of influence there started the fashion of drinking the former in preference to the latter. In America today Madeira is but little drunk, and the exportation of the wine from the island to this country amounts to less than $20,000 worth annually. Probably three times as much as this was imported by us before the rebellion.

Vintage time on the island is from the middle of September to the middle of October, and is the busiest and gayest time of the year. The peasants, when not hard at work among the heavily laden vines, are either singing, dancing or improvising doggerel poetry.

The wine industry of Madeira at present amounts to about 8,500 pipes annually, of which nearly 3,500 are exported. Before 1852, when the oidium disease first attacked the grape vines, and for the next ten years kept them almost annihilated, the yearly harvest of wine used to amount to from 25,000 to 30,000 pipes. It was by the importation of American vines, which resist the oidium disease, that the successful cultivation of the grape was resumed in Madeira. But the wine that is made there today is not to be depended on as perfectly pure unless bought from a few merchants of unimpeachable reputation. ...

LIVINGSTON HUNT.

The renowned journalist and pioneering travel writer Fannie B. Ward (1843-1913), a native of Monroe, Michigan, also visited Madeira at the end of the 19th century, and wrote several articles about this enchanted island. Next will be presented two of them. The first one, published in Pennsylvania, in 1896, seems to be the first text she wrote about Madeira. From it we just present a small excerpt where we can read her general description of the island whose hills were covered with luxuriant verdure, formed mostly by sugarcane plantations and "abounding vineyards".

THE MADEIRA ISLANDS.[537]
GARDENS OF THE SEA WHERE DISEASE IS UNKNOWN.

---

536 *The Evening Star*, June 22, 1895. (Washington, DC).
537 *The Pittsburgh Press*, February 15, 1896. (Pittsburgh, PA).

JUNE WEATHER ALL THE YEAR. ...
From a Special Correspondent.

Funchal Madeira, Dec. 30. – It seems strange that so little is known in the United States about the Madeiras, and stranger that our wealthy countrymen, who search the world over in quest of novelty in winter and summer resorts, should so long have passed unnoticed these delightful islands of eternal June. There are almost no books on the Madeiras, and we have little knowledge of them beyond a hazy notion that they belong to Portugal and are flowing with wine and honey; and also that they are a favorite haunt of consumptive Europeans and of absconding cashiers who crave seclusion. Let us first get their bearings well in mind. The two inhabited islands and three bare rocks that rejoice under the general name of "Madeiras" lie 4,000 miles due east from Charleston, South Carolina – only 350 miles from the west coast of Africa, and about twice that distance southwest from Lisbon. ...

The main island, which the discoverer named Madeira (the Portuguese word for a certain kind of building timber), on account of its mighty forests of that valuable wood – is about 35 miles long by 12 wide, with Funchal, the capital of the group and only city of consequence, on its southern coast. Like the Azores, it was thrown up from the Atlantic by volcanic forces at a comparatively recent period, and is covered with mountains; yet is bears little resemblance to those islands, having no conical hills nor apparent craters. Nevertheless, it is of magnificent outline, falling abruptly into the sea at either end, with lofty precipices and vast detached rocks of fantastic shapes and rich volcanic tints along its whole coast line. A serrated ridge, in places 6,000 feet high, deeply grooved and turreted, so that it looks like the bastions and pinnacles of a colossal fortress, extends from end to end, forming the backbone of the island. From this central mass enormous ridges run down to the shore, set at almost regular intervals, as if to buttress the principal range. Between these ridges lie deep valleys, every foot of them richly cultivated, sloping up from the sea to the central mountains. The foot of every valley is indented, forming a small semi-circular bay between the headlands, and scattered around the shores of each bay is a white-walled village. Both in the valleys and on the mountain slopes the land seems to rise in narrow, natural terraces, and all the terraces are covered with the most luxuriant verdure – the pale yellow of sugar cane, the dark green of coffee and orange groves, and the abounding vineyards from which the work and tiniest spot of soil between them being cultivated to the utmost. Sugar mills and wine presses dot the shore, and a picturesque road winds around the whole island, following the innumerable curvings of the coastline. In places it is a narrow shelf cut low down on the face of the cliff; anon it mounts far up to dizzy heights, then creeps around rocky headlands, through tunnels lighted by narrow window slits blasted out of the solid rock; and again is leaps from craig to craig, on walls of masonry at the edge of the sea. Noting this wonderful road from the shipboard, you may be sure we promised ourselves that, please heaven, when once ashore, not much time should be wasted before we traversed every rod of it. ...

Fannie B. Ward.

The second text by Fannie B. Ward, totally dedicated to the world famous Madeira Wine, was published in Pennsylvania, in 1896, and republished in other newspapers from other states, under different titles. In it she makes a brief retrospective of the history of the wine, denies that Madeira was conducive to the gout disease (an accusation that started in England and had some followers in America), mentions the blight of 1852 and its consequences, pinpoints Estreito de Câmara de Lobos as Madeira's wine district *par excellence*, describes the wine-making process and identifies several types of wine. At the end of her article there are some references that indicates that she used Charles W. March's book to get some data for this article, and we recommend a comparison of both texts.

MADEIRA WINE-MAKING.[538]
HOW THE LEADING INDUSTRY OF THE ISLAND IS CONDUCTED.
FEEDING THE WINE PRESS.
Bacchanalian Celebrations During Vintage Season – Making the Various Brands – Storage and Sales. Drunkenness Comparatively Absent From This District.
Special Correspondence.

Funchal, Madeira, Jan. 16. – It would never do to leave Madeira without paying some attention to its principal industry – that of wine making. For more than four centuries the wines of this island have been famous – ever since the introduction of the vine from Cyprus, under the patronage of the royal house of Braganza, in the year 1425. In times long past they were the favorite beverage in England, and why they are not yet it would be hard to discover. Evidently Shakespeare was acquainted with them, for he makes Poires say to Falstaff, "Jack, how agreest the devil and thee about thy soul, which thou soldest to him on Good Friday last for a cup of madeira?" Since his day, generations of Englishman continued to smack their lips and sing songs to "Old malmsey" – until about 50 years ago – when the prince regent conceived the idea that malmsey was conductive to gout, and took to drinking sherry instead, whereupon all his imitators at home and Anglomaniacs abroad immediately followed the fashion by forsaking madeira. The best physicians, however, have always maintained a contrary opinion, and among these islanders, who naturally drink most of their own beverages, the aristocratic complaint, gout, is unknown. Madeira wine has never been especially popular in the United States,[539] and within the last quarter century, since California wines have come to the front, our importation from Madeira has fallen off fully two-thirds, being now about $20.000 worth per annum. In former times the wine industry of this island yielded an annual average of 30.000 pipes; up to the year 1852, when, without warning, the blight came – a fungus on fruit and plant, called oideum tuckeri[540] – and the very next season the harvest fell to 100 pipes. That state of things con-

---

[538] *The Pittsburgh Press*, March 1, 1896. (Pittsburgh, PA); *The Daily Picayune*, March 10, 1896. (New Orleans, LA. Published anonymously and without illustrations under the titles "THE FAMOUS WINES OF MADEIRA. – The Various Vineyards of the Island and The Several Kinds and Qualities of the Product. – The Vineyards Annihilated in the Fifties. – The Importation of American Vines and the Process of Manufacturing the Wine." This source also added that this text had been written by a Funchal correspondent of the *Philadelphia Record*); *Deseret Evening News*, March 1, 1902. (Great Salt Lake City, UT. Published under the title "RURAL MADEIRA. – "Malmsey", the Celebrated Product of the Island, is Truly a Wine Fit for the Gods – The Way of Its Culture", with some minor differences in relation to the original text. Curiously this newspaper states that this text was written in Funchal on Jan. 7, 1902, which cannot be true, for it was originally published six years before.)

[539] Contrary to her statement, Madeira Wine was highly cherished in America from the 18th to the 19th century.

[540] The right spelling of the scientific name of this fungus is *oïdium tuckery*.

tinued for almost 20 years, and the vines were almost annihilated, causing untold suffering on the island from the sudden collapse of the only wealth-bearing industry. After a while the culture of sugar cane restore a portion of Madeira's lost prosperity, and later a way was found for counteracting the spread of the blight and partially resuming the production of wine. This was by blowing the powder of sulphur flowers all over the vines and grapes – a very tedious process, as may be imagined. Still later came the discovery that American vines resist the oideum disease, and a great many of them were imported to Madeira, with the best results. But the simple-hearted natives imported other things from America along with the vines, and Madeira wines are no longer to be depended upon as perfectly pure.

Figure 48. "A Madeira Freight Train". Article illustration. Author unknown.

On the north side of the island the rugged heights are too exposed to Atlantic gales for the most successful grape culture, and the little wine made on that side is changed into brandy, which is mixed with the best Madeira wines. On the south side the hills descend to the sea by easier declivities, and their sunny slopes are densely covered with vineyards that seem to fairly reel beneath their purple burden. Not only is every bit of soil given up to the vines, which are trained on trellises across the highways and byways, but on the rocky ledges where there was no soil, earth has been brought from afar, and vines planted on it. Connoisseurs declare that for richness of body, deliciousness of flavor and immunity from injury by indifferent treatment, these wines are unequaled, and in Europe they have always sparkled on the boards of those whose cellars contain the rarest brands.

Madeira wine, par excellence, is made from a mixture of white and dark grapes, and from a light claret color, it gradually pales to a rich topaz tint. The center of the vine growing region is the Estreito district, and the way thereto from Funchal is the same which leads to the Grand Curral and to San Vicento;[541] so we may kill more birds than one with the same stone. As a portion of the road cannot be traversed by horses, it is well to make the whole journey in the hammock. The sturdy beasts[542] set off at a swinging pace between a walk and a trot, and keep it up unflaggingly all day long, whatever your avoirdupois, if they are allowed to stop every three of four hours for a few minutes' rest in some wayside vanda[543] and are given the expected pour boire. Hardly has the last straggling suburb of Funchal faded from view before the village of Cama do Lobos[544] comes in sight – the whole glorious prospect dominated by the stupendous vertical cliff called Cabo Gerain,[545] 2,185 feet high,[546] with a crown of pines on top, rising straight up from the surf that dashes at its base – the very tallest sea cliff in the world.[547] Just beyond this cliff the Estreito district begins Vintage time in Madeira – from the middle of September to the middle of October – is the gayest season of the year. Then the peasants, at work all day long among the vines, are heard singing and improvising their doggerel poetry. Like New England

---

[541] The right spelling is São Vicente, a village in northern Madeira.
[542] To designate her hammock carriers as "sturdy beasts" is a pejorative, to say the least, and an almost racist remark on her part.
[543] The right spelling is venda, a small grocery shop.
[544] See Note 207.
[545] See Note 355.
[546] See Note 356.
[547] See Note 357.

husking in early days, labor is united with festive enjoyment and the season is made a half holiday. Women and girls go into the vineyards with their baskets and carefully gather the grapes, and bring them in, safely balanced on their heads. Then all the bunches must be "escalhido"[548] – that is, picked over, the good and indifferent separated, the best reserved for the costliest wine. Then they are thrown into the wine press – a wide, clumsy wooden trough, into which men jump barefooted (let us hope not unwashed), trousers rolled up, and trample out the juice. It must have been done the same way in Bible times, else why the passage, "He has trodden the wine press alone?" The advantage of expressing the juice with the feet is said to be that flesh gives way to the stems and seeds, so that their bitterness is not mixed with their pure juice. After the first expression has been drawn off, the remaining portion is put into a sack, hung up and reduced to lever pressure. The juice is conveyed to the store-houses in goatskins, which are thought to give it an additional flavor, and there emptied into casks. The process of fermentation usually occupies about five weeks. After the juice has been taken out of the wine press, water is thrown in upon the refuse, and this undergoes the same process as the pure juice, making what is called agoa-pe[549] – literally foot-water – a cheap wine which is retailed at the ventas[550] to the poorer classes. Soon as their day's work is done the peasants have a grand frolic all through the vintage time. The weather is so delightful that their dances are held in the open air, and everywhere you hear the strumming of machetas,[551] the queer little native guitars that are used to accompany the voice and dance. Everybody dances and everybody sings: and if not with perfect grace and harmony, at least with abandon and enjoyment.

The wine, having ceased fermentation, is drawn off the lees and put into sweet casks, where it is clarified with eggs or with ox blood, or usually with gypsum; a soupçon of brandy (also made of the grape), being added to each pipe to prevent the acetous fermentation. The grapes that furnish the very best wines are not those agreeable to the taste. The finest madeira wines are sercial, malmsey, bual, bergundy-maderia[552] and tinto, but several other kinds are made. Probably the best is sercial. Says one who ought to know, if experience is the best teacher: "It is called a 'dry' wine, and of a verity, if taken in full glasses the imbiber will be dry enough the morning after. It is potent, and to be treated accordingly. But its bouquet might 'create a soul beneath the ribs of death' if anything could. It sends an odor through a room sweeter than pastils. A glass of it after soup confirms the grace before, and predisposes the soul to the fullness of a gratitude – the sense of favor to come. Malmsey, too, is one of the rarest and most costly of wines, and is produced nowhere but in Maderia,[553] and nowadays not much of it here. Years may pass without a vintage. The old monks cultivate the vines with greatest care, and are said to have loved and cherished its juice. It brings $5 a bottle in the estates where it is made, and is mostly bought up before vintage time for the royal houses in Europe. Since the capital of the grape raisers is their vineyards and stored wines, they devote much time, labor and strength to the management of both. Great care is bestowed upon the selection of the cuttings, great nicety in planting and in pruning. The soil is always kept clean, properly

---

548 The right spelling is escolhido.
549 The right spelling is água-pé.
550 The right spelling is vendas. See Note 274.
551 The right spelling is machetes (plural of machete, a small stringed guitar). See Note 275.
552 The right spelling is burgundy Madeira.
553 The right spelling is Madeira.

irrigated and cleared of insects and weeds, and if by such treatment 50 pipes a year of the better class of wine is produced, the proprietor's fortune is made. Instead of keeping their wines in cobwebby cellars, the Maderia[554] merchant stores his above ground, but the sun is carefully excluded from his bodega, or warehouse, and it is kept cool and sweet. Some of them contain 1,000 pipes of wine, of different vintages and denominations, ranging in price from $2 50 the gallon to the largest sum that the most extravagant wine-bibber would care to pay. Though all the commoner wines of the island are designated abroad by the general name of Madeira, there is as much difference between them as between port and sherry. Some are dry, some full bodied, some with a fruity taste, some light, others heavy, some would have just suited our sturdy grandfathers, and others are better adapted to the weaker modern capacity. They vary in color, too, from deepest red to palest amber, and in odor as one flower differs from another. I have not yet seen a single intoxicated person in Madeira, and it is said that there is absolutely no drunkenness among the natives. The same rule seems to hold good in all wine-producing countries. Neither in Portugal, Spain nor France, nor on the Rhine, does one see a millionth part of the inebriety that disgraces the United States of America, with its "Maine laws",[555] its "local option" and prohibition parties and other futile devices for overcoming the serpent that stingeth like an adder. In Madeira, where wine is much more commonly drank than water, a person who once gets intoxicated is looked upon as something worse than a thief. They saw that necessity may compel one to steal, but nothing save his own degraded inclinations can lead a man to drunkenness. Thomas Jefferson, in one of his letters, wrote these wise words: "No nation is drunken whose wine is cheap, and none sober where the dearness of wine substitutes ardent spirits as the common beverage".[556] Christ made wine at the wedding, we are told. It is the discovery of the more modern process of distillation which has "filled the world with widows and orphans". If distillation were prohibited by law and the duties abolished on decent wines, the W. C. T. U.[557] and kindred organizations might shut up shop and retire from business.

Fannie B. Ward.

The last text of this section was published anonymously in Maine, in 1899, and presents a tourist's views of the island, where he made a stop while touring the world. Among them are his impressions of the vintage season in Madeira, as well as the description of the process of making wine, although not in complimentary terms.

IN SLOW-PLODDING MADEIRA.[558]
An Isle Not Dead but One Which Is in No Particular Hurry – Wheels Unknown and the Patient Ox Draws the Sledge.

---

554 The right spelling is Madeira.
555 See (2nd part) of Note 297.
556 See Note 296.
557 Woman's Christian Temperance Union, an organization created in 1873 at Hillsboro, OH, which aimed to create a "sober and pure world" by abstinence, purity and evangelical Christianity.
558 *Lewinston Evening Journal*, July 22, 1899. (Lewinston, ME).

"Madeira", said Mr. Frank E. Jackson of Winthrop,[559] a few days before he left home last week for another swing 'round the circle of the globe, "Madeira is a guide-book country, but it has its interesting phases for all that. ...

"The prettiest time to strike Madeira is during the vintage season. In the sunny vintage days the effervescence of the people seems to crop out and every man you meet has a smile on his lips and an added unction in his tones as he greets you with the Portuguese for 'May God grant your Lordship many good days.'

"The grape-pickers are a merry throng men and women together, and their labor is performed to the chorus of laughter and song. The grapes are picked into small baskets from which they are emptied into larger ones holding about a hundredweight of fruit. In these latter baskets the grapes are carried to the presses.

"And here your thirst for wine will cease unless your stomach is proof against anything and everything. In Madeira they still tread the wine from the grapes and, churning up and down in the purple gore, I have seen men who were not so clean that you would be over and above anxious to drink the wash of the pedal extremities.

"But the wine which is made from the first pressing of the grapes is far more palatable than that which comes after. When the crew in the lagar, or pressing trough, have squeezed out all that they can with their feet and pressure has been applied by means of a screw arrangement, water is poured over the grape skins and the liquor that results from this is called aqua pe,[560] or foot water, and that is what it literally is. It may quiet the fears of him who drinks Madeira, however, to know that this last wash does not find its way off the island, but is sold to the laboring class and by them esteemed a great delicacy.

"From the press the wine is carried to the stores where the process of fermentation is assisted and the liquid made ready for commerce. The wines of Madeira are as many as the varieties of grapes, and of these are more than a dozen. It is interesting to have seen the process of wine-making on the island but I think it is perhaps as impressive a temperance lesson as a man could have. He who can drink Madeira after having seen the barefoot gang in the lagar is blessed with a digestion that is worthy better things."

6.2. American Literature at Large (Prose)

In this section will be presented sixteen American authors and excerpts of their literary works, in which they mention Madeira Wine, portrayed in different situations and perspectives. Literature being, in a way, a mirror of society, it is no wonder that this well-known and highly reputed product in America is so often referred to in several books, published throughout the 19th century, by a wide variety of American writers. The text selection will be presented in alphabetical order, by the author's names, accompanied by brief notes about them.

---

[559] A town in Kennebec County, Maine.
[560] The right spelling is água-pé.

6.2.1. Benauly (Pseud.)

Benauly – pseudonym of Benjamin Vaughan Abbott (1830-1890), a native of Boston, MA – published in 1855, in New York, the book entitled *Cone Cut Corners: The Experiences of a Conservative Family in Fanatical Times; involving some account of a Connecticut village, the people who lived in it, and those who came there from the city*.[561] From this book we have selected an excerpt from the 16th chapter, supposedly written in 1851 and illustrated with an etching of a bottle of 1820 "South Side Madeira", in which is described, in vivid detail, a wine adulterating store in America that among other liquors, also "produced" the choicest Madeira. All this is seen through the eyes of a young boy who had applied for a job at this place. This being a controversial topic, exposing to broad daylight a misdemeanour, no wonder the author has chosen to use a fictional name to undersign this book.

Figure 49. Benjamin Vaughan Abbott. *The Railway & Corporation Law Journal*, January 28, 1888. Author unknown.

XVI.

OCTOBER, 1851.

The next morning, Paul Rundle, looking as was his wont in the columns of Wants in the morning paper, in the hope that somebody wanted him, found the following advertisement:

"Wanted, a lad to tend store and run of errands. He must come well recommended; must be steady, active, quick at figures, a good penman, understand accounts, and be a judge of money, and must be able and willing to make himself generally useful. To such an one a good place will be given, with a prospect of advance. The best of reference will be required. Wages, four dollars a week. Apply to Bagglehall, Floric & Co., 317 Broadway."

Immediately after breakfast – and Paul took his breakfast before Mrs. Stuccuppe's supper things had been cleared away – Paul started for Bagglehall, Floric & Co's., to answer the advertisement. If we should say that Messrs. Bagglehall, Floric & Co., kept a grocery and liquor store, we should do them injustice. If we should say that they were wholesale and retail dealers in family groceries, and in foreign and domestic wines, we should say exactly what their sign did. …[562]

Casting hasty glances at these features of the place, which were mostly distributed in the darkest end of the cellar, Paul followed his guide to the bench. Stored in racks upon one side were bottles of all sizes and sorts, and in great quantities. Wine bottles by the hundred; London brown stout and pale India ale bottles by the gross; Champagne bottles by the thousand; all empty, bright, and clean. On the other side was a row of hogsheads raised on a little platform, with their faucets all in a line.

---

561 BENAULY [pseud.], *Cone Cut Corners: The Experiences of a Conservative Family in Fanatical Times; involving some account of a Connecticut village, the people who lived in it, and those who came there from the city*, Mason Brothers, New York, [1855].
562 BENAULY [1855], pages 171-172.

"Now," said Mr. Hococks, producing a crumpled memorandum from the gray cap, and smoothing it out upon the rough bench, "we have got a nice order to fill. First we'll take the South Side Madeira – I think. Now Bob, we've got to make up two dozen real old South Side East India. Them's the bottles, that kind – no," said he, with his hand on the rack, suddenly interrupting himself "that ain't the kind. We haven't got one of those English bottles left."

In great apparent consternation the man ran to the foot of the stairs and called for Mr. Floric. That gentleman came to the cellar door, but being of a person not adapted to running up and down stairs as an amusement, he stood there and responded to the call, peering down the stairway, and shouting:

"What's the row?"

"I say, sir," replied Hococks, in a loud under-tone, "we haven't got any of those English Madeira bottles. He wants two dozen, and we haven't got any left; not an individual bottle."

Mr. Floric looked up to see who might be around in a position to listen, and looked down again and said, –

"The devil, Hococks."

Mr. Hococks did not notice the apposition, but continued.

"I sent down to the Drinkwater House yesterday, but they hadn't any empty yet. They're to have a dinner-party tomorrow, and we can have plenty the day after, but that won't do, I suppose. Mr. – um – he's very particular about his bottles."

"Fact!" assented Mr. Floric.

"And if we send up wrong bottles he'll make difficulty."

"Precisely," said Mr. Floric. "Can't you get 'em at Guzzling's Hotel?

"No! they supply Waters & Bungole."

"So they do. So they do," nodded Mr. Floric. "Have you got any paper labels left?"

"Oh, yes, sir," responded Hococks.

"Well, you'll have to use them."

"What bottles?" persisted Mr. Hococks.

"Oh!" cried Mr. Floric, "I have it. Stuccuppe sent down a lot this morning, just the thing; what we sent his last sherry in; they're at the back-door now. They are plain; they'll do for any heavy wine."

"Very good," said Mr. Hococks, in a tone of great relief.

"When you make that up, Hococks," added Mr. Moric, "put in a little more brandy. The last we sent him he thought was not so good a body as he'd been used to. His taste is getting that way. Put in a little more brandy."

In accordance with these instructions, Paul, who began to comprehend the art before him, was set at work to clean the empty bottles sent down from Mr. Stuccuppe's; and he wondered occasionally who it was that was to be accommodated with them next, whose eye for bottles was so sharp, and whose taste for the contents so delicately sensitive.

Mr. Hococks meanwhile calculated, according to the arithmetic of the respectable dealers, that in the usage of trade it would take just one dozen and six quarts to fill two dozen quart bottles. Then he brought forth from under the bench a large tin can which he cleaned by a whiff of his handkerchief, a puff with his breath and a shake with his hands. Placing this under a faucet which stood first and foremost in the long line of faucets, but which was not connected with any hogshead, he laid the foundation for the South Side Madeira, in about five quarts, measured by the eye, of pure, or nearly pure, Croton water. To this he added from a large hogshead, which contained the Madeira of the trade, about a dozen quarts, drawn in a gallon measure, with a little over, thrown in by way of giving himself a margin for tasting. Then he lifted the can upon the bench, and sat down by the side of it to reflect.

It must not be supposed that Mr. Hococks, in meditation, felt any compunctions at having diluted the liquid called Madeira. There was no ground for any such feeling. Rather for satisfaction. For the history of the old South Side of eighteen-twenty, and of East Indian memory, was somewhat as follows.

Not quite two years since, a dirty crew of naked natives, jumping up and down, with songs, in the wine-vats of the south side of the Island of Madeira, crushed with their feet the over-ripe and bursting grapes; and as the juice and pulp squirted from under the soles of their dancing feet, and spirted up between their brown toes, and spattered

Figure 50. A bottle of adulterated "South Side Madeira", inferred from the text. *Article illustration. Author unknown.*

upon their brawny thighs, they sang the louder and danced the faster, until the perspiration, starting in large drops, rolled down their hirsute legs, mingling with spatterings of grape, and was finally rubbed off into the vat by the hands of the retiring laborers; and thus was accomplished, at a very early period, the first dilution of the pure juice of the grape. Thence undergoing many equally pleasant courses of treatment, the final result was strengthened with brandy to enable the same to endure well the voyage, and by an imaginary trip to the East Indies, came quickly to London, and there was entered safely in bond.

Not even here, however, though safe under government care and surveillance, did its history end. For here by virtue of the authority of those convenient ordinances of the British. Government, known as Treasury Order, 20th of May, 1830, Treasury Order, 20th of June, 1830, and other like wholesome regulations, it was mixed again with not over twenty per cent of brandy and with other wines, also Madeira so called, *ad libitum,* then and there also in bond; and thence, having been racked into other casks, was brought into the city of New York, where it appeared by the oath of the respectable dealers, who imported it, (and who subsequently made a profit on it by expanding it into thirteen hogsheads out of a dozen,) that its original and true cost to them was 48½ cents a gallon. Coming from them into the hands of Messrs Bagglehall, Floric & Co., they surely did it no harm in adding what they fairly could to its quantity, since they could not injure its purity.

At any rate, so Mr. Hococks thought, and made no scruples in doing so. His next proceeding was to add a few drops of some pleasant preparations contained in certain phials conveniently kept in a shelf above the bench, the effects of which were supposed to be in every way the same as thirty years of age and a real voyage to the East Indies. Lastly he drew a quart of brandy and proceeded deliberately to work the mixture up to the standard of the customer's taste. When he had arrived so near success as to seem entirely doubtful about it, and had balanced many spoonfuls upon his tongue in long hesitation, he got up and rinsed his mouth thoroughly with cold water. He then returned to his experiments, and, making one more addition, pronounced it as good as it need be.

"But I hate," said he, "to get up these things in a hurry. I ought to have time to it, and let 'em stand, and ripen."

By this time the bottles were ready, and he instructed Paul in which box to find the labels with the right name upon them, and in which box he would find the corks with the same name branded on the end. Then he went up stairs with a wine-glass, opaque with respectable dirt, and filled with the fine old South Side Maderia of 1820 of East Indian experiences, to be tasted and approved by one of the respectable dealers.

In the course of the morning the two dozen bottles were filled, corked, sealed, labeled, and dusted with a highly respectable dust, until they presented that artistic and admirable appearance which was so pleasing to the cultivated eye of Mr. Hococks. When they had been finally arranged in two baskets, they were carried up into daylight; where the old South Side Maderia was presented – as one might almost say – in the original packages of importation, to the critical approving scrutiny of Mr. Floric.

In the counting-room, this commodity was charged to account of the customer who ordered it, at the low price of twenty dollars the dozen; a very insignificant advance upon cost, it must be confessed, when we take into account the skill and care expended by the respectable dealers, to bring it into its present excellent condition – to say nothing of the trouble of getting up foreign corks and labels, at home.

During the day too, a great many bottles of champagne were got up by the simple and ingenious process of aggravating cider into effervescence by sugar of lead, and forcing it, with a cork after it, through a machine into each bottle. Lastly Mr. Hococks, after bringing out a great many demijohns of various sizes, and filling them with various combinations of the contents of hogsheads, phials and water-fancet, checked off the last item on the crumpled memorandum, and said that job was done.

Paul that night was much gratified at receiving the approbation of Mr. Floric, and the patronizing approval of Mr. Hococks; and was still more pleased when the former called him into the counting-room and told him to come again tomorrow. Still as he went home, and as he lay awake that night, he found it very hard to decide whether he should accept a situation in the house of Bagglehall, Floric & Co., Respectable Dealers.[563]

6.2.2. Edgar Allan Poe

Edgar Allan Poe (1809-1849), a native of Boston, MA, distinguished himself in the American literary field because of his tales of mystery and gloomy poetry. However, in 1838, he published anonymously his only novel, entitled *The Narrative of Arthur Gordon Pym of Nantucket*,[564] which was printed both in New York and London. In this

---

[563] BENAULY [1855], pages 178-184.
[564] [POE, Edgar Allan], *The Narrative of Arthur Gordon Pym. Of Nantucket. Comprising the Details of a Mutiny and Atrocious Butchery on Board the American Brig Grampus, on her Way to the South Seas, in the month of June, 1827. With an Account of the Recapture of the Vessel by the Survivers; Their Shipwreck and Subsequent Horrible Sufferings from Famine; Their Deliverance by Means of the British Schooner Jane Guy; The Brief Cruise of this Latter Vessel in the Antarctic Ocean; Her Capture, and the Massacre of her Crew Among a Group of Islands in the Eighty-Fourth Parallel of Southern Latitude;*

work, which relates the incredible tale of the young Arthur Gordon Pym, who stows away aboard the whaling ship *Grampus*, there are two references to Madeira Wine, in two different chapters, the first of which in an indirect form. In the former there is a description of a fateful sea journey of a schooner from Richmond, VA, loaded with corn bound to Madeira (where it would be traded for wine, as was the fashion of the time), and on the latter, during a description of the terrible events that followed the shipwreck of the *Grampus* (butchery and starvation) one of the characters dives for food into the wreckage of the vessel and manages to find a ham and a bottle of Madeira Wine,[565] that saved him and his partners from starvation.

CHAPTER VI.

... When a partial cargo of any kind is taken on board, the whole, after being first stowed as compactly as may be, should be covered with a layer of stout shifting-boards, extending completely across the vessel. Upon these boards strong temporary stanchions should be erected, reaching to the timbers above, and thus securing everything in its place. In cargoes consisting of grain, or any similar matter, additional precautions are requisite. A hold filled entirely with grain upon leaving port will be found not more than three fourths full upon reaching its destination – this, too, although the freight, when measured bushel by bushel by the consignee, will overrun by a vast deal (on account of the swelling of the grain) the quantity consigned. This result is occasioned by *settling* during the voyage, and is the more perceptible in proportion to the roughness of the weather experienced. If grain loosely thrown in a vessel, then, is ever so well secured by shifting-boards and stanchions, it will be liable to shift in a long passage so greatly as to bring about the most distressing calamities. To prevent these, every method should be employed before leaving port to *settle* the cargo as much as possible; and for this there are many contrivances, among which may be mentioned the driving of wedges into the grain. Even after all this is done, and unusual pains taken to secure the shifting-boards, no seaman who knows what he is about will feel altogether secure in a gale of any violence with a cargo of grain on board, and, least of all, with a partial cargo. Yet there are hundreds of our coasting vessels, and, it is likely, many more from the ports of Europe, which sail daily with partial cargoes, even of the most dangerous

Figure 51. Edgar Allan Poe inserted two references to Madeira Wine in the only novel he wrote. *Photograph c. 1850. Author unknown.*

Together with the Incredible Adventures and Discoveries Still Farther South to Which that Distressing Calamity Gave Rise., Harper & Brothers, New-York, 1838.

565 Throughout the 19th century many captains of American whaling ships (mainly from New Bedford and Nantucket, two former whaling ports) used to stop at Madeira Island, following the orders of the owners of the whaling fleets, mostly Quakers, in order to purchase casks of Madeira Wine so that it could travel the world during the two or sometimes three year's long whaling voyage. By the time those ships returned to the United States, the wine would be in a perfectly matured condition and would suit the most exquisite palate. This is the reason why there was Madeira Wine aboard the *Grampus*.

species, and without any precautions whatever. The wonder is that no more accidents occur than do actually happen. A lamentable instance of this heedlessness occurred to my knowledge in the case of Captain Joel Rice of the schooner Firefly, which sailed from Richmond, Virginia, to Madeira, with a cargo of corn, in the year 1825. The captain had gone many voyages without serious accident, although he was in the habit of paying no attention whatever to his stowage, more than to secure it in the ordinary manner. He had never before sailed with a cargo of grain, an on this occasion had the corn thrown on board loosely, when it did not much more than half fill the vessel. For the first portion of the voyage he met with nothing more than light breezes; but when within a day's sail of Madeira there came on a strong gale from the N. N. E. which forced him to lie to. He brought the schooner to the wind under a double-reefed foresail alone, when she rode as well as any vessel could be expected to do, and shipped not a drop of water. Towards night the gale somewhat abated, and she rolled with more unsteadiness than before, but still did very well, until a heavy lurch threw her upon her beam-ends to starboard. The corn was then heard to shift bodily, the force of the movement bursting open the main hatchway. The vessel went down like a shot. This happened within a hail of a small sloop from Madeira, which picked up one of the crew (the only person saved), and which rode out of the gale in perfect security, as indeed a jollyboat might have done under proper management.[566] …

CHAPTER XII.

… Peters now volunteered to go down; and, having made all arrangements as before, he descended, and soon returned, bringing up with him a small jar, which, to our great joy, proved to be full of olives. Having shared these among us, and devoured them with the greatest avidity, we proceeded to let him down again. This time he succeeded beyond our utmost expectations, returning instantly with a large ham and a bottle of Madeira wine. Of the latter we each took a moderate sup, having learned by experience the pernicious consequences of indulging too freely. …[567]

6.2.3. Rev. Frederick William Shelton

Frederick William Shelton (1815-1881), a native of Jamaica, NY, and a New Jersey College graduate, took orders in the Protestant Episcopal Church in 1847. He wrote a few books during his lifetime, one of them being *Peeps from the Belfry, or the Parish Sketch Book*,[568] published New York and London, in 1856. In the first text of this book there is a curious reference to Madeira Wine used for medicinal purposes by Pettibones, a clergyman character, in order to restore his fading strength.

---

566 POE 1838, pages 61-63.
567 POE 1838, page 111.
568 SHELTON, Rev. F.[rederic] W.[illiam], *Peeps from a Belfry*, Dana and Company, New York; Sampson Low, Son and Company, London, 1856.

THE SEVEN SLEEPERS.
A TALE.

... "You want a change of air more. Both for the sake of this parish and for your own –"

"I see it, I see it," said Mr. Pettibones. "You wish to get rid of me, – me who have frequently gone into that church, and built the fires, and tolled the bell, and played the part of an underling – a sexton!" – and he began to cry.

After that, Mr. Evelyn, according to request, arrived at the study, and by his cheerful demeanour did somewhat to dispel the gloomy clouds. He brought with him a bottle of old Madeira wine, of which he advised the desponding rector to take a little, and when that was gone, he had plenty more.

Figure 52. Frederick William Shelton. *19th century illustration. Author unknown.*

Mr. Pettibones shook his head. "It will do no good, Sir. But God forbid that I should discard remedies, that I should slight the kindness of my friends. I will at last try it."

"Do so at once," said Mr. Evelyn.

"No, not now."

"Now –" replied the other.

"Mrs. Pettibones, is there such a thing as a cork-screw in this house? I don't think there is."

"Certainly," replied she; "two of them, my dear."

"Well then, get *it*. Mr. Evelyn has come to hold my hands up."

The cork came out with a pop. "Have we such a thing as a wine-glass, my love? I fear that it is broken. Have we any?"

"Six," said Mrs. Pettibones.

"Very good; then they will not be, as they have been, mere supernumerary pieces of household furniture, thanks to my worthy friend."

"This wine," said the Rector, holding up the glass to the light, after taking a swallow, and when the subtle juice had permeated through all his veins, "reluctant as I am to take it, has the colour, the taste, and the smell of a genuine cordial." He poured it out a second time, and began to sip of it, and he continued to sip of it, and to sip of it. "I say that it is a cordial, whose salutary effects I am thankful to acknowledge in the universal warmth which it diffuses through the corporeal system, driving off those black vapours which have so much troubled me of late, and persuading me that I have true friends remaining, of which you are one – of the most ardent, I dare say. I thank you, Sir, for your cordiality. I trust that I shall not stand in any need of the second bottle, to which you have made affectionate allusion. Do not send it, for if medicine of this kind will be of any service, this will be effectual. It already does me a good deal of good, and acts like a tonic upon the stomach. I may have perhaps needed something of the kind without knowing it. But we are poor ignorant creatur's, and very seldom discover what is for our own advantage – and allowing that we do, have not the means of carrying it out. My friend, give me your hand. In the interest which you have manifested for me by this little gift, and also by your pecuniary token – received at the very moment when, God forgive me, I was about to find fault with the most wide-awake man in this parish – accept my thanks. I ask your counsel. I am grateful to you for coming to lift up my hands."

Mr. Evelyn went away, sent another bottle of Madeira wine, and the next Sunday sat bolt upright in his pew again, and was not numbered among the Seven Sleepers.[569] …

6.2.4. George Little

Figure 53. "The Cruiser off Madeira, by Moonlight." *Book illustration. Author unknown.*

Captain George Little published in New York, in 1846, a novel entitled *The American Cruiser's Own Book*,[570] whose background is the War of 1812, a 32-month military conflict between the United States and the British Empire. One of the main theaters of that war was the sea, where warships and privateers of both nations attacked each other's merchant ships while the British blockaded the Atlantic coast of the United States and mounted large-scale raids in the later stages of the war. The main action of this book takes place aboard an American privateer, simply termed "the Cruiser", on which, at a given moment, after a meal, one can see several toasts being made with Madeira Wine to the success of the voyage, and the effects it had on those who indulged too much in it.

CHAPTER IV.
THE SUPPER.

… The supper being concluded and the cloth removed, the table was soon replenished with bottles of old Madeira, and glasses to each of the company.

"Come, gentlemen," said the first lieutenant, who presided at the table, "fill your glasses." This was quickly done, and he proposed a toast, which was, "Success to the noble Cruiser and her brave commander." This was drank with great satisfaction by all. Several other toasts were then drank, and the wine passed round rapidly, and soon began to make a sensible impression on the company. Some laughed immoderately, while others were discussing with great vehemence the strength and good qualities of the Cruiser. One swore they would make their fortune this cruise, while another conceived himself to be actually boarding a prize; and, indeed, nearly the whole, with the exception of the first lieutenant, lieutenant of the marines, and surgeon, boasted of their valor and prowess.[571] …

---

[569] SHELTON 1856, pages 67-70.
[570] LITTLE, Capt. Geo.[rge], *The American Cruiser's Own Book*, Richard Marsh, New York, [1846]. This book also contains several other references to Madeira Island, where she came to, and was engaged in battle with British ships. This work had other editions, under the same title, in New York, in 1849 and 1851. Entitled *The American Cruiser; or, The Two Messmates. A Tale of the Last War*, it was published in Boston, in 1846, and as *The American Cruiser; a Tale of the Last War*, it was published in the same city in 1847 and 1848.
[571] LITTLE [1846], page 43.

6.2.5. Herman Melville

Herman Melville (1819-1891), a native of New York City, is a well-known name in the American literary world for his masterpiece *Moby Dick*. At a given moment of his life, Melville joined the U.S. Navy and the experience was overwhelming for him. Later on he decided to expose to the public eye the cruel treatment given to low-ranked sailors, in the book entitled *White Jacket; or, The World in a Man-of-War*, first published in London, in 1850.[572] In this publication it is mentioned, among other things, that the *Neversink* – the fictitious name of the ship he traveled in – touched at Madeira Island and loaded a large quantity of Madeira Wine, a fact that was described as normal when American men-of-war arrived at the island, and that some officers loved to drink it, sometimes to excess.

Figure 54. Herman Melville passed by Madeira, while in the Navy, and mentions its wine as being popular among Naval officers. *Etching of Joseph O. Eaton's portrait of this author.*

CHAPTER XXX.
A PEEP THROUGH A PORT-HOLE AT THE SUBTERRANEAN PARTS OF A MAN-OF-WAR.

... After *general quarters*, it was amusing to watch his anxious air as the various *petty officers* restored to him the arms used at the martial exercises of the crew. As successive bundles would be deposited on his counter, he would count over the pistols and cutlasses, like an old housekeeper telling over her silver forks and spoons in a pantry before retiring for the night. And often, with a sort of dark lantern in his hand, he might be seen poking into his furthest vaults and cellars, and counting over his great coils of ropes, as if they were all jolly puncheons of old Port and Madeira.[573] ...

CHAPTER XXXVII.
SOME SUPERIOR OLD "LONDON DOCK" FROM THE WINE-COOLERS OF NEPTUNE.

... It must be related here that, on the passage out from home, the Neversink had touched at Madeira; and there, as is often the case with men-of-war, the Commodore and Captain had laid in a goodly stock of wines for their own private tables, and the benefit of their foreign visitors. And although the Commodore was a small, spare man, who evidently

---

[572] MELVILLE, Herman, *White Jacket; or, The World in a Man-of-War*, Vol. I., Richard Bentley, London, 1850. Until 1851 flogging was a common practice in the U.S. Navy ships and this inhumane punishment was only abolished in that year, as we can see by a newspaper article published by then: «A letter from on board the U.S. ship St. Mary's, at Madeira, Nov. 14th, referring to the fact that that vessel was the first to sail from the United States under the new act abolishing flogging in the Navy, says that, thus far, the sailors have behaved better than under the old law, and that only two or three cases of violation of discipline have been reported to the Captain, since the ship was put in commission.» *The Daily Republican*, January 13, 1851. (Springfield, MA).
[573] MELVILLE 1850, pages 196-197.

emptied but few glasses, yet Captain Claret was a porty gentleman, with a crimson face, whose father had fought at the battle of Brandywine,[574] and whose brother had commanded the well-known frigate named in honour of that engagement. And his whole appearance evinced that Captain Claret himself had fought many Brandywine battles ashore in honour of his sire's memory, and commanded in many bloodless Brandywine actions at sea.

It was therefore with some savour of provocation that the sailors held forth on the ungenerous conduct of Captain Claret, in stepping in between them and Providence, as it were, which by this lucky windfall, they held, seemed bent upon relieving their necessities; while Captain Claret himself, with an inexhaustible cellar, emptied his Madeira decanters at his leisure.[575] ...

CHAPTER XLII.
KILLING TIME IN A MAN-OF-WAR IN HARBOUR.

... One other way of killing time while in port is playing checkers; that is, when it is permitted; for it is not every navy captain who will allow such a scandalous proceeding. But, as for Captain Claret, though he *did* like his glass of Madeira uncommonly well, and was an undoubted descendant from the hero of the Battle of the Brandywine, and though he sometimes showed a suspiciously flushed face when superintending in person the flogging of a sailor for getting intoxicated against his particular orders, yet I will say for Captain Claret that, upon the whole, he was rather indulgent to his crew, so long as they were perfectly docile. ...[576]

6.2.6. James Fenimore Cooper

James Fenimore Cooper (1789-1851), a native of New Jersey, is another American renowned writer, widely known due to his novels *The Pioneers* and *The Last of the Mohicans*. In some of his novels he mentions Madeira Wine more than once. In 1823, he published his fourth novel, entitled *The Pilot, or A Tale of the Sea*, which was a tremendous literary success at the time. The subject of this historical novel is the life of a naval pilot during the American Revolutionary War. Across this book there are twelve references to Madeira Wine, which evidences that this prolific author was well aware of the existence of this treasured product and knew the value of a good "south-side" wine. Below are presented the excerpts of his text with those references, scattered by nine chapters, taken from the 1859 New York edition.[577]

---

[574] American Revolutionary War battle fought between the American army of Major General George Washington and the British army of Sir William Howe, that took place near Chadds Ford, PA, on September 11, 1777, in which the British defeated the Americans.

[575] MELVILLE 1850, pages 242-243.

[576] MELVILLE 1850, page 271.

[577] COOPER, J.[ames] Fenimore, *The Pilot: A Tale of the Sea*, W. A. Townsend and Company, New York, 1859.

CHAPTER IX.

... "Ay, ay, there is some consolation in that thought, in the midst of this dure rebellion of my countrymen. But I'll vex myself no more with the unpleasant recollections; the arms of my sovereign will soon purge that wicked land of the foul stain."

"Of that there can be no doubt," said Borroughcliffe, whose thoughts still continued a little obscured by the sparkling Madeira that had long lain ripening under a Carolinian sun; "these Yankees fly before his majesty's regulars, like so many dirty clowns in a London mob before a charge of the horse-guards."[578] ...

CHAPTER XI.

... "Ah! that may alter the case, Kit; but the ladies must have the respect that is due to their sex. I forgot, somehow, to have myself announced; but that Borroughcliffe leads me deeper into my Madeira than I have been accustomed to go, since the time when my poor brother Harry, with his worthy friend, Hugh Griffith – the devil seize Hugh Griffith, and all his race – your pardon, Miss Alice – what is your business with me, Mr. Dillon?"[579] ...

CHAPTER XIII.

The reader must not imagine that the world stood still during the occurrence of the scenes we have related. By the time the three seamen were placed in as many different rooms, and a sentinel was stationed in the gallery common to them all, in such a manner as to keep an eye on his whole charge at once, the hour had run deep into the night. Captain Borroughcliffe obeyed a summons from the colonel, who made him an evasive apology for the change in their evening's amusement, and challanged his guest to a renewal of the attack on the Madeira. This was too a grateful a theme to be lightly discussed by the captain, and the abbey clock had given forth as many of its mournful remonstrances as the division of the hours would permit, before they separated. ...[580]

CHAPTER XV.

... "I'll not deny it," said Manual,[581] more stoutly; "I have served as a marine for two years, though taken from the line of –"

"The army," said Borroughcliffe, interrupting a most damning confession of which "state line" the other had belonged to. "I kept a dog-watch myself, once, on board the fleet of my Lord Howe; but it is a service that I do not envy any man. Our afternoon parades

---

578 COOPER 1859, pages 109-110.
579 COOPER 1859, pages 130-131.
580 COOPER 1859, page 151.
581 We presume that Captain Manual was a Portuguese character in this novel. If so, the name is wrong for the right spelling is Manuel.

Figure 55. James Fenimore Cooper in his younger days, in Midshipman's naval uniform. He inserted several references to Madeira Wine in his novels. *19th century engraving. Author unknown.*

were dreadfully unsteady, for it's a time, you know, when a man wants solid ground to stand on. However, I purchased my company with some prize money that fell in my way, and I always remember the marine service with gratitude. But this is dry work. I have put a bottle of sparkling Madeira in my pocket, with a couple of glasses, which we will discuss, while we talk over more important matters. Thrust your hand into my right pocket; I have been used to dress to the front so long, that it comes mighty awkward to me to make this backward motion, as if it were into a cartridge box."

Manual, who had been at a loss how to construe the manner of the other, perceived at once a good deal of plain English in this request, and he dislodged one of Col. Howard's dusty bottles, with a dexterity that denoted the earnestness of his purpose. Borroughcliffe had made a suitable provision of glasses, and extracting the cork in a certain scientific manner, he tendered to his companion a bumper of the liquor, before another syllable was uttered by either of the expectants. The gentlemen concluded their draughts with a couple of smacks, that sounded not unlike the pistols of two practised duellists, though certainly a much less alarming noise; when the entertainer renewed the discourse.

"I like one of your musty looking bottles, that is covered with dust and cobwebs, with a good southern tan on it," he said. "Such liquor does not abide in the stomach, but it gets into the heart at once, and becomes blood in the beating of a pulse. But how soon I knew you! That sort of knowledge is the freemasonry of our craft. I knew you to be the man you are, the moment I laid eyes on you in what we call our guard-room; but I thought I would humour the old soldier who lives here, by letting him have the formula of an examination, as a sort of deference to his age and former rank. But I knew you the instant I saw you. I have seen you before!"

The theory of Borroughcliffe, in relation to the incorporation of wine with the blood, might have been true in the case of the marine, whose whole frame appeared to undergo a kind of magical change by the experiment of drinking, which, the reader will understand, was diligently persevered in, while a drop remained in the bottle. The perspiration no longer rolled from his brow, neither did his throat manifest that uneasiness which had rendered such constant external applications necessary; but he settled down into an air of cool, but curious interest, which, in some measure, was the necessary concomitant of his situation. ...

"En avant! in plain English, forward march! Well, then, the difficulty lies between women and wine; which, when the former are pretty, and the latter rich, is a very agreeable sort of an alternative. That it is not wine of which you are in quest, I must believe, my comrade captain, or you would not go on the adventure in such shabby attire. You will excuse me, but who would think of putting anything better than their Port before a man in a pair of tarred trowsers? No! no! Hollands, green-and-yellow Hollands, is a potation good enough to set before one of the present bearing."

"And yet I have met with him who has treated me to the choicest of the south-side Madeira!"

"Know you the very side from which the precious fluid comes! That looks more in favour of the wine. But, after all, woman, dear, capricious woman, who one moment fancies she sees a hero in regimentals, and the next a saint in a cassock; and who always sees something admirable in a suitor, whether he be clad in tow or velvet – woman is at the bottom of this mysterious masquerading. Am I right, comrade?"... [582]

CHAPTER XVI.

... "Court-yard! light dragoons!" repeated Borroughcliffe, in amazement; "and has it come to this, that twenty stout fellows of the –th are not enough to guard such a rookery as this old Abbey, against the ghosts and north-east storms, but we must have horse to reinforce us. Hum! I suppose some of these booted gentlemen have heard of this South-Carolina Madeira."
"Oh, no, sir!" cried his man, "it is only the party that Mr. Dillon went to seek last evening, after you saw fit, sir, to put the three pirates in irons." ...
"The amphibious dog! he was a soldier, but a traitor and an enemy. No doubt he will have a marvellous satisfaction in delighting the rebellious ears of his messmates, by rehearsing the manner in which he poured cold water down the back of one Borroughcliffe, of the –th, who was amusing him, at the same time, by pouring good, rich, south-side Madeira down his own rebellious throat. I have a good mind to exchange my scarlet coat for a blue jacket, on purpose to meet the sly rascal on the other element, where we can discuss the matter over again. Well, sergeant, do you find the other two?"[583] ...

CHAPTER XXV.

... "Come, Cecilia," she cried, after a pause of a moment, "we trespass too long on the patience of the gentlemen; not only to keep possession of our seats, ten minutes after the cloth has been drawn! but even to introduce our essences, and tapes, and needles, among the Madeira, and – shall I add, segars, colonel?"[584] ...

CHAPTER XXVIII.

... "I honour your logic, sir. Your premises are indisputable, and the conclusion most obvious. Commit, then, those worthy tars to the good keeping of honest Drill, who will see their famished natures revived by divers eatables, and a due proportion of suitable fluids; while we can discuss the manner in which you are to return to the colonies, around a bottle of liquor, which my friend Manual[585] there, assures me has come from the sunny side of the island of Madeira, to be drunk in a bleak corner of that of Britain. By my palate! but the rascals brighten at the thought. They know by instinct, sir, that a shipwrecked

---
582 COOPER 1859, pages 179-181, 183-184.
583 COOPER 1859, pages 192, 201-202.
584 COOPER 1859, page 345.
585 See Note 581.

mariner is a fitter companion to a ration of beef and a pot of porter, that to such unsightly things as bayonets and boarding-pikes!"[586] ...

CHAPTER XXX.

... "He is no more than a common Pilot after all! No true gentleman would have received so palpable a hint with such a start. Ah! here comes the party of my worthy friend whose palate knows a grape of the north side of Madeira from one of the south. The dog has the throat of a gentleman! we will see how he can swallow a delicate allusion to his faults!"[587] ...

CHAPTER XXXIV.

... All liquids in which malt formed an ingredient, as well as the deep-coloured wines of Oporto, were suffered to enter the Gulf of St. Lawrence, and were made to find their way, under the superintendence of Borroughcliffe, to their destined goal; but Manual[588] was, solely, entrusted with the more important duty of providing the generous liquor of Madeira, without any other restriction on his judgement, than an occasional injunction from his coadjutor, that it should not fail to be the product of the "South-side!" ...

About a year before this melancholy event, a quarter cask of wine had been duly ordered from the South side of the island of Madeira, which was, at the death of Manual, toiling its weary way up the rapids of the Mississippi and the Ohio, having been made to enter by the port of New-Orleans, with the intention of keeping it as long as possible under a genial sun! The untimely fate of his friend imposed on Borroughcliffe the necessity of attending to this precious relick of their mutual tastes; and he procured a leave of absence from his superior, with the laudable desire to proceed down the streams and superintend its farther advance in person. The result of his zeal was a high fever, that set in the day after he reached his treasure, and as the doctor and the major espoused different theories, in treating a disorder so dangerous in that climate; the one advising abstemiousness, and the other ad ministering repeated draughts of the cordial that had drawn him so far from home, the disease was left to act its pleasure. Borroughcliffe died in three days; and was carried back and interred by the side of his friend, in the very hut which had so often resounded with their humours and festivities! ...[589]

In 1824, James Fenimore Cooper published the book entitled *The Spy: A Tale of the Neutral Ground*,[590] in which there are also several references to toasts made with Madeira Wine, in two of its chapters.

---

[586] COOPER 1859, page 380.
[587] COOPER 1859, page 422.
[588] See Note 581.
[589] COOPER 1859, pages 481-483.
[590] COOPER, James Fenimore, *The Spy: A Tale of the Neutral Ground*, In Two Volumes, Vol. I., Fourth Edition, Charles Wiley, New-York, 1824.

CHAPTER I.

… After handing a glass of excellent Madeira to his guest, Mr. Wharton, for so was the owner of this retired estate called, resumed his seat by the fire, with another in his own hand. For a moment he paused, as if debating with his politeness, but at length threw an enquiring glance on the stranger, as he enquired –

"To whose health am I to have the honour of drinking?"

The traveller had also seated himself, and he sat unconsciously gazing on the fire, while Mr. Wharton spoke; turning his eyes slowly on his host with a look of close observation, he replied, while a faint tinge gathered on his features –

"Mr. Harper."

"Mr. Harper," resumed the other with the formal precision of that day, "I have the honour to drink your health, and to hope you will sustain no injury from the rain to which you have been exposed."

Mr. Harper bowed in silence to the compliment, and he soon resumed the meditations from which he had been interrupted, and for which the long ride he had that day made, in the wind, might seem a very natural apology.[591] …

CHAPTER XIII.

… Next came drinking with the ladies; but as the wine was excellent, and the glass ample, the trooper bore this interruption with consummate good-nature. Nay, so fearful was he of giving offence, and of omitting many of the nicer points of punctilio, that having commenced this courtesy with the lady who sat next him, he persevered until not one of his fair companions could, with justice, reproach him with partiality in this particular.

Long abstemiousness from anything like generous wine might plead the excuse of Captain Lawton, especially when exposed to so strong a temptation as that now before him. Mr. Wharton had been one of a set of politicians in New York, whose principal exploits before the war had been to assemble, and pass sage opinions on the signs of the times, under the inspiration of certain liquor made from a grape that grew on the south side of the island of Madeira, and which found its way into the colonies of North America through the medium of the West Indies, sojourning awhile in the Western Archipelago, by way of providing the virtues of the climate. A large supply of this cordial had been drawn from his storehouse in the city, and some of it now sparkled in a bottle before the Captain, blushing in the rays of the sun, which were passing obliquely through it, like amber. …

Mr. Wharton poured out a glass of wine for the lady who sat on his right hand, and pushing the bottle to a guest, said, with a low bow –

"We are honoured with a toast from Miss Singleton."

Although there was nothing more in this movement than occurred every day on such occasions, yet the lady trembled, coloured, and grew pale again, seemingly endeavouring to rally her thoughts, until, by her agitation, she had excited the interest of the whole party;

---

591 COOPER 1824, page 7.

when, by an effort, and in a manner as if she had strived in vain to think of another, Isabella said faintly –

"Major Dunwoodle."

The health was drunk cheerfully by all but Colonel Wellmere, who wet his lips, and drew figures on the table with some of the liquor he had spilt.[592]...

Another novel by James Fenimore Cooper with several references to Madeira Wine is the one entitled *Satanstoe; or, The Littlepage Manuscripts. A Tale of the Colony*,[593] published in 1845. The plot of this book is set in Colonial America, a time when this nectar of the gods was highly cherished. In four of its chapters there are allusions to this product, and the most significant of which might be the last one, which refers to an old Dutch tradition in New York associated with Madeira wine, as we had already seen in the first chapter of this anthology.

CHAPTER I.

... My grandfather met an old fellow-campaigner, at Boston, of the name of Hight, Major Hight, as he was called, who had come to see the preparations, too; and the old soldiers passed most of the time together. The Major was a Jerseyman, and had been somewhat of a free-liver in his time, retaining some of the propensities of his youth in old age, as is apt to be the case with those who cultivate a vice as if it were a hot-house plant. The Major was fond of his bottle, drinking heavily of Madeira, of which there was then a good stock in Boston, for he brought some on himself; and I can remember various scenes that occurred between him and my grandfather, after dinner, as they sat discoursing in the tavern on the progress of things, and the prospects for the future. ...[594]

CHAPTER XI.

... "As to the two that are not here, I cannot positively answer; yonder, however, is one that can speak for himself."

"I see him, Mr. Littlepage, and will answer for *him*, on my own account. Depent on it, *he* will come, But the Dominie – he has a hearty look, and can help eat a turkey and swallow a glass of good Madeira – I think I can rely on. A man cannot take all that active exercise without food."[595] ...

---

592 COOPER 1824, 204-206.
593 COOPER, James Fenimore, *Satanstoe; or, The Littlepage Manuscripts. A Tale of the Colony.*, In Two Volumes, Vol. I., Burgess, Stringer & Co., New York, 1845, page 19.
594 COOPER 1845, page 19.
595 COOPER 1845, page 164.

CHAPTER XIII.

… "Come, cousin Guert," cried Mr. Mayor, after two of three glasses of Madeira had still further warmed his heart, "fill, and pledge me – unless you prefer to give a lady. If the last, everybody will drink to her, with hearty good-will. You eat nothing, and must drink the more."

"Ah! Mr. Mayor, I have toasted one lady, to-night, and cannot toast another."[596] …

CHAPTER XV.

… It is needless to dwell on the melancholy procession we formed through the woods. Dirck and myself kept near the body, on foot, until we reached the highway, when vehicles were provided for the common transportation. On reaching Albany, we delivered the remains of Guert to his relatives, and there was a suitable funeral given. The bricked closet behind the chimney, was opened, as usual, and the six dozen of Madeira, that had been placed in it twenty-four years before, or the day the poor fellow was christened, was found to be very excellent. I remember it was said generally, that better wine was drunk at the funeral of Guert Ten Eyck, than had been tasted at the obsequies of any individual who was not a Van Rensellaer, a Schuyler, or a Ten Broeck, within the memory of man. I now speak of funerals in Albany; for I do suppose the remark would scarcely apply to many other funerals, lower down the river. As a rule, however, very good wine was given at all our funerals.[597] …

Another book by Cooper that contains a reference to Madeira Wine is *The Redskins; or, Indian and Injin: being the conclusion of the Littlepage Manuscripts*,[598] whose first edition was published in 1846.

CHAPTER I.

… "Come, let us take a glass of wine together, in the good old York fashion, Hugh. Your father and I, when boys, never thought of wetting our lips with the half-glass of Madeira that fell to our share, without saying, 'Good health, Mall! 'Good health, Hodge!'"

"With all my heart, uncle Ro. The custom was getting to be a little obsolete even before I left home; but it is almost an American custom, by sticking to us longer than to most people."

"Henri!"

This was my uncle's *maître d'hotel*, whom he had kept at board-wages the whole time of our absence, in order to make sure of his ease, quiet, taste, skill, and honesty, on his return.

"Monsieur!"

"I dare say" – my uncle spoke French exceedingly well for a foreigner; but it is better to

---

[596] COOPER 1845, pages 196-197.
[597] COOPER 1845, page 215.
[598] COOPER, James Fenimore, *Redskins; or, Indian and Injin: being the conclusion of the Littlepage Manuscripts*, In Two Volumes, Vol. I., Burgess & Stringer, New York, 1846.

translate what he said as we go – "I dare say this glass of *vin de Bourgogne* is very good; it *looks* good, and it came from a wine-merchant on whom I can rely; but Monsieur Hugh and I are going to drink together, *à l'Américaine*, and I dare say you will let us have a glass of Madeira, though it is somewhat late in the dinner to take it."

"Très volontiers, Messieurs – it is my happiness to oblige you."

Uncle Ro and I took the Madeira together; but I cannot say much in favor of its quality.[599] …

6.2.7. James Kirke Paulding

James Kirke Paulding (1778-1860), a native of New York, and 11th United States Secretary of the Navy wrote at least two books in which he mentions Madeira wine. The first one is the novel *Westward ho!: A Tale*,[600] published in 1832, in which it can be seen that the wealthy people of Virginia kept old wine, and also alludes to the American tradition of discussing the age of the Madeiras.

CHAPTER II.
A genuine Tuckahoe.

… Never were the people so rich with so little money. Plenty, nay, profusion, reigned all around them; yet many lived, as it were, by anticipation. They were almost always beforehand with their means, and the crops of the ensuing year were for the most part mortgaged to supply the demand of the present. They feared nothing but a bad season for tobacco, a deed of trust, and a Scotch merchant. They were a high-spirited race, among the best specimens of aristocracy in modern times; but they have almost all disappeared from their ancient possessions. Industry and economy, when not counteracted by laws and institutions to prevent their otherwise inevitable result, will always, sooner or later, effect a transfer of property from the rich to the poor. Here and there, however, one of these ancient lords of the soil still maintains his stage along the shores of James River;[601] and we have yet on our palates the relish of some of the sacred relics of the old Madeira which is still dispensed with open hand at their hospitable boards.[602] …

CHAPTER V.
Showing that a Gentleman will understand his affairs the better for a little Arithmetic.

… As the winter was now at hand, it was settled that Colonel Dangerfield should remain where he was until spring; and after discussing a bottle of Madeira from a vintage which I believe preceded the discovery of that island, Mactabb departed for his residence in the city of Richmond, the abode of hospitable men and bonny lasses. …[603]

---

[599] COOPER 1846, page 14.
[600] PAULDING, James Kirke, *Westward ho!: A Tale.*, In Two Volumes, Vol. I., J. & J. Harper, New York, 1832.
[601] A 348-miles long river in the state of Virginia.
[602] PAULDING 1832, pages 12-13.
[603] PAULDING, 1832, page 48.

The other work by James Kirke Paulding is *The New Mirror for Travellers; and Guide to the Springs*,[604] a guide book for foreign travellers in America, published in 1828, where there is an important reference to Madeira Wine, namely the expertise of some old *connoisseur* who had the ability of naming six different types of Madeira wine with his eyes shut.

… Besides these attractions and ten thousand more, New York abounds beyond all other places in the universe, not excepting Paris, in consummate institutions for cultivating the noble science of gastronomy. The soul of Heliogababus[605] presides in the kitchens of our hotels and boarding houses, and inspires the genius of a thousand cooks – not sent by the d–l,[606] as the old proverb infamously asserts, but by some special dispensation. … The sea green lobster of the Sound, best loved of southern invalids, a supper of whom is a sovereign cure for dyspepsia; three luscious soft crab, the discovery of whose inimitable excellence has made the city of Baltimore immortal; cat fish and flounder, slippery eel and rough shelled muscle; elephant clam, which the mischievous boys of the Sound call by a more inglorious name; – we invoke ye all! And if we forget thee, O most puissant and imperial oyster, whether of Blue Point, York River, Chingoteague or Chingarora, may our palate forget its cunning, and lose the best gift of heaven – the faculty of distinguishing between six different Madeira wines, with our eyes shut! All these and more may be seen of a morning at Fulton and Washington Markets, and the traveller, who shall go away without visiting them, has travelled in vain. …

COLONEL CULPEPER TO MAJOR BRANDE

New York, May 6, 1827

DEAR MAJOR, – I have been so occupied of late in seeing sights, eating huge dinners, and going to evening parties to matronize Lucia, that I had no time to write to you. The people here are very hospitable, though not exactly after the manner of the high hills of Santee.[607] They give you a great dinner or evening party, and then, as the sage Master Stephen Griffen is pleased to observe, "let you run." These dinners seem to be in the nature of a spasmodic effort, which exhausts the purse or the hospitality of the entertainer, an is followed by a collapse of retrenchment. You recollect –, who staid at my house, during a fit of illness, for six weeks, the year before last. He has a fine house, the inside of which looks like an upholsterer's shop, and lives in style. He gave me an invitation to dinner, at a fortnight's notice, where I ate out of a set of China, my lady assured me cost seven hundred dollars, and drank out of glasses that cost a guinea a piece. In short, there was nothing on the table of which I did not learn the value, most especially the wine, some of which mine entertainer gave the company his word of honour, stood him in eight dollars

---

604 [PAULDING, James Kirke], *The New Mirror for Travellers; and Guide to the Springs.*, By an Amateur., G. & C. Carvill, New York, 1828.
605 We presume the author meant to refer to Heliogabalus or Elagabalus (c.203-222), the 25th Emperor of the Roman Empire, serving from 218 to 222, who is famous for his life of extreme eccentricity, decadence and zealotry.
606 Abbreviation for devil.
607 Town in Orangeburg County, along the Santee River Valley, in Central South Carolina.

a bottle, besides the interest, and was half a century old. I observed very gravely, that it bore its age so remarkably well, that I really took it to be in the full vigour of youth. Upon which all the company set me down as a bore.

In place of the pleasant chit-chat and honest jollity of better wines, there was nothing talked of but the quality of the gentleman's wines, which I observed were estimated entirely by their age and prices. One boasted of his Bingham, another of his Marston; a third of his Nabob, and a fourth of his Billy Ludlow. All this was Greek to me, who was obliged to sit stupidly silent, having neither Bingham, nor Marston, nor Nabob, nor Billy Ludlow: for the fact is, as you very well know, my wines goes so fast, it has no tim to grow old.

But there was one pursy, pompous little man at table, a foreigner, I think, who my lady whispered me was worth a million and a half of dollars, who beat the others all hollow. He actually had in his garret a dozen of wine seventy years old, last grass, that had been in his family fifty years – which by the way, as a sly neighbour on my right assured me, was farther back than he could carry his own pedigree. This seemed to raise him high above all competition, and gave great effect to several of the very worst jokes I ever heard. It occurred to me, however, that his friends had been little the better for the wine thus hoarded to brag about. For my part, I never yet met a real honest, liberal, hospitable fellow that had much old wine. Occasionally the conversation varied into discussions as to who was the best judge of wine, and there was a serious contest about a bottle of Bingham and a bottle of Marston, which I was afraid would end in a duel. All, however, bowed to the supremacy of one particular old gentleman, who made a bet that he would shut his eyes, hold his nose, and distinguish between six different kinds of Madeira. I did not think much of this, as a man don't drink wine either with his eyes or nose; but politely expressed my wonder, and smacked my lips, and cried, "Ah!" in unison with this Winckelman[608] of wine bibbers, like a veritable connoisseur.[609] …

6.2.8. John Neal

John Neal (1793-1876), a native of Portland, Maine, published in 1830 a novel entitled *Authorship: A Tale*,[610] in which there are five references to Madeira Wine, in two of its chapters. On the first we can see "a dozen of Madeira" being used for a bet – a common thing in 19th century America – and in the other one there is an interesting story around some old Boston Madeira, that in the old days used to be imported by the pipe.

CHAPTER XX.
THE GAMBLERS.

…You have won – double or quits on the other card sir George, if you –
Done –
Ah, but you didn't hear me through, Sir George!

---

608 Allusion to Johann Joachim Winkelmann (1717-1768), a German art historian and archeologist, who was an ascetic aesthete by nature, and lived simply on bread and wine.
609 [PAULDING] 1828, pages 11-13, 25-27.
610 NEAL, John, *Authorship: A Tale*, Gray and Bowen, Boston, 1830, page 228.

Ha ha ha! that reminds me of a bet I heard in your country, said Sir George, addressing himself to me. A dispute occurred between two people where I was. After it had continued a good while, one of the two struck his hands together and offered a bet in the usual way there –

A beaver-hat, I suppose –

No, a dozen of madeira; but before the words were well out of his mouth, he was taken up; I'll bet you a-a-very deliberately-said one of the two, a dozen of Madei-Done! said another with a snap – Ah, but you did not take me up quick enough! replied the first.[611] ...

CHAPTER XXI.
THE WINE-CRITIC... THE PLAY... THE ARREST.

... Allow me, said Sir George, before the laugh had subsided, allow me sir, attempting to fill my glass, which I withdrew, while another of the party pushed a pack of cards up to my elbow, praying me with a very careless air, to cut for the deal –

Excuse me, said I –

Ah – you don't play?

No sir, I'd rather not.

Well well, said Sir George; do as you like about play; but being here, you'll not refuse to tap another bottle of champaign for us, I hope?

Indeed Sir George, I had rather not, I assure you. The glass you gave me is very deep and large, and after the madeira we have drunk, the best madeira I ever saw in my life, by the way –

Figure 56. John Neal alludes to Madeira Wine in one of his books. *19th century engraving. Author unknown.*

Tut man, tut! our madeira is not to be compared with your Boston madeira. Every body knows that –

Why to be sure, I have heard the Boston madeira praised by two or three of the best judges of wine that I ever met with in this country –

Are you a judge of wine – ?

I – no indeed; I hardly know madeira from sherry; and when I praised the wine we had to day, I praised it for madeira, because to tell you the truth I saw that name on the collar of a large decanter that stood near me before the cloth was removed – I tasted no other; and for all that I know, it may have been sherry or any other white wine.

Sir George bit his lip, one of the party cried bravo! bravo! and interchanged a look with Edwards who colored to the eyes, and for a minute or two appeared to be heartily ashamed of me; but the tall grave stranger with the scar in his cheek, thought otherwise of my behaviour.

Young man, said he, it requires no little courage to tell the truth in your case.

I thought so, for the words were hardly out of my mouth before I begun to feel as if I had betrayed myself in a very foolish way.

---

611 NEAL 1830, page 228.

Very true, said Sir George, very true – I do not know another man, who would dare to say that he does not know madeira from sherry; I would rather acknowledge of the two, that I do not love music.

The stranger withdrew his quiet stern eye from Edwards, and looked at Sir George without speaking a word; but I observed that Sir George grew uneasy – more uneasy than he had been while the bets were at issue, and that he took an early opportunity of whispering to Edwards, after which a sort of combined attack was made on the stranger, evidently with a view to overcome his reserve.

Very true, as you say sir, very true, continued Sir George thrusting a handful of bank-notes into his pocket, and preparing to deal as if nothing had happened – very true – So with music, so with wine, so with a multitude of things which to be ignorant of or not to like, is to be a – I beg your pardon sir; I have heard Charley-over-the-water called for by twenty voices at a time, years and years ago, when I was a young fellow; and I have been told, on asking the reason, that a particular lady present was particularly remarkable for that particular song; so I have gone up to the lady, whom I happened to know, and persuaded her to sing. The moonlight on the tufted bank, or some other pitiful affair which is never heard of now – and the whole company have been delighted with it – some declaring they were very fond of Charley-over-the-water – and others that they had never heard it half so well sung before.

I laughed heartily, and so did the major; but Edwards appeared to be lost in thought, and the stranger sat with his eye on the door, as if he expected somebody else to join the party. Meanwhile the bank-notes covered the table, and heaps of gold were passing from hand to hand with a rapidity that I never saw equalled, and with a sort of high-bred indifference which gave me the head-ache.

But speaking of your Boston madeira, said Sir George, addressing himself to me. That reminds me of a circumstance which occurred full three-and-thirty, four-and-thirty, five-and-thirty years ago, at a table in Boston. That's your sort major – pam be civil! –

Very true sir, what you said – very true – addressing the stranger – dare say you have seen a bottle of wine produced at a table sir, covered with cobwebs, decanted as if it was the elixir of life, into little glass acorn-cups, and swallowed with affected enthusiasm by grown men, who if they could have had their own way, would rather have swallowed so much cider, if not so much physic.

The stranger knitted his brow, and I began to feel rather uncomfortable for Sir George; but he proceeded with his play and his story at the same time, as if he neither knew nor cared to know what the stranger thought of him.

While I was there said he, a young chap from the city arrived with a cargo of Manchester goods to a merchant of Boston. I was invited to meet my countryman, who probably did not know that he was going to dine with perhaps the most extraordinary humorist of the age, a man of great wealth, who was a prodigal and a miser at the same time. It appeared – ah you are in luck my dear Barry, I thought my hand a sure one a minute ago – the youth had been laughing at your Yankee wines, I heard; they were not strong enough, they lacked body – they hadn't so much flavor as the Thames water, which you know is remarkable for a sort of champaign spirit, peculiar to itself – our sailors, God bless 'em! when they talk of the briskness of our Thames water have no idea of the cause of that briskness –

No, faith! – you may swear to that Sir George.

Well, there were six or eight of us. Now said Mr. G. – our worthy host – we had been sipping a variety of liquors and four or five sorts of wine, which I thought very well of, though my countryman looked as if he had never tasted such wine before –

He never had, I dare say –

– Now gentlemen said our host, I am going to fetch you a drop or two a little out of the common way; you are to be the judges – I say nothing. He left us, and there was a deal of whispering and chuckling and rubbing of hands till he came back; for he was reckoned the best judge of wines, and by far the most liberal provider of the day in America, never permitting a bottle of port – which by the way was not much drunk with you, when I was there –

– No – nor is it now – we prefer madeira; and white wines are preferred all over the country.

– To stand up or to be decanted, nor a guest to take hold of a bottle under any pretence, otherwise than by the neck – ah my dear Barry you are playing a desperate game.

Curse the cards!

Pho pho – never curse the cards; play off and fight shy, if they don't run as you wish; you are up like a bottle of soda-water just now – well sir, he came back with a set of clean glasses which he wouldn't suffer the *help* to carry.

We never say help Sir George, in the cities of America, nor in the large towns, nor any where indeed except in a small part of the back country.

I dare say not—with a bow. They were very small glasses, and richly ornamented. He put them upon the table with his own hands, wiped off the cobwebs from the bottle, drew the cork as if he were drawing a tooth, and went around with it on tip-toe, pouring a little into every glass in succession without filling any, and then going round again, till he had divided the contents of the bottle in such a way that no man appeared to have a single drop more than his neighbour. There gentlemen said he, when he had finished – there my young friend! lifting his glass with compressed lips and watching the look of my countryman – steady – steady! Full-length, cried one of the party; ay ay, full length! cried another, and up we all rose to swallow the wine. There, gentlemen, said Mr. G., I want to know your real opinion of that 'ere stuff. We looked at each other all round – we sipped a little of the sunshine, as we called it – we smacked our lips – and then we replaced our glasses very cautiously, without venturing to say a word – all eyes were upon my countryman, whose countenance was particularly solemn and thoughtful. But he did not appear inclined to speak, any more than the rest of us; and stood looking sideways at the glass before him, with a sort of expression which might be interpreted either way, as the result should require. At last however he spoke, and vowed to Gad the stuff was pure, and worthy of a duke's table. We agreed with him, smacked our lips again, protested he was right, and swore it was a mouthful worthy of a prince's table – a king's – an emperor's – liquid amber to say the least of it. And what may that wine have stood you in? said a rich na-tyve, with a sober calculating brow. No answer. How long have you had it by you? said another. We thought of the dust and cobwebs, and we smacked our lips again more heartily than before; but our host would not answer the question. It must have been a great while in the cork, said another: how long pray; do tell us; we have a curiosity to know. Guess. Did bottle it yourself? No. Ah ha! so I thought – before your time I'd swear – putting the glass to his lips with great fervor – so I thought; heard o' this 'afore: but may be you'll have no objection to say how it stood you in by the pipe. By the pipe! said Mr. G. By the pipe – no by the gallon, said the other. By the gallon sir! By the dozen I should say – beg your pardon. By the dozen! said Mr. G. – with a look which made the other throw up his hands and cry, Good God! you did not lay it in by the bottle! No –. But your father before you did; I see how it is, ah ha! Never mind who laid it in, but say what you think such wine ought to be worth now in the bottle. Why, – say about – a – a – very cautiously; eyeing Mr. G. between every two syllables – a-a-about-twelve-dollars-a-doz-en, hey? What; interest and all – bottles and all! said Mr. G. Interest! why to be sure – said the other, why to be sure, that ought to be considered; no, no – glancing at our host and then at my countryman, who sat as if he were the foreman of a jury in a matter of life and death – no, no – I did not mean interest and all; no no, interest and all indeed! excuse me. I began to feel a very uncomfortable awe upon me when I heard this, and saw a merchant of high standing, and upwards of fifty years of age, gravely calculating the interest on a small bottle of wine; I felt as if I were doing what was hardly justifiable, in partaking of so precious a liquor. Say fifteen dollars a dozen, said another, touching the glass to his lips – or sixteen, or sixteen-fifty, interest and all, which would be one twenty-five, one thirty-three-and-a-third a bottle, or one thirty-seven-and-a-half – sipping a little before every bid – interest and all. More – more! cried another, who after looking at our host, threw his head back, and shut his eyes, with an air of perplexity, and sat with his lips moving as if he were saying over the multiplication-table to himself. Ah – but I meant hard money, neighbour; sixteen dollars and fifty cents hard money; why bless your heart, only consider! one dollar and thirty-seven-cents-and-a-half – cash – ah, but you didn't say cash – cash – for a bottle of wine, why it's out of all reason! Very true, retorted the other; and so, I say two dollars a bottle; two-fifty cried another; two-seventy five, two-eighty! and a full stop. No, said our host, no! You are wide o' the mark yet; you have no idea of the actual cost o' that 'ere wine I see; you surely haven't smacked the flavor; try it again, my lads, try it again; a little o' that 'll make you fat, as the song says, all round the body O! Nantucket for ever, cried a sly old codger; what stuff it is man; say three dollars a bottle! No – said our host very positively, no! Four? – No! Five – six – seven – eight? – up went all the glasses together – no – no – no, said our host, and we felt as if every drop was a jewel. Another dead stop. – Fluid gold, as I'm a sinner, cried the youngest man at the table – eight-fifty, eight seventy-five. But still our host answered no. The company were all struck dumb. Wine had been sold – we knew that – for ten dollars a bottle in Boston; but that was at a time of great political excitement, and under very particular circumstances. And though the purchaser bought only five or six dozen, he had a supply years and years afterward.

No one dared to guess again. There was a deep dead silence – dead as that of a New-England meeting-house in the middle of a warm summer-afternoon. We looked at each other – at the wine – at our host – and then we dropped our eyes one after another, as if we had been guilty of some unpardonable sin. What had we to do with the precious ointment; what right had we to be drinking wine more costly than that in which Cleopatra dissolved the pearl –

That was vinegar, Sir George.

– And how could we drink it off with so little emotion. It was a thing never to be forgotten or forgiven. Why sir, to tell you the truth, even I – I cannot deny it – even I had begun to look upon the rich Mr. G. with singular veneration; to wonder now that he had been so prodigal, with his one little parsimonious, niggardly bottle – bottle, it wasn't a bottle! it was nothing more than a large phial; I began to reproach him for having dealt out the sunshine – the fluid gold – the liquid amber – so munificently, in the vast acorn-cups. Our glasses were nearly or quite empty; mine had been so for some time – there was only a lurking drop at the bottom, the usual-thumb-nail offering, which had been concocted from the rich exhalation of the glass, while we were engaged in estimating the total value of the treasure. I lifted the glass. I turned it up and held the edge upon the tip of my tongue, till that one thick drop had slowly trickled out – O, the flavor and fragrance of that one drop! I had never tasted the virtue of the liquid before; and while I looked about me upon the more experienced wine-bibbers, and saw their glasses not more than half exhausted, I felt ashamed of my unskilful voracity. They were voluptuaries – I a sensualist. But I was younger than they; and there was still hope for me I thought, if I should ever fall in the way of such another drop of wine while I breathed –

Here the stranger drew forth his watch, and keeping his eye upon the door, appeared to be getting very impatient. I observed him, but I did not believe that any body else did, so engaged were the whole party between the play, and the story of Sir George, who continued as follows.

I was the first to speak after the last no of Mr. G. had been articulated – the first to get my breath I believe. Now pray sir, said I, pray do tell us – I stopped, I began to fear that I was going too far, and the company sat with their heads advanced and their mouths all open, as if they were so many purchasers in a lottery, the high-prize of which would appear at the first word spoken by Mr. G. – how much did that wine cost you, interest and all, as near as you can tell? Why, said he, after a long pause, – it would be very difficult, perhaps impossible to say exactly – time – interest – compound-interest, labor, storage, leakage, breakage, agency, &c, &c, &c, but – but – as near as I am able to say – we all pressed forward, and my poor countryman gasped for breath – and I have taken some pains I promise you to arrive at the truth, knowing what sort of men were to drink it – we all bowed, my countryman lower than any body else – to arrive at the truth, and as near as I am able to say – another pause and another long breath from the whole company – and I assure you that I made the calculation myself not three hours ago, it cannot be far from twelve-and-a-half, or perhaps twelve and three-quarters – Why how you talk, Mr. G., twelve dollars and three quarters for a bottle of wine! why you ought to be, what they say you are, the richest man in America. – No sir, said Mr. G.; No sir, you are rather too lively. I did not say, nor mean to say, twelve and three-quarter *dollars* – but twelve and three-quarter *cents*.

Bravo! Sir George, bravo! bravo! cried the major, just as the door opened, and a short, square-shouldered, vulgar looking man stepped into the room and took a remote position which allowed him to reconnoitre the whole company. The moment the tall stranger saw him, his eye lighted up, and fell upon Edwards with a look which made me shiver – it was but a momentary glance, but coupling it with what followed, I am sure I never shall forget the expression, till my dying day.

Well, how do you think we behaved, how do you think we felt, continued Sir George. Mr. G. had told us nothing but the truth. It was a wine that he had picked up for little or nothing, nobody knows where, and bottled off in old weather-worn, crooked bottles, covered with dust and cobwebs. It was a good lesson to me sir – beginning to shuffle the cards, for a new deal – I have never forgotten it – I never shall forget it – there is not a day, nor an hour, in which the moral of that lesson may not be applied, one – two – three, to the every-day transactions of life, one – two – three – No sir! the value of every thing now is to be estimated by the cost in –

Here the fellow who had just entered the room drew nearer to the party, and appeared anxious to catch the eye of some one at the table –

– By the cost in pounds, shillings, and pence – a laugh, and he continued with a burlesque air of gravity – In a word sir, the prodigal and the spendthrift are followed, and the worthy are despised now –[612] …

6.2.9. John Richter Jones

Colonel John Richter Jones (1803-1863), a native of New Jersey, was killed in action during the Civil War. Three years after his death was published his book *The Quaker Soldier; or, The British in Philadelphia. A Romance of the Revolution*,[613] in which there are three references to Madeira Wine, in two chapters. In both of them can be seen some British officers toasting with Madeira, and in the second one there is an interesting comparison of it to their Port, and a character even states that this wine should be introduced at their home, i. e., in England. (This confirms the fact that Madeira Wine was widely consumed in Colonial America and that were the "Red coats" who went there to fight the rebels that took the habit of drinking Madeira to England).

CHAPTER II.
MAJOR ROBINSON AT THE OLD COFFEE-HOUSE.

A WORD, now, of the officer who had alighted at the Coffee-house.

Major Robinson was in command of a partizan corps called the "Colonial Rangers," raised from the Tory population of the Colonies, though on the regular pay-rolls of the Royal army. From the unwillingness, perhaps, of the better class of Tories to serve against their own countrymen, troops of this kind were generally *mauvaises sujets;* quite as ready to plunder and burn and rob, as to fight; and Major Robinson's command was no exception. A very little more would have made them regular banditti. Their commandant, however, was an officer bearing the king's commission; and being of a very gentlemanly address, even stood high in the service. What his real character was will appear hereafter. Against his appearance certainly not a word could be said.

The host of the Coffee-house ushered him into a private apartment, with that peculiar attention which "mine host" pays only to one who is "every inch a gentleman" in his appreciation. Major Robinson ordered refreshments; a bottle of Madeira at once; dinner as soon as possibly it could be ready, and the best in the house. He then disencumbered himself of his equipments; hip heavy silk scarf; his sword, with its belt and scabbard; a pair of pocket-pistols; and his massive silver spurs. Before he parted with the sword, he

---

[612] NEAL 1830, pages 233-242.
[613] JONES, J.[ohn] Richter, *The Quaker Soldier; or, The British in Philadelphia. A Romance of the Revolution*, T. B. Peterson & Brothers, Philadelphia, 1866.

glanced over the scabbard of black morocco, half covered with silver mountings; drew the blade, a light cut-and-thrust – too light for service, unless in the hands of one who trusted more to skill than to strength – then laid the weapon down on a small table, with the hilt carefully clear of the belt. ...

"The fellow ought to be here – ought to have been here as soon as I. Where can he be loitering? But ha, that must be he!" While he was speaking thus to himself a light knock at the door was given and repeated, and immediately a person entered.

"Ha! Captain Preston! Come at last – but late?"

"Could not be helped, major; had to take a round to avoid observation."

"Where are the men?"

"The place I cannot exactly describe, but I can have them here in half an hour."

Figure 57. Colonel John Richter Jones. In his novel, set in Revolutionary times, he mentions some "Red Coats" toasting with Madeira. *19th century photograph. Author unknown.*

"I do not want them till after dark: be sure they are in readiness then."

"Are we not always ready?"

"I do not dispute it."

"But what is in the wind now? What special duty for us to-night? To forage among the rich Quakers? I have marked several houses where I think something can be got."

"Public duty to-night, Captain Preston."

"But, major – but – you've not asked me yet to taste your Madeira," said the captain.

"Help yourself, of course; then sit down until I explain what I want done."

"Your good health, major," said the captain, pouring out a glass of the wine, and taking a seat at the table, near the bottle and wine-glasses. Major Robinson sat down on the other side, and poured out a glass for himself; but took a gentle sip, with a genteel smack of the lips, instead of the single gulph of his ruder companion.

"I have information," resumed the major, "of several noted rebels still in the town, and I know where they will lodge to-night. I mean to nab them."

Captain Preston gave a kind of smothered whistle, and quietly said: "Will it pay, major?"

"It is my duty, as a Royal officer, to arrest them."

"But will it pay ?" repeated the captain.

"I receive my pay in his Majesty's service, and that is enough pay for me."[614] ...

CHAPTER XII.
THE ROYAL ARMY IN PHILADELPHIA.

... "I do not like to hear a friend talk thus, even in joke," interposed Major Andre. "I am not rich – and so Mr. Fitzhugh's reasons do not affect me – but I am rich enough – every'man is rich enough – to be a gentleman. No gentleman can, in my opinion, enrich himself by the ruin of the colonists – rebels though they are: and I hope Government will give them an amnesty."

614 JONES 1866, pages 42–45.

Fortunately for the harmony of the company, the old major finished a spell of deep thinking, and suddenly spoke:

"Mr.Fitzhugh's toast: I am satisfied with it now: let us drink Mr.Fitzhugh's toast. 'The rich rebels!'"

"The rich rebels!" was repeated by all but Major Andre and Sir Charles, and drunk uproariously.

"Now it is my call: Major Moncrief for a song."

"I must moisten my lips first," said the old major; filled his glass, took a sip, smacked his lips, held it up between his eye and the light, took another sip and another smack: "The real stuff! If the rebel powder was half as good as their wine, we wouldn't all of us be here to-day. What do you think of this Madeira, Sir Charles?"

"Splendid! something novel; strong as our port, but more lively; we must introduce it at home. But your song; you forget your song."

The major, as little sentimental looking as the goddess Britannia herself, sung a most cloyingly sweet song, and was echoed by a chorus, more in keeping with the incongruity of the selection than the sentiment. The major then called on Major Andre for a toast.

"Our speedy return home!"

"But we are not ready," said Colonel Fitzhugh.

"Who is not?"

"Sir William Howe[615] himself. If he were, he would press the rebels and finish the war. Their army is routed – their capital in our hands – their Congress, as they call their government, broken up; they might be settled within a week."[616] ...

6.2.10. Nathaniel Hawthorne

Nathaniel Hawthorne (1804-1864), a native of Salem, MA, and a renowned American writer, published several books in which he inserted many references to Madeira Wine, but we will mention just a couple of them. In *Twice-Told Tales*[617] there is an important reference to this staple product of this far-off island, that had been kept for a long time in a cellar in America.

LEGENDS OF THE PROVINCE HOUSE.
III.
LADY ELEANORE'S MANTLE

... Our host, in due season, uncorked a bottle of Madeira, of such exquisite perfume and admirable flavor, that he surely must have discovered it in an ancient bin, down deep beneath the deepest cellar, where some jolly old butler stored away the Governor's choicest wine, and forgot to reveal the secret on his deathbed. Peace to his red-nosed ghost, and a libation to his memory! This precious liquor was imbibed by Mr. Tiffany with peculiar

---

[615] See Note 30.
[616] JONES 1866, pages 170-172.
[617] HAWTHORNE, Nathaniel, *Twice-Told Tales*, In Two Volumes, Vol. II. A New Edition, Ticknor, Reed, and Fields, Boston, 1851.

zest; and after sipping the third glass, it was his pleasure to give us one of the oddest legends which he had yet raked from the storehouse, where he keeps such matters. With some suitable adornments from my own fancy, it ran pretty much as follows.[618] …

In the book *The House of the Seven Gables, A Romance*,[619] published in 1851, Nathaniel Hawthorne praises the unique features of the Juno, a kind of Madeira Wine that was named after the ship in which it was imported into the United States.

Figure 58. Nathaniel Hawthorne in the 1860's. He loved Madeira Wine and that fact is reflected in some of his novels, where he inserted several references to it. *Photograph by Mathew Brady.*

… Pray, pray, Judge Pyncheon, look at your watch, now! What – not a glance! It is within ten minutes of the dinner-hour! It surely cannot have slipped your memory that the dinner of to-day is to be the most important, in its consequences, of all the dinners you ever ate. Yes, precisely the most important; although, in the course of your somewhat eminent career, you have been placed high towards the head of the table, at splendid banquets, and have poured out your festive eloquence to ears yet echoing with Webster's mighty organ-tones. No public dinner this, however. It is merely a gathering of some dozen or so of friends from several districts in the state; men of distinguished character and influence, assembling, almost casually, at the house of a common friend, likewise distinguished, who will make them welcome to a little better than his ordinary fare. Nothing in the way of French cookery, but an excellent dinner, nevertheless! Real turtle, we understand, and salmon, tautog, canvas-backs, pig. English mutton, good roast-beef or dainties of that serious kind, fit for substantial country gentlemen, as these honorable persons mostly are. The delicacies of the season, in short, and flavored by a brand of old Madeira which has been the pride of many seasons. It is the Juno brand; a glorious wine, fragrant, and full of gentle might; a bottled-up happiness, put by for use; a golden liquid, worth more than liquid gold; so rare and admirable, that veteran wine-bibbers count it among their epochs to have tasted it! It drives away the heart-ache, and substitutes no head-ache! Could the judge but quaff a glass, it might enable him to shake off the unaccountable lethargy which – (for the ten intervening minutes, and five to boot, are already past) – has made him such a laggard at this momentous dinner. It would all but revive a dead man! Would you like to sip it now, Judge Pyncheon?[620] …

---

618 HAWTHORNE 1851, page 44.
619 HAWTHORNE, Nathaniel, *The House of the Seven Gables, A Romance*, Tickner, Reed, and Fields, Boston, 1851.
620 HAWTHORNE 1851, pages 292-293.

6.2.11. Newton Mallory Curtis

In the book *The Patrol of the Mountain. A Tale of the Revolution*,[621] by Newton Mallory Curtis, published in New York, in 1847, there is a brief reference to Madeira Wine, in which two characters are sitting at a table discussing its qualities.

<blockquote>

CHAPTER XV.
THE MODERN BRUTUS.

WHILST this affray, the result of which had consigned Henry Robinson to a prison, had been progressing, Carleton and the Major had been seated at a table, in company with Col. St. Leger, discussing the merits of sundry bottles of Madeira, and some of the late acts of Parliament. They were in the midst of an interesting debate, when the servant opened the door and informed his master that a soldier was in waiting, who desired an audience.[622] ...

</blockquote>

6.2.12. Oliver Wendell Holmes, Sr.

In the novel *Elsie Venner, A Romance of Destiny*,[623] published in Boston, in 1861, by Oliver Wendell Holmes Sr. (1809-1894), a physician and author born in Cambridge, MA, there are three references to Madeira Wine, in three of its chapters, associated with aristocratic people.

<blockquote>

CHAPTER I.
THE BRAHMIN CASTLE OF NEW ENGLAND.

... It is in the nature of large fortunes to diminish rapidly, when subdivided and distributed. A million is the unit of wealth, now and here in America. It splits into four handsome properties; each of these into four good inheritances; these, again, into scanty competences for four ancient maidens, – with whom it is best the family should die out, unless it can begin again as its great-grandfather did. Now a million is a kind of golden cheese, which represents in a compendious form the summer's growth of a fat meadow of craft or commerce; and as this kind of meadow rarely bears more than one crop, it is pretty certain that sons and grandsons will not get another golden cheese out of it, whether they milk the same cows or turn in new ones. In other words, the millionocracy, considered in a large way, is not at all an affair of persons and families, but a perpetual fact of money with a variable human element, which a philosopher might leave out of consideration without falling into serious error. Of course, this trivial and fugitive fact of personal wealth does not create a permanent class, unless some special means are taken to arrest the process of disintegration in the third generation. This is so rarely done, at least successfully, that

</blockquote>

---

621 CURTIS, Newton M.[allory], *The Patrol of the Mountain. A Tale of the Revolution*, Williams Brothers, New York, 1847.
622 CURTIS 1847, page 96.
623 HOLMES, Oliver Wendell, *Elsie Venner: A Romance of Destiny.*, In Two Volumes, Volume I, Ticknor and Fields, Boston, MDCCCLXI [1861].

one need not live a very long life to see most of the rich families he knew in childhood more or less reduced, and the millions shifted into the hands of the country-boys who were sweeping stores and carrying parcels when the now decayed gentry were driving their chariots, eating their venison over silver chafing-dishes, drinking Madeira chilled in embossed coolers, wearing their hair in powder, and casing their legs in top boots with silken tassels.[624] ...

CHAPTER III.
MR. BERNARD TRIES HIS HAND.

... The advent of Master Langdon to Pigwacket Centre created a much more lively sensation than had attended that of either of his predecessors. Looks go a good way all the world over, and though there were several good-looking people in the place, and Major Bush was what the natives of the town called a "hahnsome mahn," that is, big, fat, and red, yet the sight of a really elegant young fellow, with the natural air which grows up with carefully-bred young persons, was a novelty. The Brahmin blood which came from his grandfather as well as from his mother, a direct descendant of the old Flynt family, well known by the famous tutor, Henty Flynt, (see Cat. Harv. Anno 1693,) had been enlivened and enriched by that of the Wentworths, which had had a good deal of ripe old Madeira and other generous elements mingled with it, so that it ran to gout sometimes in the old folks, and to high spirit, warm complexion, and curly hair in some of the younger ones. The soft curling hair Mr. Bernard had inherited, – something, perhaps, of the high spirit; but that we shall have a chance of finding out by-and-by. But the long sermons and the frugal board of his Brahmin ancestry, with his own habits of study, had told upon his color, which was subdued to something more of delicacy than one would care to see in a young fellow with rough work before him. This, however, made him look more interesting, or, as the young ladies at Major Bush's said, "interestin.'"[625] ...

Figure 59. Oliver Wendell Holmes, Sr. wrote a novel in which Madeira Wine is seen as the favorite liquor of New England's aristocracy. A.W. Elson & Co., Boston, 1894.

CHAPTER VII.
THE EVENT OF THE SEASON.

... "Well, it cost some consid'able labor, no doubt," said Mrs. Sprowle. "Matilda and our girls and I made 'most all the cake with our own hands, and we all feel some tired; but if folks get what suits 'em, we don't begrudge the time nor the work. But I do feel thirsty,"

---

624 HOLMES [1861], pages 14-15.
625 HOLMES [1861], pages 43-44.

said the poor lady, "and I think a glass of srub would do my throat good; it's dreadful dry. Mr. Peckham, would you be so polite as to pass me a glass of srub?"

Silas Peckham bowed with great alacrity, and took from the table a small glass cup, containing a fluid reddish in hue and subacid in taste. This was *srub,* a beverage in local repute, of questionable nature, but suspected of owing its color and sharpness to some kind of syrup derived from the maroon-colored fruit of the sumac. There were similar small cups on the table filled with lemonade, and here and there a decanter of Madeira wine, of the Marsala kind, which some prefer to, and many more cannot distinguish from, that which comes from the Atlantic island.

"Take a glass of wine, Judge," said the Colonel; "here is an article that I rather think 'll suit you."

The Judge knew something of wines, and could tell all the famous old Madeiras from each other, – "Eclipse," "Juno," the almost fabulously scarce and precious "White-top," and the rest. He struck the nativity of the Mediterranean Madeira before it had fairly moistened his lip.

"A sound wine, Colonel, and I should think of a genuine vintage. Your very good health."

"Deacon Soper," said the Colonel, "here is some Madary Judge Thornton recommends. Let me fill you a glass of it."

The Deacon's eyes glistened. He was one of those consistent Christians who stick firmly by the first miracle and Paul's advice to Timothy.

"A little good wine won't hurt anybody," said the Deacon. "Plenty, – plenty, – plenty. There!" He had not withdrawn his glass, while the Colonel was pouring, for fear it should spill; and now it was running over.

– It is very odd how all a man's philosophy and theology are at the mercy of a few drops of a fluid which the chemists say consists of nothing but C 4, O 2, H 6. The Deacon's theology fell off several points towards latitudinarianism in the course of the next ten minutes. He had a deep inward sense that everything was as it should be, human nature included. The little accidents of humanity, known collectively to moralists as sin, looked very venial to his growing sense of universal brotherhood and benevolence.[626]…

6.2.13. Robert Hare

In 1850, was published in New York the third volume of the book *Standish the Puritan: A tale of the American Revolution,*[627] by Robert Hare (1781-1858), a famous American chemist, born in Philadelphia, under his pseudonym, Eldred Grayson, Esq. In this work there is a reference to a Madeira toast made by one of its characters, after a dinner, when he had already drank a little too much.

---

626 HOLMES [1861] pages 142-144.
627 [HARE, Robert], *Standish the Puritan: A Tale of the American Revolution,* Volume III, Harper & Brothers, Publishers, New York, 1850.

CHAPTER VI.

... The trying moment now arrived. Dinner was announced, and, in some way, notwithstanding his utter confusion, he found himself at the head of his table, with the lady of Lord Lumberlegs on his right, and his lordship on his left. What was left undone by Mr. Snifling was supplied by the secret instructions of Mr. Dexter and his young partner. The latter had, in truth, seen much good society, not only in America, but in England.

It surely was a magnificent affair. Every gentleman attached to the army was in full uniform, and the ladies had, for the most part, been reared at court. The clear blue eye of the Saxon, and the polish of the skin, contrasted well with the tastefully powdered and frizzled hair, which, thrown upward, gave them a commanding and dignified air. The ladies cared much less for the dinner than they did for the rout that was to ensue.

Figure 60. Robert Hare. *19th century illustration. Author unknown.*

The conversation soon became general, and the master of the house occupied himself principally in recommending his wines, assuring his guests that the Port had recently been taken from the London Docks, where it had been stored for the especial use of his majesty James the Second and his favorite the Duke of Buckingham. Then he recommended his Sherry as being quite free from acids, as it was nothing but the pure juice of the grape; and as for the Madeira, it was the dearest and the oldest wine ever imported into the colonies, it having been taken out by Christopher Columbus, for sake of the sea voyage, for Ferdinand and Isabella, at the time the former discovered the American continent; and, notwithstanding several winks and nods from both Mr. Dexter and his partner, he continued on, until he convinced that portion of the company who did not know him that, of course, he must have been a wine broker. Mr. Snifling had been instructed that the test of aristocratic society was the quantity that each could drink before he was put to bed or fell under the table. He therefore partook freely of each, and so did the greater part of the company, attributing, as men of the world should do, Mr. Snifling's strange manner to the custom of the country, or as incidental to his occupation; but he who seemed the best satisfied as to the truth of Mr. Snifling's statements was General Lord Lumberlegs, if the quantity he drank was evidence of his credulity.

Every thing went on in the most satisfactory manner, and with great propriety, until the ladies, and some of the more abstemious of the gentlemen, had withdrawn. Some of them were dancing in the drawing-rooms; others ventured a short distance from the shore, aided by the light of the new moon; others were promenading and sentimentalizing in the piazza fronting the water. Those at the table were still drinking, and doing the honors of the house. Mr. Snifling had drank more than he had ever drank before, and his lordship, the general, had emptied more than three bottles.

It was now proposed that Mr. Snifling should name a toast, though his intellect was evidently much obscured. But the toast *must* be drunk. He hesitated some time, and, in hesitating, he hiccoughed; and the longer he hesitated, the more he hiccoughed; but the toast was loudly called for, and in a second effort he arose, steadying himself by grasping the collar of his lordship with one hand, and holding on to the table with the other.

"Hiccough – hiccough – gentlemen – hiccough – I give you her ladyship – hiccough – my Lady Timbertoes – hiccough;" and the toast was drunk with applause, though they did not know precisely what it meant, and therefore loudly called for an explanation, which he endeavored to give by saying, "Her ladyship is the ac–com–plished wife of my friend – hiccough – on my left – hiccough."

"Mistake! mistake! mistake!" was echoed on all sides. "It is Lumberlegs – my Lady Lumberlegs!" said a dozen voices at once. "Drink it over again!"

But Mr. Snifling grew no better. Every thing was in a state of obliquity to him. "I beg pardon – *hiccough!*" said he; "here's to – hiccough – to Lady Lumberheels – hiccough."[628] ...

6.2.14. Silas Weir Mitchell

The distinguished doctor and author Silas Weir Mitchell (1829-1914), a native of Philadelphia, was beyond all doubts a Madeira *connoisseur*, and throughout his literary career he produced several texts, either in prose or poetry, dealing with this precious wine. His short story "A Madeira Party" published in New York, in 1895, in a book under the same title,[629] is, assuredly, one of the best literary texts dealing with Madeira Wine, published in 19th century America. It depicts a gathering of a group old friends, in Philadelphia, in the 1830's, in which the main topic of conversation were the different kinds and features of Madeiras owned by a certain host, who explains them to an old acquaintance of his who had been in Europe for thirty years.

A MADEIRA PARTY

Sometime early in the second quarter of the century, in the City of Penn, and in what was then known as Delaware-Fourth street, soon after dusk in the evening, occurred the unimportant events of which I shall speak.

The room was paneled in white three feet up from the floor, and above this a fox-hunt was repeated in lively colors on every square of the paper which covered the walls. Great hickory logs, ablaze on the deep hearth, cast rosy light on a mantelpiece, in the style of the Directory, pretty with Cupids in relief dragging chariots through a tangle of roses. A similar pattern on the ceiling resembled what a visitor to the Zoological Gardens may see to-day in the small yellow house called "Solitude," where Mr. Penn is said to have been agreeably naughty and by no means solitary.

Silver candlesticks lighted a table laid for four, and their light fell on buff and gold Nankin china, glass, and glistening plate. A negro servant, well on in years, dark as the mahogany he loved to polish, with fine contrast of very white hair, moved to and fro in the room. His task was clearly grateful. To adjust a fork, snuff a wick, flick the dust off a

---

628 [HARE] 1850, pages 104-106.
629 MITCHELL, Silas Weir, *A Madeira Party*, The Century Co., New York, 1895. This book also contains another wine-related short-story entitled "A Little More Burgundy".

carved Cupid, evidently gave him a certain grave pleasure. At last, retreating a little with head on one side, artist-like, he considered for a moment the table and the setting. This final survey appeared to be entirely to his liking, for with a smile of satisfaction he turned to inspect a row of decanters on the mantel. One by one he lifted them gently, saw that the glass was clean, and for a moment looked through each decanter in turn as he held it before the light of a candelabrum on the side-table. The necessity to present a wine absolutely free from sediment he very well knew. But it is probable that he also found distinct pleasure in the brilliant garnets and varied amber tints of the several wines before him; for he possessed, like most of his race, an appreciative joy in color, and had, too, more or less artistic pleasure in the perfection of the gleaming table and its perfect appointments. At last he turned to consider the question of the temperature of the precious wines in his charge. Once or twice, when to his touch a decanter seemed too cool, he lifted it with care, moved it to the hearth, and after turning it about before the fire set it back on the mantel. Finally he looked up at the tall Wagstaffe clock in the corner, compared with it a huge silver watch which he took from his fob, and throwing open a pair of mahogany doors, stood aside as four gentlemen entered the room. Each, as he went by, spoke a kindly word to the old servant. I can fancy the party made a quaint and pleasant picture in the old-fashioned chamber, with their close-fitting nankeen pantaloons, ample shirt-ruffles, voluminous neckties, and brass-buttoned blue coats.

Figure 61. Silas Weir Mitchell was a true *connoisseur* of Madeira Wine and that expertise is reflected in his many works where he inserted references to it. *19th century photograph. Author unknown.*

"Pray be seated," said Hamilton. "Sit on my right, Chestnut. I wish to see that my good wine is not wasted. Your first Madeira-drinking will seem strange to you. Thirty years away in Europe! Why, you were but a boy when you left us! Well, we are glad to have you back again."

"And I as pleased to be at home," said Chestnut. As he spoke he noted with the readiness of a close observer of social life the gentlemen about him as they settled themselves at table with an obvious air of contentment. One, a strangely slight and very ruddy old man, after adjusting his napkin with care over his waistcoat, said, as he looked up, "Well, well, you have lost a good deal of time."

"That is sadly true," said the stranger guest. "I have tasted no Madeira these twenty years."

"Then I fear, my friend, from what Hamilton tells me, that you will hardly appreciate the charm of one of these little occasions."

"But how could I? And still, let me assure you, my dear Mr. Wilmington, that the importance of the opportunity will not be lost on me, nor the good wine either, sir."

"I trust not," said the elder man. "To consider with care some new Madeiras is – well, for that a man should have perfect health and entire tranquillity of mind. Sir, the drinking of these great wines is something more than a social ceremony or the indulgence of an appetite. It is, sir, – but I see Francis smiling – you may imagine the rest. I had an old friend who, when dying, declined to have his wine whey made out of a famous old Madeira, saying that it was a waste of a good thing on a palate which was past knowing sherry from port. That was, in my opinion, a well-bred and judicious use of conscience."

6. MADEIRA WINE IN AMERICAN LITERATURE

"There was a certain refinement of unselfishness about it," said Chestnut. "I was on the point of asking you if, in your opinion, these finer wines are apt to tempt men into coarser indulgence? I have heard it so said."

"I do not think it," returned Wilmington. "I am well aware, sir, that there are brutes who may make worse pigs of themselves with Madeira, or with anything; but as far as my memory serves me, I recall no occasion, sir, on which I have seen men who truly appreciate this wine, the worse for it."

"A pretty strong statement," laughed Francis.

"I hope, sir, you do not mean to doubt –"

"Oh, by no means," cried the other, interrupting the irascible old man. "Not I. Pardon me – a thousand pardons!"

"Enough, sir! Thank you," and he bowed formally. "I was saying, or I was about to say, when – but, no matter" – And he turned to their host:

"I hope, Hamilton, you have not arranged for a heavy supper."

"How could you suspect me of that? A trifle of terrapin, without wine in the dressing, as a friend gave them to me last week in Baltimore. Then I shall offer you the breast of a canvasback. That is all. For an honest and refined study of Madeiras which are new to the palate, one should have supped wisely and not too well."

"It seems so odd," said Chestnut, "to come back to terrapin and canvasbacks. I was unwise enough to send my French servant yesterday to buy some terrapin, never dreaming he could have any difficulty with a written order, as also he speaks English fairly. He returned with the statement that the old dealer you commended to me would not serve Mr. Hamilton's friend *parce qu'il n'avait pas des comtes*."

"Is that a true tale, Chestnut ?" asked Francis, amid the amusement of the others.

"Yes, it is true. It was explained to me later that the dealer said the terrapin were not *counts*. I believe my man came back with an obscure idea that terrapin belong to the nobility. He did fetch me some very fine ducks, however."

"Talking of ducks, my dear Wilmington," said Francis, "tell Chestnut what Wharton said of them at dinner here last week."

The gentleman addressed looked up. His face, on which were many furrows of laughter, grew slowly merry at the remembrance of the jest he was called on to repeat.

"Oh, some of us were rather heavily discussing the duck-shooting on the Chesapeake. Wharton does not shoot, and, getting tired of the talk, said quietly, 'Did it ever happen to any of you to go out after Russia duck and get nothing but canvas back?'

"For a moment we were all caught by the verbal likelihood of it; but when the laugh came it broke up the duck talk, to Wharton's delight."

"Ah, he said charming things; and now they are mostly forgotten," said the host.

"Well, well," cried Wilmington," so are the dinner and the wine of last year; but one would have been worse off without them. What was it he said of Colonel M –? Oh, yes. How the merry ghost of a jest haunts one, and at last recalls the substance! The colonel had been in the army, and later settled on a sugar-plantation. Wharton said of him, quoting Burns, "'His 'prentice han' he tried on man, and then he made the lasses O!'"

"Delightful!" cried Chestnut.

"Here is the terrapin," said Hamilton; and the supper went on with luxurious simplicity. Next came the ducks, which the host adroitly carved. Then the cloth was removed, the shining candelabra replaced on the polished mahogany table, and a crust of bread on a plate set by each guest. Meantime the talk continued, while Chestnut looked on, much amused at the gravity which of a sudden fell upon the party.

"Olives?"

"No," said Wilmington, declining. "Nothing cleans the palate like bread. For red wines, a peach helps one's taste. Your table is perfect, Hamilton;" and, turning to the servant, "It does you credit, Uncle John. How many a fellow must have rolled under it when it was young! Ah, your old decanters and those coasters could tell some queer tales."

Figure 62. Madeira decanting utensils. *Book illustration. Author unknown.*

"A pretty word, 'coaster,'" remarked Chestnut. "Coasters delivering wine at the human harbors around the table."

"It is not in the dictionaries," said Francis.

"Odd, that," returned Hamilton. "You may like to know, Chestnut, that at this table Washington, Lafayette, and Franklin have dined."

"All Madeira men, I doubt not," said Wilmington; "that accounts for a good deal."

"Perhaps," said the host, smiling. "Ah, I see you glancing at the cigars, Chestnut. But, alas! they are forbidden until the Madeira has been tasted."

"Cigars!" exclaimed Wilmington. "The mere odor in a room destroys the palate."

"I have never held to this belief," said Francis, addressing Chestnut. "But it is common among the lovers of wine. I would like to put Wilmington on oath as to this strange opinion. At least he will permit me to ask him if he believes that smoking affects the taste of all wines?"

"There is but one wine," returned Wilmington.

"And his name is Madeira, of course," laughed Francis. "But there are other juices of the grape which cannot be quite set aside as bastards."

"I might give a little corner of esteem to the highest grades of Burgundy," said the old gentleman. "No other, not even the finest claret, but is underbred compared to this aristocrat."

"I can't go quite so far as that," said Francis. "Ah, me! Do you remember, Hamilton, that gay day at Dijon,[630] long years ago, in the Hôtel Jura, and the way that old innkeeper fell in love with you, and lavished on us a varied harem of wines ever better and better, until at last you admitted, as to a famous Beaune, that it was equal to any Madeira –"

"What – what – I, sir? No, sir! My judgment must have been disturbed."

"Oh, it is true."

"Well, maybe; but – it is not so to-day," said Wilmington. "There is but one wine. I loved it when I was young; no new mistress can disturb my affections. I never touch it now without a thought of the friends at whom I have smiled a health across it in days long past. For the fool, a wine is wine and nothing more."

"True, true," said Francis. "For me too, it is a magician. I never lift to my lips a glass of this noble wine without seeing faces that are gone, and hearing the voices and the laughter and the jests that are no more."

"Wine makes poets of us all!" exclaimed Hamilton. "Once I asked Wilmington what

---

630 A city in eastern France, the capital of the Côte d'Or département and of the Burgundy region.

he saw, for he was staring down into his glass, and he said he saw memories. By George! we were all as still as mice for a moment. But he is right; there is but one wine, and that, like tobacco, is an American discovery."

"I can talk tobacco with you all day," said Chestnut. "Wine is another matter. We should have a monument to that unknown Indian brave who evolved the pipe. How did he do it? There is the simplicity of genius about it. I can understand the discovery of America, and the invention of printing; but what human want, what instinct, led up to tobacco? Imagine intuitive genius capturing this noble idea from the odors of a prairie fire! Surely, Lamb's roast pig was nothing to the discovery of the gentle joy of a wholesome pipe."

"What a droll fancy!" said Francis. "I envy that fellow his first smoke – the first pipe of man."

" My envy," said Chestnut, "is reserved for that medieval priest who by happy chance invented champagne. His first night in the convent wine-cellar with the delicious results of his genius must have been – I wonder no poet has dwelt on this theme."

"We were talking about Madeira," remarked Wilmington, impatiently. "You were about to say, Hamilton, –"

"Only that I am not quite so clear as to our credit for discovering Madeira," said their host.

"No? It is all in Smith's 'Wealth of Nations.'[631] Great Britain allowed no trade with France or Spain; but as to what were called non-enumerated articles we were permitted to trade with the Canary and Madeiras. We took staves and salt fish thither, and fetched back wines. It so happened that the decisive changes of weather our winter and summer afford did more to ripen this wine than its native climate. The English officers during the French war found our Madeiras so good that they took the taste to England."

"And yet," said Chestnut, "Madeira is never good in England. Is it climate, or that they do not know how to keep it?"

"Both – both," returned Wilmington. "They bottle all wines, and that is simply fatal. Madeira was never meant to be retailed. It improves in its own society, as greatness is apt to do."

"I myself fancy," said the host, "that despite English usage, even port is better for the larger liberty of a five-gallon demijohn. I tried this once with excellent result. The wine became pale and delicate like an old Madeira."

"How all this lost lore comes back to me as I used to hear it at my father's table!" said Chestnut. "I recall the prejudice against wine in bottle."

"Prejudice, sir ?" retorted Wilmington, testily. "Your demijohn has one cork; your five gallons in bottles, a dozen or two of corks, and the corks give an acrid taste. Some wise old Quaker found this out, sir. That is why there is so little good wine in Charleston and Boston. They bottle their wine. Incredible as it may seem, sir, they bottle their wine."

"That is sad," returned Chestnut, gravely.

"Keep it in demijohns in moderate darkness under the roof," returned Francis. "Then it accumulates virtue like a hermit. I once had a challenge from the Madeira Club in Charleston to test our local theory. They sent me two dozen bottles of their finest Madeira. When we came to make a trial of them, we were puzzled at finding the corks entire, but not a drop of wine in any of the bottles. At last I discovered that some appreciative colored person had emptied them by the clever device of driving a nail through the hollow at the base of the bottles. I found, on experiment, that it could easily be done.

---

631 Shortened title of the book *An Inquiry into the Nature and Cause of the Wealth of Nations*, the most famous work by Adam Smith (1723-1790), a Scottish moral philosopher, first published in 1776.

A letter from my friends forced me to tell the story. I fancy that ingenious servant may have suffered for his too refined taste."

"But he had the Madeira," said Wilmington grimly, glancing at the old servant. "I have no doubt Uncle John here has a good notion of Madeira."

The old black grinned responsively, and said, with the familiarity of an ancient retainer, "It's de smell ob it, sar. Ye gets to know 'em by de smell, sar."

"That is it, no doubt," laughed Francis. "By and by we shall all have to be content with the smell. It is becoming dearer every year."

"I found yesterday," said Hamilton, "an invoice of fifty-eight pipes of Madeira, of the date of 1760. The wine is set down as costing one dollar and four cents a gallon. I should have thought it might have been less, but then it is spoken of as very fine."

"My father," returned Wilmington, "used to say that the newer wines in his day were not much dearer than good old cider. They drank them by the mugful."

"I remember," said Francis, "that Graydon[632] speaks of it in his 'Memoirs.'"[633]

"Who? What?" cried Wilmington, who was a little deaf. "Oh! Graydon – yes, I know the man and the book, of course, but I do not recall the passage."

"He says: 'Our company' – this was in 1774 – 'our company was called "The Silk-Stocking Company." The place of rendezvous was the house of our captain,[634] where capacious demijohns of Madeira were constantly set out in the yard, where we formed for regular refreshment before marching out to exercise.' He was most amusing, too, as to why the captain was so liberal of his wine; but I can't quite recall it, and I hate to spoil a quotation.[635] You would find the book entertaining, Chestnut."

"How delightful!" exclaimed Chestnut. 'Capacious demijohns in the yard, and the descendants of Penn's Quakers – anti-vinous, anti-pugnacious Quakers – drilling for the coming war! By George! one can see it. One guesses that it was not out of such fairy glasses as these they drank the captain's Madeira."

"I am reminded," cried Hamilton, "that I have a letter of the captain's brother, Colonel Lambert Cadwalader, to Jasper Yeates, at Lancaster, in 1776. It is interesting. Wait a moment; I will get

---

[632] Alexander Graydon (1752-1818), a native of Bristol, PA, who was a captain in the Revolutionary Army.

[633] Allusion to Alexander Graydon's book *Memoirs of a Life, Chiefly Passed in Pennsylvania, Within the Last Sixty Years; with occasional remarks upon the General Occurrences, Character and Spirit of that Eventful Period*, first published in Harrisburg, PA, in 1811, where one can find some references to Madeira Wine.

[634] AN: Afterward General John Cadwalader. [John Cadwalader (1742-1786), a native of New Jersey, who distinguished himself as a commander of the Pennsylvania troops during the American Revolutionary War.]

[635] The right quotation is as follows: «They went so far as to form a company of light infantry, under the command of Mr. Copperthwaite, which was called *The Quaker Blues*, and instituted in a spirit of competition with *The Greens*, or, as they were sneeringly styled *The silk stocking company*, commanded by Mr. John Caldwalader, and which having early associated, had already acquired celebrity. This nickname evinced that the canker worm jealousy already tainted the infantile purity of our patriotism. The command of this company consisting of the flower of the city, was too fine a feather in the cap of its leader to be passed by unenvied; it was therefore branded as an aristocratic assemblage, and Mr. (since general) Mifflin, had the credit of inventing the invidious appelation. To this association I belonged. There were about seventy of us. We met morning and evening, and from the earnest and even enthusiastic devotion of most of us to learn the duty of soldiers, the company, in the course of a summer's training, became a truly respectable militia corps. When it had some adroitdness in the exercises, we met but once a day. This was in the afternoon, and the place of rendez-vous the house of the captain, where capacious demi-johns of Madeira, were constantly set out in the yard where we formed, for our refreshment before marching out to exercise. The ample fortune of Mr. Cadwalader had enabled him to fill his cellars with the choicest liquors; and it must be admitted, that he dealt them out with the most gentlemanly liberality.» [GRAYDON, Alexander], *Memoirs of a Life, Chiefly passed in Pennsylvania, within the last Sixty Years; With occasional remarks upon the General Occurrences, Character and Spirit of that Eventful Period*, Printed by John Wyeth, Harrisburg [PA], 1811, pages 107-108.

it." And so saying, he left the table, and presently returning said, "I will read only the bit about the wine. It shows how much store they set by their good wine even in those perilous days.

"Take particular care of the red chest clampt with iron herewith sent, which contains some bonds and mortgages which I could not take out, the key being lost; and also that you would be kind enough to let the two quarter-casks of Madeira, painted green, be deposited in some safe place under lock and key in your cellar, if possible where you keep your own liquors in a safe place, as I value them more than silver and gold in these times of misfortune and distress.

"Then he goes on to tell the news of Washington's victory at Trenton."

"What a glimpse at the life of those days!" said Chestnut.

During the chat the servant had placed before the host a half-dozen quart decanters filled with wine of various hues and depths of color.

"And now for the wine! We have been losing time," exclaimed their host.

As he spoke, the servant set on either side of the fire a brass-bound, painted bucket in which were a number of decanters – the reserve reinforcements to be used if the main army gave out. Meanwhile the desultory chat went on as the servant distributed the glasses. These were arranged in rather an odd fashion. In the center of the table was set a silver bowl of water. The notches in the rim received each the stem of an inverted glass. Before every guest a glass bowl, much like a modern finger-bowl, held also two wine-glasses. Thus there was to be a glass for each wine, or at need the means for rinsing a glass.

The talk had been more entertaining to the younger men and their host than to Wilmington. He had come for the purpose of tasting wines, and was somewhat annoyed at the delay.

"Dined with Starling last week," he said. "Never was more insulted in my life, sir. Had his after-dinner wine – all of it, sir –in pint decanters!"

"Not, really?" said Francis, with a seriousness by no means assumed. "In pints! You are quite sure you are correct?"

"Fact, sir."

"I –!" exclaimed Chestnut. "Pardon me; but I fail to see the insult."

"What! You, sir ! Your father's son! Gentlemen do not serve wine in pints after dinner. They don't do it; and the wine was bad – sick, thick!"

"Ah, I see. I have been long enough away to have forgotten many things. As to these wines you all discuss so critically, I have tasted some of them of late, and they seemed to me much alike."

"Alike, sir! You surprise me," said Wilmington. "I pity you. What a waste of opportunities! But it is not too late to reform – to learn. I know one man who made a quite correct palate at the age of forty – not a gentleman, either; and that's rather remarkable."

"And is that so rare?" cried Chestnut, much delighted.

"Oh, very," said Francis.

"I knew the man," returned Hamilton. "He died somewhat early. However, I have noticed that the acquisition of a taste for Madeira in middle life is quite fatal to common people."

"Is that so?" said Chestnut, greatly enjoying it all. "Upon my word, I still have a dim memory of all this stuff about wine, as I used to hear it when a lad. I thought it had gone with other superstitions. To be frank, I have so little trust in the tales I hear every day after dinner, about wine and wine-tasting, that –"

"Pardon me," interrupted Wilmington. "Of course you can hear much that is foolish; but to my mind the real facts are very often interesting."

"Such as –?" asked Chestnut. "Pray tell me."

"Hamilton will indorse this as an illustration. He was one of eight gentlemen – of whom three are now here – who were asked to give judgment on certain wines. Each man wrote his opinion as to the value, age, and quality of each specimen, and folding over the paper passed it with the wine. Finally, Hamilton read aloud each statement. The estimated price, or value, of a demijohn – that is of five gallons – of each was given; the age, the character, the defects, and so on. The prices assigned to the grape-juices varied much, because most of us cared for them but little. As to the Madeiras pure and simple, the conclusions as to value, age, and quality were so very much alike as even to surprise some of us."

"It is, I suppose," said Chestnut, who began to take a more serious interest, "a matter of habit – acquired habit – and attention."

"No," said Hamilton. "Far more is it a gift. Some women have it wonderfully."

"But, after all," said Francis, "why should appreciative delicacy of palate amaze us more than sharpness of vision or delicacy of touch?"

"Only because a fine taste is, of all forms of sensory acuteness, the rarest," returned Hamilton. "It is still more uncommon to have a perfect memory of taste, while odors are so easily remembered.

"I have known certain persons in whom refined delicacy of palate was accompanied with an almost incredible remembrance of past impressions as to the taste of things. Our old friend Mr. C–, as we all know, could recall a particular coffee or tea he had tasted years ago; could say what wines had been by accident mixed in the Madeira he drank; and was able to declare, as a test of his singular skill, in which of two clean wine-glasses a boiled egg had been placed a day or two before."

"It is interesting," said Chestnut; "but to me, if not incredible, it is at least made almost so by my own deficiencies."

"Well, now, to reeducate you," said Hamilton, "let us exchange theory for practice." So saying, he put on his spectacles, and began to scan the silver labels on his decanters, and to rearrange the order of the row of wines, so as to present them somewhat as opinions are given in a council of war – the least esteemed first. Meanwhile he said: "Wilmington likes his wine cool. It is a grave question. I prefer it a trifle above the temperature of the room. It insures a more perfect presentation both of taste and smell. A little chill may cloud wine, or repress its bouquet. We are all agreed that the wine should be at rest in a warm room some days, or longer, before it is drunk. Nothing mellows a wine like that. And then one must be careful not to have wine shaken; that bruises it. But this is commonplace, Chestnut; I am merely giving you a preliminary education. I think you will find these Madeiras in good condition, carefully drawn and bright. I ought to add that they are all drawn with the siphon, so as not to disturb the salts which crystallize on the sides of the demijohn, or the deposit every wine lets fall, as a good man drops his faults as he goes on in life."

"Just a word before we take our wine," said Francis. "I saw Chestnut smile at the idea of a wine being bruised. I can tell him a story about that. We were dining at the Quoit Club, in Germantown, and were at table when Wilmington, who was in the habit of riding out to the club, arrived somewhat late. We came by and by to the Madeiras. I saw the general taste a wine, as if in doubt. At last he looked up, and said: 'Wilmington, this wine is bruised; you brought the bottle out in your coat-tail pocket – the left pocket.' We were soon convinced as to the wine having been thus shaken out of health; but his inference as to the left pocket puzzled us all, until the general asked some one to stand up, and to put a bottle in his own coat-tail pocket. Then the reason of my friend's conclusion became clear enough – however, I delay the wine."

"Well, here it is," said Hamilton, filling his glass. Then he passed the decanter to Wilmington, on his left, saying, "With the sun, gentlemen."

"A fair grape-juice," said the latter; "but a trifle too warm."

"And what," said Chestnut, "is a grape-juice? All wines are merely that."

"Oh, usually it is the product of the south side of the island, sometimes of one vineyard, but untreated by the addition of older wines; sweet, of course; apt to be pale. When a Madeira-drinker speaks of a grape-juice, that is what he means. But a Madeira – what we call simply a Madeira – is apt to be dry, and usually is the result of careful blending of wines and some maturing by natural heat."

"But in time," said Chestnut, "your grape-juice becomes a Madeira. Certainly this is delicious! How refined, how delicate it is!"

"Ah, you will learn," cried Wilmington. "But wait a little. A grape-juice never becomes what we denominate a Madeira."

"I don't agree with you," said the host.

"We are in very deep water now," laughed Francis. "I, myself, think the finest of the old dry Madeiras were once sugary maidens."

"Nonsense," said Hamilton, passing the next wine. "With the sun."

"Why with the sun?" said Chestnut, infinitely delighted by these little social superstitions and the odd phrases.

"Because it sours a wine to send it to the right," said Wilmington, dryly. "That is a fact, sir, – a well-known fact."

"Droll, that," returned Chestnut. "I wonder whence came that notion."

"It is a pretty old one; possibly Roman. The Greeks passed their drink to the right. Wine is a strange fluid. It has its good and its bad days."

"I am willing to say its moods," added Hamilton.

"I suppose," continued the older man, "that you will be entirely skeptical if I assure you that for women to go into a wine-room is pretty surely to injure the wine."

"Indeed, is that so?" returned Chestnut. "I am not surprised. In France women are not allowed to enter the great cheese-caves."

"Wine is very sensitive," said Francis. "I give you this story for what it is worth:

"A planter in the South told me that once two blacks were arranging bottles in his wine-room, and quarreled. One stabbed the other. The fellow died, and his blood ran over the floor; and from that day the wines in that room were bitter. You know that bitterness is one form of the sicknesses to which Madeira is liable."

This amazing tale was received with entire tranquillity by all save Chestnut, whose education was progressing. Meanwhile another decanter went round.

"I congratulate you," cried Wilmington, as he set down his glass. "A perfect grape-juice – new to me too. High up, sir; very high up"; and refilling his glass, he sent on the coaster. "Observe, Chestnut, the refinement of it; neither the sweet nor the bouquet is too obvious.

It is like a well-bred lady. Observe what a gamut of delicate flavors; none are excessive. And then at last there remains in the mouth a sort of fugitive memory of its delightfulness."

"As one remembers the lady when she is gone," said Francis.

"Thanks," said the old gentleman, bowing.

"Am I wrong," said Chestnut, "in fancying that there is here a faint flavor of orange-water?"

"Well, well!" said Wilmington. "And this man says he has no palate! That is the charm of these lovely wines: they are many things to many lovers – have for each a separate enchantment. I thought it was a rose-water taste; but no matter, you may be correct. But Hamilton can give you a better wine. No grape-juice can compete with the best Madeiras. In wine and man the noblest social flavors come with years. It is pure waste to ask to dinner any man under forty."

"And now fill your glasses," said Hamilton. "Are you all charged? Your health, gentlemen! I waited for this wine;" and he bent his head to each in turn.

"That good old formula, 'Are you all charged?' is going out," said Chestnut. "I used to hear it when I came in to dessert at my father's table."

"One rarely hears it nowadays," remarked Francis. "But at the Green Tree Insurance Company's dinners it is still in habitual use. When the cloth is off, the President says, 'Are you all charged, gentlemen?' and then, 'Success to the Mutual Assurance Company.' You know, Chestnut, its insurance sign – still to be seen on our older houses – is a green tree. The Hand in Hand Insurance Company refused to insure houses in front of which were trees, because in the last century the fire-engines were unable to throw a stream over or through them. The Mutual accepted such risks, and hence has been always known popularly in Philadelphia as the Green Tree. After a pause, the Vice-President rises and repeats the formal query, 'Are you all charged?' The directors then stand up, and he says, 'The memory of Washington.' We have a tradition that the news of the great general's death in 1799 came while the Board of Directors was dining. From that time until now they have continued to drink that toast."

"I like that," said Chestnut. "These ancient customs seem to survive better here than elsewhere in America."

"That is true," returned Hamilton. "And what you say reminds me of some odd rules in the Philadelphia Library, which Franklin founded in 1731. We have – at our own cost, of course – a supper of oysters roasted in the shell at a wood fire in the room where we meet. A modest bowl of rum punch completes the fare. Old Ben was afraid that this repast would degenerate into a drinking-bout such as was too common in his time. He therefore ingeniously arranged a table so high that it was impossible to sit at it, and this shrewd device seems to have answered."

"When I became a director of the library," said Francis, "my predecessor had been ill for two years. As a consequence, he was fined a shilling for non-attendance at each meeting. This, with the charges for suppers, and for the use of the library as a stockholder, had accumulated a debt of some fifty dollars. Now, as Franklin found it difficult to collect such debts from estates, he made it a rule that the new director, while pleased with the freshness of his novel honor, should pay the bill of the man he succeeded; and accordingly I paid my predecessors debts."

"How like Poor Richard!" said Wilmington.

"I was consoled," added Francis, "by the reflection that I always had the sad privilege of leaving my successor a similar obligation."

"Agreeable, that," murmured Wilmington. "But we are trifling, my dear Francis. What is next, Hamilton? Ah, a new wine. That is a wine indeed! A Madeira. Stay! I have drunk it before. A Butler wine, isn't it?"

"Yes. I misplaced the decanters; this should have come later."

"I see now," said Chestnut. "What is that curious aftertaste? Prunes? Isn't it prunes?"

"Certainly," cried Hamilton. "You are doing well, Chestnut. These noble old wines have a variety of dominant flavors, with what I might call a changeful halo of less decisive qualities. We call the more or less positive tastes apple, peach, prime, quince; but in fact these are mere names. The characterizing taste is too delicate for competent nomenclature. It is a thing transitory, evanescent, indefinable, like the quality of the best manners. No two are alike."

"Yes," said Hamilton; "and this same wine, in bottles, after a few years would quite lose character. Even two demijohns of the same wine kept in one room constantly differ, like two of a family."

"As you talk of these wines," said Chestnut, "I dimly recall the names of some I used to hear. 'Constitution,' a Boston wine, was one –"

"And a good vintage, too," said Hamilton. "It was the class wine of 1802."

"The class wine?" queried Chestnut.

"Yes. At Harvard each class used to import a tun of wine, which, after it was bottled, was distributed among the graduates.[636] I still have two of the bottles with '1802,' surrounded by 'Constitution,' molded in the glass."

"A good wine it was," added Francis. "I know of no other which has been so little hurt by being bottled."

"There were others I used also to hear about. One, I think, was called 'Resurrection' – a wine buried for protection in the war; but some of the names of these wines puzzle me."

"The Butlers," returned Francis, "of course represent in their numbering the successive annual importations of Major Pierce Butler for his own use. Some wines were called from the special grape which produced them, as Bual, Sercial, Vidogna. As to others, it was a quality, as in the case of the famous apple-wine; or the name of the ship in which the wine came to us, as the Harriets (pale and dark), the Padre; others again were wines long held by families, as the Francis, Willing, Butler, and Burd Madeiras."

"Might I ask how long may a Madeira live, and continuously gain in value for the palate?"

"Ah, that depends on the wine," said Hamilton. "I never drank a wine over seventy years old which had not something to regret – like ourselves, eh, Wilmington?"

"I have nothing to regret," returned the elder man, smiling, "except that I cannot live my life over precisely as it was. I have neglected no opportunity for innocent amusement, nor–" and he paused.

"For some others," added Francis, amid a burst of laughter.

"I fancy," said Chestnut, "that Mr. Wilmington is of the opinion of Howell.[637] You will find it in those letters of his[638] which Walpole loved."

---

636 This is a fact, and we found evidences of this in other sources. On section 9.5. of this anthology, for instance, there is a newspaper article, published in 1895, that refers that the grandson of the secretary of the Harvard Class of 1802 still possessed his grandfather's bottle of Madeira he had been given by that prestigious university about a century before, and that the wine was apparently in excellent condition.

637 James Howell (1594-1666), an Anglo-Welsh historian and writer.

638 Published in a book entitled *Epistolae Ho-Elianae: Familiar Letters, Domestick and Foreign, Divided into Four Books:*

"And what was that?"

"It is long since I read it. I am not quite sure I can repeat it accurately. He contends in a humorous vein for the moral value of wine – I think he is speaking of Canary. 'Of this,' he says, 'may be verified that merry induction – that good wine makes good blood; good blood causeth good thoughts; good thoughts bring forth good works; good works carry a man to heaven: *ergo*, good wine carrieth a man to heaven.'"[639]

"It sounds like one of Shakespeare's fools," said Hamilton. "I should like to read that book," added Wilmington.

"It is at your service," replied Chestnut; "and what else he says of wine is worth reading."

"Then let us get nearer to good works," laughed their host. "Here is a pleasant preacher. Try this."

"Ah," said Wilmington; "a new friend! Curious, that. Observe, Chestnut, the just perceptible smoke-flavor – a fine, clean-tasting, middle-aged wine – a gentleman, sir, a gentleman! Will never remind you to-morrow of the favor he did you last night."

"Needs time," said Francis, "and a careful fining – a little egg-shell and the white of one egg."

"One might risk it," said Wilmington. "But I would rather use a milk fining. It is more delicate, and the wine recovers sooner, unless the dose of milk be too large. But above all, Hamilton, be careful about the moon. A summer fining might be better, but touch it lightly."

"What on earth has the moon to do with it?" said Chestnut.

"If you want to spoil a Madeira," answered Wilmington, "fine it at the change of the moon. I spoiled my dark Harriet that way. Always fine a wine during the decline of the moon."

"I shall call this wine 'Smoke,'" said Hamilton. "Its name is really Palido. Certainly it has a great future. No better wine ever coasted along the shores of this table, and it has seen many vinous voyages. And now for a very interesting vintage. A little more bread, John. 'With the sun.'"

Wilmington ate a morsel of bread, rinsed a glass in the bowl before him, filled it to the brim, and slowly emptied it. Then he set it down deliberately.

"That is not Madeira, Hamilton; that is sherry. Some mistake."

"What!" cried Francis. "Wrong for once! It is Madeira, and old, – too old, I should say." Hamilton laughed.

"I thought I should puzzle you. I have but little of it left, and it is new to all of you. Two generations have disputed its parentage."

"I might be mistaken," said Wilmington. "There are Madeiras so like some rare sherries as to puzzle any palate."

"I myself," said Hamilton, "have an inherited belief that it is Madeira. It is difficult to tell, at times, a very old Madeira from a very aged sherry. The Burd wine was remarkable because no one could decide this question. I have heard an old friend remark that the age of all great wines brought them together as to taste. Thus a certain Charles March grape-juice and Blue Seal Johannisberger were scarcely to be told apart."

"I leave you to settle it," said Chestnut, rising, well aware how long the talk would last. "The knowledge I have acquired has, of a verity, gone to my head, – I suppose because, as Miss M– says, nature abhors a vacuum. Thank you for a delightful evening."

Partly Historical, Political, Philosophical: Upon Emergent Occasions, printed in London, in 1713.
639 Quote from Book II of the afore mentioned work.

"But sit down for five minutes." said Hamilton, who had risen with his guest. "There is a beautiful story about this wine. I must tell it, even if it be familiar to Wilmington as his own best joke."

"Delighted," said Chestnut, resuming his place.

"Well," said Hamilton, "I will not keep you long. This wine came ashore on Absecom Beach[640] from a Spanish wreck, about 1770. Then it was brought to Trenton,[641] and my great-uncle bought it. All but a demijohn was buried in his garden at the old house, not far from Princeton,[642] to keep it out of British stomachs. The one demijohn kept for use made the mischief I shall tell you of.

"Try that grape-juice, Wilmington. No? Then let Francis have his cigar. My Cuban friend shocks me with the late rise of prices. Eighteen dollars a thousand makes one hesitate."

"It does, indeed," said Francis. And soon the room was hazy with delicate smoke, as Hamilton continued:

"It was during the war, you know. My great-uncle Edward, who was with Washington, heard that his wife was ill. He got leave, managed to cross the Delaware, and in citizen's clothes made his way to his own country-house near Princeton. There he learned that she was not seriously ill, and as the country was full of British scouts, he resolved to go back next day to his duties in Washington's camp. The friend who had aided his adventure and was to set him across the Delaware again, came in about nine of the evening; and to aid them with the wisdom which is in wine, the demijohn of this disputed wine was brought out. Also a noble bowl of rum punch was brewed, and divers bottles were allowed their say, so that when Mr. Trent departed, Uncle Ned retired in some haste lest he should not be able to retire at all. It is probable that he left the candles to burn, and the hall door to close itself. About three in the morning, having snored off his rum and some wine, and hearing a noise, he put on his boots and a wrapper, and taking his pistols, went downstairs. As he entered the dining-room there were candles burning, fresh logs on the fire, and facing him sat an English captain, with his dirty boots on my aunt's best Chippendale arm-chair, and in act to swallow a glass of wine. Uncle Ned stepped through the open door and covered the unexpected guest with his pistol, at the same time remarking (and he was really the most imperturbable of men), 'Perhaps you are not aware that you are making free with my best Madeira, and really –"

"'Don't shoot, I beg you, until I finish my glass,' said the captain, calmly. 'Did I understand you to say Madeira? Madeira! It's sherry – unmistakably sherry! Of course, I don't dispute the ownership.'

"'Very kind of you,' remarked Uncle Ned. 'There seems to have been a considerable transfer of ownership.'

"'That is so,' replied the captain. 'I am like Mary after she ate her lamb. "Everywhere that Mary went that lamb was sure to go." Permit me to apologize. The sherry –'

"'I have had the honor to assure you that it is Madeira.'

"'Madeira! Great George !'

"Now Uncle Ned hated the king, and loved his wife, and greatly honored his own taste in wine. Both his prejudices and his affection had been lightly dealt with, so he

---

[640] Former name of the present-day area of Atlantic City, in Atlantic County, NJ.
[641] Capital of the state of New Jersey.
[642] A New Jersey borough, best known for its university with the same name, established in 1756.

said tartly: 'There is only one Great George, and he is across the Delaware, and the wine is Madeira, and you have soiled my wife's chair; and I wait, sir, to learn your errand.'

"'I grieve, sir, to say that you will quite too soon know my errand, when I call up the troopers who are back of the house; or if you are in haste a shot from you will do as well. Meanwhile permit me most humbly to apologize to Mrs. Hamilton. I regret to continue to differ concerning the wine. As to your George, he is a very small rebel George. And now I am obliged most reluctantly to finish my unfortunate business; perhaps, however, we had better see the last of the wine; you may not have another opportunity.'

"These remarks somewhat sobered Uncle Ned, and he became of a sudden aware of the trap he was in. So he sat down, with his pistols convenient, and saying, 'With all my heart,' began to push the bottle. The Britisher was good company, and his temper was already so mellowed by wine that he was fast nearing the stage of abrupt mental decay which mellowness naturally precedes. He graciously accepted a tumbler of punch, which my uncle contrived to make pretty strong, and then numberless glasses of wine, enlivened by very gay stories, at which my uncle was clever. At last the captain rose and said with some gravity, 'The glasses appear to be all t-twins. We have made a night of it. When you make a n-night of it you improve the s-shining hours. And now my painful duty –'

"'One glass more,' said my uncle; 'and about that story. Pray pardon me, I interrupted you.'

"'Oh, yes,' said the captain, emptying a very stiff glass of rum punch, which by no means put its own quality into the lessening vigor of his legs. 'As I was saying, I knew a man once – very clever man; loved a girl – very clever girl. Man consumedly fond of liquor. Girl didn't know which he liked best, the wine or the woman. One day that girl – he told her a very foolish story about not askin' for wine if she would put a k-kiss in the glass. And that day, instead of a k-kiss she put a little note inside the decanter; and when he had drunk up the wine, and the men were laughing at this f-fashion of billet-doux, he broke the decanter with the poker and r-read the note. Give you my word, he never drank a drop after that; and the note, it was a very c-clever note, and it just said –' But at this moment the captain made a queer noise in his throat, and slipped down, overcome with rebel rum and much Madeira. Uncle Ned humanely loosened his cravat and swordbelt, and lost no time in creeping through the dark to his friend's house, where he found clothes and a good horse. He was back in camp next day."

"And so this was the wine," said Chestnut; "and the man and the maid are gone, and the wine is still here. But the end of the story? – what the girl said in her note?"

"Ask the wine," laughed Hamilton, "or ask some good woman. No man knows. We shall find Mrs. Hamilton and my daughters in the drawing-room. They must be at home by this time. You can ask them."

"With all my heart," said Chestnut.

"That is, if you have had enough tobacco," added the host.

"Just one more glass from the disputed bottle," said Wilmington, rising with the rest, and holding his glass between his face and the lights. "As our old table-customs seem to interest you, Chestnut, I give you a toast which I have drunk now these fifty years. Once it was a present joy; it is now but a sad remembrance. Quite often I say it to myself when I take my last glass in company; and always when I dine alone I say it aloud, or it seems to say itself of long habit."

With these words, the spare little, ruddy old gentleman bowed in turn to each of his fellow-guests, and last to his host, and then said, with a certain sad serenity of manner: "Here is to each other," – and with a slight quaver in his voice, – "and to one other."

With this they turned from the table to follow Hamilton.

John gravely divided the mahogany doors opening into the drawing-room, and as Mr. Wilmington passed, murmured under his breath, "Dat wine's a sherry, sar, sure's ye're born."

"Uncle John," replied Wilmington, "you are a great man. Here is a dollar," and slowly followed his host, humming under his breath the old drinking-song:

"The bottle's the mistress I mean, I mean."[643]

Besides this short story, Silas W. Mitchell also published two other novels in which he refers Madeira Wine. In the first one, *Dr. North and His Friends*,[644] published in New York, in 1900, there are four references to Madeira Wine, in three different chapters, the most important of which is some of this nectar being brought to a certain dinner table after the removal of the cloth.

I

… We had a glad welcome at that first dinner. He was particular about his diet, and had the peculiarity of giving but one wine during the dinner. It might be a Burgundy, a claret, or a vintage champagne, but we were given no other until, after our good old fashion, the cloth was removed and the decanters of Madeira were set on the well-rubbed mahogany table. Vincent and I had often remonstrated with our friend on his disregard of the tastes of his guests. He replied that the Jews had the sense not to mix wines when they drank. Vincent remarked that a too generous use of texts would probably leave us neither drink nor diet, and certainly would forbid champagne. We did not change Clayborne's ways, and he continued, I do not why, to limit us to the one wine he that day fancied. …[645] …

X

… We dined merrily, discussing the woman movement and less serious matters. When we came to my father's old Madeira, we fell upon the war, as Clayborne had predicted. …

"A little Smoke," I said, pushing toward him the wine we call "Smoke Madeira," because of its singular smoke-like bouquet.

"A great wine," said Vincent, "and a fine story. Were you not caught after Antietam? Tell us about it, Haro, I have heard it only at second-hand."

"Certainly, if you would like."[646] …

---

[643] MITCHELL 1895, pages 3-60.
[644] MITCHELL, Silas Weir, *Dr. North and His Friends*, The Century Co., New York, 1900.
[645] MITCHELL 1900, pages 4-5.
[646] MITCHELL 1900, pages 168, 171-172.

XIX

… Then again the talk became gay and general.

When we came to the end of a pleasant hour and a half, the cloth was removed, and the butler set on the table two decanters of old Madeira.

"A grape-juice," said our host, as he passed the wine to the left. After it had gone round the table he added in his old-fashioned way: "Absent friends and your own good selves."

"Here, next," he said, "is the wine with a story. It is the Rose Madeira, Vincent."

"Indeed! I fear your ancient wines; but I must taste this. It is not quite perfect, Clayborne, – on its last legs, as our fathers used to say, – and yet it is still very fine. How old is it?"

"It was put in demijohn in 1798, and was before that in cask. You can detect the taste of the wood. You must all of you admit that I rarely tell stories, but –"

"Well," interrupted St. Clair, "for an historian, that is a crammer."

"Do not mind him," said my wife. "Please to go on."

"Vincent has heard it. It is a family legend. My great-uncle Rupert commanded the privateer *Rose*, out of New London.[647] She was lucky, and during a West Indian cruise sent home several prizes, from one of which she supplied herself with provisions and several hogsheads of the wine you are now drinking. …[648] …

The other literary work published by Silas W. Mitchell containing a few references to Madeira Wine, *In War Time*,[649] was also published in New York, in 1900, just as his previous book. In this one this wine is mentioned thirteen times, in five different chapters, and in one of them we can see it being used to make a toast, during a dinner conversation.

VI.

… "Oh, that's just one of the many advantages of being a woman! Don't you think I am horribly disloyal? I talked so to old Wilmington, the other night, that he says I am dangerous, and to-day he would hardly speak to me; but then he had been taking a great deal of the major's madeira, and his nose shone like a cheerful lighthouse!"[650] …

VII.

… "What a lovely day!" said Mrs. Westerley.

"Yes, the day seems quite lovely," assented Wilmington.

"But we want rain."

"Yes, we want rain very much."

"Our wells are nearly dry" –

"Indeed, mine is quite dry."

---

[647] A Connecticut seaport city.
[648] MITCHELL 1900, page 324.
[649] MITCHELL, S.[ilas] Weir, *In War Time*, The Century Co., New York, 1900, page 91.
[650] MITCHELL 1900, page 91.

"But luckily weather does not affect wine, at all, I am told; at least, not madeira."

"No, I don't think weather affects wine, but the moon does."

"And when are you coming over to taste my madeira, Mr. Wilmington? I am told it is good; but Major Morton said, last spring, that it needed care, – like myself, he was kind enough to add. [651] …

VIII.

… "Three o'clock, then. Good-by," and she drove away. "Gracious," she exclaimed, "what an escape! If I had to leave my doctor to talk madeira with Wilmington! What nice eyes the man has!" …

Then Mr. Wilmington shifted his seat to the place she had left, and the servant put in front of him, on silver coasters, four or five tall, slender, antique decanters.

The old gentleman, with his head on one side, looked through massive gold eyeglasses at the silver labels, and very deliberately rearranging the bottles, filled his glass, and passed the wine to Wendell. "With the sun, if you please," he said. "A little cold, John, this wine," upon which, to Wendell's amazement, he clasped the wine-glass in both hands, and shut his eyes with a tranquil expression of such utter satisfaction as the coming pleasure, and with so much of a look of devotion, that the doctor conceived for a moment the idea that nothing less than a thankful prayer for a good dinner could be in the old man's mind; but presently he drank off his wine, and remarked, "A good grape juice. '28, I think. I didn't suppose there was any of it left."

Wendell certainly found it good.

The second wine was dismissed with, "I wouldn't advise you to take that. It wants a good fining, Colonel Fox."

The colonel was of like opinion.

"There is no label on this; but women take no care of their wines. Hem," he said, as he set down his glass, "I remember that wine well. It is precisely my own age. It's getting just a little shaky, like myself; it is smoke! No better wine, Dr. Wendell; do you know it?"

"I can't say that I do," said Wendell, rather puzzled at the appelation. "I know little or nothing of wines."

"Well," remarked Fox, "Mr. Wilmington is a good instructor. I advise you to begin your education."

"But what on earth is smoke?" asked the doctor.

"Don't you taste it?" returned Wilmington. "There is no better madeira. I don't know many as good. A little eggshell would help it."

"Yes, a little eggshell," repeated Fox, with equal gravity.

"I am glad you still like it," exclaimed the old gentleman; "the taste is going out. I don't know five lads who can tell sherry from a fine madeira. My Jack says he likes cider. 'Likes cider,' – good heavens! Will you take another glass, doctor, or a cigar?"

"Unless you want to be excommunicated vinously," said Fox, laughing, "you can't drink after your smoke;" and so the cigars were brought an there was more talk, during which Fox slipped away to chat with Mrs. Westerley, and the doctor was left alone with Mr. Wilmington.

---

651 MITCHELL 1900, pages 100-101.

Wendell very soon found that any discussion which did not involve wine talk was, at this stage of the dinner, quite out of the question, and he therefore wisely yielded, and as a consequence rose many degrees in the old gentleman's favor. What he learned as to wines it is perhaps not worth while to inquire. "And when I say wines," said Mr. Wilmington, " I mean madeiras, sir. There are other drinks; but excepting now and then a rare claret, – a very rare claret, – there are no wines except madeira. None, sir!" said the old gentleman, with unusual warmth, – "none, sir!"

He talked of wines as people talk of other people, of their vices and virtues, their births and decays. His dinners were gossips about wines. Such was the fashion of his day, and he and a very few old friends held to it with the tenacity of age. The friends were dropping fast, but the wines remained, and through them more than in any other way were aroused his pleasantest memories of departed feasts and the comrades at whom he had smiled above some golden south side vintage, in days when manners were more courtly an healths were drunk.

At last, when Wendell timidly remarked that all this care about wines must take up a good deal of time, Mr. Wilmington said, "Yes. It was quite true; they were like women and needed a good deal of attention, and that was just why Morton's wines had all gone to the devil. And a very pretty cellar he might have had, too, if he had only looked after it."

Sunday afternoon, he added, he himself had found a good quiet time to see to his madeiras; and, as Wendell learned later, any Sunday the old gentleman was to be found in his wine garret, contemplative and surrounded by demijohns, and eggshells, and what not.[652] …

XIII.

… "Well, go and dress for dinner. And mind that you are very attentive to the old gentleman, – you know he likes it; and don't leave him alone with Dr. Wendell and the madeira."

"Oh, no, of course not; and as to madeira, I haven't heard it mentioned for a year!"[653] …

XVIII.

… "Disagreeable business, all this!" said Wilmington, vaguely, – "death of Lincoln, and all that. There is a passage in the Spectator which applies to it, – something about rebels; but it might be in Milton."

"I don't recall it," replied Wendell.

"Nor I. My memory isn't at all what it was. Bless me, how sharp the air is!"

"Yes, it is rather biting for the season. And how is the gout, Mr. Wilmington?"

"Well enough, if I don't drink madeira. But you see, doctor, if you don't drink madeira, why, life really isn't worth much in the latter part of the day, you know."

"I wouldn't take a great deal, or habitually," said Wendell.[654] …

---

652 MITCHELL 1900, pages 109, 123-126.
653 MITCHELL 1900, page 193.
654 MITCHELL 1900, page 289.

Other than these works, Silas Weir Mitchell also inserted some references to Madeira Wine in other books of his published in New York, in the early 20th century, namely in *The Red City; A Novel of the Second Administration of President Washington*, [The Century Co., 1908]; *The Guillotine Club and Other Stories*, [The Century Co., 1910]; and *Westways; A Village Chronicle*, [The Century Co., 1913].

6.2.15. William Gilmore Simms

The novel *The Partisan - A Romance of the Revolution*,[655] by William Gilmore Simms (1806-1870), a native of Charleston, SC, was published in New York, in 1852. Its plot is set in the South, during the Revolutionary War, where Madeira Wine was widely known and consumed, and in two chapters of this book there are three references to this precious wine in that time period.

CHAPTER XII.

... "And what of the Britons, Humphries? are they yet in saddle, and when may we hope to approach the dwelling? I have not been used to skulk like a beaten hound around the house of my mother's brother, not daring to come forward; and I am free to confess, the necessity makes me melancholy."

"Very apt to do so, major, but you have to bear it a little longer. The horses of the officers have been brought up into the court, and the boy is in waiting, but the riders have not made their appearance. I suppose they stop for a last swig at the colonel's Madeira. He keeps a prime stock on hand, they say, though I've never had the good fortune to taste any of it."

"You shall do so to-night, Humphries, and grow wiser, unless your British major's potations exceed a southern gentleman's capacity to meet them. But you knew my uncle long before coming down from Santee[656] with him."[657] ...

CHAPTER XIV.

... Thus impressed, silent and unobserving, it was a relief to all, when Major Singleton, shaking off his sadness with an effort, reminded Humphries of the promise which he had presumed to make him, touching the old Madeira in his uncle's garret. He briefly told the latter of the circumstance alluded to, and the prompt orders of Colonel Walton soon brought the excellence of his wines to the impartial test to which Humphries proposed to subject them.

The lieutenant smacked his lips satisfactorily. It was not often that his fortune had indulged him with such a beverage. Corn whiskey, at best, had been his liquor in the swamps; and, even in his father's tavern, the tastes were not sufficiently high, of those

---

[655] SIMMS, William Gilmore, *The Partisan - A Romance of the Revolution*, New and Revised Edition, W. J. Widdleton, Publisher, New York, [1852].
[656] See Note 607.
[657] SIMMS [1852], page 131.

who patronized that establishment, to call for other than the cheapest qualities. A brief dialogue about the favorite wines – a sly reference on the part of Singleton to the drinking capacities of his British guests, and a hypocritical sort of condolence upon the privations to which his uncle must be subjected, in consequence of the proclamation, soon brought the latter back to the legitimate topic. …

"What, Gates! that is brave news, truly – brave news – and we shall do well to wish him success in another glass of Madeira. Come, Mr. Humphries – come, sir – you see Proctor has left us some of the genuine stuff yet – enough for friends, at least."

"Ay, sir," said Humphries, drinking, "and this news of the continentals promises that we have enough also for our enemies."

"Bravo! I hope so; I think so. Nephew, drink; drink – and say, what has been the effect of this intelligence upon the people? How has it wrought upon the Santee?"[658]

Figure 63. William Gilmore Simms inserts a few references to Madeira Wine in his novels set in the South, during the American Revolutionary War. *Photo by Mathew Brady, c.1860.*

"Everywhere well, uncle, and as it should, unless it be immediately in your neighbourhood, where you breathe by sufferance only. Everywhere well, sir. The people are roused, inspired, full of hope and animation. The country is alive with a new sentiment. …"[659]

In another novel, *The Sword and the Distaff: or, "Fair, Fat, and Forty." – A Story of the South, At the Close of the Revolution*,[660] published in Philadelphia, in 1853, William Gilmore Simms presents four references to old Madeira Wine, in three different chapters.

CHAPTER XLVII.
THE CORPORAL PUTS THE CAPTAIN FAVORABLY FORWARD.

… Mrs. Eveleigh seized the occasion to invite her guests to take refreshment, and led the way for them into the dwelling. As Porgy followed, Millhouse nudged him with his elbow.

"How could you do it?" he murmured – "Show jest that leetle heap when I was a-spreading you out?"

"Pshaw, fool!" was the muttered thunder which saluted the sergeant in reply, the captain fiercely pressing forward, and completely covering the entrance as he did so.

"Fool!" growled the sergeant to himself. "Well, that's for sarving a pusson what don't desarve it."

"Here is some old Madeira, captain, and some Jamaica. Please show the way to your friends – my son does not drink."

"Why, ma'am," quoth Millhouse, possessing himself of a beaker, and approaching the widow – "you don't mean to let the young man go without a sodger's education."

---

658 See Note 607.
659 SIMMS [1852], pages 157-159.
660 SIMMS, William Gilmore, *The Sword and the Distaff: or, "Fair, Fat, and Forty." – A Story of the South, At the Close of the Revolution*, Lippincott, Grambo, & Co., Philadelphia, 1853.

"His father was a soldier, sir, yet it was his dying injunction that Arthur should never drink."

"Well, that's mighty strange, I swow! 'Twouldn't ha' done in *our* sarvice, where the only way to forgit that you had nothing to eat, was to git r'yal drunk on what you had. Here's your health, ma'am, and my sarvice to you, ma'am, for ever."

The lady bowed, and Porgy, having refreshed himself with such a glass of Madeira as he had not often enjoyed for years, withdrew, at a motion from Mrs. Eveleigh, to an adjoining room.

"Why, whar's the cappin!" cried Millhouse, who had been lingering over his liquor.[661] ...

CHAPTER LVII.
COUP DE THEATRE.

... The sheriff noted the man's air and manner, and was impressed accordingly. The conduct of Lance Frampton, who was singularly quiet, was yet of a sort to fix his attention. In this young man he beheld a fixed confidence in his superior, and a readiness to obey orders, which showed that, at a wink, he would be prepared to act, and without any regard to responsibilities. After awhile the wine began to circulate, though the sergeant still confined himself to the Jamaica. Even when, at the summons of the captain, he emptied his glass of Madeira, he was sure to swallow a good mouthful of the rum after it, as if to prevent any evil consequences from the more aristocratic liquor. The dishes were cleared away, and Tom gave the party a rice-pudding, which was voted good on all hands. Its removal was followed by the introduction of raisins, ground-nuts (*peanuts* or *pindars*), and black walnuts. Over the wine and walnuts, the chat grew more and more lively. It passed from topic to topic; the town and country; the camp and court; civil life and that of the soldier; but there was one lurking trouble in the mind of the sheriff which invariably brought him back to the peculiar condition in which he found the household. ...

"None to me! Don't you see, my dear colonel, that I am prepared to sacrifice my life with my property, and that law can in no way, exact a higher forfeit? But d–n the law! We've had enough of it for the present. Fill up your glass. You will find that Madeira prime. It is from an ancient cellar!"

"Thank you! [Fills.] Well, my dear captain, suffer me to hope for you an escape from the clutches of the law by legitimate means!"[662] ...

CHAPTER LVIII.
LEGAL REGIMEN.

... The day passed and the party of four had not left the table. They had raised their clouds around it; all being smokers except the lieutenant. Coffee was served by Tom, in the midst of the cloud. When the coffee disappeared, the Jamaica and the Madeira were restored. Cards followed, and at twelve o'clock at night, the sheriff rose a loser of some thirty shillings to sergeant Millhouse, who played through the hands of Frampton, and

---

661 SIMMS 1853, page 389-390.
662 SIMMS 1853, pages 493-494.

who became more and more reconciled to the suspicious guest with every shilling which the latter yielded. When, next morning, after the colonel's departure, – which took place soon after an early breakfast – he was discoursing of his good qualities, his companionable virtues, and so forth, the captain of partisans laid his hand on his shoulder –[663] ...

There is still another novel by William Gilmore Simms, *Eutaw - A sequel to The Forayers; Or, The Raid of the Dog-Days. A tale of the Revolution*,[664] published in 1856, in New York, where there are ten references to Madeira Wine, in six different chapters. In one of them there is a reference to an old Madeira, of the vintage of 1758.

CHAPTER XVII.
GAMES OF PEACE AND WAR.

... And had it not been for a timely fate that interposed for Rawdon's safety, the Gamecock of the Santee[665] would probably have happened upon a conquest which he never hoped for at the beginning of his march. But we must not anticipate. The several parties were everywhere in motion, on the indicated routes, while Rawdon was sipping Madeira with old Sinclair, and Fitzgerald was drinking in delicious draughts of love from the bright eyes of Carrie Sinclair, as they sat together over the chess-board, or as she played for him upon the venerable harpsichord.

Lord Rawdon secured for him every opportunity for pressing his attentions profitably. He soon engaged Colonel Sinclair in the important topics of the country, the condition of the war, tho case of his rebel son, and the future prospects of the struggle. Absorbed in subjects of this sort, the old loyalist colonel almost forgot he had a daughter; and, while Rawdon kept his mind busy on these matters, in the supper-room, long after the meal was over – the Madeira taking the place of the tea and coffee urns – the young lover was free to exhibit all his resources and attractions, with no restraint except that which is inevitable from the modesty of a bashful Irishman.

... "Let me beg you to fill, my lord. I must drink his majesty's health, and the success of his arms."

And they drank. The brief interruption over, old Sinclair proceeded; –

"'Willie Sinclair, my dear lord, bating this monomania of liberty which has made him a rebel, is yet no foul, sir – but a cool, shrewd, thoughtful, long-headed young fellow – and as brave, sir, as Julius Caesar."

"I know his character, my dear colonel. I have heard the same report of him from far less partial sources. In these respects, at least, he proves his legitimacy."

"Ah! my lord, I could have been, I was proud of this likeness to myself, until he became a rebel. But, no more of that – no more of that."

And unconsciously the old man refilled and swallowed another glass of his favorite Madeira, while Rawdon beheld another and bigger tear crawling down his cheek. ...

---

663 SIMMS 1853, page 499.
664 SIMMS, William Gilmore, *Eutaw - A sequel to The Forayers; Or, The Raid of the Dog-Days. A tale of the Revolution*, W. J. Widdleton, Publisher, New York, [1856].
665 See Note 607.

"Is it so? Is it come to this? The arms of Britain can no longer give me protection on my own grounds." And he sighed from the bottom of his heart.

"Oh, Willie Sinclair! Willie Sinclair! you have helped to bring this dishonor on your country's flag!"

And the baron hastily gulped down another stoup of Madeira, thrusting the decanter to his lordship, who followed his example without a word. Rawdon then resumed the dialogue.

"I must leave the country, colonel; you see my condition. I am worn out – exhausted. Another campaign will kill me. My whole system is out of tone. I have no energies. I only remain to see the army put in order – to adjust the affairs of my military government with the civil authorities; do what I can, by some severe examples, to discourage treason and desertion, and then leave the future administration in hands that will, I trust, prove more efficient than mine." [666] …

CHAPTER XVIII.
HOW THE SOLDIERS WENT ONE WAY, AND THE LADIES ANOTHER – HOW HELL-FIRE DICK TAKES TO LITERATURE.

… He, following Rawdon, was followed in turn by Major Jekyll, of the British army, who was instantly introduced to Colonel Sinclair. The old gentleman took the opportunity, immediately after, to introduce the Madeira.

"You have had some warm work of it, my lord; will you be pleased to take a glass of Madeira. Gentlemen, will you be so good as to grace us in a little Madeira."

His lordship filled, and the other gentlemen followed. Rawdon bowed to the colonel and said: –

"We owe this brush to your son, colonel. It is he who has been beating up our quarters!"

"My son! ah! my lord, spare me. This is a great humiliation to a father." …

As Jekyll was about to retire, Colonel Sinclair arrested him

"One moment, Major Jekyll; one moment. My lord, I have had a demijohn of rum put in readiness, thinking you might desire to serve out a ration of it to the brave fellows in your escort."

"Thank you, my dear colonel; it will prove grateful enough, I warrant."

"And, if you will permit me, my lord, I should like to join yourself, my Lord Edward, and Major Jekyll, in a much better liquor."

"I can answer for it, colonel, that my two friends will be as well pleased as myself to do justice to your Madeira."

They drank, and Jekyll at once retired. The Lords Rawdon and Fitzgerald lingered an hour later, and the bottle was emptied; unobservedly, by all parties, as a very interesting conversation ensued, upon the affairs of the war.[667] …

---

666 SIMMS [1856], pages 192-193, 196-198.
667 SIMMS [1856], pages 206, 208.

CHAPTER XXVIII.
SHOWING HOW COLONEL SINCLAIR, SENIOR, CONFOUNDED TWO VERY DIFFERENT KINDS OF FISH.

… "To be sure, Captain Porgy, to be sure. Come and see us. Though you are a rebel, sir, like my son, you are a gentleman, I believe, and a man of honor; and all that I have ever heard of you is grateful. Nothing, I assure you, will give me more pleasure, in a social way, than to have you at my board; and I promise you, if you will come, to put some old Madeira before you, of the vintage of 1758, such as is seldom broached now-a-days in Carolina. I pray you, sir, to believe that I am sincere, and forgive that stupid blunder of mine in taking your name in vain."

All this was said very heartily, and in just the tone and strain to make its way to Porgy's heart.

"To be sure, you are sincere, Colonel Sinclair. A man with the taste to keep Madeira twenty years in his house must be an honest man; and to broach it freely to his guest, proves him a gentleman. You may look to see me, should occasion ever offer. As for your mistake in my name, sir, let it never trouble you. I never take offence where I am assured it is unmeant; and, when we look at the facts, you really conveyed a compliment. …"[668] …

CHAPTER XXX.
STRANDED ON THE KING'S HIGHWAY.

… "But he is *not* shot – not hurt – as I understand you!"

"To be sure not! God was merciful! I missed him; had I slain him, my lord, be sure, I had not been here to answer you to-night. I had kept one pistol for myself."

"My dear colonel, dismiss these thoughts. I hope to drink many a good glass of that old Madeira with you yet. But suffer me to send my surgeon to you. He is an able man, and may, no doubt, afford you some relief."[669] …

CHAPER XXXV.
EVERYWHERE THE SERPENT UNDER THE VINES.

… Sam Peter Adair, that day, entertained a single guest, in a person who, in South Carolina, enjoys a certain amiable reputation, as one of the few British officers who exhibited traits of courtesy, tolerance, and magnanimity, in dealing with his foes. This was Major John Marjoribanks, a fine-looking gentleman, of middle age, then commanding a flank battalion, and stationed, for a time, at Monck's Corner which post Rawdon had re-established. His duties calling him to the neighborhood of Wantoot and Pooshee, Adair eagerly sought out Marjoribanks, and made him his guest while in the vicinity. Hence the dinner-party of which Griffith has told us; the officers at Wantoot and Pooshee being invited to meet with Marjoribanks. He remained, after they had gone, and though but a portion

---
[668] SIMMS [1856], page 352.
[669] SIMMS [1856], page 372.

of the guests suffered from the wine, in the manner reported at Griffith's, yet all of them were made sufficiently to approve of the host's old Madeira.[670] ...

CHAPTER XLVII.
DENOUEMENT.

... How the war still lingered, and with what petty strifes in Carolina, we need not report in these pages. Enough, perhaps, as we may never meet with him again, in fiction, to report, that our brave boy, Henry Travis, obtained a cornetcy of dragoons, under Sinclair, and served with great spirit, zeal, and promise, to the end of the war. "We all know what was the good result of that training which he then received, from the high distinction which he won subsequently, and long after, in the West, when, as Colonel Travis, he went through the Creek and Seminole campaign, and in the war of 1812, fully displayed the admirable uses of the lessons which he had acquired in that of the Revolution.

The baron lived to a good old age, in spite of gout and Madeira. He and Mrs. Travis were equally fortunate and happy, in being able to dandle numerous grandchildren upon their knees.[671] ...

6.2.16. William Taylor Adams

Figure 64. William Taylor Adams, known in the literary world as 'Oliver Optic'. *Photo inserted in the book* The Who-When-What, *published in 1900.*

William Taylor Adams (1822-1897), a native of Medway, MA, was a noted academic, author and Massachusetts state legislator. He was a teacher and traveled extensively, crossing the Atlantic four times and visiting each European country. He used the knowledge acquired from the contact with his young students, and from his travels abroad to convey reality to his books – he published over a 100 – most of which were written for boys, under the pseudonym Oliver Optic. In 1877, he published, in Boston and New York, the book entitled *Isles of the Sea; or, Young America Homeward Bound*,[672] the sixth and last volume of the Second Series of "Young America Abroad", in which he describes a homeward bound voyage of the academy squadron, a group of young American students who had gone to Europe. In two chapters of this novel there are some references to Madeira Wine. In chapter X it is mentioned during a lecture directed to the boys about the island, and in the following one, in the form of a dialogue between two characters, there are allusions to the transportation of wine in goatskins and to the disease that had affected the vines decades earlier, and also a reference to its shortage and adulteration.

---

[670] SIMMS [1856], pages 437-438.
[671] SIMMS [1856], page 581.
[672] ADAMS, William T., (Oliver Optic, pseud.), *Isles of the Sea; or, Young America Homeward Bound. A Story of Travel and Adventure*, Lee and Shepard, Publishers, Boston; Charles T. Dillingham, New York, 1877.

CHAPTER X.
SOMETHING ABOUT THE MADEIRA ISLANDS.

… While this conversation was going on, the signal, "All hands attend lecture," had been displayed on board of the steamer. All the boats were in the water, and the students were soon assembled in the American Prince. As usual, there was a large map of the country to be described, hung where all the pupils could see it. In this instance it was a map of the Madeira Islands, drawn on a large scale by the professor himself. Mr. Mapps stood by it with a long pointer in his hand, when the students took their places.

"The Madeiras are a group of five islands," the professor began, flourishing the pointer over the map to attract the attention of his audience. …

"Funchal is the principal town, and has about twenty thousand inhabitants. Its principal business is in wine and fruit. In later years the vine has failed to a great extent, and the commerce of the island has been greatly reduced. Many of the inhabitants are in a state of destitution; and beggars are more common here than in most of the countries of Europe.[673] …

CHAPTER XI.
BUDDING VINES AND ORANGE-GROVES.

… "This looks like Spain," said Wainwright, pointing to a lot of men from the country, who were driving three or four donkeys each, loaded with skins filled with wine. "They leave the legs of the goats on for handles."

"Those sacks look something like a goat," added Murray. "I wonder how they can sew them up tight enough to prevent them from leaking."

"They can roll the edges of the skins together a little when they join them, and sew through four thicknesses of the skin, replied the doctor.

"Is that Madeira wine in those sacks?" inquired Murray.

"Probably not; for that is a scarce article, even in this island, at the present time. Porto Santo, or Holy Port, was the first island discovered and settled. Columbus lived there for a time; and his house is still shown. He married his wife there. The discovery and settlement of Madeira followed soon after; and two years later the Portuguese brought from Candia or Crete a vine which proved to be admirably adapted to the climate. The wine made from it became celebrated all over the civilized world. Like port and sherry, it obtained its peculiar flavor from the kind of grape of which it was made. Ten years ago, owing to the failure of the vine-crop, there were only four hundred pipes of it remaining in the island, while twenty-five thousand pipes had once been the average quantity manufactured in a year. The disease attacked the vine nearly twenty years ago; but the people are doing their best to replace it, and doubtless the commerce and reputation of the island will be fully restored. Probably the greater portion of all the wine sold for Madeira is not such; and not a little of it is manufactured in the shops where it is sold, in England and America."[674] …

---

673 ADAMS 1877, pages 145-146.
674 ADAMS 1877, pages 154-155.

6.3. American Poetry

Last but not least, in the last section of this long chapter will be presented some poems honoring Madeira, published by a few 19th century American poets, listed in alphabetical order.

6.3.1. James Gates Percival

James Gates Percival (1795-1856), a native of Berlin, CT, wrote a poem that might be termed, more than a tribute, a true anthem to Madeira Wine. It was published originally in 1821, in New Haven, CT, and its stanzas speak for themselves.

BALMY JUICE OF RICH MADEIRA[675]

Figure 65. James Gates Percival, author of one of the best poems ever written about Madeira Wine. *19th century illustration. Author unknown.*

Balmy juice of rich Madeira –
How thy amber bubbles shine,
How thy fragrance charms the wary,
Soothing like a song divine.

When thy nectar gaily flushes,
And thy hues the goblet stain,
How the mounting spirit rushes
Lightly through the dancing brain.

Every scene of sadness brightens,
All is rob'd in vestment fair,
How the cloud of sorrow lightens,
As we sip, and banish care.

Now the patriot bosom throbbing
Swells to deeds of high renown,
And the lover ceases sobbing,
Though beneath his mistress' frown.

Now, his eye with frenzy rolling,
How the poet sweeps his lyre,
While no hand his fire controlling
Madness thunders o'er his wire.

---

[675] PERCIVAL, James G.[ates], *Poems*, Published for the Author, New Haven, 1821, page 54; *The Poetical Works of James Gates Percival. With a Biographical Sketch.*, In Two Volumes, Vol. II., Ticknor and Fields, Boston, 1863, pages 417-418; *Daily Eastern Argus*, April 3, 1866. (Portland, ME, under the title "RICH MADEIRA").

Fir'd by thee he grasps the lightning,
Hurls it fiercely through the air,
And a wreath of glory brightening
Flames around his waving hair.

When my fancy faintly drooping
Loses all its fire divine,
Let me o'er thy fountain stooping
Quaff the richly mantling wine.

6.3.2. Philip Freneau

Philip Freneau (1752-1832), a native of New York City, was widely known in his days as the "Poet of the American Revolution" due to the patriotic poems he wrote supporting it. In 1803, he became shipmaster of the brig *Washington*, which was engaged in Madeira Wine trade, sailing between Charleston, SC, and Madeira, and came to the island in that year, leaving it for that American city, on July 14, 1803. While in Madeira Island he wrote an interesting poem depicting an encounter he supposedly had with Bacchus, with whom he had to negotiate a cargo of wine. This poetical composition was originally published in an American newspaper, a few months after his return to the United States.

COMMUNICATED FOR THE DAILY ADVERTISER.
BENEVOLENT BACCHUS.[676]
WRITTEN BY CAPTAIN PHILIP FRENEAU, AT THE ISLAND OF MADEIRA, JULY, 1803.[677]

Arrived at Madeira, that favourite isle,
Renown'd for the choicest of wine,
Her Genius approach'd me, and said with a smile,
What I'll tell you in subsequent lines:

He said, with a sneer, (and I trembled with fear
As I roved by her fountains and springs)
He said, you Columbian,[678] how dare you come here,
You hater of despots and kings?

---

676 *The Daily Advertiser*, September 17, 1803. (New York City, NY).
677 In July 1803 Freneau was at Madeira, as shipmaster of the brig *Washington*, from Charleston, SC. He had arrived on June 23rd of the same year and left the island, bound for Charleston, on the 14th of July.
678 Native of Columbia, the state capital and largest city of South Carolina. As we have seen before he was not born in Columbia but rather in New York. As we have referred on the previous Note, he had come from South Carolina and was taking this wine cargo for the same destination, hence perhaps the reason why Bacchus referred to himself as "Columbian".

Figure 66. Philip Freneau, who described in verse a dialogue he allegedly had with Bacchus while on the island to buy wine, in the early 1800's. *Engraving by Frederick Halpin.*

Do you know that a prince,[679] and a despot indeed,[680]
Whose sway not a climate confines,
Is monarch of all, and a regent decreed
To preside in this island of wines?

Haste away with your barque – on the foam of the main
To Charleston I bid you repair,
And drink your hot whisky that maddens the brain,
You shall have no Madeira, I swear.

Dear Bacchus, I answer'd – (for Bacchus is was
That spoke in this menacing tone;
I knew by the smirk and the flush in his face
It was Bacchus, and Bacchus alone) –

Dear Bacchus, (I answered) ah, why so severe –
Since your nectar abundantly flows,
Allow me one cargo – without it, I fear
Columbians will soon come to blows.

I left them in wrangles, disorder, and strife,
Political feuds were so high,
I was sick of the people, and sick of my life,
They so wrangled – and few can tell why.

The monarch you mention, no doubt, he combines
Some traits of yourself with his power;
So, to me, he is only the monarch of wines,
He cannot be savage or sour.

Permit me to take the produce of grape,
And long may he govern your isle,
This prince, or this king – and my course I will shape
For Columbia, and change the old style.

Though still democratic, two kings I adore,
That monarch of monarchs, the sun,
He guides me at sea, and lights me on shore,
Director of all that is done.

No eye can avoid him, no action escape,
To him is all nature consign'd:

---

[679] John VI (1767-1826), who was Prince Regent of Portugal from 1799 to 1816, who ruled the country due to the mental illness of his mother, the Queen. Later on he was crowned King, ruling from 1816 to 1826.
[680] As Prince Regent he possessed absolute powers, being one of the last representatives of absolutism in his country.

He scorches, he burns – but the king of the grape
Illumines and softens the mind.

With a nod he assented, and said, I forgive
Your visit from far to my shore;
Haste; fill up your vessel, and when you arrive,
Bid Charleston old Bacchus adore:

Let Washington[681] waft them that nectar divine
Which may hush them to peace and repose:
On the wings of the winds, with this present of wine,
You shall travel, and tell them – here goes!

A health to that Bacchus, who sends them the best
Of the wine he extracts from the soil:
Whith this essence of grapes, if they will not be blest,
I forbid you hereafter my isle.

You may go to Fayal,[682] and the island more south,
Teneriffe, and her Pico[683] of Fame;
But wine like my own never moisten'd a mouth
Or kindled so noble a flame.

In a poetry book Freneau published in New York, more than ten years later, we found a second version of this poem, under a different title, containing a few differences, both in the number of stanzas as in the verse's word choice, therefore we decided to present it as well, so that the curious reader might compare both versions.

A BACCHANALIAN DIALOGUE.[684]
WRITTEN 1803.

Arrived at Madeira, the island of vines,
Where mountains and vallies abound,
Where the sun the mild juice of the cluster refines,
To gladden the magical ground.

As pensive I stray'd in her elegant shade,
Now halting and now on the move,

---

[681] AN: The name of the vessel.
[682] An Azorean island in mid Atlantic.
[683] Another Azorean island, facing Fayal, dominated by the imposing Pico, the tallest Portuguese mountain, and where good wine was also made and exported to the United States, under the name of "Fayal Madeira" or "Pico Madeira".
[684] FRENEAU, Philip, *A Collection of Poems, on American Affairs, and a variety of other subjects, chiefly moral and political; Written between the year 1797 and the Present Time*, Vol. I., New York, 1815, pages 169-171.

Old Bacchus I met, with a crown on his head,
In the darkest recess of a grove.

I met him with awe, but no symptom of fear
As I roved by his mountains and springs,
When he said with a sneer, "how dare you come here,
You hater of despots and kings? –

Do you know that a prince, and a regent renown'd
Presides in this island of wine?[685]
Whose fame on the earth has encircled it round
And spreads from the pole to the line?

Haste away with your barque: on the foam of the main
To Charleston I bid you repair:
There drink your Jamaica,[686] that maddens the brain;
You shall have no Madeira – I swear."

"Dear Bacchus," (I answered) for Bacchus it was
That spoke in this menacing tone:
I knew by the smirk and the flush on his face
It was Bacchus, and Bacchus alone –

"Dear Bacchus, (I answered) ah, why so severe? –
Since your nectar abundantly flows,
Allow me one cargo – without it I fear
Some people will soon come to blows:

I left them in wrangles, disorder, and strife,
Political feuds were so high,
I was sick of their quarrels, and sick of my life,
And almost requested to die."
The deity smiling, replied, "I relent: –
For the sake of your coming so far,
Here, taste of my choicest – go, tell them repent,
And cease their political war.

With the cargo I send, you may say, I intend
To hush them to peace and repose;
With this present of mine, on the wings of the wine
You shall travel, and tell them, here goes

A health to old Bacchus! who sends them the best

---

685 See Note 679.
686 Allusion to the Jamaica rum, largely consumed in the United States at the time, especially by the lower classes.

Of the nectar his island affords,
The soul of the feast and the joy of the guest,
Too good for your monarchs and lords.

No rivals have I in this insular waste,
Alone will I govern the isle
With a king at my feet, and a court to my taste,
And all in the popular style.

But a spirit there is in the order of things,
To me it is perfectly plain,
That will strike at the sceptres of despots and kings,
And only king Bacchus remain."

6.3.3. Silas Weir Mitchell

Silas Weir Mitchell, mentioned in the previous section, also wrote two poems related to Madeira Wine, the first one in 1887, and the second one, later in life, in 1914. In both of them he pays a special tribute to this famous wine, of which he was a true *connoisseur*.

A DECANTER OF MADEIRA.[687]
A Decanter of Madeira, aged 86, to George Bancroft, aged 86, Greeting:
OCTOBER 3, 1886. NEWPORT.
BEAULIEU.

I.
GOOD MASTER, you and I were born
In "Teacups days" of hoop and hood,

---

[687] MITCHELL, S.[ilas] Weir, *A Masque and Other Poems*, Houghton, Mifflin and Company, Boston and New York, 1887, pages 61-63; *The Collected Poems of S. Weir Mitchell*, The Century Co., New York, 1896, pages 347-348; *Selections from The Poems of S. Weir Mitchell*, Macmillan and Co., London, 1901, pages 173-175; *The Complete Poems of S. Weir Mitchell*, The Century Co., New York, 1914, pages 411-412. This poem was also revealed in several American newspapers: *The Macon Telegraph*, October 17, 1886. (Macon, GA. Published under the titles "HISTORIAN BANCROFT – How His Birthday Was Honored With a Poem and a Bottle of 86-Year Madeira.", preceded by this introduction: «NEWPORT, October 7. – At a dinner given on the 3d of October by Mrs. Astor in honor of the 86th birthday of George Bancroft, the historian, the following poem was read. It was the hit of the evening. Copies of it have been in great demand, but few have been able to obtain them. The author modestly withholds his name:»); *The Washington Critic*, October 20, 1886. (Washington, DC); *Springfield Republican*, October 25, 1886. (Springfield, MA. Published under the titles "THE VINTAGE OF 1800. – Wine on George Bancroft's Birthday" and preceded by the following introduction: «At Mrs. Astor's dinner in honor of George Bancroft's birthday anniversary, October 3, a poem was read from "A decanter of Madeira, aged 86, to George Bancroft, aged 86, greeting." The author is said to be Mrs. Astor herself, and the verses are as follows:»); *Deseret Evening News*, August 27, 1904. (Salt Lake City, UT. Published under the title "With a Decanter of Maderia" at the section 'Literature – Poems Everybody Should Know', accompanied by the following note: «This poem which bears date Oct. 3, 1886, is published in Dr. Mitchell's "A Masque and Other Poems," 1887, and when first written accompanied a decanter of Madeira wine aged 86 years old, which was presented to George Bancroft, the historian, on the day he was 86 years old.»). This was also briefly reported in another source, namely in the *Oshkosh Daily Northwestern*, November 9, 1886. (Oshkosh, WI. Published in the section "POINTS ABOUT PEOPLE.", in these words: «Dr. S. Weir Mitchell contributed a dust-covered bottle of Madeira and a poem to the birthday festivities of Bancroft, the historian, the other day.»).

And when the silver cue hung down,
And toasts were drunk, and wine was good;

II.

When kin of mine (a jolly brood)
From sideboards looked, and knew full well
What courage they had given the beau,
How generous made the blushing belle.

III.

Ah me! what gossip could I prate
Of days when doors were locked at dinners!
Believe me, I have kissed the lips
Of many pretty saints – or sinners.

IV.

Lip service have I done, alack!
I don't repent, but come what may,
What ready lips, sir, I have kissed,
Be sure at least I shall not say.

V.

Two honest gentlemen are we. –
I Demi John, whole George are you;
When Nature grew us one in years
She meant to make a generous brew.

VI.

She bade me store for festal hours
The sun or south side vineyard knew;
To sterner tasks she set your life,
To statesman, writer, scholar, grew.

VII.

Years eighty-six have come and gone;
At last we meet. Your health to-night.
Take from this board of friendly hearts
The memory of a proud delight.

VIII.

The days that went have made you wise,
There's wisdom in my rare bouquet.
I'm rather paler than I was;
And on my soul, you're growing gray.

IX.
I like to think, when Toper Time
Has drained the last of me and you,
Some here shall say, They both were good, –
The wine we drank, the man we knew.

AN OLD MAN TO AN OLD MADEIRA[688]

When first you trembled at my kiss
And blushed before and after,
Your life, a rose 'twix May and June,
Was stirred by breeze of laughter.

I asked no mortal maid to leave
A kiss where there were plenty;
Enough the fragrance of your lips
When I was five-and-twenty.

Fair mistress of a moment's joy,
We meet, and then we parted;
You gave me all you had to give,
Nor were you broken-hearted!

For other lips have known your kiss,
Oh! fair inconstant lady,
While you have gone your shameless way
'Till life has passed its heyday.

And then we met in middle age,
You matronly and older;
And somewhat gone your maiden blush,
And I, well, rather colder.

And now that you are thin and pale,
And I am slowly graying,
We meet, remindful of the past,
When we two went a-maying.

Alas! while you, an old coquette,
Still flaunt your faded roses,

---

[688] *The Complete Poems of S. Weir Mitchell*, The Century Co., New York, 1914, pages 355-356; FUESS, Claude Moore; STEARNS, Harold Crawford, *The Little Book of Society Verse*, Houghton Mifflin Company, Boston and New York, 1922, pages 254-256; *San Jose Mercury Herald*, May 11, 1913. (San Jose, CA. Published in the section "Recent Verse – Selected from New Magazines."); "The Atlantic Monthly", Volume 111, 1913.

The arctic loneliness of age
Around my pathway closes.

Dear aged wanton of the feast,
Egeria of gay dinners,
I leave your unforgotten charm
To other younger sinners.

6.3.4. Anonymous Poems and Songs

In this section will be presented a selection of some anonymous poetical compositions, from different sources, whose main topic is Madeira Wine, or in which this wine is mentioned in a special manner.

A PARODY
On the famous Song "THE WILLOW," ... to the same tune.
MADEIRA WINE.[689]

O fill me up another glass of that Madeira Wine,
O fill me up another glass… for 'tis extremely fine,
I like the taste… so pray make haste,
A bumper fill for me;
For here I sit… not quite drunk yet,
Altho' I've drank so free.

The Power of Madeira.[690]

Ah what is the bosom's commotion,
On a sea of ill luck when 'tis tost;
While the heart on misfortune's wide ocean,
Finds e'en the last dollar is lost.
Oh Madeira! thou art my dearest:
My heart thou hast never deceived,

---

689 *Federal Republican & Commercial Gazette*, October 17, 1808. (Baltimore, MD).
690 "The Port Folio", Vol. 2 for 1816, Harrison Hall, Philadelphia, 1816, page 353; *Franklin Monitor And Charlestown General Advertiser*, May 22, 1819. (Charlestown, MA). This poem is an adaptation from a song of Act I, Scene II, of the romantic drama "The Forty Thieves", by Richard Brinsley Sheridan, an Irish-born playwright and poet. In the play it was sung by the character Ganem to his beloved Morgiana. Here we transcribe it so that it can be compared: «Ah! what is the bosom's commotion,/ In a sea of suspense while 'tis tost,/ While the heart in our passion's wild ocean,/ Feels even hope's anchor is lost./ Morgiana, thou are my dearest,/ For thee I have languish'd and griev'd;/ And when hope to my bosom was nearest,/ How oft has that hope been deceiv'd./ Morgiana my hope was deceived.// The storm of despair is blown over;/ No more by its vapour deprest,/ I laugh at the clouds of a lover,/ With the sunshine of joy in my breast. Love, made by a parent my duty,/ To the wish of my heart now arriv'd,/ I bend to the power of beauty,/ And every fond hope is revived./ Morgiana, my hope is revived.»

And when fate show'd her frown the severest,
My care thou hast kindly reliev'd,
Oh! MADEIRA my cares were reliev'd!

Now releas'd from the dullness of thinking,
Of wit and good humour possest;
I laugh at the evils of drinking,

With a glass of old wine in my fist.
Care flies from the joyous potation,
Ill humour retires subdued,
And the heart in the plenteous libation,
Feels every fond hope is renew'd;
Oh! MADEIRA my hopes are renew'd.
   J.H.

FOR THE HERALD.
THE WINE-GLASS.[691]

Let Woodworth[692] sing sweetly in praise of the Bucket,[693]
That nothing but water can bring to our lips;
I sing of the Glass, and will venture a ducat
That Woodworth sometimes from this Helicon sips.
Oh! bring me a glass with Madeira o'erflowing –
My mirror I'll give to some pretty-fac'd lass;
Ne'er more view reflected, a countenance glowing
With the bright rosy tints that flow from the glass,
From the pleasure-crown'd wine-glass, the care-killing wine-glass,
The Madeira fill'd glass my lips love to kiss.

---

691 *Connecticut Herald and General Advertiser*, June 6, 1820. (New Haven, CT).
692 Samuel Woodworth (1784-1842), a native of Scituate, MA, was an American author, literary journalist, playwright, librettist and poet.
693 Allusion to his most famous poem "The Bucket", in three stanzas, which we transcribe next: «How dear to this heart are the scenes of my childhood,/ When fond recollection presents from them to view!/ The orchard, the meadow, the deep-tangled wildwood,/ And every loved spot which my infancy knew!/ The wide-spreading pond, and the mill that stood by it,/ The bridge, and the rock where the cataract fell,/ The cot of my father, the dairy-house nigh it,/ And e'en the rude bucket that hung in the well –/ The old oaken bucket, the iron-rod bucket,/ The moss-covered bucket which hung in the well.// That moss-covered vessel I hailed as a treasure,/ For often at noon, when returned from the field,/ I found it the source of an exquisite pleasure,/ The purest and sweetest that nature can yield./ How ardent I seized it, with hands that were glowing,/ And quick to the white-pebbled bottom it fell;/ Then soon, with the emblem of truth overflowing,/ And dripping with coolness, it rose from the well –/ The old oaken bucket, the iron-bound bucket,/ The moss-covered bucket, arose from the well.// How sweet from the green mossy brim to receive it,/ As poised on the curb it inclined to my lips!/ Not a full blushing goblet could tempt me to leave it,/ The brightest that beauty or revelry sips./ And now, far removed from the loved habitation,/ The tear of regret will intrusively swell,/ As fancy reverts to my father's plantation,/ And sighs for the bucket that hangs in the well –/ The old bucket, the iron-bound bucket,/ The moss-covered bucket that hangs in the well!» WOODWORTH, Samuel, *Melodies, Duets, Trios, Songs, and Ballads, Pastoral, Amatory, Sentimental, Patriotic, Religious, and Miscellaneous. Together with Metrical Epistles, Tales and Recitations*, James M. Campbell, New York, 1826, pages 12-13.

"The mirror of nature" it truly discloses,
Virtues and vices that adorn or disgrace;
Like the philosopher's glass, the heart it exposes –
Of hypocrisy's garb, it leaves not a trace.
Those rays of the mind, that before were diverging,
To a focus are brought, the focus of wit;
Their source, from the dark clouds of languor emerging,
Fondly smiles on the fire his sun-glass has lit –
This, the pleasure-crown'd wine-glass, &c.

The seaman may safely relinquish his spy-glass,
And nasal relief be afforded to age,
The lady abandon for ever her eye-glass,
The telescope drop from the hand of the sage;
For the wine-glass, 'tis known, will make us see double –

The dandies, who glasses for ornament wear,
Themselves may relieve from a portion of trouble;
Yet a bright ruby splendour their noses will share,
With the pleasure-crown'd wine-glass, &c.

The glasses of Venice I'd give not a rush for;
Poison is harmless when taken in wine;
In such glasses or not, I always shall blush for
The man who's afraid of such liquor as mine.
Fill up to the brim this the choicest of glasses,
That doth of all others the uses supply:
Ne'er may this, that all its kindred surpasses,
Or we who can prize it, a moment be dry.
Oh! the pleasure-crown'd wine-glass, &c.
Stop! stop! – there's the *Hour-Glass*, I'd even forgot it,
And rarely those think of't, who oft think of mine –
I've seized at Time's forelock, but never have caught it,
To empty his hour-glass and fill it with wine:
Then, stopping to drink, he'd neglect his vocation,
And suffer his scythe to be stole from his arm:
That he still holds his scythe, forbids my libation:
The thought, tho' unwelcome, has broken the charm
Of the pleasure-crown'd wine-glass, the care-killing wine-glass,
The Madeira fill'd glass my lips lov'd to kiss.
                                        EDWIN.

Dithyrambic. – A College Lyric.[694]

I.
There needs should be reasons for thinking,
To the eyes that are evermore winking;
But when eyes gleam with fire,
What fool would require
A plea or a reason for drinking?

II.
Leave books to the sages that make 'em,
And laws to the scoundrels that break 'em,
But in wine we have saws,
That are better than laws,
And we're infidels if we forsake 'em.

III.
These teach us that thinking is trouble,
That your glory is only a bubble,
And that study and care,
Will but end in a snare,
Making innocent students see double.

IV.
We have doctrines more genial and better,
Writ in crimson and not in black letter;
Madeira, for ink,
Gives us freedom, I think,
While your thought only finds us a fetter!

V.
The devil take Blackstone and Vattel;
Here's the wisdom that's born of the bottle;
And the student who drains
The last drop, for his pains,
Shall never have pains in his throttle!
COLUMBIA, S.C.   BLOX.

---

[694] *The Charleston Mercury*, July 8, 1859. (Charleston, SC).

THE HONEST DEACON.[695]
AN OLD STORY PUT IN RHYME.

An honest man was Deacon Ray,
And though a Christian good,
He had one fault – the love of drink,
For drink he often would.

On almost every Sunday, too,
He would, at dinner time,
Indulge to quite a great extent
In good Madeira wine.

At church, in front, upon the side
The deacon had his pew,
Another worthy, Squire Lee,
He had a seat there too.

One Sunday morn, the sermon done,
The parson said he'd talk,
In language plain, that afternoon,
Of sins within his flock.

He warned them that they must not flinch,
If he should be serene;
Each thought their neighbor'd get dressed down,
So all turned to hear.

The church at early hour was full;
The deacon, some behind,
Came in quite late, for he had been
Indulging in his wine.

And up the long and good broad aisle
He stiffly tottered on,
And by the time he'd reached his seat
The sermon had begun.

The parson of transgressors spoke,
And of the wrath to flee,
And soon he to this query came,
"The drunkard, where is he?"

---

[695] *The Anderson Intelligencer*, February 22 and March 15, 1877. (Anderson Court House, SC).

A pause – and then the deacon rose,
And answered like a man,
Though with a hiccup in his voice:
"Here, parson – hic – 'ere I am."

Of course the consternation
Was great on every side
For who'd have thought the deacon
Would thus aptly have replied!

The preacher, not the least disturbed,
With his remarks kept on,
And warned him to forsake his ways.
The deacon then set down.

'Twas soon another question came,
With no more welcome sound,
"Where is the wicked hypocrite?"
This made them all look round.

Some looked at this one, some at that,
As if they would inquire
Who 'twas that now the person meant;
His eyes were on the squire.

The deacon, noting how things stood,
Turned round and spoke to Lee:
"Come, squire – hic – come you get up,
I did when he called me."

7. Madeira Wine in American Reference Books

This chapter presents a few texts related to Madeira Wine compiled from several American reference books – encyclopedias, wine-related books, trade-related publications, Government-related books, and other sources, – organized, in each section, by date of publication, which shows different perspectives about this famous insular product.

7.1. Encyclopedias

A large number of encyclopedias published in the United States throughout the 19th century contain entries about Madeira. In them, a common topic used in the description of the island is its wine. A peculiar feature of some of these texts is that they were transcribed from British sources. Next will be shown eleven different examples, so that we can see which approaches were made about Madeira Wine, by different authors, from 1808 to 1855.

Madeira,[696] an island of the Atlantic Ocean, 120 miles in circumference, and 240 N by E Teneriffe. In 1419, the Portuguese, under the patronage of Prince Henry, discovered this island, uninhabited, and covered with wood. Prince Henry, the next year, settled a colony here, and furnished it with the seeds and plants, and domestic animals common in Europe, and procured slips of the vine from Cyprus, and plants of the sugar cane from Sicily, into which it had been lately introduced. These throve so prosperously, that the sugar and wine of Madeira soon became articles of some consequence in the commerce of Portugal; but its wine, in particular, is in the highest estimation, especially such as has been a voyage to the E or W Indies, for it matures best in the hottest climate. The scorching heat of summer and the icy chill of winter, are here equally unknown; for spring and autumn reign here continually, and produce flowers and fruits throughout the year. …

AFRICAN ISLANDS.[697]

Situation. The principal islands are Madeira and the Canary islands in the northwest; …
Owners. The Azores, Madeira and Cape Verd islands belong to Portugal; …
Madeira. Madeira is a small island, only 54 miles long, and 21 broad, consisting of a collection of lofty mountains, the highest of which rises upwards of 5000 feet above the level of the sea. On the declivity of these mountains the vine is cultivated, which produces

---

[696] MORSE, Jedidiah; Parish, Elijah, *A New Gazetteer of the Eastern Continent; or, A Geographical Dictionary: containing, in alphabetical order, a description of all the Countries, Kingdoms, States, Cities, Towns, Principal Rivers, Lakes, Harbors, Mountains, &c. &c. in Europe, Asia, and Africa, with their adjacent islands, carefully compiled from the best authorities*, Second Edition, Thomas & Andrews, Boston, 1808.
[697] MORSE, Jedidiah; Morse, Sidney Edwards, *A New System of Geography, Ancient and Modern, for the Use of Schools, accompanied with an Atlas, Adapted to the Work*, Twenty-Fourth Edition, Richardson & Lord, Boston, 1824, pages 268-269.

the famous Madeira wine. The commerce of the island consists almost entirely in the export of its wine, the annual amount of which is about 16,000 pipes. The population is estimated at 90,000....

BOOK LXXIV.
AFRICA.
Continuation of the Description of Africa. – The Western African Islands.[698]

... The *sugar* of Madeira was formerly much esteemed for its violet odour and aromatic flavour; at the present period, they prepare only a small quantity of molasses and syrup. The cultivation of the sugar-cane has given way altogether to that of the vine, which in fact constitutes the wealth of the island. The vineyards, for the watering of which much industry has been used, rise on the southern sides of the mountains, to the height of nearly two leagues. The grapes ripen in the shade of the vines, and are gathered when half dried. The precious Malmsey wine is produced from plants brought originally from Candia. According to Staunton,[699] five hundred pipes are made annually. The other and most abundant kind, is known by the name of dry Madeira. The produce varies annually from between fifteen and twenty-five thousand pipes; the exportation amounts to twelve or fifteen thousand. Five thousand five hundred are sent to England; five thousand five hundred to the East Indies, three thousand to the West Indies, and two thousand to the United States of America, where wine of an inferior quality is purchased.[700] ...

The government of *Machico*, formerly fertile in sugar, and which now also produces the best malmsey wine, contains a borough of the same name, situated on the eastern coast, and having a bad open road-stead....

Madeira and Teneriffe wines.[701] To the Madeira and Canary islands we are indebted for some excellent white wines. Of these, *Madeira* wine is considered by far the most valuable, particularly after it has been ripened by conveyance into a hot climate. The number of pipes of Madeira annually made in that island is about 30,000. The grapes when gathered, are put into wooden vessels, and the juice is extracted by persons treading upon them. ...

---

[698] MALTE-BRUN, M., *Universal Geography, or A Description of All the Parts of the World, On a New Plan, According to the Great Natural Divisions of the Globe; Accompanied with Analytical, Synoptical, and Elementary Tables, Improved by the addition of the most recent information, derived from various sources*, Volume IV, Containing the Description of Africa and Adjacent Islands, likewise additional matter, not contained in the European Edition, and Corrections, Wells and Lilly, Boston; E. Bliss and E. White, New York, 1825, pages 479-481.

[699] Sir George Staunton (1737-1801), a native of Ireland, author of the book *An Authentic Account of An Embassy from the King of Great Britain to the Emperor of China; […]*, in Two Volumes, published in London, in 1797. His references to Madeira are inserted on the first volume of his book.

[700] AN: Barrow, Voyage to Cochin-China, ch 1.

[701] GOODRICH, Charles A., *A New Family Encyclopedia; or Compendium of Universal Knowledge: comprehending a plain and practical view of those subjects most interesting to persons, in the ordinary professions of life*, Second Improved Edition, Philadelphia, 1831, page 65.

Wines, Ancient and Modern.[702] Our limits will only permit us to touch upon this part of the subject. ... Madeira, so called from the island which produces it, is much used in this country. There is a great difference in the flavor and other qualities of the Madeira wines: the best are produced on the south side of the island: they may be kept for a very long period, and, as is well known, are often sent long voyages in warm climates, to mellow them. They are naturally very strong, but commonly receive an addition of brandy when racked off. The Madeira wines retain their qualities unimpaired in both extremes of climate, suffering no decay, and constantly improving as they advance in age. Indeed, they are not in condition until they have been kept for ten years in wood, and afterwards allowed to mellow nearly twice that time in bottle; and even then they will hardly have reached the utmost perfection of which they are susceptible. When of good quality, and matured as above described, they lose all their original harshness, and acquire that agreeable pungency, that bitter sweetishness, which was so highly prized in the choicest wines of antiquity, uniting great strength and richness of flavor with an exceedingly fragrant and diffusible aroma. The nutty taste, which is often very marked, is not communicated, as some have imagined, by means of bitter almonds, but is inherent in the wine. The following statement of wines imported into the U. States for the years ending (Sept.) 1829 and 1831, indicate the quantity used in this country.

Year ending September, 1829.

	Gallons.
Madeira	282,660
Burgundy, Champagne, Rhenish and Tokay	23,562
Sherry and St. Lucar	62,689
Wines of Portugal and Sicily	325,350
Teneriffe and Azores	61,467
Claret, &c., in bottles or cases	356,332
Other wines, not in bottles or cases	1,838,251
	2,977,311

Year ending September, 1831.
(Treasury Report, May 4, 1832.)

	Gallons.
Madeira	114,625
Sherry	78,905
Red, of France and Spain	934,451
France, Spain and Germany, not enumerated	1,888,355
Sicily, &c., not enumerated	663,725
	3,680,062

---

702 LIEBER, Francis; Wigglesworth, Edward; Bradford, Thomas Gamaliel, Encyclopaedia Americana. *A Popular Dictionary of Arts, Sciences, Literature, History, Politics and Biography, brought down to the present time; including A Copious Collection of Original Articles in American Biography; on the basis of the seventh edition of the German Conversations-Lexicon*, Vol. XIII., Carel, Lea, & Blanchard, Philadelphia, 1833, pages 216-217.

7. MADEIRA WINE IN AMERICAN REFERENCE BOOKS

MADEIRA.[703] A wine brought from the island of that name. It is more stimulant than port; it agrees well with the stomach, and is excellently adapted for debilitated constitutions, and for rousing the nervous energy in the weakness of typhoid diseases. But good Madeira wine is difficult to be procured; it is no longer made of the same excellence as formerly; and the trade, according to Mr. Brande,[704] overflows with a variety of inferior and mixed wines, of all prices and denominations, to which the name of Madeira is most undeservingly applied. In its purest form, Madeira generally is more acid than either port or sherry, and is consequently not so well adapted to stomachs inclined to acidity, where it is generally found peculiarly heating and irritating.

MADEIRA,[705] a famous island in the N. Atlantic ocean, belonging to Portugal, ...
Agriculture is chiefly confined to the raising of vines. ...
... But its wine is the great glory of Madeira. The grape is not indigenous to the island; and it is said to have received its first plants from Crete, carried thither by order of the famous Prince Henry of Portugal, under whose auspices it was settled by the Portuguese in 1421. Many other varieties of the grape have since been carried to the island, its mild climate and volcanic soil being especially suitable for their growth.

The steepness of the hill-sides, on which the vines chiefly grow, and the necessity of economizing valuable space, have led to the practice of raising the vinebeds on successive terraces, supported by retaining walls. The vines are trellised on bamboo and other supports for the purpose of exposing the grapes to the ripening influence of the sun, and the bunches are frequently of enormous aze. The usual method of cultivation is to trench the ground from four to seven feet deep, according to the soil, and to lay a quantity of loose or stony earth at the bottom, to prevent the roots from reaching the clayey soil beneath, which would otherwise hinder their growth. The ground is watered three times, if the summer be very dry, and each time it is thoroughly saturated; but the less it is watered the better is the wine, though the quantity, of course, be diminished.

The N. side of the island, though sufficiently fertile, being the most exposed to cold winds and fogs, is not so favourable to the culture of the vine as the S., where all the finest growths are raised. The best Madeira - malmsey, or *Malvoisia*,[706] is produced on rocky grounds exposed to the full influence of the sun's rays, the grapes being allowed to hang till they are dead ripe. The *Sercial* grape will, also, only succeed on particular spots. The wine made from it is, when new, harsh and austere, and requires to be long kept. The best Madeira wine is produced on the S. side of the island; but it is alleged that not less than two-thirds of the wine grown even in this quarter is of secondary quality; so that in Madeira, as in all wine countries, the first growths *(premiers crus)* are both scarce and dear. The

---

[703] BLAKE, Rev. J.[ohn] L.[auris], *The Family Encyclopedia of Useful Knowledge and General Literature*, Peter Hill, New York, 1834, page 549; BLAKE, Rev. John Lauris, *The Parlor Book; or, Family Encyclopedia of Useful Knowledge and General Literature.* [...], Fourth, New and Improved Edition, John L. Piper, New-York, 1837, page 549; BLAKE, Rev. John L.[auris] Blake, *A Family-Text Book for the Country; or The Farmer at Home: being a Cyclopaedia of the More Important Topics in Modern Agriculture, and in Natural History and Domestic Economy, adapted to Rural Life,* C. M. Saxton, Agricultural Book Publisher, New York, 1853, page 258.

[704] William Thomas Brande (1788-1866), a reputed English chemist who published, among other works, the *Manual of Chemistry*, in 1819.

[705] M'CULLOCH, J. R., *M'Culloch's Universal Gazetteer, A Dictionary, Geographical, Statistical, and Historical, of the Various Countries, Places, and Principal Natural Objects in the World,* New York, 1855, pages 265-266.

[706] The right spelling is *Malvasia*.

process of making the wine is very simple. The grapes are picked from the stalk, thrown into a vat, pressed, first with the feet, and afterwards with a weighted wooden lever. The proprietor of the land, and the collector of taxes for the crown, both attend at the press; the latter takes out of the tub his *tenth* of the whole *must*, the remainder being equally divided between the landowner and the tenant. Each takes with him a sufficient number of porters to carry away their respective shares, sometimes in barrels, but more frequently in goat skins, *borrachas*,[707] to the cellars in Funchal, where the English merchants have extensive yards and vats for storing the wine, and carrying it through the different processes of fermentation, mixture, &c. They usually advance money beforehand to the growers, to enable them to defray the expenses of cultivation. (*Barrow's Voyage to Cochin China*,[708] p. 22.)

Though naturally strong, a quantity of brandy is added to Madeira wine when racked from the vessels in which it has been fermented, and another portion is added when it is about to be exported. The demand for Madeira wine in the E. and W. Indies, where it is highly esteemed, first led to a knowledge of the improvement it derives from being carried to a warm climate; and it has long been customary for ships outward bound for India and China to touch at Madeira, and take large quantities of wine on board, which they bring home to England. But it must not be supposed that all the Madeira wine that has gone to Calcutta and Canton is necessarily better than any brought direct from the island, as much must obviously depend on the quality of the wine sent to the east. But, if due care be taken in the selection of the wine sent to India and China, it is very much improved and matured by the voyage; and it not only fetches a higher price, but is in all respects superior to the direct importations. Most of the adventitious spirit is dissipated in the course of the Indian voyage, and the full flavour of the wine is evolved.

Madeira wines may be kept for a very long period.

"Like the ancient vintages of tho Surrentine hills, they are truly *firmissima vina*, retaining their qualities unimpaired in both extremes of climate, suffering no decay, and constantly improving as they advance in age. Indeed, they cannot be pronounced in condition until they have been kept for ten years in the wood, and afterward allowed to mellow nearly twice that time in bottle; and even then they will hardly have reached the utmost perfection of which they are susceptible. When of good quality, and matured as above described, they lose all their original harshness, and acquire that agreeable pungency, that bitter sweetishness, which was so highly prized in the choicest wines of antiquity; uniting great strength and richness of flavour with an exceedingly fragrant and diffusable aroma. The nutty taste, which is often very marked, is not communicated, as some have imagined, by means of bitter almonds, but is inherent to the wine." (*Henderson*,[709] p. 253.)

The wines of Madeira have fallen of late years into disrepute in England. The growth of the island is very limited, not exceeding 15,000 or 18,000 pipes, of which a considerable quantity goes to East and West Indies, and America. [...]

The commerce of Madeira is very considerable; the exports consist principally of wine. ...

---

[707] The right spelling is *borrachos*.
[708] Sir John Barrow's book *A Voyage to Cochinchina, in the Years 1792 and 1793;* ..., published in London, in 1806.
[709] Alexander Henderson (1780-1863), a Scottish physician, author of the book *The History of Ancient and Modern Wines,* published in London, in 1824.

SUBSECT. 5. – Wines of Madeira and the Azores.[710]

3372. The Island of Madeira is almost entirely of volcanic origin, and the soil produced by decomposing lava is found to be very favourable to the growth of the vine. This, added to the warmth of its climate, renders this place celebrated for the excellence of its wines. The vine was planted there soon after its first settlement by the Portuguese in 1421; but the introduction of the wines of Madeira into England is of more modern date than those of Portugal, and they were first brought here about the middle of the last century from the West Indies, which had been supplied from the island where they are made.

3373. *Madeira produces several kinds of wine.* The finest is *Sercial,* a red wine obtained from a grape much like the Malvasia, but which will only succeed on certain spots. The quantity of this wine produced does not exceed forty or fifty pipes in the year; it is harsh and austere when new, but is mellowed by being kept long.

3374. *The white wine usually known in England by the name of Madeira* is made in the greatest proportion; and, when genuine, is one of the richest wines in the world, having great strength, dryness, and delicacy of flavour. It is extremely durable in all climates, and is improved by age. It is meliorated in a remarkable manner by a sea voyage, a circumstance which was observed when it was first exported to North America. In consequence of this improvement, it has been the custom to prepare it for the European markets by sending it purposely to the East and West Indies, which, of course, must very considerably enhance the price. But it is by no means the case that the wine which has been on a voyage to India is the best Madeira, for inferior wines have been sometimes supplied for this speculation; and it has been discovered lately that by keeping the wine in a certain warm temperature, particularly with agitation, it is nearly as much improved as by a sea voyage, and in a much shorter time. Accordingly, it is the practice at present to ripen the wine in stoves in the island, where it is kept in a heat of 90°.

Madeira, being a strong wine naturally, has, least of all, occasion for the addition of brandy; yet it is the constant practice to add some of this spirit previous to exportation, which time incorporates. In other respects the first sorts are very little sophisticated; but the inferior kinds, of which there is a large proportion, are made up with almonds and various additions.

3375. The English wine-merchants who reside in Madeira consign their wines to agents in London, from whom it may be had genuine; and there is no other way of getting it good; but the great demand of late is said to have exhausted the island of all the finest old wine. Madeira should not be kept in a cold under-ground cellar, but in a warm part of a dwelling-house. To have it in perfection, it should be kept several years in wood, and nearly as much in bottle.

3376. *A Malmsey* wine of the first quality is also produced in Madeira from the Malvasia grapes, which are kept till over-ripe and partly shrivelled by hanging a month longer than

---

[710] WEBSTER, T.; PARKES, Mrs., *The American Family Encyclopedia of Useful Knowledge, or Book of 7223 Receipts and Facts: A Whole Library of Subjects Useful To Every Individual; such as Planning, Building, Warming, Ventilating, and Lighting Houses; Household Furniture, Servants, Selecting and Cooking of Food of Every Kind; A Catalogue of Fruits and Vegetables of Every Variety, Pastry, Preserves, Confectionary, Beverages; Receipts for English and French Cookery; The Selection of Clothing, Dress, and the Toilet, Jewelry; The Laundry, Carriages, Driving and Managing of Horses; The Dairy and Domestic Animals, Bees and Fish; The Preservation of Health; Receipts for Domestic Medicines; &c., &c., Illustrated with nearly One Thousand Engravings.*, J. C. Derby, New York, 1856, pages 622-623.

the other grapes. This wine was much in request in England before the use of tea, when a few glasses were drunk after a meat breakfast: it is now little imported.

3377. Part of the red grapes are employed in making a wine called *tinta*, which is extremely astringent, and, when new, resembles Burgundy; but when it has been kept some time, it becomes pale, like tawny port, or even paler, and acquires, in part, a rich Madeira flavour.

3378. All the best wines are grown on the south side of the Island of Madeira; those from the north side are very inferior, and are chiefly used for distilling brandy, which is not very good; these are too often exported instead of the best wines; and they alone, well brandied, are sent to Russia. But even on the south side the wines are not all of the same quality; about one half is inferior to the rest, but are usually passed off as some of the best.

Madeira wines have lately got much out of fashion, and the prejudice against them has been considerably increased by a supposed discovery that they contain a little more acid than sherry, which is now generally preferred; but this opinion is disputed, having been derived from the inferior Madeiras. So difficult is it to distinguish all these varieties of wine, that a large portion of the inferior Madeiras are now sold for sherry; and even the best Cape wine passes for Madeira. It is stated in Holman's Travels[711] that the wine trade of Madeira is rapidly declining; and that, in consequence, the planting of coffee has become very general in the island.

3379. The *Azores* produce a Malmsey, called *vino passado*, and also a dry wine; but both are inferior to Madeira wines.

3380. *The Canary Islands* formerly produced a great deal of sweet wine, which was formerly imported into England.

3381. *Teneriffe* has the best wines of all these islands: what is called Vidonia is a dry wine, much resembling Madeira.[712] The Malmsey of Teneriffe is excellent: common Teneriffe wine is inferior. The wines of these islands were formerly, in England, called *Sack*, as well as sherry and Malaga. Orotava is a wine so called from the port where is shipped.[713]

Madeira.[714] The Madeira Isles are a group in the Atlantic Ocean, belonging to Portugal, from the southwest coast of which they are distant 660 miles southwest. They consist of the islands of Madeira and Porto Santo, and the islands called the Desertas …

It is said that plants of the vine were conveyed from Crete to Madeira in 1421, and have since succeeded extremely well. There is considerable difference in the flavor and other qualities of the wines of Madeira; the best are produced on the south side of the island. The method of cultivation most generally followed is to trench the ground from three to seven and seven to nine feet deep, according to the nature of the soil, and lay a quantity of loose and stony earth at the bottom, to prevent the roots from reaching the clayey soil beneath, which would otherwise oppose their growth. The ground is watered three times

---

711 James Holman (1786-1857), a native of Exeter, England, known as the "Blind Traveller", was an adventurer, author and social observer, best known for his writings on his extensive travels. In 1834 he published, in London, a travel book containing references to Madeira and its wines, under the title *A Voyage Round the World, including Travels in Africa, Asia, Australasia, America, Etc. Etc., From MDCCCXXVII to MDCCCXXXII*.

712 In America this wine was sometimes termed Teneriffe Madeira.

713 Port of the municipality of La Orotava, in the northern coast of the island of Teneriffe.

714 HOMANS, I.[saac] Smith; Homans, Jr., I.[saac] Smith, *A Cyclopedia of Commerce and Commercial Navigation, with Maps and Engravings*, Second Edition with recent statistics, Harper & Brothers, Publishers, New York, 1860, pages 1299-1300.

if the summer has been very dry, the sluices being left open until the ground is pretty well saturated; the less the ground is watered, the stronger the wine, but the quantity is diminished in proportion. The vines are found to bear fruit as high as 2700 feet, but no wine can be made from it. ...

The manufactures of Madeira are insignificant; their chief object being to satisfy some of the simple wants of the poorer classes. Baskets, straw hats, coarse linen and woolen articles, and shoes, are the principal objects. Artificial feathers, flowers, and sweatmeats are made for sale by the nuns. A good deal of needlework embroidery has been executed of late years by the women of Funchal for exportation, and a few fancy articles are made of the fibre of the *Agave Americana*.[715] The bulk of the laboring population is employed in agricultural pursuits. Wine has hitherto been the chief article of export, but this branch of trade will soon cease. The rearing of the cochineal insect has been lately undertaken, in the hopes of its supplying the loss of the grape. Many of the coopers employed during the existence of the wine trade have emigrated; the rest earn a precarious subsistence. The casks they made possessed repute for excellence of construction....

... In 1843 the imports from the United States amounted to $59,900, and the exports from Madeira to the United States to $2750, employing 38 vessels, with an aggregate tonnage of 8533 tons. The commerce of this island with foreign nations, and especially with the United States, is declining, and must continue to decline so long as the vines remain diseased, as wine is the only article of export from Madeira.

MADEIRA[716] ... For nearly 4 centuries previous to 1852 the staple product of the agriculture of Madeira was the vine, which yielded the celebrated wine bearing the name of the island, of which the annual export averaged 5,000 pipes, each pipe containing 92 gallons. In that year disease began to infect the vines, which soon stopped the production of wine, and has at length nearly destroyed the vines themselves. The rearing of the cochineal insect has been introduced to give occupation to those thrown out of employment by the failure of the grape crop. The commerce of the island depended almost entirely on the wine, and was chiefly in the hands of resident British merchants. The entrances at Funchal (the only port) in 1855 were 75 British and 117 other vessels, and the clearances 77 and 107. The value of imports in 1855 was £110,210, and of exports £75,280. The customs duties on imports in 1855-6 were £13,119, 16 per cent more than in the preceding year. The imports of Madeira wine into the United States in the year ending June 30, 1859, were valued at $55,000, about one third of which came direct from Madeira and the rest through France, Spain, England, and other countries. ...

---

[715] Commonly known as the century plant, maguey, or American aloe, is an agave originally from Mexico but cultivated worldwide as an ornamental plant, which grows wild in Madeira.

[716] RIPLEY, George; DANA, Charles A., *The New American Cyclopaedia, A Popular Dictionary of General Knowledge.*, Vol. XI., Macgillivray-Moxa., D. Appleton and Company, New York and London, 1861, page 32.

Madeira,[717] an island off the NW. coast of Africa, from which it is distant about 400 miles, subject to Portugal. It is 54 miles in length by 21 in breadth, containing 1110 square miles. The island consists of a collection of mountains, the highest of which rises 5068 feet above the sea. The productions of the island are raised on the declivities of these mountains. On the summits are forests of pine and chestnut. The lower slopes are covered with vines. Wheat, barley, and oats are raised in small quantities; but two thirds of the consumption of grain by the inhabitants, is supplied from the Azores and from America. Goats and hogs abound in the mountains. The commerce of Madeira consists principally in the export of the wine of the island, famed all over the world for its superior excellence and peculiar qualities. The quantity annually made is about 20,000 pipes, two thirds of which are exported to Great Britain and her colonies. In 1830, about 1200 pipes were sent to the United States; but a considerable quantity reaches the latter country in an indirect manner. The best vines grow on the south side of the island, whence the term "south side" is applied to wines made in that quarter. There are several varieties of wines, viz. 1. London particular; 2. London market; 3. India market. The fourth is for the New York market, and the fifth, or most inferiour kind, is called cargo.

The wines are generally supposed to improve much by a long sea voyage, and are frequently carried to the East Indies, and then sent to England and the United States. The inhabitants are supplied, in part, with manufactures from England, and provisions and lumber from the United States. The people are generally of Portuguese descent, negro slavery not being permitted. …

7.2. Wine-Related Books

In this section will be shown excerpts from two wine-related books, both published in New York, one in 1832 and the other one twenty years later. The former provides an accurate insight into the history of Madeira Wine, mode of production and details the features of various kinds, whereas the latter presents two ways of improving Madeira Wine and also describes its production.

CHAPTER IX.[718]
OF THE WINES OF MADEIRA.

INTRODUCTION OF THE VINE – MADEIRA WINE DISTINGUISHED FOR ITS EXTRAORDINARY DURABILITY AND SUPERIORITY – MALMSEY – SERCIAL – BUAL – TINTO – TINTA – VERDELHO.

---

[717] *The Treasury of Knowledge, and Library of Reference: containing an English Grammar, English Dictionary, Universal Gazetteer, Chronology and History, Classical Dictionary, Law Dictionary, with Various Other Useful Information*, Parts I, II & III, Fifth Edition, Enlarged and Corrected, Conner & Cooke, New York, 1834, page 173; *Treasury of Knowledge and Library of Reference. Vol. I. Containing a New Universal Gazetteer or Geographical Dictionary, describing the various countries, states, provinces, cities, towns, villages, seas, harbors, rivers, lakes, mountains, capes, and islands, of the Known World, with Population and Other Statistical Tables, and an Appendix, containing numerous additions, bringing geographical and historical information down to the present time, to which is added an Epitome of Chronology and History, and a compendious Classical Dictionary,* New and Revised Edition, J. W. Bell, New York, 1855, page 173.

[718] McMULLEN, Thomas, *Hand-Book of Wines, Practical, Theoretical, and Historical; with a description of Foreign Spirits and Liqueurs,* New York, 1852.

7. MADEIRA WINE IN AMERICAN REFERENCE BOOKS

The island of Madeira is said to have been stocked with plants brought from Cyprus, by order of Prince Henry, under whose auspices the first colony of the Portuguese was established there, in the year 1421. The mildness of the climate and the volcanic soils with which that island abounds, were so favorable to their growth, that if we may credit the report of the Venetian traveller, Alvise de Mosto,[719] who stopped there on his voyage to Africa, in 1455, they produced more grapes than leaves, and the clusters were of extraordinary size. For a long time sugar was the principal commodity which Madeira supplied; and it was not until a comparatively recent period that its wines became generally known, and acquired that distinction to which their many valuable qualities so justly entitle them. From a very early period, Madeira wine has been in extensive use in this country; it is on record, that wines were exported from the island before 1460. The first colonists of North America were no sooner settled there, than they carried staves, corn, and other produce to the island, and exchanged them for wine. It appears to have been little used in England, until the middle of the last century, and owed its introduction to the British officers who had served in the West Indies, and had become acquainted with the excellence of the wines. The demand considerably increased from the suspension of commercial intercourse with other wine countries, during the European war (Madeira being then looked upon as an African settlement). This led to importations of all the inferior grades, and these being sold for above their value, necessarily brought the whole into disrepute, at least among those who were not aware of the distinctions existing. None but the very highest grades can now be sold for consumption in that country.

The north side of the island, though sufficiently fertile, being exposed to cold winds and fogs from the sea, is necessarily less suitable to the culture of the vine than the south side, where all the best vineyards are accordingly situated. The soil most commonly met with, consists of pumice-stone, mixed with a portion of clay, sand and marle; on several of the lower hills, nothing but black or gray volcanic ashes are seen, and the higher lands are generally covered with a soft lava, which rests upon a stratum of black ashes. As the acclivities are often very steep, they are partly formed into terraces, to prevent the loose earth from being washed away; and to counteract the effects of the summer droughts, watercourses are constructed along the sides of the mountains, which enable the farmers to irrigate their vineyards as occasion may require.

Among the various species of grape cultivated those called *verdeilho*,[720] *negra, molle*,[721] *bual, malvazia*,[722] and *sercial,* yield the best wines. They are propagated by quicksets or cuttings, and planted in rows; the ground being always trenched sufficiently deep to allow the roots to penetrate into the substratum of volcanic ashes. Some are left without support, and kept low by frequent pruning; others are trained on square frames or trellises, from twenty to thirty inches high; while others, again, are disposed on a sloping lattice work, formed of canes, and supported by poles, the tallest of which rise about seven feet from the ground. The fruit is generally ripe about the first week in September; for the best wines, it

---

719 Alvise Cadamosto or Alvide da Cà da Mosto (c.1432-1483), a Venetian explorer hired by Prince Henry the Navigator to travel alongside the coast of Africa. He depicted those journeys on a book originally published in Italy in 1507, which had several editions in other languages. The English version was published in 1811 under the title *Original Journals of the Voyages of Cada Mosto and Piedro de Cintra to the Coast of Africa, the former in the years 1455 and 1456, and the latter soon afterwards.*
720 The right spelling is verdelho.
721 The right denomination and spelling is negra mole.
722 The right spelling is malvasia.

is gathered at different times, and carefully picked, the unripe and damaged portion being set apart for the manufacture of an inferior wine. Most of the red grapes are consumed in the manufacture of white wines; but a portion of them are converted into *tinta*.

The demand for Madeira wines, in this country, to which, at one period, they were alone exported, first led to a knowledge of the benefit they derive from removal to a warm climate, and since they have come into use among the nations of Europe, it has been usual to prepare them for particular markets, by a voyage to the East or West Indies. The wines which have been thus matured, necessarily sell for much higher prices than those which have been imported directly from Madeira; but it does not follow, that the wines which have made the longest voyage, and been transplanted to the hottest country, are always the best. Much will depend on the original quality of the wine, on the degree of fermentation which it had previously undergone, and on the quality of brandy which had been used with it.

The great additional expense attending this mode of improving Madeira wines, has occasioned the adoption of various artificial methods, by which a similar effect may be obtained. It has, for many years, been the practice to subject a certain portion of the vintages to the continued influence of a high temperature, by placing them in rooms heated by stoves and flues, like the *apotheca* or *fumarium* of the ancients. The wine thus treated is said to acquire, in the course of a few months, the same degree of mellowness, and the same tint, which it would take as many years to produce by the ordinary method of keeping, or by a voyage to a hot climate; but it generally wants that delicacy of flavor, which nothing but time will give. Delicate high grade wines are generally exempted from this course of treatment, and are allowed to attain maturity by time, unassisted by these artificial means. Various additions are used to bring up the character of the inferior growths to the standard of the first, and palm them upon the world for that which they are not. Some imagine the character of the wines to have deteriorated of late years, but such is not the case – indeed there is no reasonable ground for the supposition. The demand for the cheap wines of all countries, has been so great that the Madeira merchants have been compelled to send cheaper, and, consequently, inferior wines, especially to this country, and these qualities, in many instances, being sold to consumers for the finest, naturally caused a reaction, which must be the case with all wines, from the same cause.

Madeira.

Fine Madeira wines are distinguished for their extraordinary durability. Like the ancient vintages of the Surrentine hills, they are truly "*firmissima vina,*" retaining their qualities unimpaired in both extremes of climate, suffering no decay, and constantly improving as they advance in age. Indeed they cannot be pronounced perfect until they have been kept eight or ten years in wood, and afterwards allowed to mellow for the same time in bottle; and even then, they will hardly have reached the utmost perfection of which they are susceptible. When of good quality, and matured in the manner described, they lose all their original harshness, and acquire that agreeable pungency, that bitter-sweetness, which was so highly prized in the choicest wines of antiquity – uniting great delicacy and richness of flavor, with an exceedingly fragrant and diffusible aroma. The nutty taste which is often very marked, is not communicated, as some have imagined, by means of bitter almonds, but is the result of superior quality and great age, and, consequently, becomes inherent in the wine. It is scarcely necessary to remark, that the preceding observations apply exclusively to wines of a high order, for Madeira, like all other wine countries, furnishes, along with a few superior growths, a great many of indifferent quality.[723]

Malmsey.

The term Malmsey is merely a corruption of Malvasia,[724] or rather Monovasia, the name of a small fortified town in the bay of Epidaurus, Limera,[725] where the grape was originally derived.[726] It is grown on rocky grounds, which are exposed to the full influence of the sun's rays, and like all other luscious wines, is made from grapes allowed to remain on the vine until they are over-ripe, or partially shrivelled. Malmsey is universally admitted to be one of the finest and most delicious sweet wines, a portion of which is usually reserved for the royal table of Portugal – the quantity produced is very limited.

Sercial

Is an excellent and highly esteemed dry wine, obtained from a grape, which, like the Malvasia, will only succeed on particular spots. When new it is very harsh and austere, and requires to be kept a great length of time before it is thoroughly mellowed. It possesses all the requisites of a perfect wine, being extremely delicate, with a rich aromatic flavor, quite peculiar to itself, combining with the ordinary properties of the finest Madeira, an agreeable nutty flavor, an aërative property and stimulancy, that leaves nothing to be desired. It holds the same rank among Madeira wines that Amontillado does among Sherries. The grape which yields it is the Johannisberg, transplanted from the Rhine.

Bual.

An extremely delicate soft wine possessing a high flavor, and reckoned among the most superior on the island. It is supposed to have descended from a Spanish or the Burgundy grape.

Tinto, or Pure Juice Madeira,

Is a south side wine, made from purple grapes and some white mixed; the husks being excluded in making the wine, renders it not astringent; it is an excellent table drink, and improves much in this country with age and proper treatment.

---

[723] Most of this paragraph is quoted from Alexander Henderson's book, as we have seen previously.
[724] The name Malvasia is generally thought to derive from Monemvasia, a Venetian fortress off the coast of Laconia.
[725] Epidaurus Limera, located at the north of the town of Monemvasia, in Greece, was one of the most important towns in ancient Laconia.
[726] Another theory, the most commonly referred to, states that this name derives from the district of Malevizi, near the city of Heraklion, known to the Venetians as Candia or Crete.

Tinta, or Burgundy Madeira,

Resembles Burgundy, from which vine it is produced, and is the only red wine made on the island – it is a fine wine of a ruby color and astringent in its character, and very agreeable as long as it retains its fragrancy and color, though it generally wants the high aroma for which the white sorts are distinguished. When old it may be compared to tawny Port; after a few years it loses its color entirely, and is apt to turn into a delicate but rather an ordinary Madeira.

Verdeilho[727]

Is produced from the white grape, and when made from the growth of the South side is the most potent wine of Madeira: it requires great age to mature and attain celebrity.

Nearly all the fine wines are produced in the district of Cama de Lobos,[728] Estreito, St. Roque[729] and St Antonio.[730] In the district of Companio[731] a very delicate flavored white wine is made, possessing a high aroma and esteemed on the island; little of this is exported.

TO IMPROVE MADERIA[732] WINE, No. 211.[733]

Maderia wine is a very strong wine, and is in great repute in this country; yet this wine requires age full as much as any other, for the reason that many merchants send their wines by the way of the West Indies home, that it may become mellow, and also be fine, and bring a better price; this wine however, sometimes will want to be fed with a little good brandy, but to save the merchant the expense of a voyage round by the West Indies, let him have some particular Teneriffe wine, and fine it down with three quarts of sweet milk, and the whites and shells of a dozen eggs, broken small, and stir it well up to a froth; and the improvement will be such that the oldest wine dealers will not perceive the difference, without a real knowledge of the fact.

TO FINE MADERIA WINE, NO. 212.

For one pipe take two ounces of isinglass dissolved in the wine, and three eggs, the whites and shells, beat well up together, and mix with your wine....

---

727 The right spelling is Verdelho.
728 See Note 207.
729 The right spelling is São Roque.
730 The right spelling is Santo António.
731 The right spelling is Campanário.
732 The right spelling is Madeira. The same applies to the other occurrences in this text.
733 [Old Distiller, By an], *The Complete Grocer: being a Series of Very Valuable Receipts, For Distilling and Mixing Cordials of All Kinds, Brandy, Rum and Gin, with a Variety of Information Respecting the Making and Treatment of Both Foreign and Home Made Wines, and Other Things too Numerous to Mention., Particularly Dedicated to Merchants, Wine Dealers and Others Engaged in the Business,* Published for the Author, John H. Turner, Printer, New York, 1832, page 101.

MALMSEY WINE, NO. 215.

This wine is a sweet flavored wine, and is in great repute among different classes of society, it is a full bodied wine, and of a delicious flavor, and should be managed, and bottled in the same way as old Madeira.[734] ...

PORTUGAL WINES, No. 275.

MADEIRA.

This is an excellent wine, the produce of an Island[735] of the same name in the Atlantic Ocean, belonging to Portugal, and is made of a variety of dry grapes, among which are the Verdello,[736] Listan,[737] Vindonia,[738] and Negramullo.[739] In the culture, pressing, fermentation and making up, the planters and merchants, are very attentive, and have been more particularly so of late years, since the inhabitants of Teneriffe, have so much improved their wine. The genuine Madeira wine, is naturally the color of oil, and will tinge the glass with a light bluish hue, on which it hangs in proportion to the richness of wine; it has a kernelly taste, somewhat like the walnut flavor, the juice is enriched by the grapes being suffered to hang on the vines, until they wrinkle, and look like half dried raisins, they make however, a commoner kind, and tinge it in the wine press. The planting, culture, and growth of the vine, is very particularly attended to by those who undertake the management of a vineyard, on this Island. The vines, are mostly placed on the side of a hill, of a south or southern aspect, or on inclined plains, at the foot of such hills, sometimes from cuttings, but mostly from layers which is much the best mode of propagating the plant. The manner of preparing the ground differs, something according to the situation: one way on mountainous, and another on moderate hills, and different still when on plains: on some estates, they erect walls breast high, or dry stone dug out of the trenches, and the vines are planted in rows, from east to west, their walls, trenches, and vine rows, ranged at proper distances, resemble a magnificent staircase, and have a charming effect, the wall, answers several purposes, they uphold the earth, they hinder the vine rows being laid bare, they withhold the rain water, which would otherwise run down the hills, without soaking in the earth, they defend the blossoms and fruit, from the violence of the winds, and increase the reflection of the sunbeams, they occasionally admit of poles of a proper length, being suspended from wall to wall, to defend and support the fruit, the principal stakes, to which they bind each vine, are strong, and are about four feet above the ground, the smaller ones to which they attach the young shoots are more slender, the wild cane is employed for this last purpose, and from laying from stake to stake, to suspend the fruit upon, for its exposure to the sun, and to reflect heat from the soil, they are then generally cropped at

---

734 [Old Distiller] 1832, pages 101-102.
735 AN: Bullion's Journal.
736 The right spelling is Verdelho.
737 The right spelling is Listão.
738 The right spelling is Vidonia. This grape was not cultivated in Madeira, but in Teneriffe.
739 The right spelling is Negra Mole.

right angles, forming a square lattice work, and so support the different clusters of the grape. The season for the vintage, mostly depend upon the weather, during the Spring and Summer, which makes it sooner or later by about fifteen or twenty days, and is usually about the last of September, or the beginning of October; the weather being suitable, they are brought to press, they are pressed without taking off the stems: these Islanders throw in a substance they call yesso;[740] the liquor is then drawn off into pipes, in which it finishes its fermentation; after four months, the wines are racked from those casks, when a suitable quantity of French brandy is added, and they are then set aside for improvement by age.[741]

7.3. Trade-Related Publications

This section contains a set of eight texts concerning Madeira Wine, published in American trade-related publications, from 1834 to 1883, in which can be seen different aspects of this product, such as the export/import, the duties levied upon the wine, trends of its consumption in the United States and its characterization, among other topics.

CHAP. VIII[742]
WINES.

1. A great number of vegetable substances may be made to afford wine, as currants, cherries, &c.; but that obtained from the fruit of the vine is the best and most drank. There are many sorts of wine, because there are many countries where the vines grow luxuriantly; and each has its own peculiar flavor. Sometimes this excellence is confined to a single hill; and sometimes it extends over a whole country....
3. MADEIRA. The true Madeira wine is made at Madeira, an island lying northwest of the coast of Africa. As the wine of Madeira stands so high in repute, a little account of the vineyards in that island, and the mode of cultivation, may amuse you. In every spot, where the soil is suitable, and a due exposure to the sun affords sufficient warmth, the vines are planted. Low stone walls enclose the several walks, which cross each other from one side of the vineyard to the other. These walks have a kind of trellis-work of laths and bamboos, which almost meet at the top, and render them delightfully shady. It is the ripening of the grapes in the shade, which is said to give them their peculiar flavor. The vines are thus supported; and the keepers can clean the ground of every weed with the utmost ease. Every vineyard has a plantation of bamboos adjoining, as the grapes will not prove excellent without this shade and support. The external hedges

---

740 The right spelling is gesso, or plaster. Contrary to what this author states, Madeira Wine was never plastered.
741 [Old Distiller] 1832, pages 139-141.
742 *The Book of Commerce by Sea and Land, exhibiting its connexion with Agriculture, the Arts, and Manufactures, to which are added A History of Commerce, and a Chronological Table; designed for the use of schools*, Boston, 1834, pages 32-33; *The Book of Commerce by Sea and Land, exhibiting its connection with Agriculture, The Arts, and Manufactures, to which are added A History of Commerce, and a Chronological Table.*, Uriah Hunt, No. 101 Market Street, Philadelphia, 1837, pages 32-33; *The Book of Commerce by Sea and Land, exhibiting its connection with Agriculture, The Arts, and Manufactures, to which are added A History of Commerce, and a Chronological Table.*, Uriah Hunt & Son, 44 N. Fourth Street, Philadelphia, Applegate & Co., Cincinnati, 1857, pages 32-33.

which defend these vineyards are composed of the prickly pear, myrtles, brambles, and wild roses: so that the whole country has the appearance of a garden.

4. Besides what may be consumed at home, the islanders export sometimes forty thousand pipes of wine in a year; each worth from one hundred to two hundred dollars. Some of our East-India ships take a great quantity in their outward voyage, and bring it back to America. The voyage and the warmth ripen and improve the wine much. In its native state, as brought immediately from the island, Madeira wine is worth very little. There are, besides this description of the wine, Burgundy Madeira, Sicily Madeira, and Malmsey Madeira, a white, luscious, and highly palatable wine. The wine which produces malmsey wine, properly so called, is a native of Malvasia, a small Grecian island[743] where its cultivation is at present but little attended to....

6. In Madeira, the grapes are gathered when ripe, and put into wooden vessels. Then, to press out the juice, the vintagers strip off their jackets, and their shoes, and get into the vessels; there, working with their hand and feet, and elbows, they press and squeeze, till every grape is crushed.

7. When they have obtained the juice clear from the stalks, it does not want sugar; for the grapes are so very ripe and sweet, that the liquor presently ferments. It is the sugary substance in the grape, which, by fermenting, evolves a vinous spirit, and produces, after long standing, (which ripens and clears it) the liquor we call wine.

ESSAY No. XI.[744]
FEBRUARY 3, 1830.

Trade between the United States and Madeira. Influence of high duties upon wine, in diminishing exports, as well as imports. Effects upon consumption of a small increase in price.

The commerce between the United States and the island of Madeira, affords one of the most fatal examples of the folly of tampering with trade, and of the ruinous consequences of high duties, which is afforded by our custom-house returns. Our exports, which were once two millions three hundred and thirty-six thousand six hundred and fifty six dollars in a year, have dwindled away to one hundred and eleven thousand nine hundred and thirty three dollars, as will appear from the following statement, which shews the amount exported in the following years: –

1798	332,625	1814	32,540
1799	203,185	1815	613,942
1800	522,728	1816	353,342
1801	528,344	1817	448,832
1802	481,053	1818	486,186
1803	370,878	1819	320,875
1804	586,869	1820	223,928

---

743 See Notes 724 and 726.
744 RAGUET, Condy, *The Principles of Free Trade, illustrated in a series of Short and Familiar Essays.* Originally published in the *Banner of the Constitution,* Second Edition, Philadelphia, 1840, pages 30-33.

1805	479,213	1821	193,414
1806	519,213	1822	186,952
1807	528,375	1823	117,685
1808	131,102	1824	315,896
1809	2,336,656	1825	122,840
1810	1,587,641	1826	119,058
1811	961,733	1827	100,153
1812	700,225	1828	111,933
1813	361,719		

The above table commences with the first year in which an account was kept of the exports to Madeira, separate from those to the other Portuguese dominions, and up to 1802, inclusive, comprises the articles of foreign as well as of domestic growth. Since that year the exports include none but domestic productions, of which the principal were flour, corn, corn meal, ship bread, lumber, fish, oil, spermaceti candles, beef, pork, butter, lard, hams, bacon, rice, bees' wax, tallow, candles and soap. Now if we can perceive a great falling off in the amount of these exports, since the increase of the duties upon Madeira wine, it is very fair to conclude, that a great part, if not the whole of it, has resulted from that increase. By the act of 1794, the duty on London Particular was fifty-six cents, and upon other Madeira, 40 cents per gallon. By the act of 1816, the duty, which had been raised by the war act, was retained at one hundred cents upon all kinds of Madeira, and continued at that rate until 1828, when it was reduced to fifty cents, to take effect from the 1st of January, 1829.

To those who have not been accustomed to reflect upon the great influence upon consumption, of a small change in the price of a commodity, the foregoing revolution in our commerce with Madeira will hardly appear to have been brought about by so slight an increase of duty. To such we would remark, that in some articles of luxury, a resort to a diminished quantity is had upon the most moderate rise in price, or the use of it is abandoned altogether. An increase of sixty cents in the duty on one gallon of Madeira wine, would occasion an increase of price, by the time it reached the hand of the consumer, of seventy-five cents, inasmuch as each vender charges a profit upon his advance of the amount of the duty. Wine, which used to be three dollars, must be sold at three dollars and seventy-five cents; and our wine merchants know, that the great mass of persons who used to purchase common Madeira wine, regarded three dollars as the maximum price which they would consent to give. We understand that, in Philadelphia, there is not now a gallon of Madeira wine drunk, where formerly there was a demi-john, and we have the authority of an extensive dealer in wine for asserting, that many, who were formerly liberal consumers of wine, are now drinkers of brandy. The misfortune of this too is, that after new habits are formed, it is no easy matter to change them, and one of the lamentable effects flowing from the American System is, that it has converted drinkers of wine into drinkers of spirits. If any one doubts our position, as to the influence of a small rise of price upon consumption, let him inquire of his next door neighbour, whether he does not, in marketing for his family, establish in his own mind a limit for articles of luxury, such as butter, eggs, lamb, asparagus, cream cheese, lobsters, young chickens, strawberries and other delicate fruits, beyond which he will not purchase, and he will soon ascertain, that there is not an individual whose consumption of luxuries is not regulated by very arbitrary laws.

That we should import more wine from Maderia than we pay for with our exports, which is the case at present, is one of the consequences of our own acts. Madeira, at one time, took from us forty thousand barrels of flour per annum, besides large quantities of corn. She paid us in wine, of which we took from her, at that time, about five thousand pipes. We then resolved, by increasing the duty on wine, to diminish the extent of our trade, and we now import only two thousand five hundred pipes, for a population nearly double. This step drove Madeira to find out another market for bread. She found it in Sardinia, from which country she now derives the supply which she formerly drew from the United States, and at a much cheaper rate; and as Sardinia takes no wine from her, she pays for her bread with the funds which we pay her for wine. This roundabout commerce is now the most profitable for Madeira. How soon our reduction of duties will bring back trade into its old channels, time will determine. The taste and fashion for wine, will gradually return with its cheapness, and as the vessels which bring it to this country will be able to carry outward cargoes at a very low freight, there cannot but be a revival, to some extent, of the export trade. The nation, however, has lost by its folly millions which can never be regained, and has driven thousands from the consumption of a wholesome and innocent liquor, to inebriating substitutes, which they can never be induced to abandon.[745]

MADEIRA,[746] so called from the island of that name, is a wine that has long been in extensive use in this and other countries. Plants of the vine were conveyed from Crete to Madiera[747] in 1421, and have succeeded extremely well. The trade in Madeira wine is carried on at Funchal, the capital of the island....

MALMSEY WINE: a very rich species of the Madeira. It is made from grapes grown on rocky grounds, exposed to the full influence of the sun's rays, and allowed to remain on the vine till they are over-ripe.

MADEIRA.[748] – A fine island near Africa, in the Atlantic Ocean, 180 miles in circumference; population, 150,000; Funchal, the capital, has 16,000 inhabitants. Discovered by the Portuguese, A. D. 1419, to whom it belongs. The surface is alternated with lofty mountains and rich valleys, and the soil produces choice grapes. The annual exports of wine are 30,000 hogsheads, of which the kind called "London Particular" is esteemed the best. No part of the world is more beautiful or healthy; the rose, the myrtle, jasmine and honeysuckle adorning even the fields, while the mountain-sides are covered with vines. Canary-birds

---

[745] AN: Since the reduction of the duty on the wine of Madeira, the exports to that island have been as follows – 1829 - $175,074; 1830 – 155,719; 1831 – 171,563; 1832 – 145,667; 1833 – 119,341. This statement shews an increase, but one so small, as to prove, incontestably, the difficulty of restoring a commerce once lost.

[746] GOODRICH, Samuel Griswold, *Peter Parley's Illustrations of Commerce*, H. H. Hawley & Co., Hartford [CT] and Hawley, Fuller & Co Utica [NY], 1849, pages 65-66.

[747] The right spelling is Madeira.

[748] *The World in a Pocket Book, or Universal Popular Statistics; Embracing the Commerce, Agriculture, Revenue, Government, Manufactures, Population, Army, Navy, Religions, Press, Geography, History, Remarkable Features and Events, Navigation, Inventions, Discoveries and Genius of every nation on the Globe. [...]*, Third Edition, Greatly Enlarged and Improved; with a Copious Appendix of changes and events, down to the present time, George S. Appleton, Philadelphia, D. Appleton & Co., New York, 1845, pages 66-67.

and goldfinches make the woods vocal with their songs. The British factory[749] settled on this island, is said to have more trade than the Portuguese.[750] Religion, Catholic.

Garblings: or, Commercial Commodities Characterized.[751]
Number V.
Alcoholic Liquors.
WINE.

… Madeira wines, were first taken to England from the West Indies, only about a century ago. But the vine was introduced into Madeira by the Portuguese soon after its first settlement, in the early part of the fifteenth century. Ever since that time, Madeira has been distinguished for producing some of the finest wine in the world. This wine, however, is found to improve in a remarkable manner by a sea voyage, in a hot climate, a fact which was first discovered by its exportation to the West Indies.

In consequence of this, it is the custom in Madeira to improve every opportunity of giving their wines such a voyage, by which its value is much enhanced. The very best Madeira wines, however, are frequently matured on the island, by keeping them in warm upper rooms, and frequently agitating them, while much inferior wine is sold on the faith of a tropical sea voyage. It is durable and improves by age in every variety of climate, but thought to keep best in wood, in warm rooms instead of underground cellars. The Madeira wine proper is a strong wine, at best, notwithstanding it is always *brandied* before exportation.

Sercial is a red wine obtained from a grape much like the Madeira. When new it is disagreeably rough to the taste, but it improves by age, and is the finest variety of Madeira. There is, however, very little of it made – not over forty or fifty pipes a year. A very fine *Malmsey* is also produced in small quantity, from the same species of grape as the sercial. This is made from the grapes partially dried, by permitting them to hang on the vines a month longer.

The variety called *tinta* is, when new, a red astringent wine, somewhat resembling Burgundy. But if kept long it loses color, and acquires the taste of Madeira – for which it is sometimes brandied and exported. …

MADEIRA WINE.[752]

A Funchal correspondent says that it is not an open question whether any more Madeira wine will ever be produced. None has been made since 1851, and there are now only some 7,000 or 8,000 pipes upon the entire island. All recent attempts to manufacture this wine have utterly failed, and pumpkin vines now adorn the old grape arbors once covered with abundant clusters of rich grapes.

---

749 A corporation formed in Madeira on the 2nd half of the 17th century, by several prominent merchants, with the intention of settling the shipping prices of wine, according to its demand and other fluctuating circumstances. And once a price was established, every merchant should follow it in their mercantile transactions.
750 It is a fact that for a long time the British dominated the island's wine export business.
751 "Merchant's Magazine and Commercial Review", Volume Thirty-Eight, From January to June, Inclusive, 1858, New York, 1858, pages 49-50.
752 *Ibidem*, page 765.

IX.[753]
MADEIRA WINES.

MADEIRA, to which the vine was transplanted in 1421 from Candia, produced formerly some 30,000 pipes; but at present only about 20,000 pipes of common wines and about 500 pipes of Malvasie, of which about the half goes to England, North America, and the West Indies; the balance is consumed on the island itself. The vines are mostly planted upon sandy and stony soil; and some vine-trunks can be seen there which the extended arms of three men are unable to compass. They have three kinds of wine: 1. Malvasie; 2. Dry white; and 3. Tinto.

The Madeira Malvasie, from the variety of Candian grapes, is the most exquisite sort of Malvasie, sweet, very delicious, and full of a balsamic fragrance. It occupies a prominent place among the first-class wines. It becomes with age more pleasing, and sells, at the place of its growth, for $200 per pipe; but, in order to enable it to hold out a sea-voyage, alcohol or brandy must be added.

The Dry Madeira, or *Madère sec,* is still more dry than the white Burgundy, though without having the piquantness of the Rhine wines. This is amber-colored, spirituous, aromatic, and often of a walnut taste.

The Red Madeira (Tinto) has a great deal of astringent matter, and can not be used alone without injury to the health.

In the interior of this island they raise the vines on trees, under the shade of which the grapes attain so little of maturity that they must be subjected to a crushing process in order to press out the juice; but this, of course, gives only a watery, poor wine; that does not bear keeping.

The Dry or Harsh Madeira is often mixed with the Tinto, and thus exported. It improves by passing the equator; and Englishmen ship it and re-ship it for this purpose to the East Indies and back. But now the same result is attained in Madeira by keeping such wines in heated rooms, where they will become, in a few months, as good as if kept in a cellar for five or six years. They have had in Madeira, for some fifty years, such apartments, of enormous sizes, heated with large stoves and heat-conducting tubes, filled with barrels and hogsheads, for the above purpose.

ON THE PRESERVATION OF GRAPE JUICE.[754]

… The due adjustment of the alcohol to the sugar and the antiseptic quality of the former preventing any further change in the latter, is the whole secret involved in the manufacture of the wines of Madeira, Xeres and Oporto; while the wines of France and Germany purport to be made from the unadulterated juice of the grape, as it comes from the vineyard. Such may be true, but there is a large consumption of brandy and starch sugar in

---

[753] HARASZTHY, Agoston, *Grape Culture, Wines, and Wine-Making, with notes upon Agriculture and Horticulture,* Harper & Brothers, Publishers, New York, 1862, pages 184-185. This segment was taken from Appendix A of this book, related to "Wines and their Varieties", which, by its turn, had been extracted from Johann Carl Leuchs' *Treatise on Wines and Wine-Making*, published in Nuremberg in 1847.

[754] De BOW, J. D. B., "De Bow's Review, Industrial Resources, Etc.", New Series, Vol. VII, Nos. I & II, January & February 1862, New Orleans, pages 272-273.

the wine regions, which may be used to strengthen the wines which are to be exported to England and the United States. The employment of brandy and sugar to construct a good wine is notorious; and it may truly be said, if these materials are omitted, the wine is weak and acid, and not adapted to the English or American taste; but when they are skillfully "fretted in" and judiciously proportioned, we have a wine worthy of the highest laudation. The unrivalled Madeira, so esteemed in South Carolina, so early introduced – for Mr. Peter Purry[755] commended its virtues in 1731[756] – and so long continued as the favorite of the state, is a compound of this description. I have already shown that no natural grape juice ever contained the quantity of alcohol and sugar which is found in Madeira, sherry or port wine; hence, from whence was it derived? Simply by additions made to the must previous to fermentation, or to the wine after fermentation. Both practices are common; and so long as art can improve nature and produce such an article as "old Madeira," the pure and unsophisticated wines of France and Germany will remain undesirable. Aiken[757] may choose her own standard of wine. She can avoid both extremes. Neither make the weak and acid wines of France and Germany, nor yet the strong and sweet wines of Spain, Portugal and Italy. There is a medium which may suit all tastes, and that medium can be reached by science, by experiment, and by practice.

We can select methods from all the European wine makers, and adapt them to our circumstances, to our tastes, and to our habits. We are habitually an "ardent spirit" drinking people, and this habit can only be cured by substituting a more moderate and pleasanter beverage than whiskey or brandy. It is the alcohol of the wine or whiskey that charms the world, and acetic acid cannot be substituted for it even if it be the fermented juice of the grape. The conversion of grape juice into wine is an art, and he who can prepare the most palatable wine is considered to be the best and most successful artist, and the question is not whether he adds sugar to the recent must, or brandy to the weak, fermented wine – one or the other is done, and the amended wine is pronounced to be good; and no charge of adulteration has ever been sustained against the wine-houses of Funchal, where the last complement to the thirtieth gallon of brandy is added to each pipe of Madeira wine before it is considered worthy to sustain the reputation of the exporting house in a foreign market. That a great deal of this added brandy evaporates there is no question; but experience has taught the merchants that this quantity is requisite to supply deficiencies, and still to retain a sufficiency to secure durability to the wine. Adulteration implies something not only foreign, but injurious; and the world has never decided that sugar and brandy are either foreign or injurious to wine. They are the natural primary and secondary productions of the grape; and if one gallon of juice cannot furnish a sufficiency to make and preserve one gallon of wine, two gallons are used with the suppression of half of the water. A weak juice may be concentrated by boiling: that is, by removing half the water we virtually double the quantity of sugar; but there is an objection to the process, for with the water we abstract the aroma, and thus lose an important element in the composition of wine. By distilling an inferior wine we obtain not only the alcohol that was in the wine, but the

---

[755] Jean-Pierre de Pury, a native of Switzerland, and founder of Purrysburg, a colonial town located on the South Carolina bank of the Savannah River.
[756] In his book entitled *Proposals of Mr. Peter Purry, of Newschatel, For Encouragement of Such Swiss Protestants as Should Agree to Accompany him to Carolina*. In this work Purry wrote that no wine but Madeira was drunk in South Carolina, although there were wild vines there bearing five or six sorts of grapes.
[757] City in and the county seat of Aiken County, in South Carolina.

aroma also; and if this be added to another wine, we concentrate in one portion the valuable constituents which were previously distributed through both. We accumulate what is valuable, and reject what is valueless. We make one good article out of two inferior ones, which under no construction of language can be called an adulteration. The Madeira wine drinkers scarcely know that in the consumption of one glass of wine they are consuming the constituents of three, and possibly four glasses of grape juice, less the water which has been removed; and yet it is expected that the normal juice of an Aiken grape can make a wine to compete with Madeira under the judgment of these amateurs....

CHAPTER XIV
SWEET WINES – FORTIFIED WINES ...[758]
MADEIRA.

Making. – In the island of Madeira it is the practice, according to Mr. Vizitelli,[759] to tread the grapes thoroughly in a large, square wooden trough, or lagar, in which they are also pressed, as in sherry making. A great part of the juice is extracted by treading, being strained through a basket as it runs off into casks. After the grapes have been thoroughly trodden, the pomace is gathered together and piled in the centre of the lagar, and pressed and patted with the hands to extract the must, and this is repeated three times, and finally the pomace is again raised in a mound, wound with a rope, and pressed by means of a heavy beam suspended over the lagar. This primitive method, however, can have but little interest for the wine maker, as the essential practice in making Madeira, or rather in the aging of it, is the application of heat.

Casks, Treatment. – The must is fermented, the wine racked and heated, in casks holding 130 gallons. After heating, it is stored in casks holding about 400 gallons. It is fermented in these smaller casks with the bung open, simply covered by a leaf, till the month of November. Either before or after the fermentation, a small quantity of brandy is added, varying in quantity according to the quality of the must, but seldom exceeding three per cent. When the wine has well cleared, it is racked and lotted, according to quality, and forwarded to the heating house, or estufa.

Heating House, Heating. – One of these at Funchal, described by Vizitelli,[760] consists of a block of buildings of two stories, divided into four compartments. "In the first of these, common wines are subjected to a temperature of 140º F., derived from flues heated with anthracite coal, for the space of three months. In the next compartment wines of an intermediate quality are heated up to 130º for a period of four and a half months, while the third is set apart for superior wines, heated variously from 110º to 120º for the term of six months. The fourth compartment, known as the 'calor,' possesses no flues, but derives its heat, varying from 90º to 100º, exclusively from the compartments adjacent; and here only high-classed wines are placed." They receive a further addition of spirit, after leaving the estufa, varying in quantity from one to three gallons per cask, presumably to supply

---

[758] RIXFORD, E. H., *The Wine Press and the Cellar. A Manual for the Wine-Maker and the Cellar-Man*, Payot, Upham & Co., San Francisco; D. Van Nostrand, New York, 1883, pages 113-115.

[759] The right spelling is Vizetelly. We present the illustrations of his book *Facts about Port and Madeira* on section 13.2.3. of this anthology.

[760] The right spelling is Vizetelly.

what has evaporated during the heating. Wines are also heated by exposing them to the rays of the sun in glass houses. In the day time a temperature of 120° to 130° is secured, which becomes considerably less during the night, which change is by many considered detrimental. Some again, put the casks out of doors in the full sunshine. In the estufas mentioned, the pipes are placed on end in stacks of four, with smaller casks on the top, a gangway being left between the different stacks. The casks are vented with a small hole during the process. Leaking is common during the exposure to so great a heat, and it is necessary to inspect the casks once during every day and once during the night.

Each compartment is provided with double doors, and after it is filled with wine, the inner door is plastered so as to stop all the cracks. In entering the estufa, only the outer door is opened, entrance through the inner one being made through a small door for the purpose. The man who examines the casks, coming out after a stay of an hour, drinks a tumblerful of wine, and cools off in a tight room provided for the purpose. From 10 to 15 per cent of the wine is lost by evaporation while it remains in the heating house.

General Treatment – Alcoholic Strength. – The solera[761] system is somewhat in vogue in Madeira, as in the sherry country. The practice also of leaving the casks in ullage prevails – a vacant space of ten or a dozen gallons is left. On the south side of the island 5 per cent is the largest amount of alcohol added, and on the north side a little more, which is added at different times. Most Madeira is dry, or nearly so, and contains about 18 per cent of alcohol on the average. …

7.4. Government-Related Books

In this section will be presented six different texts, from different government-related sources, published between 1856 and 1867. The first one was extracted from the second volume of Commodore Perry's official report to the House of Representatives, in which can be found the "Report Made to Commodore Perry on the Agriculture of Madeira, the Cape of Good Hope, Mauritius, etc.," written by D. S. Green, M. D., the USN surgeon attached to the frigate *Mississippi* during the expedition to Japan. In this important report are found some impressions about Madeira wine and the island's vineyards, then recently affected by the blight. It is also interesting to underline the way in which the author compares the reality of the island's wine production to what could be done in America in order to improve the domestic wine production. In the other texts one can find official reports by three U.S. Consuls in Funchal, John Howard March,[762] George True[763] and Charles A. Leas,[764] on the subject of Madeira Wine, a text about the grape disease in Europe and another one about Madeira wine production.

---

[761] See Note 382.
[762] John Howard March, a native of New Hampshire, was U.S. Consul in Funchal for forty five years, from 1816 to 1861.
[763] George True, a native of Ohio, was U.S. Consul in Funchal from 1862 until the day he died, in Madeira, on February 24, 1864.
[764] Charles A. Leas, a native of Maryland, was U.S. Consul in Funchal from 1866 to 1870.

AGRICULTURAL NOTICES AND OBSERVATIONS
MADE DURING
A CRUISE IN THE UNITED STATES STEAM FRIGATE MISSISSIPPI
FROM THE UNITED STATES TO JAPAN, DURING THE YEARS 1852, 1853, AND 1854.[765]

MADEIRA.

This island presents much of interest to the visitor. Besides its salubrious and delightful climate, its beautiful views, and picturesque scenery, its wine, of world-wide repute, would make it ever memorable; not Scian nor Falernian are more famous. But, alas for the island and the people! a blight had swept over their vines a short time before our arrival, and we found them anticipating not only scarcity, but even famine, from the failure of wines thence resulting. Nor is this their greatest calamity; as their immediate wants could be, as they have been, relieved by the humane assistance of foreigners; but the probability is, that this blight, like that of the potato, will continue for an indefinite time, and no period can be assigned for the island's return to prosperity.

This apprehension is further strengthened by its extending (again like the potato pestilence) over France and other vine countries of Europe, and even to the vineyards on the banks of the far-distant Ohio. Its cause and nature will be investigated in Europe; it is sufficient to state here, that it is a white, downy, or fungous growth, showing itself upon the branches of the plant, and upon the fruit, and preventing its due nutrition, in a manner analogous, probably, to the rust in wheat.

From the preceding cause alone, the vintage was decreased, in 1852, from about three hundred to thirty pipes of wine. Now, when it is considered that this is almost the only article given in exchange for foreign breadstuffs and manufactured goods, an idea may be formed of the magnitude of the misfortune, especially should it continue from year to year.

In connection with the wine, it may be remarked, that although much of the quality of wine depends upon the climate where made, and its mode of manufacture, yet much also depends upon the character and nature of the soil on which it grows. In Madeira, as far as observed, the wine-growing region consists of a friable, red, argillaceous soil, darkened by the admixture of humus. It is confined chiefly, if not exclusively, to the lower portions, bordering upon the sea-shore; as you ascend higher, the soil, losing its humus and richness, assumes a lighter red color, but is still formed principally of clay, with small black pebbles intermixed. It is very similar to the red-clay lands lying at the eastern foot of the Blue Ridge,[766] in the United States, extending from beyond the Susquehanna,[767] upon the one hand, and the James river[768] upon the other; and probably, from their nearly exact resemblance, they are of the same geological formation. A specimen was secured for comparative analysis. Doubtless this region in our country is adapted to the Madeira vine, as to soil; but will the climate answer well?

---

[765] [Perry, Matthew Calbraith], *Narrative of the Expedition of an American Squadron to the China Seas and Japan, performed in the years 1852, 1853, and 1854, under the command of Commodore M. C. Perry, United States Navy, by Order of the Government of the United States.*, Volume II, A. O. P. Nicholson, Washington, 1856, pages 2-4. This frigate arrived at Madeira on December 11, 1852, as we have seen in section 6.1.1.16. of this anthology.

[766] Mountain range located in the eastern United States, in the territory of two states, Georgia and Pennsylvania.

[767] The longest river on the American east coast, which flows through three states: New York, Pennsylvania and Maryland.

[768] River in the state of Virginia.

The most experienced and most extensive wine-growers with us are abandoning foreign grapes, in despair of their successful culture, and are improving our own varieties; but has this vine been tried in the above indicated region, where (in South Carolina) the tea-plant grows and flourishes? Nearer the sea it has been, but there the soil is generally sandy. It is worthy of a trial. …

Upon entering the town of Funchal, one is struck with the cleanliness of the streets and their neat pavements. They are narrow, and bordered either by houses or stone walls, which latter extend with them, in some directions, into the country. These roads, in passing along steep places, are graded, by cutting down from the upper side, and embanking from below, which is faced and supported by stone-work. While walking upon this raised side, it is frequently observed that vines grow out horizontally, *i. e.*, at right angles with the facing, and are received upon frames. By keeping them properly trimmed, and not planting too close, the earth beneath is occupied by culinary vegetables or grass, and the vines require and receive neither cultivation nor tending, &c. In what manner the necessary atmospheric influences penetrate to, and the necessary moisture is retained at the roots, may be a question, seeing they spread out under the beaten road and along the land face of the wall. However this may be, the vines are healthy and flourishing. Might not a hint be taken from this, to construct a vineyard upon a moderate declivity, by laying it out in wide terraces, facing them with stone, training the vines from the walls, either horizontally or perpendicularly, at pleasure, and cultivating the level plots as indicated above – the whole to be regularly manured, &c.? No grass or weeds could ever encumber or choke the roots and stem of the vine in this way, and the labor of attendance would be greatly lessened, and more than repaid by the other produce, leaving the grapes for wine as net profit. By-the-by, though no opportunity presented itself of visiting any regular vineyard, yet it was noticed that the usual close trimming of Europe was not followed here, and that around very many cottages or huts the frames were so made as to lean over, and at a few feet from their rooms, and rising nearly to the ridge poles, upon which vines were trained and embowered the houses – rivaling in size and extent those of Mr. Miller, of North Carolina. This observation corroborates the growing opposition in our country to very close cutting. …

FUNCHAL, MADEIRA.[769]
JOHN H. MARSH, *Consul.*

JUNE 10, 1854.

I have the honor to acknowledge the receipt of your circular of the 15th of March, and to reply. The trade of Madeira with foreign countries is very small. It is wholly regulated by the mother country, and no new regulations have been made for many years past that have influenced its commerce with the United States.

ANSWERS. …
SECOND SERIES.

---

[769] FLAGG, Edmund, *Report on the Commercial Relations of the United States with All Foreign Nations,* (Prepared and Printed under the Direction of the Secretary of State, in Accordance with Resolutions of the House of Representatives.), Volume III, Cornelius Wendell, Printer, Washington, 1857, pages 168-169.

1ˢᵗ. Within the limits of my consular district there is only one port of entry, and the only commodity exported is wine. It is generally bought by the merchants raw from the presses, and afterwards exported by them. The cost of a pipe of wine of the last vintage was from $15 to $60 per pipe of 23 almudes,⁷⁷⁰ or 109¾ gallons, according to quality.

2ᵈ. The freight of a pipe of wine hence to the United States averages from $5 to $7 a pipe, and the insurance charged is from 1 to 1½ per cent. according to the season. The wine being exported either on account of the shippers or the parties ordering it, no commission is ever charged.

3ᵈ. Good wines, when new, are sold for cash, or on a credit of a month or two, but old, inferior wines are usually sold on a credit of from 24 to 48 months; that is to say, the amount is received in 24 to 48, and sometimes in 60, equal monthly instalments.

4ᵗʰ. As bills of exchange are never passed, nor any money transactions ever made between this island and the United States, no average rate of exchange can be estimated with reference to either place; the value of American coin here, however, is upon a par of dollar for dollar.

5ᵗʰ. The duty levied on the exportation of wine is $5 53 per pipe, and on the imports from the United States, which consist of flour, corn, rice, staves, and lumber, the following: duty on flour, $1 per barrel; on corn, 6¾ cents per bushel; on rice, 1 cent per lb.; on staves, $1 60 per 1,000 for pipes, $1 30 per 1,000 for hogsheads, and 75 cents per 1,000 for barrels; on lumber, $1 90 per M. feet.

6ᵗʰ. No internal taxes whatever are levied on any of the imported commodities. The only article of export, which is wine, is subject to a tenth, levied at the time of the vintage. ...

The commerce between the United States and Madeira must continue to be unimportant as long as the vines remain diseased, as wine is the only article of export from Madeira.

PORTUGAL – MADEIRA.⁷⁷¹

... The island of Madeira is a colony of Portugal, and far excels the mother country in the quality, if not the quantity, of its wines. It was discovered in 1419 by the Portuguese, and colonized two years later. It is probable that the vine was introduced contemporaneously with the first settlements. Wines were exported from the island prior to 1460. Its hills are high and picturesque, and covered with vines. There are several varieties of grapes. The Malvasia, or Malmsey, believed to have been first introduced, is said to have been brought from Candia, but more probably from Portugal. Single clusters of grapes in this island have been known to weigh twenty pounds. The Jesuits formerly owned nearly all the Malvasia wines, which were embraced in one extensive vineyard. It is said that Madeira wine was extensively exported to North America and the West Indies more than a century and a half ago. Many varieties of grapes grow in Madeira.

The island produces from twenty to thirty thousand pipes of wine annually, of which a very small portion is considered first quality. Madeira wine has to be retained for many

---

770 An obsolete unit of measurement of liquids used in Portugal in the past, whose name derives from the Arabic word *al-mudd*. An almude used to be the equivalent of 16,8 liters, or 4.44 gallons.

771 *Report of the Commissioner of Patents for the year 1860. Agriculture.*, Government Printing Office, Washington, 1861, page 393.

years to arrive at perfection, or it must be sent on a long sea voyage to warm latitudes. In twenty years it attains to perfection, but none has ever been known to deteriorate by age. …

ANNUAL REPORT ON FOREIGN COMMERCE[772]
FUNCHAL, (MADEIRA.) – GEO. TRUE, *Consul.*

JANUARY 1, 1862.

I avail myself of the general regulation requiring consuls to send information of a statistical character, to forward to the department the following items respecting the district embraced in my consulate.

The commerce of this port has been almost entirely prostrated during the past ten years. Up to 1851 wine was the great article of produce and export. The failure of the wine in that[773] and the succeeding years was a great calamity to this island and to its commerce, and to no part of the latter more than to the prosperous trade then in existence with the United States. …

ANNUAL REPORT FROM UNITED STATES CONSULATE, FUNCHAL. – GEORGE TRUE, *Consul.*

OCTOBER 30, 1862

1. The trade of this consular district during the year 1861 was less than the average of the past five years. …

The most of the people use the coarsest food, and there is, occasionally, a scarcity even at that. A considerable amount of wheat is raised on the island, and the quantity thus grown has slowly increased of late years, as the old vineyards were abandoned; the limits of cane cultivation being much more circumscribed than that of the vine. Indeed, after a most prosperous cultivation of the vine for hundreds of years, its failure has not only changed the entire routine of agriculture among the people slow to change anything, but it has, in addition, ruined the only basis of the commerce of the island, and greatly reduced the actual productive power of the soil under cultivation.

The sugar-cane, which, to a limited extent, has taken the place of the vine requires more nourishment than can long be afforded it, while the wheat fields also require more, and return but a scanty harvest.

It can safely be said that nothing cultivated by man returns him more, in proportion to what it takes from the soil, than the vine. It may be inferred, therefore, that unless the vine can be restored to fruitfulness here, Madeira can never again be what she once was.

I have not been here long enough to have examined the diseased vines thoroughly, but I have made diligent inquiry respecting the disease, believing that *in its remedy* was the only source of improving the commerce of our country in this direction; and I find that the efforts made to ascertain the precise nature of the disease have, apparently, been

---

[772] *Executive Documents printed by order of The House of Representatives, during the Third Session of the Thirty-Seventh Congress, 1862-'63, In Twelve Volumes,* Government Printing Office, Washington, 1863, pages 242-243, 252-253.
[773] The failure of the wine in Madeira occurred in 1852 and not in 1851, as implied here.

inadequate, when the interests at stake are considered; and that, so far from scientific and persistent endeavors having been made to remedy the evil, the very *preliminaries* to such endeavors have yet to be taken.

Overlooking the fact that the same stock of vines has been cultivated on the same soil for hundreds of years, and not even conjecturing that some element of the soil necessary to the continued thrift and health of the vine *might* in that time have been exhausted, and that the vine might thus have become predisposed to disease, contagious or otherwise, the people generally accept the *fact* in a spirit of fatalism, or contend that the disease is entirely in *the air*; yet, healthy American vines brought here[774] by Mr. March's[775] enterprise, a few years ago, resisted the disease almost entirely for several seasons, and then showed gradually increasing indications of succumbing to the "blight."

I have noticed that the soil here seems to be entirely lacking in one element, which in many countries is found in good vineyard soils, viz: sulphate of lime. The experiment of sending to Cypress[776] and other points whence the grape first came to this island, and procuring healthy plants, and preparing the soil with a view to the proper elements required, remains yet to be tried; and no effort of mine shall be wanting to secure it a fair test.

Just in proportion to the prosperity of the island in its old product, (wine,) will be its imports of breadstuffs and other articles of American production.

The loss to the commerce of the island, consequent on the failure of the vine, may be estimated from the fact that the average yearly export of wine from Madeira from 1832 to 1842 was 8,193 pipes per annum. Taking the very low figure of $150 per pipe as the average shipping price, (the real average, I think, would be much higher,) and the value of the wine thus exported would be $1,228,950, or about $12 *per capita* of the population – about two-thirds *per capita* of the exports of *Great Britain*. Now, however, the exports are almost nothing, and so far as wine is concerned, it must soon altogether cease, except, perhaps, very small quantities of spurious stuff drugged out of apple-juice into a temporary semblance of Madeira. …

THE GRAPE DISEASE IN EUROPE;[777]
ITS
ORIGIN, HISTORY, PHENOMENA AND CURE.
BY HENRI ERNI, M. D., DEPARTMENT OF AGRICULTURE.

The grape disease being with us a growing evil, threatening the total destruction of some of our native American varieties of vines, like the Catawba, I have deemed it important to give a brief history of the destructive malady which has prevailed of late in European vineyards, hoping it may to some extent aid in understanding the character of diseases of the grape which are beginning to prevail in this country. …

---

774 The Isabella and Catawba, brought from the banks of Ohio.
775 John Howard March, the former U.S. Consul, and True's predecessor.
776 We presume the author meant to refer to Cyprus.
777 *Report of the Commissioner of Agriculture for the Year 1865,* Government Printing Office, Washington, 1866, pages 324-330.

Its prevalence in Madeira, where, probably in consequence of the isolation of the country, it did more damage than anywhere else, is thus described in the report of Dr. H. Schacht.[778] The oïdium first appeared in Madeira in 1852, soon after the flowering season in June, attacking both leaves and the young grapes, and destroying the first year nearly the total crop. In the following year it was scarcely less injurious in its effects, and, with the exception of the summer of 1856, no wine was produced on the island from 1852 to 1857. As late as 1850 the wine crop, according to the tax levied upon it, amounted to 12,964½ pipes, though in the judgment of those best informed it was double this quantity, yet in 1856 only 200 pipes were raised. No kind of grape escaped in Madeira, even the American grape, *Vitis vulpina*,[779] which before 1856 did not suffer, likewise became affected. From an oral statement of Mr. Acevede,[780] major of the engineer corps at Funchal, the disease had shown signs of its presence long before this time in Madeira, since old leases from the west of the island Ponta do Sol contain this article of agreement: that if the grape should become diseased with a white bloom, the contract should be considered annulled. In Portugal, also, some evidence of the grape disease has been perceived, but to a less extent. The vine is raised in the southwest of Madeira upon espalier frames, formed with canes fastened horizontally, four or five feet above the ground, to wooden beams or wall posts. Under the shadow of this vine roof sweet potatoes and other useful vegetables are planted. Before 1852 the largest portion of the country around Funchal, as well as the western portion of the island, is said to have been covered with vine espaliers. In 1857 these were seen only here and there. Still later, the wine stock has been entirely neglected, and in its stead sugarcane and cochineal have been planted. In the northern portions of the island, producing an inferior kind of wine, and, where, consequently, less labor was bestowed upon its culture, the vine climbs upon trees, mainly chestnut. Vine espaliers were never seen here, and although the disease affected some isolated leaves, it never attacked the grape. The 200 pipes mentioned as the product of 1856 were derived exclusively from this portion. It will thus be seen that the consumption of Madeira wine has rapidly diminished, and that that which is now sold as such is not genuine.

In 1831, Great Britain imported 209,127 gallons or 3.57 per cent, of her total wine consumption from Madeira, while in 1861 it amounted to only 28,749 gallons or 0.27 per cent. Schacht[781] calculated the annual loss of the island from the oïdium to be 1,137,990 dollars. The Madeira is replaced in part by the various wines of the South Canary islands, or the proper Canaries, viz: Teneriffe, Canary, Lanzerote, Fuerteventura, Palma, Gomera, and Ferro. ...

---

778 AN: Dr. Wm. Hamm's Weinbuch, Leipzig, 1865, p. 321. [Hermann Schacht (1814-1864), a German botanist who lived in Madeira for two years, due to his pulmonary condition, and author of a book, published in Berlin, in 1859, about the vegetation of two Atlantic islands, entitled *Madeira und Tenerife mit ihrer Vegetation*.]

779 Commonly known as frost grape, winter grape, or fox grape.

780 The right spelling is Azevedo. His full name was António Pedro de Azevedo (1814-1889). He was a native of Caminha, in northern Portugal but lived for many years in Madeira, where he was the director of the Public Works department. He is also known for having drawn the charts of Porto Santo, Madeira and Desertas, together with the officers of the British steam frigate *Styx*.

781 See (2nd part of) Note 778.

THE PRODUCTION OF WINE.[782]

After the appearance of the grape-blight sugar cane was introduced, and has succeeded very well; but now that the blight is more thoroughly understood and can be pretty effectually prevented by the agency of sulphur during the months of May, June and July, some of the cultivators are pulling up their cane and replanting the vine. The limited supply of water on the is island is an inducement to the cultivation of the grape, the vine being capable of subsisting for months without rain, and that is supposed to be one of the reasons of the fair quality of Madeira wine, while cane, on the contrary, requires regular irrigation.

The vintage which is now coming off promises a good yield, the general calculation being that about four thousand pipes of 110 gallons of wine will be secured against some three thousand last year.

There are several varieties of wine made here from grapes grown upon this island, viz: sercial, bual, tinta, malmsey and Madeira. These derive their names from the grape from which they are made, except Madeira, which is manufactured from the verdelho grape.

The sercial is a fine, light, dry wine, requiring at the least seven years of age before using. There is but a limited amount produced, and the old now on hand commands about seven hundred dollars a pipe.

The bual grape is now nearly extinct, and but little of the wine is to be met with. It is a light sweet wine; not so much so, however, as the Malaga. It is much admired by many. The price now asked for the remaining stock is seven hundred dollars the pipe.

The tinta is a dark wine, somewhat heavier than claret, and resembling in some respects Burgundy.

The malmsey is a dark sweet wine, resembling in taste the Malaga, but in quality a much richer wine. The supply is somewhat limited, and the price demanded is seven hundred dollars the pipe.

The Madeira wine is obtained, as before stated, from the verdelho grape, which is by far the most abundant in the island. There are two varieties of this grape, the light and the dark. Hence, wine made from either one or other of these grapes will be dark or light, according to the grape from which it is obtained. Frequently, however, it happens that a producer will have a portion of each, and will throw them together, forming a union of Madeira colors. So that the color of Madeira wine is no indication of quality.

Madeira wine is not usually regarded drinkable until it has attained at least three years of age; though it is frequently offered to purchasers at the end of six months to a year, by having the characteristics of age forced into it through a high degree of artificial heat. This manufactured wine is easily distinguished from that allowed to mature in the natural way. An imitation of Madeira wine has been, and probably now is, to some extent, manufactured from apples, having a trace of the fine old Madeira mixed with the apple juice, and exported to foreign markets and palmed off on consumers for Madeira wine. This article is readily detected by its burnt-apple taste. As the yield of grapes is, however, becoming more abundant, and the supply of pure wine greater, the temptation to thus imitate the genuine article becomes less and less.

---

[782] *Letter of the Secretary of State, Transmitting a Report on the Commercial Relations of the United States with Foreign Nations, for the year ended September 30, 1866*, Washington, Government Printing Office, 1867, pages 258-259. This text is an excerpt of a report by Charles A. Leas, U.S. Consul in Funchal, written on September 5, 1866.

There is not a very large stock of old Madeira wine on hand, but still a very good article of pure wine can be purchased for $150 to $300 the pipe of 110 gallons, free on board ship, and at the latter price will be warranted fifteen years old. That at the former price, probably, three to five years old. But the finest old dry southside, of, say, from thirty to fifty years old, cannot be purchased for less than seven hundred dollars the pipe.

The shipments of Madeira wine to the United States this year, so far, have amounted to $24,780.

7.5. Other Sources

In this last section of the chapter will be presented seven texts, published between 1808 and 1863, the first of which was written by Charles Jared Ingersoll (1782-1862), an American lawyer from Philadelphia and Democratic member of the U.S. House of Representatives, concerning Madeira Wine trade to the United States before and after the Revolution, two generic texts about this product, a letter from Daniel Webster to his friend Charles March ordering some Madeira, an excerpt from a book about the Madeira Exiles[783] where some prejudice against the islanders is perceived and, last but not least, a short text giving instructions as to how properly decant Madeira.

Figure 67. Charles Jared Ingersoll. 19th century illustration. Author unknown.

Mr. Pinkney to Mr. Canning[784]

Great Cumberland Place, Feb. 23, 1808.

… Beer, ale, and porter are prohibited by the non-importation act. There is no particular in which British monopoly is more glaring, than in what are called articles incidentally imported from Great Britain. These amount to the enormous sum of eight millions.

> Brandy and Geneva 2,700,000
> Wines 2,900,000
> Teas 2,300,000

The greater part of this sum is literally paid to Great Britain, in preference to incurring all the risks her navies oppose to importing those articles direct from the places of their production. The brandies are smuggled from France, the geneva from Holland; the wines carried from Madeira, Portugal, France, Spain, and Italy, and the teas from Canton. All the difference between the prime cost of these articles, and their inordinate enhancement in England, is paid by the United States, for the greater security of getting them from England,

---

[783] See Note 334.
[784] INGERSOLL, Charles Jared, *A View of the Rights and Wrongs, Power and Policy, of the United States of America*, Philadelphia, 1808, pages 147-149.

and is therefore nothing less than so much duty from the United States. In Madeira wine, this may be made peculiarly palpable. Before the revolution, the mother country permitted these colonies to trade with no part of Europe northward of Cape Finisterre, which is an extreme southern boundary. The island of Madeira, though attached to European dominion, being excluded by this colonial regulation, America sought the opportunity thus presented of communicating directly with a region distinct from the mother country: the consequence was the introduction of Madeira wine, and that prevailing taste for it which distinguishes the inhabitants of the United States. Though this trade was open before the revolution, and has always been nominally open since, that is, as open as the universal restrictions of England will allow, and though Madeira wine is not drank as a prevailing beverage in England, yet is a large proportion of what we receive actually purchased in London, and imported thence, with all the impositions of a double trade, double duties, and ignorant adulterations, down to the very nomenclature of the London market; most of the wine we consume being not only imported from England, but sold and know by the appelations of London particular, and London market wine. …

LETTER FIRST, TO THE EDITOR[785]
QUAEDAM DE VINO.[786] ON WINE.

… But enough of the ancients; let us follow Horace's model of a good epic poet, *In medias res semper festinat*:[787] shew me at once the way to your cellar; if it be not as well furnished as Mr. Paymaster Rigby's or old Q's,[788] we will suppose it to be so. What is this? Malmsey: good.

"Come broach me a bottle of rich Malvoisie,[789]

"Tis the boast of the Marmion tavern."

But this, like the Constantia, (the cape wine), Tokay, &c. is good only as a cordial or to give flavour to other wines, particularly the north side Madeira. It does not equally improve the south side wine. I think it is better kept in bottles than in casks.

When a wine is kept in a cask, three things are to be considered: what is the wine: what is the cask: where is it kept? …

Madeira, Sherry, White Port, Lisbon, Malaga are improved by warmth; they bear also exposure to alternations of weather; by gradual evaporation they become stronger, richer, mellower; and a garret is better for them than a cellar. …

Having thus made en passant, some general, and I hope useful observations, I return to Malmsey, which the French (who have no wine so good) call Malvoisie.

---

785 *The Emporium of Arts and Sciences,* New Series Conducted by Thomas Cooper, Esq., Volume I, Kimber and Richardson, Philadelphia, 1813, pages 484-487.
786 Latin expression meaning "on wine".
787 Latin expression meaning "always eager to get in the middle of things".
788 AN: The duke of Queensbury, lately deceased.
789 AN: Malvoisie. This is a name given to three different kinds of wine. 1st, It is the wine of Malvasia, the ancient Epidaurus, but better made in the island of Candia. 2dly, It is a Muscat wine from a grape grown in Provence. 3dly, It is the Malmsey of the island of Madeira. Malvasy, Malvisy, Malmsey, are names synonimous. There is a French Muscat grape also, called Malvoisie, a table fruit, of which wine is not usually made. It is not uncommon in the hot-house vineries of England. The Malmsey-Madeira, is the wine to which the name Malmsey ought to be confined.

It is too rich to be drink alone. From one twentieth part to one tenth part of old Malmsey, very greatly improves the common Madeira wine. The vinho tinto, a coloured wine, a Tent wine of Madeira, is *I believe*, a species of Malmsey not old enough to have yet lost its colour. I consider this as the old sacramental wine of the church of England.

Common Madeira may be greatly improved, and is so when wanted for immediate drinking, by a small quantity, (a dessert spoonful to a bottle) of well clarified syrup of the finest loaf sugar. I believe in addition to this, it is not unusual to put a teaspoonful of a filtered vinous solution of isinglass in good Madeira. These give a fullness, a richness, and a silkiness to the wine, that to my palate is very grateful. But the isinglass is apt to precipitate on standing and exposure to the air.

Your next cask is Madeira. Is it London particular? Is it bill wine or barter wine? Is it Cercial?[790] From the north, or the south side of the island? The London particular, is the highest priced wine for the London market; next to that is the bill wine, sold for bills of exchange; next to that is the barter wine, exchanged for goods. The wine of the south side of the island, as the Cercial[791] wine, is much the richest; the northern side is comparatively harsh. Wine is made up in Madeira, by mixing, 1st, a certain quantity of old with new wine; 2d, a certain quantity of Malmsey with the common wine; 3dly, a certain quantity of north side with south side wine. The more old the more Malmsey, the more south side wine, the better and dearer is the mixture. Clarified syrup is a frequent substitute for Malmsey. Teneriffe is, I believe, lately, introduced as an adulteration.

All wines are vinegars as you say. But the older, the fuller, the richer the wine, the more wholesome is it, and the less apt to produce indigestion, heart-burn, and of course gout.

Madeira should not be bottled; frequently the ullage is the best part of it. Madeira is adulterated, by Teneriffe, by Sherry, by Lisbon, by Malaga, by Fayal. Sherry hurts the quality of the wine least, but the Sherry flavour cannot be disguised. Teneriffe spoils it in flavour, and in body. The twang of common Lisbon is detestable; so is Malaga unless very old and very dry. Fayal does not deteriorate the flavour, but it renders the wine meagre.

The harsh, subacid Madeira commonly met with, is extremely unwholesome. A good judge, will prefer the smooth, full, silky wine; though I confess this is a sensation frequently given as I have said before, by a slight admixture of clarified sugar. It approaches however nearest to the full rich south side wine; and is less apt to disorder the stomach.

The clarified sugar, should be of the best double refined, dissolved in clear pure water, boiled with the white of egg, and filtered through a flannel jelly bag. The isinglass addition, I suspect only, from my own observations and experiments, but I think I have detected it. A solution of terra japonica,[792] will always throw down isinglass or any other animal gelatine. …

---

790 The right spelling is Sercial.
791 The right spelling is Sercial.
792 Catechu or Japan earth, is an extract of any several species of Acacia, especially Acacia catechu, produced by boiling the wood in water and evaporating the resulting brew.

From a Merchant at Madeira, to one in Philadelphia, directing an Exchange of Goods.[793]

MADEIRA, JULY 2D, 18–.

Sir – I hereby send this letter of advice to say, that on the 24th of June, I shipped on board the Jane, Captain Williams, ten pipes of Madeira, marked X, which you will be good enough to dispose of; and with the produce, after deducting a proper commission for your trouble, purchase such goods as you may imagine will be most likely to find a good market here (observing also to complete the enclosed order.) These you will be good enough to ship by the first vessel from Philadelphia to this port.

Not doubting but you will select the best and cheapest article you can procure of American manufacture,
    I am, sir, your humble servant.
    Mr.

The answer.

Philadelphia, Sep. 20th, 18–.

Sir – I received yours in due time. The ten pipes of wine, marked X, were safely lodged in the custom-house. I lost no time in advertising them for sale, in consequence of which I disposed of them for $–. This sum, agreeably to your commands, I have laid out to the best advantage; and yesterday I shipped on board the Adrian, Captain White, seven bales for you, marked IOI, which I hope you will receive in good order, and find them to be such as you desire to have.
    I am, sir,
    Your very obedient servant.
    Mr.

VINUM.[794] U.S.[795]
Wine.

… *Properties.* Wine, considered as the name of a class, may be characterized as a spirituous liquid, the result of the fermentation of grape-juice, and containing colouring matter, and some other substances, which are either combined or intimately blended with the spirit. All its other qualities vary with the nature of each particular wine. The wines used for medicinal purposes are the officinal wine, sherry, together with madeira, teneriffe, port, and claret. …

Madeira is the strongest of the white wines in general use. It is a slightly acid wine, and, when of proper age and in good condition, has a rich, nutty, aromatic flavour. As it occurs

---

[793] TURNER, R., *The Parlour Letter-Writer, and Secretary's Assistant: consisting of Original Letters on Every Occurrence in Life, Written in a Concise and Familiar Style, and Adapted to Both Sexes, to which are added Complimentary Cards, Wills, Bonds, &c.*, Thomas, Cowperthwait, & Co., Philadelphia, 1845, pages 44-45.

[794] Latin word for wine.

[795] WOOD, M.D., George Bacon; BACHE, M.D., Franklin, *The Dispensatory of the United States of America,* Eighth edition, Grigg, Elliot, and Co., Philadelphia, 1849, pages 737-738.

in the market, however, it is of very variable quality, on account of the adulterations and mixtures to which it is subjected after importation. The madeira consumed in this country is generally better than that used in England; its adulteration being practised to a less extent with us, and our climate being more favourable to the improvement of the wine. ...

MR. WEBSTER TO MR. CHARLES MARCH.[796]

WASHINGTON, FEBRUARY 5, 1849.

MY DEAR SIR, – At that poor place called Marshfield,[797] which you have never thought it worth your while to visit, and I am afraid never will, there are a few bottles, though but a few, of good old Madeira wine, introduced in the country through your agency, and some of it the fruit of your bounty. But here, in this great city, I have not a single drop of such wine as I have now mentioned. Not having fallen into the Sherry heresy, I take a glass of Madeira sometimes myself. But that is not important. There comes our new President,[798] however, and I should like to be able to offer to him and his attendants. A glass of what you and I regard as fit to drink.

Therefore, I will be obliged to you to send me a dozen or two of such a quality of wine as you think likely to make a favorable impression on the taste of the chief magistrate elect, and I will cheerfully defray cost and charges.

Mr. Edward Curtis[799] is now with us, with health marvellously improved.

Yours, with constant regard,
DAN'L WEBSTER.[800]

Figure 68. Daniel Webster ordered some bottles of Madeira Wine to be served to the new President-elect Zachary Taylor. *Illustration from the frontispiece of the book* Daniel Webster and his Contemporaries, *(New York, 1852).*

---

796 WEBSTER, Fletcher, *The Private Correspondence of Daniel Webster,* In Two Volumes, Volume II, Little, Brown and Company, Boston, 1857, page 297. We presume this Charles March was his friend and the author of the Madeira-related book we presented in section 6.1.1.15. of this anthology, and who also wrote the book *Daniel Webster and his Contemporaries,* published in New York, in 1852.

797 A town in Plymouth County, MA.

798 Zachary Taylor (1784-1850), a native of Virginia, was the 12th President of the United States, serving from 1849 to 1850. He was also a planter based in Baton Rouge, LA, and a military leader, known as "Old Rough and Ready", with a 40-year military career in the United States Army, serving in the War of 1812, the Black Hawk War, the Second Seminole War, and achieved fame leading the American army to victory in the Battle of Palo Alto and the Battle of Monterrey, during the Mexican-American War.

799 Edward Curtis (1801-1856), a lawyer and Representative from New York for two terms, from 1837 to 1841, and a Collector of the Port of New York, from 1841 to 1844.

800 See Note 72.

CHAPTER I.[801]

Figure 69. Wine carriers. This etching has some similarities with the one in Figure 24. *Book illustration. Author unknown.*

Figure 70. Wine making in Madeira. This etching has some similarities with the one in Figure 25. *Book illustration. Author unknown.*

A few slips of the grape-vine were brought from the Isle of Cyprus and planted in Madeira. They grew, and from them have grown the celebrated vineyards of the Isle of Wines. The wealth of Madeira is chiefly derived from its vineyards. ...

The stranger who never saw any old fashioned bottles is amused to see the sheep-skins filled with wine, and carried on the shoulders of peasants to the market. Of course they know better than to put "new wine into old bottles." It might not be very pleasing to a wine-bibbler to look on the men in their bare feet treading the grapes in the press, especially in a warm, sweating day. ...

A few years ago[802] the vineyards began to fail. The traveller could no longer pass along under the shadow of the vines, and have rich clusters of grapes hanging over his path. The fruit was cut off! It brought a famine on the island. ...

The Christians of the United States took a deep interest in the famishing people of Madeira. They sent them the "finest of the wheat," and induced them to cultivate such eatables as we raise in our fields and gardens. ...

The famine made many people poor. The women of the island, who have always done most of the labour, began to turn their skill to good account. They made fancy articles of a very superior quality, such as laces, edgings, paper-cutters, card-cases, work-boxes, and writing-desks. They took the dark Til-wood of the old wine-presses, and made beautiful articles for foreign parlours.[803]

---

801 BLACKBURN, Rev. William Maxwell, *The Exiles of Madeira,* Presbyterian Board of Publication, Philadelphia, [1860], pages 11, 13-15.
802 In 1852.
803 BLACKBURN [1860], pages 15-16.

DECANTING MADEIRA AND CLARET.[804]

A frequent error is that of decanting Madeira wine and leaving the stopper out; it is a barbarous system and cannot be sufficiently reprobated. The fine nutty flavor so much prized by the gastronomic planters, the indescribable aroma, the nosegay in short, is destroyed by this senseless process; your pseudo judge says it renders the wine soft and silky, for which read *fiat and vapid*.[805] Above all, never put your Madeira into a decanter – it is little short of sacrilege. Keep it in the black bottle, and never take the cork out but to replenish your glass. The error just pointed out as regards Madeira applies also to Claret; …

---

804 WELLS, David Ames, *Things Not Generally Known: A Popular Hand-Book of Facts Not Readily Accessible in Literature, History, and Science,* D. Appleton and Company, New York, 1863, page 318.
805 Latin words meaning so be it and spoiled.

8. Generic Texts about Madeira Wine in American Magazines

Throughout the 19th century several American magazines revealed a wide variety of articles dealing with Madeira Wine, some of them signed by their authors, and some others published anonymously. Shown here is a selection of eleven of the most important texts we could find dealing with this subject, organized by date of publication, from 1817 to 1871. One will see themes already tackled in other sources, but which complement them, such as the history of Madeira Wine, its different types and production, among other topics.

ART. II. – *Wine*.[806]

… The wine of the island of Madeira, is well known and greatly esteemed in France, and with good reason: but it should be dry, with a very slight bitter, a pleasant odour, and a slight taste of pitch from the skins in which it is transported. The Malmsey-Madeira, is a delicious wine,[807] greatly esteemed by connoisseurs, and is very wholesome. …

GRAPE-VINE - VITIS[808]

… The island of Madeira was planted with the vine from cuttings brought from Cyprus, by Prince Henry, son to John the First of Portugal, in the year 1420, when the island was first discovered; and it now affords about 30,000 pipes of wine annually. The Rhenish vine has also been planted in Madeira, and produces a very superior wine, known by the name of Cerciel[809] Madeira; this island also affords us a sweet wine, called Malmsey Madeira, but the genuine Malmsey wine is the produce of Malvisia, and is now very rare. The ancients sometimes ripened particular wines, by placing them in the smoke above a fire, or in an upper part of their houses; and it is well known to the moderns, who are curious in their Madeira wines, how much they improve by being kept in a garret, instead of a vaulted cellar. Good West-India Madeira that has been exposed to the frost, as well as the heat of summer, will be found to have ripened, as well by a voyage to the East Indies. …

---

[806] IRVING, Washington, "The Analectic Magazine", Vol. 10, From July to December, 1817, M. Thomas, Philadelphia, 1817, page 475.

[807] AN: In France, where a glass or two only of these wines are drank at dinner, or at the desert, they may deserve the commendations here given: but they will not do to be used, as the English and Americans use wine.

[808] SKINNER, John S., "American Farmer, containing Original Essays and Selections on Rural Economy and Internal Improvements, with Illustrative Engravings and the Prices Current of Country Produce", Vol. IV, J. Robinson, Baltimore, 1823, page 203. This article had been originally published in the edition of September 20, 1822, of this magazine. It is a transcription of the same text published at the *Pomarium Britannicum: an Historical and Botanical Account of Fruits, known in Great Britain*, by Henry Phillips, published in London, in 1820. Vitis is the Latin word for grape-vine.

[809] The right spelling is Sercial.

[For the N. Y. Farmer and Horticultural Repository.][810]
ART. 97. – *Adlum's Catawba Wine.* – *Extract of a letter from* JOHN ADLUM, *Esq. of Columbia District, author of an instructive Memoir on the Cultivation of the Vine,*[811] *to Dr.* MITCHELL, *dated at his Vineyard, near Georgetown, May 21, 1828.*

I send for your acceptance two bottles of Catawba wine, and a book on the cultivation of the vine and making wine in America. The wine was made by myself; and the book contains all my practice in both branches of the business, with large extracts from other authors. ...

If, after dinner, I drink three glasses of either Madeira or Sherry, I have to rise in the course of the night, wash my mouth, and drink water frequently. Whether the wines imported now are not so good as they were forty years ago, I do not certainly know; but I do not believe they are; for then I could drink the best part of a bottle after dinner without feeling any unpleasant sensation of thirst after I went to bed: but it is now otherwise.

When the indolent Portuguese had the wine-vaults of the island of Madeira in their hands, the wine was suffered to get old by time; but now it is made old in a fifth or sixth part of the time it formerly took, by the foreigners who have monopolized the wine trade there, especially the English. An eminent wine merchant informed me some days since, that the present exporters from Madeira told him, on his complaining that they did not sell or send such good wine as they formerly used to do, that such was actually the fact. The old wine that was in the vats when the present proprietors purchased them from the Portuguese, was used up by mixing it with wines of a more recent state; and of course they were obliged to send him such as they had. ...

To the Editors of the "New-York Farmer and Horticultural Repository."

Sir, – In perusing an article entitled "Adlum's Catawba wine," in the June number of your useful miscellany, I was struck with the remark therein made, that the Madeira wine imported at this day, was not of as good quality as that of forty years since, and the cause there assigned, though correct in part, yet is not wholly true. The great material reason for this deterioration is as follows: The wine merchants, as Mr. Adlum justly observes, formerly let their wine remain in large vaults or tanks, to ripen by age, and improve by time; but the present dealers, generally, to realise a quicker return for their investment in this trade, force the wine, by the process they have adopted, of what is termed "*stoving*," which is somewhat of the following manner: Instead of having wine vaults, as formerly, they now have large store houses, of two, three or four stories high, in which they store their wine in pipes, piled in open tiers, having no floors intervening between the different lofts. At the bottom, or on the ground floor, large furnaces are erected, with flues carried through the whole building, which furnaces are kept continually heated for a length of time, thereby creating an extra degree of heat, and forcing the

---

[810] "The New-York Farmer and Horticultural Repository. Devoted to Practical Husbandry and Gardening, and embracing the most important information in the sciences, intimately connected with rural pursuits. Under the Patronage of the New-York Horticultural Society," Volume I, New-York, 1828, pages 132-133, 204-205. The first letter was published in the issue of June 1828 of this magazine, whereas the second one was inserted on its September edition.

[811] ADLUM, John, *A Memoir of the Cultivation of the Vine in America, and the Best Mode of Making Wine,* Davis and Force, Washington, 1823.

ripening of wine. The consequence of this process is, that one year old wine will obtain the flavour of three years; but the subsequent improvement in the quantity of the wine is forever checked, because the true vital principles are destroyed. In order however, to regulate the age of the wine for importation, they mix wine of different ages qualities, and according to the mixture, is the quality and age of the vine commercially stated. This information I obtained from personal observation, during a short residence in that Island, some years since. – I have no doubt but that the quality of the Madeira wine has much deteriorated from what it formerly was, in consequence of the mode above described being adopted in preparing it for market. I resided in the Island of Teneriffe for many months, and paid some little attention to their manner of preparing wine for exportation. The wine merchants do not stove their wine, but mix the same of different ages and quality, according to the character they wish to stamp it with in shipping it; from London particular to India market, superior cargo, and common cargo wine. Should there be any connoisseurs in wine in your place, who have observed the difference in Madeira no doubt they could state, that in some Madeira wine, they could perceive no improvement whatever; which is owing to the treatment before stated. I have drank wine of a purer quality and better flavor in Teneriffe, than any Madeira wine that I have ever tasted. It gives me much pleasure to observe that great attention is beginning to be paid to the cultivation of the grape generally, and the making of wine in our country. I sincerely hope that the time is not far distant, when the American public can be as independent in the production of good wine, as they are in many other articles of foreign aid. If the above remarks, in your opinion, are worthy of publication, you are welcome to them.

I am respectfully, yours &c.
J. O. D.
Albany, Aug. 1828.

Madeira Wine.[812] – The Island of Madeira is said to have been stocked with plants brought directly from Candia, by order of Prince Henry, under whose auspices the first colony of the Portuguese was established there in 1421. The mildness of the climate, and the volcanic soils with which the island abounds, were so favourable to their growth, that in 1455, the manufacture of wine was already commenced, from grapes whose beauty and size commanded the admiration of the traveller.

The best vineyards are found on the south side, which is least exposed to cold winds and fogs from the sea. The soil is generally composed of pumice stone mixed with a portion of clay, sand and marl – and as in Germany, it is often necessary to form terraces, in order to prevent the soil from being washed away from the acclivities.

The grapes are propagated by quicksets or cuttings, and planted in rows, the ground being trenched sufficiently deep to allow the roots to penetrate into the sub-stratum of volcanic ashes. Some are left without support, and kept low by frequent pruning; others are trained on square frames from twenty to thirty inches high; while others again are disposed on a sloping lattice work, formed of canes, and supported by poles, the

---

[812] "The North American Magazine", Vol. III, Philadelphia, 1834, pages 433-434. Article written by a correspondent of the *Albany Gazette*.

tallest of which rise about seven feet from the ground. In January or February, the vines are pruned, and the first dressing is given: in April or May, they are in flower, and by the first week in September, the fruit is generally ripe. It is very carefully picked – all unripe and damaged clusters being set apart for the manufacture of an *inferior wine*. The grapes are tread in a trough, and the juice thus obtained is called *vinho da flor*. The bruised grapes are again taken and subjected to the action of a press, which gives the second quality of must. On account of the mountainous nature of the country, the grapes are sometimes pressed in one place, and fermented in another, to which they are conveyed on men's backs, either in goats' skins or small barrels. By the first or second week in November, the wine is expected to be clear.

The celebrated Malmsey wine is also grown on certain rocky grounds, (in this island) exposed to the full influence of the sun's rays. As the grapes from which it is procured require to be overripe, or partially shrivelled, they are allowed to hang about a month later than those used in the manufacture of dry wines.

The grapes most preferred in the Island, are the *Malvazia* and the *Sercial*. They will only succeed in particular spots. The *Sercial* is very dry and austere, when new, but becomes thoroughly mellowed by age. It then has a rich aromatic flavour quite peculiar to itself, and combines all the requisites of a perfect wine. The quantity of Sercial produced does not exceed forty or fifty pipes in the year.

Most of the red grapes are consumed in the manufacture of white wines, but a portion of them are converted into *tinta* or red wine.

Some twenty or thirty years since, Barrow,[813] the traveller, estimated the quantity of Madeira annually exported from the Island at fifteen thousand pipes.

The wines receive an addition of brandy previous to exportation. The effect of this is injurious to the flavour of the better kinds, but it is supposed necessary to enable them to bear the high temperature to which they are exposed. The demand for Madeira in America, to which it was at first alone exported, led to a knowledge of the benefit derived by removal to a warm climate. It does not however follow, that because Madeira wine has been on a voyage to the East or West Indies, therefore, it is better. Many of the cargoes sent to the East Indies, are purchased on speculation and on long credit, or in barter for goods. Hence the best growths are not always furnished, and the wine in question is sometimes contemptuously distinguished in the London market, by the name of truck, or barter Madeira.

Exposure to heat in regulated rooms, or under the roof of a house in summer answers most of the advantages obtained from a voyage.

When kept eight or ten years in wood, and afterwards allowed to mellow nearly twice that time in the bottle, Madeira wines acquire "that agreeable pungency, that bitter sweetness, which was so highly prized in the choicest wines of antiquity, emitting great strength and richness of flavour, with an exceedingly fragrant and diffusible aroma. The nutty taste, which is often very marked, is not communicated, as some have imagined, by means of bitter almonds, but is inherent in the wine."

---

813 See Note 708.

EXPERIENCES OF A MODERN PHILOSOPHER.[814]
Dans les petites boites les bons onguen[t]s.[815]
LESSON THE SECOND.

… XV. If you are dyspeptic, drink Madeira. It possesses a more delicate flavor than Sherry, but is equally spirituous, and very little more acidulous. It is not in condition unless it has been kept for ten years in wood, and for twice that time in bottle. Madeira wine cannot be too old. Sea voyages assist to mellow it, but age can alone deprive it of the original harshness, and bestow that agreeable pungency, that bitter sweetishness, and nutty flavor, which is so much admired. It is too often spoiled by the addition of brandy when racked off; and an adulterating compound of burnt almonds and tansey is frequently added, to give it some of its wonted peculiarities.

A CHAPTER ON GASTRONOMY.[816]

… One of the most gentlemanlike hobbies a man can indulge in, is a good cellar; for I know not a truer gratification than being enabled to give a friend a bottle of fine wine. To me it is the *ne plus ultra* of enjoyment. I need scarcely say, that great judgment and experience are required in laving the foundation of your stock; and if you be diffident of your power of taste, confide implicitly in a respectable wine merchant, and he will do you justice. Of all wines, Madeira demands the nicest discrimination in its selection; the deservedly high place it once held in the estimation of connoisseurs, has been usurped by Sherry, and it is to be lamented that it should have grown into comparative desuetude; for of the two it is incomparably the finer wine. An error has long prevailed regarding this long neglected nectar, whish, in justice to my brother "*bons vivants*," I must expose.

The unwary are led to believe that East India Madeira is the best – this is decidedly wrong, as I shall presently show. The West India Madeira is the wine par excellence – immeasurably superior in every respect. The authority I can quote in support of my argument is not to be disputed, for this important and little-known fact was communicated to me on the Island of Madeira itself, by one of its most influential merchants, under whose hospitable roof I was living some few years ago. He told me that the West India planters are the very best judges in the world of Madeira wine, and purchase none but of the very best description, and whether consigned to them, or sent on speculation to the several islands, the very first quality only is shipped – the distance is nothing – a three weeks' run, and if wine of an indifferent kind were submitted for sale, it would be returned on the merchant's hands. Not so with the commodity sent to the East India market under the attractive cognomen of "London Particular," – it is a thin acid potation, a second-growth wine in fact, and as unlike the rich, fruity, nutty beverage of occidental celebrity, as a horse-chesnut is to a chesnut horse. Of course I do not allude to private orders from governors-general, commanders-in-chiefs,

---

814 BURTON, William E., "The Gentleman's Magazine.", Volume I., From July to December., Charles Alexander, Philadelphia, 1837, page 93.
815 French expression meaning "the good ointments are (kept) in small boxes".
816 "The Evergreen: A Monthly Magazine of New and Popular Tales and Poetry.", Volume I., January to December, 1840, J. Winchester, Publisher, New York, 1840, pages 401-404. We presume this text was transcribed from an English source, namely "The New Montly Magazine and Humorist", published in London, in the same year and under the same title.

and nabobs, but to the common run of wine with high sounding title, exported by captains of free traders, either on their own account, or that of the retailers and keepers of stores at the various presidencies.

During my short stay at Madeira on a voyage to the West Indies, I discovered that there was a great difference in the price as well as the quality of the wine shipped to the East – that for the West averaging fifty guineas and fifty-four pounds, while the latter could be had at thirty-eight and forty pounds per pipe. The contented citizen in the innocence of his heart imagines, that a pipe of Madeira stowed away in the hold of the Neptune or Polly, of London, and which has been to *Ingy* and back, must be superior, forgetting that if the wine itself be not originally good, all the voyages from the days of Lord Anson[817] to the present time will never impart richness and flavor to any juice of the grape of a poor and thin body: – a genial climate and perpetual motion may accelerate the progress to maturity, but fifty tropical suns and as many trips round the Cape will never make fine Madeira. Lady Duberly's elegant axiom may be justly quoted in this case, when snubbing her lord, she says, "You cannot make a silk purse out of a sow's ear."[818] You might as well attempt to convert table-beer into brown stout. With the exception of private stocks in the cellars of the East India connoisseur, there is no Madeira equal to that to be met with in every island in the West Indies, and to have it in perfection it should be drunk upon the spot.

Another popular error, and one which makes a thoroughbred West Indian shudder, is that of decanting old Madeira wine, and leaving the stopper out: it is a barbarous system and cannot be sufficiently reprobated. The fine nutty flavor so prized by the gastronomic planters, the indescribable aroma, the nosegay in short, is destroyed by this senseless process – your pseudo judge says it renders the wine soft and silky, for which read *flat and vapid*.[819] What would the genuine porter-swigger say to having his favorite beverage left standing exposed to the action of the air for some three or four hours before his dinner? Why, he would write the man down an ass who committed such an atrocious act. The cases are parallel, and in both instances the spirit and flavor of the liquid are destroyed.

The principal firms of Madeira have adopted the plan of giving their wines the benefit of the motion of a vessel by manual application. Whole gangs of Portuguese are employed on the beach in rolling pipes and hogsheads of Madeira, thus saving the expense of a voyage, and with the same beneficial result – the undulating motion of the vessel being tolerably imitated on this vine-flourishing island. The merchants there also bring on premature age by means of artificial heat, and it is astonishing how soon the wines ripen under the sweating process, as it is termed. In the West Indies, as soon as a pipe of Madeira is bottled off, the planter stores it in a loft of his dwelling, with nothing between his dearly-prized supernaculum, and the broiling sun but the shingled roof. The heat in these lofty cellars is intense beyond conception. In two years the wine is ready for drinking – rich, and ripe, and of a flavor unimaginable to those who have never visited the Antilles.

One house at Madeira has adopted this plan, and they have a very extensive stock of the finest old bottled wine. The name of the firm is Leacock, and without prejudice, I am

---

[817] George Anson (1697-1762), British Admiral of the Fleet and wealthy aristocrat, noted for his circumnavigation of the globe and his role overseeing the Royal Navy during the Seven Years' War.

[818] Quote from Scene II, Act III, of the play "The Heir at Law", by George Colman the Younger (1762-1836), in which the character Lady Duberly states: «I wish you could learn him to follow my example, and be a little genteel: – but there is no making a silk purse out of a sow's ear, they say.»

[819] See Note 805.

of opinion that their wines are the very finest that are exported from the island. This may be accounted for by their vineyards being more favorably situated than their competitors, for we all know that, on any large slope of a hill tilled for the growth of vines, one particular site will often yield a finer flavored juice than the surrounding ones; but be this as it may, the Madeiras of the Messieurs Leacock are in high repute throughout the West India Islands, and deservedly so, for finer wine it is impossible to meet with; and were I to lay in a stock for my own consumption, I should send to them for as many dozens as they could spare of their bottled nectar. The climate of this country is ill-suited to this generous wine: the cold is its greatest enemy – and it would be impossible to recognize the same wine in London that you were in the habit of drinking in Barbadoes. I can give a case in point:

Some years ago I sent a few dozens of superlatively fine old Madeira to a near and dear relative of mine in this country – my late father. This wine was renowned throughout the West India Islands, being part of the stock of the late Mr. Probyn,[820] Governor of St. Christopher's.[821] I bought it at a sale which took place after his death, and paid a very high price for it, at much as twenty-eight dollars the dozen – but then it was such wine! Well, I sent it home, where a heavy duty was superadded to the original cost; *n'importe*. It arrived safe, and was glorified beyond measure. The late Sir Herbert Taylor[822] and Sir Henry Torrens[823] (no bad judges) pronounced it the very finest they had ever tasted; but notwithstanding such high authority, I can assure the reader that it was very inferior to what it had been before it left the West Indies – it was not like the same wine. The best plan I know of is, to construct a large cupboard as near your kitchen-chimney as possible, line it with sheet or plate iron, pass a flue through the top of it, and keep this wine-press at an unvaried temperature of ninety-six or a hundred. Keep your Madeira in it, and by these artificial means you will have your wine in drinkable order. *I* have tried it, and have found it to answer marvelously well. Some old East and West India acquaintances have followed my advice, and have thanked me for the hint. Above all, never put your Madeira into a decanter – it is little short of sacrilege. Keep it in the black bottle, and never take the cork out but to replenish your glass.

There is very little really fine Madeira to be purchased in London. The best I know of is at Messrs. Calrow's, of St. Mary's Hill, Thames street. It comes nearer to the Leacocks' wine of any I have met with (purchaseable I mean) in England. – If Madeira is but little understood in this country, that amphibious delicacy, the turtle, is still less. …

To resume: the error I have pointed out as regards Madeira applies to claret; for some unthinking persons will pour it into glass jugs, if not decanters. It makes one's flesh creep on one's bones to witness such profanation …

For dinner wines, hock and sherry are to be preferred, a little champaign, of course; Madeira and claret after the meal is concluded. …

Sans adieu, then, kind reader! if the foregoing observations may have the effect of adding one iota to your stock of gastronomic knowledge I shall be more than repaid for my pains; and if in the course of human events, we should chance to meet at the table of a mutual acquaintance, I will pledge you with all sincerity in a bumper of the best his cellar affords.

---

820 Thomas Probyn, who served as the Governor of St. Christopher from 1816 to 1821.
821 Saint Christopher Island, known today more formally as Saint Kitts, in the West Indies.
822 Sir Herbert Taylor (1755-1839), Lieutenant-General of the British Army who was the first Private Secretary to the Sovereign of the United Kingdom, William IV.
823 Sir Henry Torrens (1779-1828), Major-General of the British Army who was an Adjudant-General to the Forces.

EXPENSIVE DRINKING.[824] – Madeira wine is the grand beverage of the United States, whenever it can be got – in perfection, if possible, but in any condition rather than not at all. An American thinks of his finest Madeira, what an Englishman and a Frenchman think of their port and claret, or what a dweller by the Rhine thinks of his hock; and he will pay a far greater price for it, than all these together will disburse for the beverage they prefer. We had more than one opportunity of tasting, at the table of an American millionaire, white Madeira wine, for which the enormous price of sixteen dollars (£3. 6s. 8d. in English currency) per bottle had been given – something very much like 5s. 6d. per glass; and the princely donor remarked, that if he knew where it was possible to procure more, he would willingly give the same sum for any quantity of it. – *Bunn's Old England and New England.*[825]

"MADEIRA, PORT AND SHERRY"[826]

They who go down upon the waters in ships see the wonders of the Lord; but they who go down on schooners, it is also said, see – a place not to be mentioned to ears polite. Whomever unkind fate has driven upon the reckless waters in a vessel of ridiculous tonnage, let him be pitied, by all at least who have no stomach for the sea. The author of this book, commissioned to explore the countries that bear the vines whose products serve as caption to this article, undertook to reach Madeira in a schooner numbering less than 200 tons. …

… In spite of storms, hurricanes, or calms, he arrived in Madeira in twenty days from Southampton.

… What a change greeted the new-comer! Winter had become glorious summer; the naked trees had put on luxuriant and varied foliage, and flowers of every kind enlivened and scented the air. Hills covered with the verdant vine, and gardens loaded with the ripening fruit, gladdened the eye, while the picturesque costume of the inhabitants, and their earnest welcome, delighted the mind; …

… It is its wine, however, for which Madeira is world-famous – a wine redolent of great facts. For under its inspiration what epics, acted or written, have not been achieved! It has inspired the poet's brain, it has warmed the speaker's tongue, and has thawed the miser's heart. One glass of it makes the whole world kin; strangers, meeting at abrupt angles of life, never before encountering, have embraced and sworn eternal amity over its rosy goblets. It decorates prosperous days, and takes the sting from misfortune.

Sometimes when the carriers are bringing the juice to market, or rather to the store-houses, in their goat-skins, they grow fatigued beneath the burden, and place it on some fortuitous rock or auxiliary stump or tree. Here they pull out the stopper from the mouth of the *bota*,[827] or skin, and stop it by another mouth, which is found to facilitate evaporation

---

[824] LITTELL, E., "Littell's Living Age", Second Series, Volume IV, (From the beginning, Volume XL), January, February, March, 1854, Massachusetts, page 358.

[825] Alfred Bunn (1796-1860), an Englishman who published this book containing his impressions of America. See section 10.13. of this anthology.

[826] "Harper's New Monthly Magazine", Volume 12, Issue 71, New York, April 1856, pages 601-602. This article is a review of the book *Sketches and Adventures in Madeira, Portugal, and the Andalusies of Spain*, by Charles W. March, which we present in section 6.1.1.15. of this anthology.

[827] Bota is the Portuguese word for boot, and not for skin.

very much. Of course the lighter burden the lighter the spirits; and sometimes by the time they arrive in Funchal the skin of the animal and the skin of the man seem to have changed functions. A safer way of getting it along is by oxen on sledges; no wheel carriages can be used in the island from its precipitous formation, and the other fact that the streets are paved with a flat smooth stone, necessary to prevent the roads from being broken up by the raging inundations that sometimes occur, one of which some years since carried houses and all their occupants into the unreturning sea.[828] These inundations are terrible when unchecked, and their ravages sometimes obliterate the former pathways.

Figure 71. "Bringing wine in skins." This illustration is similar to Figure 28. Article illustration. Author unknown.

Over these smooth stones the smooth-worn sledges glide almost as easily as sleighs upon the snow-covered earth. The cattle, however, have none of the ambition of our 2 40's, but move along slowly, sedately, and with a consciousness of their priceless cargo.

The language used by these *burroqueros*,[829] or ox-drivers, to their four-legged companions is a dialect unwritten, but most expressive. The beasts evidently understand and obey it. But to an "outsider" it has a shrill, and almost unearthly sound. Indeed it has a fearful influence upon the animals themselves, for they start at it more than at the puncture of the goad.

Figure 72. "Hauling wine on sledges." This illustration is similar to Figure 29. Article illustration. Author unknown.

[Untitled][830]

Madeira wine, once so popular in England and in India, has long become a drink of the past. The grape disease destroyed the famous vineyards of the island, and the peasantry, thrown out of work, emigrated to the West Indies, whence a few of them returning, substituted the cultivation of the sugarcane for that of the grape. But Messrs. Cossart, Gordon, and Co., write from Funchal, to the Times, to announce that the vines of Madeira are recovering from the plague by which they have been smitten; that the vintage of 1867 amounted to 2,300 pipes, of which 1,600 were of prime quality; and that the yield of the present year promises to surpass that of 1867. So cheered are the Madeiras by their prospects that in many parts of the island they are rooting up the sugar-canes and replanting vines.

---

828 Reference to the big flood that devastated downtown Funchal in October 1803. See 1st article of section 9.5. of this anthology.
829 See Note 437.
830 "Every Saturday: A Journal of Choice Reading selected from Foreign Current Literature", Vol. VI., July to December, Fields, Osgood, & Co., Boston, 1868, page 286; *New York Commercial Advertiser*, August 12, 1868. (New York City, NY. Published under the title "MADEIRA WINE." adding that it had been transcribed from the *Pall Mall Gazette*); *Massachusetts Weekly Spy*, August 14, 1868. (Worcester, MA. Published, untitled, without the last sentence).

Madeira Wine.[831] – The Hamburg *News* gives a report on the wine of the Island of Madeira, from which we condense the following: Soon after 1850 the grape disease (Oidium) destroyed nearly all the vineyards of the Island, leaving only a few on the south side, so that it seemed as if the Madeira wine would entirely disappear from the market. The small quantity produced commanded exceedingly high prices. After turning out all grapevines, sugar cane, tobacco and corn were planted, but with little success. Those plantations seemed not to agree with soil and climate, except on the north side, and about eight years after the grape disease had broken out, the land-owners returned to planting grape vines. Although the disease had not entirely disappeared, favorable results were obtained, and from 1860 to 1862, the crop amounted to 500 tierces[832] yearly; in 1863, to 1000 tierces, and increased steadily to 4000 tierces in 1867; in 1868, to 8000, and the same quantity was produced this year. It will be some time yet before the regular yield of 25,000 tierces a year will be obtained at former prices; but the quality produced from the new plantations is equal to the best before the disease made its appearance.

Wine.[833]

Wine is the *fermented* juice of the grape, though the term is frequently used to designate any saccharine solution, the sugar of which has been wholly or partially converted into alcohol. This definition, however, cannot be very strictly construed, for if so, the most popular wines of our day would be excluded, viz: Madeira and Sherry. These wines both contain *distilled* liquors, added to give them body, to please the taste of consumers, and to preserve them from acetous fermentation. The custom in Madeira is for the merchants of Funchal to purchase the wine from the manufacturers, distil a portion into brandy, which they add to the wine at the rate of twenty-four to every one hundred and ten gallons. The wine of Madeira originally is very little if any stronger than the wines of Germany and France, and is only made so by the addition of brandy. When it is considered that for every per cent, of alcohol in any given wine there must have been in the grape juice two per cent, of sugar, you will readily perceive that no grape can yield a must sufficiently rich in saccharine matter to produce wine containing from 17 to 19 per cent, of alcohol, and from 3½ to 5 per cent, of unconverted sugar, and yet such is the average composition of the Madeira and Sherry, most prized by connoisseurs.

Mr. Henderson, in his work on the history of wine, published in London in 1824,[834] gives a table prepared by Mr. Brande,[835] showing 22.27 per cent, alcohol, as the average of four specimens of Madeira. Prof. Wm. Hume[836] in more recent analyses found from 17 to 19 per cent, of alcohol and from 3½ to 5 per cent, sugar. To produce such wine would require a must containing from 38 to 43 per cent, of saccharine matter. The richest grape

---

[831] "The Friend. A Religious and Literary Journal", Volume XLIII, William H. Pile, Philadelphia, 1870, page 164.
[832] A tierce is an old English unit of volume that corresponds to 42 US gallons (about 159 liters).
[833] JACQUES, D. H., "The Rural Carolinian; An Illustrated Magazine, of Agriculture, Horticulture and the Arts", Walker, Evans & Cogswell and D. Wyatt Aiken, Charleston, S. C., 1871, pages 159-160.
[834] Alexander Henderson's book, entitled *The History of Ancient and Modern Wines,* Baldwin, Cradock and Joy, published in London, in 1824.
[835] See Note 704.
[836] Professor William Hume, a native of Charleston, SC, who was passionate about chemistry and discovered a new method of making wine without fermentation.

that I have met with yielded a must whose specific gravity indicated 22.50 saccharine matter, which would have given a wine of 11.25 alcohol, if *all* the sugar had been converted into alcohol by fermentation. …

… The difficulty of producing a pleasant combination of brandy with wine, has been partially overcome by the merchants of Funchal, who have learned to prepare their wines for particular markets, by a voyage to the East or West Indies. The explanation is evident – that a new fermentation is brought about by removal to a warmer climate, and thereby a blending of the wine and brandy effected. The nutty flavor of Madeira is not communicated like Sherry, by means of bitter almonds, that is inherent in the wine. …

9. Madeira Wine in the American Press

In the 1800's Madeira Wine is widely mentioned in the American press, and that is not to be wondered, since until the first half of that century it was widely advertised and referred to in a million ways. This chapter is dedicated to displaying a wide array of newspaper articles related to this special wine, enabling us to perceive the way in which Americans saw and used it in their own country. From our extensive research we have selected the most interesting texts, from different sources across the United States, dealing with several topics involving Madeira Wine, such as its production, transportation to America, press advertisements, general articles and curious facts about this wine, Madeira used as Medicine, the vine blight of 1852, its consequences and the ensuing relief from America, the subsequent vine failures, phylloxera and the gradual recovery of the vines, Madeira wine adulteration in the U.S. and abroad, Madeira, a cherished product to wine *connoisseurs*, old Madeira wines in America, Madeira Wine auctions across the United States and, last but not least, a selection of amusing episodes involving Madeira Wine.

As it will be seen, it was usual, back then, for the American press to quote some of these texts from other American sources – other newspapers, magazines or books – and even from similar foreign sources, mostly from England. Some of the articles presented in this chapter were widely revealed in several newspapers, either within the same state or in the neighboring ones, usually in an East-West direction, thus helping to make Madeira Wine, its features, related facts and stories widely known to a vast audience across the United States.

9.1. Wine Production

In this section are nine texts dealing with Madeira Wine production, published between 1833 and 1888, through which an in-depth view of this topic can be seen, from different perspectives and by different authors, most of them unknown.

[Untitled][837]

The vintage at Madeira has this season been so extraordinary, especially in the north part, that for want of casks it had been necessary to put some of the new wine into boxes well caulked.

Madeira Wine.[838] – Commander Wilkes, in his report of the Exploring Expedition,

---

[837] *Republican Compiler*, April 16, 1833. (Gettysburg, PA).
[838] *The Southern Patriot*, July 17, 1845. (Charleston, SC); *The Daily Morning Post,* July 19, 1845. (Pittsburgh, PA); *The Norfolk Democrat,* September 12, 1845. (Dedham, MA. Published under the title "MAKING MADEIRA WINE – *Interesting to Wine bibbers.*", preceded by the following text: «Commander Wilkes, in his narrative of the Exploring Expedition, gives the following account of the process of making Madeira wine, which he witnessed while stopping at the island

stopped at the Island of Madeira.[839] He visited with the U.S. Consul[840] a wine factory – a kind of shed – and thus sketches the process: – "On our approach we heard a sort of a song, with a continued thumping, and on entering saw six men stamping violently in a vat of six feet square by two feet deep, three on each side of a huge lever beam, their legs bare up to the thighs. On our entrance they redoubled their exertions till the perspiration freely poured from them; the vat had been filled with grapes, and by their exertions we were enabled to see the whole process. After the grapes had been sufficiently stamped, and the men's legs well scraped, the pulp was made into the shape of a large bee-hive, a rope made of the young twigs of the vine being wound around it. The lever was then used, which has a large stone or rock attached to it by a screw. The juice flows off and is received in tubs. The produce of the press is on an average 50 gallons daily. Each gallon requires about two bushels of grapes. The general average is from one to three pipes of wine per acre annually." The south side of the island produces the finest wines. The common Madeira is made of a mixture of three kinds of grapes. After being expressed, the wine is put into casks, ferments, and is clarified with gypsum or isinglass, after which two or three gallons of brandy are added to each pipe.[841]

Grape-growing in Madeira.[842]

In the Island of Madeira, the grape-vine is not a native plant, and, after growing well a few years, the fruit begins to degenerate and makes inferior wine. The expense of new plantations being very great, as they are usually taken from the hock vineyards of Germany, every expedient has been tried to keep them healthy as long as possible, but no manuring, pruning or attention, is of much avail, and the only remedy is found in deep cultivation. I once happened to see the process: Nearly a score of laborers were working in a trench as deep as they were tall, throwing the soil out that depth. On inquiry, I was told that they were preparing an old vineyard for fresh planting. Trenching nearly six feet deep. Some months afterwards, a merchant, in taking me over his wine stores, pointed out, in some casks that were being opened, a mineral incrustation, about the sixteenth of an inch in thickness, and as brittle as glass, which he called tartrate of lime, adding that it was commonly deposited by the wine, especially when new. I afterwards ascertained that soda and potash existed in the deposit. Now these minerals are so deficient in the soil of the Island, that even that required for medicinal purposes is all imported. Here, then, was reason good for the deep trenching. The vine, to supply its mineral wants, robbed the soil so fast of what little alkali it contained, that nothing but opening a great depth to the action of the roots, would keep up a supply for many years. – Farmer and Gardener.[843]

---

of Madeira. It would seem (says the Louisville Journal) that this favourite drink is not made in the most unexceptionable way:» After the sentence ending as "till the perspiration freely poured from them" this source added this peculiar remark: «[We presume this contributes to the *peculiarity* in the flavor of 'Old Madeira.']»; *Sangamo Journal*, March 12, 1846. (Springfield, IL. Published under the title "INFORMATION FOR WINE-BIBBERS.", preceded by the following introduction: «The following account of the manner of expressing the juice of the grape is respectfully submitted to the attention of wine-bibbers who are so very particular in their choice of a pure article:»).
839 Where he arrived on September 16, 1838. See section 6.1.1.6. of this anthology.
840 John Howard March.
841 Excerpt from Chapter I of Charles Wilkes' book.
842 *California Farmer and Journal of Useful Sciences*, March 8, 1861. (San Francisco, CA).
843 Quote from an article by C. W. H., published in the magazine "Pennsylvania Farmer and Gardener", of January

CURRENT TOPICS.[844]

The St. Louis Republican States: "Our Consul at Funchal,[845] Island of Madeira, in a communication to the State Department at Washington, gives a detail of the process by which the Madeira wine is prepared for the United States market. He says that the Madeira wines now mostly sent to this country are prepared by the method he describes. These are generally the low priced article which find the readiest sale in this country, such as do not bear a greater market value where produced than from one hundred to one hundred and fifty dollars the pipe of one hundred and ten gallons. Many of these wines, though pure, are brought to a marketable state by a process of artificial heat or cooking, and are known in the market where prepared as *estufed wines*. The result of the *estufed* process is to make a wine which is only one year old appear as if it were three years old, or as if it had acquired the flavor of a three year old wine in the natural way. The cooking process is after this fashion: The wine is put in casks in which the bung or stopper is left out. In this condition the liquid is subjected for several months to an artificial heat of about one hundred and fifty degrees Fahrenheit, during which period a kind of second fermentation takes place. After, the wine has remained in the *estufa*, or heated room, a sufficient length of time to have acquired a marketable age in taste, it is racked off, and then offered for sale, or shipped to foreign countries; and much of the wine shipped to the United States is said to be of the *estufed* kind, doubtless the most of it. This wine, when offered for market or shipped, is in no respect adulterated other than by the process indicated, which can scarcely be called adulteration. If adulterated at all, such of it as is shipped to this country, it is done after it gets into American hands, and there is little doubt that this is done to considerable extent by some American liquor dealers so as to increase the quantity at the expense of the quality. Such, at least, is the prevailing notion. The flavor of the *estufed wine* is said to be quite different from that which is left untouched, and allowed to acquire mellowness and flavor by the lapse of time alone. The difference, it is said, may be readily detected by an expert. But as there are comparatively few experts in our country, because the opportunities to test the aged article are very few the *estufed* wine passes current. It would be well if this were the only *doctoring* which our Maderia wine gets."

The Madeira Wine Crop.[846]//
From the London Times, January 27th.

Messrs. Cossart, Gordon & Co., of Madeira, write us from that island, under date of the 16th instant, as follows: "The cutting of grapes, owing to an exceedingly mild Spring and Summer, did not occur until three or four weeks later than usual, so much so, that had we had our usual wet season toward the end of October, the 'mostos'[847] from the upper districts would not have been gathered in perfection. The 'oidium', or grape disease, which almost excluded Madeira from the list of wine-producing countries, has now

---

1861, pages 213-214.
844 *The Charleston Daily News,* October 7, 1867. (Charleston, SC).
845 The U.S. Consul at Funchal in this time period was Charles A. Leas. See Note 764.
846 *Daily Alta California,* March 5, 1872. (San Francisco, CA).
847 Portuguese word for musts.

all but entirely disappeared, and we trust from the excellent quality and abundant quantity of the vintage of 1871 – amounting to some 8,000 or 9,000 pipes – to see the wine restored in some degree to its former position. In 1869 we stated, from the favorable supply of that year and the increased quantity of land planted with vines, our expectation that in a few years the island would produce some 4,000 to 5,000 pipes annually. Our anticipations have been more than realized, the quantity produced during the past year being nearly double that amount."

MADEIRA WINE.[848] – Two years after its final settlement by the Portuguese, the wine was imported into Madeira from the island of Candia or Crete, and found so congenial a soil that its wine became renowned as the most delicious beverage it has been granted man to taste. Madeira has been a household word in every language of Europe, but in 1860 there were only four hundred pipes remaining on the island; and though Madeira is still offered for sale in every city of the United States at reasonable rates, it is not difficult to imagine its sources. The Madeira wine of commerce was itself a compound of the various productions of the island, known by the special names as Bual, Sercial, etc., each possessing a distinctive character. At one time the production amounted to twenty-five thousand pipes a year, but in 1852 the same terrible disease which spread over the other Atlantic islands appeared among the vineyards, and destroyed its culture, ruining thousands of wretched people, and depriving man of a blessing; for since man will yield to the craving nature has implanted in him, and everywhere furnished him the means of gratifying, it is a blessing when he can drink of wine like this rather than some vile substitute. Fortunately the *oidium* appears to have been destroyed or to have disappeared, and new plants introduced from the United States and Europe are thriving with every promise of restoring to the island its former celebrity among wine-producing countries. The mildew which attacked the vine has not impaired the fertility of the island in any other respects. Its lofty mountain-sides are covered with valuable timber. Pines are of extraordinary quick growth. The *Juglans regia*[849] – the fruit of which is termed by some of the Persian and by others the English walnut, better known as the Madeira nut – here attains its highest development. Spice trees flourish, the red pepper excelling in flavor the product of Cayenne. Oranges and other tropical fruits thrive without care, and strawberries ripen in February in the open air. – *Harper's Magazine for March*.

FACTS ABOUT PORT AND MADEIRA[850]
Funchal and Some Famous Wine Stores – Past and Present

---

[848] *The New York Times,* February 18, 1877. (New York City, NY); *The Anderson Intelligencer,* February 22, 1877. (Anderson County House, SC); *Evening Daily Bulletin,* February 24, 1877. (San Francisco, CA). This is an excerpt of the beginning of the text "A Summer cruise among the Atlantic Islands," by Dr. A. L. Gihon, which we have already presented on the section 6.1.2. of this anthology.

[849] Scientific name of the Persian or English walnut.

[850] *The Sun,* December 25, 1882. (New York City, NY). Contrary to what the title of this article may indicate, it contains no reference whatsoever to Port wine. The title was borrowed from a book written by Henry Vizetelly, *Facts About Port and Madeira, with Notices of the Wines Vintaged Around Lisbon, and the Wines of Tenerife,* published in London and New York in 1880. The text reproduced in *The Sun,* transcribed from another publication, is nothing more than a selection of excerpts taken from the fifth chapter, "Some other Funchal Wine-Stores", of the afore mentioned book.

Productions of Madeira.
From Boufort's Wine and Spirit Circular.

On a subsequent occasion we had the satisfaction of tasting some Porto da Cruz,[851] vintaged in 1829 and bottled in 1842, of remarkable lightness and delicacy of flavor, together with a rare vinous Sao Martinho[852] Verdelho, boasting a wonderful perfume, and already more than half a century old. This was one of the most perfect old Madeiras we ever tasted, far surpassing in flavor, although it failed to rival as a curiosity, a wine of the year 1760, of which it is sufficient praise to say that, although but a phantom of its former self, it had not in the slightest degree turned acid, as many another robust growth would have done at least half a century earlier.

The firm of Leacock and Company was established more than a century and a quarter ago. The business has descended from father to son through successive generations, and there seems every prospect of its continuing to do so. This firm and that of Cossart, Gordon, and Co. are the only two houses remaining in Madeira who were members of the once-important British factory,[853] which had almost a monopoly of the wine trade of the island, annually fixing the price to be paid for mosto purchased of the growers, as well as the prices at which wines were to be shipped.

The house of Henry Dru Drury, formerly Rutherford, Drury & Co. was originally established in Madeira soon after the commencement of the present century. Its armazens, situated in the western quarter of Funchal, and entered upon a narrow court, comprise a couple of large buildings, not much under 200 feet in length, of two stories each, and connected on the first floor by a wooden gallery arched over with trellises of vines left to grow at their own sweet will. On the one side mosto is store while it completes its fermentation, while the other are the matured and grand old wines of the firm, the latter being kept by themselves in ancient-looking pipes on the upper floor. This little vineyard is bounded on one side by an old nunnery to which seven venerable nuns – the youngest being aged about 70 – were installed at the time of our visit.[854] The suppression of conventual establishments having been decreed by the Portuguese Legislature,[855] additions are no longer made to the venerable sisterhood. At Mr. Henry Dru Drury's stores we tasted a powerful Cama de Lobos[856] wine of 1874 which had never been to the *estufa*, and one of the year 1870, which had been matured by exposure to the sun; also a delicate and fresh-tasting Bual of 1876, a splendid Campanario[857] with fine bouquet, pale in color, soft, slightly sweet, but of

---

[851] Wine produced at Porto da Cruz, a village located in the northeastern coast of Madeira.
[852] The right spelling is São Martinho.
[853] See Note 749.
[854] In 1877, as the author mentions further on. By then there were still three nunneries in Funchal, all of them belonging to the Order of the Poor Claires: the Santa Clara convent, the Encarnação convent and the Mercês convent. The first two were closed in 1890, with the death of the last professed nuns, but the latter continued to exist until 1910, the year in which it was forced to close its doors, on October 13, by a decree issued five days before by the newly-established Portuguese Republic. By then its Mother Superior was Madre Virgínia Brites da Paixão (1860-1929), a mystical nun, favored with innumerable divine apparitions and revelations, whose Beatification and Canonization Process is under way, at this moment, at the Funchal's Diocese.
[855] In 1834 the immediate closure of all convents existent in Portugal was decreed. The male monasteries were closed at once and had their properties confiscated by the Government, but the female ones were allowed to remain in existence, until the death of the last professed nun, a time when their properties would pass into the hands of the Portuguese State.
[856] See Note 381.
[857] The right spelling is Campanário.

remarkable fine flavor. In our judgment the best Campanario[858] growths surpass the more powerful and more generally prized Cama de Lobos[859] vintages by reason of their greater delicacy of flavor and more fragrant bouquet. The older wines comprised of a Sercial of 1820, with a powerful bouquet and a dry but scarcely pungent flavor; a Bual of about the same age exceedingly pungent and powerful – an essence of wine, so to speak; and some deep-tinted luscious Malmsey of the same period. We further tasted some wine the casks of which were marked "Roda"[860] to indicate that they had voyage either to the East or West Indies and home again. They were not particularly deep in color, but remarkably powerful, and with that indefinable flavor which Maderia acquires after being subjected to the combined head and motion of a voyage to the tropics in a ship's hold.

At Messrs. Henriques and Lawton's we passed through a dilapidated porte-cochère, with tall stone pillars on either side, into a spacious paved courtyard, where the dismantled mansion reared its massive façade, pierced with numerous large ornamental windows on our left hand, and a lower range of stores, partially overgrown with vines, rose up in front. Through the house a second paved court is reached, roofed in with leafy vines trained in corridors, beneath the shade of which numerous coopers are at work. The estufas of the firm which include an estufa warmed by artificial heat and an estufa do sol, deriving its warmth, as its name implies, exclusively from the sun, and the two holding together 350 pipes, are situated in another part of the town in full view of the open sea.

We tasted at Messrs. Henriques & Lawton's stores numerous fine wines, going through the customary scale of Cama de Lobos,[861] a series of vintages of the highest character. We then were shown some dry and aromatic Santo-Antonios, aged six, seven, and nine years respectively; a pungent light-colored wine, formed by the blending of a Sao Roque[862] and a Sercial five years old; a Sercial, aged twelve years, a great wine in full perfection; some rich oily Bual of 1872 – too sweet, however, to be drunk excepting as a dessert wine; with a venerable Malmsey, vintage forty-five years ago, of ruby brightness and rich liqueur-like flavor, and possessing an admirable bouquet. Five per cent, is the largest amount of spirit which Senhor Henriques adds to wines vintage on the south side of the island, while wines from the north receives a slightly larger quantity. This spirit is invariably added by degrees. As in all the other Funchal stores, the pipes here remain with a vacuum equivalent to ten or a dozen gallons, which is something less than the Jerez shippers allow in a butt of sherry. The yearly loss from evaporation averages about 5 per cent, which of course tends to increase the alcoholic strength of the wine; still, Madeira is shipped at an average strength of 32 degrees of proof spirit.

The largest of the native shipping houses at Funchal is that of Meyrelles, Sobrinho e Cia., in which Senhor Salles, whose vineyard at Santo Antonio[863] we have already described, is a leading partner. The numerous stores of the firm are scattered in different parts of the town. The central establishment is in the vicinity of the cathedral, while another range of stores is close to the palacio,[864] and facing the sea, and others, again, are situated more

---

858 The right spelling is Campanário.
859 See Note 381.
860 Allusion to the "Vinho da Roda", the wine that had endured a long sea-voyage, in order to mature itself, a process repeated over and over, for decades, before the introduction of the *estufas*, or hothouses, with the same purpose.
861 See Note 381.
862 The right spelling is São Roque.
863 The right spelling is Santo António.
864 Palácio de São Lourenço, an imposing military fortress and palace located in Funchal's waterfront.

in the centre of Funchal. The firm also possess an estufa do sol[865] constructed of iron an glass, in which a temperature of 130º is secured. Highly picturesque are the ancient central stores with their rows of venerable butts filled with grand old wines, and the improvised galleries running round the walls immediately under the blackened rafters, where wine of fabulous antiquity, in bottles covered with dust and wound round about with cobwebby festoons, is stowed away. To enumerate all the remarkable wines shown us at these stores is impossible. Suffice it to say that they comprised Cama de Lobos[866] of different years, always full of character, sometimes even a little rich, though generally lightly pungent, and not unfrequently exceeding potent. We remember, too, a delicate, fine old Bual, an archaic Verdelho with some of the characteristics of a liqueur, a Bastardo combining a certain sweetness with peculiar freshness of flavor, a youthful and astringent Tinta, an aromatic Malmsey of fabulous value, with other growths, which in flavor and bouquet ran through all the keys of the gamut.

Another Portuguese shipper, holding a considerable stock of high class Madeiras, is Senhor Henrique J. M. Camacho, who matures his wines principally in an estufa do sol perched on the summit of one of his stores, and in which he obtains a temperature of 150º. Among the curiosities which we were invited to taste were some old Sao Martinhos,[867] with a curious collection of high class Buals from Cama de Lobos,[868] Campanario[869] and Santo Antonio;[870] also a Ponta do Pargo from fifteen to twenty years old, powerful, yet refined in flavor, a rare Bastardo, and a Malmsey – with a slight blend of Bual to give it character and roundness – in which "false, fleeting, perjured Clarence"[871] might well have been content to drown.

The firm of Viuva Abudarham e Filhos has its stores in the old Funchal Post Office, near Cossart, Gordon & Co.'s principal establishment. The Campanarios of this firm are of a high class. One of 1871, which had been matured by six month's exposure to the sun, was remarkably fine in flavor and possessed a peculiar and delicate bouquet. Their Cama de Lobos[872] was also distinguished for its bouquet, and we were struck with a very soft old wine, the result of a slight blend of Malmsey with a fine Verdelho.

The Madeira vintage in 1877, the year I visited the island, was estimated not to exceed 7,000 pipes, one half of which, however, with due allowances for the unfavorable season, would be first class wine. This yield is about one-fourth less than the average annual production of recent years, with the exception of 1876. The falling off was due partly to the phylloxera, but more especially to the excessive dampness of the preceding spring and summer, which caused much fruit to rot. Small as the yield was calculated to be, it would still be equivalent to double the annual shipments, although these have been steadily increasing since the vineyards which have suffered so severely from the oïdium came into bearing again. Ninety years ago, the earliest date of which we have available records, Madeira used to ship upwards of 10,000 pipes of wine annually. At the commencement of the present century this quantity had increased to 17,000 pipes, and rose during the year 1813 to

---

[865] Literally translating means a sun hothouse.
[866] See Note 381.
[867] São Martinhos, designation of wines produced in this Funchal's parish.
[868] See previous Note.
[869] The right spelling is Campanário.
[870] The right spelling is Santo António.
[871] Excerpt of a line from Act I, Scene IV, of Shakespeare's play "King Richard III".
[872] See Note 381.

as many as 22,000. A variety of circumstances conduced to this result, of which one was the general turbulent state of Europe and the closing of certain wine ports, and another the great consumption of the wine in the East and West Indies, whither it was sent in time of war with the periodical convoys. In the good old times fleets of war-vessels, as well as convoys of merchantmen, used constantly to touch at Madeira and take in large supplies of wine, the orders for which the merchants often found it difficult to execute during the short time the ships remained in port. On these conditions it frequently happened that whilst the merchants were entertaining the officers above stairs, and dancing was being kept up until the small hours of the morning, the clerks and cellarmen were as busy as bees down below getting the required wine ready for shipment.

It has been stated that the substitution of sherry for Madeira by George IV drove the latter wine out of fashion and caused its greatly reduced consumption; but this can scarcely have been the case, since it was not until the "First Gentleman in Europe" had been interred in the Royal vault at Windsor that any great falling off in the importation of Madeira occurred. In 1842 the shipments of the wine to England were under 1,000 pipes; and subsequently a severe blow was dealt to a failing trade by the oïdium, when production altogether ceased, and existing stocks became gradually exhausted, while prices rose, as the latter diminished, from £25 to £75 per pipe for the lowest qualities. This enhancement of the price of Madeira naturally operated unfavorably with regard to the consumption, more especially as the shippers of sherry and marsala succeeded in keeping the English market supplied with these last-named wines at almost one-fourth of the rate demanded for common Madeiras. The consumer of Madeira, thus forced to fall back upon sherry and marsala, in many instances never returned to his old love. The East India market, too, had become affected first by the dissolution of the East India Company, which imported the wine largely to their possessions, and subsequently by the construction of the Suez Canal, which opened a more favorable route to the East, so that ships no longer called at Madeira on their outward voyage for their half-dozen or half-score pipes of wine according to ancient custom; two things of which the wine-drinking portion of the British public can scarcely be aware: Madeira has fallen considerably in price, and the stocks of matured wines in the island are altogether unprecedented, so that everything is favorable to an increased consumption. The wine has certainly a special character. It boasts of a refined high flavor, combined, when duly matured, with remarkable softness, to which it moreover unites exceptional keeping powers. As an accompaniment to soup, or many of the lighter *plats*, its drier varieties are especially suitable; while the French have long since taught us the richer qualities are essential to dessert.

The present stocks of Madeira on the island are estimated at fully 30,000 pipes; so that any deficiency in production arising from phylloxera, oïdium, or atmospheric influences is not likely to make itself felt for some years to come. Moreover, the phylloxera spreads but slowly in Madeira, it having confined its ravages during the five years preceding our visit to a comparatively small area; whereas a single department of France in the same space of time had its vineyards ravaged to the extent of the entire cultivated area of the island. Madeira-drinkers may rest assured that never was finer wine procurable than at the present moment, every variety of vintage or blended growth – dry, sweet, soft, or pungent – being held by the shippers, whose prices range from as low as £26 to as high as £300 a pipe; an excellent medium wine being procurable at from £50 to £80. Madeira can, therefore, be retailed as low as 30s. a dozen, and all but very choice varieties at from 60s. to 70s.

QUEER THINGS IN TRADE.[873]

… Consul Charlesworth[874] shows that the wine trade of Madeira has steadily decreased in exports to the United States from $30,363 in 1880 to $17,216 in 1884. Last season's grapes were finely matured, and the wine said to be of better quality than for years past. It may shock tender stomachs to learn that the very ancient practice of treading out the wine with the feet is still in vogue. Consul Charlesworth says the grapes are placed in a large wooden or stone vat, in which the peasants, with legs bare to the knees, travel in a circle to the cadence of an extemporized song – the sentiment of which is suited to the occasion – until the grapes are reduced to a pulp. This is placed in a primitive press with a long sweep and wooden screw. If not too far from shore, the must – as it is now called – is put in the casks and conveyed by boats to the merchant in Funchal, in whose hands it undergoes the various operations of racking and fermentation. It then receives the necessary amount of spirit, and either undergoes the artificial heating process or is stored in warehouses until it has acquired the proper age for use. The Consul adds, by way of solace, perhaps, that all the wine firms have steadily refused to handle any adulterations, and their brands may always be relied upon. …
Washington Cor. St. Louis Globe-Democrat.

OLD MADEIRA.[875]
The Rise, Fall, and Rejuvenation of that Noble Liquid – Strange Procedures of Manufacture.
From the London Standard.

For the first six months of 1888 the shipments of Madeira have already reached 3,636 pipes, the correct total for 1887 having been 4,247 pipes, and for 1886 5,227. These figures are small enough when compared with the averages of the years from 1788 to 1838, during which time the wine may he said to have had its day.

The largest exports were recorded in 1800, 16,981 pipes; in 1801, 16,732 pipes, and in 1807 16, 701 pipes. In 1801 the island was taken by the English, and in 1807 it was again captured by them. British tars – or, at any rate, their officers – were familiar with the quality of the wine; for an old bill of landing shows that my Lords of the Admiralty were accustomed to order it for victualing his Majesty's navy so long ago as 1793. In the quaintly worded document, which is still preserved, they stipulate that a cargo intended for Barbadoes, per the good ship Providence, should consist of "120 London-made pipes bound with 12 iron hoops each, both heads painted dark chocolate color, and branded upon the heads, bungs, and spiggots, N. G. L." The original of an order of 500 pipes for Savannah

---

873 *The Huntingdon Journal,* July 3, 1885. (Huntingdon, PA); *The Hazel Green Herald,* July 8, 1885. (Hazel Green, KY).
874 Firth Charlesworth, a native of Kansas, who served as U.S. Consul in Funchal from 1884 to 1886.
875 *The Sun,* August 27, 1888. (New York City, NY).

can be seen dated May, 1780. In 1801 the agents in the island reported to London: "There are not 100 pipes of old wine in the hands of the natives for sale; the exports of the year 1800 exceeded all previous exports, being upward of 17,000 pipes, and should the demand for our wine increase as much as it has done for some years, the island will not be able to supply the requisite quantity." During the succeeding quarter of a century the demand was fairly maintained, rising in 1825 to over 14,400 pipes, but in the following year the export fell to 9,398. A decline, occasionally broken by a good year, however, set in, and the totals more than once were short of 6,000. In 1851 the aggregate was 7.301, and that number has never since been attained.

It was in 1852 that the wine of Madeira was at a crisis of its history. The vineyards were devastated by the oïdium, a fungus which attacks the grapes when the skins are very thin. For eleven seasons not a pipe of wine was manufactured, and the stocks were gradually depleted, although the exports were reduced to less than 1,000 pipes per annum. It took more than ten years to discover that the fungus could be treated with sulphur, and since then the vintage has by degrees been to some extent recovered, a steady improvement having been especially noticeable since 1879.

A trade subject to such fluctuations owes its preservation to one or two leading houses. In the good old times, when East and West Indiamen outward bound called at Madeira, there were quite thirty English firms, each of which had its own flag. Their number has now been reduced to five or six. Whenever the ships hove in sight and displayed the colors of the merchants there was activity at Funchal, the capital of the island, to prepare the freights and to entertain visitors. Those times have gone, and no shipper now would consign his wine per a vessel which was bound to complete a voyage to the Indies before it could sail for home. A cask of Madeira which had been carried round the world and matured in the hot atmosphere of the hold was a prize indeed. There is not the same romance, but there is something of interest about the Madeira wine of to-day.

It is the soil of the favored island which gives character to its grapes. The districts of vine culture fringe the coasts, the interior of the island rising to mountain peaks of 5,000 feet and 6,000 feet altitude. Different varieties of grape are grown, but the Malmsey, Sercial, and Bual are termed specialties. They, as well as the Tinta, a small black Burgundy, are giving way before the Verdelho, "a small oval grape, hardly as large as a coffee berry, when ripe of a rich, golden hue, full of flavor and saccharine." The produce of a vineyard is frequently purchased before the grapes are pressed. The "mosto," or raw wine, is transported to Funchal in Canteiro[876] pipes, holding 130 gallons each, old measure. These great barrels are drawn about by oxen yoked to a kind of sled. Fermentation goes on until November, a small quantity of brandy being added. The stores in which the processes are carried on are of most picturesque appearance – trellised vines stretching from shed to shed, and scarlet geraniums giving color to the stores, which may occupy several acres. The method of maturing the wine by sending it in a heated temperature to the West Indies and back has had to give place to a more practical system. In the country districts it is still the custom to put the butts in the open air under the direct sun, or store them in a glass house with the same object. But the large shippers are provided with estufas, or buildings of two stories, divided into four compartments.

---

[876] Canteiro is a Portuguese word that designates the wooden rack where the pipes are left for a long time so that its wine might age and mature.

"In the first of these," an eyewitness relates,[877] "common wines are subjected to a temperature of 140 degrees Fahrenheit – derived from flues heated with anthracite coal – for the space of three months. In the next compartment wine of an intermediate quality are heated up to 130 degrees for a period of four and a half months, while a third is set apart for superior wines, heated variously from 110 to 120 degrees for the term of six months. The fourth compartment, known as the 'calor,'[878] possesses no flues, but derives its heat, varying from 90 to 100 degrees, exclusively from the compartments adjacent, and here only high class wines are placed. The object of this heating of the wine is to destroy whatever germs of fermentation still remain in it, and to mature it more rapidly, in order that it may be shipped in its second and third year without any further addition of spirit. Each compartment is provided with double doors, and after it is filled with wine the inner doors are coated over with lime, so as to close up any chance apertures.

"When it is necessary to enter the estufa the outer doors only are opened, and a small trap in the inner door is pushed back to allow of the entrance of the man in charge, who passes between the various stacks of casks, tapping them one after the other to satisfy himself that no leakage is going on. On coming out of the estufa, after a stay of a full hour, he instantly wraps himself in a blanket, drinks a tumblerful of wine, and then shuts himself up in a closet, into which no cool air penetrates." During the time the wines are in the estufa they diminish by evaporation 10 to 15 per cent. The wine is put into butts, each holding 400 gallons, and when ready for shipment is transferred to casks, which are made by coopers with the adze, of American oak staves, and cost perhaps £2 apiece. The casks are measured, branded, scalded, and steamed. They are seasoned with water, and then charged with common wine for two or three months. After this careful preparation they are considered fit for use.

While a quantity is sent to England for home consumption, it is stated that the people who drink most Madeira are the French, although until recently they were rivaled by the Russians.

9.2. Transportation of Madeira Wine to the United States

Throughout the first half of the 19th century, as it had been done on the 18th, Madeira Wine reached the American shores by sailing ships, that took, on average, a month to reach their final destination. The long sea journey, the heat of the cargo hold, and the continual rocking movement of the vessel helped to improve the qualities of the Madeiras in a special way that some wines ended up being associated with them, in America, like the Juno Madeira, to name one example.

In this section is an excerpt of a text published in 1877, telling the story of an old ship engaged in Madeira Wine trade, fifty years before, from the island to Charleston and Savannah, two of the main importing markets in America.

---

877 Henry Vizetelly.
878 Portuguese word for heat. In this context it means the heat room.

TALES OF MY GRANDFATHER[879]
VANDERBILT FIFTY YEARS AGO.
THE COMMODORE AT THE HELM – ... – REMINISCENCES OF FORMER TIMES.

"My first acquaintance with Vanderbilt dated from about 1826. Steam-boating never was in my line, though I had no objection to taking a venture in a sailing craft. It might have been in 1825 that Stephen Girard, of Philadelphia, had an old brig for sale, which some four or five of us bought. She was of teak, and might have been fifty years old when we purchased her. We owned her for 29 years, then sold her for more than we paid for her, and I remember to have followed her up in the papers with a certain amount of interest, and if my memory serves me rightly, I think I read she came to grief some time in 1856, in the China seas. We were in the habit of sending the old brig to Madeira, and she brought back wine on ship's account, and did quite well. She was so slow that the wine acquired, generally, age on the voyage. Some of you may remember a particular pale Madeira. No you don't. Dear me! I am forgetting myself. If you boys never had a chance at it, very certainly your fathers punished it severely. It was a remarkable sound wine, and such as you can't buy to-day. About from $1 50 to $2 a gallon would buy the choicest Madeira in those times. Our best market was in Charleston and Savannah, and the consumption was so large that we would occasionally send a part of a cargo there direct, and bring back rice. Southern planters in those days must have bathed in Madeira."

"But, grandfather, what about Commodore Vanderbilt?"

"Oh! I am coming to it straight. You all know that Vanderbilt ran steamers from New York to Amboy. One Spring morning, when there was something of a fog, our brig was coming in from Madeira. When just beyond Fort Hamilton one of the steamers ran into the brig, and a precious lot of damage was done to our vessel. ...

9.2.1. Madeira Wine Arrivals to America

For many years it was a tradition among the American wine sellers to advertise in the press new Madeira Wine arrivals, informing the eventual customers in which ship it had been brought, and sometimes specifying the commercial house of Funchal where it had been purchased from or the quantity or type of Madeira imported. The following are twelve examples of those ads, published between 1800 and 1840, presenting this kind of data.

MADEIRA WINE.[880]

The Subscriber, has just received a quantity of HILL's First Quality *London Particular Wine*, in Pipes, Hhds.[881] and Quarter Casks.
GIDEON HILL WELLS.
Philadelphia, Nov. 15.

---

879 *The New York Times,* February 11, 1877. (New York City, NY); *The Atlantic Telegraph,* May 2, 1877. (Atlantic, IA. Published under the title "Vanderbilt Fifty Years Ago. – Grandfather's Story.").
880 *Gazette of the United States, and Philadelphia Daily Advertiser,* January 6, 1800. (Philadelphia, PA).
881 Abbreviation for hogsheads. A wine hogshead contains about 300 liters (79.25 gallons).

MADEIRA WINE.[882]

Just received per Ship Charlotte Murdoch, Six pipes 4 hhds, and 8 qr.[883] casks London particular Madeira Wine. For Sale by HENRY SADLER & CO.

MADEIRA WINE[884]

Just Received per brig Dove, capt. Childs from Madeira, 36 pipes 30 half-pipes 16 q'r casks all of very first quality, and years old.

ALSO IN STORE,

Pipes, half-pipes and quarter-casks of five years old, L. P. Madeira Wine,[885] the quality of which is universally approved, and now ready for immediate use. …
All the above articles will be sold on moderate terms by HENRY THOMPSON.

MADEIRA WINE.[886]
A CHOICE PARCEL.
Pure old Madeira Wine,

In pipes, half pipes and qr. casks, of the brand Murdoch, Yuille, Wardorss & Co. received per schooner Sheperdess, Samuel Carr, master, from Madeira – for sale by *Foulke & Karrick,* Spear's Wharf.

OLD MADEIRA WINE.[887]

SIXTY pipes (in pipes, half pipes, qr. casks and half qr. casks) MADEIRA WINE, fit for immediate use, and warranted genuine, and of a superior quality, just received by the ship Howard.
And on hand of a former importation, a few pipes New Madeira Wine, for sale by MARCH & BENSON,[888] 71 Washington-st.

---

882 *Commercial Advertiser,* May 12, 1802. (New York City, NY).
883 Abbreviation for quarter.
884 *The North American, and Mercantile Daily Advertiser,* August 19, 1808. (Baltimore, MD).
885 Abbreviation for London Particular Madeira Wine.
886 *Federal Republican & Commercial Gazette,* September 30, 1809. (Baltimore, MD).
887 *New-York Gazette & General Advertiser,* December 15, 1809. (New York City, NY).
888 Commercial partners of John Howard March, the U.S. Consul at Funchal, and wine merchant.

Superior L. P. Madeira Wine.[889]

The Subscribers have received and offer for sale, One pipe MADEIRA WINE, having had the benefit of two sea-voyages, via Bombay and Calcutta, and of which the best recommendations can be given of its purity and good quality. ...
NICOLSON & HOLMES,
No. 234 East Bay.

Murdock, Yuille, Wardrop & Co's.[890]
Finest old L. P. Madeira Wine.

Received by the brig Hebe from Madeira, a full supply of the finest old wine from that House, in pipes, hogsheads and quarter casks, which with their former stock, will be sold on reasonable terms.
A. C. CAZENOVE & Co.

OLD MADEIRA WINE.[891]

GEO L. DEBLOIS & CO. 39, India-street, have just received, 5 half pipes of superior old Madeira Wine, which has been one voyage to Bombay and Calcutta, is warranted pure, and considered of the first quality. ...

London particular Madeira Wine.[892]

The Subscribers have received per schr[893] *Mary*, direct from Madeira. 10 pipes 10 half pipes 20 qr. casks very CHOICE OLD WINE. Which they offer for sale, on a liberal credit.
MAGWOOD, PATTERSON & CO.

PURE WINES. – MADEIRA GRAPE JUICE.[894] – The subscribers have received per brig Enterprize, a further supply of Madeira Wine, *entirely free from distilled spirits*. A part is entitled to debenture. It is made from grapes raised on the south side of the Island, and has a delicacy of taste and flavor, which the ordinary Wines (containing 12 to 14 gallons of brandy to the pipe,) do not possess. ...
Orders from any part of the country will be promptly attended to.
They add the following certificate to those heretofore published.

---

[889] *City Gazette and Commercial Daily Advertiser*, January 23, 1821. (Charleston, SC).
[890] *Alexandria Gazette*, October 23, 1821. (Alexandria, VA).
[891] *Boston Commercial Gazette*, May 30, 1822. (Boston, MA).
[892] *City Gazette and Commercial Daily Advertiser*, July 27, 1826. (Charleston, SC).
[893] Abbreviation for schooner.
[894] *New York Commercial Advertiser*, June 27, 1832. (New York City, NY).

New-York, March 8th, 1832.
POMEROY & BULL, 64 Waterstreet.
COPY.

We the undersigned Portuguese Merchants in the Island of Madeira, do solemnly swear that one butt, one pipe, and twelve quarter casks, we have shipped per order of Messrs. Pomeroy & Bull, of the city of New-York, on board the brig Enterprize, Timothy Lewis, master, and now going to that city, branded Robert Leal, and marked Pomeroy & Bull, contain the pure juice of the grape, perfectly free from brandy, or any admixture of any other ingredient whatsoever: and furthermore declare, that said wine was so prepared by the order of the said Messrs. Pomeroy & Bull. To the truth of which we have this day taken our oath before George Perigal, Esq. Pro-Consul of the United States of America, the 23^d day of December, 1831.
[Signed] LEAL & ARAUJO,
Consulate of the United States.

MADEIRA, 23D DECEMBER, 1831.

I, George Perigal, Pro-Consul of the United States of America for the Island of Madeira, and its dependencies, do hereby certify, that on the day of the date hereof personally appeared before me Carlano Alberto d'Araujo, partner of the firm of Leal & Araujo, Merchants of this Island, who solemnly make oath to the foregoing statement: in testimony of the truth of which I have hereto subscribed my name and affixed my consular seal of office at Ternschal,[895] Island of Madeira, the day and date before written.
[Signed] GEORGE PERIGAL,
Pro-Consul of the United States

MADEIRA WINE.[896]

The subscribers have received, per the schr. Village, from Madeira, 10 half pipes 20 quarter casks of finest old high colored Madeira Wine, from the house of Murdoch, Shortridge & Co. *And have in Store, of previous importation,* 5 pipes and 20 half pipes of the finest wine of Murdoch, Yuille & Co., part of which has had the benefit of a voyage to the East Indies. All old, and warranted of the very best quality.
aug 6
A. C. CAZENOVE & CO.

MADEIRA WINE.[897]

The subscribers have lately received by the Brig Kentucky, from Madeira, 80 quarter casks of very superior old Madeira Wine of the Murdoch brand, equal to any imported. And have in store of the importation of 1834, a few pipes, half pipes and quarter casks, also 50 boxes containing one dozen bottles each of old Reserve, all of which is for sale, and will be delivered to any part of the District, on the reception of orders by mail, at importation cost.

Tinta Madeira in 16 gallon casks, first quality Sicily Madeira, St. Lucar, fine Sherry, and Port in wood, superior Port in cases, Champagne, &c., &c.,
A. C. CAZENOVE & Co.

---

895 The right spelling is Funchal.
896 *Alexandria Gazette,* August 7, 1834. (Alexandria, VA).
897 *Alexandria Gazette,* March 28, 1840. (Alexandria, VA).

9.2.2. Madeira Wine Aboard U.S. Navy Ships

We presume that 95% of Madeira Wine imported into America was transported aboard merchant vessels and the other 5% was carried in the Navy ships that frequently called at the island during their Atlantic, Mediterranean or African missions, either in the outward or homeward bound trips. This wine was usually bought by the officers of the crew for personal use, or to be drunk during the long voyages, or even to be presented to foreign dignitaries. This wine was usually termed Navy Madeira. The next five articles about this topic, published between 1872 and 1898, indicates the effects of indulging too much in Madeira Wine while on duty at sea and how sometimes this wine was unloaded in America avoiding Customs and the payment of duties levied upon it.

THE FLOATING BASTILE.[898]
Voyage of the Guerriere with the Corpse of Sumter's Hero
– A Cargo of Wine – Drunken Officers Carousing in the Face of Death –
Incendiariam near a Powder Magazine.

The letter published in The Sun of yesterday from Patrick Donagher, a marine on the United States frigate Guerriere, receives emphatic corroboration, as regards the brutality of the officers, from Alexander McChesney of Harlem, N. Y., who was steerage steward on the last voyage from Europe to Norfolk, Va. A few days since he visited the SUN and gave some details of his experiences, which he says will be endorsed by any of the ship's company.

He says the Guerriere was sent from New York eighteen months ago to a Mediterranean station. Capt. Thomas H. Stevens in command. She was stranded on the Veido reefs, off the coast of Italy, and was repaired at Spezzia[899] at a cost of about $380.000. Capt. Stevens was superseded in command by Capt. J. Blakely Creighton, and ordered to report to Norfolk, and with John J. Reed, navigator, and Duncan Kennedy, Lieutenant-Commander, has since been arraigned before a court martial for allowing the ship to be stranded and injured.

THE CARGO OF WINE.

On the 26th of December, 1871, the Guerriere sailed from Cadiz with the remains of Sumter's hero, Gen. Anderson,[900] on board. Capt. Creighton was in command, and Capt. Stevens, under suspension of duty, was a passenger. In seven days they reached Madeira, where they laid in a large stock of wines. Then began a general carousal among the officers, which continued during the remainder of the voyage. From Maderia[901] they reached St. Thomas in eighteen days, and when five days out from the latter point they arrived off Cape Hatteras,[902] on a stormy evening. Fearful gales were blowing, which dashed the heavy

---

[898] *The Sun*, February 2, 1872. (New York City, NY).
[899] La Spezia, capital city of the province of La Spezia, located between Genoa and Pisa, on the Ligurean Sea.
[900] Robert Anderson (1805-1871), a native of Kentucky and a West Point graduate, was a Union Army officer in the American Civil War, known for his command of Fort Sumter, at the start of the conflict. At the end of his life he went to Nice, France, seeking a cure for his ailments, but ended up dying there, on October 26, 1871.
[901] The right spelling is Madeira.
[902] Cape on the coast of North Carolina.

seas over the decks, thoroughly drenching and almost freezing the men as they attempted to execute the orders, which were innumerable and contradictory.

THE OFFICERS WERE TOO DRUNK

to comprehend the danger, and for two nights and a day they were constantly tacking, running before the wind, and beating off the Cape. During the second night Capt. Stevens became sober enough to get frightened, and addressed Capt. Creighton in an excited manner, saying, "If you do not put the ship about to sea, and immediately, I will report you to the Department, if I ever live to get ashore."

Capt. Creighton replied: "I am in command of this ship, and capable of taking charge of her." and then ordered Stevens back to his cabin and not to interfere with the management of his ship. They quarrelled about other matters, and during the remainder of the voyage held no intercourse. By putting to sea the dangers would have been avoided and the sufferings of the crew prevented. …

Those "Smuggled" Goods.[903]

WASHINGTON, October 21. – Speaking to-day of the alleged importation of wine, etc., by the officers of the United States ships *Saratoga* and *Portsmouth*, Commodore Schley, Chief of the Equipment Bureau, said that there was no attempted smuggling on board the training ship. The officers did bring over a considerable quantity of wine with them from Madeira, intended for friends on this side, who had sent for it with the express understanding that the duty, whatever it be, should be paid. If the commanding officers had been given an opportunity, Commodore Schley said he would have sent to the customs authorities, and asked for an inspector to come aboard to make an appraisement of such goods as might be dutiable. But the officers were treated as smugglers caught in the act, almost before the vessel had anchored, and did not have an opportunity to show their intentions.

NEWPORT, R.I., October, 21. – The matter of smuggling on the training ships *Saratoga* and *Portsmouth* was settled this afternoon by a deputy collector boarding the vessels and collecting from the officers the duty on the contraband goods by inspectors who had been on board the vessels ever since their arrival and possession, of which they had severally made depositions. The collection amounted to nearly $600. The money was not paid without a protest, but it was paid, as the ships leave here to-morrow. The protests will be referred to the Secretary of the Treasury.

WAR SHIPS AS SMUGGLERS.[904]
Made to Serve an Ignobile Purpose for High Officials.
A Cargo of Wine, Carpets, Silks, Laces, Etc. Brought from Europe by the Saratoga Marked as Consigned to Secretary Thompson, General Sherman and Others.

---

903 *Salt Lake Daily Herald,* October 22, 1886. (Salt Lake City, UT).
904 *Columbus Enquirer-Sun,* October 27, 1886. (Columbus, GA); *Wheeling Register,* October 27, 1886. (Wheeling, WV. Published under the titles "WAR SHIPS AS SMUGGLERS. A Costly Cargo From Europe Consigned to Secretary Thompson, Gen. Sherman, et. al.").

WASHINGTON, October 26. – Although the prominent officials in the navy department have made light of the recent disclosures of smuggling by naval officers as brought to light by the seizures on the Saratoga, the rank and file in the service know that these apologies by certain officers of high rank are made merely to mislead the secretary of the navy and the public and prevent unpleasant disclosures. Seamen and marines who have been on European voyages and think they can talk without fear of detection, view the case very differently. An ex-corporal of the marine corps, who resigned in 1882, and who is now in business in this city, gave a reporter the following chapter on smuggling in the navy as it came under his own observation:

"In 1880 I served on board the United States ship Saratoga," he said, "in a subordinate capacity while the vessel made a European cruise for the purpose of instructing Admiral Luce's babies in the art of seamanship. The opinion generally expressed, however, by the crew upon our arrival in the Mediterranean was that the Saratoga was sent across to bring home a cargo of goods belonging to high officials in Washington. …

"Sailors and marines," he replied, "are not in the habit of expressing their opinions when on board ship. Whatever we thought we kept to ourselves. Upon the return trip we stopped at Funchal, where the ship's launch was lowered for the purpose of assisting in taking on board our last cargo, viz., wine. The exact amount of wine stowed away here I am not unable to state, but I have no hesitation in saying that it exceeded the quantity usually purchased by importers at one time. Paymaster's stores were broken out of the hold and piled around deck to make room for the cargo. The brig was given up for the time being and converted into a wine store room. In fact, every available place was used until the berth deck became uncomfortably crowded. Upon arriving in the United States instead of putting into an important port we anchored in Hampton roads[905] and were not troubled by a visit from the collector of customs. The first transfer of cargo made was to a lighthouse tender which came into the roads, and to it were transferred the casks of wine which were marked 'Babcock.'

"A few days later the Tallapoosa came down from Washington to Hampton Roads and made it convenient to come alongside the Saratoga after dark. The crew was at once put to work rigging whips and tackle to aid in taking the cargo out of the hold. An estimate of the amount of goods, consisting of wines, carpets, laces, silk goods, etc., transferred to the Tallapoosa may be formed from the fact that the time occupied in unloading the vessel consumed about five hours. In justice to the officers attached to the Saratoga it is proper to state that their portion of the cargo was reasonable, one or two casks of wine each to ship to friends in distant parts of the country, a couple of dozen pairs of gloves and several bolts of silk. The bulk of the cargo, however, was marked as consigned to such humble citizens as Secretary of State Thompson, General Sherman, Commodore English and others of the same standing. Of course, an improper use might have been made of their names by the real smugglers to daunt prying custom officials. Next year, while still on the Saratoga, I went to Halifax. There we purchased the same amount of bottled goods and brought back an equally valuable cargo."

"This statement regarding the smuggling propensities of our prominent naval officers can be vouched for and is not the spiteful outpourings of a disgruntled sailor," said a navy department official today.

---

905 Located on southeastern Virginia, being one of the world's longest natural harbors, where there is a USN base.

LIVE TOPICS ABOUT TOWN.[906]

The United States ship Essex has left the Brooklyn Navy Yard for a long cruise, and she took with her a lot of Madeira wine the memory of which still lingers in the yard. Although the Essex is now badly outclassed by the new cruisers, she is a comfortable old boat, with an easy-going way that lengthened her last cruise from the Madeira Islands to New York to forty-six or forty-seven days, the extra day being in dispute. Nothing stronger than sherry is allowed in the wardroom of a United States fighting boat, and light wines that are really good are at a premium. Before the Essex left the Madeira Islands the officers of the wardroom laid in some Madeira wine of an excellent quality. It is generally believed that a sea voyage improves a wine of this character, and the longer the voyage the better the wine is supposed to be. If this theory of the improvement of wine be true, it is safe to say that since the introduction of steam vessels no such Madeira wine has ever been landed here by a United States boat. The officers of the Essex are a jolly lot of men, and when the quality of their Madeira had been tested they found that officers on all the other boats were anxious to cultivate their acquaintance. Their Madeira was worthy of the reputation that it acquired, and its flavor was a guarantee of the statement that it came from the right side of the island, whichever that may be.[907]

"If we had brought the wine on one of the fast cruisers," said a Lieutenant, "it wouldn't have had this flavor. Nothing like a long sea voyage to give it tone."

"Yes," said a man from the Puritan, "your trip to Madeira was forty-seven days, wasn't it? I suspect that if you shipped table d'hôte claret in New York, by the time the Essex reached Liverpool[908] you would find that it had become high-grade Burgundy."

SPREE ON WINE[909]
A Bit of U.S. Navy History Told as a Story.
FIRST TRIP OF THE OMAHA
Casks Filled With Light Liquor. More Than Half the Crew "Laid Out" – In the Wet.

"Did you ever hear of the drunk of the U.S.S. Omaha, or rather the spree of the Omaha's crew? Well, it's a stock naval yarn, but a good one, and with the extra rare merit of being true."

The speaker was a gentleman who as an officer had paced the decks of many American warships in many waters. He continued:

"It was one of the earlier trips of the cruiser. The orders were for Rio, after putting into Madeira for supplies. The season was pleasant and the 350 officers and men were enjoying the voyage immensely. As the Omaha scudded along, her machinery working beautifully

---

906 *The Sun,* January 16, 1897. (New York City, NY).
907 The south side, where the best Madeira Wine was made.
908 City and metropolitan borough of Merseyside, in England.
909 *Hawaiian Gazette,* January 21, 1898. (Oahu, HI); *The Sun,* February 20, 1898. (New York City, NY. Published under the title "THE BIGGEST NAVAL SPREE. Half the Omaha's Water Casks Filled with Wine and 150 Men Drunk at One Time." adding that it had been transcribed from the *Pacific Commercial Advertiser.*). Under the titles "THE BIGGEST NAVAL SPREE. Half the Omaha's Water Casks Filled with Wine and 150 Men Drunk.", this text was published in these sources: *Sycamore True Republican,* March 19, 1898. (Sycamore, IL); *Muskogee Phoenix,* May 5, 1898. (Muskogee, Indian Territory, OK). Under the titles "THE BIGGEST NAVAL SPREE. Cruiser's Water Casks Filled With Wine and 150 Men Drunk." and stating that it had been transcribed from the *Chigaco Chronicle,* this text was published in the *The Kansas City Journal,* April 1, 1898. (Kansas City, MO).

and sea easy as a bay, all felt satisfied with the service. There would be a number of warships with acquaintances aboard at Rio, and we knew their officers and crews would welcome us and admire the Omaha. We had her neat as a lady dressed for a reception.

"While we were taking on meat and vegetables in Madeira our captain conceived the idea of saving coal by filling up the water tanks from shore. From the Island we could stand into a trade wind and would with half luck be able to make a fine run into Rio.

By doing no condensing and taking advantage of all sailing chance it was calculated to make a fuel showing that would gain a few effective credit marks at Washington.

"A watering party of about fifty, in charge of petty officers, handled the casks. They filled themselves with Madeira wine, then made a common purse and bought enough of it to load about half the casks. The scheme was to have Madeira on tap till we reached Rio. As usual, though, Jacky overreached himself.

"On a man-of-war, you know, the halyards are so laid that all the canvas can be spread at once. Well, it was done this time in a fashion that nearly drove the captain crazy. He was on the bridge and cursed a blue streak that poisoned the air and polluted the sea. He cursed officers and men, the service and the ship, all countries and the earth and the universe.

"First the men talked as they tangled the halyards about. For this they were mildly and then sharply reproved. Next they sang. Then the officers were compelled to swear drown the voice of the captain. The men staggered around and did all sorts of maudlin things. They fell and rose and fell again. They tried to fight amongst themselves. They talked back to the officers, cursed the non-coms and shouted badinage to the captain. It was a pronounced case of general certain jag, and no remedy to be suggested. At least 150 of the men were paralyzed drunk and those able to stand still drinking till the supply was cut off.

"It is a blessing there was no weather. Not a thing in the way of handling ship was done after she was once headed. It did rain. It was quite a down pore, but the helpless drunks, lying on the decks, slept right through it. From them during the night there were groans and growls and an occasional attempt at a rally. Several times bo's'ns blew their pipes in a confused, halting way, without knowing what was wanted.

"At daybreak all hands able assisted in driving the carousers back to duty. The spree left them stupid, blear-eyed, with aching heads and sore bodies and a wondering on what the punishment was going to be. They had a mighty long day of it after the remainder of the wine was run over the sides.

"There was no court martial. No one was cited or charged or place in the brig. The task of inflicting punishment was too great and the captain had to wink at the Omaha's big drunk.

"Bringing liquor aboard ship is the chief of minor offenses, yet the Jackies are at it constantly. I once saw a smuggler caught in the act in such a peculiar and striking way that even the dominie sympathized with him. He was assisted with supplies. Every article was inspected as usual when handed up. The corporal of marines stuck his nose into a can of milk, followed it up with his fingers and brought out a whiskey bottle label that was floating in plain view. The firewater container was anchored at the bottom of the can. I call this a pretty good hard luck story, myself."

Back in the 19th century not everyone was allowed to carry alcoholic beverages aboard USN ships. Officers could, for their own use or even to be used in US diplomatic actions in Asia, and we found several examples of Madeira Wine being loaded aboard Naval units anchored in Funchal bay. But low-ranked sailors could not do it, and we found an interesting testimony, published in 1841, reporting how it was brought, concealed, into a Navy ship there, an action that involved a complicity between the buyers and the sellers.[910]

9.3. Madeira Wine Advertised in the American Press

Madeira Wine was advertised in the American press at least since the 1720's. In this section there is a selection of fourteen interesting advertisements of this precious commodity, published in different 19th century American newspapers, from 1808 to 1884, where the sales and consumption of Madeira were most prevalent, namely in South Carolina, Georgia, Virginia, Maryland, Washington, New York and Boston.

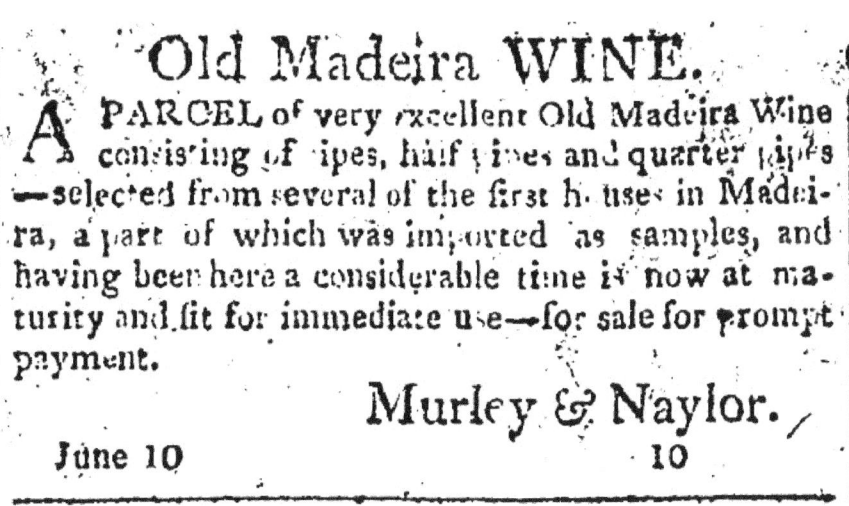

Charleston Courier, June 10, 1808. (Charleston, SC).

---

[910] «The old frigate that I was an inmate of last cruise, came to anchor one morning at the Island of Madeira; as is customary the *bum-boats* came alongside with fruit, bread, eggs, &c., and amongst other things they offered for sale some very handsome covered straw baskets; – it was astonishing to see how great was the demand for those articles, although the price was a dollar each; but straw baskets were the rage from the mizen-top to the berth-deck; three times a day would the boats come alongside, half full of those fragile things, and as quick as lightning would they be all dispose of: for know, gentle reader, half a gallon of liquor was stowed securely in the inside; – and we left the Island without an officer on board having the slightest suspicion how well those baskets were lined.» [MERCIER, Henry James; GALLOP, William], *Life in a Man-of-War, or Scenes in "Old Ironsides" during her cruise in the Pacific. By a Fore-Top-Man.*, Lydia R. Bailey, Printer, Philadelphia, 1841, page 158.

MADEIRA WINE.
A CHOICE PARCEL
Pure old Madeira Wine,

IN pipes, half pipes and qr. casks, of the brad Aburdoch, Yuille, Wardross & Co. received per schooner Shepherdess, Samuel Carr, master, from Madeira—for sale by

Foulke & Karrick,
Spear's Wharf.

WHO HAVE ALSO FOR SALE,

CODFISH, in boxes and hhds.
AMERICAN GIN, very first quality
MANUFACTURED TOBACCO
And a quantity of NICARAGUA WOOD, &c.
July 13.   dtf

Federal Republican, August 30, 1809. (Baltimore, MD).

MADEIRA WINE, &c.

FRANCIS BARRETTO offers for sale, at No. 14 Hudson-street, a few hhds. and quarter casks of Old Madeira Wine, that has been to the Brazils, imported in the ship Susannah, Bunce, master, from Madeira.

ALSO,

20 pipes of former importations.
Old Malmsey, fresh Madeira.
Citron in boxes or by the lb.
Sherry and Teneriffe Wines, of superior quality.
Old Cognac Brandy
Holland Gin, with a general assortment of Groceries.   march 18.

Commercial Advertiser, May 2, 1811. (New York City, NY).

Madeira Wine.

A FEW Pipes, half pipes and quarters of choice Madeira Wine—Also, a few dozen in boxes, which have been in bottles twelve years. For sale by
KETCHUM & BURROUGHS.

The above Wine will be sold, entitled to debenture.

Bryan County, Dec. 1.
dec 2   7—L

The Georgian, December 2, 1829. (Savannah, GA).

CHOICE WINES.

THE Subscribers, agents for J. Howard March & Co. of Madeira, have on hand a large stock of old L. P. Madeira Wine, imported into the United States in the ship Brahmin, after having performed a voyage to the East Indies with her cargo of wines. It is in boxes containing two dozen bottles each, and they offer it at the cash price per gallon, with the addition of the cost of bottles and corks. Also, Sherry and Burgundy, in qr. casks, Old Port, in half pipes. The pure juice of the Madeira Grape, in boxes containing two dozen bottles each, and in quarter and half quarter casks. All of which they offer for sale on the most accommodating terms.
S. M. & S. H. JANNEY.
Alexandria, Nov. 8—tf

Daily National Intelligencer, November 8, 1830. (Washington, DC). John Howard March & Co. was the commercial firm owned by the U.S. Consul in Madeira, which dealt mostly in Madeira Wine exports.

CHOICE OLD MADEIRA WINES.—The subscriber has just received, in addition to his old stock of Wines, a few pipes and quarter casks south side India Madeira, per the "Golconda," via Canton, by special order, from the house of Newton, Gordon, Murdock & Scott.

This Wine is confidently recommended to be of superior quality, and fully equal, if not superior, to any former importation from this house. For sale by

may 26   RICH'D. WILLIAMSON, 19 Malden lane.

Commercial Advertiser, June 6, 1834. (New York City, NY). In this add can be seen Madeira Wine that had gone to India before being imported into the United States. The long sea voyage that this wine had endured made sure that it was a unique product.

MADEIRA WINE.

THE subscribers have received, per the schr. Village, from Madeira,
10 half pipes
20 quarter casks of finest old high colored Madeira Wine, from the house of Murdoch, Shortridge & Co.

And have in Store, of previous importation,
5 pipes and 20 half pipes of the finest wine of Murdoch, Yuille & Co., part of which has had the benefit of a voyage to the East Indies. All old, and warranted of the very best quality.

aug 6   A. C. CAZENOVE & CO.

MADEIRA WINE.

7 Pipes
3 half pipes
30 qr do
33 half qr do

Consisting of Sercial, Tinto, Burgundy, Grape Juice, fine old London Particular, and a few casks of "extra good" old London Particular Madeira Wine.

The above mentioned Wines are from the well and favorably known house of J. Howard, March & Co. who state that this collection of Wines is equal to any ever sent to the port of Alexandria. For sale on accommodating terms.

8 mo 5—eo7t   PHINEAS JANNEY.

☞ Nat. Int. eo7t; Winchester Rep. and Fredericksburg Arena 3t.

OLD L. P. MADEIRA WINE.

2 Pipes
4 qr casks
4 eighth do

Old high colored L. P. Madeira Wine, of "G. D. Welsh's" brand

Received per schr. Village, Newcomb, master, direct from Madeira, for sale by

aug 5   W. FOWLE & CO.

MADEIRA WINE.

50 Cases, containing 1 to 2 dozen bottles each, of Newton, Gordon, Murdoch & Co's superior old L. P. Madeira Wine.

4 qr casks
8 half qr casks } Grape Juice

Just received per schr. Village, from Madeira, and for sale by

aug 5   S. MESSERSMITH.

MADEIRA WINE.

THE subscriber is now receiving, and offers for sale, an importation of Madeira Wine, per "Iyanough," via New York, consisting of
6 hhds
6 qr casks
4 half qr casks

Of the finest old L. P. Madeira Wine, of Newton, Gordon Murdoch & Co.'s celebrated brand; and he will receive and forward orders for their Old L. P. Madeira, superior Bual, Tinta, Burgundy, Malmsey, and Grape Juice.

aug 2   S. MESSERSMITH.

Alexandria Gazette, August 7, 1834. (Alexandria, VA). Sometimes the Madeira Wine was imported into the United States via the East Indies, and due to the tropical heat the wine endured during the long sea trip it was rendered excellent. Usually this wine was known in America as East India Madeira.

ORDERS FOR MADEIRA WINE.—The subscribers, agents for the old established house of George and Robert Blackburn & Co. of Madeira, are now receiving orders for Wines to be shipped direct to this port.

One of the above firm is now here, and can give persons disposed to order, every information as to quality. Besides the other obvious advantages of a direct conveyance to Baltimore, all expenses of transshipment from another port are avoided.

FOR MADEIRA.—The fast sailing copper fastened and coppered brig MARY, Capt. Parker, will sail for Madeira on the 3d of June next, and return direct to this port; for passage only, apply to
WM. & THOS. ADAIR,
may 25—3t   South Charles Street, Baltimore.

Daily National Intelligencer, May 29, 1838. (Washington, DC). In this interesting add the Madeira Wine agent in the political capital of America, where this product was highly appreciated and consumed, is calling for orders next to his customers.

CHOICE OLD WINES AND LIQUORS, IN GLASS AND WOOD.—
25 dozen Miranda's South-side Madeira, vintage 1830
25 do Monteiro Madeira Wine, vintage 1830
25 do Bual   do   do 1826
25 do Sercial   do   do 1826
50 do Old Reserved do   do 1815
(This collection embraces the finest wines made on the Island of Madeira.)
50 dozen fine Pale and Gold Sherry Wines, Duff Gordon and Co.
25 dozen Tinta and other Madeira Wines
50 do Virgin Brandy, vintage 1830
100 do old Cognac Brandy, vintage 1830.
  IN WOOD.
1 pipe fine Old Reserved Madeira wine, vintage 1815
1 do   do Bual   do vintage 1826
4 half pipes do Blackburn's do
5 butts fine old Brown Sherry do
2 do do Pale do   do
1 pipe Pure old Port   do
20 half and quarter pipes Teneriffe Wines
20 do   do   Sicily   do
50 baskets Champagne Wines, Beaver, Gold Medal, and Grape brands
2 puncheons superior Jamaica Rum
2 do   Irish Whiskey
8 pipes fine old Rye Whiskey
  ALSO,
100,000 superior Havana Cigars, Regalia, Industria, Principe, and other brands.
A few boxes very choice Chewing Tobacco
These wines and liquors are confidently recommended to the public as being pure as imported, and unsurpassed in quality by any in the country.
Demijohns loaned, and goods sent to any part of the city free of porterage.
MIDDLETON & BEALL,
Pa. avenue, opposite the National Hotel.
Nov 29—eo2w

The Globe, December 2, 1839. (Washington, DC). Up to a certain time Madeira Wine was sold in America in casks, quarter casks or hogsheads but from this time onwards it was advertised as being sold in bottles, by the dozen.

OLD MADEIRA WINE.
110 Packages Welsh Brothers' OLD MADEIRA WINE, of various qualities, in quarter and eighth casks, for sale in bond or duty paid, by
o 24 MWS2m   FOSTER & TAYLOR, 115 Broad st.

Boston Evening Transcript, November 2, 1859. (Boston, MA). George Day Welsh, a native of Philadelphia, had his own wine exporting company in Madeira.

MADEIRA WINE.

The attention of the trade and consumers is respectfully called to the sale of a choice lot of Madeira wine, to be sold this day at W. B. Griffin's Auction rooms, commencing at 10 o'clock, A. M. It is imported, and can be relied on as an excellent wine.

Daily Constitutionalist, June 11, 1862. (Augusta, GA). After the shortage of Madeira Wine supply in America, due to the blight that attacked the vines of the island in 1852, the best opportunities to purchase good Madeiras in America arose when auctions like these were advertised in the press.

Estate Sale, by order of Executor—Very Old and Superior Leacock Madeira Wine.
BY THOMAS FARR CAPERS.
Will be sold, at my Office, Vanderhorst's Wharf, next east of Captain Welsman's, on FRIDAY next, 27th instant, at 11 o'clock,
Eight dozen SUPERIOR OLD LEACOCK MADEIRA WINE.
Conditions cash.
The above may also be treated for at Private Sale.
March 25

The Charleston Mercury, March 25, 1863. (Charleston, SC). Madeira Wine was often part of the estate received by the heirs after the death of a wine collector. When they did not want to keep the wine, as seems to be this case, it was sold by an Executor, to settle the estate, and distribute the money by the descendants.

WINE! WINE!

IN PRIVATE HANDS, AND FOR SALE REASONABLE, the remainder of a cask of

MADEIRA WINE,

(About twenty gallons,) imported five years ago. Apply at this Office.   February 14

Charleston Daily Courier, February 19, 1868. (Charleston, SC).

SUPERIOR MADEIRA WINE.

A RARE opportunity is afforded to the lovers of choice Madeira Wine, to obtain a pure article; which has not only been carefully selected at Madeira, but greatly improved by a voyage thence to Calcutta, Madras, and Philadelphia—where it is now deposited in the custom-house stores, to remain till sold, to guard against the possibility or doubt of adulteration. This wine is in the possession of one of the first houses in Philadelphia, who intend keeping a regular supply, and to stand on reputation. These are safe guarantees to the purchaser.
Further information will be given, and orders received, at the office of the subscriber in 15th street.
march 31—eo2w   JAMES H. CAUSTEN.

Daily National Intelligencer, April 10, 1884. (Washington, DC). Here is another example of a superior Madeira Wine that had travelled all the way to India and back to the States.

9.4. General Articles about this Commodity

In this section we have gathered five texts, published between 1825 and 1897, dealing with general thoughts about Madeira Wines, from the discrimination of its different kinds to the art of keeping a good cellar, to how Madeira was seen and consumed in Philadelphia and in New York.

MADEIRA WINES.[911]

Some of the London periodicals have of late treated, *apparently* with great learning, in fact very *ignorantly*, of Madeira Wines. The following letter from Mr. Samuel Alexander, a merchant in Philadelphia, to the Editor of the National Gazette, exposes some gross blunders in an article which was recently copied into that paper, we believe from the New Monthly Magazine.[912]

Mr. Editor, – In the third number of the article of "Wines," from the London Magazine, published in the National Gazette, there appears an error which I beg leave to point out and correct. Of Madeira Wines, it is stated, "The Tinta is an indifferent wine." "There are four distinct wines produced here" (Madeira) – "the Madeira is well known, the Tinta, or red Madeira, the Malmsey and the Sercial." Now sir, there are to my knowledge *seven* different wines made on the island of Madeira, which are as follow, Verdelho, Negro Mol,[913] Negrinho, Tinta, Bual, Sercial, and Malmsey, five of which I have for sale. The three first, with a little Tinta and Bual, are, in the south, generally planted in certain proportions in the same vineyard, and being fermented together, form the wine usually shipped. Indeed, the Sercial, Malmsey and Tinta, (the latter so far from being "indifferent wine," is very choice) are the only wines made separately in any quantity. – Of the Bual it is difficult to obtain many casks by itself, really fine; so also of South Verdelho.

I find, in another passage, these remarks, which are also incorrect. "The English and East India demand, include the best class, and the cant name of *London particular* is familiar. America, it is equally understood, is treated with the worst wines." I know not from what source the writer obtained his information, but from my own experience and personal observation at Madeira, I know that America is treated with as great a proportion of the best wine, as any country in the world. The name of London particular does not infer that that is the best wine, as will appear by the following gradation of Madeira wines, and their prices to each for the present year, from one of the best and oldest houses in Madeira. Cargo wine, 22*l*. per pipe; India market, 30*l*.; London market, 34*l*.; London particular, 38*l*.; select Old Wine, 40 a 50*l*.; Tinta, Sercial and Malmsey, 80*l*. per pipe.

Besides the grapes used for making wines at Madeira, there is a great variety of eating grapes; the Muscatel, Alicant red and white, Listrao,[914] Lady's Finger, Grapes of the Land of Promise, being in immense clusters, Bastardo, Esganacao;[915] – in short, all kinds

---
911 *The Portsmouth Journal of Literature & Politics,* December 10, 1825. (Portsmouth, NH).
912 The "New Monthly Magazine and Literary Journal" was an English publication, printed in London.
913 The right spelling is Negra Mole.
914 The right spelling is Listão.
915 The right spelling is Esganação.

of grapes will grow there, and every one who has had the curiosity to procure any thing uncommon, and stick it in his garden, has preserved it.

FOREIGN MISCELLANY.[916]

THE WINES OF MADEIRA. – 1. *Madeira* – commonly so called – which is the produce of a variety of grapes – Verdelho, Bual, Tinta, Negrinha, &c, which are all pressed together and make the choicest wine, or London Particular.

2. *Malmsey.* A very rich sweet wine, highly esteemed. It derives its luscious flavor from the grapes being permitted to hang in a considerable time after they are ripe before they are gathered. It is greatly improved, and acquires a darker color by age.

3. *Tinta.* A delicious red wine, very seldom exported. When new, the color is as deep as that of claret and it is then usually drunk; when older it becomes about the color of tawny port. It is the produce of a particular grape; and the color is fixed and peculiar flavor acquired by permitting the skins of the grapes to remain in the cask during the process of fermentation.

4. *Sercial.* This is a dry wine, and possesses much body, flavor, and fine aroma. It is the most expensive of the Madeira wines, of a lighter color than Malmsey, and requires to be kept a considerable time before it arrives at perfection.

5. *Bual.* An agreeable light wine, not possessing so much body as the others.

6. *Verdelho.* A pleasant full bodied wine, the produce of white grape. The grape is much used as one of the component parts of Madeira, and the wine is seldom exported.

7. *Negrinha.* A rich cordial wine, made from grapes dried in the sun.

8. *Bastardo.* A wine of very rare occurrence, being made from a peculiar grape seldom pressed separately.

The whole quantity of wine produced on the island is about 25,000 pipes annually; of which not more than 6000 are of the best quality. During the war time there was an immense demand for wine, from the large number of vessels calling, so that all the fine wines were soon disposed of, leaving in the stores the wines of the North, which are very acid and poor, and not worth more than $100 per pipe. The demand, however, continued and the temptation of obtaining $300 per pipe, which was readily offered, was irresistible, so that the merchants were content to pass off these inferior wines for the best, keeping them previously for three months in *estufas*,[917] or rooms heated to 100 degrees which diminishes in some degree the acidity and newness of flavor, imparting an artificial age to wine.

Prices of Madeira. – The export price of the best Madeira is $230 or 240 per pipe, and it can be deposited in a cellar in London, for $12 per dozen; and yet this, or an inferior kind is often retailed at $20 per dozen. The export price of Malmsey and other wines averages at least $390 per pipe.

---

[916] *The North American and Daily Advertiser,* October 10, 1840. (Philadelphia, PA); *Alexandria Gazette,* October 21, 1840. (Alexandria, VA. Published under the title "THE WINES OF MADEIRA.").

[917] Portuguese word for hothouses.

CONCERNING GASTRONOMY[918]
The Art of Giving a Perfectly Good Dinner.
… A GOOD CELLAR.

One of the most gentlemanlike hobbies a man can indulge in is a good cellar, for I know not a truer gratification than being enabled to give a friend a bottle of fine wine. To me it is the greatest enjoyment. I need scarcely say, great judgement and experience are required in laying the foundation of your stock, and if you be diffident of your power of taste, confide implicitly in a respectable wine merchant and he will do you justice. Of all wines Madeira demands the nicest discrimination in its selection; the deservedly high place it once held in the estimation of connoisseurs has been usurped by sherry, an it is to be lamented that it should have grown into comparative desuetude, for, of the two it is incomparably the finer wine. A popular error regarding this long neglected nectar is that of decanting old Madeira wine and leaving the stopper out. It is a barbarous system and cannot be sufficiently reprobated. The fine nutty flavor so prized by the gastronomic planters, the indescribable aroma, the nosegay in short, is destroyed by this senseless process. Your pseudo judge says it renders the wine soft and silky, for which read fiat and vapid.[919] What would the genuine Bavarian beer drinker say to have his favorite beverage left standing exposed to the action of the air for some three or four hours before his dinner? Why he would write the man down an ass who committed such an atrocious act. The cases are parallel, and in both instances the spirit and flavor of the liquid are destroyed. The principal firms of Madeira have adopted the plan of giving their wines the benefit of the motion of a vessel by manual application; whole gangs of Portuguese are employed on the beach in rolling pipes and hogsheads of Madeira, thus saving the expense of a voyage, and with the same beneficial result – the undulating motion of the vessel being tolerably imitated on this wine flourishing island. The merchants there also bring premature age by means of artificial heat, and it is astonishing how soon the wines ripen under the sweating process, as it is termed. In the West Indies, where the planters are supposed to be the best judges in the world of Madeira wine, as soon as a pipe of Madeira is bottled off, the planter stores it in a loft of his dwelling, with nothing between his dearly prized supernaculum and the broiling sun but the shingled roof. The heat in these lofty cellars is intense beyond conception; in two years the wine is ready for drinking, rich and ripe, and of a flavor unimaginable to those who have never visited the Antilles. The climate of our Northern States is ill suited to this generous wine; the cold is its greatest enemy, and it would be impossible to recognize the same wine in New York that you were in the habit of drinking in Barbadoes. The best plan would be to construct a large cupboard as near your kitchen as possible, line it with sheet or plate iron, pass a flue through the top of it, and keep this wine press at an unvaried temperature of ninety-six or a hundred. Keep your Madeira in it, and by these artificial means you will have your wine in drinking order. Above all, never put your Madeira into a decanter; it is a little short of sacrilege. Keep it in the black bottle and never take the cork out but to replenish your glass. …

---

918 *The Brooklyn Daily Eagle,* August 17, 1884. (Brooklyn, NY). This text is an excerpt of the article "A Chapter on Gastronomy", inserted in section 8 of this anthology.
919 See Note 805.

HALF A CENTURY AGO.[920]
Philadelphia Gentlemen Drank In a Way to Astonish Their Descendants.

Among Americans up to 1855 the use and abuse of strong drink were almost universal, but it certainly affected their health less injuriously than at the present time. The worry and strain of modern business and social life shatter nerves now and lead to dram drinking to repair them. On the contrary, most of the excesses in the old times came after a solid dinner, and three of four hours were spent in rest and conviviality, but the amount drank was enormous. When the exchange was completed, in 1832, a dinner was given, and there was some apprehension that the wine would run out, and a well known broker on the committee expressed his surprise, as the company had not averaged more than three bottles apiece. This would be thought a very large allowance of strong Madeira in these times.

In 1853 the final audit of the accounts of the United States bank was completed, and on behalf of the government James A. Bayard of Delaware, John M. Mason and a Kentucky gentleman named Dukes appeared. It was a mere formality, as the matter had been settled ten years before. John Young acted as clerk. The party met in the northwest chamber of the bank building – now the custom house – at 11 o'clock. A bottle of brandy and six of Madeira were on the table, and after a short inspection of papers the wine was opened, and by 1 o'clock was drank. The day was warm, and a bowl of bishop was ordered, and this was made by the servant with the brandy and a flask of Curacoa.[921]

This was drank, and the three committeemen went to dine with Charles J. Ingersoll about 5 o'clock. They returned, bringing a friend. A dozen Madeira were at hand, and smoking, drinking and whist were in order until 12, when the last bottle was drank, and then Prosser, the cook, brought in cold ducks and a mighty lobster salad. A gallon bowl of brandy punch was made as conducive to digestion. A tumbler of this finished the clerk, who went to sleep and was aroused at daybreak to drink a cup of coffee, and then all went down the steps and walked away in the fresh morning air, none the worse in appearance from the night's potations.

It is apparent that in a life like this it was the survival of the fittest. The steady ones carried off the honors, but gout, gravel and dropsy played havoc with the others, and these complaints were charged to port and Madeira by the doctors, and so the habit of drinking claret and light wines came into fashion.

Gambling was almost universal, and many fortunes of old Philadelphians disappeared in this way. – Philadelphia Times.

---

[920] *The Roanoke Times,* June 1, 1895. (Roanoke, VA); *Lima Times Democrat,* June 8, 1895. (Lima, OH); *Harrisonburg Rockingham Register,* July 26, 1895. (Harrisonburg, VA); *The Hawaiian Star,* August 5, 1895. (Honolulu, HI).
[921] The right spelling is Curação, a liqueur made on the island of Curaçao.

NEW YORK SOCIETY AND WINE DRINKERS.[922]

… Having had your champagne from the fish to the roast, your vin ordinaire through the dinner, your burgundy or johannisburg or fine old tokay, with the cheese, your best claret with the roast; then, after the ladies have had their fruit and have left the table, comes on the king of wines, your madeira, a national wine, a wine only well matured at the south, and a wine whose history is as old as that of your country.

I may here say that madeira imparts a vitality that no other wine can give.

After drinking it, it acts as a soporific, but the next day you feel ten years younger and stronger for it. I have known a man whose dinners were so famous by reason of his being always able to give at them a faultless madeira to disappear with his wine. When his wine gave out he collapsed. When asked "Where is Mr. Jones?" the ready answer was always given. "He went out with his 'Rapid madeira.'"

Nothing is more important than the serving of your wines for the success of a dinner. …

9.5. Curious Facts Related to Madeira Wine

Madeira Wine is associated with an endless number of curious facts in America or abroad. In the following twenty-two articles, published between 1803 and 1896, they can be seen. Here is a short summary of their subjects: thousands of casks of Madeira wine destroyed in the island's terrible deluge of 1803, Madeira used to toast the Louisiana Purchase, a bottle of Madeira used to baptize the U.S. frigate *Constitution* in 1797, a curious bet made by Nathaniel Hawthorne involving Madeira Wine, this wine as the favorite of the Justices of the Supreme Court, the origin of the fortune of the Blandy family – English wine merchants in Madeira, – old Madeira wine discovered during the demolition of old mansions, bottles of Madeira Wine being given to Harvard students in the early 1800's, a curious episode occurring in Madeiran waters during the early Norse immigration to the United States, and a curious story of some Japan Madeira, among others.

CALAMITY AT MADEIRA.[923]

---

922 *The World,* December 19, 1897. (New York City, NY).

923 *New-York Gazette & General Advertiser*, December 9, 1803. (New York City, NY); *American Citizen,* December 10, 1803. (New York City, NY); *The Spectator,* December 10, 1803. (New York City, NY); *Gazette of the United States,* December 10, 1803. (New York City, NY); *Weekly Museum,* December 10, 1803. (New York City, NY); *Aurora General Advertiser,* December 12, 1803. (Philadelphia, PA); *Federal Gazette & Baltimore Daily Advertiser,* December 12, 1803. (Baltimore, MD); *New-Jersey Journal,* December 13, 1803. (Elizabethtown, NJ); *Alexandria Daily Advertiser,* December 14, 1803. (Alexandria, VA); *The Connecticut Courant,* December 14, 1803. (Hartford, CT); *Republican Watch-Tower,* December 14, 1803. (New York, NY); *Mirror of the Times & General Advertiser,* December 14, 1803. (Wilmington, DE); *Alexandria Expositor,* December 15, 1803. (Alexandria, VA); *Boston Gazette,* December 15, 1803. (Boston, MA); *Connecticut Journal,* December 15, 1803. (New Haven, CT); *American Mercury,* December 15, 1803. (Hartford, CT); *The Albany Gazette,* December 15, 1803. (Albany, NY); *Columbian Courier, or Weekly Miscellany,* December 16, 1803. (New Bedford, MA); *The Albany Register,* December 16, 1803. (Albany, NY); *The Salem Gazette,* December 16, 1803. (Salem, MA); *Washington Federalist,* December 16, 1803. (Georgetown, DC); *The Albany Centinel,* December 16, 1803. (Albany, NY); *Republican Advocate,* December 16, 1803. (Fredericktown, MD); *Newport Mercury,* December 17, 1803. (Newport, RI); *Gazetteer,* December 17, 1803. (Boston, MA); *Philadelphia Repository,* December 17, 1803. (Philadelphia, PA); *The Oracle of Dauphin, and Harrisburg Advertiser,* December 17, 1803. (Harrisburg, PA); *Independent Chronicle,* December 19, 1803. (Boston, MA); *The Reporter,* December 19, 1803. (Brattleboro, VT); *The Balance, and Columbian Repository,* December 20, 1803. (Hudson, NY); *Oracle Post,* December 20,

This extraordinary event, happened on Sunday the ninth of October,[924] at eight in the evening. The day had been previously very cloudy and a continual rain had fallen, accompanied with squalls, which were not violent, until the sun had sunk beneath the horizon, when the sea appeared to be unusually agitated, and such a darkness prevailed, that an object was not discernible at a yard's distance – during this progress, every person remained within their houses, in seeming security, and wholly unconscious of that approaching horror which was destined so shortly to sweep them from the earth!

The clock of the cathedral was striking eight, when an instantaneous storm of terrible lightning and thunder began, and the rain fell in such torrents, that all the cross streets of the eastern part of the city of Funchal, were suddenly filled with mud and water above the first floors of the houses, which was occasioned by its being impeded, in some measure, from its furious descent from the ravines of the mountains into the sea. At this shocking period the stoutest heart felt appalled; nothing was to he heard but the din of ruin working in every direction: hundreds of huge stones, that had been torn from their quarries on the hills three miles above the town, were tumbling over each other in stupendous concussion, carrying with them, in conjunction, with the deluge, churches, convents, streets, trees, bridges, battlements, and eight hundred human beings into the bottom of the deep. Whenever a flash of lightning penetrated the gloom, were seen mothers wading through the streets, up to their chins in water, holding their infants on their heads with one hand, and endeavoring to catch security with the other, while those who attempted to assist them, were frequently maimed or killed, by the beams of timber or wine pipes which floated around them; …

Thus, in so short a space of time as a few minutes, were many hundred individuals carried to their eternal home, in the very plenitude of an apparent security; and several thousands reduced from affluence to poverty; and many of them, it is probable, in the indulgence of those imperfections, which constitute our criminality of our folly, and sent to their account, "unblanched, unannointed, unannealed." Ten thousand pipes of wine and brandy were destroyed, and the sea shore was skirted on the ensuing morning with millions of fragments, among which the mourning survivors of the calamity were eagerly seeking for the dead remains of their relations or friends. …

It was remarkable that this deluge, in its course, swept away twenty-nine vineyards that were situated on the south west side of the city; and so decisive was the ruin, that it tore

---

1803. (Portsmouth, NH); *The Hive,* December 20, 1803. (Northampton, MA); *The New Hampshire Gazette,* December 20, 1803. (Portsmouth, NH); *Columbian Minerva,* December 20, 1803. (Dedham, MA); *The Federal Spy,* December 20, 1803. (Springfield, MA); *Virginia Herald,* December 20, 1803. (Fredericksburg, VA); *The Maryland Herald, and Elizabeth-Town Weekly Advertiser,* December 21, 1803. (Elizabethtown, MD); *Republican Farmer,* December 21, 1803. (Bridgeport, CT); *The Courier,* December 21, 1803. (Norwich, CT); *National Aegis,* December 21, 1803. (Worcester, MA); *Kline Carlisle Weekly Gazette,* December 21, 1803. (Carlisle, PA); *The Adams Centinel,* December 21, 1803. (Gettysburg, PA); *Courier of New Hampshire,* December 21, 1803. (Concord, NH); *Rhode-Island Republican,* December 22, 1803. (Newport, RI); *Windham Herald,* December 22, 1803. (Windham, CT); *Otsego Herald; or, Western Advertiser,* December 22, 1803. (Cooperstown, NY); *Rutland Herald,* December 24, 1803. (Rutland, VT); *Providence Phoenix,* December 24, 1803. (Providence, RI); *Vermont Mercury,* December 26, 1803. (Rutland, VT); *Farmer's Register,* December 27, 1803. (Lansinburgh, NY); *Vermont Gazette,* December 27, 1803. (Bennington, VT); *Hornet,* December 27, 1803. (Fredericktown, MD); *Hudson Gazette,* December 27, 1803. (Hudson, NY); *The Western American,* December 30, 1803. (Bardstown, KY); *The Patriot,* January 2, 1804. (Utica, NY); *The Green Mountain Patriot,* January 3, 1804. (Peacham, VT); *Weekly Wanderer,* January 4, 1804. (Randolph, VT). This text was also published at "The Literary Magazine, and American Register", for 1803-4, from October to March, Vol. I., edited in Philadelphia and other major American cities, in 1804, on pages 238-239.

924 1803. This was perhaps the worst natural disaster in Madeira's history, in which hundreds of people perished, and many properties were destroyed by a terrible flood. Many people still retains in memory the drastic images of the flood of February 20, 2010 that devastated the island and made news worldwide. The flood of 1803 was at least ten times worst, and this article depicting it was revealed in an endless number of American newspapers, as we just have seen.

up all the trees by the roots, and bore away not only them, but all the cottages, with their inhabitants, the ground, cattle and an appurtenances, and left the rocky basis, as bare of vegetation as the cliffs of Norway. ...

All the vessels that arrived at Funchal, for several weeks after this miserable occurrence, gave an account of the dead bodies, casks, and boxes which they had seen floating many leagues off at sea; and it is believed that some of the crews were considerably enriched by the contents of many of the trunks. ...

This is admitted to have been the greatest civic evil, that has happened since the earthquake of Lisbon in 1754, and was the most tragical, of its nature, that ever happened. Had the younger Pliny[925] been on the spot, it would have been adequately detailed.

The property destroyed has been estimated at upwards of a million of pounds sterling.
Lang and Co.'s Gazette.

Translated for the National Intelligencer, from the Moniteur of Louisiana.[926]

NEW-ORLEANS, Dec. 21, 1803. The work was at length consummated – Louisiana changes her government for the last time; and the flag of the United States has throughout this city every where replaced that of the French republic.

The following account of the three last days will complete the history of these events, which mark an epoch, destined to be one of the most memorable in the history of America. ...

At three o'clock the company seated themselves at the table of the colonial Prefect who gave a dinner to the commissioners of the United States, followed by a tea party in the evening. The Festival was splendid. On the dinner table were ninety two covers; and there were from four to five hundred guests at supper. ... The toasts commenced after the first course, and continued till the end of the repast, which was prolonged by the firing that followed them. They were given in the following order: – *The United States and Jefferson*, in Madeira. *Charles the 4th and Spain, in Malaga and Canary; The French Republic and Bonaparte*, in Red and White Champagne. Each of these toasts was announced by sixty three discharges of artillery; of which twenty one were fired from the fort; twenty one from the French battery before the prefecture; and twenty one from the French brig L'Argo. After these toasts, given by citizen Laussat, the Spanish and American commissioners gave the *French Comissioner and his family* and the French Commissioner then gave, *to the friendship and indissoluble unions of the three powers whose Comissioners are present*. Additional discharges were heard, and others repeated on the Colonial Prefect announcing as the last toast. TO THE ETERNAL HAPPINESS OF LOUISIANA! Acclamations, transports, and huzzas accompanied each of these toasts. ...

---

925 Gaius Plinius Caecilius Secundus (61AD-ca.112AD), better known as Pliny the Younger, was a lawyer, author and magistrate of Ancient Rome. He witnessed the eruption of the Vesuvius on August 24, 79AD, and about 25 years later he wrote two letters containing minute details of this tragic event.

926 *Alexandria Daily Advertiser*, January 30, 1804. (Alexandria, VA); *The Maryland Herald, and Elizabeth-Town Weekly Advertiser*, February 8, 1804. (Elizabeth-Town, MD). This article depicts the toasts that celebrated the Louisiana Purchase, in 1803.

Extract of a letter from a Baltimorean to his friend in this city, dated Funchal, Madeira, May 30, 1815.[927]

"In honor of the Bishop of this Island,[928] there was a Portuguese ship last Sunday, dressed very handsomely with the colors of the different known nations; and although there were *two* British and *one* Swedish sloops of war in the Roads, the *star-spangled banner* was most conspicuously hoisted at the *main* and the *English* and other flags promiscuously placed underneath. However unimportant this might appear to many, it nevertheless had its effect on the feelings of every *true* American in port. At Mr. –' table yesterday, amongst many toasts that gentlemen gave, we had the pleasure of drinking "The commander of Fort M'Henry,"[929] in 30 years old Madeira; from which you will infer that a knowledge of the manly defence of that post is not confined to an ordinary space."

[The writer of the above letter participated in the defence of Fort M'Henry.][930]

[Untitled][931]

A bottle of Madeira was picked up recently from the wreck of the Royal George sunk at Spithead[932] in 1780, having been 54 years under water. It was in excellent condition, though covered with sea shells.

[Untitled][933]

It is positively stated by the Journal that wine – "Madeira wine" – probably south side Madeira – was "introduced and used at the commencement dinner in Cambridge!" Gov. Briggs[934] was at that dinner; his feelings can be better imagined than described. We cannot trust our pen to add another word. – [Post.]

---

927 *Baltimore Patriot,* July 12, 1815. (Baltimore, MD); *The Mechanic's Gazette; and Merchant's Daily Advertiser,* July 13, 1815. (Baltimore, MD); *American Watchman,* July 22, 1815. (Wilmington, DE); *Vermont Republican,* July 24, 1815. (Windsor, VT). Quoting the *Baltimore Patriot* this text was revealed in these sources: *Providence Patriot and Columbian Phenix,* July 22, 1815. (Providence, RI); *American Advocate and Kennebec Advertiser,* July 22, 1815. (Hallowell, ME); *New-Hampshire Patriot,* August 1, 1815. (Concord, NH); *Columbian Patriot,* August 2, 1815. (Middlebury, VT).
928 Right Reverend Joaquim de Meneses e Ataíde.
929 George Armistead (1780-1818), a native of Virginia, was an American military officer who served as the commander of Fort McHenry during the Battle of Baltimore, in the War of 1812.
930 Fort McHenry, in Baltimore, MD, a coastal star-shaped fort best known for its role in the War of 1812, when it defended Baltimore Harbor from an attack by the British navy in Chesapeake Bay, on September 13-14, 1814. It was during this bombardment that Francis Scott Key (1779-1843) was inspired to write the poem "Defence of Fort McHenry", later on renamed "The Star-Spangled Banner", which is the present-day American anthem.
931 *New Bedford Mercury,* October 31, 1834. (New Bedford, MA); *New Bedford Gazette and Courier,* November 3, 1834. (New Bedford, MA. Published under the title "Old Wine"); *Adams Sentinel,* November 3, 1834. (Gettysburg, PA. Published under the title "Old Wine").
932 An area of the Solent and a roadsted off Gilkicker Point, in Hampshire, England.
933 *New Bedford Register,* September 9, 1845. (New Bedford, MA).
934 George Nixon Briggs (1796-1861), who served as the 19th Governor of Massachusetts, from 1844 to 1851.

[Untitled][935]

Among Commodore Hull's[936] wines, of Philadelphia, is some very old Madeira, taken from the British ship Macedonia[n],[937] when captured by Commodore Decatur,[938] and purchased of him by Commodore Hull.

Figure 73. The *USS Constitution* was baptized in 1797 with a bottle of Madeira Wine and still sails today, being the world's oldest commissioned naval vessel afloat. *Painting attributed to Michel Felice Corné, ca. 1803-04.*

HISTORY AND EXPLOITS[939]
OF THE
United States Frigate Constitution.

... The Constitution was launched on the 20th day of September, 1797, from Hart's ship-yard, now known as Constitution wharf, Boston. The late Com. James Sever stood on the heel of the bowsprit, and according to the usage of the time, baptised the ship with a bottle of choice old Madeira wine, furnished from the cellar of the Hon. Thomas Russell, a leading merchant of Boston. "Brave men and fair women" stood on the deck as witnesses of the ceremony, which inaugurated her advent as a national ship.[940] ...

[Untitled][941]

...Workmen employed in altering the residence[942] of the late David Sears[943] for the use of the Somerset club,[944] at Boston, a few days since, discovered a large room, the entrance to which had been for many years so carefully concealed that no one knew of the existence of such a room. Within this room were found 131 dozen of Madeira wine, which must be at least 40 years old. It will no doubt bring $10 a bottle, making a total of $15,720.[945] ...

---

935 *Burlington Hawk-Eye,* May 16, 1850. (Burlington, IA).
936 Isaac Hull (1773-1843), a native of Connecticut, who commanded several U.S. naval ships, including the USS Constitution, and saw service in the Quasi-War, the Barbary Wars and the War of 1812. At the end of his career he commanded the Washington Navy Yard and later the Mediterranean Squadron.
937 *HMS Macedonian,* a 38 gun frigate of the Royal Navy, captured by the *USS United States* during the War of 1812.
938 Stephen Decatur, Jr. (1779-1820), a native of Maryland, was a United States naval officer notable for his many victories in the early 19th century.
939 *Boston Semi-Weekly Courier,* October 10, 1859. (Boston, MA).
940 This episode was told, in other words, on another source, adding interesting details about the Madeira used in this occasion: «At 12:30 all was in readiness. A few ladies and gentlemen, with Commodore James Sever, who was to perform the act of the christening, at their head, stood on the deck./ The signal was given, and the vessel slided gracefully into the water, a bottle of rare old Madeira wine, which had been thrice around the Cape, from the cellar of Hon. Thomas Russell, one of Boston's foremost merchants, being broken over her bows by the commodore. ...» *The Boston Herald,* March 27, 1893. (Boston, MA. Published in the article entitled "JUST NINETY-NINE YEARS AGO – George Washington Signed the Bill for a Navy.").
941 *Springfield Republican,* August 19 and 25, 1871. (Springfield, MA. Published at the rubric 'Eastern Massachusetts' of the section "New England News Items").
942 Located at 42 Beacon Street, on Beacon Hill, in Boston.
943 David Sears II (1787-1871), a prominent 19th century Boston philanthropist, merchant and landowner.
944 This private social club still exists, in Boston, on the same location.
945 This text was also published, untitled, in other words, in the following sources: *Salem Register,* August 21, 1871. (Salem, MA. Published in the section "ITEMS AND INCIDENTS"); *Jackson Daily Citizen,* August 23, 1871. (Published in

Sumner's First Days in Washington.[946]
[Correspondence of New York Graphic.]

Senator Sumner[947] recently met an old friend who enjoyed the honor of being the only man in Washington to live in the same house with him when in 1834 the future Senator first visited the capital. This was Dr. Blake, President of the Metropolitan Bank, and a member of the Board of Public Works. Dr. Blake was boarding at the house of Mrs. Pleyton, at the corner of the avenue and Four-and-a-half street, when young Sumner, tall, fresh and Bostonian, came there to lodge. He had just seen the first slave on the stageroad between Baltimore and Washington, regarded him with wonder, curiosity and indignation.[948] Before the guests had made up their minds what kind of a young he might be, the Marshall of the Supreme Court stopped with his carriage, and left the cards of all the Justices for him, a formality which made no little talk. This courtesy was due to Judge Story,[949] whose pupil Sumner was, and who had advised him at the termination of his studies to attend the Supreme Court, and get the spirit and association of that tribunal. At that time, all the Judges messed together in Mrs. Carter's boarding-house, which was recently torn down to extend the Capitol grounds. They drank what was called the Judicial Maderia,[950] an importation direct from Maderia[951] Island, which George Washington ordered through the port of Alexandria, and seeing his world-famed name in the order, the shippers picked out quite a superior pipe. When General Washington died, his nephew, Bushrod, who was a Justice in the Supreme Court, continued the annual order, and next John Marshall[952] fell heir to it, so that to hear Sumner relate the sequence gave one a kind of musty hilarity such as might have been felt at the tomb of Washington, if the old General had got up by request to join us in a glass of the original importation. The justices of the Court used their dining-table for consultation, and after they had messed together, the cloth was removed, and with nothing but the Judicial Maderia[953] and the laws of the republic, they tempered justice with mercy in their decisions.

Figure 74. Charles Sumner, who recounted the story of the Judicial Madeira, the wine cherished by the Justices of the U. S. Supreme Court. *Daguerreotype taken in 1855.*

Jackson, MI); *Massachusetts Spy*, August 25, 1871. (Worcester, MA. Published quoting the *Boston Journal*); *Newport Mercury*, September 2, 1871. (Newport, RI); *Sacramento Daily Union*, September 2, 1871. (Sacramento, CA).

946 *Sacramento Daily Union*, March 20, 1874. (Sacramento, CA); *Los Angeles Herald*, March 26, 1874. (Los Angeles, CA); *The Weekly Kansas Chief*, March 26, 1874. (Troy, KS. Published under the title "THIRTY-NINE YEARS AGO. The Late Senator Sumner's First Days in Washington.", adding that it had been written by the correspondent of the *New York Graphic*).

947 Charles Sumner (1811-1874), was an American politician and senator from Massachusetts.

948 It is not to wonder, since Sumner was the leader of the antislavery forces in Massachusetts.

949 Joseph Story (1779-1845), a native of Massachusetts, was an American lawyer and jurist who was appointed by President Madison as Chief Justice of the Supreme Court of the United States, where he served from 1811 to 1845. He is known for his magisterial work entitled *Commentaries on the Constitution of the United States*, first published in 1833, and which is considered a cornerstone of early American jurisprudence.

950 The right spelling is Madeira.

951 The right spelling is Madeira.

952 See Note 88.

953 The right spelling is Madeira.

"JIM" PARKER, OF THE ASTOR.[954]

More than a hundred thousand people who have been travellers will say, "Dear old 'Jim' Parker; he was a jolly good fellow," when they are now told of the death at New Bedford of James S. Parker, who was ten years manager for Stetson, of the Astor House.[955] When that – and now oldest – hotel in this city changed hands "Jim Parker" went "hoteling" on his own account, and has since kept the Vineyard House, near New Bedford, and hotels at Plymouth and Springfield. He was the first manager of the Stewart House at Garden City. "Jim" was known as a good manager for the "beginnings" of hotels, or under their "forlorn and worn-out circumstances." Although a rolling stone he gathered some moss. He was probably the best judge of Madeira wine in the United States, and could detect any acidity in it with the first whiff from the cork. As the hundred thousand travelers well knew, he knew how to be obliging without seeming to be conscious of that fact.

A Reminiscence of Hawthorne.[956]
Bowdoin College Correspondence N. Y. Tribune.

Figure 75. Jonathan Cilley made a bet with Nathaniel Hawthorne involving "a barrel of the best old Madeira wine". He won the bet but did not collect his wine because he was shot in a duel. Etching by J. B. Sears, ca. 1838.

In response to a call from Mr. Benson, Commodore Bridge[957] read an original document signed by Hawthorne and Cilley, of the class of 1825. Outside was the inscription:

"Mr. Horatius Bridge is requested to take charge of this and not open it until November 14, 1836, unless by the wish of both the undersigned.

(Signed.)   NATHANIEL HAWTHORNE.[958]

JONATHAN CILLEY.[959]

Dated Nov. 14, 1824.
Within was written:

"If Nathaniel Hawthorne is neither married nor a widower in 1836, I pledge my honor to pay him a barrel of the best old Madeira wine. Witness my hand and seal.

---

[954] *The World,* February 25, 1879. (New York City, NY).

[955] A luxury hotel in New York City, that opened in 1836 and soon became the most famous hotel in America. It was originally built by John Jacob Astor. In the late 1830's, in this hotel's wine list, there was a wide variety of Madeiras, that could be had by its guests, from $2 to $12 a bottle, as Frederick Marryat refers on his travel book. See section 10.8. of this anthology.

[956] *Cincinnati Daily Gazette,* July 14, 1875. (Cincinnati, OH).

[957] Horatio Bridge (1806-1893), a US Naval Commodore and author of the book *The Journal of an African Cruiser*, an excerpt of which we present on section 6.1.1.13. of this anthology.

[958] Nathaniel Hawthorne (1804-1864), who wrote several novels on which he included references to Madeira Wine, as we have seen on section 6.2.10. of this anthology.

[959] Jonathan Cilley (1802-1838), a native of New Hampshire and member of the House of Representatives, who died in office, at Bladensburg, MD, during a duel with Congressman William J. Graves. He had attended Bowdoin College, being a member of the famed class of 1825, which included future literary giants such as Nathaniel Hawthorne and Henry Wadsworth Longfellow.

"JONATHAN CILLEY."

"If I am, in 1836, either married or a widower, I pledge my honor to pay Jonathan Cilley a barrel of the best old Madeira wine. Witness my hand and seal.

"NATHANIEL HAWTHORNE.
"Nov. 14. 1824."

"To be delivered to Horatius Bridge and, if living, he shall, in 1836, transmit intelligence to the loser, and the bet shall be paid within a week.   "N. H. and J. C."

In 1836 Mr. Bridge opened the paper, and Cilley was making arrangements to pay the wager when his sudden death occurred.[960]

CAN INSECTS BE DROWNED?[961]

As an instance how long some insects may retain life when immersed in a fluid, I have been assured by a very ingenious and accurate gentleman that, being present at the opening of a bottle of Madeira wine which had been brought from Virginia to London, three flies were found in it.[962] He immediately observed that they had a fair opportunity

---

[960] This episode was widely spread in the American press years later, thus making it well known to the American readers, in four different versions. The first one, published untitled, presented this contents: «A curious document was produced at the Bowdoin College commencement dinner, last week, by one of their fellow classmates of 1825, in the shape of a wager between Nathaniel Hawthorne and Jonathan Cilley, November 14, 1824, Cilley betting a barrel of old Madeira wine that twelve years from that day Hawthorne would be married or a widower. Cilley lost, and was preparing to pay the forfeit when he fell in a duel.» *New York Commercial Advertiser,* July 15, 1875. (New York City, NY. Published in the section "GOSSIP OF THE DAY"); *Massachusetts Weekly Spy,* July 16, 1875. (Worcester, MA). In the second one, we can read the following text: «Nathaniel Hawthorne made a curious wager with Jonathan Cilley when both were in college in 1824. The memorandum in writing, dated Bowdoin College, November 14, binds Cilley to pay Hawthorne a barrel of the best old Madeira wine if Hawthorne marries before November 14, 1836. Hawthorne, who was a bashful youth, pledging himself in turn to pay Cilley the wine in case Hawthorne should still be a bachelor. Cilley lost, but was killed by Graves in a duel before he could pay the bet.» *St. Lawrence Republican,* January 13, 1892. (Ogdensburg, NY. Published under the title "Personal"); *Davenport Morning Tribune,* January 24, 1892. (Davenport, IA). Untitled and inserted in the section "A Batch of Remnants", this text was published in the following newspapers: *Oak Park Reporter,* January 22 and February 19, 1892. (Oak Park, IL); *Belleville Telescope,* February 12, 1892. (Belleville, KS). Under the title "A Curious Wager" this text was also revealed in these sources: *The Sunday Advocate,* January 17, 1892. (Ironwood, MI); *The Princeton Union,* January 28, 1892. (Princeton, MN). The third version was published in *The Boston Daily Globe,* July 12, 1875, (Boston, MA), under the title "Nathaniel Hawthorne's College Bet.": «Horatio Bridge of Washington, one of the famous class of 1825 at Bowdoin, produced a curious document at commencement, containing the terms of a bet between Nathaniel Hawthorne and Jonathan Cilley, a classmate. The bet was made, November 14, 1824, Cilley agreeing to give Hawthorne one barrel of old Madeira wine if the latter was not married or widower twelve years from that time, or November, 14, 1836, while if he did marry before that date, Hawthorne was to give Cilley the wine. Mr. Bridge was the custodian of the agreement, and at the appointed time notified Cilley that he had lost, but within the month allowed him to pay the forfeit, he died. He was regarded as one of the most brilliant members of his class, and had he lived would have had a public reputation equal to any of them.» The fourth text about this subject was printed in other sources, under a different title, "Why the Bet Was Not Paid": «Jonathan Cilley, the congressman who was killed in a duel, met his fate before he could discharge a singular obligation. A Maine man has discovered among his papers the articles of agreement of a wager between Jonathan Cilley and Nathaniel Hawthorne, dated at Bowdoin College Nov. 14, 1824. Hawthorne wagered a barrel of old Madeira that he would not be married twelve years later. He won, but Cilley was slain before he could pay.» *The Democratic Standard,* January 29, 1892. (Coshocton, OH); *Oshkosh Daily Northwestern,* January 30, 1892. (Oshkosh, WI); *Bismark Daily Tribune,* February 3, 1892. (Bismark, ND); *The Olean Democrat,* February 4, 1892. (Olean, Cattaraugus Co., NY). This text was also published, untitled and without the first sentence, in the following sources: *Galveston Daily News,* February 15, 1892. (Galveston, TX); *Daily Gazette and Bulletin,* March 16, 1892. (Williamsport, PA. Published in the section "THE WRITERS' SCRAP-BOOK"); *The Evening Times,* April 11, 1892. (Monroe, WI. Published in the section "MISSING LINKS").

[961] *California Farmer and Journal of Useful Sciences,* July 15, 1875. (San Francisco, CA).

[962] This famous episode happened to Benjamin Franklin, as we have seen before.

of trying the truth of the common opinion that a fly can not be drowned, and desired the company to lay the flies in the sun, the day being very warm: The flies were accordingly laid on a china plate, and in less than an hour two took wings. M. de Reumer kept bees under water nine hours, and all of them came to life. – *Old History*.

Washington Society in 1830.[963]

In former years the wildest gentlemen used to spend their evenings in decorously playing whist, with frugal suppers of broiled oysters, bread and cheese, and a glass or two of madeira. …

Assemblies were held once a week between Christmas - day and Ash-Wednesday, to which all the respectable ladies in the city who danced were invited. It was also customary for those of the Cabinet officers and other high officials who kept house to give at least one evening party during each session of Congress, invitations for which were issued. …

At ten the guests were invited to the supper table, which was often on the wide back porch which every Washington house had in those days. The table was always loaded with evidences of the culinary skill of the lady of the house. There was a roast ham at one end, a saddle of venison or mutton at the other end, and some roasted poultry or wild ducks midway. A great variety of some baked cake was a source of pride, and there was never any lack of punch with decanters of madeira. The diplomats gave champagne, but it was seldom seen except at the legations. …

TEA TABLE GOSSIP.[964]

Old Madeira wine has always been popular in Washington, especially on the tables of the Justices of the Supreme Court. For many years supplies were obtained from old mercantile houses in Alexandria, which had made direct importations prior to the Revolution, and in November 1852, many Washington cellars were replenished at the sale of private stock of the late Josiah Lee of Baltimore. Fifty demijohns of various brands of Madeira were struck off at prices ranging from $24 to $49 per gallon, and one lot commanded $15.50 per bottle, which, at five bottles to the gallon, is at the rate of $77.50.[965]

---

[963] *The Wellsboro Agitator*, April 6, 1880. (Wellsboro, PA); *Sacramento Daily Record-Union*, April 10, 1880. (Sacramento, CA).
[964] *The St. Paul Daily Globe*, November 17, 1884. (Saint Paul, MN); *Daily Alta California*, November 24, 1884. (San Francisco, CA. Published under the title "Madeira Wine."); *The Brooklyn Daily Eagle*, December 7, 1884. (Brooklyn, NY. Published under the title "Madeira Wine", adding that it had been transcribed from the *Pittsburg Dispatch*). As the first chapter of the text "Reminiscences of Public Men.", it was published in these sources: *The Daily Gazette*, December 18, 1884. (Fort Wayne, IN); *The Evening Sentinel*, January 6 and 8, 1885. (Le Mars, IA); *The Independent*, January 8, 1885. (Calliope, Sioux Co., IA); *The Malvern Leader*, January 8, 1885. (Malvern, Mills County, IA); *Palo Alto Reporter*, January 9, 1885. (Emmetsburg, IA).
[965] This article was also published in other sources, but containing a few more interesting sentences at the end: «Several pipes of fine Madeira were taken aboard Commodore Perry's fleet on its way to Japan, during the Fillmore administration, and President Fillmore brought many cases of it back to Buffalo when he retired from office. We believe there was none of it found when the inventory of Mr. Fillmore's cellar was taken, after the decease of his widow, and there is probably none of it in existence today.» *Plain Dealer*, November 21, 1884. (Cleveland, OH. Published under the title "Genuine Old Madeira." And reporting that it had been transcribed from the Buffalo Commercial Advertiser); *The Sun*, November 26, 1884. (Baltimore, MD. Published under the title "FINE OLD MADEIRA WINE.", adding that it been transcribed from the *Buffalo Courier*).

[Untitled][966]

George Coggswell, of Westernville, has brought to this office, says the Rome Sentinel, a black quarter bottle having upon its side a glass seal inscribed "W. Floyd, 1790." It was originally the property of one of the signers of the declaration of independence, whose name it bears. Nearly a century ago it undoubtedly contained a part of the pipe of Madeira wine which was awarded to Gen. Floyd[967] as his share of a prize captured by him as a privateer in the revolution. The more recent contents of the bottle were now cider.

THE LAST MAN CLUB.[968]
Only About Half a Dozen Members Left in the Organization.

There are about half a dozen members left in the famous Last Man Club. There were thirty-three members when the club was formed on Saturday, February 16, 1856, the membership being regulated by the number of States which at that time comprised the Union. Of the members twenty-nine were of the old inquirer office, three were of the *North American* office, and the remaining member was a young friend of Lafayette Horter, the West Philadelphia real estate man, who was only elected after much persuasion on the part of Mr. Horter, and who was the first member of the club to die.

Figure 76. William Floyd, one of the signers of the Declaration of Independence owned a bottle of Madeira Wine from 1790. *Oil painting on canvas by Ralf Earl, 1793.*

During the forty-four years of the club's existence, annual meetings or reunions have been held on the third Saturday of each February. There have been no new members admitted. As various ones of the original thirty-three have passed away, their names and the dates of their death have been duly recorded on the archives of the club. For many years the annual banquet table was laid with the customary thirty-three plates, and the chairs of the dead members set at their places around the festive board, but as the number dwindled this grew expensive and the practice has of recent years been discontinued.

It is one of the customs of the club when a member dies to have upon the table at the ensuing reunion a handsome bouquet of flowers, which is subsequently presented to the family of the departed one.

Stored away in the archives, kept under lock and key by Secretary and Treasurer Dyball, is a bottle of rare Madeira wine, which at the first meeting in 1856 was sealed in the presence of the entire thirty-three members. This old, dust-covered bottle is brought out at each reunion, but the seal has never been broken, nor will it be until all of the members are dead but one, and the last man will then drink the wine in silence and alone, pouring

---

966 *Watertown Daily Times,* October 31, 1885. (Watertown, NY).
967 William Floyd (1734-1821), an American politician from New York and a delegate for his homestate at the Continental Congress, from 1774 to 1776, and a signer of the Declaration of Independence.
968 *The Philadelphia Inquirer,* February 23, 1890. (Philadelphia, PA).

down a mental bumper to each of his old companions whom he has successfully distanced in life's race.

The forty-fourth reunion and dinner of the club was held last Saturday night at the residence of Robert Dyball, 926 Spring Garden street, where the occasions have been celebrated years past. Mr. Dyball is the oldest member of the club, and Walter W. Bell, the South Broad street real estate man, who has for several years been president of the club, the youngest.

William Lowrey, who has been employed continuously in the inquirer office since 1856, is one of the members, and confidently expects, although he will do so with great regret, to drink the wine so religiously preserved.

ORIGIN OF A FORTUNE.[969]
The Wealth of a British Peeress Comes from Wine.

Figure 77. Sir William Thomson, who inherited, through his second wife, part of the superb Madeira Wine stock of Charles R. Blandy. *19th century photograph. Author unknown.*

Inasmuch as Americans are the greatest appreciators and connoisseurs of Madeira wines, says the New York Record, it may interest them to learn that Lady Thomson, the wife[970] of the eminent scientist, Sir William Thomson,[971] who was created a peer of the British realm last New Year's day, is the daughter[972] of the well-known Funchal wine merchant, Charles R. Blandy,[973] now dead. When the oidium attacked the Madeira vineyards in 1852 Mr. Blandy, under the impression that the vines would never recover, invested over five hundred thousand pounds sterling in buying up all the good wine that he could lay his hands upon and eventually accumulated some eight or ten thousand pipes of choice varieties, ranging in value from two hundred dollars to two thousand dollars apiece. To lodge his wines Mr. Blandy was forced to purchase no less than forty buildings, among them being the Funchal theater,[974] which he ruthlessly transformed into a storehouse. It was here that I had an opportunity of tasting when last at Funchal a Madeira of the year 1760. The gem of the entire collection, however, was a rare Sao Martinho[975] Verdelho, rather more than fifty years of age, and possessed of a wonderful perfume. Old Mr. Blandy, who was a man of most genial and hospitable

---

969 *Muskegon Daily Chronicle,* March 10, 1892. (Muskegon, MI); *Middletown Daily Press,* March 12, 1892. (Middletown, NY); *The News Herald,* April 7, 1892. (Hillsboro, Highland Co., OH).
970 She was Thomson's second wife. His first wife, Margaret Crum, died on June 17, 1870, and he married Fanny four years later, on June 24, 1874.
971 Sir William Thomson (1824-1907), born in Belfast, the capital of Northern Ireland, was a mathematical physicist and engineer. For his work on the telegraphic project he was knighted by Queen Victoria, the first scientist upon which was bestowed such an honor, thus becoming the 1st Baron Kelvin.
972 Fanny Blandy, one of the three daughters of Charles R. Blandy, and 13 years younger than Thomson.
973 Charles Ridpath Blandy (1812-1879), an important member of the Blandys of Madeira, a family long associated with Madeira wine trade. Due to misunderstandings with his sons, Charles R. Blandy disinherited them and left his fortune in priceless wines to his daughters.
974 Teatro Esperança, once located then at Rua dos Aranhas, in Funchal.
975 The right spelling is São Martinho.

disposition, has now been dead for several years, and it is the fortune realized by him in the Madeira wine trade, and which he bequeathed to his daughter, Lady Thomson, that will enable her husband, the learned president of the Royal society, to maintain with befitting dignity his new title.

NINETY-THREE-YEAR-OLD WINE.[976]
Uncovered by Workmen While Demolishing the Old Van Rensselaer Mansion.
(Special to The World.)

ALBANY, Oct. 21. – Workmen engaged in tearing down the old Van Rensselaer manor house this week discovered a quantity of fine Madeira wine that had been hidden in the vaults for nearly a century.

The furniture and furnishings of the old house were removed about ten years ago, and the structure has been gradually falling into decay in the district now given up to foundries and factories. When it was finally decided that the old house would have to be dismantled the building was thoroughly searched from garret to cellar, so that no little odds and ends should be left behind. One result of this search was the finding of the old wine.

In one corner of the cellar is the old wine vault where were stored the sparkling liquors with which the patrons were wont to entertain their guests in the lavish hospitality of old Dutch Albany. It was thought that this had been cleared out years ago, but the workmen, poking into every nook and corner, discovered at last, snugly stored away in one of the bends, covered an inch thick with dust and cobwebs, a row of big, old-fashioned demijohns.

Figure 78. Stephen Van Rensselaer III, one of the wealthiest Americans of all times, had some precious demijohns of Madeira Wine of the year 1800 hidden in the cellar of his mansion, which were only discovered when it was being demolished. *Engraving by G. Parker, from a miniature by C. Fraser, c. 1835.*

With small regards for the traditions of the old house the men pried out a cork or two and started to enjoy their find. They found it, however, thick and not pleasant to their uncultivated taste, and the demijohns reached the heirs of the original owner with very little of the contents impaired. There were about fifteen demijohns of the wine left, some of them having become uncorked, allowing their contents to evaporate.

The jugs were labelled, and so far as the dusty tags could be deciphered the wine was Madeira, and had been laid down about the year 1800. This was during the time of the third Stephen Van Rensselaer.[977] The mansion has been untenanted for more than twenty years, since the death of Mrs. Stephen Van Rensselaer.[978]

---

976 *The World,* October 22, 1893. (New York City, NY). A shorter version of this text was published, untitled, in another source, in these terms: «Workmen engaged in tearing down the old VanRensselaer manor house at Albany NY the other day discovered a quantity of fine Madeira wine that had lain hidden in the vaults for nearly a century.» *The Wellsboro Agitator,* November 1, 1893. (Wellsboro, PA).

977 Stephen Van Rensselaer III (1764-1839), a native of New York, was the 2nd Lieutenant Governor of his homestate, as well as a statesman, soldier, land-owner and heir to one of the largest estates in New York, which made him the tenth richest American of all time.

978 Cornelia Paterson, his second wife.

The wine was at once carefully moved to a place of safety, and an expert wine-taster was brought from New York to pass judgment upon it. His report has not been received yet. It is estimated that there is enough of the wine to furnish twenty-two bottles for the representative of each of the twenty-seven heirs.

[Untitled][979]

Whenever one is presented with wine, it is always Madeira.

[Untitled][980]

The late William Minot,[981] of Boston, preserved a bottle of Madeira which had belonged to his father, William Minot,[982] the Secretary of the Harvard class of 1802,[983] and the bottle is now in the possession of William Minot, the third of the name, who was graduated from the Harvard Law School in 1868. The wine is apparently in excellent condition, and it is to be kept until 1902, when it will be drunk to the health of the class in whose year it was bottled. As all the class will be comfortably dead by that time, their health won't be visibly affected by the drinking. But the men who drink the wine may be particularly if they order enough large cold bottles to accompany the Madeira.

EARLY NORSE IMMIGRATION.[984]
A Spree at Funchal – Generous United States Proconsul.

The sloop "Restauration" plays pretty much the same part in the history of the Norwegian immigration of the nineteenth century as did the "Mayflower" two centuries earlier in the English immigration. The Restaurationer left Stavanger,[985] Norway, July 4, 1825, with fifty persons on board, and arrived at New York Oct. 9, the same year, with fifty-three persons on board, a baby girl having been born Sept. 2. This must now be looked upon as a well established historical event. But before it an incident connected with this voyage which borders on the mythical, and at least one Norwegian-American student of history is inclined to discredit it in toto.[986]

The story is briefly as follows: In some way which has not yet been accounted for the Restaurationer drifted out of its course as far south as the Madeira island. Before reaching this island a pipe of wine was found floating in the sea. The fluid was hoisted on board

---

[979] *The Bath Independent,* September 14, 1895. (Bath, ME. Published at the "Drift" section).
[980] *The World,* September 23, 1895. (New York City, NY. Published in the "Personal and Pertinent" section); *Newport Daily News,* September 28, 1895. (Newport, RI. Published but incomplete).
[981] William Minot (1817-1894), a Harvard graduate, from the class of 1836.
[982] William Minot Sr. (1783-1837), a Harvard graduate and Boston lawyer, who lived at 58 Beacon Street.
[983] Silas Weir Mitchell mentions in his text "A Madeira Party", also published in 1895, the fact that a bottle of Madeira Wine had been given to every Harvard student of this class. It all indicates that in the early 1800's it was a Harvard tradition to present a bottle of Madeira Wine to each student of any class, as a reminder of their graduation year.
[984] *The Saint Paul Daily Globe,* March 22, 1896. (St. Paul, MN).
[985] Norwegian city and municipality, being the third largest urban zone and metropolitan area.
[986] The writer should have meant to say "in total".

the sloop, and the emigrants drank so freely of its contents that they became unable to manage the sloop, which drifted into the harbor of Funchal without colors. Fearing that the sloop might bring some contagious disease, the commander of the fortress[987] ordered a cannon to be aimed at it. But just in the nick of time one of the emigrants hunted up a Norwegian flag, which he ran up to the top of the mast, thus averting danger of having the sloop shelled. The matter was now explained, and the Norsemen received much attention at Funchal. The American consul gave them a large quantity of provisions, including grapes, and before leaving the whole party was invited by the consul to a magnificent dinner.

O. N. Nelson,[988] who has spent several years of patient work in preparing a history of the Scandinavians of the United States, the first volume of which work appeared three years ago, has scrutinized the accounts of this story very carefully, and has come to the conclusion that additional light on the subject would not be amiss. Some one having expressed doubt as to the existence of an American consulate at Funchal at the period in question.[989] Nelson some time ago wrote to the secretary of state for information on that point.

THE KENNEDY WINE.[990]
Major Hancock Tells How the Madeira Was Brought to This Country.
COMMODORE'S PERRY'S SCHEME.
It Was Made to President Fillmore[991] and His Cabinet.
And All Agreed to Take a Cask – Major Hancock Was Consul of the United States at Malaga from 1831 Until 1879 – He Drank Some of the President's Wine and Also Some of Mr. Kennedy's.

The publication in the Sun of Tuesday of some interesting facts concerning the history of the rare old "Japan" madeira wine[992], which once belonged to the late John Pendleton

---

[987] Forte de Nossa Senhora da Conceição, located at the top of "Loo Rock".
[988] Olof Nickolaus Nelson (?-1917), author of the book *History of the Scandinavians and Successful Scandinavians in the United States*, published in Minneapolis, MN, in 1893. This book had several other editions, in 1897, 1900 and 1969.
[989] The U.S. Consulate in Funchal was established in 1790, being the first one created in Portuguese territory, due, in large part, to the extensive wine trade between the island and America.
[990] *The Sun*, December 24, 1896. (Baltimore, MD).
[991] Millard Fillmore. See Note 117.
[992].This article referred to a disputed auction sale of Madeira wine and was published under the title "RARE OLD WINES. Once Owned by John Pendleton Kennedy, of Maryland, and by Charles Bruce, of Virginia." From it we selected this excerpt: «About 500 bottles of rare old Madeira and sherry wines were sold yesterday at the auction rooms of Matthews and Kirkland, 32 and 34 South Charles street. The prices ranged from $1 90 to $6 50 per bottle, and the total amount obtained was $1,561 30. for 525 bottles./ The wines came from two estates. Three hundred and twenty-seven bottles and a five-gallon demijohn of "lees," all of it Madeira, came from the wine cellar of the late John Pendleton Kennedy, the Maryland novelist and statesman, who was secretary of the United States Navy during the administration of President Fillmore./ One hundred and thirteen bottles of Madeira, 67 bottles of sherry and 17 other bottles, whose character was not determined, came from the estate of the late Charles Bruce, of "Staunton Hill,"Va., father of State Senator William Cabell Bruce, of Baltimore./ The Kennedy wines have several interesting stories connected with them. Mr. Kennedy died in the summer of 1870 at Newport, R. I., and his wine cellar passed into the possession of his widow. Mrs. Kennedy died in 1889, and the Kennedy home, at 12 West Madison street, became the property of her sister, Miss Martha E. Gray. Miss Gray died in the spring of 1895, and after the furniture in the house had been sold for the purpose of settling up her estate, her executors, Messrs. Reverdy Johnson and John D. Donaldson, unexpectedly discovered this wine in a wine-cellar underneath the house. It was in demijohns and last fall the two gentlemen had it "racked off" into bottles./ Two of the varieties were of well-known brands, 27 bottles of "Dun & Co." of the vintage of 1833, and 50 bottles of "Blackburn" vintaged in the same year. Three other varieties were discovered, one of the vintage of 1837, to which the name of "Thomas" was given, and two of unknown dates, which were labelled "Japan" and "Washington." Of the "Thomas" there were 36 bottles, of the "Washington" 5 and of the "Japan" 207./ The "Japan" wine has a link which binds it to one of the noted events in the history of this country. Mr. Kennedy was Secretary of the

Kennedy[993], the Maryland statesman and novelist, and which was purchased Monday by Mr. W. W. Spence, has led to the discovery of other facts in relation to it through the recollections of Major A. M. Hancock.

It was stated at the sale that the wine was part of a cask brought back from the Island of Madeira by Commodore Perry when he returned from his famous Japan expedition in 1853, and by him given to Mr. Kennedy, who had been Secretary of the Navy in the cabinet of President Fillmore at the time when Commodore Perry had set out, and had been active in furthering the ends of the expedition.

Major Hancock was a close friend of both President Fillmore and Mr. Kennedy, and the history of Commodore Perry's wine was told to him on several occasions by both of these gentlemen, but more particularly during the winter of 1864-5, when President Fillmore was the guest of Major Hancock at Malaga, Spain, and during the winter of 1868-9, when Mr. Kennedy was his guest at the same place. Major Hancock was United States consul at Malaga from 1861 until 1879.

Figure 79. John Pendleton Kennedy, the 21st United States Secretary of the Navy, possessed a rare Madeira Wine that had been purchased by Commodore Perry, in 1852, and had travelled to Japan and back to America. In 1896, a lot of that wine still existed and was sold at a high price. *19th century engra-ving. Author unknown.*

The story, as Major Hancock had it from the lips of the two famous men, was that Commodore Perry[994] had been present at the last cabinet meeting in Washington prior to his departure. As he was making his adieux he said to President Fillmore that he expected to stop at the Madeira Islands, either on the outward or return voyage, and that he would be glad to bring back a cask of the wine if the President would order it. President Fillmore never drank wine himself and rarely served it to his guests. "I gave the order to the Commodore," he afterward said to Major Hancock, "without thinking what I was doing. He turned to the members of my Cabinet, and they, too, told him to obtain a cask of the wine for them."

Commodore Perry's stop at Funchal, in the Island of Madeira, was made on the outward voyage,[995] according to the best recollection of Major Hancock, and the casks of wine which he bought there were taken to Japan on his ship and thus mellowed by the tropical heat to which it was exposed. It was probably a number of years old when bought in 1853, so that its present age is not far from fifty years.

When the Commodore returned from Japan, Fillmore was no longer president. He was living in Buffalo, and one day he was surprised to receive from a New York customs broker a bill for a cask of wine, duties and commission upon it. For several days he was deeply puzzled to remember, where he had ever ordered any wine, but finally he recalled

---

Navy in 1852, when Commodore Perry was sent with a fleet for the purpose of trying to open up commercial relations with Japan. Mr. Kennedy took such an active part in furthering the expedition that Commodore Perry on his return voyage, having met with entire success, stopped at the Island of Madeira and purchased a cask of wine for the Secretary as a token of personal thanks for his valuable aid in opening up the Oriental Empire. [...]» The Sun, December 22, 1896. (Baltimore, MD). Contrary to what this article states at the end, this wine was bought on Perry's outward voyage to Japan.

993. John Pendleton Kennedy (1795-1870), a native of Baltimore, MD, was an American novelist and whig politician who served as United States Secretary of the Navy between 1852 and 1853, during President Fillmore's administration.
994 See Note 298.
995 This is correct. See sections 6.1.1.16. and 6.1.1.17. of this anthology.

the suggestion of Commodore Perry and his assent to it. He paid for the wine and stored it away in the cellar of his home. Major Hancock drank some of it on the occasion of a visit to President Fillmore a year before the President's death in 1874.

"I was never told that Mr. Kennedy's wine was obtained in a different way from Commodore Perry," said Major Hancock, "and I always believed that he had bought and paid for it. I drank some of it at Mr. Kennedy's home on several occasions. I remember very well one dinner at which he gave me some of it shortly after he had been my guest at Malaga. The narratives of President Fillmore and himself were gone over by us at that dinner.

"During the civil war Mr. Kennedy removed the wine from the original cask and put it into demijohns in order to transport it with others of his rare wines for safe keeping in New York city."

9.6. Madeira Wine used for Medicinal Purposes

Throughout the 19th century Madeira Wine was also used in America for medicinal purposes and it was common to see it in some hospitals, to be administered to convalescent patients. Here are a few examples of it, two of which are ads advertising pure Madeira Wine "fit for medicinal use". This section starts with a recipe for a treatment to two conditions, one of them being gout, using Madeira Wine. This is interesting since, specially in the second half of the 19th century, some people in America accused this product of causing gout, which was utterly denied by others.

CURE FOR THE RHEUMATISM OR GOUT.[996]

Take 4 ounces of Colchicum Seed, steep it in one quart of Madeira wine; let it stand ten days, when it will be fit for use; strain it through a flannel, and take from one to one and a half tea spoons full three times a day until relieved. Should it sicken the stomach, either stop taking or take less quantity. The same seed will answer to steep once more with the same quantity of wine

PURE MADEIRA WINE.

THE subscriber has imported in the Mexican Capt. Deming, direct from the respectable house of *George & Robert Blackburn & Co, Madeira*, a supply of their best Madeira, "the produce of the best situations on the island." It can safely be recommended as pure, and fit for medicinal use.
87   E. W. BULL,
july 13—6md&w]   Sign of the "Good Samaritan."

The Connecticut Courant, December 21, 1839. (Hartford, CT).

---

996 *Daily National Intelligencer*, May 1, 1833. (Washington, DC).

A DOCTOR OF SPIRIT.[997]

We find the following spirited card in the Chicago Tribune, of August 5:
To the Editors of the Tribune:
I learn from various sources, that the Board of Health officers complain of my using Madeira wine and brandy too freely at the City Hospital. I am willing to admit that I use all that I deem necessary for the sick, (and also for myself,) and I shall continue to do so as long as I remain in my present condition. I must be faithful to the trust confided in me and conscientiously perform every duty it imposes. If this course does not meet the sanction of the Board of Health they are at perfect liberty to supply my place at any time.
DR. W. B. GREENMAN, City Hospital.

OLD MADEIRA FOR THE SICK.[998] – J. B. Couret, the well-known proprietor of the Ruby, 118 Common street, has for sale by the bottle or gallon, some very superior Madeira wine (over twelve years old), which is exactly right for convalescents. He is selling this wine at moderate prices and solicits a call.

9.7. Oïdium Tuckery – The Madeira Vine Disease of 1852 and its consequences

In 1852, a severe blight – the *oïdium tuckeri* – fell upon the vineyards of Madeira, which resulted on an almost total failure of the wine production of that year. From tens of thousands of pipes produced on previous years, in 1852 the yield was reduced to just a few hundreds, which left everyone in despair on an island where wine was the staple product and the main article of exportation, and also a source of revenue to many people. Without wine to sell, the landowners would face bankruptcy and the peasants destitution and famine.

By then the United States was one of the main importers of Madeira Wine and news of this tragic occurrence were soon revealed by its main newspapers. Next we present a selection of twenty-one articles dealing with this topic, published between 1852 and 1853, and arranged chronologically, in which it will be seen how the Americans learned about this terrible event that caused a widespread panic both in Madeira and in America.

[Untitled][999]

We learn from Madeira that the wine growers are much alarmed by the appearance of blight among the vines.[1000]

---

997 *Alexandria Gazette,* August 14, 1854. (Alexandria, VA).
998 *The Daily Picayune,* August 25, 1878. (New Orleans, LA).
999 *The Charleston Daily Courier,* August 13, 1852. (Charleston, SC).
1000 Seven days later, the same source reiterated this fact, in other words: «There has been a complete failure of the vintage in the Island of Madeira.» *The Charleston Daily Courier,* August 20, 1852. (Charleston, SC).

9.7. OÏDIUM TUCKERY – THE MADEIRA VINE DISEASE OF 1852 AND ITS CONSEQUENCES

Items by the Franklin.[1001]

… Most disastrous accounts had been received from Madeira, and it seemed not improbable that the celebrated wine of Madeira will be a matter of history. A blight of some sort has entirely destroyed the vintage for this year, and seems likely to destroy the vines themselves. It appears in the shape of a thick white powder, which entirely covers the clusters of grapes. The inhabitants have memorialized the Portuguese Government to be permitted to cultivate tobacco.[1002] …

Madeira.[1003]

A complete failure in the vines and vintage of the Island of Madeira is announced.

WINE FAILING.[1004] – From Madeira we learn that the wine-growers are much alarmed by the appearance of blight among the vines.

THE VINE ROT.[1005] – Accounts from Madeira, Italy, Sicily, various parts of France, and the neighborhood of Lisbon, mention the appearance of a disease in the grape, called by some "Mangra,"[1006] by others "Oidium," which at first appears like small dust on the green berry, causing the fruit to burst and ultimately to become putrid – and something similar has affected the currants, in the islands of the Levant.[1007]

LATE FOREIGN ITEMS.[1008]

… The grape crop of Madeira has failed. …

1001 *Albany Evening Journal,* August 17, 1852. (Albany, NY). Under the title "Madeira Wine", and with some slight differences in the first sentence, this text was published in the following sources: *Daily Evening Transcript,* August 19, 1852. (Boston, MA); *The Sun,* August 19, 1852. (Baltimore, MD); *The Daily Picayune,* August 26, 1852. (New Orleans, LA); *Albany Evening Journal,* September 17, 1852. (Albany, NY). This text was also published, untitled, in other newspapers: *Alexandria Gazette,* August 20, 1852. (Alexandria, VA); *The Portsmouth Journal of Literature & Politics,* August 21, 1852. (Portsmouth, NH); *Daily National Intelligencer,* August 28, 1852. (Washington, DC.)
1002 A similar article was published, later on, in other newspapers, on the section of the news from Portugal: «Application had been made to the Cortes by the people of Madeira, praying them to grant permission for the free growth of tobacco in that Island, as the grape crop had entirely failed.» *Albany Evening Journal,* September 6, 1852. (Albany, NY); *North American and United States Gazette,* September 7, 1852. (Philadelphia, PA); *Pennsylvania Inquirer,* September 7, 1852. (Philadelphia, PA).
1003 *North American and United States Gazette,* August 18, 1852. (Philadelphia, PA. Published in the "Foreign News" section).
1004 *Weekly Wisconsin,* August 18, 1852. (Milwaukee, WI).
1005 *The Sun,* August 23, 1852. (Baltimore, MD); *The Daily Picayune,* September 2 and 3, 1852. (New Orleans, LA).
1006 Portuguese word for oidium.
1007 Designation of the eastern Mediterranean litoral between Anatolia and Egypt.
1008 *Green Bay Spectator,* August 24, 1852. (Green Bay, Brown County, WI).

[Untitled][1009]

The vine disease is making great ravages in France and Spain, and at Madeira fears are expressed of the total destruction of the vines on the island.

News of the Day.[1010]

… Extract from a letter dated Madeira, August 3^d: – We much regret to inform you of the entire failure of the Vintage this season – the grapes having been destroyed by a disease, similar to what which appeared in France in 1847. Wines have advanced at least 30 per ct., since our last advices to you. …

ADVANCE IN WINES AND BRANDIES.[1011] – The *Express* states that there has been quite an advance in wines and brandies within the last week or ten days, owing to the reported short grape crops in France, Spain, &c., and a further material rise is predicted soon. All through the Island of Madeira it is said that the vine has suffered severely, and in some parts wholly destroyed; so that there will be little if any wine for export next year. This will be a severe blow to the inhabitants, as the grape is to them what potatoes are to a large part of Ireland – the principal support.

[Untitled][1012]

The grape disease which has done so much mischief to the vineyards in the island of madeira, is not confined to that region alone. An article in the German papers, dated Turin,[1013] August 6th, says, that it is very common in Sardinia.[1014] It has been known in that kingdom for several years past, but now it is said there is not a corner in the whole land which is free from it. All the methods taken to check its progress have proved ineffectual, or at best are mere palliatives.

The Madeira Vintage.[1015]
Extract from a letter received per ship Versailles, 9th inst., dated

FUNCHAL, ISLAND OF MADEIRA,
20th July, 1852

MESSRS. W – & B – , Richmond, Va.

1009 *The Pittsfield Sun,* August 26, 1852. (Pittsfield, MA).
1010 *Alexandria Gazette,* August 30, 1852. (Alexandria, VA).
1011 *Newark Daily Advertiser,* September 10, 1852. (Newark, NJ).
1012 *The Charleston Daily Courier,* September 11, 1852. (Charleston, SC); The Daily Picayune, September 16 and 17, 1852. (New Orleans, LA).
1013 City of northern Italy, capital of the Piedmont region.
1014 A former independent island in the Mediterranean, who joined Italy in 1861, of which it is nowadays an autonomous region.
1015 *Alexandria Gazette,* September 16, 1852. (Alexandria, VA).

9.7. OÏDIUM TUCKERY – THE MADEIRA VINE DISEASE OF 1852 AND ITS CONSEQUENCES

DEAR SIRS – "We regret to inform you that the prospects of our coming vintage have been completely destroyed by the visitation of a devastating disease, technically called *Oidium Tuckeri*, which attacks the fruit in the form of a minute white fungus, covering the grape so thickly that its growth is completely blasted. – The whole island, from North to South and from East to West, is affected by this disease, and our season is now sufficiently advanced to enable us to assert that not a gallon of Wine will be produced in Madeira this year. A similar calamity has never before been felt here, and its effect on the farmers and peasantry is distressing to contemplate. Holders of Wine have already increased their prices 25 per cent.
Yours very truly,
OLIVEIRA & DAVIES.

THE PLAGUE IN MADEIRA.[1016] – The Boston *Journal* says: The following extract from a letter written by an eminent physician at Funchal, Madeira, to a friend in Boston, disproves the reports[1017] which have been published, of the presence of the plague in that Island.

MADEIRA, FRIDAY, JULY 30, 1852.
Until your letter arrived, I had no idea of the ridiculous report circulated in some American papers. The whole tale is a pure fiction. There is no plague nor any disease of malignity in the Island. Madeira is well known to be remarkably exempt from severe calamities of the kind. The Brazil steamers calling off the Island, and always put into quarantine, have had a few cases of yellow fever on board; but as to the existence on shore, the whole tale is unfounded.

Some dreadful disease has attacked the grapes, which all appear shriveled up. The vintage is entirely lost, and some report that the vine itself is deceased. Should this prove true, we may have the unhappy experience of a visitation in this place equal to the potato disease in Ireland. The poor and rich will all suffer; the proprietors from the failed crops – the poor laborers from want of employment.

This Island, to its shame be it spoken, produces only about three month's consumption of food.

The thermometer to-day, noon, (July 30,) stands at 65° Fahrenheit. So temperate is our Summer.

1016 *The New York Daily Times*, September 22, 1852. (New York City, NY). This newspaper assumed its present-day denomination – *The New York Times* – in 1857. Another version of this text was published in another source: «NO PLAGUE IN MADEIRA. – A letter has been received in N. Y., dated Gibraltar, from Dr. F. J. Bumstead, of Boston, who passed the winter in the Island of Madeira. In reference to a report that went the rounds of the papers some two months since, that the plague had broken out in Madeira, he writes: "Madeira is the last place in the world for the plague to make its appearance. They have never had even the cholera there, notwithstanding the tendency to bowel complaints on the island." Madeira, according to Dr. B., is blessed with one of the most agreeable, balmy, and healthy climates that is known to exist, and is eminently adapted to persons subject to pulmonary complaints, as a winter residence.» *State Gazette*, May 29, 1852. (Trenton, NJ).

1017 One of the earliest news about this subject was published in Virginia, and reported the following: "THE PLAGUE. It is stated that much apprehension is felt in New Orleans of the approach of a new disease which is called the plague, and is now said to be prevailing in some of the West India Islands./ We see by the papers that a disease called by the same name, has made its appearance in some parts of the West. It is said to be like the cholera, but more fatal./ Whether it is the same disease as that which goes by the name of plague in the East, is not stated./ The Boston Medical Journal alludes to the subject as follows: "It is very certain, from the accounts received both here and in England, that the true plague has been introduced into Madeira, and the work of death has been really appalling. [...]» *Alexandria Gazette*, March 18, 1852. (Alexandria, VA). This report indeed circulated afterwards in several other American newspapers, from March to July, thus spreading these fake news about the island, even after the publication of Dr. Bumstead's text, which was also duplicated in other sources for quite some time, until October of the same year.

9. MADEIRA WINE IN THE AMERICAN PRESS

[Untitled][1018]

The news from Madeira is, that almost all the fine vines of that island have been destroyed, and some persons say, that the wine of that name will soon only be a matter of history.

[Untitled][1019]

Advices from Madeira represent the island to be in a lamentable state of destitution, owing to the entire failure of the grape harvest.

Great Distress at Madeira.[1020]

From a communication addressed to the *London Times* by a prominent mercantile firm at Liverpool, we learn that much suffering exists at Madeira, in consequence of the failure of the grape crops.[1021] A circular from the Governor of the Island, makes the following representations and appeal:

"Deeply lamenting the calamitous loss which this island has suffered by the entire destruction of its vintage, occasioned by the blight which has unfortunately annihilated its principal production, I think it proper to call your attention to the disastrous effect which this loss will have on the landholders, farmers, and laboring classes of this island. The landed proprietors and farmers have this year thus suffered most heavily from the annihilation of their crops; and the laboring classes will suffer equally with them, by the entire cessation of the labor which the preparation and treatment of the wines have hitherto required. In consequence of this calamity these classes will be reduced to the greatest distress, and their subsistence become almost impossible, if not extraneous succors be provided for their relief. I feel entire confidence in the solicitude of Her Most Faithful

---

1018 *Albany Evening Journal,* September 27, 1852. (Albany, NY).

1019 *North American and United States Gazette,* October 19, 1852. (Philadelphia, PA. Published in the "Foreign Items" section).

1020 *The New York Daily Times,* October 22, 1852. (Published in New York City, NY); *North American and United States Gazette,* October 23, 1852. (Philadelphia, PA). A summary of this text was published in other sources, in these terms: «GREAT DISTRESS AT MADEIRA. – The failure of the vintage, resulting from the recent blight upon the grape, has produced the greatest distress among the inhabitants of Madeira, and threatens with absolute starvation large masses of the laboring classes. Ribeiro, the Civil Governor of the Island, has issued a circular acknowledging the impotence of the Portuguese Government to meet the emergency, with any thing like adequate relief, and appealing to the Christian sympathies of foreign nations for aid to avert the impending calamity. He invokes the instrumentality of the Funchal merchants to make known the distressed situation of the country to their correspondents in Europe and America. Landed proprietors and laborers are alike victims of the calamity, the one from the annihilation of their crops, and the other from the entire cessation of the labor which the preparation and treatment of the wines have hitherto required. [*Journal of Commerce*]» *Daily National Intelligencer,* October 25, 1852. (Washington, DC); *Alexandria Gazette,* October 27, 1852. (Alexandria, VA); *The Georgia Telegraph,* November 9, 1852. (Macon, GA); «The failure in the vintage crop of Madeira, has caused great distress and threatens starvation to large masses of the laboring classes. Don Ribeiro, Civil Governor of the Island, has issued a circular acknowledging the impotency of the Portuguese Government in the matter, and appealing to foreign nations for sympathy and aid. Landed proprietors and laborers are alike the victims of this calamity – annihilation of the former, cessation of labor to the latter.» *The Boston Daily Atlas,* October 25, 1852. (Boston, MA. . Published untitled).

1021 This first sentence was revealed in another source, namely at the *Pennsylvania Inquirer,* on October 23, 1852. (Philadelphia, PA).

Majesty's[1022] Government to relieve as much as in their power, the suffering population of this island; but the distress is so great, and presses so heavily on every class, that it will find it impossible to extend commensurate relief. Particularly as the extraordinary defalcation in the revenue hitherto derived from this island will tend still further to embarrass the already attenuated circumstances of the general treasury. Under these circumstances, I have thought it my duty to call the benevolent attention of the principal mercantile establishments of Funchal to the distressing crisis now impending over so large a portion of the unfortunate inhabitants of the island, in order that they, being in constant communication with the wealthy cities of Europe and America, may make known abroad the present distressed situation of the country, and solicit the liberality of their correspondents and connections in behalf of its unfortunate population, now threatened with all the horrors of starvation. I abstain from making a more direct application; but I am convinced that those whom I now address, who have at all times shown the greatest solicitude in all that tends to the general welfare of the island, will now do all in their power to contribute to the relief of a community suffering under so severe a dispensation.

"Palace of the Civil Government in Funchal, Aug. 24, '52.[1023]

"JOSE SILVESTRE RIBEIRO,[1024] Civil Governor.

Figure 80. José Silvestre Ribeiro, the Civil Governor of Funchal in 1852, who sent a circular to the prominent Funchal foreign merchants urging them to write to their acquaintances and business partners at home, both in Europe and America, asking them to provide relief for the distressed Madeirans, threatened by starvation, due to the dreadful failure of the grape crop, their only means of subsistance. *Litograph by António Joaquim de Santa Bárbara.*

By Telegraph to the Transcript.[1025]
FROM OUR N. Y. CORRESPONDENTS, ABBOT AND WINANS.

… **DISTRESS IN MADERIA.**[1026] The failure of the vintage, resulting from the blight upon the grape, has produced the greatest distress among the inhabitants of Madeira, and threatens with absolute starvation large masses of the laboring classes. …

1022 Queen Mary II of Portugal (1819-1853), a member of the House of Braganza who was Queen of Portugal for two terms, from 1826 to 1828 and from 1834 to 1853.
1023 The Portuguese version of this Circular was published in the Madeiran newspaper *A Ordem,* of November 27, 1852.
1024 José Silvestre Ribeiro (1807-1891), a native of Idanha-a-Nova, Portugal, who served as Civil Governor of Madeira from 1846 to 1852, being one of the most cherished Governors the island had in the 19th century, due to his energetic actions, in several fields, while in office.
1025 *Daily Evening Transcript,* October 23, 1852. (Boston, MA).
1026 The right spelling is Madeira.

[Untitled][1027]

Great distress is said to exist in Madeira in consequence of the failure of the vintage, and in consequence of the inability of the Portuguese Government to provide relief the sympathy of foreign nations is invoked.

[Untitled][1028]

The failure of the vintage, resulting from the recent blight upon the grape, has produced the greatest distress among the inhabitants of Madeira, and threatens with absolute starvation large masses of the labouring classes. Ribeiro, the civil governor of the Island, has issued a circular acknowledging the impotence of the Portuguese government to meet the emergency with anything like adequate relief, and appealing to the Christian sympathies of foreign nations for aid to advert the impending calamity. He invokes the instrumentality of the Funchal merchants to make known the distressed situation of the country to their correspondents in Europe and America. Landed proprietors and laborers are alike victims of the calamity, the one from the annihilation of their crops, and the other from the entire cessation of the labor which the preparation and treatment of the wines have hitherto required.

MADEIRA WINE CROP.[1029] New York, Dec. 26. By the arrival of the brig Eliza Waite, 30 days from Madeira, we learn that the quantity of wine produced by this year's crop will fail short of the usual quantity, and consequently the operatives are in considerable distress.

THE DISTRESS on the Island of Madeira.[1030] – This famous Island contains 100,000 inhabitants – most of whom are now on the verge of starvation, as their harvest has fallen for the first time in two hundred years.

The culture of the vine has been the chief occupation of the inhabitants of Madeira for more than two centuries; in many parishes, from the nature of the soil, the warmth of the climate, and the want of water, nothing else can be advantageously grown.

The vintages average from twenty five to thirty five thousand pipes, and up to the present year, *never* failed. But the last vintage was almost a total failure; in many districts where thousands of pipes of wine had annually been made, not a grape was gathered; and in the whole island the vintage did not amount to a hundred pipes of good wine. The condition,

---

1027 *The Charleston Daily Courier,* October 27, 1852. (Charleston, SC).
1028 *Illinois State Register,* November 15, 1852. (Springfield, IL).
1029 *Daily Evening Transcript,* December 27, 1852. (Boston, MA); *The Boston Daily Atlas,* December 27, 1852. (Boston, MA); Similar articles, under the title "FROM MADEIRA", were published in these other sources: *Public Ledger,* December 27, 1852. (Philadelphia, PA); *Boston Semi Weekly Courier,* December 30, 1852. (Boston, MA. Adds that the brig's name was *Eliza Wait* and it was oriented by Capt. Hutchinson); *The Daily Picayune,* January 4, 1853. (New Orleans, LA. It also states that the brig was named *Eliza Wait* and its Capt. was Hutchinson). Under the title "MADEIRA WINE CROP" this telegraphic dispatch was published in these sources: *Daily Evening Transcript,* December 27, 1852. (Boston, MA); *The Boston Daily Atlas,* December 27, 1852. (Boston, MA).
1030 *Weekly Wisconsin,* February 2, 1853. (Milwaukee, WI).

therefore, of the Madeira people – those who were formerly in good circumstances, as well as the poor laborer – is woeful in the extreme; and unless foreign assistance be given them, many of them must die of starvation.

The Island of Maderia.[1031]

The following statement of deplorable condition of the inhabitants of the island of Maderia, is communicated to the New York *Commercial Advertiser* by E. T. BUNSTEAD, Esq:

"These poor Islanders are oppressed by the corrupt Government of Portugal, and hampered by the old Metayer system[1032] of division of land, which deprives them of all incentive to a far-sighted cultivation of their grounds, and to the execution of improvements, which, in a short time, might render them independent of any such reverse in their crops as has been their lot in the past season.

The labor which they are obliged to undergo, under the most unfavorable circumstances, to earn their daily bread, is almost incredible. A more hard-working and industrious people I have never known. Constantly, during my ride about the island, I saw bands of men, women, and children, coming down from the high barren mountains with immense loads of brush on their heads, and dragging after them an equal quantity attached to their waists by means of cords. To procure one such load, they were obliged to walk, including going and coming, from ten to twenty miles, over the steepest and most rugged paths; they must be up early and go to bed late to accomplish their tasks within a day; and yet, from ten to twenty cents a day was all they obtained for it.

Often have I gone out at midnight, on one of the little terraces that clothe the sides of the amphiteatre of mountains about Funchal, and, under the magnificent starry sky of that latitude, listened to the stroke of the pickaxe of some laborer, who was still working on his small plot of land, with the consciousness that by far the larger number of those strokes went to enrich others, and not to feed and clothe his half-starved wife and children.

The cheapness of labor astonishes every visitor to the island. A good seamstress can be hired for ten cents a day, and a mere trifle is paid for the most beautiful embroidery and artificial flowers. A man is obtained to take care of your horse, and follow, clinging to his tail, in your daily drives, for from two to four dollars a month, not including food. And yet that the cost of living is not proportionally cheap is shown by the fact that good board can nowhere be obtained for less than fifty dollars the lunar month.

The records of the hospital at Funchal for the year 1847, of which I have a copy, show that during the year, twenty-one patients were brought there for no other reason than they were in a state of starvation;[1033] and to what extremity they were reduced before seeking this asylum, may be inferred from the fact that nineteen of the twenty-one died at the hospital. This number at first sight may appear small out of a population of 108,000; but it must be observed that the hospital is difficult to access to the inhabitants of other parts of the island, requiring patients to be borne on litters over the high central ridge of mountains; and, moreover, that poverty and exposure in most cases induce active diseases,

---

1031 *The Alton Weekly Courier,* February 25, 1853. (Alton, IL). The right spelling is Madeira.
1032 The Metayer system refers to the cultivation of the land for a proprietor by one who receives a proportion of the produce, as a kind of sharecropping.
1033 In 1847 the potato crops failed in Madeira, which lead the island to a starvation crisis.

which would be admitted to the hospital under their appropriate names, so that their cause would not so clearly appear on the books. Looking at it in this light, the fact is an index of great general want during an ordinary season.

The larger part of the arable land at Madeira is occupied by the vine. The island produces only three month's consumption of food, under its present cultivation.

Let this fact be known, and the present condition of the island will be better understood. Food for the other nine months is imported, and paid for out of the small wages earned by labor on the vineyards.

This year, the grapes have entirely failed from disease of the vines, and the inhabitants are cut from employment, and all means of earning their daily bread.

It is not that there is not import flour there for sale; provisions are really cheaper on the island this season than usual; but the poor have no means of obtaining money wherewith to buy them.

It is not that there are not more wealthy merchants on the island, with generous hearts and open hands, as every stranger who has visited the island and experienced their noble hospitality can testify. They have done much, and are constantly doing much, to relieve the distress, though they themselves have suffered severe losses by the failure of the crops; but, even if they impoverished themselves, they could not adequately relieve the present want, without assistance from abroad. To add to the umprofitableness of this season, a panic seems to have seized those who usually resort to the island for health, in Winter, at the report of a "failure" existing there, and, from ignorance of the fact that a person with money can live as well and cheap as ever, and the number of visitors is very much less than usual; thus another means of employment, in the service of strangers, is cut off.

A letter in behalf of Madeira was recently published, from the lady of one of our late most distinguished naval officers, now spending the Winter at Funchal; and I conversed yesterday with a gentleman who has just arrived from the island, and confirms the numerous reports that have reached us of the present wretchedness of the poor inhabitants.

A ship is now fitting out to carry them relief in provisions and money. Let those who are able contribute their part, and they may be assured of blessings from the poor Madeirese,[1034] who never receive a penny in charity without pressing it to their lips and kissing it."

9.7.1. United States' Relief for Madeira

The United States of America was one of countries to which aid was requested in order to mitigate the menace of famine that threatened the impoverished Madeirans, due to the failure of the grape. John Howard March, the American Consul, played a key role in the entire process of securing relief for Madeira, by writing to his influential acquaintances in America, among which were Jacob A. Westervelt, Mayor of New York, and John Adams Dix, a distinguished politician, who had visited Madeira some years before. His appeal was heard and funds and food would be gathered and sent to the island from three important cities (which were also large importers of Madeira Wine), New York, Boston and Philadelphia, each of which dispatched a ship with provisions, a synonym of the philanthropic heart of the Americans.

1034 The right spelling is Madeirense(s).

Below is a set of eighty-eight articles, from different sources, published between 1852 and 1854, organized in chronological order, containing the appeals sent from Madeira and those published in Philadelphia, New York and Boston on behalf of the poor Madeirans, and many others about the relief gathering process in these three main cities, through which we can see how the entire process was developed, with a special emphasis on New York, where a Madeira Relief Committee would be created. These articles are complemented, in footnotes, with data from Madeiran newspapers.

The Sufferers of Madeira.[1035]

It will be seen by the following brief appeal that an effort is in progress in this city to raise contributions in behalf of the suffering and the poor of the Island of Madeira. It is to be hoped that the response will be prompt and liberal. Donations of money and provisions should be sent directly to the citizens below, who have kindly consented to appropriate them in the proper manner: –

TO THE BENEVOLENT. – The entire failure of the crop of the celebrated Grape of the Island of Madeira has produced a state of unexampled distress among a large portion of its inhabitants. The poor classes, who derive from the exportation of the famous wines the only means by which they can garner the necessities of life, are by this visitation of Providence reduced to a deplorable condition. Those among them as cannot manage to leave the Island should perish, if aid be not extended sufficient relief enabling them to live through the coming winter. The spring will, no doubt, restore them to their usual state and bring back the means of subsistence. Under these circumstances the undersigned Frederick Stoever, F. J. Figueira,[1036] S. A. Martinez who have voluntarily formed themselves into a committee for the purpose of making collections of money to be applied in the purchase of useful and necessary articles of food, here to be shipped from this port for the relief of the poor of Madeira, make an earnest appeal in their behalf to the humane and charitable of their fellow citizens in Philadelphia. They guarantee the faithful application of any sums that may be subscribed for the above purpose, and will most cheerfully, not only contribute to the fund, but give their time to the proper discharge of the duties of the Trust they assumed, so managing as to make it available in the uttermost most extent, for those for whose benefit it is designed.

1035 *Pennsylvania Inquirer*, November 18, 1852. (Philadelphia, PA). This appeal, the first one published in America in behalf of the island's sufferers, was translated into Portuguese and published in the Madeiran newspaper *O Progressista*, of April 6, 1853, preceded by the following introduction: «We publish today the following appeal to the charity of the inhabitants of Philadelphia in behalf of the Madeirans afflicted by so many evils; an action spontaneously taken in our benefit by Mr. Fortunato Joaquim Figueira, a son of Madeira, as soon as he was informed of this calamity by his Brother-in-law, the landed proprietor Mr. Joaquim José de Faria Bettencourt, through a letter written on August 1st 1852./ The date of the appeal for subscriptions, that yielded the large alms recently arrived at our port on the bark *Aaron* [J. Harvey], is previous to the knowledge in that city of the appointment of any Committee by the American Consul in this land./ The cargo consists of 4720 bushels of corn, 220 barrels of crackers, 100 barrels of flour, 25 ditto of corn flour, and other objects of small value, all adding up to 5,800$000 réis, the result of the subscriptions./ Due to the lack of time we do not add the comments of some of the circumstances that accompany this shipment. But on the next edition, after the due acknowledgements to such notorious act of our fellow countrymen, we will make some reflections.»

1036 Fortunato Joaquim Figueira was a Madeiran merchant who lived in Philadelphia. He was very instrumental in getting the help that was gathered in that city for the benefit of his distressed fellow countrymen.

They cannot but hope in this laudable and disinterested effort, they will be kindly encouraged and cordially aided by all who have in their power to give, and who sympathize with the sufferers. A statement of the amount received and the manner of its distribution, will be at a proper season communicated to the contributors.
Philadelphia, 1852.[1037]

SUFFERING IN MADEIRA.[1038] – A voluntary committee of citizens of Philadelphia has been formed to collect money to purchase food to be shipped for the relief of the poor in the Island of Madeira, where the failure of the crops is producing suffering.[1039]

We invite attention to the following
Appeal to America.[1040]
DISTRESS IN THE ISLAND OF MADEIRA.

1037 On the following week another newspaper from Pennsylvania gave a brief account of the discovery of the island, on these terms: «MADEIRA. This beautiful and fertile Island, now desolated by famine, to relieve whose wants our benevolent citizens are now making collections to purchase and ship provisions for their relief, was first discovered by Gonzalves Zarco, a Portuguese, in the year A. D. 1419. He commanded two small vessels, fitted out for the occasion, by the Infant Don Henry, of Portugal. Zarco reared a Cross, and a Priest consecrated the ground as "Santa Cruz." Funchal is named after mountains covered with *Fennel*, which is *Funcho* in Portuguese. The Island was destitute of inhabitants Zarco called his discovery "Madeira," or the "Island of Wood." In the following year, 1419, he again sailed for Madeira, to plant a Colony, carrying with him animals of various kinds – cuttings of the Vine and Olive, and Lemons and Oranges. The discovery of Madeira, is attributed to a Moor, who was the pilot of Gonzalves Zarco, named Juan, and who acted as the pilot of his vessels, who had been made a captive, and carried into Fez when four or five years old, in company with an English sailor, who had been the mate of a ship, that was foundered in the Atlantic; and who had been able to reach Madeira; so that the real discoverer of the Island, was Robert Machin, an Englishman, whose mate imparted the knowledge to the pilot Juan.» *Public Ledger*, November 23, 1852. (Philadelphia, PA).
1038 *The Sun*, November 22, 1852. (Baltimore, MD); *The Charleston Daily Courier*, November 26, 1852. (Charleston, SC); *Daily Alabama Journal*, November 27, 1852. (Montgomery, AL).
1039 A summary of this article was published in other sources, on these terms: «Citizens of Philadelphia are now making a collection to purchase and ship provisions to Madeira, to alleviate the famine there prevailing.» *State Gazette*, November 27, 1852. (Trenton, NJ); *The Charleston Daily Courier*, November 29, 1852. (Charleston, SC); *The Dixon Telegraph*, December 18, 1852. (Dixon, IL).
1040 *The Evening Post*, December 28, 1852. (New York City, NY). Under the title "DISTRESS IN THE ISLAND OF MADEIRA", and preceded by the following introduction – «Our readers are already aware of the fact that the vintage of Madeira has been almost a total failure the past season, and that, instead of 20,000 pipes of wine – the average harvest – scarcely 1,000 will be produced. The failure of this harvest, combined with the rot in the potatoes, has caused great suffering amongst the laboring classes of the Island, and we cheerfully comply with the request to publish the following appeal, wishing that our citizens will respond to it with their characteristic and usual liberality:», – this text was published in these sources: *Semi-Weekly Courier and New York Enquirer*, December 31, 1852. (New York City, NY); *Pennsylvania Inquirer*, January 7, 1853. (Philadelphia, PA). Under the same title but without the short introduction, this appeal was published in the following sources: *Daily National Intelligencer*, December 31, 1852. (Washington, DC); *The Charleston Daily Courier*, January 1, 1853. (Charleston, SC); *North American and United States Gazette*, January 5, 1853. (Philadelphia, PA). In this last source the appeal was preceded by the following introduction: «WE HAVE ALREADY furnished the details of the calamity which has befallen the island of Madeira; and we trust that the appeal which is inserted below will meet a ready response in this community. Donations will be received by Messrs. Robert Adams & Co., north side of Walnut street, above Fourth.» This appeal was also revealed in the Madeiran press, namely in *A Ordem*, of December 4, 1852, both in English and Portuguese, under the titles "DISTRESS IN THE ISLAND OF MADEIRA" and "MISERIA NA ILHA DA MADEIRA". Other than only sending this appeal to America, it was also sent to different people in Great Britain (London, Liverpool, Manchester and Bristol), in France (Paris), in Russia (St. Petersburgh) and Germany (Berlin and Hamburg). The English version of this text was also published in two other Madeiran newspapers of that time, namely *O Amigo do Povo*, of December 4, 1852, and *O Progressista*, of December 11, 1852. The Portuguese version of this appeal was republished, two months later, on a supplement of *A Ordem*, of February 26, 1853.

9.7. OÏDIUM TUCKERY – THE MADEIRA VINE DISEASE OF 1852 AND ITS CONSEQUENCES

A calamity has fallen on Madeira unparalleled in its history. The vintage, the revenue of which furnished the chief means of providing subsistence for its inhabitants, has been a total failure, and the potato crop, formerly another important article of their food, is still extensively diseased. All classes, therefore, are suffering, and as there are few sources in the island to which they can look for food, clothing and other necessities of life, their distress must increase during the winter, and the future is contemplated with painful anxiety and apprehension.

Under such appalling prospects, the zealous and excellent civil Governor, Senr.[1041] José Silvestre Ribeiro, addressed a circular letter to the merchants of Madeira on the 24th of August last,[1042] for the purpose of bringing the unfortunate and critical position of the population under his Government to the notice of the benevolent and charitable classes in foreign countries, and in the hope of exciting their sympathy with, and assistance to, so many of their fellow-creatures threatened with famine. His Excellency's appeal having been responded to by various parties to a limited extent, and expectations having been raised that, with a systematic organization and management, very considerable succors would be forthcoming, he has named us, in an alvara[1043] of the 22^d inst., as a committee to receive and superintend the distribution of all such money and other articles as may be placed at our disposal, towards the alleviation of the suffering and indigent classes in the island.

We willingly accept the trust with which his Excellency has charged us, with an earnest desire to promote the laudable work of charity which he has so much at heart; and although we do so with a fervent determination to use all the means in our power to discharge it to the advantage of the distressed, and to the satisfaction of the philanthropic contributors toward their relief, we undertake the duty with a full knowledge of its difficulty, in the hope that we can calculate upon the counsel and co-operation, when applied for, of the numerous persons in the island possessing intelligence and local knowledge, and in the full reliance of experiencing, in all our actions, every necessary indulgence. The undernamed parties have kindly undertaken to receive subscriptions, and to transmit them to the island:

IN AMERICA.
Messrs. Boorman, Johnson & Co.,
Messrs. March & Benson,
George M. Lewis, Esq., New York
William Depew, Esq.,
Messrs. Robert Adams & Co., Philadelphia

Geo Stoddart,[1044] Richard Davies

1041 Abbreviation for Senhor, or Mister, in English.
1042 Published in the *London Times,* as we have already seen.
1043 Portuguese word for charter.
1044 George Stoddart, the English Consul in Funchal, was appointed by the Civil Governor of Madeira, José Silvestre Ribeiro, President of a Committee officially created by him on the 22nd of November 1852, who was in charge of receiving and distributing whatever funds that were gathered abroad on behalf of the poor of Madeira. He and the other members of this Committee, in which was included the American Consul, John Howard March, and George Hasche, Richard Davies (treasurer) and Nuno Alexandre de Carvalho (secretary) signed this Appeal.

J. Howard March, Nuno A. Carvello.[1045]
Geo. Hasche.
Madeira, Nov. 25, 1852.

MADEIRA.[1046] – The inhabitants of the island of Madeira are said to be in a deplorable condition. There has been an almost total failure of the vintage this year, depriving them of their principal means of subsistence. In addition to this the potato crop is nearly destroyed by the rot. A number of gentlemen in New York have formed themselves into a committee to receive subscriptions for their relief.

RELIEF FOR MADEIRA.[1047] An appeal has been made in New York in behalf of the inhabitants of the ill-fated island of Madeira, just now severely suffering from famine, in consequence of the total failure of the vintage, the revenue from which furnished the chief means for providing their subsistence. The potato crop is also extensively diseased, and we can readily believe, therefore, that the situation of the people is deplorable in the extreme.[1048]

MADEIRA.[1049] An appeal is made to the benevolent of this country, in behalf of the people of Madeira, who are suffering from the almost total failure of the crops. The vines generally yield 20,000 pipes of wine. This year they will not yield over 1000, and the potato crop is also a failure. The people of Madeira are poor, and starvation threatens them. Let this appeal to the humane not be without its fruits.

MADEIRA.[1050]

1045 Nuno Alexandre de Carvalho.
1046 *Albany Evening Journal,* December 29, 1852. (Albany, NY).
1047 *Daily Evening Transcript,* December 30, 1852. (Boston, MA); *Alexandria Gazette,* December 30, 1852. (Alexandria, VA. Published untitled).
1048 Another version of this text was also revealed in the American press: «RELIEF FOR MADEIRA – Subscriptions are being taken up in New York for the relief of the inhabitants of the ill-fated island of Madeira, in consequence of the total failure of the vintage, the revenue from which furnished the chief means for providing their subsistence.» *The Sun,* December 30, 1852. (Baltimore, MD).
1049 *Daily Evening Transcript,* January 1, 1853. (Boston, MA).
1050 *New York Daily Tribune,* January 7, 1853. (New York City, NY); *Milwaukee Daily Sentinel,* January 13, 1853. (Milwaukee, WI. Published without the last four paragraphs). Under the title "FAMINE IN THE ISLAND OF MADEIRA", and divulging only the second and third paragraphs (the latter incomplete), this text was printed in the following sources: *The Sun,* January 13, 1853. (Baltimore, MD); *The Adams Sentinel and General Advertiser,* January 17, 1853. (Gettysburg, PA); *The Charleston Daily Courier,* January 17, 1853. (Charleston, SC); *Daily National Intelligencer,* January 17, 1853. (Washington, DC). Published under the title "FAMINE IN MADEIRA" and preceded by the following text: «We published lately an article briefly describing the suffering to which the people of Madeira have been reduced, and the still greater degree of suffering with which they are threatened – even to absolute starvation – by the unprecedented failure of the last year's grape crop – wine being the staple product of the island, and on which alone the population depended for subsistence – all their breadstuffs being brought from abroad, and chiefly from the United States. We add to-day, on this subject, so interesting to our humanity, a letter from CHARLES W. MARCH, Esq., a well-known American gentleman, at present visiting Madeira. The letter of Mr. March makes a strong appeal to the sympathy of our country in favour of an honest and simple and Christian people, who have dealt constantly and largely with us for more than half a century past, and been purchasers and consumers of our produce to the amount of millions of dollars. We insert the letter in the hope

Fearful Destitution.

Correspondence of The N. Y. Tribune.

ISLAND OF MADEIRA, Dec. 5, 1852.

You doubtless have heard of the failure of the Grape this year in Madeira: but you cannot know the extent of suffering already caused by the failure, nor the fearful apprehensions of still greater calamities it naturally excites.

The Wine is the staple and almost sole production of the Island. The annual vintage has afforded for many years past an average of twenty-five to thirty-five thousand pipes of Wine. *There has not been produced this year one hundred pipes of salable wine on the whole Island.* It needs but this statement to afford you a definite idea of the awful calamity that has fallen upon these people.

None, it is true, thus far have died of famine; there are few, however, but have felt its menace or its actual presence. The wealthy curtail their expenditures; those of sufficient means heretofore practice a stringent economy; persons of more cramped resources sell day by day whatever ornaments they may have of better days, at ruinous prices, while the poorest class fill the streets and beg. And this is but the beginning of the days of Famine. How many months of misery, of agony, of starvation, indeed to thousands, are yet in reserve, no man can foresee. Without aid from abroad, death alone can terminate the sufferings of the population. For, destitute of provisions, destitute of all save their trust in God, what hope can they have in life but an early death?

They are a mild, patient, laborious, devout people; kind to each other, careful of and attentive to strangers; obedient and reverential toward their priests. They respect man and fear God. In a population of upward of one hundred and thirty thousand souls, I know not where you will find so much contentment and so little vice.

I enclose you a copy of the appeal put forth at the instance of the Governor, and signed by the English and American Consuls and other gentlemen of consideration in this place.[1051] It is short and comprehensive, and will, I doubt not, meet with a full response.

The Portuguese, it is true, have no influence upon the elections in the United States; they cannot aid in political demonstrations there, nor determined by their numbers and union the success of either of the great political parties of our country. But they are Christians – they are men – they are sufferers, and I know my countrymen too well not to feel what such an appeal will be signally responded to.

It is well remembered here and often repeated, that when some years since famine in a less fearful form threatened the neighboring Cape de Verd Islands, the Americans rushed to their rescue; an from full hands, scattered among the starving population, money and provisions; recalling thousands to a grateful existence.

The inhabitants of these islands, with greater claims to our sympathies, because under greater sufferings, hope for equal charity. They, besides, are not unmindful that, for nearly two centuries, an intimate social and mercantile relationship has subsisted between their

---

that it may give rise to some active measures amongst us to raise assistance for our suffering fellow-creatures in a distant land:»). The very same portion of this text was also published untitled in *The Washington Reporter,* of February 2, 1853. (Washington, PA. Published in the section "GENERAL NEWS.", preceded by this introductory sentence: «A letter from the Island of Madeira, dated Dec. 5, referring to the failure of the vintage, says:»).

1051 Already presented on this section, under the title "APPEAL TO AMERICA".

island and our country; that the first colonies of North America had hardly escaped European tyranny and the rage of the seas before they sent to this island the products of their labor – staves, and corn and other food – to receive in return the product of the vine. Our country, too, is as well known to the world for its acts of beneficence as for its deeds in arms, and rescued Ireland blazons its history no less than conquered Mexico. I hope that our countrymen will not be tired in well-doing, but will now come forward and sustain, in so good a cause, their well deserved reputation; that these poor people may also feel how great in disinterested kindness is the heart of the GREAT REPUBLIC; and then, though the fig-tree has not blossomed, neither is there fruit in the vine; though the labor of the olive has failed, and the fields have yielded no meat, yet shall they rejoice in the Lord, and in their prayers of thanksgiving invoke blessings upon the American name!

With the hope that you will publish the inclosed statement, and lend some portion of your great influence in furtherance of its views. I remain, ever very respectfully and faithfully, your friend and servant.

HORACE GREELEY, Esq.[1052]
CHS. W. MARCH.[1053]

[Untitled][1054]

The people of the Island of Madeira are said to have great distress, owing to the shortness of the vintage this year. We notice that Messrs. Boorman, Johnston & Co., of New York, and other gentlemen of that city and Philadelphia, have been appointed to receive contributions in behalf of the famishing inhabitants of the island.

MADEIRA.[1055]

The people of this small but delightful island are on the brink of starvation; the fact is beyond doubt. We have published the circular announcing it of a number of the most respectable mercantile firms of our City, as also the more circumstantial letter of our friend Charles W. March, now on a visit to that island… The cause simply is the dependence of the population almost wholly on the cultivation of the Vine, and the utter failure of the Grape harvest in 1852. With Wine they have been accustomed to buy most of their food and all their clothing; and, the Grape having failed, they have nothing wherewith to pay; and while the wealthy and forehanded are pinched, the poor are reduced to the last

---

1052 Horace Greeley (1811-1872), to whom this letter was addressed to, was the founder of the *New York Daily Tribune*, America's most influential newspaper from the 1840's to the 1870's. Charles W. March was, himself, a member of the editorial staff of this paper, although he does not mention it on his letter.

1053 This article was written by Charles Wainwright March, a former journalist of the *New York Daily Tribune* and nephew of the American Consul in Funchal, Madeira, who had arrived at the island two months before.

1054 *The Daily Picayune*, January 7 and 8, 1853. (New Orleans, LA). A similar article to this one was printed in another source: «An unparalleled calamity has visited Madeira. - The vintage on which the inhabitants mainly depended for their means of subsistence is a total failure, and the potato crop an important article of food for them is extensively diseased. All classes are suffering for food, and the distress is increasing with the advance of the winter. An appeal is made to the merchants and people of other countries for contributions to alleviate this distress, and committees are designated in New York and Philadelphia to receive and forward contributions.» *Illinois Daily Journal*, January 14, 1853. (Springfield, IL).

1055 *New York Daily Tribune*, January 10, 1853. (New York City, NY).

extremity. Of the 80,000 inhabitants of the island, probably 60,000 are to-day needy, while 40,000 must perish unless assisted from abroad.

They must be helped; and our City must do her part toward it. The cost of one good cargo of Flour would never be felt by our men of property, and it should be made up before the week is out. We trust there will be a meeting held at the Exchange forthwith, and a numerous Committee appointed, who will canvass the business portion of our City vigorously promptly. Meantime, let none who can give hesitate to send their money at once to Messrs. Boorman, Johnson & Co., March & Benson, or some others of the Committee already named in our columns.

When this money shall have been raised, and the dire necessities of the sufferers relieved, we may proffer one more remonstrance against the fatal system which has now (and by no means for the first time) reduced the Madeirans to this extremity – the system glorified by our present Governor[1056] in his late Agricultural Address as '*Commercial* Farming'[1057] – that system, namely, which devotes an entire farm, district, county, island, or country, to the production of some one, two or three great staples to which it seems peculiarly adapted, to the neglect of everything else. It is a system which makes rich merchants and extensive commerce, but a squalid, dependent, miserable Laboring Class, at times reveling in luxury, then suddenly plunged into famine and despair. Madeira could support *all* her people if she sedulously developed all her resources and grew her own food; it is the inordinate extension of her wine-producing industry that is now starving her. She must mend her hand after being lifted over this chasm, or the benevolent will grow weary of helping her.

THE ISLAND OF MADEIRA.[1058] The recent accounts from the Island of Madeira represent the inhabitants as on the brink of starvation, and these accounts have been confirmed, in a circular of a number of respectable mercantile houses in New York. The cause of this destitution is the utter failure of the grape harvest of 1852, the cultivation of which is their sole dependence for support. With wine they have been accustomed to buy most of their food and all their clothing; and, the grape having failed, they have nothing wherewith to pay, and while the wealthy and forehanded are pinched, the poor are reduced to extremity. Of the 80,000 inhabitants of the island, probably 60,000 are today needy, while 4,000 must perish unless assisted from abroad.

The New York Tribune, in speaking on this subject, calls upon the merchants of that city to take immediate steps to contribute for the relief of these starving inhabitants, and says, very truly, that "the cost of one good cargo of flour would never be felt by our men of property, and should be made up before the week is out."

It seems to us that the condition of the inhabitants of Madeira calls upon our merchants as well as New York, for prompt assistance. A large business has been done between this island and Boston, and we can see no reason why we should be backward in lending a helping hand to relieve the great suffering which now prevails in Madeira. Shall there not be a move in the right quarter in Boston immediately?

[1056] Horatio Seymour (1810-1886), who served as Governor of New York from 1853 to 1854 and from 1863 to 1864.
[1057] Presented at the State Fair of Utica, NY, in 1852, in which he divided the history of farming into two eras, that of the axe, and that of commercial farming.
[1058] *Daily Evening Transcript,* January 11, 1853. (Boston, MA); *Daily Missouri Republican,* January 24, 1853. (St. Louis, MO. Published under the title "THE MADEIRA SUFFERERS." and presenting only the first paragraph).

RELIEF FOR THE MADEIRA SUFFERERS.[1059] – The present condition of want and suffering among the inhabitants of the Island of Madeira, consequent upon the almost entire failure of the fruit and grapes, their chief product, with the potato and some other crops, the past season, must awaken concern in every Christian community, and lead to the bestowal of prompt and efficient aid. The accounts which we have from time to time published from the island, show that the greatest distress already prevails especially among the poor, over whom starvation impends, and the richest even can obtain a bare subsistence in the midst of so great a scarcity. In some of our cities steps have already been taken to forward relief, and it cannot be doubted that the citizens of Baltimore on this, as on similar occasions heretofore, will gladly respond to any practical scheme of benevolence for supplying the wants of the unfortunate people of the island. An opportunity for doing this presented by P. Tiernan & Son, No. 5 North Charles, near Baltimore street, who have been requested by our Consul at Madeira and the committee there to solicit donations from the citizens of Baltimore "All the resources of the people having failed, unless we have aid from abroad, (write the committee,) death alone can terminate the sufferings of the populations." Any donations made, will be duly acknowledged and immediately remitted by the gentlemen above named.

THE STARVING OF MADEIRA.[1060]
To the Editors of the Advertiser:

Permit me to call attention through your columns to wants which some of our townsmen may be willing to aid in relieving.

It has already been made known in general terms that great distress has been produced in Madeira by the complete failure of the last year's vintage. But it has not yet been brought home to us that thousands of the inhabitants of that island are in danger of starvation. So entire has been the interruption to their usual employments, so scanty are the resources upon which they can fall back for assistance, that they are daily approaching the very extremities of destitution and suffering.

A circular signed by the leading merchants of the island, amongst others, by our highly esteemed Consul, J. Howard March, Esq., makes the following statement: "A calamity has fallen on Madeira, unparaleled in its history. The vintage, the revenue of which has furnished the chief means for providing subsistence for its inhabitants, has been a total failure, and the potato crop, formerly another important article of their food, is still extensively diseased. All classes, therefore, are suffering, and as there are few sources in the island to which they can look for food, clothing, and other necessaries of life, their distress must increase during the winter, and the future is contemplated with painful anxiety and apprehension." This sad story is confirmed by private letters. One says, "It will be necessary to

---

1059 *The Sun,* January 14, 1853. (Published in Baltimore, MD).
1060 *Boston Daily Advertiser,* January 17, 1853. (Boston, MA). A summary of this article was also published, on the same day, on another Boston newspaper, under the same title, in these words: «Mr. Samuel Eliot, No. 2 Channing street, in a communication to the Advertiser, calls attention to the sufferings of the inhabitants of Madeira, which we mentioned last week; and requests those who are disposed to contribute to their relief to send it to his office, and he will promptly forward it. We have been surprised that some action has not been taken by our merchants.» *Daily Evening Transcript,* January 17, 1853. (Boston, MA).

ask for aid from abroad. I fear without this, many must perish from hunger. – Another says, "The distress is not exaggerated." – A third says, "The condition of the people, – those who were formerly in good circumstances, as well as the poor laborers – is woeful in the extreme; and unless foreign assistance be given to them, many of them must die of starvation. It is feared that the hospital and the poor houses must be closed, as the sources of their maintenance are nearly exhausted.

In view of this alarming condition in which the inhabitants of Madeira are placed, in view, likewise, of the excellent character which they have always borne amongst those acquainted with them, it has seemed to me that an appeal in their behalf, might reasonably be made to the humanity of our citizens.

Whatever any one may contribute to the relief of this afflicted people, shall be promptly forwarded, if left at my office, No. 2, Channing street.
SAMUEL ELIOT.[1061]

Figure 81. Samuel Eliot, a famous Boston historian, was very influential and active in the process of securing relief for Madeira from his city. Litograph published in the Boston Athenaeum, 1907.

[Untitled][1062]

The barque Nautilus is chartered to carry supplies to the starving inhabitants of Madeira. The public are invited to send any articles of food, or of light clothing, to the vessel, lying at India wharf. Notice of the articles thus sent may be left at 39 India wharf.

Distress in Madeira.[1063]

The beautiful island of Madeira is threatened with the most appalling visitation. Last year the vine crop, almost the sole resource of the people, failed, and distress amounting almost to a general famine was the result. It is feared that another failure of the grape crop will succeed to the former, and the condition of the inhabitants be still more deplorable. The Governor of the Island has issued a circular, appointing agents in European and American cities, to receive and forward such aid as may be extended to the poor famishing people. Messrs. MARCH & BENSON, at No. 5 New street, New York, are the agents for that city and this State. They are connected with a house at Funchal, Madeira.

1061 Samuel Eliot (1821-1898), a native of Boston, MA, and a Harvard graduate, was an historian, educator and public-minded citizen, who played a key role in securing relief from his city to the Madeiran sufferers, in 1853.
1062 *The Boston Daily Atlas,* January 21, 1853. (Boston, MA); *The Boston Herald,* January 21, 1853. (Boston, MA. Published under the title "RELIEF FOR MADEIRA." and complemented by the following sentence at the end – "We trust the unfortunate inhabitants of Madeira will be cheered by liberal donations from our citizens."); *Boston Semi-Weekly Courier,* January 24, 1853. (Boston, MA. Published under the title "RELIEF FOR MADEIRA." and complemented with another sentence at the end: "The whole grape crop of the island has been cut off this season, and the people have been left in a state of abject poverty.").
1063 *Albany Evening Journal,* January 21, 1853. (Albany, NY).

Judge Denio,[1064] of Utica, spent some months upon the island a few years since, and thus speaks of it and its inhabitants: –

"Madeira lies about 600 miles from the coast of Spain, the nearest civilized country. It contains about 100,000 inhabitants, the greatest part of whom are engaged in cultivating the vine, from which the Madeira wines are produced. They have no other article of export. The island being a volcanic rock, with a scanty though fertile soil, interspersed with ravines and rising into lofty elevations – only a very small amount of breadstuffs and edible vegetables can be raised. It is reckoned that the whole annual produce of the island, exclusive of the vintage, would not support the population for more than two months. The residue of their subsistence, which has never been abundant, has been obtained in the shape of flour and meal, received in exchange for their wines, from the United States and Europe. This residue being cut off, and the means of the merchants of Funchal crippled from the same cause, it is difficult to see how the poor people can escape starvation, unless the wealthy and charitable of other lands shall be induced to come to their relief in their sore calamity.

"During a residence of about five months in the island in the winter of 1849-50, I acquired a very favorable opinion of the laboring population of Madeira. They are, it is known, of Portuguese origin, and attached to the Roman Catholic Church. They are faithful to their engagements, industrious in their habits, and mild and amiable in their dispositions."

Touching appeals have been made in behalf of the starving population of Madeira, but have they been responded to? We have heard of no movements. The population of that Island is not so large but that it might be relieved from this state without inconvenience.

THE STARVING POPULATION OF MADEIRA.[1065] – We are glad to learn that benevolent men in our community have already come forward in a considerable number to aid in the relief of the sufferers at the island of Madeira. We have seen a subscription paper bearing the names of seven or eight of our liberal merchants for a hundred dollars each, and a larger number for smaller sums. A very short space of time remains before the sailing of the Nautilus, which we learn must sail on Wednesday, the 25th last – *Advertiser*.

FOR MADEIRA.[1066] Alluding to the fact that a vessel has been chartered at Boston to sail for Madeira with supplies for the suffering people of that island, the Providence Journal remarks: "A ship load of food sent to Madeira will be a better propagandist of republican principles than a ship load of arms sent to any part of the world. This kind of foreign intervention is better than Kossuth's.[1067] It will carry the American name to the homes and hearts of thousands, and send it up in grateful prayers to Heaven."

1064 Hiram Denio (1799-1871), a native of New York, was an American lawyer and judge, being chief judge of the New York Court of Appeals from 1856 to 1857 and from 1862 to 1865.
1065 *The Boston Herald,* January 24, 1853. (Boston, MA).
1066 *Daily Evening Transcript,* January 24, 1853. (Boston, MA).
1067 Lajos Kossuth de Udvard et Kossuthfalva, better known as Louis Kossuth (1802-1894), was an Hungarian lawyer, journalist, politician and Regent-President of the Kingdom of Hungary during the Revolution of 1848-49.

9.7. OÏDIUM TUCKERY – THE MADEIRA VINE DISEASE OF 1852 AND ITS CONSEQUENCES

Sufferers in Madeira.[1068]

We observe that the barque Nautilus is now loading at Boston, with provisions, &c., for the relief of the sufferers by the famine which has prevailed for some time past in the Island of Madeira. Our readers will remember that a similar movement is in progress in this city, and we trust Philadelphians will in this case exhibit their characteristic generosity by giving of their abundance a little food to the starving inhabitants of that lovely but unfortunate island.

DISTRESS IN THE ISLAND OF MADEIRA.[1069] – The undersigned having received from friends in Madeira authentic intelligence of the fearful destitution, so suddenly and severely brought upon the inhabitants of that Island, by the destruction of the vine and potato, – and some of them having personal knowledge of the facts, – respectfully invite the benevolent citizens of New-York to assemble at the Astor House,[1070] Monday evening, the 24th inst., at 7 o'clock, to take measures for the relief of those unfortunate sufferers.

(Signed) Jacob A. Westervelt,[1071] John A. Dix,[1072] Jon Van Buren,[1073] Henry M. Burden,[1074] Clement D. March,[1075] Moses H. Grinnell,[1076] Simeon Draper,[1077] J. Prescott Hall,[1078] Junius T. Stagg,[1079] Charles A. Stetson,[1080] Robert B. Coleman.[1081]

NEW-YORK, Jan. 22, 1853.

1068 *Pennsylvania Inquirer,* January 24, 1853. (Philadelphia, PA); *Daily Alabama Journal,* January 31, 1853. (Montgomery, AL. Published under the title "Sufferers of Madeira", with some changes in the second sentence).

1069 *The New York Daily Times,* January 24, 1853. (New York City, NY). News about this meeting, written by a New York correspondent, on the 24th of January, were also revealed in another state: «There is to be a meeting at the Astor House this evening, to take measures for the relief of the distressed citizens of Madeira, who are suffering for the want of food. The call for the meeting is signed by quite a number of our most influential citizens, and it can hardly fail to be productive of favorable results. It certainly is a cause worthy of support.» *Pennsylvania Inquirer,* January 25, 1853. (Philadelphia, PA).

1070 See Note 955.

1071 Jacob Aaron Westervelt (1800-1879), a native of New Jersey, was a renowned and prolific shipbuilder, having constructed over 247 vessels during his career. From 1853 to 1855 he served as Mayor of New York City.

1072 John Adams Dix (1798-1879), American politician, who had visited Madeira in 1842, and author of the book *A Winter in Madeira and a Summer in Spain and Florence,* in which he also expressed his views on Madeira Wine, which we previously presented, on section 6.1.1.12. of this anthology.

1073 John Van Buren, (1810-1866), American lawyer and politician. He was also the second son of the U.S. President Martin Van Buren and a Yale College graduate.

1074 Henry John Burden, a long-time British resident in Madeira and recently arrived at New York.

1075 Brother of the American Consul in Funchal, John Howard March, and father of Charles Wainwright March, who visited Madeira at the end of 1852, and years later published the book *Sketches and Adventures in Madeira, Portugal, and the Andalusias of Spain,* in which he dedicated an entire chapter to the topic of Madeira Wine, which we present on section 6.1.1.15. of this anthology.

1076 Moses Hicks Grinnell (1803-1877), a native of New Bedford, MA, who moved to New York at an young age, becoming a successful merchant and shipper, being also appointed as president of the New York Chamber of Commerce.

1077 Simeon Draper (1804-1866), a native of Massachusetts, who established himself in New York as a merchant and politician.

1078 Jonathan Prescott Hall, an eminent New York lawyer and author, descendant of two signers of the Declaration of Independence. At the end of 1852 he was a United States District Attorney.

1079 Junius T. Stagg, Esq. was, at the end of 1852, the Treasurer of the Third Guard, a military corps.

1080 Co-proprietor of the Astor House, located at the west side of Broadway, and one of the fanciest and largest hotels in New York at the time, along with Robert B. Coleman.

1081 Robert B. Coleman (1828-1857), a native of New York, was the owner of the Astor House and also of a fifty acres farm at the Flatlands, adjacent to Jamaica Bay, on the easterly side of Long Island, filled with luxuriant crops, abundance of fruit, a large number of trees, and vines of the Isabella and Catawba varieties. On January 1853 the American Institute awarded him the first premium for the best cultivated farm of fifty acres. *Transactions of the American Institute of the City of New York, for the year 1852,* Charles Van Benthuyen, Albany, 1853, pages 45-49.

News of the Morning[1082]

A meeting of influential citizens was held in the Astor House last evening, to provide measures for the relief of the inhabitants of Madeira, who suffer from a failure of the vine crop. A committee was appointed to collect subscriptions.

Relief for Madeira.[1083]

In pursuance of a call, published yesterday morning, and signed by Mayor Westervelt and several distinguished citizens, a meeting was held in the Astor House, last evening, to take measures for the relief of the unfortunate sufferers in Madeira, who had been rendered destitute by the failure of the Vine and Potato. Among those present we observed His Honor Mayor Westervelt, Hon. John A. Dix, Hon. John Van Buren, Hon. Horace Greeley,[1084] Wm. Depew, Stephen A. Whitney,[1085] Robert Kelly, Clement March, Esqs., &c., .

On motion of Robert Kelly, Esq., His Honor Mayor Westervelt took the Chair. Stephen A. Whitney, Esq., was appointed Vice-President, and Phillip W. Engs, Esq., was requested to act as Secretary.

The President read the call of the meeting, and the following letter, from Archbishop Hughes, enclosing a check for $50:[1086]

NEW YORK, Jan. 24, 1853.

SIR: – The Most Rev. Archbishop HUGHES[1087] being still confined to his room by illness, and therefore unable to attend your meeting this evening, has directed me to express his very deep and earnest approval of your charitable work, and to send you the enclosed check as his contribution to the same. The Archbishop has received a letter from the Bishop of Funchal,[1088]

1082 *The New York Daily Times,* January 25, 1853. (New York City, NY).
1083 *The New York Daily Times,* January 25, 1853. (New York City, NY).
1084 See Note 1052.
1085 Stephen Whitney (1776-1860), a native of Connecticut, who became one of the wealthiest merchants of New York, in the 1st half of the 19th century, whose fortune was considered second to that of John Jacob Astor.
1086 On a newspaper article it was stated that the $50 contribution by Archbishop John J. Hughes seemed rather small to a New York's Protestant Society, (that had helped bringing to America a large number of Madeira exiles, followers of Robert Reid Kalley, some years before), which urged him to give ten times more, adding that, if he did so, a member of his organization would contribute with $500 as well. Next we present that interesting text, entitled "Famine in the Island of Madeira – A CARD FROM THE AMERICAN AND FOREIGN CHRISTIAN UNION": «The Christian Public will remember that a few years since several hundred men, women and children, natives of this Island, in consequence of having read and endeavoring to obey the Holy Scriptures, were subjected to the most cruel persecution by the Romish Priests there, who, assisted by the civil power, imprisoned many of them, strip them of their little all, and finally drove them into exile. This Society expended $12.000 in rescuing a large part of them from starvation, clothing and bringing them to this country, where they are now settled comfortably in the State of Illinois, highly respected, and most worthy citizens. It appears from the letter of the Archbishop Hughes read to the Committee in behalf of the sufferers from famine in the island, that he is now in correspondence with those Priests, and is moved to contribute $50 to the fund. We submit that, under the circumstances, this contribution is rather small, and would now propose to the "most reverend" that he increase it to $500, being the amount which he contributed to the fund in aid of the late attempted revolution in Ireland; upon his doing this, one of the members of our Board stands ready to make up the amount to $1,000, which will give substantial aid to the starving people. ROBERT BAIR, E. R. FAIRCHILD, Secretaries. ANSON C. PHELPS, Jr., Treasurer.» *The New York Daily Times,* January 28 and 29, 1853. (New York City, NY).
1087 John Joseph Huges, (1797-1864), was an Irish-born clergyman of the Roman Catholic Church, being the fourth Bishop and the first Archbishop of the Archdiocese of New York, serving from 1842 to 1864.
1088 Bishop Manuel Martins Manso. According to the Madeiran newspaper *O Progressista,* of December 11, 1852, this letter had been written by him, in Latin, upon request of the U.S. Consul in Funchal, John Howard March. This source also praised and thanked all the efforts the Consul had done so far to promote in his Fatherland a subscription

in the Island of Madeira, which leaves no doubt of the calamity which has fallen upon the inhabitants of that island, and which can only be alleviated by the charitable interference of benevolent persons in other countries.

I remain, with sincere respect, your obedient servant,
J. R. BAYLEY,
Sect'y to Archbishop of New-York.
HENRY JOHN BURDEN, Esq., New York.

Hon. JOHN A. DIX rose and said – The objects of the meeting had been set forth in the call convening the meeting, to adopt measures for the relief of the suffering inhabitants of the Island of Madeira. It was probably known that the vintage of last year had totally failed, and that this calamity, with the total failure of the potato crop, had reduced the inhabitants to the greatest destitution. Independent of their physical sufferings, the actual loss had been $1,000,000. That their condition might be better understood, he would read a letter received from J. HOWARD MARCH, Esq., their Consul there for many years, who was deservedly beloved and respected for his open hospitality and kindness of heart.

MADEIRA, Thursday, Dec. 2, 1852.[1089]

MY DEAR SIR: – When we had the pleasure of your company in Madeira, a few years ago, the Madeira people, though poor and laborious, were contented with their lot, for their great industry enabled them to obtain the means of subsistence.

But a sad change has lately come over great numbers of them. As you well know, the culture of the vine has been the chief occupation of the inhabitants of Madeira for more than two centuries, in many parishes; from the nature of the soil, the warmth of the climate and the want of water, nothing else can advantageously be grown.

The vintages average from twenty-five to thirty-five thousand pipes, and up to the present year never failed. But the last vintage was almost a total failure; in many districts where thousands of pipes of wine had annually been made, not a grape was gathered; and in the whole Island, the vintage did not amount to a hundred pipes of good wine. The condition, therefore, of the Madeira people – those who were formerly in good circumstances, as well as the poor laborers – is woeful in the extreme; and unless foreign assistance be given to them, many of them must die of starvation. It is feared that the hospital and the poor-houses must soon be closed, as the sources of their maintenance are nearly exhausted.

Figure 82. Jacob A. Westervelt, the Mayor of New York in 1853, was the Chairman of the Madeira Relief Committee established on that city in order to raise funds for the sufferers on the island. *19th century engraving. Author unknown, c. 1845.*

Now it appears to me to be beyond a doubt, that many of the charitable and benevolent in the United States, would be happy to give some little assistance to the poor of Madeira, upon being made acquainted with their sad condition, and the channel through which their donations would be transmitted.

I am told a committee may be organized in New-York for this purpose; and should such be the case, I hope, my dear sir, you will say a good word to your friends in favor of the starving people of Madeira. You can truly represent them as being a very hard working, kindly disposed, extremely temperate and religious people; and let me add, that a gift of the value of a barrel of flour, or of even a couple of bushels of corn, might be the means of preserving the lives of a whole family.

---

in benefit of the poor in Madeira.

1089 A few days later the Madeiran press, namely *O Amigo do Povo*, of December 11, 1852, reported that, according to a reliable source, the American Consul had written to America in order to get relief for the Madeiran people, praising his attitude and tireless efforts to help them. This is that letter.

With great regard I am, my dear Sir,
faithfully yours, J. HOWARD MARCH.
Hon. JOHN A. DIX, New-York.

In addition to this statement, he had a letter in his hand setting forth the condition of the inhabitants, but as it was confirmatory of that from Mr. MARCH, he would not detain the meeting by reading it. To the truth of what Mr. MARCH had said as to the moral character of the people, he could bear witness, having spent two months in the island. A more kindly disposed, temperate, and industrious people, he had never seen. During his sojourn there, he could not remember having seen one drunken person, and he was certain he had not witnessed a drunken brawl. The appearance of the island was striking and beautiful, rising boldly in portions to a height of 3,600 feet above the level of the sea. The southern face of the island, where the vine was successfully cultivated, consisted of sloping acclivities, where it was impossible for carriages, and in many instances, for horses, to be of use. The burdens of the island had, therefore, to be carried by the people on their heads. It was difficult to find in any country persons who earned their bread more laboriously. The cultivation of the vine was their only profitable source of employment, and on the south of the Island they had no other means of earning, on the failure of the vine crop. Beautiful as the Island was in all its aspects; favored as it was in climate, it had nevertheless very little wealth. A system of commercial restrictions had contributed to this result. They might imagine to what a situation people so circumstanced would be reduced upon the failure of their only productions. They asked us to give of our abundance enough to sustain them through the Winter; and he was sure their appeal would not be in vain. If those of the gentlemen present who were known in the City, exerted themselves, through their acquaintance, they would be able to obtain sufficient. We were surrounded by evidences of prosperity – our docks crowded with ships, unloading their rich freights – our streets so incumbered with men and merchandise as to be at times almost impassable – gold flowing in from California, – in a word, wealth and enterprise filling up every channel; these were the pregnant evidences of our unexampled prosperity. From all this abundance the destitute Islanders asked for a small contribution to relieve them. He had no doubt this City would respond, in a liberal spirit; and, in this view, he had drawn up some resolutions, which he would read for the meeting:

Whereas, A large portion of the inhabitants of the Island of Madeira, by a failure of their crops, are in imminent danger of starvation; and whereas, the civil Governor, the Consuls of the United States and Great Britain, and other distinguished residents, have appealed to the liberality of foreign countries for the relief of the suffering Islanders; therefore,

Resolved, That a Committee of thirty be appointed by the chairman, to solicit contributions from the inhabitants of this City, and that the citizens be requested, without waiting to be called on by such Committee, to deposit such sums as they may be disposed to give, with Messrs. Coleman & Stetson, at the Astor House, or either of the members of the Committee, with whom a subscription book will be left, for the purpose of registering all such contributions.

Hon. Horace Greeley said a few words in seconding the resolutions, not to add force to the appeal, but to the energy with which they would respond to it. This was not to be looked upon as a great undertaking, as when Europe was in destitution, and Ireland stretched out her hands for bread. It seemed to him that $100,000, which would be only the profits of one day's business in New-York, would be sufficient, and when it was known to the citizens that one day's profits only was required, they would not deem it hard. Again, when

Ireland was in destitution, it was said she is part of a great and rich nation, let her give of her abundance; but in the present instance this plea could not be put forward, for the country was a poor one. Our relations with Madeira were as intimate as with any other place; she was a kind of half-way house in the Atlantic. The appeal came to us with the utmost force. He trusted the Committee to be appointed would act promptly, as it was now the severest part of the season, and it would be important to be ready to lend their contribution with the general relief, by a vessel which was chartered to sail from Boston for that purpose. If this City could give assurance of forwarding $100,000, there were merchants in Madeira who would advance the money until it was forwarded. He trusted they would be prompt and liberal, and no man would feel the poorer for having contributed to saving a whole population from starvation.

Figure 83. John Van Buren, the son of a former U.S. President, was also a distinguished member of the Madeira Relief Committee. *Photograph by Mathew Brady, 1855.*

Mr. John Van Buren said he had lived some time in Madeira,[1090] and had occasion to know something of the character of that simple, unpretending, industrious population. They worked laboriously, but accumulated little or nothing; and living in a climate which did not caution them to provide for the future – where at all times, they could escape the inclemency of the weather by changing their position, – the consequence was what we could call improvidence. They labored for the day, and for the hour, and provided not for the future. They were, as already stated, mainly employed in cultivation of the vine, which was their great reliance, and for two hundred years it had never failed until the past year. He believed the branches did not manifest any appearance of decay; they blossomed and then died. They again done so the second year, and it was feared would not bear again. The people were exceedingly hospitable, and after their wants were supplied, gave away without reserve; so that the calamity found them totally unprepared. It was, he knew very difficult for us, who had several branches of industry to embrace, to imagine that the failure of any one employment could so affect the entire people. Madeira was, perhaps, the only place to which the invalid could go with a certainty of serving his health, and at the same time bring his friends, in health, without fear of injury; and was, therefore, a place which invalids would always seek. We who lived in this rugged climate, did not know how

---

1090 He traveled to Madeira in December 1843 or January 1844, for the sake of his wife's health, as can be inferred from a widely circulated New York's newspaper article of the time: «JOHN VAN BUREN. – The friends of John Van Buren, Esq., in this city, will be glad to hear of his safe arrival at the Island of Madeira. The Charles Carroll, in which he sailed, made the passage from New York, in nineteen days. The health of Mrs. V. B., the restoration of which was the chief inducement to the voyage, was materially improved, and no doubt is now entertained of her entire recovery. – *Albany Atlas.*» *The Evening Post,* January 26, 1844. (New York City, NY); *Albany Argus,* January 26, 1844. (Albany, NY. Quotes the *Atlas* of the previous day); *New-York Spectator,* January 27, 1844. (New York City, NY. Also quotes the *Albany Argus*); *Daily National Intelligencer,* January 29, 1844. (Washington, DC); *The Southern Patriot,* February 3, 1844. (Charleston, SC); *The Daily Picayune,* February 9, 1844. (New Orleans, LA). Despite the winter sojourn at Madeira, his wife ended up dying at the end of 1844, as the press reported: «We regret to learn the death of Mrs. John Van Buren, at Albany. This lady was the daughter of the late Judge Vanderpoel, and was much admired for her amiable character and a high poetical talent. She passed the last Winter at Madeira, for the benefit of her health, and it was hoped by her friends that it was entirely re-established. These hopes have been blasted, and she is now the early tenant of the tomb. – *True Sun.*» *New-York Spectator,* November 23, 1844. (New York City, NY).

soon we might require to seek its inviting refuge; and how delightful it would be to reflect that he would find the kindest feelings extended towards the United States, growing out of their prompt action in relieving them from an unforeseen calamity.

ROBERT KELLY, Esq., moved that the persons who signed the call, should compose a portion of the Committee, and that the Mayor act as Chairman. The following were then appointed by the Chair:

Jacob A. Westervelt,	Wm. De Pew,
John A. Dix,	Henry H. Elliott,
John Van Buren,	Geo. M. Lewis,
Henry J. Burden,	Stephen Whitney,
Clement March,	Phillip W. Engs,
Moses H. Grinnell,	Charles O'Conor,
Simeon Draper,	Thos Tileston,
J. Prescott Hall,	Geo. Griswold,
Junius. T. Stagg,	Augustus Schell,
Charles A. Stetson,	Horace Greeley,
Robert B. Coleman,	Robert Benson,
Edward K. Alburtes,	Ambrose C. Kingsland,
Henry S. Leveridge,	J. P. Phoenix,
Robert Kelly,	Charles W. Elliott,
Sheperd Knapp,	Schuyler Livingston,
Wm. S. Wetmore	Myndert Van Schaick.

Hon. JOHN A. DIX presented the following, which was adopted:

Resolved, That the Committee now appointed be authorized to use their discretion as to the mode in which the amount collected shall be appropriated for the benefit of the people of Madeira.

It was resolved that the proceedings of this meeting be published in the Madeira papers.[1091]

Senor[1092] FIGANIERE,[1093] a Portuguese Minister, returned grateful thanks to the meeting for the prompt and benevolent action taken in behalf of the distressed inhabitants of Madeira. A request had that day arrived to the Portuguese Consul, to interest the inhabitants of New-York; but he was happy to see they had anticipated any foreign appeal.

1091 A summary of this article was published in the Madeiran newspaper *O Amigo do Povo*, of March 1, 1853 (who wrongly reported that this meeting had been published in the *New York Daily Times* of January 18, 1853, a few days before this meeting effectively took place), and a complete translation into Portuguese was published, two days later, in *O Progressista*, (who got the date right, January 25, 1853). This newspaper also added an article about the situation in Madeira, which contained an excerpt of the letter written by the American Consul in Funchal, translated from the edition of January 18, 1853 of the *Mobile Daily Advertiser* (Mobile, AL).

1092 The right spelling is Senhor, the Portuguese word for Mister.

1093 Cesar Henrique Stuart de la Figanière, Portuguese Consul General in New York. On the Madeiran newspaper *O Progressista*, of March 31, 1853, we can find a copy of an official document issued by the Portuguese Queen Mary II, on the 14th of December 1852, ordering him to open up a subscription in New York on behalf of the suffering Madeirans, but he did not do it. On a reply sent back to Portugal, on the 26th of February 1853, he stated that the British subject Henry John Burden had anticipated him and that he had done everything he could and knew to help him and the [Madeira Relief] Committee established in New York. This allegation is denied on a anonymous communication published four months later on the same newspaper, of July 23, 1853, which denounces his shameful behavior and reports that he did not contribute with a single penny to the subscription and only attended this meeting because he had been summoned to it. Furthermore it is also stated that if it wasn't for the tireless efforts of Henry John Burden [in New York] and Fortunato Joaquim Figueira [in Philadelphia] no relief whatsoever would be gathered on these states. And last but not least he is also accused of charging a ten pesos' fee to dispatch a relief ship to Madeira, when he was asked not to do so by Mr. Burden.

A resolution of thanks was passed to Messrs. Stetson & Coleman, for their kindness in giving the use of their House, and the meeting adjourned.

Distress in the Island of Madeira.[1094]

A meeting of a number of the prominent citizens was held last evening, at the Astor House, to take into consideration the intelligence of the fearful destitution of the inhabitants of the Island of Madeira, in consequence of the destruction of the vine and potato crops, and to take measures for the relief of the unfortunate sufferers.

The meeting was organized by choosing Mayor WESTERVELT, Chairman; STEPHEN WHITNEY, Vice-President, and PHILIP W. ENGS, Secretary. A call of the meeting was read by Mayor Westervelt. Mr. HENRY J. BURDEN, of Madeira, then presented the following letter, which he had received from Archbishop HUGHES, in which was enclosed a check for $50, to be applied for the benefit of the sufferers at Madeira.

NEW-YORK, January 24, 1853.

SIR: – The most Rev. Archbishop being still confined to his room by illness, and therefore unable to attend your meeting this evening, has directed me to express his very deep and earnest approval of your charitable work, and to send you the inclosed check as his contribution to the same. The Archbishop has received a letter from the Bishop of Funchal, in the Island of Madeira, which leaves no doubt of the calamity which has fallen upon the inhabitants of that Island, and which can only be alleviated by the charitable interference of benevolent persons in other countries.

I remain, with sincere respect, your obedient servant.

J. R. BAYLEY, Secretary to Archbishop of New-York.

HENRY JOAS[1095] BURDEN, Esq., New-York.

Hon. JOHN A. DIX then stated the objects for which this meeting had been called; the vintages of the past year, together with the potato crop, had failed, leaving the inhabitants destitute; it is estimated that the loss exceeds $1,000,000. Mr. Dix then read the following letter which he had received from Mr. J. HOWARD MARCH, of Madeira:

MADEIRA, Thursday, Dec. 2, 1852.

MY DEAR SIR: When we had the pleasure of your company in Madeira, a few years ago, the Madeira people, though poor and laborious, were contented with their lot, for their great industry enabled them to obtain the means of subsistence.

But a sad change has lately come over great numbers of them. As you well know, the culture of the vine has been the chief occupation of the inhabitants of Madeira for more than two centuries; in many parishes, from the nature of the soil, the warmth of the climate and the want of water, nothing else can advantageously be grown.

The vintages average from twenty-five to thirty-five thousand pipes, and up to the present year never failed. But the last vintage was almost a total failure; in many districts where thousands of pipes of wine had annually been made, not a grape was gathered; and in the whole island the vintage did not amount to a hundred pipes of good wine. The condition, therefore,

---

1094 *New York Daily Tribune*, January 25, 1853. (New York City, NY). There are several differences between this article and the precedent one, published on the same day by the *The New York Daily Times* and therefore we decided to present this one as well, so that both could be compared by the curious reader.

1095 The right spelling is John.

of the Madeira people – those who were formerly in good circumstances, as well as the poor laborers – is woeful in the extreme; and unless foreign assistance be given to them, many of them must die of starvation. It is feared that the hospital and the poor-houses must soon be closed, as the sources of their maintenance are nearly exhausted.

Now it appears to me to be beyond a doubt, that many of the charitable and benevolent in the United States would be happy to give some little assistance to the poor of Madeira, upon being made acquainted with their sad conditions, and the channel through which their donations would be transmitted.

I am told a Committee may be organized in New-York for this purpose; and should such be the case, I hope, my dear Sir, you will say a good word to your friends in favor of the starving people of Madeira. You can truly represent them as being a very hard-working, kindly disposed, extremely temperate and religious people; and let me add, that a gift of the value of a barrel of flour, or of even a couple of bushels of corn, might be the means of preserving the lives of a whole family.

With great regard, I am, my dear Sir,
Faithfully yours. J. HOWARD MARCH
Hon. JOHN A. DIX, New-York.

Figure 84. John Adams Dix, who had visited Madeira in 1842, played a key role in the Madeira Relief Committee. 'Carte de visite', by M. B. Brady, c. 1861, showing him in his general military uniform.

Mr. Dix said, that a few years since he passed several months at the Island of Maderia, and could vouch for the sobriety, industry, and integrity of the inhabitants. He was some time at Funchal, the Capital, containing over 25,000 inhabitants, and never saw a drunken person or a brawl during his stay. The formation of the island makes it most laborious for persons engaged in the vineyards or agricultural pursuits, in consequence of the unevenness of the country, as some of the mountains rise to a height of 6,200 feet, and carriages or mules are seldom used; all articles transported over the island are carried by the inhabitants upon their heads; and in no country are the people more industrious. There is, however, very little wealth amongst them, the chief cause of which is owing to the commercial restrictions. They now ask of us sufficient aid to sustain them through the winter. If gentlemen well acquainted in the City will take an interest in this matter, and represent their conditions to our wealthy citizens, no doubt, abundant means to relieve the wants of these distressed people, will be furnished. The speaker then submitted the following preamble and resolutions which were adopted:

Whereas, A large portion of the inhabitants of the Island of Madeira, by a failure of their crops, are in imminent danger of starvation, and whereas, the Civil Governor, the Consuls of the United States and Great Britain, and other distinguished residents, have appealed to the liberality of foreign countries for the relief of the suffering Islanders – therefore

Resolved, That a Committee of 30 persons be appointed by the Chairman to solicit contributions from the inhabitants of this City, and that the citizens generally be requested, without waiting to be called on by said Committee, to deposit such sums as they may be disposed to give, with Messrs. Coleman & Stetson, at the Astor House, or either of the members of the Committee, with whom a subscription book will be left for the purpose of registering all such contributions.

Resolved, That the Committee appointed be authorized to use their discretion as to the mode in which the amount collected shall be appropriated for the benefit of the people of Madeira. Mayor Westervelt then announced the following named gentlemen said Committee:

Jacob A. Westervelt,	Stephen Whitney
John A. Dix,	Philip W. Engs.
John Van Buren,	Chas. O'Connor,
Henry J. Burden,	Thos. Tileston,
Clement March,	Geo. Griswold,
Moses H. Grinnell,	Myndert Van Schnick,
Simeon Draper,	Ausgustus Schell,
J. Prescott Hall,	Horace Greeley,
Jas. T. Stagg,	Robt. Benson,
Chas. A. Stetson,	Ambrose Kingsland,
Robt. B. Coleman,	J. P. Phoenix,
Edw. K. Alburtis,	Robt. Kelley,
Henry S. Leveridge,	Shepard Knapp,
Henry H. Elliott,	Wm. S. Wetmore,
Geo M. Lewis,	Wm. Depew,
Chas. W. Elliott,	

Mr. Greeley made a few suggestions. He said the aid required by the inhabitants of Maderia was much less than that required in Ireland at the time of the famine. Many argued that the large landholders, who owned the lands of Ireland, should provide for the wants of their tenants, while in this case it was far different. There are in the Island of Madeira about 100,000 inhabitants; they would probably not require over $100,000 from New-York. This would be comparatively a small sum for this City to raise. If the profits of the business of this City for one day (estimated at $160,000) were appropriated, it would be sufficient. They are certainly deserving of our aid, and we cannot act too promptly. A vessel is to sail from Boston in a few days for that Island, mainly to carry out provisions. I trust the committee appointed will take hold of this matter, and should the citizens of New-York give $100,000, I trust they will not be any poorer at the end of the year.

John Van Buren arose and said, he had spent some four months in the Island of Madeira; the people there, are honest, simple, independent and industrious; they accumulate but little property, and owing to the peculiarity of the climate, require but little. By changing their location from one part of the Island to another, they can always be in a climate where no houses, and but light clothing is required. The crops of the vineyard have never before failed in 200 years. It is true, their vineyards have varied from 15,000 to 50,000 pipes per year. This last season, the vineyards have entirely failed. This is the only means they have for support, and unless they should receive foreign aid, many of them must starve.

Several hundred dollars were subscribed by gentlemen present.

Figure 85. Horace Greeley, the owner of the *New York Daily Tribune*, also played an important role in securing relief for the Madeirans at the beginning of 1853. *Photograph by Mathew Brady, taken between 1844 and 1860.*

Previous to the adjournment it was resolved that the proceedings of this meeting be published in the various papers of the Island of Madeira. The meeting was then adjourned.

The Committee are to hold a meeting at the Mayor's Office on Wednesday, at 4 P. M., to take further action in this matter.

MADEIRA RELIEF MEETING.[1096] – The meeting at the Astor House, New York, was not numerously attended, but those present determined to act efficiently. Gen. Dix, Mr. Greeley, John Van Buren, &c., appealed warmly in favor of extending immediate Relief. A strong Committee was appointed. Contributions may be sent to the Hon. Jacob A. Westervelt, Mayor of New York.

RELIEF FOR MADEIRA.[1097] A public meeting was held in New York at the Astor House, on Monday evening, to take measures for the relief of the sufferers at Madeira. The Mayor presided. Hon. John A. Dix read a letter[1098] dated Madeira, Dec. 2d, which said:

As you well know, the culture of the vine has been the chief occupation of the inhabitants of Madeira for more than two centuries, in many parishes, from the nature of the soil, the warmth of the climate, and the want of water, nothing else can advantageously be grown. The vintages average from twenty-five to thirty-five thousand pipes, and up to the present year never failed. But the last vintage was almost a total failure; in many districts where thousands of pipes of wine had annually been made, not a grape was gathered; and in the whole island the vintage did not amount to a hundred pipes of good wine. The condition, therefore, of the Madeira people – those who were formerly in good circumstances, as well as the poor laborers – is woeful in the extreme; and unless foreign assistance be given to them, many of them must die of starvation. It is feared that the hospital and the poor-houses must soon be closed, as the sources of their maintenance are nearly exhausted.

In remarking upon these facts, Mr. Dix spoke of the temperance habits, the liberal hospitality and the industry of the inhabitants, and of the general aspect of the country. The physical conformation of the island renders the inhabitants laborious.

It rises boldly from the ocean attaining the height of the White Mountains of New Hampshire. The genial heat of the climate renders the cultivation of the grape almost the only resource for agricultural labor. In the whole southern part of the country no rain falls from June to September, rendering it highly favorable to the cultivation of the vine. Beautiful as the island is, it has, notwithstanding, very little wealth. You may readily imagine the utter destitution of a people thus circumstanced, when the grape – their chief support and their only article of commerce – fails. Many of them are in danger of starvation for the want of bread, and they ask us, of our abundance, enough to sustain life through the winter. I trust that this appeal will not be made in vain.

Horace Greeley and John Van Buren followed Mr. Dix in remarks appropriate to the occasion. The former said that one million of dollars would suffice for the effectual relief

---

1096 *Albany Evening Journal,* January 25, 1853. (Albany, NY).
1097 *Daily Evening Transcript,* January 26, 1853. (Boston, MA).
1098 From the U.S. Consul in Funchal, John Howard March.

of that whole population;[1099] and though we cannot expect that New York will give it all, yet surely she will raise $100,000.

LOCAL AFFAIRS.[1100] – ... – At the meeting of the Madeira Relief Committee yesterday, an encouraging state of the subscriptions was shown. ...

RELIEF FOR THE CITIZENS OF MADEIRA.[1101] – The subscriptions in Boston to purchase a cargo of food, to send by the barque Nautilus, to the starving inhabitants of the island of Madeira, have been pretty successful. Over $2,000 have been raised. Nine gentlemen subscribed $100 each, and many others $50 and $25 each. At the relief meeting held in New York, the other evening, John Van Buren stated that he had spent some four months in the island of Madeira; the people there are honest, simple, independent and industrious; they accumulate but little property, and, owing to the peculiarity of the climate, require but little. By changing their location from one part of the island to another, they can always be in a climate where no houses, and but light clothing is required. The crops of the vineyard have never failed before in 200 years. This last season the vineyards have entirely failed. This is the only means they have for support, and, unless they should receive foreign aid, many of them must starve.

Relief for the starving inhabitants of the Island of Madeira.[1102]

We observe by the New York papers that a large meeting of the citizens of that city was held at the Astor House, on the 24th instant, to take measures for the relief of the suffering inhabitants of the Island of Madeira, at which Mayor WESTERVELT presided, and which was addressed by several distinguished citizens. Energetic measures were taken to afford prompt relief to the sufferers. Want of space puts it out of our power to publish the proceedings in full.

We, whose good fortune it is to dwell in a land where want is hardly known, and where all the blessings a beneficent Providence can bestow upon man are heaped upon us, cannot surely hear the wail of distress from abroad without hastening to afford relief to those from whom it comes.

We understand a committee, consisting of Mayor MAURY,[1103] Mr. SEATON,[1104] and Major B. B. FRENCH,[1105] have already made some collections in this city to aid the destitute inhabitants of Madeira, and that the subscription paper is in Major FRENCH's hands, to whom any one so disposed can contribute.

1099 Horace Greeley never mentioned the sum of one million dollars but rather of $100.000.
1100 *New York Daily Tribune,* January 27, 1853. (New York City, NY).
1101 *The Sun,* January 27, 1853. (Baltimore, MD); *Charleston Courier,* February 1, 1853. (Charleston, SC. Published untitled).
1102 *Daily National Intelligencer,* January 27, 1853. (Washington, DC).
1103 John Walker Maury (1809-1855), a native of Virginia, who served as Mayor of Washington, D.C. from 1852 to 1854.
1104 We presume he was William Winston Seaton (1785-1866), a former Mayor of Washington, D.C. and one of the owners of the *National Intelligencer,* a newspaper published in that area.
1105 Benjamin Brown French (1800-1870), the Commissioner of Public Buildings in Washington, D.C.

Relief for the Sufferers in Madeira.[1106] – At a meeting of the committee to obtain relief for the suffering people of Madeira, held at the Mayor's office, on the 26th of January, the following resolution was passed:

Resolved, That a Committee of three be appointed to advertise a vessel for the Island of Madeira, and to solicit donations of corn, rice, flour, and other provisions, to be forwarded by said vessel, for the use of the sufferers there.

The following gentlemen were appointed [to] said Committee, and will receive and dispose of all such donations: GEORGE M. LEWIS, No. 61 Front-st.; WILLIAM DEPEW. No. 115 Pearl-st.; HENRY J. BURDEN, Astor-House.

[Signed.] JACOB A. WESTERVELT, Chairman.

P. W. ENGS, Secretary

The Committee referred to in the above resolution, beg leave to call upon the benevolent to send in their contributions, as a vessel will be dispatched without delay.

ISLAND OF MADEIRA SUFFERERS.[1107] – Yesterday efforts were made in the business circles down town for the relief of the destitute poor on the Island of Madeira, who are now suffering from the failure of the grape crop and scarcity of provisions. The Corn Exchange Association[1108] subscribed $500; and although the Stock Board declined, in their associate capacity, to contribute a given sum, the members of the Board expressed a readiness to join other business men in the good work.

Relief for Madeira.[1109] – A number of citizens of New York assembled at the Astor House on Tuesday evening for the purpose of taking measures to relieve the people of Madeira during their present destitution and distress in consequence of the failure of the Wine crop on that island. Mr. Westervelt, the Mayor, was called to the Chair and Mr. Stephen Whitney acted as Vice President. Speeches were made by the Hon. John A. Dix, John Van Buren and Mr. Greeley of the Tribune; after which a committee of highly respectable gentlemen was appointed to obtain subscriptions. We trust the subscription will be a large one, and that relief will be promptly sent. A stronger claim upon the humanity of the American people was never presented, and it is gratifying to see how emphatically it is felt. There will, we hope, be a generous rivalry between New York and Boston and the other large cities, in seeing which shall be the most liberal in responding to this call. If *every* call upon American philanthropy were as well grounded as this one, there would be a good deal *less* ground for the operation of hypocrisy and fanaticism, and much less of the public means would be expended upon foreign adventurers and maudlin agitators.

1106 *The New York Daily Times*, January 28, 29 and 31, 1853. (New York City, NY).

1107 *The New York Daily Times*, January 28 and 29, 1853. (New York City, NY).

1108 A few days later this Association would be in the basis for the foundation of a new bank, the Corn Exchange Bank. According to *The New York Daily Times* of February 1, 1853, this bank started to operate on that very same day, being located at 67 Pearl St., and presided by E. W. Dunham.

1109 *New-London Daily Chronicle*, January 28, 1853. (New London, CT).

THE FAMINE AT MADEIRA.[1110] – The Nautilus, says the Boston Atlas of the 26th, is nearly ready to sail for the island of Madeira, with the assistance subscribed here for the distressed population of that island. To-day was fixed as her day for sailing, but it may not yet be too late to add to her cargo of benevolence. The following extract from a letter from Charles W. March, Esq., well known in this community, written from Madeira on the 5th ult., gives a more distinct view of the existing suffering than we have seen elsewhere. …[1111]

[Untitled][1112]

Boston is in first with relief for the Island of Madeira. The brig Nautilus has sailed with Flour and Corn.

FOOD FOR THE STARVING.[1113] The bark Nautilus, which was chartered to carry supplies of food for the destitute inhabitants of Madeira, sailed from this port Thursday on her benevolent errand. Liberal donations were received from a number of our citizens. The cargo consists of 367 bushels of beans, 2 barrels bread, 1188 bushels corn, 192 barrels corn meal, 333 barrels flour, 412 barrels potatoes, 546 bushels do., and 16,906 lbs. rice.

Distress at Madeira.[1114]

One of our citizens has furnished us the following extract of a letter from a lady of this State, who is spending the winter in the Island of Madeira. A meeting was held in New York on Monday to take measures to relieve the suffering in that Island, and a large committee headed by the Mayor, appointed to solicit subscriptions. A vessel has also been chartered in Boston to carry provision, &c. The letter from which the extract is taken was written at Funchal in November.

"The weather is warm and has been very rainy; it is now like June; thermometer at 70 or 72. The vintage having been completely cut off through the whole island, there is and will be immense suffering; instead of 30,000 pipes of wine not one is made – the distress is very great – fruits are abundant but there is apprehension now that the vegetable on which all the poor live, the Yam, will also fail – if that is the case there will be almost a famine."

AID FOR THE MADEIRA SUFFERERS[1115] – The Committee who have in charge the

---

[1110] *The Barre Patriot,* January 28, 1853. (Published at Barre, MA).

[1111] In this article were transcribed the first three paragraphs of Charles W. March's letter to the New York *Daily Tribune* – which we have already presented on the previous section of this book – but the last one was incomplete, ending at "the sufferings of the population".

[1112] *Albany Evening Journal,* January 28, 1853. (Albany, NY).

[1113] *The Boston Herald,* January 29, 1853. (Boston, MA).

[1114] *The Connecticut Courant,* January 29, 1853. (Hartford, CT).

[1115] *The New York Daily Times,* January 29, 1853. (New York City, NY). At the section "News of the Morning" of the same edition of this newspaper there is a summary of this article, in these terms: «The Committee to collect funds for the relief of the Madeira sufferers, met yesterday afternoon at the Mayor's office, and reported the collection of $4,500. They hope to collect as much more and to dispatch a vessel laden with provisions, to the famine-stricken island next week.»

business of collecting money to be applied to the relief of the destitute inhabitants of Madeira met yesterday afternoon in the Mayor's office and reported that their collections up to that time amounted to $4,500,[1116] and the Committee hoped to raise as much more, and believed they could load a vessel to sail for that "Isle of beauty," on Monday, or at any rate at a very early day next week. The Committee have been exceedingly active and the result of their labors shows their success.

AID TO MADEIRA.[1117] – The Committee appointed on Monday evening last, and at a subsequent meeting, to solicit aid for the starving inhabitants of the Island of Madeira, met yesterday afternoon at 4 o'clock, to report progress. In the absence of the Chairman, Mayor Westervelt, Mr. Kelly was chosen Chairman *pro tem*.[1118]

The Committee made the following report of moneys, &c., collected on Thursday and Friday:

Collected by Committee on 'Change	$800 00
Board of Stock Brokers	700 00
Corn Exchange	500 00
By Mr. Leveridge	234 50
By H. H. Elliott	400 00
Mr. Burden	160 00
Mr. Lewis	25 00
Mr. Depew	132 00
Mr. Greeley	15 00

There were also ten barrels of flour and a number of barrels of rice contributed on 'Change.

The whole amount received up to last evening was $4,500. About as much more is required, in order to fit out a vessel with a cargo of provisions.

Mr. Depew reported that a vessel of 1.800 barrels capacity could be obtained upon reasonable terms.

The Committee appointed to procure a vessel were accordingly empowered to make such contract for a vessel, to carry out provisions to Madeira, as they may deem advisable. Also that they be empowered to purchase provisions, and the bills for the same be paid by the Treasurer, after being audited by them.

The Committee appointed at the last meeting, will meet again on Change, to solicit further contributions for the sufferers of Madeira, as the Committee are exceedingly anxious to raise some $4,000 or $5,000 at the earliest possible moment, in order that a vessel may be dispatched at once with provisions to the sufferers in Madeira.

The Committee adjourned to meet on Tuesday next, at 4 o'clock, at the Mayor's office.

1116 As a curiosity we add that an article, from January 27 and published on the same day as the present one in the neighbor state of New Jersey presented another figure, much lower than this one: «The Madeira Relief Committee announce that only $1,328 has been contributed so far, and renew their urgent appeals for aid. – They also advertise for a vessel to take out clothing and provisions and other comforts.» *Trenton State Gazette,* January 29, 1853. (Trenton, NJ. Published in the section "Things in New York").

1117 *New York Daily Tribune,* January 29, 1853. (New York City, NY). The right spelling is Madeira.

1118 Abbreviation of the Latin expression *pro tempore,* meaning "for the time being", which is often used to describe a person who acts as a place holder in the absence of a superior.

News of the Day.[1119]

The destruction of the Vine and Potato crops on the Island of Madeira has produced a famine, so general and so fearful that hundreds have died for want of food. On the reception of the news in New York and Boston, Public Meetings were called, Relief Committees appointed to solicit subscriptions, and a vessel chartered, to be freighted with Provisions for gratuitous distribution amongst the sufferers. The vessel will have quick dispatch from Boston.

MADERIA.[1120] – Of the 100,000 inhabitants of the Island probably 60,000 are to-day needy, while 40,000 must perish unless assisted from abroad. – Such is the statement of the New-York papers, and an urgent appeal is made in behalf of the destitute inhabitants of the Island.

The Island of Madeira is in a starving condition; its 100,000 inhabitants have failed of their annual crop for the first time for 200 years. All its arable land has been occupied with the culture of the vine, which an insect has lately destroyed. Heretofore "a land of corn and wine – a land of bread and vineyards," now its inhabitants "lament for the wine;" they stagger, but not with strong drink. – Unless relief goes from this country, thousands must starve; subscriptions are open to the benevolent in New York.

FOR SUFFERING MADEIRA.[1121]

The People of Madeira are suffering the horrors of famine – the fact is certified to us by the American Consul on that island, as well as by the authorities thereof and by many Americans now there. The facts have been fully set before our readers. Suffice it here that an almost total failure of their last year's harvests have deprived probably 100,000 of the 120,000 Madeirans of any chance of independent subsistence. They must starve if not aided from abroad. But Madeira is an isolated rock in the Atlantic, dependent on the very poor Kingdom of Portugal, whence she can expect little help.

In this exigency, an appeal has been made to the men of business and wealth in our city; most respectable and well known citizens have sanctioned and enforced it; and the result is a collection at the outside of some beggarly $8,000 – not so much as has been made in a day by individuals in a single speculation – not so much as has been realized in an hour from the rise in Breadstuffs and Stocks. Reader! if you have done your duty in the premises, or had none to do, you will not take to yourself our remark that the meagerness of this collection strikes us as deeply disgraceful to New-York.

THE MADEIRA SUFFERERS.[1122] – By the active exertions of Mr. Brodhead, Secretary

---

1119 *Daily Commercial Register,* January 29, 1853. (Sandusky, OH).
1120 *The Portsmouth Journal of Literature & Politics,* January 29, 1853. (Portsmouth, NH).
1121 *New York Daily Tribune,* January 31, 1853. (New York City, NY).
1122 *New York Daily Tribune,* January 31, 1853. (New York City, NY).

of the Board of Brokers,[1123] subscriptions to the amount of $900 have been raised from members of the Board. The entire subscription for Madeira amounts to about $7,000.

[Untitled][1124]

Upwards of five thousand dollars have been collected in New York for the relief of the inhabitants of Madeira. The Board of Brokers contributed $900 on Saturday.

[Untitled][1125]

A subscription has been commenced in Providence for the people of Madeira. … The provisions sent from Boston to Madeira amounted in value to $5,500.

PORTUGAL.[1126]

… On account of the distress caused in Madeira by the failure of the vine crop, a Royal Decree is published permitting, for one year from Nov. last, vessels, whether sailing ships or steamers, to land passengers and call for supplies at Funchal, exempt from payment of custom house clearance, as well as from the charges of the Health Office and Government visits. The import duty on salt fish is also reduced to 15 per cent, *ad valorem;* and potatoes and pearl barley are admitted duty free, through the custom-house at Funchal.

[Untitled][1127]

The brig Nautilus sailed from Boston, on Friday last, for Madeira, with 200 barrels of flour, and filled up with corn – all the product of free contributions to the starving inhabitants of that island. A vessel will also shortly be despatched from New York. The members of the Corn Exchange of that city, a new organization,[1128] have subscribed $500 to the relief fund.

AID FOR MADEIRA.[1129] Upwards of $7000 has been contributed at New York as relief

---

[1123] New York Board of Brokers, the former denomination of the New York Stock Exchange.
[1124] *The Boston Herald,* January 31, 1853. (Boston, MA).
[1125] *The Sun,* January 31, 1853. (Baltimore, MD).
[1126] *The New York Daily Times,* January 31, 1853. (New York City, NY); *The Boston Daily Atlas,* February 1, 1853. (Boston, MA); *North American and United States Gazette,* February 1, 1853. (Philadelphia, PA); *Boston Courier,* February 3 and 4, 1853. (Boston, MA); *The Weekly Herald,* February 5, 1853. (New York City, NY); *The Daily Picayune,* February 8, 1853. (New Orleans, LA).
[1127] *Alexandria Gazette,* February 1, 1853. (Alexandria, VA. Published in the section "News of the Day."). Under the title "Relief for Madeira." and published in other words, this article was revealed in this source: *Charleston Courier,* February 3, 1853. (Charleston, SC).
[1128] See Note 1108.
[1129] *Daily Evening Transcript,* February 1, 1853. (Boston, MA).

to the sufferers at Madeira. The Board of Brokers contributed $900. A vessel, with food for the destitute, will be despatched in a few days. In the meanwhile, the Nautilus, from this port, will have had a fair start of some two weeks, and we trust by the time of the sailing of the New York ship, she will be nearing the Island of Madeira, with her cargo of aid to that suffering people.

RELIEF FOR MADEIRA.[1130] – The food sent from Boston for the relief of the starving inhabitants of Madeira, consisted of 867 bushels beans; 2 barrels of bread; 1188 bushels of corn; 192 barrels of corn meal; 338 barrels flour; 412 barrels potatoes; 548 bushels do, and 16,903 lbs. rice.

AID FOR THE SUFFERERS AT MADEIRA.[1131] – The Committee who have charge of the business of collecting contributions for the relief of the inhabitants of Madeira, have chartered the brig *Tally Ho*, which vessel is to be laden with provisions, and despatched on her mission of mercy on Saturday next. One half the means necessary to accomplish this object are already obtained, and the Committee are not doubtful of their success in raising the balance during the week. Contributions of corn, flour, rice, beans, potatoes, salt provisions, &c., are solicited by the Committee, who meet from day to day at the Mayor's Office. The relief, to be effective, must be immediate, for the horrors of famine are already upon the poor islanders.

AID FOR THE STARVING.[1132] – John A. Dix, Horace Greeley, and John Van Buren were among the speakers at the meeting in New York in aid of the starving people of Madeira. Archbishop Hughes contributed $50. Mr. Greeley thought New York would contribute $100,000.

SUFFERING IN MADEIRA.[1133] – A considerable amount of money has been subscribed in this city for the relief of the suffering poor in the Island of Madeira, but not sufficient to enable the gentlemen who have the matter in charge to procure and load a vessel with provisions. As New York has forwarded a large sum in cash, and Boston has despatched a ship with supplies, it is to be hoped that Philadelphia will not be backward in this charitable work, and that her citizens will prove themselves not less liberal than their neighbors. Donations will be received by Messrs. Adams & Co., Walaut street, above Fourth.

1130 *The Sun*, February 1, 1853. (Baltimore, MD); *Charleston Courier*, February 4, 1853. (Charleston, SC. Published untitled).
1131 *The New York Daily Times*, February 1, 1853. (New York City, NY). A summary of this article was published in the same edition of this newspaper, at the section "News of the Morning", in these words: «… The Committee on collecting money and provisions for the relief of the sufferers in Madeira, have chartered the brig *Tally Ho*, and will dispatch her, if possible, on Saturday next, laden with flour, corn, rice, beans, potatoes, salt provisions, &c. …»
1132 *Daily Commercial Register*, February 1, 1853. (Sandusky, OH).
1133 *North American and United States Gazette*, February 1, 1853. (Philadelphia, PA).

Cheeryble Brothers.[1134]

This justly renowned and joy-giving firm is not confined to its original London. It has branches of greater or less degree in every commercial city. New-York has its Cheeryble Brothers. One of the members of the house put down his $400 or $500 for the Madeira sufferers; and we have reason to know it is only one of the many acts of similar kindness. His brothers, too, are scattered all through South, and Front and William, and Beaver and Wall-streets. Aye, in Wall-street, where sins of omission and commission are sometimes rated in a geometrical proportion to the capital it wields. The Wall-street stock brokers alone made up $1,100 or $1,200. They were asked in their associate capacity to give only $500. They declined to trench upon a found reserved for objects peculiar to their own purposes of charity and liberality; but individually they told out more than double the sum.

All this is nothing remarkable for New-York. Her merchant interest has ever been prompt to respond to the cause of suffering humanity in every clime. It ought to be nothing remarkable for any city of American growth and American enterprise and prosperity. Of him who hath, we are told by the good Book,[1135] much shall be required. It is eminently proper that our enlarged benevolence in seasons of prosperity shall be freely indulged. We should have hands and hearts as open as the day to melting charity. One of our co[n]temporaries thinks that the Madeira fund is therefore stinted. Perhaps it is and, if so, will no doubt be increased when the real state of things on the Island is better understood. Thus far, we take it, most persons have gone into the charity without this information. As in the first apportionment of a new fancy in Wall-street, they take their *shares* blind, waiting for time and the newspapers to develop where the concern is located, and what its deserts. Any stock in the great interest of Humanity, they consider "must pay," whether in Madeira or the Cape de Verde.

It is well we should advert to and cherish occasions like the present, as calling forth the kindlier sentiments of a community eminently practical and mercantile. It is a comfort and consolation against a wicked world, at least equal to that which Mr. "Graves," in the play, finds in the thought that "it will one day be burnt up!" Before that good time comes, let us enjoy the few green spots in the waste of sin and sorrow, afforded by these manifestations of charity and made doubly attractive by the CHEERYBLE BROTHERS, who "POINT TO BETTER THINGS, and lead the way."

FOR MADEIRA.[1136] The subscription raised in this city for the relief of Madeira have already reached the respectable sum of $600, which has been remitted. Further subscriptions are expected. Providence Journal, 2d.

1134 *The New York Daily Times,* February 3, 1853. (New York City, NY). The Cheeryble Brothers are the twin characters Charles and Edwin, from Charles Dickens' novel *Nicholas Nickleby.* Excessively cheerful and benevolent, these characters were based upon the rich and philanthropic Manchester merchants David and William Grant.
1135 The Bible.
1136 *Daily Evening Transcript,* February 2, 1853. (Boston, MA).

By Telegraph to the Transcript.[1137]
[FROM OUR N.Y. CORRESPONDENT – BY HOUSE'S LINE.]

New York, 2ᵈ.

... MORE AID FOR MADEIRA. The amount collected up to yesterday noon by the Committee on behalf of the sufferers at Madeira, was $7500. The brig Tally ho, has been chartered and is now loading with provisions for that island. ...

News of the Morning.[1138]

... The Brig *Tally Ho*, chartered to take out the provisions contributed for the relief of the inhabitants of Madeira, cleared yesterday. She has on board 6,635 bushels of Corn, 291 barrels [of] Flour, 400 pounds of Rice, and quite a number of packages of other provisions. ...

[Untitled][1139]

A meeting of the Madeira Relief Committee was held at the Mayor's Office, Feb. 10, 1853.

In the absence of his Honor the Mayor, Hon. John A. Dix was appointed Chairman, *pro. tem.*[1140]

On motion, Mr. Robert Kelly was appointed Secretary, *pro. tem.*

The Treasurer reported that the amount received by him to this date, is $8,681 25.

The Committee appointed to charter a vessel and purchase cargo of Provisions, presented the following account.

Account of Cost of Shipment to Madeira per brig Tally-Ho, Capt. Higgins, viz:

280 barrels Flour (Middlings) at $5		$1,400 00
2,972 bushels Corn at 72c	$2,146 05	$1400 00
Less given in on Lighterage	12 52	2,127 51
3,283 bushels Corn at 70c		2,298 32
2,212 Cotton Bags at 14½		620 74
Extra Labor and Cartage on do		6 00
1,500 Heavy W. O. Ilhd Staves at $55		82 50
Half Culling at 36c		54
Delivering at 50c		75
Freight, as per Charter	$1, 200	
Less 3½ per cent off for cash advanced	42 -	1,158 00
Marine Insurance on $6,859 99, at 1½ pr. ct.		85 75
Ditto on Freight, $1,260, at 1½ pr. ct		15 00
Total		$7,495 11

[Errors Excepted] – New York, Feb. 10, 1853.
GEO M. LEWIS,
HENRY JNO.[1141] BURDEN,
WM. DEPEW

1137 *Daily Evening Transcript,* February 2, 1853. (Boston, MA).
1138 *The New York Daily Times,* February 12, 1853. (New York City, NY).
1139 *New York Daily Tribune,* February 12, 1853. (New York City, NY).
1140 See Note 1118.
1141 John.

List of gratuitous donations shipped per brig Tally Ho:
Gibson, Stockwell & Co., 5 bhls. Flour; Abbott, Dodge & Co., 5 bhls. Flour; S. Freeman & Co., 1 bhl. Flour; Wheeler & Co., 1 bhl. Rice; Sam'l Van Benachoten, 1 tierce and 1 bhl. Rice, 1 bhl. Corn Meal; George Haws, 1 bhl. Beef; Mrs. Cape, 1 bhl. Hams.

The amount of the above account of disbursements deducted from the sum received by the Treasurer, will leave a balance in his hands of $1,186 14.

It was reported by various gentlemen of the Committee, that sundry sums had been subscribed which were not yet collected, amounting to, probably, $400.

The following resolutions were adopted:

Resolved, That Hon. Jacob A. Westervelt, Chairman of this Committee, P. W. Engs. Secretary, R. B. Coleman, Treasurer, and the Committee on purchases, Messrs. G. M. Lewis, Henry J. Burden, and Wm. Depew, constitute an Executive Committee, to receive such further subscriptions as may be handed in, and expend the whole balance of funds in the purchase of provisions to be shipped by a vessel from this or some other port hereafter, or to make such other disposition of said balance for the benefit of the sufferers at Madeira as they may deem expedient.

Resolved, That the Executive Committee publish a statement of the whole subscription obtained, when it shall be completed, with the names of the contributors.

Mr. Henry J. Burden, long a resident of Madeira, who has left the island since the failure of the Vine and Potato crop, and has been highly instrumental in awakening the interest of our citizens in the relief of its suffering inhabitants, desired, before the Madeira Relief Committee be dissolved, to express, in the name of the people of Madeira, the thanks that they would themselves more abundantly and appropriately render hereafter, to those citizens of New York who had contributed the very considerable aggregate of material relief which had gone forward in money and provisions from this City, and to those who had devoted their time and exertions in this service of benevolence.

The Committee then adjourned, sine die.[1142]

John A. Dix. Chairman, pro. tem.[1143]

Robert Kelly, Secretary, pro. tem.

NEW YORK RELIEF FOR MADEIRA.[1144] We learn from the New York papers that the brig "Tally Ho," chartered by the committee for the relief for the sufferers in Madeira, has obtained her clearance, and will sail immediately. She has on board 6636 bushels of corn, 291 barrels of flour and 400 pounds of rice, besides small quantities of other provisions. This vessel will probably reach her port of destination, wind and weather permitting, after the "Nautilus," with the Boston contributions, shall have arrived, and her cargo been distributed to the starving inhabitants. – *Transcript*.

1142 Latin expression meaning "adjourned for an indefinite period" (anticipating that this particular committee would never meet again).

1143 See Note 1118.

1144 *Daily Evening Transcript,* February 12, 1853. (Boston, MA); *Boston Recorder,* February 17, 1853. (Boston, MA . Quotes the former source).

RELIEF FOR MADEIRA.[1145] Mr. Nathll Barney publishes in the Nantucket Inquirer a statement of the amount subscribed in that place for the suffering people of Madeira amounting to $267 50.[1146]

[Untitled][1147]

Nearly nine thousand dollars had been subscribed in New York, on the 5th inst., for the relief of the suffering inhabitants of Madeira.

FOR MADEIRA.[1148] Brig Tally Ho cleared at New York on Thursday, with 6336 bushels corn, 291 bhls. flour, 400 lbs. rice, besides other articles, for the relief of the starving people of Madeira. It is proposed to send another vessel soon.

RELIEF FOR MADEIRA.[1149] – The brig *Tally Ho* has gone on her mission of mercy, bearing food to the hungry inhabitants of Madeira, and the Relief Committee report that they have still on hand $1,186 14. It is to be hoped that this sum will soon swell to an amount sufficient to freight another vessel, which shall follow *Tally Ho*.

The Sufferers at Madeira.[1150]

We learn that the barque "Aaron J. Harvey" is now loading at Lombard street wharf, and will sail without delay for Madeira. Such of our citizens as are charitably disposed are earnestly invited to send on board any articles of food which they may deem calculated to assist the suffering inhabitants of the island. The officers on board will receipt for the same, while any funds to be invested for the benevolent object, will be received with pleasure by Robert Adams & Co., No. 123 Walnut street, or by Messrs. Figuera,[1151] Stoever & Longstreth, No. 45 Walnut street.

1145 *Daily Evening Transcript,* February 12, 1853. (Boston, MA).
1146 A similar article was published, untitled, in other sources, adding also the amount gathered in Providence, RI, in these words: «NANTUCKET Mass., has raised $267 50 for the relief of the people of Madeira. Providence has contributed about $600 for the same worthy object.» *The Boston Herald,* February 14, 1853. (Boston, MA); *The Sun,* February 16, 1853. (Baltimore, MD); *Charleston Courier,* February 19, 1853. (Charleston, SC); *Daily Zanesville Courier,* February 24, 1853. (Zanesville, OH). A similar article was published in another source, adding a peculiar remark: «NANTUCKET AND MADEIRA. – The Inquirer states that $267 have been collected in that town for the relief of the people of Madeira. This is truly the act of the good Samaritan, who poured *oil* upon the sufferer.» *Newport Mercury,* February 19, 1853. (Newport, RI. The fact that the word "oil" is presented in italics could have something to do with the fact that back then Nantucket was well know as a whaling port).
1147 *The Daily Picayune,* February 13, 1853. (New Orleans, LA).
1148 *The Boston Herald,* February 14, 1853. (Boston, MA).
1149 *The New York Daily Times,* February 15, 1853. (New York City, NY).
1150 *Pennsylvania Inquirer,* February 15, 1853. (Philadelphia, PA). On the following day the same newspaper published a summary of this article under the title "Relief for the Madeira Sufferers", in these words: «The barque Aaron J. Harvey is now loading at Lombard street wharf, and is receiving on board a considerable quantity of food, &c., for the sufferers of the Island of Madeira.»
1151 Figueira. See Note 1036.

Relief for the Island of Madeira.[1152]

An appeal is being made in behalf of the Starving Population of the Island of Madeira. Upon the Vineyards of this Island all its laboring People rely for support. This year the Vines are barren, and without relief the inhabitants must starve. New York and Boston have done something for their relief. Will not Albany add its contribution? The sum required is not large, for the number of sufferers is limited. But relief is greatly needed and it should go quickly.

FOR MADEIRA.[1153]

The bark Aaron J. Harvey has been taken up to load with provisions at Philadelphia for the distressed inhabitants of Madeira. The Committee here have determined to send on the balance of the funds in hand to be invested there and sent by that vessel. As there is money still required to complete the cargo, the benevolent are still called upon to contribute, so that the vessel may be dispatched by the end of the present week.

RELIEF FOR MADEIRA.[1154] – The brig Tally Ho has just sailed from New York for Madeira with 5636 bushels of corn, 291 barrels of flour, and 460 pounds of rice, besides small quantities of other provisions. Her cargo is consigned to the U.S. Consul at Funchal, who will superintend the distribution of the provisions. It is proposed to send out another vessel on the same mission, and sums of money have been raised in various quarters for this object, but the amount is as yet inadequate.

[Untitled][1155]

At the request of the donor, Mr. Robert Adams acknowledges the receipt through Blood's Despatch, of ten dollars for the Madeira sufferers.

AID FOR MADEIRA.[1156] The bark Aaron J. Harvey, has been taken up to load provisions at Philadelphia, for the distressed inhabitants of Madeira, and the New York committee have determined to send on the balance of their funds in hand to be invested in the shipment by that vessel.

1152 *Albany Evening Journal,* February 15, 1853. (Albany, NY).
1153 *New York Daily Tribune,* February 16, 1853. (New York City, NY).
1154 *North American and United States Gazette,* February 16, 1853. (Philadelphia, PA).
1155 *Pennsylvania Inquirer,* February 17, 1853. (Philadelphia, PA).
1156 *Daily Evening Transcript,* February 17, 1853. (Boston, MA); *The Boston Herald,* February 17, 1853. (Boston, MA. Published incomplete). The content of this brief article was revealed, in other words, on another source: «The Madeira Relief Committee, in New York, are to apply the balance of the funds on hand to aid in getting out the bark Aaron J. Harvey, now loading at Philadelphia, with provisions for the sufferers.» *The Daily Picayune,* February 24, 1853. (New Orleans, LA).

Relief of the Madeira Sufferers.[1157] – We learn that the bark "Aaron J. Harvey," left this port yesterday, for Madeira,[1158] having on board the following articles contributed by benevolent individuals, in aid of the sufferers at that island: 4,730 bushels Corn, 220 barrels Navy Bread, 100 barrels Middling Flour, 25 barrels Corn Meal, 5 do Pork, 2 do extra superfine Flour, 1 do Rice, 1 do Fish. Great credit is due to the gentlemen who were instrumental in getting up this noble contribution – and particularly to Messrs. Robert Adams & Co, Figuera,[1159] Stoever & Longstreth, and S. Morris Waln & Co.

Items.[1160]

… – In addition to the prompt and handsome contribution sent from Boston, New York will send about $50,000[1161] worth of provisions to the starving people of Madeira. – …

AID TO MADEIRA.[1162] – The Committee appointed at a meeting held at the Astor House, on the 24th of January last, "to solicit contributions from the inhabitants of this City," and to "use their discretion as to the mode in which the amount collected shall be appropriated for the benefit of the suffering people of Madeira," having concluded the duties assigned to them, respectfully present to the donors and the public the following synopsis of what has been done, referring those who would desire further information to the books of subscription and account, in possession of the Treasurer, Mr. ROBERT B. COLEMAN.

The total amount collected up to this date is $9,725 25.

This sum has been disposed of in the following manner:

The brig *Tally Ho* was chartered, loaded and dispatched on the 11th February, with a cargo consigned to JOHN HOWARD MARSH.[1163] Esq., Consul of the United States at Madeira, to be distributed at his discretion, consisting of Corn, Flour, &c., and amounting, together with freight and insurance on the same, $7,495 11.

After paying for the *cargo* and *charter* of the *Tally Ho,* further subscriptions were received enhancing the balance of funds, so as to justify the Committee in appropriating $1,699 34.100ths, to the purchase of freight and insurance part of a cargo, to be shipped by the bark *Aaron J. Harvey,* from Philadelphia; and we are indebted to Messrs. ROBERT

1157 *Pennsylvania Inquirer,* February 24, 1853. (Philadelphia, PA); *The New York Daily Times,* February 26, 1853. (New York City, NY. States that the article had been transcribed from the former source).
1158 According to the information published at the section related to the movement of the Port of Funchal in the Madeiran newspaper *A Ordem,* of March 28, 1853, the American bark *A. J. Harvey,* captained by Captain Barnes, had arrived from Philadelphia on that very same day, after a crossing of 30 days, bringing as cargo 100 barrels of wheat, 225 barrels of biscuits and several products for the relief of the poor.
1159 Figueira. See Note 1036.
1160 *Democratic Banner,* February 25, 1853. (Davenport, IA).
1161 This amount is exaggerated since it did not reach the $10.000 by then.
1162 *The New York Daily Times,* March 1, 1853. (New York City, NY). A summary of this text was published in another source, in these terms: «AID TO MADEIRA. The benefactions received in New York to the present time, amount to $9725 25, on the strength of which a vessel freighted with provisions has been promptly forwarded to the scene of distress, amounting together with value of cargo and insurance to $7495 11. Further subscriptions enabled the committee to freight another vessel in part, to the full extent of the collection, viz $9725 25. The actual amount transmitted from the city, including cash and provisions, has been 14,000.» *Daily Evening Transcript,* March 3, 1853. (Boston, MA).
1163 His surname was March.

ADAMS & Co, and Mr. F. I. FIGUERA,[1164] of that city, for making purchases, shipping the articles, and doing all that was necessary therewith, the same being consigned to the Committee appointed in Madeira to solicit aid, and consisted of the following: 50 barrels Navy Bread; 50 barrels Middlings Flour; and 687 bags Corn, containing 1.374 bushels.

The liberality of our citizens having furnished means beyond what the Committee had anticipated when they arranged for a shipment *via* Philadelphia, they are enabled to remit to Madeira, in cash, $530 80, which closes the trust confided in them, and disposes of the whole amount collected, making an aggregate of $9,725 25, for which they would return thanks to the kind donors, on behalf of those who are to be the recipients of their bounty.

Previous to the call of a public meeting, gentlemen who were appointed by the committee of Madeira to solicit aid had promptly acted in the premises. And as we are informed remitted in cash funds about $4 500, thus making a total of contribution from this City, of over $14.000, an amount which we consider speaks well of the readiness of New-Yorkers to respond to the demands of distressed Humanity from any quarter.[1165]

JACOB A. WESTERVELT, Chairman.
R. B. COLEMAN, Treasurer.
P. W. ENGS, Secretary.
NEW-YORK, Feb. 28, 1853.

[Untitled][1166]

On Sunday, $220 were contributed in St. Peter's Protestant Church for the relief of the starving inhabitants of the Island of Madeira.

1164 Figueira. See Note 1036.

1165 The will of New Yorkers in helping distressed people at home and overseas was underlined in an article, entitled "The Sunny Side", published in New York three months later, from which we present a brief transcription: «... And leaving these purely local aspects, there is much to be proud of in the cordial beneficence of our people; enough certainly to set off, if not cancel, the mortifications and wrongs we have enumerated. Let none of us hang his head. Nowhere else in the world is a charitable appeal so promptly and munificently answered. The need has only to be well authenticated, and thousands seem anxiously ready to supply it. There are people seeking for such opportunities of bestowing wealth. The history of a year attests immense outlays, derived from voluntary contributions, and applied to pious purposes. There are a hundred societies dependent upon such support. Charitable, sectarian, missionary, churches, hospitals, dispensaries, refuges, asylums, relief societies; and so through a long special vocabulary of benevolence. These are established channels; and they are always filled. Nor are they used as excuses for evading less methodic claims. The occasional demand is never repulsed. A famine to be alleviated in Ireland or Madeira; the disastrous result of a conflagration at Pittsburgh, or Albany, or Montreal, to be mitigated; a runaway negro to be bought; a temporary benevolent scheme to be expedited; emigrants to be sheltered, and fed, and sped on their way; searches to be made for hopeless navigators; and so on through an endless and incessant list of applications; to all of which the people of New-York respond with a cordial willingness and liberality, which we venture to plead as a fair set off against all, and the very worst, that may be alleged to their disadvantage. The benevolence of the New-Yorker is not posthumous; nor is it exhausted in few startling sums, such as endow the Cooper Institute. It is a constant and abundant stream fed by the daily contributions of thousands; tithes levied upon the sole authority of the Golden Law. ...» *The New York Daily Times*, June 2, 1853. (New York City, NY).

1166 *The Sun*, March 2, 1853. (Baltimore, MD. Published in the section "THINGS IN PHILADELPHIA"). The same fact was reported in another source, through different words: «At the Offertory of the Communion at St. Peter's Protestant Episcopal Church, Philadelphia, of which the Rev. Mr. Odenheimer is Rector, on Sunday morning last, the large sum of two hundred and twenty dollars was received for the relief of the sufferers by famine in the Island of Madeira. This is truly a noble example, and cannot be too widely imitated.» *Alexandria Gazette*, March 3, 1853. (Alexandria, VA. Published in the section "News of the Day.").

MADEIRA SUFFERERS.[1167] – L. W. TINELLI[1168] will deliver a lecture on Portugal at the Brooklyn Institute, this evening. The proceeds will be appropriated for the benefit of the inhabitants of Madeira.

Aid for Madeira.[1169] The N. Y. Committee appointed January 24th, to solicit contributions for the suffering inhabitants of Madeira, have closed up their work and made their report. They have collected about ten thousand dollars for this object; about nine thousand five hundred of which had been laid out in provisions, chiefly corn, flour and rice, and forwarded to the Island; and in addition, they have sent about $500 in money. Besides these liberal donations, about $4,500 had been collected and remitted in cash, to Madeira, previously to the appointment of this committee; making in all, from the city of New York, more than fourteen thousand dollars for this single object. – *Traveller*.

RELIEF FOR MADEIRA.[1170] The fast sailing barque Nautilus, Capt. Lincoln, which it will be remembered was dispatched hence by the Relief Committee with food material for the famishing of the Island of Madeira, has arrived out after a very fine passage of 22 days.[1171]

1167 *The New York Daily Times,* March 8, 1853. (New York City, NY).
1168 Luigi Walter Tinelli (1799-?), a native of Milan, was an Italian politician who arrived in America in 1836 as a political exile. In this country he distinguished himself as a New York militia commander and as an industrialist, being linked to the silk production in New Jersey. Moving well in the American political arena, he was appointed U.S. Consul General to Portugal, in 1840, and lived in Oporto. While he was there he published a book, in 1843, entitled *A Arte de Cultivar a Seda*. Six years before, in 1837, he had published a similar book, in New York, entitled *Hints on the Cultivation of the Mulbery: With some General Observations on the Production of Silk*.
1169 *Boston Recorder,* March 10, 1853. (Boston, MA).
1170 *Daily Evening Transcript,* March 26, 1853. (Boston, MA); *The Boston Herald,* March 28, 1853. (Boston, MA. Published under the same title but incomplete and reporting that it was quoting the *Transcript*); *The New York Daily Times,* March 30, 1853. (New York City, NY. Quotes the *Boston Evening Transcript* and presents just the first sentence of the text).
1171 According to the information published on the section related to the movement of the Port of Funchal in the Madeiran newspaper *A Ordem*, of February 26, 1853, the American bark *Nautilus*, captained by Captain Lincoln, had arrived from Boston on the 23rd, after a crossing of 26 days, bringing as cargo different products for the relief of the poor. On the other hand, the gazette *O Amigo do Povo*, of March 1, 1853, published in the front page the following notice: «A ship just arrived to this port bringing a portion of food that our brothers in America sent to the needy inhabitants of this Province. Our ills were known there and the benefactors were elucidated so well as to which miserable conditions the poorer classes endured, after the total loss of the wines last year, that the efforts of Mr. March, the worthy Consul of the United States of America in this island, were crowned with the best results. …» Together with the relief sent from Boston was also sent two precious letters addressed to the American Consul in Funchal, John Howard March. They were translated into Portuguese and published in the edition of March 3, 1853, of the Madeiran newspaper *O Progressista*. We translated them back into English and present them next. The first one, written by the Boston historian Samuel Eliot, contained the following message: «Dear Mr. March. – I send this [letter] through the bark «Nautilus», chartered to take provisions to the poor inhabitants of that island./ As soon as I received your letter I had its contents published at the gazette I am sending you enclosed. The news attracted the attention of several people, among which is our friend and relative, Mr. A. S. Ballard, that is also writing you./ It is especially to him that I owe the call of being able to provide you this service. It is therefore to him that you should be thankful to./ The provisions the bark is carrying, were bought through general subscriptions, of the importance of five to six thousand dollars./ It is the gift the inhabitants of Boston are sending to the Madeirans./ I cannot explain to you, my dear Sir and friend, how pleasant it was to provide you this service, and the sincere satisfaction I have in announcing its results to you./ May this relief produce all the benefits we wish!/ There was a great divergence about how this donation should have been made; however I thought that the best expedient was to send you merchandise to be distributed among the poor, and not money./ And it was specially for that reason that I sought to make the subscription more extensive, by loading up a ship and to sending you a bill of exchange./ I cannot forget the kindness you had towards me, when I was at Madeira. – I also cannot forget the hospitality with which I was welcomed by other people. – May the Bark «Nautilus» prove that I am not ungrateful!/ Mr. Ballard, who supervised the purchase and shipment of the provisions, writes you about it, as well as about its distribution when they get there. I recommended to Mr. Ballard to consign the ship to you, since you are the American Consul

The Nautilus belongs to Messrs. Wm. Worthington & Sons, of this city, and very rarely do we see a vessel which sustains her reputation as a fast sailer better than the N. but it cannot be otherwise while she is commanded not only by a gentleman, but a thorough bred sailor.

BOSTON RELIEF TO THE MADEIRA SUFFERERS.[1172] – The Boston *Advertiser* says; It may gratify those who contributed to pay for the cargo of provisions sent to Madeira by the bark *Nautilus*, to read the following letter just received from our Consul, J. HOWARD MARCH, Esq., under date of the 28th February:

"It is with infinite satisfaction I announce to you the arrival of the *Nautilus*, and the delivery of her cargo in good condition. It is the first succor the starving inhabitants of Madeira have received from abroad in the shape of provisions, and the very sight of them has already gladdened the hearts of thousands. On their behalf permit me to offer to you and the other generous benevolent donors, their warmest heartfelt thanks. Had an unlimited credit been placed at your disposal, the cargo would not have been sent forward with greater expedition; and long after those who will be kept alive by it shall have gone to their last homes, the very name of Boston will be almost worshipped by Madeira. * * *

Again returning you my thanks, and those of the Government and inhabitants of Madeira, for sending us the *Nautilus*. I am, my dar Sir, with great regard and respect, faithfully yours."

---

there./ With the loudest recognition, I am truly your Friend, *Samuel Eliot*. – Wildwood January 24, 1853.» The other letter, by A. S. Ballard, contained the following message: «Mr. J. Howard March./ Boston, January 26, 1853./ Dear Sir./ The Harvest Shortage in Madeira, and the ensuing misery that fell on many poor inhabitants of that Island, induced some people of this City and vicinity to contribute to the purchase of the load of provisions sent aboard the Bark «Nautilus», Captain Lincoln, consigned to you, on the terms of the enclosed invoice and conditions./ The will of the subscribers is that these provisions or relief be distributed to those Madeirans that, not having any means of subsistence, are in urgent need./ Should these provisions be in greater portion than what is necessary for immediate distribution, the surplus can be stored or sold (in the case its conservation does not face any risk) or exchanged for some other articles more adequate to the needs of the people they are destined to; this or any other expedient that you would have to adopt to extenuate, in the largest possible extension, the needs of the people who suffer, would have our sincere and cordial approval./ The charter of the ship, as you will see by the enclosed copy, will be paid in Boston, when you would inform us that the cargo had been safely unloaded; and I would appreciate if you could send us the news of that fact on the shortest possible time./ As the owners of the ship want to receive, in full, the price of the service they provide, the usual port charges will be received by her agent, however we trust that the Government would prescind of its payment, as well as of any other expense that might result from the cargo./ Trusting on your benevolent cooperation to help us relieve the largest number of unhappy people of that island, to whom may reach the benefit of our donations, we are/ Your faithful servant/ A. S. Ballard, for himself and on behalf of the subscribers.»

[1172] *The New York Daily Times*, March 31, 1853. (New York City, NY); *Boston Semi-Weekly Courier*, April 4, 1853. (Boston, MA. Published without referring which newspaper it was quoting). This letter of the U.S. Consul at Funchal was also published in another source, under a different title and preceded by a different introduction: «FOOD FOR THE STARVING IN MADEIRA. – The American consul at Maderia acknowledges the receipt of the relief sent from Boston for the starving inhabitants of that island, in the following letter, dated February 28th:» *The Oregonian*, June 11, 1853. (Portland, OR). A different version of this text was published in other sources: «THE BOSTON RELIEF FOR THE MADEIRA SUFFERERS. A letter from the American Consul at Madeira, J. Howard March, dated 28th of February, states that the Nautilus, from this port, with relief for the Madeira sufferers, had arrived, and delivered her cargo in good condition. He adds that "it is the first succour the starving inhabitants of Madeira have received from abroad in the shape of provisions, and the very sight of them has already gladdened the hearts of thousands. Long after those who will be kept alive by it shall have gone to their last homes," says Mr. March, "the very name of Boston will be almost worshipped by Madeira."» *Daily Evening Transcript*, March 30, 1853. (Boston, MA); *The Boston Daily Atlas*, March 30, 1853. (Boston, MA); *The Boston Herald*, March 30, 1853. (Boston, MA. Adds the it had been transcribed from the *Atlas*); *The Daily Picayune*, April 6, 1853. (New Orleans, LA. Published in a slightly different form). Another summary of this text was published in another American newspaper: «RELIEF FOR THE MADEIRA SUFFERERS. – The ship Nautilus, which left Boston some time since, freighted with provisions for the hungry poor of Madeira, has arrived out, and the succour has been acknowledged by a letter from the American Consul laudatory of the donors.» *Daily National Intelligencer*, April 1, 1853. (Washington, DC).

THE FAMINE IN MADEIRA – *Arrival of the Nautilus.*[1173] – The following is an extract from a letter dated Madeira, Feb. 27, 1853:

"The Nautilus, from Boston, with the generous offering from Nantucket, has arrived. As yet, no one to my knowledge has died from starvation, though there are thousands whose pale and meager faces too plainly indicate their unhappy, miserable condition. Nearly all the coopers, numbering between five and six hundred, with their families, have had no employment or means of subsistence for several months past, and their pressing wants have been answered as far as possible, but it has not been in the power of three or four individuals to do much for the help of thousands! Your succor is the first in the way of provisions, and I am happy to say to you, that our solicitations abroad have been most kindly answered. From Russia, Hamburg and England, donations are coming in, and from our happy country they are, and they will be such as to make the Madeira people almost worship the name of an American. Flour will gladden the hearts of the destitute ones.

RETURNING THE COMPLIMENT.[1174] – Mr. March, speaking of the relief sent to Madeira from Boston, says:

"Long after those who will be kept alive by it, shall have gone to their last homes, the very name of Boston will be almost worshipped by Madeira."

This is only returning the compliment, for the name of Madeira has, for a long time, been almost worshipped by the solid men of Boston. – *Providence Journal*.

[Untitled][1175]

The amount of contributions at Providence for the sufferers by famine at Madeira was $700 – showing that the "solid" men of that town don't "worship Madeira" much.

THE DISTRESS AT MADEIRA.[1176] – Mayor Westervelt, of New York, has received letters from the Hon. J. Howard March, United States consul at Madeira, and from Antonio Goncalves d'Almeida,[1177] president of the Municipal Chamber of Funchal,[1178] expressing warm thanks for the aid sent to the island from New York.

1173 *New York Daily Tribune,* April 4, 1853. (New York City, NY); *The Boston Herald,* April 13, 1853. (Boston, MA); *North American and United States Gazette,* April 16, 1853. (Philadelphia, PA); *The Daily Picayune,* April 23 and 24, 1853. (New Orleans, LA. Published under the title "The Famine in Madeira." and presenting some slight changes in the introductory note: «A letter dated Madeira, February 27, 1853, after noticing the arrival of the Nautilus with provisions, from Boston, says:»).

1174 *Daily National Intelligencer,* April 5, 1853. (Washington, DC); *Alexandria Gazette,* April 6, 1853. (Alexandria, VA); *Daily Evening Transcript,* April 8, 1853. (Boston, MA); *Illinois State Register,* April 9, 1853. (Springfield, IL); *Salem Register,* April 11, 1853. (Salem, MA); *Zanesville Daily Courier,* April 15, 1853. (Zanesville, OH); *Fremont Journal,* April 30, 1853. (Fremont, Sandusky Co., OH).

1175 *The Daily Picayune,* April 29 and 30, 1853. (New Orleans, LA. Published in the section "Splinters from the Boston Post.").

1176 *The Sun,* May 2, 1853. (Baltimore, MD); *The Boston Daily Atlas,* May 2, 1853. (Boston, MA. Published untitled in slightly different words).

1177 The right spelling of his name is António Gonçalves d'Almeida.

1178 Funchal City Hall.

9. MADEIRA WINE IN THE AMERICAN PRESS

THE RELIEF TO MADEIRA.[1179] – Mr. HOWARD MARCH, Consul of the United States at Madeira, has addressed a letter to Mayor WESTERVELT, enclosing a letter of thanks from the Municipal Chamber of Madeira, in reference to the liberal aid furnished towards the support of the famishing population by the recent subscription in New-York. Mr. MARCH states that the cargo of provisions sent in the ship *Tally-Ho*, has been delivered in good condition, and that its distribution has greatly mitigated the wants of several hundred families, who, before its arrival, were in the last stage of destitution. "The vines," adds Mr. MARCH, "are now beginning to bud, which induces us to hope that the next vintage may restore the island to its former state of prosperity." The following is a copy of the letter addressed to Mayor WESTERVELT, by the President of the Madeira[1180] Chamber:

MADEIRA, March 17, 1853.

To the Hon. John A. Westervelt, Mayor of the City of New-York:
SIR: On the part of the Municipal Chamber of the Concelho[1181] of Funchal, over which I have the honor to preside, I have to acknowledge the arrival of the American brig *Tally-Ho*,[1182] with its most welcome freight of corn, flour, rice, &c., the munificent donation of the generous citizens of New-York to alleviate the distress – the deep distress – of the unfortunate inhabitants of this island, consequent on the entire failure of last year's vintage from the universally prevalent disease among the vines.

In behalf of our fellow-countrymen, the inhabitants of Madeira, we have to offer our thanks, the warm expression of grateful hearts, for the generous assistance now extended to us. In doing this, we are not unmindful of the many previous occasions in which the inhabitants of the islands of the Atlantic have been relieved from the pressure of death and famine by the compassionate intervention of the citizens of the United States.

It is by such generous deeds that men are taught to regard each other as brethren, and distant communities to sympathise with others in all that affects their welfare or their woe. Accept then our most grateful thanks, and with them receive our warmest wishes for the continued well-being and prosperity of your great, generous and free country.

To you, sir, the honored delegate of your country's generosity, we beg to tender our most grateful acknowledgements, and with sentiments of most profound respect and esteem, I am, sir, your most obedient servant,

---

1179 *The New York Daily Times*, May 3, 1853. (New York City, NY). A short summary of this article was published in other sources: «Major Westervelt has received a letter from Mr. March, U.S. Consul at Madeira, and from the President of the Municipal Chamber of Funchal, expressing warm thanks for the aid sent to the Island by the American Brig Jaloe [Tally Ho].» *Daily Commercial Register*, May 2, 1853. (Sandusky, OH). «THE DISTRESS AT MADEIRA. – Mayor Westervelt, of New York, has received letters from the Hon. J. Howard March, United States consul at Madeira, and from Antonio Goncalves d'Almeida, president of the Municipal Chamber of Funchal, expressing warm thanks for the aid sent to the island from New York.» *The Sun*, May 2, 1853. (Baltimore, MD); *Alexandria Gazette*, May 4, 1853. (Alexandria, VA. Published untitled). «Mayor Westervelt of New York, has received letters from Mr. March, U.S. Consul at Madeira, and from Antonio Goncalves d'Almeida, President of the Municipal Chamber, at Funchal, expressing the warmest thanks for aid sent to the Island by brig Tally Ho.» *The Boston Daily Atlas*, May 2, 1853. (Boston, MA); *Springfield Daily Republican*, May 2, 1853. (Springfield, MA); *The Daily Picayune*, May 7 and 8, 1853. (New Orleans, LA).
1180 Funchal.
1181 Portuguese word for Municipality.
1182 According to the information published at the section related to movement of the Port of Funchal in the Madeiran newspaper *A Ordem*, of March 12, 1853, the American brig *Tally Ho*, captained by Captain J. C. Higgins, had arrived from New York, consigned to the Consul, after a crossing of 29 days, bringing a cargo of flour and corn for the poor of this island, and six passengers, five of which to Madeira. On the same newspaper it was also published the following notice: «On today's afternoon (12) arrived at our port an American Brig, from New York, loaded with provisions that the philanthropic citizens of the United States of America sent to the illustrious Committee of Public Relief, to be distributed among the poor inhabitants of Madeira.» Another local newspaper, *O Progressista*, of March 24, 1853, also announced the arrival of the *Tally Ho*, in its section related to the Port of Funchal.

(Signed) ANTONIO GONCALVES D'ALMEIDA,[1183]
President of the Municipal Chamber of Funchal.[1184]

The Madeira Distress.[1185]

We mentioned on Saturday that Mayor Westervelt had received from Madeira letters acknowledging the receipt of the Tally Ho's cargo of provisions. The subjoined is the interesting correspondence, which will be a sufficient reward to those who contributed to aid the people of Madeira in their hour of need. – [N. Y. Com. Adv.]

[COPY.]

CONSULATE OF THE UNITED STATES,
MADEIRA, March 17, 1853.

Hon. JACOB A. WESTERVELT, Mayor of the City of New York:

MY DEAR SIR – I have the honor to acknowledge the receipt of your most welcome letter, accompanying a bill of landing of a cargo of provisions by the Tally-Ho, for the distressed inhabitants of Madeira.

The cargo has been delivered in good condition, and the distribution already made of a portion of it has greatly mitigated the wants of several hundred families, who, before its arrival, were in the last stage of destitution. On their behalf permit me to convey to you, and to the other benevolent donors, their humble heartfelt thanks.

It is true that I had led some of the poor Madeiran people to hope that a small sum of money might be collected for them through the influence of a few gentlemen of high standing in New York, who having resided a short time on their island, and being thus acquainted with their habits and resources, could comprehend the extent of the calamity which the failure of their vintage had brought down upon them, but no one could have supposed that so munificent an offering as a whole cargo of provisions would be made to them by your city.

A letter of thanks from the Madeira Camera,[1186] I have the honor herewith to enclose.

As you have been so charitable and benevolent as to take an interest in the welfare of the poor Madeira people, permit me to make known to you that, though their distress is very great, no one to my personal knowledge has died of hunger; for like the Irish, the natives of Madeira, how poor soever they may be, never refuse to give a part of their scanty morsel to a poorer neighbor.

The vines are now beginning to bud, which induces us to hope that the next vintage may restore the island to its former state of prosperity.[1187]

With the greatest regard and consideration, I have the honor to be, my dear sir,
very respectfully,
your obedient faithful servant.
(signed) J. HOWARD MARCH,
Consul of the United States at Madeira.

1183 See Note 1177.
1184 See Note 1178.
1185 *Albany Evening Journal,* May 3, 1853. (Albany, NY).
1186 See Note 1178. As we have seen, this letter is presented on the previous article.
1187 It did not, since it took about ten years for that to happen, as will be seen on the next section.

The Sufferers at Madeira.[1188]

The Philadelphia contributors to the Relief Fund on behalf of the suffering inhabitants of Madeira, will read the following with pleasure.

MADEIRA, 2ᵈ April, 1853.

Gentlemen: – I have received, and had the greatest satisfaction in laying before the Relief Committee for distributing contributions among the poor of this Island, and of which I am Chairman, your esteemed letters of the 23ᵈ and 28ᵗʰ of February, and 8ᵗʰ ultimo;[1189] and the gratifying task devolves upon me of conveying to you, in our name, and on behalf of the distressed population around us, heartfelt, grateful and thankful acknowledgments for your benevolent and successful exertions in promoting subscriptions and liberally affording succour towards the mitigation of wide-spread and severe destitution. You will also have the goodness of undertaking the duty of expressing these our sentiments of deep obligation, as speaking for the suffering Madeira inhabitants, to the numerous generous contributors to this charitable cause, in which we are earnestly engaged.

The barque "Aaron J. Harvey" arrived here on the 27ᵗʰ ultimo,[1190] and the provisions which you shipped by her, subject to our control, as specified in two invoices, amounting to Rs.[1191] 1,699$34, and Rs.[1192] 3,515$18, have been landed; and we are in possession of Messrs. Robert Adams & Co.'s draft on Messrs. John Blandy & Sons for $291 54, being the balance, as per statement with which you also furnish us, of collections made, by your joint indefatigable and laudable efforts, in aid of our destitute fellow creatures, after paying for the shipment of provisions made therefrom.

Our earnest endeavors will be used to relieve, as far as in our power, the most necessitous, and if, in the administration of the responsible trust committed to our charge, we should be fortunate enough to give satisfaction to the philanthropic donors, and do the amount of good we desire with their generous donations, we shall have great reason for thankfulness.

Gentlemen, your most obedient humble servant,   GEO. STODDART,[1193]
Chairman of Relief Committee for distressed inhabitants of Madeira.
P. S. – I inclose a note of thanks to the Rev. W. H. Odenheimer.[1194]   G. S.

PLEASANT.[1195] – A letter from an officer in the U.S. Navy, dated Funchal, Madeira, May 1ˢᵗ,[1196] is published in the Portland *Advertiser*. The following is an extract:

The hill sides of Madeira appear pictures of fertility, and it is to be hoped a year of

---

[1188] *Pennsylvania Inquirer,* May 3, 1853. (Philadelphia, PA); *North American and United States Gazette,* May 3, 1853. (Philadelphia, PA. Published under the title "THE MADEIRA SUFFERERS" and a different introductory note: «The following letter from Madeira, acknowledging the arrival there of the barque Aaron J. Harvey, from Philadelphia, and the receipt by her of the provisions sent thither for the relief of the distressed inhabitants of the island, possesses a peculiar interest in this locality, where so many of our benevolent citizens contributed liberally of their means in aid of so deserving a cause:». At the end of the letter it is mentioned its addressees, namely Messrs. Robt. Adams & Co., and Messrs. Figueira, Stoever & Langstroth, Philadelphia).

[1189] Portuguese word for last.

[1190] See previous Note.

[1191] Abbreviation for Réis, the Portuguese currency of the time.

[1192] See previous Note.

[1193] English Consul in Funchal.

[1194] Rector of St. Peter's Protestant Episcopal Church, in Philadelphia, who during one of his Sunday services was able to collect $220 for the sufferers of Madeira. See Note 1166.

[1195] *The New York Daily Times,* June 13, 1853. (New York City, NY). Under the title "Madeira." this text was published on the following sources: *Daily National Intelligencer,* June 13, 1853. (Washington, DC,); *Bangor Daily Whig and Courier,* June 17, 1853. (Bangor, ME); *The Daily Picayune,* June 20 and 21, 1853. (New Orleans, LA).

[1196] This letter was certainly written by an officer of the U. S. ship *Macedonian* for *The New York Daily Times* of June 9, 1853, reports that a letter dated at Madeira, on May 1ˢᵗ, had been received from on board that Navy vessel.

fruitfulness is to succeed the last year of famine. As we approached our anchorage this morning, the fishermen in the boats, as we passed them, saluted us by doffing their hats and crying "a good nation," "a good nation," showing that the charity of Boston and New-York had been felt and appreciated, and fulfilling an old saying "that the way to the people's heart is down their throat."[1197]

HOW IS THIS?[1198] – A letter written at Madeira, March 6, on board the U.S. steam frigate Powhatan,[1199] says of the famine: "We have seen nothing of the kind; and I heard that the provisions that had arrived to be given to the poor, were locked in the custom house, and probably would not be delivered, unless we pay the duties upon them.[1200] The mother government has sent nothing here, and I fear out people have thrown away their sympathy and money." – *Boston Post.*»

FAMINE IN MADEIRA.[1201] – A paragraph, purporting to be an extract from a letter written at Madeira, on board the United Stated steam-frigate *Powhatan*, is floating through the press, which denies the existence of any famine on the Island, and insinuates that the provisions and money sent from this country would both be thrown away, or, at all events, not applied to the benevolent uses for which they were contributed. This statement is wholly without warrant, for we have seen letters to a most respectable merchant of this city, from parties resident in Madeira, Americans and others, in which the writers acknowledge with warm expressions of gratitude the timely relief afforded to the suffering poor, whose condition, they say, but for the aid thus afforded, would have been very

---

1197 This fact was reported, in other words, in other sources: «NOT UNGRATEFUL. – One effect of the aid sent by Philadelphia, New York and Boston, to Madeira, as that when an American vessel approaches the island, the fishermen and others salute her with cries of "A good nation – a good nation."» *Public Ledger*, June 24, 1853. (Philadelphia, PA. Published in the section "Varieties."); *The Sun*, June 25, 1853. (Baltimore, MD); *North American and United States Gazette*, June 27, 1853. (Philadelphia, PA); *Cleveland Daily Plain Dealer*, June 28, 1853. (Cleveland, OH). «One effect of the aid sent to Madeira, from New York, Boston and Philadelphia, is, that when an American vessel arrives there, it is said – "there come a ship from the good nation."» *Illinois Daily Journal*, July 11, 1853. (Springfield, IL).
1198 *The Richmond Whig and Public Advertiser*, June 3, 1853. (Richmond, VA); *Newport Mercury*, June 4, 1853. (Newport, RI. Published untitled and preceded by the following sentence: «A LETTER written at Madeira, March 6 aboard U.S. steam frigate Powhatan, says of the famine.»); *Cleveland Daily Plain Dealer*, June 6, 1853. (Cleveland, OH. Published under the title "THE MADEIRA FAMINE.", preceded by the same sentence as in the previous source). Other bogus reports, published before and after this one, also mentioned that the situation in Madeira was not that bad after all: «From Madeira. From the N. Y. *Commercial Advertiser*. U.S. Ship MACEDONIA, Madeira, May 1, 1853. – … The people on the islands are not so badly off, after all, for provisions. They appear in about the same condition as when I was in Madeira last.» *Pennsylvania Inquirer*, June 2, 1853. (Philadelphia, PA); *Richmond Whig and Public Advertiser*, June 7, 1853. (Richmond, VA. Published under the title "NAVAL."); *The Daily Picayune*, June 9, 1853. (New Orleans, LA. Published under the title "The U.S. Ship Macedonian."). «Late accounts from Madeira, where a famine was said to prevail, represent the citizens to be well supplied with provisions.» *The Sun*, June 3, 1853. (Baltimore, MD); *Daily National Intelligencer*, June 4, 1853. (Washington, DC).
1199 This Navy ship arrived at Madeira on the 2nd of March, as we learn from the edition of *The New York Daily Times* of April 1, 1853. She was on its way to Japan. A Madeiran source, namely the newspaper *A Ordem*, of March 5 and 12, 1853, also refers, in its section of the movement of the Port of Funchal, that this ship had arrived at Funchal on the 2nd of March, from Norfolk, and left the island on the 8th, for China.
1200 This is a false statement since the Portuguese government had exempted from taxation all donations from abroad.
1201 *North American and United States Gazette*, June 8, 1853. (Philadelphia, PA); *Daily National Intelligencer*, June 10, 1853. (Washington, DC). Quoting the *North American and United States Gazette*, this article was published in these sources: *Alexandria Gazette*, June 11, 1853. (Alexandria, VA); *The New York Daily Times*, June 13, 1853. (New York City, NY); *Richmond Whig and Public Advertiser*, June 14, 1853. (Richmond, VA); *Newport Mercury*, June 18, 1853. (Newport, RI); *Oshkosh Weekly Courier*, June 29, 1853. (Oshkosh, WI).

destitute, and refer to the action of the Government, which at once remitted all duties on the articles forwarded, and ordered an address of thanks to be made to the donors through the American Consul, thus officially recognizing the existence of the calamity, and their appreciation of the means adopted to alleviate it.[1202]

The Madeira Sufferers.[1203]
TO THE EDITOR OF THE HERALD.

NEW YORK, July 20, 1853.

The proprietor of the HERALD kindly published a letter from a lady in Madeira last winter, the postage of which she was not able to pay; she now encloses it, with many thanks for his courtesy.

The prompt and generous assistance which was sent from New York and Boston for the sufferers of that island was most gratefully received by them, and with astonishment by the Portuguese government; every resident expressed the warmest surprise and admiration at such spontaneous liberality.

There is still very great destitution and suffering in Madeira, and the prospect is there will be still greater; but every one must feel the propriety and the absolute necessity of their being relieved by their own government, and the English merchants who have enriched themselves by its products.

America has done nobly, and all the world acknowledges it.

1202 Other articles were also published, denying the facts mentioned on that letter from the *Powhattan*: «MADEIRA. We noticed a few days since an extract from a letter, purporting to have been written from aboard one of our U.S. vessels at Madeira, stating that the provisions and other necessaries sent by our citizens to the destitute there, had never been distributed, but held under custom house lock by the government. We consider it due to ourselves – we being the only house that publicly solicited contributions – to state, that we have received contrary information from a member of the House of J. Howard March & Co., who was here a few days since; he states that not only had our donations been received, but by them thousands had been saved from absolute starvation. Baltimore, June 7. P. TIERNAN & SON.» *Alexandria Gazette*, June 8, 1853. (Alexandria, VA). «*The Famine at Madeira*. – A letter dated on board a U.S. vessel-of-war, then at Madeira, spoke of the famine which had been reported to exist there as chiefly an affair of imagination; and intimated that the provisions sent from this country might be unavailable for lack of the payment of duties, or to that effect. The N. Y. Journal of Commerce says it has good reason to believe that these representations are incorrect; and that conclusive evidence of their incorrectness will soon be laid before the donors and the American people. The Journal is in possession of a circular of 27th March last, signed by the consuls of the United States, Great Britain, and Prussia, at Madeira, acting with other persons as a committee for the management and distribution of contributions from foreign countries, which speaks of the succour which had been received as "timely, although they fear inadequate," and expresses the hope that other charitable individuals will follow the example of those who have already given. It also speaks of "the unprecedented calamity to which this island has been a victim, occasioning almost universal suffering." The Journal of Commerce has also a petition to the Queen by the authorities of Funchal, praying for the remission of all duties upon said cargoes on account of the charitable object of the importation; and it was not doubted that the petition would be granted. It is dated February 24.» *The Daily Picayune*, June 18, 1853. (New Orleans, LA). Posterior reports from Madeira informed that the situation was still critical in the island: «A letter from the Island of Madeira states, that a day of great suffering hangs over the peasantry of that island. Those before rich cannot now relieve them. Charitable contributions must come from the States, or pestilence will be added to the horrors of famine.» *Illinois Daily Journal*, June 18, 1853. (Springfield, IL); «We are informed that the great destitution and suffering still exist in Madeira, and the prospect is that there will be still greater. The assistance sent from New York and Boston was received with gratitude by the people.» *State Gazette*, July 28, 1853. (Trenton, NJ); *The Weekly Herald*, July 30, 1853. (New York City, NY).

1203 *The Weekly Herald*, July 30, 1853. (New York City, NY).

The Condition of Madeira.[1204]
[For the Evening Post]

Anonymous statements having appeared in the newspapers, calculated to create an impression that the accounts of distress in the Island of Madeira, caused by the failure of the vintage last year, had been misrepresented, or at least greatly exaggerated, the following letter will not only refute such statements, but, we trust, convince those who so generously and promptly responded to the appeal in behalf of the unfortunate but industrious and truly deserving inhabitants of Madeira, that their sympathy was not wasted, nor their contributions misapplied.

This year again has the vine been attacked by the blight; there will be a total failure of the vintage, and, as may be imagined, the situation of the inhabitants of Madeira is indeed deplorable.

The undersigned[1205] have not been requested, therefore it is not their intention to solicit aid for these sufferers, but they will most cheerfully receive and forward such remittances as the charitable may place in their hands for that purpose, following the donors directions, in regard to any special disposal thereof.

GEORGE M. LEWIS, 61 Front street.
WILLIAM DEPEW, 135 Pearl street.

1204 *The Evening Post,* August 5, 1853. (New York City, NY); *Pennsylvania Inquirer,* August 6, 1853. (Philadelphia, PA. Informs that the copy of this correspondence had been submitted to the newspaper by Messrs. Robert Adams & Co.); *North American and United States Gazette,* August 6, 1853. (Philadelphia, PA. Published under the title "Famine at Madeira.", preceded by the following introductory note: «On the authority of letters received by several respectable merchants of this city, we contradicted, a short time since, an assertion that the misrepresentations of the distress of this people of the Island of Madeira from famine were exaggerated. The following letter from Capt. Mayo, commander-in-chief of the United States naval forces on the West Coast of Africa, to the U.S. Consul at Madeira, confirms our opinion that the reports of the dearth on the Island were entirely true, and that the charitable contributions from this country for its relief were not misappropriated.»); *Daily National Intelligencer,* August 8, 1853. (Washington, DC. Published under the title "THE ISLAND OF MADEIRA." and preceded by the following statement: «Commodore Mayo, of the U.S. Naval forces on the coast of Africa, writing from Funchal, Madeira, July 2d, expresses his entire conviction that the general representation of the terrible poverty and suffering brought upon the laboring class on this Island by the successive failures of the vintage has been in no degree exaggerated. He says:»); *Daily Chronicle & Sentinel,* August 9, 1853. (Augusta, GA. Published under the title "The Distress Madeira." preceded by this note: «The following letter from Com. Mayo confirms the worst accounts that have been received of the distress and destitution of the people of Madeira. It has been transmitted to us by Messrs. George M. Lewis, 61 Front street, and Wm. Depew, 185 Pearl street, who "will most cheerfully receive and forward such assistance as the charitable may place in their hands for that purpose, following the donors' direction in regard to any special disposition thereof:"»); *The New York Daily Times,* August 15, 1853. (New York City, NY. Published under the title "From Madeira. *From the Boston Advertiser*", preceded by this sentence «The following letter will be of interest to those who have contributed to the relief of the suffering people of Madeira:», and ending with a *post scriptum,* also written by Isaac Mayo: «P. S. – I am usually unwilling to permit any letter of mine to appear in print, but if you believe that the publication of what I have written will be of any service to the charitable cause in which your feelings are so warmly interested, you are at liberty to make any use of it you may deem proper.»). We should also add that the Commodore Mayo's letter, without his P.S. but accompanied by the previous note, subscribed by two members of the New York's Madeira Relief Committee, was also published, in English and in Portuguese, in the Madeiran press, namely at *O Progressista,* of September 17, 1853, under the titles "DISTRESS IN MADEIRA./ To THE EDITORS OF THE EXPRESS".

1205 Members of the New York's Madeira Relief Committee.

[COPY.]

FLAG SHIP CONSTITUTION,[1206]
Funchal, 2ᵈ July, 1853.

DEAR SIR: A letter, purporting to come from the United States steamer *Powhatan*, dated Funchal, March 6, has recently gone the rounds of the American papers.

This communication, coming from one of our national vessels, may create an impression upon the public mind at home, and serve to repress that active sympathy manifested towards the starving poor of Madeira by our generous countrymen.

I desire, therefore, peremptorily to contradict the statements of the anonymous writer, and as the commanding naval officer on this station, to express my entire conviction that the general representation of the terrible poverty and suffering brought upon the labouring classes in this island by the successive failures of the vintage has been in no degree exaggerated.

I am in possession of the most authentic proofs that the contributions from the United States have not only alleviated much distress, but have saved many persons from starvation.

The Portuguese authorities, so far from throwing impediments in the way of those charged with distributing the provisions sent from our country, have most promptly suspended their tariff, and admitted the donations free of duty; and these donations seem to have been distributed with admirable judgment by the committee to which they have been entrusted.

In passing over the island, I have been forcibly impressed by the gratitude exhibited towards our people, for the prompt and efficient aid extended to Maderia in her sore necessity. And I have felt most proud of that far-reaching charity that knows no limit of nation or language, but has sought out the famine stricken sufferers in this distant island.

There is every reason to fear that the distress of the coming year will be even greater than that which is past, and our countrymen may still find most worthy objects of their charity in this island, so beautiful, but by the visitation of Providence, so full of misery.[1207]

I am, dear Sir, with great regard,
faithfully yours,
[Signed.] T. MAYO,[1208]
Commander in Chief U.S. Naval Forces,
West Coast of Africa.[1209]
J. HOWARD MARCH, Esq.,
U.S. Consul, Madeira.

1206 According to the section of the movement of the Port of Funchal, in the Madeiran newspaper *A Ordem*, of June 25 and July 9, 1853, this U.S. Navy ship had arrived at Funchal on the 18th of June, from Gibraltar, and left the island on the 3ʳᵈ of July, for the Coast [of Africa].

1207 Some passages of Commodore Mayo's letter were transcribed in another source, under the title "THE DISTRESS IN MADEIRA", preceded by the following introduction: «It will be recollected that after contributions were made in this country to relieve the famished inhabitants of the island of Madeira a letter was published, purporting to come from on board the U.S. frigate Powhatan, in which the existence of distress on the island was denied, and it was asserted that the contributions supplied had been wasted and misapplied. Commander Mayo, of the U.S. African Squadron, gives these statements an unqualified denial. He says –». *Publid Ledger,* August 17, 1853. (Philadelphia, PA).

1208 Commodore Isaac Mayo (1794-1861), a native of Maryland, was a renowned American Naval Officer who at the end of 1852 had been assigned to command the U.S. African Squadron, aboard the Flag Ship *Constitution*, with the intention of stopping the slave trade to America.

1209 A brief summary of this letter was published in another source, in these terms: «FAMINE IN MADEIRA. – Com. Mayo, of the U.S. African squadron, writes to New York, confirming the reports of famine in Madeira last year, and expressing fears that it will be worse this year, on account of the failure of the vintage.» *The Sun,* August 6, 1853. (Baltimore, MD); *Cleveland Daily Plain Dealer,* August 10, 1853. (Cleveland, OH); *The Daily Alton Telegraph,* August 17, 1853. (Alton, IL. Published untitled at the "News Items." section).

Madeira.[1210]

The relief sent by the charitable of Boston and New York to the sufferers from famine in Madeira, was properly distributed, and is stated not only to have alleviated distress, but to have saved many persons from starvation. The Portuguese authorities promptly suspended their tariff and admitted these donations free of duty. The Commander of our Naval Forces on the West Coast of Africa has traversed the Island, and reports that every where the greatest gratitude was felt for the very prompt and liberal aid from America. He says that there is every reason to fear that the distress of the coming year will be even greater than that of the past, for the grape crop is still blasted. If so, our generosity may be again needed.

RELIEF FOR MADEIRA.[1211] – Our latest advices states that there is yet a good deal of suffering in Madeira. The following correspondence has taken place between the purser of the brig Perry and the United States consul at Madeira:

U.S. BRIG PERRY,
FUNCHAL, July 12, 1853.
Sir: The officers and crew of the Perry, availing themselves of the opportunity offered by their visit to this place at a time when want and suffering prevail to a considerable extent among the inhabitants of Madeira, beg leave, through you, to tender to those who are intrusted with the distribution of voluntary contributions, a very small sum of money, which they requested may be received and appropriated to the benefit of such hospital and asylum for the poor as may need is most.
Very respectfully,
Your obedient servant,
(Signed) WM. W. KELLY,[1212] Purser,

To J. Howard March, Esq., U.S. Consul at Madeira.
MADEIRA, July 13, 1853.
Wm. W. J. Kelly, Purser, United States brig Perry. – My Dear Sir: It is with great satisfaction I acknowledge the receipt of your letter of the 14th instant, and the very generous gift of $70 from the captain, officers and crew of the Perry, for the sick and poor of Madeira.[1213]
This most liberal donation will relieve the urgent wants of a great number of our fellow-creatures, and cause the name of the Perry to be long remembered here.
The money has been divided between the hospital and poor-house, according to your instructions, as you will see by the enclosed receipts; and permit me on behalf of the sick and poor of Madeira, to offer to every person on board the Perry, their most grateful and heartfelt thanks. With the greatest regard and esteem,
(Signed) J. HOWARD MARCH.
Consul of U.S. at Madeira.

1210 *The Connecticut Courant,* August 13, 1853. (Hartford, CT).
1211 *The Evening Post,* September 9, 1853. (New York City, NY).
1212 William Washington Jones Kelly (1814-1878), a native of North Carolina, better known for being the 1st Lieutenant Governor of Florida, a position he held for three years, from 1865 to 1868. Some years before, he had joined the U.S. Navy as a purser and served on various ships and at the Pensacola Navy Yard for nine years.
1213 This fact was also reported in another American newspaper: «The officers and crew of the U.S. brig *Perry*, during their recent visit to Funchal, contributed $70 for the relief of the suffering inhabitants of Madeira.» *The Charleston Daily Courier,* September 12, 1853. (Charleston, SC).

The Suffering in Madeira.[1214] By the report of the Madeira Relief Committee, recently published in pamphlet form,[1215] it appears that the contributions in aid of the sufferers on the Island, prevented a large amount of distress which could not otherwise have been avoided. The report also exhibits the gratifying fact that the aggregate amount of subscriptions made in the United States nearly double those of Great Britain, and surpasses those of all other places combined.

Figure 86. William W. J. Kelly promoted a subscription among the officers and crew of the U.S. Brig *Perry* in behalf of the poor Madeirans, during his passage by the island on July 1853. *19th century engraving. Author unknown, c. 1865-68.*

THE FAMINE IN MADEIRA. – CONSULATE GENERAL OF PORTUGAL, New York, May 5.[1216] – For the information and satisfaction of all the humane contributors who in this country so liberally subscribed money, provisions, and effects, for the relief of the unfortunate inhabitants of the Island of Madeira, reduced to want and penury in consequence of the dreadful visitation of the "vine disease," the undersigned has the pleasure publicly to announce that, in addition to acknowledgements of the authorities and inhabitants of that island, (already transmitted and published in this country,) he has received the commands of his Majesty the King Regent of Portugal,[1217] to tender, in expressive terms, his Majesty's thanks to all and every contributor for the sentiments of humanity and evident proof of sympathy manifested by them on the occasion, and for the generous cooperation of the citizens of the United States in relieving that hopeless people.

C. H. S. DE LAFIGANIERE,[1218]

Consul General of Portugal.

The relief-gathering process in the United States was very swift and efficient. From the publication of the "Appeal to America", at the last day of December 1852, to the gathering of all the funds and purchase of goods to be sent to Madeira, and the arrival of the first ship to the island, only two months elapsed. And if we consider that a voyage from the United States to Madeira, on a sailing ship back then, took about a month, on average, we can infer how fast the philanthropic Americans worked in this humanitarian cause.

The *Nautilus*, with relief from Boston, arrived in the island on February 23, 1853, the *Tally Ho*, from New York, on March 12th and the *Aaron J. Harvey*, from Philadelphia, on March 28th. Curiously enough, the last ship to arrive, was from the place that first started the fund gathering, organized, among others, by a Madeiran merchant who

---

1214 *Boston Semi-Weekly Courier,* June 19, 1854. (Boston, MA).
1215 Published anonymously in London, in 1854, under the title *Report of the Madeira Relief Fund Committee; Established in the Year 1853.* Due to its utmost relevance we present some excerpts of it at the end of this anthology, under the form of an attachment. See section 13.1. of this anthology.
1216 *The Daily Globe,* November 28, 1854. (Washington, D.C.).
1217 Ferdinand II (1816-1885), husband of Queen Mary II, who ruled from 1837 to 1853.
1218 See Note 1093.

lived and worked there, Fortunato Figueira. The food sent to the island was distributed among the poor, by a committee created for that purpose, especially among those from the wine districts of Madeira, and instead of distributing money at random among them, and thus promoting idleness, it was used instead to hire teams of men from all over the island to be used in a major public work, the opening of the New Road, as it was called back then, or Estrada Monumental, linking Funchal, the capital of the island, to Câmara de Lobos,[1219] and a set of other public works, including the opening of *levadas* (water channels) or a construction of a bridge at Ponta do Pargo, a village in southwest Madeira.[1220]

As we can also infer from the last texts of this section, the impressive and fast relief sent from America surprised its promoters on the island, among them the U.S. Consul, who were unaware of the fact that the American press had done a massive campaign on behalf of the sufferers of Madeira who were at the verge of famine, due to the failure of the wine crops. The quick response sent to the island is due, in our view, to the prestige Madeira Wine had in the United States at that time. By sending all this help, the philanthropists, most of whom were fond lovers of this wine, secretly hoped that the vine plague would soon disappear, and they could enjoy their Madeiras as before. But this did not happen, since it took quite a few years for the vines to recover, as will be seen on the next section.

Due to the generosity of hundreds of Americans, who contributed for this cause, the United States was beyond any doubt the main contributor to remedy the calamitous situation arisen in the island as a consequence of the failure of the grape. Such kindness, shown in a time of utter need, instilled in the islanders an enduring feeling of gratitude towards America and the Americans.

9.7.2. Consecutive Failures of the Wine Crops

In this section there are twenty-nine articles, published between 1853 and 1864, dealing with the consecutive failures of the wine crops in Madeira, for over ten years,

---

1219 When Charles W. Thomas, the Chaplain of the African Squadron visited Madeira in 1855 he mentioned this fact in Chapter III of the travel book he published five years later: «On the New Road, as the road between Camera de Lobos and Funchal is called, the American may walk feeling that he has a right there, for it was, in part, constructed by American benevolence; … Many of the applicants for bread were able-bodied adults, and to keep such from contracting habits of indolence during the famine, it was determined by the committee that a small amount of daily labor should be demanded for daily bread. It was thought that by appropriating this labor to the formation of a good road in this part of the island, a double purpose could be accomplished: that by making a good road between Funchal and a densely populated district, a permanent benefit would be bestowed on the poor of that district; and at the same time such a road would form a pleasant *promenade* for visitors to the island, most of whom are from the countries which contributed. The American or English visitor to Madeira, as he enjoys a breezy walk on this beautiful and gravelled way, finds sufficient reason to approve of this application of the labor which his benevolence supported, …» THOMAS 1860, pages 438-439. Years later, in 1871, a Funchal correspondent of an American paper also mentioned the United States' contributions for the opening of this road: «After the failure of this crop, as noticed, the distress on the island became very great, and you will remember food was sent the people from the United States. At this time a beautiful new road of about six miles in length, on the south side of the island, was laid out and built, payment to the laborers being made in part from these provisions. The idea was an excellent one, as the road is a benefit to stranger and citizen, and produced upon the laborers an impression of earning the food, which if given would naturally induce careless idleness and consequent eventual miscontent.» *Salem Register*, May 8, 1871. (Salem, MA).

1220 On that bridge, which still exists, was inscribed the following stanza: "Esta ponte é de memória/ Por ser oferta estrangeira/ América, tens a glória/ De socorrer a Madeira." English translation: This bridge is memorable/ For being a gift from abroad/ America, you have the glory/ Of relieving Madeira.

which caused a lot of suffering in the island, either in the form of massive unemployment or resorting to begging in order to survive. This unfavorable conjuncture led to a mass migration of islanders to foreign destinations, many of whom were formerly engaged in wine-related jobs. In Madeira the vineyards would be rooted up and substituted by the sugar cane, the wine stocks diminished at a fast pace, and to avoid the total destruction of the island's vines the American Consul imported, at his expense, around 1857, cuttings of Catawba and Isabella vines, from Ohio, to be grafted in Madeira.

[Untitled][1221]

The grape disease, it is feared, will this year cause much distress in the island of Madeira. The ordinary exports of the island (chiefly wine,) are in value £300,000. Those to England amount to £130,000. Should the disease again prove destructive, a repetition of the misery which took place in Ireland, on the failure of the potato crop, may be expected in the island of Madeira.

THE ISLAND OF MADEIRA.[1222]

This ill-fated island, whose destitution experienced a partial and temporary relief from the contributions of this country last spring, is still, we are sorry to learn, in a state of extreme suffering. The following is an extract of a private letter from a gentleman of Madeira, travelling for this health, to his friend in Washington. It is dated but four days ago:

"I have letters from Madeira, to the 22d June. Alas for the dear island! There will be no wine this year. I am persuaded it will be necessary to root up all the vines and get fresh cuttings from abroad, so that many years may elapse ere good wine be made there again. I fear the glory of the place has departed; certainly for a season. The people can only be relieved by emigration. Without this outlet being opened for them, *hundreds will perish*. The letters that have lately appeared in the papers will prevent much more aid being sent from this country, unless vigorous efforts be made to counteract the false impressions and put before the public the plain facts: that the means which chiefly supported the population of the island (125,000) have been swept away suddenly, completely; that the produce of the vineyards supported the people for nine months out of the twelve; that there is no immediate means of restoring the vines to health; to root them up seems the only plan and plant fresh cuttings, involving the necessity of waiting for at least three years ere they can get any return."

1221 *Charleston Courier,* April 20, 1853. (Charleston, SC); *North American and United States Gazette,* April 21, 1853. (Philadelphia, PA); *Illinois State Register,* April 29, 1853. (Springfield, IL).

1222 *Daily National Intelligencer,* August 3, 1853. (Washington, DC); *Public Ledger,* August 4, 1853. (Philadelphia, PA. Quotes the former source); *Albany Evening Journal,* August 6, 1853. (Albany, NY. Published under the title "Madeira.", preceded by the following sentence: «The generous aid extended to the Island of Madeira has alleviated but not removed its misfortunes. A correspondent of the National Intelligencer writes under the date of June 22^d: –»); *The Daily Picayune,* August 13 and 14, 1853. (New Orleans, LA).

THE GRAPE FAILURE[1223] – A letter written by a gentleman who is at present on the Island of Madeira, states that there is no hope of a grape crop. Indeed, the wines are blighted beyond recovery, and it will be necessary to root them up and plant new cuttings, which will require three years to come to bearing. In the meantime, the inhabitants of the island will be deprived of their usual means of support and must either emigrate, or subsist upon the charity of the rest of the world.

The suffering of Madeira may be a lesson to other States, not to depend upon a single crop – for that may fail, and then they are ruined.

Latest from Madeira – Distressing News.[1224]

By the arrival of the steam yacht North Star,[1225] we have received advices from Madeira to Aug. 12. The grape crop was entirely destroyed by a blight. The destruction was universal. The inhabitants are in a worse condition than ever. Unless aid reached them from other countries, starvation was inevitable.

RETURN OF THE NORTH STAR.[1226]
Com. Vanderbilt's Pleasure Party at Home Again.

Commodore VANDERBILT's steam-yacht North Star returned to this port yesterday, from her pleasure-cruise in European waters. …

We learn from the officers of the *Star* that the condition of affairs at Madeira is melancholy in the extreme. The grape crop is again a total failure, and much suffering is feared when the Winter sets in. During the Summer months there is nothing to be feared, as the Island abounds in vegetables, and the inhabitants can easily obtain their sustenance therefrom. But in the other months of the year there are no such facilities, and sorrow accounts may be again looked for from the unfortunate Madeirans, unless timely aid be given them. …

FAMINE IN MADEIRA.[1227] – It is stated that in consequence of the entire destruction of this season's grape crop in Madeira, the inhabitants are in a worse condition than ever. Unless aid reaches them from other countries starvation is inevitable.[1228]

1223 *Weekly Wisconsin,* August 17, 1853. (Milwaukee, WI).
1224 *The New York Daily Times,* September 24, 1853. (New York City, NY); *Albany Evening Journal,* September 24, 1853. (Albany, NY).
1225 This yacht had arrived at Madeira on September 12, 1853, where it had its last stop during Vanderbilt's European tour, as we have seen on section 6.1.1.18. of this anthology.
1226 *The New York Daily Times,* September 24, 1853. (New York City, NY).
1227 *The Sun,* September 26, 1853. (Baltimore, MD); *Charleston Courier,* September 29, 1853. (Charleston, SC. Published untitled); *The Daily Picayune,* October 5, 1853. (New Orleans, LA); *The Star and Banner,* October 21, 1853. (Gettysburg, PA. Published untitled); *The Farmer's Cabinet,* November 3, 1853. (Amherst, NH. Published untitled).
1228 During the summer of 1853 the situation in the island was dreadful, and in order to escape misery hundreds of islanders were compelled to emigrate, as we learn from the article entitled "Madeira", revealed on another source: «The following picture of the poverty, want and suffering among the poorer classes of the inhabitants of Madeira, which we find in a letter from that island, dated August 23, and published in a Newfoundland paper, is corroborated by all the accounts received from the island for the last year and a half. The people of this and other countries will undoubtedly be called upon to contribute again for the relief of the suffering poor of Madeira:/ "A vessel is coming next week

LATER FROM AFRICA.[1229]
... – Madeira.

... At Madeira, as is already known, the vine crop has failed. Their usual export has been about 25,000 pipes, but it is expected that it will not this season reach three pipes; and the poorer inhabitants are in consequence, in a state of great suffering. The cause of this failure arises from the mildew having got into the plant just as it was budding, and occasioning the rotting of the buds. During the last two years Madeira has been visited by constant and heavy rains, so that the vine has not ripened. The vines, however, are not supposed to be permanently injured. Dr. Ross,[1230] one of the passengers home, who came from Madeira, states that he found a solution of spirits of wine and sugar, and also a solution of sulphur, very effective in removing the mildew.

FROM MADEIRA.[1231] By the schooner Sarah Maria at New York, thirty-two days from Madeira, we learn that there was another entire failure of the wine crop, owing to the blight having again appeared on the vine and grape. The following is an extract of a letter dated July 12th, 1854: –

I am sorry to inform you that the grape crop has again failed. I was informed by many intelligent wine-growers that they do not think the present vine will ever produce; but where are they to get others? All countries are alike afflicted. What is the cause of this blight? Is it the prayers of the temperance people? Many growers are digging up the vine and planting grain and vegetables, the latter they will grow in great quantities, and I have no doubt that if the New York and Marseilles Steam Company will make the Island a stopping place, it will become the market garden of the United States; the invalids with their companions will flock there in great numbers; it is the finest climate in the world for the afflicted with consumption. Many persons far gone in that disease have been relieved by resorting to this Island.[1232]

---

to carry off 400 laborers (including their families), passage free to Jamaica, but they are still unwilling to go. It is an infatuation that is upon them; they will rather starve than 'passar o mar' (cross the sea); and they must starve by hundreds if they remain here, for we (i. e. the upper classes) cannot support them – we are all too poor ourselves. I do not think more than one cottage that we have been into has a bed, nor one individual a change of raiment. When they get a shirt they wear it till it drops off their back, and they sleep on a little dirty straw. One cottage we saw was so damp that ferns were growing out of the walls, an one of the children, in consequence, was so diseased that at seven years old she was too weak to stand. How they get food at all is more than we have been able to find out; and yet nothing we can say moves them. One woman to-day did make an objection. She said she did not like to go where they would have no Church and Priest of their own. I have not been able to make out that there is any spiritual provision for them. By far the best plan would be for them take a Priest of their own, if that would be allowed. The Priests are starving here, pretty nearly as much of the people, and ought to be anxious to go."» *North American and United States Gazette,* October 19, 1853. (Philadelphia, PA).

1229 *The New York Daily Times,* October 3, 1853. (New York City, NY); *Daily Ohio Statesman,* October 7, 1853. (Columbus, OH).

1230 Archibald Colquhoun Ross (?-1856), an English physician who lived in Madeira for about 20 years. He died in Madeira, in 1856, victimized by the terrible cholera outbreak that had appeared on the island, on that year, originating a huge death toll.

1231 *Boston Semi-Weekly Courier,* August 17, 1854. (Boston, MA).

1232 This text ended with a description of the 4th of July celebrations in Madeira: «It is the principal resort for the Europeans so afflicted. The climate here in the winter is like the climate of May in the United States. I was here on the 4th of July, the national day of the Americans. The United States ship Marion was here, and I cannot tell which was the most pleased, the Americans or the Portuguese, at the exchange of courtesy. At sunrise the Marion hoisted her national standard at the mast-head, and fired twenty-one guns. The corvette and fort on Loo Rock joined in. The Brazilian steamer could not fire, she only mounting two guns. Lieut. Gardner, an officer of standing in the navy, returned the

From the African Squadron[1233]

NORFOLK, Tuesday, Sept. 12.

... The U.S. practice ship *Preble* has arrived from Madeira, and reports the grape crop again failed. ...

MADEIRA WINE.[1234]

The following extract of a letter from an old resident of Madeira confirms the previous advices as to almost the cessation to the production of Madeira wine for a number of years, and those who fortunately have a supply of this wine here will have the more reason to congratulate themselves:

"The stocks of old wine on the island of Madeira are diminishing, without any prospect of more being produced to supply their place, after the total loss of the last vintage and the destruction of at least three-fourths of the vines. The remaining fourth has little or no strength to produce more for many years, even in the unexpected event of the wine disease disappearing. The best vine lands are being turned to the cultivation of sugar, cotton, and green crop."

[Untitled][1235]

Intelligence from the Island of Madeira says that the stocks of old wine on the Island are diminishing, without any prospect of more being produced to supply the place. The vines appear to be nearly destroyed by the prevalent grape disease.

MADERIA.[1236]

Advices from Madeira give an unsatisfactory account of the condition of the Island. The vines are completely withered, and there is no other culture on which to rely for the means of subsistence.

THE HERMANN'S MAILS.[1237]

The United States Mail steamship *Hermann* arrived at her dock about 11 o'clock last evening, with dates from England to the 15th inst., 266 passengers, and a full cargo. ...

---

salute and thanks for the honor.»
1233 *The New York Daily Times,* September 13, 1854. (New York City, NY).
1234 *Daily National Intelligencer,* May 1, 1855. (Washington, DC); *Alexandria Gazette,* May 2, 1855. (Alexandria, VA); *The Massachusetts Spy,* May 9, 1855. (Worcester, MA. Adds that it had been transcribed from the *Boston Chronicle*). This extract, without these introductory words, was published in other sources, under the title "GENUINE MADEIRA WILL BE VERY SCARCE." *Weekly Wisconsin,* May 23, 1855. (Milwaukee, WI); *Democratic Standard,* May 30, 1855. (Janesville, WI).
1235 *The New York Daily Times,* May 7, 1855. (New York City, NY).
1236 *The New York Daily Times,* August 23, 1855. (New York City, NY). The right spelling is Madeira.
1237 *The New York Daily Times,* August 30, 1855. (New York City, NY).

The vintage in the Island of Madeira has again failed – being the fourth consecutive year; much destitution prevails in the island, from so many persons, in consequence, being thrown out of employment. …

[Untitled][1238]

The vintage in the Island of Madeira has again failed – this being the 4th consecutive year. It will be borne in mind that a year ago the people of Madeira were rescued from starvation by the liberality of the people of the United States and this recent failure will be calamitous indeed.

News from Madeira.[1239]
THE JAMESTOWN AT MADEIRA – … – AFFAIRS AT MADEIRA.
Correspondence of the New-York Daily Times.

UNITED STATES SHIP JAMESTON,
FUNCHAL, Madeira, Sunday, May 18, 1856.

This ship arrived here on the 16th inst., twenty days from Porto Praya,[1240] having encountered strong N. E. trade winds for most of the passage. …

The Island of Madeira looks very well, but the grape crop is still a failure. They have suffered from very heavy rains during the past Winter, and the weather has been unusually cold. Most of the strangers have returned home, and the next packet will take what few remain. There are a few American ladies here. No American vessels in port. The weather now is delightful, and everything looks green and fresh.

Interesting from the African Coast Squadron.[1241] – Our attentive correspondent, who is attached to the U.S. sloop-of-war St. Louis, on the African station, writes us as follows:

U.S. SHIP ST LOUIS,
PORTO PRAYA, Cape de Verde, Aug. 9, 1856

…On our arrival at Madeira I was very much pleased with the town of Funchal. Everything vegetable in its neighborhood appeared to be under the most elaborate cultivation, excepting the grape, which has failed throughout the island for the last five years. As a natural consequence of these repeated failures there is considerable destitution, and one meets many beggars. Our consul, Howard March, Esq., has a regular set of them pensioned, paying each so much every week. He is very popular here, and when he leaves town and returns again the people turn out to welcome him. …

1238 *Daily Hawk-Eagle & Telegraph,* September 15, 1855. (Burlington, IA).
1239 *The New York Daily Times,* June 30, 1856. (New York City, NY).
1240 Praia is the capital and largest city of Cape Verde, an archipelago in the Atlantic, off the coast of Senegal, which in the 19th century was a Portuguese possession. Many Navy ships of the African Squadron used to often stop there at this time.
1241 *Evening Star,* October 9, 1856. (Washington, DC).

From Madeira.[1242]

... In a country so densely populated as Madeira, however advantageous it might be to change the crop, more or less suffering would inevitably take place. Now, they have no article to export. The wine crop employed vast numbers of the inhabitants in taking care of the vineyards, in irrigating and dressing them, and in making casks for wine, as well as preparing it for market. At present there is no wine made in the island. The vineyards have all gone to decay; also sugar cane. Grain and vegetables have taken the place of the culture of the vine; but these do not by any means supply the failure of the wine crop.

The city of Funchal has dwindled down to a fishing town. A few steamships resort to the island, and in smooth weather are supplied with some coal.

No effort has been made to renew the grape up to this time, and, probably, in our day, will not. ...

It is ascertained by letter from an intelligent merchant long resident in Madeira, that the grape growing commenced in the year 1420, when sugar cane was also introduced. The quantity of wine annually made from the year 1820 to the time the blight first appeared in 1852, was from 35,000 to 40,000 pipes. Since the blight it has gradually diminished, and is of an inferior quality, so that now there is none made. The importation of brandy to the island was prohibited in 1822. Madeira had a population of 125,000, and Porto Santo 1,200 persons. The produce of the island now is sugar cane, grain, vegetables, and fruit. The probable quantity of wine now on hand at the island is about 12,000 pipes of former crops.

[Untitled][1243]

Letters from Madeira state that there are symptoms of improvement in the vines, and it is hoped that they may continue, so that the surplus of wines may be kept up. The failure of the wine crops has had the effect of turning the native industry of Maderia into other profitable channels.

THE UNITED STATES AND MADEIRA.[1244] – A correspondent of the Washington Union at Funchal, Madeira, writes that there is now very little commerce between the United States and Madeira, owing to the total failure of the vintages in Madeira since 1851, and to there being only one article of export, namely wine.

1242 *Alexandria Gazette,* November 1, 1856. (Alexandria, VA).
1243 *Racine Daily Journal,* December 1, 1856. (Racine, WI. Published in the section "Last Foreign Intelligence by the Persia").
1244 *Memphis Daily Appeal,* September 17, 1857. (Memphis, TN).

From Madeira – The Grape Failure – Introduction of the Catawba.[1245]
Correspondence Boston Traveler.

Madeira, Saturday, July 25.

Madeira has lost much of its prestige since the cholera of last Summer, which carried off ten thousand persons.[1246] The English avoid it this year, which is a drawback to its gaiety. The failure of the grape has given it another blow, and produced a great deal of poverty and distress. The Portuguese say, however, that it has been of service to the island, as the people have turned their attention to the production of grains and the sugar cane, and are no longer under the dominion of English wine merchants. This year there is not a *grape on the island*, and all hopes of overcoming the blight are given up. No one comprehends the disease and no remedy can be found. The grapes when two months old collect a mould on the shady side, as large as a pin's head, which bursts and shoots out the seed – in a few days they are dead. Mr. MARCH has introduced the Catawba, which he thinks will flourish, and produce in a few years as much wine as the island has ever done, and of a very fine quality. On the 25th of August he gives a *fete* to ten thousand of the poor, on the occasion of the dedication of a church which he has built for them.

The Foreign Wine Crop.[1247]

... Letters from Madeira, of the latest dates – July 25th – convey the information that the grape crop there has wholly failed. This year there is *not a grape on the Island*, and all hopes of overcoming the blight are given up. No one comprehends the disease, and no remedy can be found. The grapes when two months old collect a mould on the shady side, as large as a pin's head, which burns and shoots out the seed – in a few days they are dead. Mr. March has introduced the Catawba, which he thinks will flourish, and produce in a few years as much wine as the Island has ever done, and of a very fine quality. Says a letter to the *Boston Traveller*, alluding to the present depressed condition of Madeira: "The failure of the grape has given it another blow, and produced a great deal of poverty and distress. The Portuguese say, however, that it has been of service to the Island, as the people have turned their attention to the production of grains and the sugar cane, and are no longer under the dominion of English wine merchants."[1248] ...

Madeira Wine.[1249] – A gentleman lately arrived from the Island of Madeira, confirms the statement in our last publication, as far as regards the non-production of Madeira wine since 1851, but states, of his own knowledge, that there is no more than 3000 pipes

---

1245 *The New York Daily Times,* September 28, 1857. (New York City, NY).
1246 This is a fact. According to Madeiran sources, this cholera epidemic ravaged Madeira from July to October 1856, killing ten thousand people, as states the author of this text.
1247 *Daily Alta California,* October 26, 1857. (San Francisco, CA).
1248 Madeira Wine trade was, in a large extent, controlled by the British Factory. See Note 749.
1249 *Charleston Courier,* February 16, 1858. (Charleston, SC); *The Portsmouth Journal of Literature & Politics,* March 13, 1858. (Portsmouth, NH).

of wine left on the island; and that this, in consequence of the demand grown up for it in Russia, since the war, is fast being shipped to that country. – *New York Journal of Commerce*.

NO MORE MADEIRA.[1250] – A Funchal correspondent of the Philadelphia Ledger says that it is not an open question whether any more Madeira wine will ever be produced. None has been made since 1851, and there are now only some seven or eight thousand pipes upon the entire island. All recent attempts to manufacture this wine have utterly failed, and pumpkin vines now adorn the old grape arbors once covered with abundant clusters of rich grapes.

Madeira.[1251]

A correspondent of the Journal of Commerce, writing from Funchal, under date of January 4, says:

"I have made special inquiry respecting the vine, its disease, and the prospect of renewing the grape culture. The vine was introduced from the island of Cyprus in the year 1425, but was not extensively cultivated till the first part of the 16th century, say about 1525. The Jesuits went largely into the production of wine, and excelled all others in the fine qualities of their varieties. The abundant supply furnished by the island is shown by the fact, that about the year 1720, when the trade with the island was by barter, an Englishman bought one pipe of wine for *two half-worn suits of clothes*, and another for *three second hand rings!* The culture went on increasing, till, as Mr. March informs me, who has resided here at intervals, for about 30 years, the quantity of wine produced amounted to 51,000 pipes in the most favourable seasons, while the average production was about half that quantity. In 1825 it was fully 25,000 pipes, and the price about $400 per pipe. One pipe per acre of vineyard was an average yield, while sometimes four pipes were produced. The vine is not cultivated more than 1,500 feet high on the mountain sides, as the grape does not ripen above that elevation.

"The vine disease first appeared in the year 1852, the cause and nature of which still remain a profound mystery. All that is known is this, that a minute fungus, called by botanists *oidium*, appears in the shape of a white powder upon both the leaves and the fruit; but whether this fungus is the *cause* of the disease, or only *symptom*, has not been ascertained. Various remedies have been tried, but without effect, the vines still being unproductive, or the fruit decaying and becoming worthless, and the vines dying out, till at last in despair,

---

1250 *The Charleston Mercury*, February 15, 1858. (Charleston, SC); *Evening Star*, February 16, 1858. (Washington, DC); *Farmer's Cabinet*, February 17, 1858. (Amherst, NH); *The Massachusetts Spy*, February 17, 1858. (Worcester, MA); *Wisconsin Weekly Free Democrat*, February 24, 1858. (Milwaukee, WI); *The Compiler*, March 1, 1858. (Gettysburg, PA); *The Daily Wisconsin Patriot*, March 2, 1858. (Madison, WI. Published without referring its source); *Berkshire County Eagle*, March 5, 1858. (Pittsfield, MA); *Lewis County Banner*, March 6, 1858. (Lowville, NY); *The Eastern Texian*, March 13, 1858. (San Augustine, TX); *The Weekly Independent*, March 13, 1858. (Belton, Bell County, TX); *Superior Chronicle*, March 23, 1858. (Superior, WI); *Philadelphia Inquirer*, March 25, 1858. (Philadelphia, PA). A similar article to this one, bearing the same title but with slight changes and a bit longer was published in other sources. It referred that it had been written by a Funchal correspondent of the London *Times* and added another sentence at the end: «The New York *Evening Post* has the best authority for saying that instead of 7,000 or 8,000, there are not more than 3,000 pipes on the Island.» *Racine Daily News*, March 26, 1858. (Racine, WI); *Richland County Observer*, April 6, 1858. (Richland Center, Richland County, WI).
1251 *The Charleston Mercury*, February 19, 1858. (Charleston, SC).

they were rooted up by the owners, and the land occupied with other crops. So complete has been the agricultural revolution, that Mr. March states that not above *five* pipes of wine were produced last year in the whole island. It is worthy of being remembered, that at the same time a disease attacked the potato and even the chestnut. About 200 varieties of grape were cultivated,[1252] and went in combinations to make the different wines.

"It is stated by Mr. March that the American Isabella or Catawba vines which have been introduced here, have succeeded admirably. Should they continue to prosper, the grape culture may revive in Madeira; otherwise the hills will soon be denuded of the last vine. It should be added, that though much suffering followed from the first year's grape failure to the peasantry, who make the mass of the people, sufficient time has now elapsed from the substitution of other vegetables and fruits, and the peasantry were never in a better condition."

MADEIRA WINE.[1253] – Recent advices from Madeira furnish the intelligence that the grape vines are almost wholly destroyed by a fatal disease which has been on the increase for several years on that island. It is stated, on the authority of Mr. March, a large wine producer, as well as an eminent merchant there, that the whole produce of the last year did not exceed five pipes of wine, and the great probability now is, that the vine will become totally extinct. We were perfectly aware of this fact some time ago. Very little pure Madeira Wine has been imported into the markets of the United States during the last five years, for the conclusive reason, that it has not been produced, and probably never will be, certainly not while the whole vine culture of the island remains in the hands of the inhabitants who are neither enterprising, industrious, nor frugal. The soil needs renewing; it requires manuring, the same as other soils, with guano or other strengthening substances, and the total neglect of these essential and all important safeguards has resulted in the destruction of the natural nutriment of the soil. The island of Madeira has furnished the world with more rich and delicious wines than any similar piece of ground in the universe. It has been under constant cultivation for about *one thousand years*;[1254] and, at one time its delicious wines were preferred to any other produced, by the great emperors, kings, princes and monarchs of the world. The wine originally produced was sweet, rich, and resembled sweetened cream, and was much used by all classes of invalids for its highly nutritious and strengthening properties. This species has been entirely extinct for many years, and the last sample that ever reached this country was presented to the late Henry Clay[1255] by some American merchants, then resident in Madeira; and a sample of this elegant and valuable wine is now in our possession, and, we are inclined to believe, the only specimen in this market. So, from this state of facts, it will be seen that the old Madeira, which has for so many years graced the tables of the opulent and extravagant of the land, will now pass into history as among the luxuries of former times. At one time, more than 50,000 pipes of this wine were annually produced.

1252 This is an exaggerated figure. 20 varieties would be closer to the truth.
1253 *The Washington Reporter*, June 21 and July 21, 1858. (Washington, PA).
1254 This sentence is clearly exaggerated, since the island was only officially discovered and settled in the 15th century, therefore the vine could only have been planted in Madeira for four centuries by the time this article was published.
1255 Henry Clay (1777-1852), a native of Virginia, was a lawyer, politician and skilled orator, who represented Kentucky in both the Senate and the House of Representatives. He was also Secretary of State, from 1825 to 1829, and ran three times for President but was never elected.

9.7. OÏDIUM TUCKERY – THE MADEIRA VINE DISEASE OF 1852 AND ITS CONSEQUENCES

Intemperance in Madeira.[1256] – The Hon. James O. Putnam,[1257] in a recent letter, makes the following statement:

"When in the Island of Madeira I saw a few cases of intoxication among the poorer people. And I had from a nine years' resident, this explanation: That before the failure of the wine crop in Madeira, (formerly the annual yield was about 15,000 pipes of wine, now five or six hundred,) there was scarce any drunkenness on the island, but the failure had placed wine beyond the reach of the poor; they now cultivated the sugar cane, from which was manufactured a strong spirit now in common use; and the result was, drunkenness had appeared as the wine disappeared."

MADEIRA WINE.[1258] – The grape crop of Madeira has for some years been a failure. This product having been for a long time the principal support of the island, its failure has brought general distress to the inhabitants; and a year or two since, caused a famine, which the citizens of the United States contributed largely to relieve. We learn that as yet no remedy has been found to eradicate the disease of the vine. New cuttings from Europe, and those of the Catawba from the United States, have been imported, but were attacked by the existing disease shortly after their importation.

INTERESTING FROM THE COAST OF AFRICA.[1259] – By the Vanderbilt we learn that the African mail steamer Athenia had arrived at Liverpool, bringing interesting news from the West Coast of Africa, from the 30th of June up to the 25th of July, inclusive. …

At Madeira, the cochineal and sugarcane plantations were looking well, but the vines were almost extinct.

The Madeira Wine Crop.[1260] – A Washington correspondent says:

Official reports from the United States Consul at Madeira[1261] show that the wine crop there is so small that "Old Madeira" will soon command fabulous prices. The average yearly imports from 1832 to 1842 were 8193 pipes per annum, worth say $1,228,950 – now not a dozen pipes of genuine wine leave the island. Even a few healthy American vines brought to Madeira a few years since by Mr. March, have gradually succumbed to the blight which covers the surface of the vines and gradually absorbs the wine juices. The same disease has manifested itself in France, Southern Italy and Greece.

Due to the abrupt shortage of Madeira Wine supply in America, from 1852 onwards, the wines already existing there for sale and the island's wine stocks would suffer a 30%

1256 *The Adams Sentinel*, May 2, 1859. (Gettysburg, PA); *Banner of Liberty*, May 11, 1859. (Middletown, NY).
1257 James Osborne Putnam (1818-1903), a native of New York and Yale graduate, he was an American lawyer and politician, being the U.S. Minister to Belgium from 1880 to 1882.
1258 *Milwaukee Daily Sentinel*, February 17, 1860. (Milwaukee, WI).
1259 *Oconto Pioneer*, September 8, 1860. (Oconto, Oconto County, WI).
1260 *The Daily Picayune*, February 27, 1864. (New Orleans, LA).
1261 George True. See Note 763.

increase in price. For many Madeira Wine *connoisseurs* in America money was not an issue, and in order to get good wine the aristocrat's attention was turned to the auctions of old Madeiras, kept for decades in dark cellars across the eastern states, and to the large stocks of century-old Madeiras kept in the South. On the other hand, the sudden disappearance of Madeira Wine from the American wine market led to the consumption of other wines, especially sherry and champagne, and slowly Madeira went into a kind of oblivion, only revived, once and awhile, by the old timers' taste and demand for this excellent product.

9.8. Gradual Recovery of the Madeira Vines

After the blight of the vines in 1852, the yield of Madeira Wine was drastically reduced for over a decade, and only around 1865 the production started to achieve satisfactory figures. In this short section are three articles, published in that year, dealing with this new reality, that shed some hope into Madeira Wine trade.

[Untitled][1262]

The vines at Madeira are reviving this year, and we may again hope to drink pure Madeira wine.

[Untitled][1263]

The Madeira wine crop, which for several years was destroyed by a disease of the vines, is this year a success. About 4,000 pipes of wine will be made, and the prospect of the next crop are even more favorable.

The Grape Crop in the Madeira Islands.[1264]

The following letter has been received at the State Department:

"UNITED STATES CONSULATE,
FUNCHAL, MADEIRA, Nov. 20, 1865.

"SIR: I beg to inform you, as a matter of general information, that the grape crop of this island has just been gathered, and the amount of yield is about 4,000 pipes of wine, which is nearly double that of last year, and the belief is that the crop will be still greater next year. The blight still continues to a considerable extent, but the grape is saved from utter destruction

---

1262 *The Cincinnati Daily Enquirer,* August 12, 1865. (Cincinnati, OH. Published at the "FOREIGN NOTES." section).
1263 *Jackson Daily Citizen,* December 20, 1865. (Jackson, MI. Published at the "General News." section); *The Cincinnati Daily Enquirer,* December 22, 1865. (Cincinnati, OH); *The Memphis Daily Avalanche,* January 6, 1866. (Memphis, TN).
1264 *The Cincinnati Daily Enquirer,* December 30, 1865. (Cincinnati, OH).

by the use of sulphur, which can not, however, be thoroughly washed from the grape, or extracted from the juice, hence the wine is not so good as before the blight.

"There is but little old wine on the island, and as the new will not come into the market for three years to come, the price will still keep up, but after that the price of Madeira wine must go down considerably, from the double fact of the increased yield and the planters again planting the vine instead of the sugar-cane. Many are pulling up their cane and planting vines instead. Hence, again, the yield of sugar in the island will decrease in quantity. The yield of sugar the present year has been about 500,000 pounds, English.

"With great respect, I have the honor to be your most obedient servant,
"CHARLES A. LEAS,[1265]
"United States Consul."

9.9. Phylloxera - The Second Blow to the Island's Vineyards

The normalization of Madeira Wine production was short-lived since another blight, the phylloxera, attacked the island's vineyards in 1872. According to the Portuguese agronomist F. de Almada e Brito, this new disease had been brought to the island in the Isabella cuttings brought from America years before, in order to restore the *oidium*-affected vineyards. But the news about this new disease were not widely published in the American press in the way the former had been, three decades before, and that may be due to the fact that by then Madeira Wine had somehow gone out of fashion in America, as a result of the abrupt supply shortage from 1852 onwards. But after some years of struggle with the phylloxera the Madeirans devised a way to overcome it and gradually Madeira Wine production started to thrive, although the vineyards had to compete with the sugar cane plantations. The next four articles deal with this vine disease.

EDITORIAL AND OTHER ITEMS[1266]

Madeira wine is likely to become scarce, as the vines in that island are said to be dying.

PRODUCTION OF MADEIRA WINE.[1267] – It is well known that for some years past Madeira wine has been almost unknown in the trade on account of the extinction of the crop of the island consequent upon a long series of bad vintages. The old vineyards were rooted up, and new ones planted; but of course a long time would have to elapse before any great yield could be expected, and those having in their possession genuine Madeira held it as a great prize. The least period of production extended from 1853 to 1857; and from 1860 to 1863 but 500 pipes were produced. At present the production has risen to an average of 10,000 or 12,000 pipes, which is about one-third that of former years. It is

---
1265 See Note 764.
1266 *The Morning Star and Catholic Messenger,* December 6, 1874. (New Orleans, LA).
1267 *Evening Daily Bulletin,* March 27, 1876. (San Francisco, CA).

not thought however, that the quantity will ever much exceed this, since a great deal of the Island which formerly was planted with vineyards is now used for corn and other crops, which are said to pay the proprietors better than wine.

[Untitled][1268]

British consular reports from Spain and Portugal announce the remarkable success of the system of grafting American on native vines, which results in preventing phylloxera and producing a good wine. The Consul at Madeira[1269] writes that a large amount of new wines, mostly American, have been planted in the districts most celebrated for their wine and produces a superior quality. On the north side of the island, where all the vines were destroyed by phylloxera years ago, the new vines have given their first fine crop.[1270]

THE VINTAGE OF 1892.[1271]

… It has rarely happened in history that a wine-growing district has ceased to be wine-growing. In the course of wars wines have been uprooted and vintages destroyed. But when peace followed war the vines were replaced and soon regained their productiveness. The wines of Italy, Greece and the Greek islands, which the Romans drank, is made to this day, and uncommonly poor wine it is. There is one instance of a vine-growing region ceasing to figure as a source of supply – that is Madeira. At the time the oidium disease broke out there forty years ago, Madeira wine was even more popular than champagne and was fully as expensive. Abroad no good dinner was served without it, and at the tables of many people who were well to do in this country the decanter of Madeira was as indispensable as knives and forks. The oidium caused the destruction of every vineyard on the island, and when the vines were replanted the phylloxera appeared and protracted the battle of the vine-growers for ten years more. In the meantime wine-drinkers had been compelled to replace their favorite wine with the vintages of France and Germany, and when the islanders succeeded in growing wine once more it had gone out of fashion. The two islands now produce less wine than is raised in Alameda County,[1272] and there is no demand for it. The Madeira which is sold by wine-merchants is mostly made in London out of the sweet wines of Spain and Portugal. …

1268 *Evening Capital Journal,* April 28, 1891. (Salem, OR).
1269 In 1891, the American Consulate in Madeira was occupied by John F. Healey, a native of Minnesota, who served from 1890 to 1893.
1270 It is worth mentioning that one of the two vines whose grafts John Howard March brought to Madeira, the Isabella, is still widely cultivated on the island, producing the *vinho americano,* as it is termed by the natives, or, American wine, in English. Although it is cultivated all over the island, the wine produced at Porto da Cruz, in the northeastern coast of the island, has been for a long time very appreciated by the locals. Despite all this, this wine is, at the present-day, considered as non-valuable in commercial terms, and is only consumed on the island, either privately, or retailed on some countryside bars.
1271 *The Morning Call,* April 10, 1893. (San Francisco, CA).
1272 A California county, which occupies most of the East Bay region of the San Francisco Bay area.

9.10. Madeira Wine Adulterated in the U.S. and abroad

Adulteration of Madeira Wine in 19th century America was a fact, even during the time of its continual supply to the American market, since the consumption largely outnumbered the importation to the United States. Due to the high demand and to the prestige bestowed upon the real Madeira Wine, several unscrupulous people were more than willing to provide their customers adulterated wine. In the following articles, published between 1839 and 1868, in several sources, will be found a thousand and one ways of "making Madeira" in America and abroad, using all sorts of ingredients, some more disgusting and lethal than others, with the intention of getting an easy profit. More serious than that there were even some books published in the United States that taught how to imitate some liquors, including Madeira. This unlawful and reprehensible practice raised a lot of criticism in America, especially from some Temperance societies and doctors that alerted the wine bibbers to the serious consequences of drinking adulterated wine. A set of thirteen articles related to this shameful practice will be presented in this section.

WINE.[1273] – An officer in our navy,[1274] writing from Madeira, June 5, 1838, says: "There are about thirty thousand pipes of wine produced here annually, and of that, not more than ten thousand pipes are ever sent to the United States; and it is no less true that strange, that at least fifty thousand pipes are annually served up at the United States hotels, under the name of Madeira." The extent to which wines are manufactured is astonishing. The question whether ardent spirit is a *poison* has been often discussed (and very unprofitably;) but if sugar of lead, arsenic, &c. are poisons, it will not be difficult to settle the question respecting our wines. It is well ascertained that the most deleterious drugs are often used in making imitation wines. Indeed, an alarm should be publicly sounded respecting this source of danger, aside from the general alarm respecting the dangers of alcohol. Imitation wines combine the two evils – poisonous drugs and alcohol. – *N. American*.

REMARKS ON WINES BY C. A. LEE,[1275] M. D. NEW-YORK.[1276]
Published in the American Temperance Intelligencer,[1277] July, 1836.

… The Island of Madeira must have a fruitful soil, if it produces all the wine imported under this name. Madeira wine is most frequently adulterated by mixing it with Marseilles, Lisbon, Teneriffe, and other cheap wines. By mixing those, which can be bought at about

---

[1273] *Examiner and Democratic Herald,* November 21, 1839. (Lancaster, PA). Under the title "Deleterious Wines", this article was published, in other words, in the following sources: *Madison Express,* March 7, 1840. (Madison, WI. States that it had been transcribed from the Philadelphia *North American*); *Wisconsin Enquirer,* April 1, 1840. (Madison, WI. Published *ipsis verbis* as in the previous source).

[1274] John H. Belcher. See section 6.1.1.4. of this anthology.

[1275] Charles A. Lee, M.D., then Professor of General Pathology and Materia Medica at the Geneva Medical College, in New York.

[1276] *The Enquirer,* December 1841. (Albany, NY).

[1277] A monthly paper published in Albany, NY, by the Executive Committee of the New York State Temperance Society, from 1834 to 1836.

forty cents per gallon, with real Madeira, an article is furnished which even the best judges of wine cannot distinguish from pure Madeira. Writers inform us, that a portion of brandy is always added to Madeira wine immediately after fermentation, and another before exportation. A cheap Madeira is made here by extracting the oils from common whiskey, by passing it through carbon, then adding a small proportion of genuine wine; supplying the want of color by Caramel or burnt sugar, and the nutty flavor by hickory nuts or almonds. There are immense establishments in this city, where the whiskey is thus, (without a miracle,) turned into wine; in some of these, devoted exclusively to this branch of business, the whiskey is rolled in in the evening, but the wine goes out in the broad day light, ready to defy the closest inspection.

The trade in empty wine casks in this city, with the custom house mark and certificates is immense; the same cask being replenished again and again, and always accompanied by that infallible test of genuineness, the certificate! An empty quarter cask readily brings three dollars, and I have heard of a pipe being sold as high as twelve. There are persons employed whose sole business consists in hunting up these casks. A wholesale grocer, not long since, under an examination at court as a witness in this city, was asked by the judge how many empty wine casks he had known sold with the custom house mark and certificate? He replied "not one." A friend of mine, who is known to keep a well stored wine cellar, was applied to a short time ago by one of those itinerant cask buyers, for empty wine casks. He told him he had one or two which he would sell cheap, as he had no farther use for them. He was then asked if he sold a certificate with them. He said no. "Then," says the cask merchant, "I don't want them." There is also an extensive manufactory of wine casks in the neighborhood of New-York, which are made so closely in imitation of the foreign, as to deceive experienced dealers; the custom house mark is easily counterfeited, and certificates are never wanting. I could relate a great many similar facts, all going to prove that great quantities of fictitious wines are manufactured among us; but I believe the public are already convinced that a great proportion of the wines sent into the country, are spurious compounds. ...

TEMPERANCE.[1278]
Adulteration of Liquors: A Sermon Preached by Rev. A. F. Bourns, at the Broad Street M. E. Church, Adrian, on Sunday, March 22, 1874.[1279]
SERMON.

We have observed that there is quite a general impression among the people of our day that many of the wines and liquors which are sold are not genuine – that they are imitations only. We occasionally hear people speak in rather severe terms of what they call adulterated liquors – speak as though they are manufactured from injurious articles, and sometimes poisonous drugs. But the more unsuspecting portion of the community do not really believe this. They cannot quite believe that men will put injurious drugs into liquors, and then sell them to people who will drink them the next minute. Or, if there should be

---

[1278] DWIGHT, William T., *The Work and the Workmen. A Discourse in behalf of the American Home Missionary Society, preached in the city of New York, May 8, 1859.*, American Home Missionary Society, New York, 1859.

[1279] This text was inserted in the book above mentioned, stating that it had been "Published by Request", at the *Times and Expositor Pioneer Print*, on Adrian, Mich., in 1874, on its pages 2-3.

a few who are so unscrupulous as to do this, many people are very slow to believe that such a practice is at all common.

But there is another portion of community who know very well that the practice of adulterating liquors is very common – and that in the majority of cases, the compounds which are used are of a pernicious and poisonous character. While this art seems to have been brought to a higher degree of perfection by the men of our day, still history informs us that it was practiced thousands of years ago. From our text and other portions of the scriptures it appears that the Hebrews were in the habit of using "mixed wines" – wines which were characterized as the "poison of dragons and the cruel venom of asps."[1280]

… If the people only knew the facts, their notions of "pure wines" would be greatly modified. The wine consumers of this country talk much about pure wines, port, Maderia[1281] and Champagne; whoever bought a bottle of wine, either for medical or other purposes, who was not told, and perhaps made to believe, that it was a "genuine article," "direct from France or Portugal, or the Island of Madeira." But how they are deceived. …

Then, take Madeira wine. Dr. Nott[1282] states, on reliable authority, that the sum total of wine produced on the Island of Madeira, is only about 30,000 barrels. And yet the American people alone claim to consume 50,000 barrels,[1283] and all the rest of the nations, you know, have plenty of "Madeira wine," and so they have, if the name were any indication of the quality. But, not one in ten of the wine consumers of this country ever saw a bottle of pure Madeira wine. The same is true of what is called port wine. …

SHAMEFUL DISHONESTY.[1284] – As a proof of the dishonest adulteration of liquors in this country, the New York Sun says, that more Port Wine is drank in the U. States in one year than passes through the custom-house in ten; that more champagne is consumed in America alone than the whole champagne district produces; that cognac brandy cost four times as much in France, where it is made, than it is retailed for in our grocery shops; and that the failure of the whole grape crop in Madeira produced no apparent diminution in quantity or increase in the price of wine.

LIFE IN MADERIA.[1285] – **SCARCITY OF MADEIRA WINE IN ITS NATIVE ISLAND.**[1286] – The Rev. Henry Wood, a chaplain of the United States Navy, accompanied Gen. Pierce

---

[1280] Deut. 32:3.

[1281] The right spelling is Madeira.

[1282] Rev. Dr. Eliphalet Nott, President of the Union College, in Schenectady, NY, whose book we quote on the following Note.

[1283] This is the original quotation: «Correspondent to this, was that letter from Madeira by an officer of our navy, stating that but thirty thousand barrels of wine was produced on the island, and fifty thousand claimed to be from thence, drank in America alone.» NOTT, Eliphalet, *Lectures on Temperance*, Sheldon, Blakeman & Co., New York; Gould & Lincoln, Boston; S. C. Griggs & Company, Chicago; Trubner & Co., London, 1857, page 176.

[1284] *The Star and Banner*, October 20, 1854. (Gettysburg, PA).

[1285] The right spelling is Madeira.

[1286] *Nashville Union and American*, May 13, 1858. (Nashville, TN); *Charleston Courier*, May 18, 1858. (Charleston, SC. Published under the title "Scarcity of Madeira Wine in its Native Island."); *Albany Patriot*, June 10, 1858. (Albany, Dougherty County, GA. States that it had been transcribed from the *Mobile Advertiser*).

in the *Powhattan* to Maderia,[1287] from which place he has written a number of interesting letters, an extract from one of which we give below:

"We left Madeira with a good deal of regret, indeed with something of melancholy, and that for various reasons. Funchal is a neat and picturesque city, and Madeira a charming island in climate, fruits and scenery.

"Nor should I forget J. H. March, Esq., our noble hearted consul who kept a free table at his elegant house, a mile or two out of the city,[1288] and an open house in the city, whose spacious and well-furnished rooms were at the service of any of our company who choose to occupy them, whether by day or by night, by the week or the month. I never saw such princely living, elegant with luxuriousness, and most ample without intemperance and sensualism. He takes no care of his table; he knows nothing about it till he sits down to it, as he has some forty of fifty servants at his three distinct establishments, the head men of whom not only do his bidding, but do everything he needs without his bidding or even his knowledge; and were a dozen of strangers to appear at dinner without notice, their presence would occasion no inconvenience, and all to be done would be for them to sit up to the table.

"Mr. March has resided on the island for about thirty years, I believe, and had been a large wine merchant and wine producer, in which business he has accumulated an ample fortune. In other times, as he told me, above 50,000 pipes were made annually on the island; but the last few years, since the appearance of the vine disease, only a few pipes, and the last year not above five, as he positively knew; and yet Madeira wine is abundant both in the United States and elsewhere! Think of this, ye wine-bibbers and sinners! Where is it made, of what is it made?

"I ought to add that Mr. March, though he has the most perfect knowledge of wines, and some of the most delicate qualities of wines, of which he has varieties dating back to our revolutionary war, yet practices the most perfect temperance, indeed absolute abstinence, never raising the glass to his lips, while he allows his guests to act their own pleasure."

It is contemplated to establish a line of steamers between New York and Genoa; if the purpose should be carried out, Madeira will be a most delightful half-way stopping place, where one can "lay by" during the winter months.

MADEIRA WINE – WHERE IT COMES FROM.[1289] – A travelling correspondent of the *New Hampshire Patriot*,[1290] writing of Maderia,[1291] says:

"Mr. March, U.S. Consul at Madeira, is a native of the fine agricultural town of Greenland, N.H., whose ample and cheerful hospitality amazed others as well as myself. It was absolutely princely; at the same time it was without ostentation or boast. Not only he keep a free table, spread with all the delicacies of the island, at his house out of town, where ample rooms and chambers were at the disposal of our party, with attendants to do the waiting,

---

1287 The right spelling is Madeira.
1288 At Quinta Magnólia. See Note 279.
1289 *The Daily Ohio Statesman,* September 12, 1858. (Columbus, OH); *Alexandria Gazette,* September 13, 1858. (Alexandria, VA); *Anti-Slavery Bugle,* October 2, 1858. (New-Lisbon, OH); *Galveston Weekly News,* October 5, 1858. (Galveston, TX. Published without the last sentence of the text); *The Weekly Georgia Telegraph,* November 2, 1858. (Macon, GA).
1290 Rev. Henry Wood, also quoted on the previous text.
1291 The right spelling is Madeira.

and servants to provide our breakfasts. Indeed, we 'were lords of all we surveyed,' whether house, beds, servants, fruits, books, or food. Mr. March has been for many years largely engaged in the wine culture and wine trade, in which he has made a princely fortune. I wish that all the 'wine bibbers, publicans and sinners,' would remember the statement Mr. March made to me, that not five pipes of wine are now made a year in all the Island of Madeira! And yet it is abundant in the United States, and as delicious as abundant. The American crop never fails, though blight and mildew have killed all the vines in Madeira. Strychnine does not fail either, if the wine does."

LOOKING IN THE WINE CUP.[1292]

"Look not thou upon the wine cup when it is red, when it giveth his color in the cup, when it moveth itself aright. At the last it biteth like a serpent and stingeth like an adder." – *Proverbs* 23: 31, 32.

Hiram Cox,[1293] M. D., of Cincinnati, has made the following statement:

"I analized a lot of liquors for some conscientious gentlemen of our own city, who would not permit me to take samples to my office, but insisted upon my bringing my chemicals and apparatus to their store, that they might see the operation. I accordingly repaired to their store, and analyzed samples of sixteen different lots. Among them were Port wine, Sherry wine and Madeira wine. The wines *had not one drop of the juice of the grape.* The basis of the Port wine was diluted sulphuric acid, colored with elderberry juice, with alum, sugar, and neutral spirits. …

The basis of the Madeira was a decoction of hops with sulphuric acid, honey, spirits of Jamaica rum, &c. …

1292 BROWN, Simon; HOLBROOK, Frederick; FRENCH, Henry F., "The New England farmer; A Monthly Journal, devoted to Agriculture, Horticulture, and their kindred Arts and Sciences; and Illustrated with Numerous Beautiful Engravings.", Volume XI., Nourse, Eaton & Tolman, Boston, 1859, pages 396-397. A summary of the first two paragraphs of this text was also published in the press, under the alarming title "POISON IN LIQUORS.", in these words: «Dr. Cox, Ohio liquor inspector, lately made an analysis of a number of samples of the "genuine article."/ A bottle of what was sold by an importer of genuine champagne, contained *one-quarter of an ounce of sugar of lead.* – The same gentleman analysed sixteen samples of wine – Port, Sherry and Madeira – in which *not one drop of the juice of the grape* was found. The base of the Port wine was diluted sulphuric acid, colored with elderberry juice, with alum sugar and neutral spirits. The basis of the Sherry wine was a pale malt, sulphuric acid from bitter almonds, with a percentage of alcoholic spirits from brandy. The Madeira was a decoction of hops, sulphuric acid, honey, Jamaica spirits, etc.» *Gazette and Sentinel,* June 16, 1860. (Plaquemine, LA). Ten years later some parts of this text were duplicated in another book, on the chapter related to the Adulteration of Liquors, in these words: «… Take that of Madeira. Dr. Nott states on reliable authority that but 30,000 barrels of wine were produced on the island of Madeira, and yet 50,000 are claimed to be from there drank in America alone./ …/ … Prof. C. A. Lee, of New York, says: "A cheap Madeira is made here by extracting the oils from common whisky, and by passing it through carbon. There are immense establishments in this city where the whisky is thus turned into wine; in some of those devoted to this branch of business, the whisky is rolled in the evening, but the wines goes in the broad daylight, ready to defy the closest inspection. A grocer, after he had abandoned the nefarious traffic, assured me that he had often purchased whisky one day of a country merchant, and before he left town he sold the same whisky back to him turned into wine, at a profit from 4 to 500 per cent."/ This methamorphosis is not even excelled by the French wine merchant, who said, "Give me six hours' notice of what wine you like, and you shall have it out of those two barrels."/ …/ Of sherry, madeira, muscadel, etc.," he [Dr. Cox] says they are all, or at least all he has inspected, either mixed or have a basis water, cider, wort made of pale malt, or a mixture of sulphuric acid and water to the acidity of weak vinegar, with brown sugar, honey, orris-root, and neutral spirits to give it alcoholic percentage; …» DUNN, Rev. James B., *The Adulteration of Liquors, with A Description of the Poisons Used in their Manufacture,* National Temperance Society and Publication House, New York, 1869, pages 5-7.

1293 The celebrated chemist and Inspector of liquors for Hamilton County, Ohio.

Prof. C. A. Lee,[1294] of New York, makes the following statement:

"A cheap Madeira is made here, by extracting the oils from common whisky, and passing it through carbon. There are immense establishments in this city where the whisky is thus turned into wine; in some of those devoted to this branch of business, the whisky is rolled in in the evening, but the wine goes out in the broad daylight, ready to defy the closest inspection."

Prof. Lee further states, "The trade in empty wine casks in this city, (N. Y.) with the Custom House mark and certificate, is immense; the same casks being replenished again and again, and always accompanied by that infallible test of genuineness, the Custom House certificate. I have heard of a pipe being sold for twelve dollars."

"There is in the neighborhood of New York an extensive manufactory of wine casks, which are made so closely to imitate the foreign, as to deceive experienced dealers. The Custom House marks are easily counterfeited, and certificates are never in wanting."

"I have heard," says Dr. Lee, "dealers relate instances in which extensive stores had been filled with these artificial wines, and when merchants from the country have asked for genuine wines, these have been sold them as such, with assurances that there could be no doubt of their purity."

The late Rev. T. P. Hunt, of Wyoming, Penn., wrote: "While I lectured in Philadelphia, I became acquainted with a man who was engaged extensively in making wines, brandy, &c. Through my influence he abandoned the horrid traffic. He informed me, that in order to produce the "nutty flavor" for which Madeira was so much admired, he put a bag of cockroaches into the liquor and let it remain there until the cockroaches were dissolved. I have been informed by several that this is no uncommon practice.[1295] If any wine drinker doubts it, he can soon settle the question by experiment. Cockroaches are plenty, and many much more nauseous and poisonous substances are known to be employed by the makers and venders of intoxicating drinks. I would give you the name of the person who gave the recipe for using cockroaches, but he gave it in confidence, and is now occupying a much more moral and useful station than that of poisoning his customers."

Says President Nott,[1296] in his admirable lectures, "I had a friend who had been himself a wine dealer, and having read the startling statements, some time since made public, in relation to the brewing of wines, and the adulteration of other liquors generally, I inquired of that friend as to the verity of these statements. His reply was: "God forgive what has passed in my own cellar, but the statements made are true – all true, I assure you."

"That friend," says President Nott, "has since gone to his last account, as have doubtless many of those whose days on earth were shortened by poison he dispensed. But I still remember, and shall long remember, both the terms and the tone of that laconic answer, "The statements made are true – all true, I assure you."

"But not on the evidence of that friend does the evidence of these frauds alone depend. Another friend informed me that in examining, as an assignee, the papers of a house in that city, which had dealt in wine, and which had stopped payment, he found evidence of

---

1294 See Note 1275.

1295 This practice was confirmed in other sources, namely in some newspapers, in this untitled short text: «The nutmeg flavor of Madeira wine, is caused by *spicing* it with cockroaches. These creatures, while living, prey on man's *victuals*, and, after death, on his *vi-tals*.» *Daily Free Democrat*, April 21 and 23, 1851. (Milwaukee, WI); *Gloucester Telegraph*, May 3, 1851. (Gloucester, MA).

1296 See Note 1282.

the purchase, during the preceding year, of hundreds of casks of cider, but none of wine; and yet it was not cider, but wine, which had been supposed to have been dealt out by that house to its confiding customers."[1297] – *Michigan Farmer*.

Something About the Wine we Drink.[1298]

It is generally supposed that the world consumes a great deal of wine, whereas, of the vast quantities of liquids used as such, very little is wine. The usual run of statistics are ignorant, and therefore silent, on the subject of adulteration. Cheating has become so respectable and popular that if we were suddenly to stop, many departments of trade and commerce would dry up for want of material. It is, therefore, the safest to let the sharp practices go on, or, at farthest, emancipate the people from them very gradually. It will do no harm to expose a few tricks that are played with wines, especially some of the famous foreign productions that pass for wines, but are entirely innocent of grapes. Many have seen the old conjurer's trick of pouring a dozen different kinds of wines and liquors out of the same bottle. The wine makers have a trick that performs the same miracle on a grand scale, and the wine drinkers willingly pay for without the fun of seeing it done.

The leading wines are Port, Madeira and Champagne. Claret, Sherry and Malaga take the second rank, and Hock is still lower in the scale. Malmsey from Madeira is produced in such small quantities that the best of it is never sold. Madeira wine should be ten years in pipe and ten years in bottle to reach perfection. They now make twenty-year old Madeira in a year or two at most, by extra heat, which may be applied to produce any required age.

No wine suffers so much abuse as Madeira. It is adulterated to much an extent that the wonder is it has any good name left. It is vilely fabricated in Germany. Austrian white wines, alcohol and an extract of walnut hulls are the materials there used in its manufacture. In France, apple cider and honey distilled from the basis, which is dosed with brandy and then bottled, and in six months the compound is old Madeira. The product of real Madeira is so small and the demand so great, that all sorts of substitutes had to be invented, or the consumers would have been miserable.

… Madeira once produced 25,000 pipes of wines. In 1852, the vines were destroyed; in 1856, only 200 pipes were produced, and now the annual exportation is 4,000 pipes at the outside. …

… The old English wine-drinking doctrine is: "Good wine makes good blood, good blood causes good humors, good humors cause good thoughts, good thoughts bring forth good works, good works carry a man to Heaven; *ergo*, good wine carries a man to

---

1297 Some of the chapters of this article were also published in another source, which contained another interesting episode regarding the fortification of Madeira Wine with brandy, at Madeira Island before its exportation to America: «A friend of mine ordered some wine from Madeira, for sacramental purposes, with the positive injunction that no ardent spirit should be put in it. The wine came, but as strong as ever. The question was asked of the shipper, "Did you comply with my order?" The answer came, "We complied with the letter, but not with the spirit of your order; we put no ardent spirit in the wine, but we put wine into the ardent spirit; had we not made the addition, the wine would have spoiled before reaching you." It is now a well ascertained fact, that no wine, in its natural state, can cross the Atlantic without spoiling it: it must be boiled down, or be enforced by drugs, or ardent spirits.» DELAVAN, Edward C., *Letter to the Bishops of the Episcopal Church on the Adulteration of Liquors, &c.*, C. Van Benthuysen, Albany [New York], 1859, page 10. In the United States some authors considered Madeira Wine fortification process as adulteration, but as it is plain to see by this quote, it was something necessary for the wine to endure a long sea voyage.

1298 *The Daily Phoenix*, October 10, 1872. (Columbia, SC).

Heaven." At present the probabilities of getting pure wine are so remote that mankind in general had better try some other system of salvation than the above prescription.

IMPORTED WINES.[1299] – We noticed recently the fact, that a large portion of the wines introduced into this country, were innocent of the presence of the juice of the wine grape – in proof of this we see it stated by the late Dr. Nott, on reliable authority, that only 30,000 barrels of wine were produced yearly in the island of Madeira; and yet, after supplying the continent of Europe with unknown thousands, 50,000 barrels of what is called Madeira wine are annually sold in this country. ...

Article II. Liquors and their Adulterations. By Frederick Stearns,[1300] Pharmaceutist.[1301]

... In our own country is this art of *manufacturing* liquors carried to its greatest perfection – and it is the purpose of the writer to show, in his article, some of the methods employed.

The high ruling prices of imported wines and liquors, caused by the scant vintages of late years, has been the great incentive to the artificial production of them here. ...

Madeira wine, in a *pure* state, it is asserted, is exported to our shores in greater quantities than to any other country, because Young America likes this wine for its flavor, rather than strength. In a pure state, and when old, it has a pungent, bitter-sweet taste and nutty flavor; it is very fragrant, and is generally admired by wine drinkers. It is considered one of the most valuable medicinal wines. It is *manufactured* from neutral spirit, to which a portion of good Madeira or sherry is added, with sugar, coloring matter, and flavoring, denominated "Ether of Madeira Wine," sold by importers of these flavors. It is also *made* by fermenting a mixture of malt and sugar, and adding Cape wine, brandy, sherry and port. ...

No. 329.
How to imitate Madeira Wine. No. 1.[1302]

Take of white Havana sugar 30 pounds, water 10 gallons, white tartar 6 ounces; boil the whole half an hour, and skim it well; let it stand until cool; then add 8 gallons strong beer-wort from the vat while working; stir it well together, and let it stand until next day; then put it into a sweet cask; then add to it 6 pounds bruised raisins, 1 quart French brandy, ½ pound brown rock-candy, 2 ounces isinglass. After the wine is put into the cask, put a piece of muslin over the bung-hole; and when it has done working, which will be in about 6 weeks, then add 2 green citrons; let them remain until the wine is bottled; it will be ready for bottling in about 6 months.

1299 *The Daily State Journal,* August 12, 1873. (Alexandria, VA).
1300 Frederick K. Stearns, a native of Detroit, MI, was the founder of the Stearns Pharmaceutical Company, established in 1855.
1301 GUNN, Moses; ROBINSON, L. G., "The Medical Independent: a Monthly Review of Medicine and Surgery", Volume 3, Detroit, 1857, pages 307 and 313-314.
1302 MARQUART, John, *600 Miscellaneous Valuable Receipts, Worth Their Weight in Gold. A Thirty Years Collection, to which is added Two Simple Gauging Tables, to enable merchants to take inventory of their stock.,* Christian Henry, Lebanon, PA, 1860, pages 154-155.

No. 330.
Another Imitation of Madeira Wine. No. 2.

Take 10 gallons prepared cider, 1½ gallons pure imported Madeira wine, 3 quarts sweet liquor, 1 ounce tartaric acid, ½ drachm oil of bitter almonds cut in alcohol, 2 pounds bruised raisins, 2 quarts brandy; let stand 10 days; then rack and fine until clear.

RECEIPTS FOR MAKING WINE AND BRANDY[1303]

MADEIRA WINE.	COGNAC.
20 gals. prepared Cider, add	20 gals. pure Spirits,
5 gals. Madeira Wine,	5 gals. pure Cognac Brandy,
1 ½ gals. pure proof Spirits,	1 ½ ozs. Oil of Cognac,
2 ozs. Tartaric Acid,	¾ oz. Ocnanthic Acid,
1 ½ drs. Essential Oil of Bitter Almonds cut in a half pint Alcohol.	¾ oz. Actic Ether,
1 gal. good Brandy,	1 ½ oz. Tincture of Kino,
2 lbs. Raisins,	1 pt. Simple Syrup,
¼ lb. Lean Beef.	2 oz. Salt.

The above are receipts used in France and other wine producing countries, where nearly all, if not all, liquors for sale are adulterated; for making the *best* Madeira and the *best* Cognac. It will be observed, that they contain only five gallons of the pure articles in twenty-five gallons. In this country the pure are not to be had, and the French manufactured liquors are substituted in their place. As these have but five gallons in twenty-five, or one in five, the American, made after similar receipts, contains but one gallon in twenty-five, and an increased proportion of the acids and drugs. But the liquors thus made, are sold as the first qualities of wines and brandies. The inferior and cheaper kinds, as they descend in grade in proportion to the cupidity of the manufacturer, have less and less of the real articles, until they disappear altogether and their places are supplied by sharp acids, and mineral vegetable and animal poisons, of the most disgusting and dangerous characters, as will appear in the following pages. All other brandies, wines and fermented liquors, it will be seen, are subjected to similar or worse adulterations, to enable the manufacturer to administer poisons in disguise, under the names of well known beverages, and to sell for dollars what cost only a few cents. Few persons will hesitate to believe the following statements, as it is a well known fact, that the wine growing countries do not produce one-fifth of the quantity sold and consumed as such in those countries, and that not one-tenth of that sold in the United States is imported. It follows that it is a composition made to resemble nearly in taste the real article. The same is true of brandies and other liquors.

1303 S., P. S. T., *Astounding Disclosures and Frauds in the Liquor Traffic.*, Tract Society, Philadelphia, 1860, pages 7-8.

III
ARTICLES USED FOR FLAVORING WINES, LIQUORS, AND CORDIALS.[1304]

The great secret of success in the manufacture of liquors consists in imparting to the imitation the precise aroma of the genuine, and thus obtain an article of spirit as near reality as possible, at a far less cost. ...

PURE LIGHT OIL OF WINE

Is a colorless, oily liquid, having an aromatic odor, and imparts a greasy stain to paper. This is the product by distillation of alcohol, sulphuric acid, and potassa. It is used for imitating foreign brandies; it is first dissolved in alcohol; the proportion is from one and a half ounces to five hundred gallons of clean spirit. We have nothing better than the oil of wine, as this is the article that imported brandies are indebted to for their aroma, and it is the perfume that we are endeavoring to imitate.

The objections to be urged against the oil of wine by the manufacturer are, the high price, and almost all that is found contains extensive adulterations. And now it is rarely, if ever, used, having found so very many excellent substitutes. But in the manufacture of brandy on a small scale, oil of wine is preferable, and also for the imitation wines, viz. madeira, teneriffe, sherry, port, &c. It is used in the same quantities for wines as for brandies; the spirit to which it is added must be free of grain oil. The oil of wine is highly useful in bottling imitated wines and brandies, for these packages are examined with greater scrutiny than they would otherwise be. It is also used in the fancy whiskeys, when they are put up in small packages. ...

VALERINATE OF AMYLIC OXIDE

Is produced from grain oil by distillation; its odor recalls that of sweet apples, and is known as apple oil. It is used in flavoring plain spirit in imitation of apple brandy, and also in champagne cider. Apple oil, combined with butyric ether, is used for *old reserve, pathetinho*,[1305] *south side*, and *East India madeira*; and when combined with Jamaica rum, it is used in making imitations of rum from neutral spirit. The apple oil and oil of wine form one of the finest perfumes that we have for the conversion of clean spirit into peach brandy; and with acetic ether it is used, giving a fine, and at the same time, natural aroma to the juices of fruits, fruit cordials, and syrups prepared from fruits for use: it is dissolved in clean alcohol, in the proportion of one part to four of spirit. ...

RAISIN SPIRIT.

This is produced by the destillation of raisins. This spirit can be manufactured at that season of the year in which the previous year's stock of raisins have deteriorated from age. Spirit of raisins occupies a position, from its properties, near oil of wine, as they

---

1304 LACOUR, Pierre (of Bordeaux), *The Manufacture of Liquors, Wines, and Cordials, Without the Aid of Distillation. Also the Manufacture of Effervescing Beverages and Syrups, Vinegar, and Bitters. Prepared and Arranged Expressly for the Trade,* Dick & Fitzgerald, Publishers, New York, 1868, pages 50, 54-57, 60-61, 204, 206, 214-215.
1305 We assume that the author meant to say palhetinho, a type of old Madeira Wine.

are obtained from the same sources, only under different circumstances; and as much of the original flavor of the raisin has been dissipated from age, this spirit is extensively used by all classes of manufacturers, and probably to a greater extent in France than elsewhere in flavoring clean spirit for brandies; and, also, for flavoring madeira, sherry, teneriffe, and all of the different brands of champagne. The process consists in using any well managed champagne, and adding the raisin spirit to the neutral spirit intended for the champagne. ...

XII.
WINES.

... *Division and Nomenclature.* – Wines, according to their color, are divided into white and red, and according to their taste and other qualities are either spirituous, sweet, dry, light, sparkling, rough, or acidulous. ...

Wines are known in commerce by various names, according to their sources; thus Portugal produces Port and Lisbon; Spain, Sherry, St. Lucar, Malaga, and Tent; France, Champagne, Burgundy, Hermitage, Vin de Grave, Sauterne, and Claret; Germany, Hock and Moselle; Hungary, Tokay; Sicily, Sicily Madeira and Lissa; the Cape of Good Hope, Constantia; Madeira and the Canaries, Madeira and Teneriffe. ...

DIRECTIONS FOR THE MANUFACTURE OF WINES.

... *Madeira Wine* is the strongest of the white wines in general use. It is a slightly acid wine, and when of the proper age and in good condition, has a rich, nutty, aromatic flavor.

Madeira Wine. – Take white wine, ten gallons; honey, ten pints; of equal parts of rum and neutral spirits, ten pints; five ounces of hops, one fourth pound of bitter almonds, mashed; one pint of flour paste; mix and allow it to stand for five days, then fine with a pint of boiled milk.

Madeira Wine – Cheap and good. – Water, twelve gallons; honey, one gallon; clean spirit, five quarts; hops, five ounces; bitter almonds, three ounces. Boil for twenty-five minutes, and allow to ferment by the addition of a quart of yeast; allow the fermentation to continue until the liquor tastes pleasantly acid, then fine with milk, and add three quarts of rum and four ounces of mustard – allow it to stand for a few days – the mustard should be inclosed in a thin piece of muslin and be suspended in the wine. If this wine should need more body, it can be given by the addition of clean spirit, or when it is only to be kept for a short time, the body may be given by the aid of tincture of paradise. Those preferring it, can use for making Madeira, thus: – Sherry, ten parts; port, four parts; raisin spirit or tincture of prunes, one part; and ten drops sulphuric acid for every gallon.

9.11. Madeira, a Cherished Product to Wine *Connoisseurs*

This section shows a selection of five texts, from different sources, published from 1886 to 1897, in which can be seen how this unique wine was cherished by several *connoisseurs* that were very proud of their Madeiras, kept in their cellars to be drunk on special occasions, and were very learned about the origin and features of every kind of wine, which they would convey to their hosts while drinking it.

Justice Miller and His Friends.[1306]

Says yesterday's New York *Sun*: "Justice Miller[1307] of the United States Supreme Court likes to run over from Washington and eat a good dinner with some of his legal friends in New York. The Justice leaves his bench manners on the bench when he quits it. He is now stopping at the Victoria, and though nearing his seventieth year, whisks the tails of his always-worn swallow-tail around as lively as a young fellow in a waltz. Justice Miller dearly loves a good story and can tell one, is a connoisseur of Madeira wine, and can stew a dish of terrapin better than any chef in Washington. A good many politicians think he is the brainiest Republican in Washington. Justice Miller is thought to resemble President Andy Johnson[1308] in feature, and he does very greatly resemble the late President in having a profound admiration for Maxwell Evarts."[1309]

CHAPTER XX.[1310]
Madeira the King of Wines – It took its Name from the Ship it came in – Daniel Webster and "Butler 16" – How Philadelphians "fine" their Wines – A Southern Wine Party – An Expert's shrewd Guess – The Newton Gordons – Prejudice against Malmsey – Madeira should be kept in the Garret – Some famous Brands.

Having had your champagne from the fish to the roast, your *vin ordinaire* through the dinner, your Burgundy or Johannisberg, or fine old Tokay (quite equal to any Johannisberg), with the cheese, your best claret with the roast, then after the ladies have had their fruit and have left the table, comes on the king of wines, your Madeira; a national wine, a wine

---

1306 *The Washington Critic,* September 30, 1886. (Washington, D.C.).
1307 Judge Miller (1816-1890), a native of Kentucky, was a statesman, jurist, and a Justice of the United States Supreme Court.
1308 See Note 129.
1309 Maxwell Evarts (1862-1913), a Yale graduate and student at Harvard Law School, for two years, after which he worked for the law office of Sward, DaCosta & Guthrie, until the summer of 1889.
1310 McALLISTER, Ward, *Society as I Have Found It,* Cassell Publishing Company, New York, 1890, pages 267-275. This book contains several references to Madeira Wine but we have selected only this chapter for it praises Madeira Wine, once highly consumed in Savannah and Charleston. Samuel Ward McAllister (1827-1895), a native of Savannah, GA, was the self-appointed arbiter of New York society from the 1860's to the early 1890's. He succeeded as a lawyer in California during the Gold Rush, and used his earnings to travel extensively throughout Europe. Upon his return to the United States he settled in New York and married the heiress Sarah Taintor Gibbons, and using his wife's wealth and his own social connections, he sought to become a tastemaker among New York's aristocracy, formed mostly by old merchant and landowning families. He is also known for coining the phrase "the Four Hundred". According to him this was the number of people in New York that really mattered, in other words, the people that felt at home in the ballrooms of high society. Popularly this number was supposed to be the capacity of Mrs. William Backhouse Astor Jr.'s ballroom.

only well matured at the South, and a wine whose history is as old as is that of our country. I may here say, that Madeira imparts a vitality that no other wine can give. After drinking it, it acts as a soporific, but the next day you feel ten years younger and stronger for it. I have known a man, whose dinners were so famous by reason of his being always able to give at them a faultless Madeira, disappear with his wine. When his wine gave out, he collapsed. When asked, "Where is Mr. Jones?" the ready answer was always given, "He went out with his 'Rapid' Madeira."

Families prided themselves on their Madeira. It became an heirloom (as Tokay now is, in Austria). Like the elephant, it seemed to live over three score years and ten. The fine Madeiras were fine when they reached this country. Age improved them, and made them the poetry of wine. They became the color of amber and retained all their original flavor. But it is an error to suppose that age ever improved a poor Madeira. If it came here poor and sweet, it remained poor and sweet, and never lost its sweetness, even at seventy or eighty years, while the famous Madeiras, dating as far back as 1791, if they have been properly cared for, are perfect to this day. We should value wine like women, for maturity, not age.

Figure 87. Samuel Ward McAllister inherited the priceless Madeiras of his father-in-law and was a true wine *connoisseur. Photo taken from his book* Society as I Have Found It. *Author unknown.*

These wines took their names generally from the ships in which they came over. There is no more sensitive wine to climatic influences. A delicate Madeira, taken only a few blocks on a cold, raw day, is not fit to drink; and again, you might as well give a man champagne out of a horse bucket, as to give him a Madeira in a thick sherry or claret glass, or a heavy cut glass. The American pipe-stem is the only glass in which Madeira should be given, and when thus given, is, as one of our distinguished men once said, "The only liquid he ever called wine." This ought to be given as was done by the Father of the Roman Lucullus,[1311] who never saw more than a single cup of the Phanean wine[1312] served at one time at his father's table.

A friend of mine once gave the proprietor of the Astor House,[1313] for courtesies extended to him, a dozen of his finest Madeira. He had the curiosity years after to ask his host of the Astor what became of this wine. He replied, "Daniel Webster came to my house, and I opened a bottle of it for him, and he remained in the house until he had drunk up every drop of it." This was the famous "Butler 16."

As in painting there are the Murillo and Correggio schools, the light ethereal conceptions of womanhood, as against the rich Titian coloring; so in Madeira, there is the full, round, strong, rich wine, liked by some in preference to the light, delicate, straw-colored, rain-water wines. Philadelphians first took to this character of wine. They judiciously "fined" their wine, and produced simply a perfect Madeira, – to be likened to the best Johannisberg, and naturally so, it having similar qualities, as it is well known that the

---

1311 Lucius Licinius Lucullus (118-57/56BC), a politician and general of the late Roman Republic, known for his luxury life style.
1312 Once produced in Chios, the most celebrated Greek island for the character of its growths.
1313 Robert B. Coleman. See Note 1081.

Sercial Madeira, the "king pin" of all Madeiras, was raised from a Rhine grape taken to the Island of Madeira. And here let me say, that "fining," by using only the white of a perfectly fresh egg and Spanish clay, is proper and judicious, but milk is ruinous. The eggs in Spain are famous, and are thus used.

In Savannah and Charleston, from 1800 up to our Civil War, afternoon wine parties were the custom. You were asked to come and taste Madeira, at 5 p.m., *after your dinner.* The hour of dining in these cities was then always 3 p.m. The mahogany table, which reflected your face, was set with finger bowls, with four pipe-stem glasses. in each bowl, olives, parched ground nuts and almonds, and half a dozen bottles of Madeira. There you sat, tasted and commented on these wines for an hour or more. On one occasion, a gentleman, not having any wine handy, mixed half "Catherine Banks" and half "Rapid." On tasting the mixture, a great wine expert said if he could believe his host capable of mixing a wine, he would say it was "half Catherine Banks and half Rapid." This was after fifteen men had said they could not name the Madeira.

A distinguished stranger having received an invitation to one of these wine parties from the British Consul, replied, "Thanks, I must decline, for where I dine I take my wine."

The oldest and largest shippers of Madeira were the Newton Gordons, who sent the finest Madeiras to Charleston and Savannah. From 1791 to 1805, their firm was Newton Gordon, Murdock, & Scott. One hundred and ten years ago, they sent five hundred pipes of Madeira in one shipment to Savannah. These wines sent there were the finest Sercials, Buals, and Malmseys. All those wines were known as extra Madeiras. The highest priced wine, a Manig[a]ult Heyward[1314] wine, I knew forty years ago; it was ninety years old – perfect, full flavored, and of good color and strength.

In Charleston and Savannah from 1780 to 1840, almost every gentleman ordered a pipe of wine from Madeira. I know of a man who has kept this up for half a century.

There is a common prejudice against Malmsey, as being a lady's wine, and sweet; when very old, no Madeira can beat it. I have now in my cellar an "All Saints" wine, named after the famous Savannah Quoit Club, imported in 1791; a perfect wine, of exquisite flavor. My wife's grandfather imported two pipes of Madeira every year, and my father-in-law[1315] continued to do this as long as he lived. When he died he had, as I am told, the largest private cellar of Madeira in the United States. All his wines were Newton Gordons. He made the fatal mistake of hermetically sealing them in glass gallon bottles, with ground glass stoppers, keeping them in his cellar; keeping them from light and air, preventing the wine from breathing, as it were. It has taken years for them to recover from this treatment.

Madeira should be kept in the garret.[1316] A piece of a corn cob is often a good cork for it. Light and air do not injure it; drawing it off from its lees occasionally, makes it more delicate, but, if done too often, the wine may spoil, as its lees support and nourish it.

The great New York Madeiras, famous when landed and still famous, were "The Marsh and Benson, 1809," "The Coles Madeira," "The Stuyvesant," "The Clark," and "The Eliza." In Philadelphia, "The Butler, 16." In Boston, The "Kirby," the "Amory 1800," and "1811," "The Otis." In Baltimore, "The Marshall," the "Meredith," or "Great Unknown," "The Holmes Demijohn," "The Mob," "The Colt." In Charleston, "The Rutledge," "The Hurricane," "The

---

[1314] William Manigault Heyward (1789-1820), a native of Charleston, SC, who married to Susan Hayne Simmons.
[1315] William Gibbons (1781-1845), father of Sarah Taintor Gibbons (1829-1909), the heiress to whom Ward McAllister married with, in New York, in 1853.
[1316] Usually the majority of Americans kept their Madeiras on cellars.

Earthquake," "The Maid," "The Tradd-street." In Savannah, "The All Saints" (1791), "The Catherine Banks," "The Louisa Cecilia" (1818), "The Rapid," 1817, and "The Widow."

THIS WEEK IN SOCIETY.[1317]...
... A Sportsman and Connoisseur in Wines, Aged Seventy-two, is in Our Midst – ...

... A most interesting man is now visiting us, Mr. William Neyle Habisham. He is on his way to the Restigouche Club to indulge in salmon fishing. His grandfather was Postmaster-General in Geo. Washington's Cabinet. The house of Robert Habisham & Son, of which he is a member, has done business in Savannah, Ga., for one hundred and fifty years. Mr. Habisham is seventy-two years of age. He is to-day the best amateur flute player in this country, the best salmon-fisher and one of the best judges of wine to be found anywhere. He is supposed to have had at one time in his cellar, $75,000 worth of Madeira wines. He has himself personally sold nearly $50,000 of this rare wine. There is but one wine cellar in America that approaches his, it is that of Mr. Hartman Kuhn,[1318] of Philadelphia, who died a few months ago. Last week Mr. Habisham was asked to taste eight famous New York Madeiras, dating from 1791 to 1830. He found them all perfect and assured their possessor they would retain their excellence for at least twenty-five to thirty years more. ...

FAMOUS WINE CELLARS[1319]
George Gould[1320] Has the Finest One in the World.
HOW BOTTLES ARE STORED.
... – Rare Vintages Stored in Locked Cellars and No One but the Master Visits Them – ...

The finest wine cellar in this country belongs to George Gould. It is a divided wine cellar. Part of it is up in the Catskills and Furlough Lodge. A second portion is under the residence at Lakewood. But the great bulk of it lies in the vaults of his new town house in Fifth avenue.

Every man wealthy enough to own a wine cellar has one. He may not drink the wine himself. ...

George Gould's wine cellar is fitted out with racks hung against the wall. These racks were put up at great expense. They are of three kinds – wood, metal and sewer pipe. ...

GOULD WINE CELLAR.

In George Gould's cellar there is a long shelving of these short links of sewer pipe. In each link he hides a rare bottle. Some of the wine is of the vintage of 1791, which is the oldest claret known. It is worth $200 for a case of a dozen bottles.

Mr. Gould's famous Bordeaux and Madeira are the talk of the Old World. When they were at Cowes Mr. Gould took over a mixed case to the Prince. ...

1317 *The World,* June 5, 1892. (New York City, NY).
1318 Hartman Kuhn (1784-1860), a native of Pennsylvania, and a graduate of the University of Pennsylvania, was a member of the American Philosophical Society and a Trustee of his *alma mater,* from 1836 until his death.
1319 *The Salt Lake Tribune,* August 30, 1896. (Salt Lake City, UT).
1320 Justice of the Supreme Court of New York.

No man drinks wine that is under 25 years old – no man who has a wine cellar. As a matter of fact, he knows from personal experience the age of his wines. Every man has a favorite vintage. ...

When a man buys a vintage he marks it and puts it away. His son some day reads the date and knows the age of the wine. In the course of years the bottles are taken away one by one, but so large is a wine cellar, so many are the bottles and so careful is the owner of them that in no case do the rare bottles diminish more than a bottle a year. Owners of rare wine become like coin collectors. They want to keep their possession to look at it. ...

A WINE CONNOISSEUR

... The wine connoisseur is up on all wines. He knows their years, their ratings, their prices and how many bottles there are on the market. A man who is contemplating the stocking of a wine cellar will save money by consulting an expert upon wine. Gould wine is like a diamond. You can always realize your money upon it. Better than a diamond, it can never be flooded upon the market by a Cecil Rhodes[1321] of wines, and your investment will increase in value. The only two drawbacks are that the bottles are perishable, and that you drink them up. They are harder to keep than a diamond would be.

The presence of cobwebs upon a bottle is not a guarantee of age. Webs are often dragged over bottles that are to be brought to the table. Or, at a pinch, a host who wants to put on much assumption of style will set a wine bottle in a wooded arbor where spiders are thick and allow them to spin a web over the bottle in a night.

Spider webs are prized, but from another reason. Wine must never be shaken up. In the cellar it lies upon its side for years, and when brought up to the table it should not be disturbed. It spoils good wine to shake it. When it is taken from the shelves it is laid flat in a basket and carried up to the table. The master of the house does this. He takes the bottles as gently as though they were eggs and places them side by side, without removing the dust or the webs. At the table the butler lifts the bottle tenderly, dusts it off gingerly with a soft cloth and pulls the cork. The honored guests sees that the wine is brought up for him unshaken from its long habitation of its own notch. ...

No man except Henry Clews[1322] has ever gone in the Clews wine cellar, which lies under the city house. Mr. Clews used only the wooden shelving in his cellar. And no man except Mr. Fair ever stepped into the mysterious depths of his wine-room. But Mr. Gould

Figure 88. "No One Except the Master Ever Visits the Wine Cellar." *Article illustration. Author unknown.*

1321 Cecil John Rhodes (1853-1902), an English-born South African businessman, mining magnate and politician, who was the founder of the De Beers diamond company.
1322 Henry Clews (1836-1923), a native of England, he emigrated to the United States around 1850, where he became a successful financier and author, having published a book entitled *Fifty Years in Wall Street*.

is either lazier or more trusting, for he allows his man to visit the wine cellar with the wine list and make selections. All wine cellars have an addendum, where the every-day table wine is kept, but no one except the master ever goes into the big wine cellar.

... An Englishman talks a great deal about his wines, but the American likes to think he has got them. He will take you for a walk through his cellar and open a bottle for you, once in your life. But he says little about the cellar, and unless you happen to have done him a favor you will never know that this wine cellar is more than a little shelf from which the butler draws a bottle of table claret for dinner.

HARVEY WILLIAMS.

OLD NEW YORK GOURMETS.[1323]
MEN NOTED AS HOSTS AND THE GUESTS AT THEIR TABLES.
The Pre-eminences of New Yorkers as Dinner Givers and as Diners-Out Long Acknowledged – Three Eras of Dinner Giving and the Men Who Have Been Conspucious in Them.

No European visitor to New York who came with a social passport ever quitted it without bearing testimony to the excellence of its private dinners and to the charm of the guests participating in them. For instance, the late George Augustus Sala,[1324] in his pleasant volume of reminiscences touching his two visits to this city in the years 1864[1325] and 1881,[1326] has left such testimony in most complimentary terms. The pre-eminence of New Yorkers as dinner givers and as diners-out was acknowledged even in the colonial-infancy of New York society; for on their return in 1783 to London many English officers who had resided here as enemies, expressed themselves in published letters or diaries as delighted with the Knickerbocker[1327] hospitality of that era. But, substantially, it was not until the later twenties that dinner giving among Knickerbockers took rank as a gastronomic art on a place with the dinner giving in creole New Orleans (that boasted its Cherrystone oysters, Caribbean pompano, and gumbo okra soup); or in cavalier Charleston, with its delicate broiled ricebirds; or in aristocratic Baltimore, with its matchless terrapin. In this comparison Philadelphia and Boston did not demand important place.

The seventy years past of Knickerbocker dinners may be divided into three eras – the Madeira era, the claret and burgundy era, and the champagne era. The last named is in the nowadays; the first named existed through the thirties; and the second through the quarter century succeeding. ...

It was a quaint fashion among the dinner givers of a half century ago sometimes to ask each guest to send a bottle of Madeira to the giver of the feast, who would mark it

---

1323 *The Sun,* July 11, 1897. (New York City, NY).
1324 George Augustus Sala (1828-1895), an English journalist and author of several travel books.
1325 In 1865 he published a book, in London, describing his first visit to the United States, entitled *My Diary in America in the Midst of War,* in two volumes. On Volume II Sala inserts three minor references to Madeira Wine.
1326 In 1882 he published, in London, another book, in two volumes, depicting his second visit to this country, entitled *America Revisited: From the Bay of New York to the Gulf of Mexico, and From Lake Michigan to the Pacific.* This illustrated work had several editions. On Volume I there is a minor reference to Madeira Wine.
1327 A term to designate Manhattan's aristocracy "in the early days", composed mostly by old merchants and landowners who could trace their lineage back to the days of colonial New Amsterdam. Nowadays it is an obsolete general term for a New Yorker.

when decanted for his private knowledge. The various wines would be tasted in turn and a vote solemny taken as to which decanter held the choicest brand, and it was great fun to frequently find the giver of the wine innocently condemning his own boasted brand. …

9.12. Old Madeira Wines in America

In this section can be found a set of twenty-five texts, published between 1859 and 1900, in which can be seen some concrete examples of old Madeiras that existed in America during this time frame. As we have already mentioned, since the abrupt supply shortage of Madeira Wine to the United States from the early 1850's onwards, a special attention was dedicated to the old privately owned Madeira Wine collections across the United States, kept mostly in the cities that used to largely import this appreciated product in the past, as was the case with Boston, New York, Philadelphia, Savannah and Washington. These texts will reveal, among other topics, references to different types of old Madeiras and their owners, which were some of the most prominent people of the time, old wines being served in special occasions such as marriages and political gatherings – in one of them would be served some Madeira from the cellar of Thomas Jefferson –, and a special focus is given to the old Madeiras kept for generations in the South, some of which were over a hundred years old. We will also have a look at some references to several fortunes in wines, acquired over the years by their owners, who stored them away, for decades, in the cellars of New York City.

OLD WINES.[1328] – … Most of the old Madeira wine for sale in this country formerly belonged to families in Boston. The "Judge Story"[1329] brands are $4 a bottle, Isaac P. Davis's "Eclipse" is $8 a bottle, "Gov. Philips, 1820" and "Edward Tuckerman,[1330] 1820," are $10 a bottle, "Francis Amory" Madeira bottled in 1800 is sold at $12 a bottle!

A GRAND DINNER.[1331]

It was in 1851, when Millard Fillmore[1332] ruled this land, and times were slow. There were two clubs of good-livers, one in New York and the other in Philadelphia, and they spent one day in every year and all their spare cash in trying to rival each other's annual banquets. On the 19th of April, in the year just mentioned, the competition culminated in one of the grandest dinners that ever was eaten. Fifteen New Yorkers were brought by fifteen Philadelphians to a just appreciation and full understanding of what

---

1328 *Boston Evening Transcript*, April 20, 1859. (Boston, MA). Quoting this source, this article was published in the following newspapers: *Lowell Daily Citizen & News*, April 21, 1859. (Lowell, MA); *Alexandria Gazette*, April 25, 1859. (Alexandria, VA); *Salem Register*, April 25, 1859. (Salem, MA); *The Charleston Mercury*, April 27, 1859. (Charleston, SC); *Lancaster Examiner and Herald*, May 4, 1859. (Lancaster, PA); *Daily Chronicle & Sentinel*, May 4, 1859. (Augusta, GA).
1329 Joseph Story. See Note 949.
1330 Edward Tuckerman (1817-1886), a native of Boston, MA, was a botanist and professor.
1331 *The Andrew County Republican*, October 2, 1874. (Savannah, MO).
1332 See Note 117.

constitutes a dinner, properly so called. The caterer was John W. Parkinson,[1333] since then the author of a series of articles on "American Cookery." A survivor of the New York delegation, in a letter to the Philadelphia *Press*, tells the story as follows: As this dinner was given in April, it took the caterer greatly at a disadvantage as to both game and vegetables. It was "between seasons." He could only obtain what he did by special use of both telegraph and express. His lettuce, green peas, cauliflowers, etc., had to be ordered from Georgia. His reed birds came from South Carolina. He sent anglers and hunters to the woods and waters of Virginia. The salmon of the occasion were swimming the night before in the Kennebec,[1334] in Maine. The dinner consisted of seventeen distinct courses. Each course was a perfect banquet in itself. Every separate course of viands was accompanied with its own appropriate course of wines. The expensiveness and rarity of the liquors will be inferred when I say the opening "Cognac" cost $6 a pint at wholesale. Before every one of the thirty guests was a wine-cooler. Behind each guest was a waiter (colored), in the full evening party-dress of the day – black pantaloons and swallow-tail coat, with white vest and white cravat. The gloves of the waiters were not cotton or berlin, but the newest and best of white kid. Among the choice and voluntary contributions to the common feast were two bottles of Madeira wine, which were brought by Joshua Price, a citizen who was as well known in Philadelphia at that day as Independence Hall. These bottles had come down to him from his great-great-grandfather. They had been in the family for over 150 years. Their great age was attested by the accumulation of dust, cobwebs, and what not. These incrustations on the glass were half an inch thick. Enchained to our seats by this long and brilliant succession of culinary enticements, interspersed, of course, with that "feast of reason and flow of soul," in the way of wit and song, poetry, eloquence, and anecdote which such bountiful good cheer is sure to inspire, we sat so long at the table that the sun in the meantime had both set and risen again. It was precisely 6 o'clock in the evening when we sat down, and it was high 6 in the morning when we arose. The Philadelphia papers of the day spoke of this entertainment as "the $1,000 dinner." The fact is, that our Philadelphia entertainers paid the caterer $1,500 for the banquet - $50 a plate. And yet such was the expense incurred in providing so great a variety of such rare and costly viands that the purveyor made no profit even at that. Indeed, he stated to the committee that while he asked a carte blanche, he would employ a special clerk who should keep an accurate account of all the outlays, and he would add no profit for himself. "All that he asked was the pleasure of showing to our friends from New York what the culinary and confectionery art could do in his native city of Philadelphia."

1333 John W. Parkinson (?-1895), a native of Philadelphia, whose parents owned a successful confectionary store. In 1844 his mother published the book *The Complete Confectioner, Pastry, Cook and Baker*, in the afore mentioned state. In this book there are two recipes using Madeira Wine as one of its ingredients, of which we present one, in section 11.1.6. of this anthology. For 20 years James Parkinson published culinary-related articles at the Confectioner's Journal and, in 1874, he published the book entitled *American Cookery at the Centennial*, at his homestate. With the preparation of the dinner alluded to in this text, in 1851, responding to a challenge from Delmonico's restaurant, in New York, he gained national attention due to his 17-course $1000 dinner.

1334 A 170-mile-long river that crosses the state of Maine.

[Untitled][1335]

Mr. Henry R. Mygatt,[1336] of Oxford, N. Y., has a quart bottle of old Madeira wine in his possession which was put up and hermetically sealed by Robert Morris,[1337] of Revolutionary Treasury fame, in 1774. He will have it on exhibition at the Centennial Exhibition at Philadelphia in 1876.[1338]

SOME SHERRY.[1339]
AMONG THE WINE-TASTERS.
LIEBIG AS A WINE EXPERT – THE OLD MADEIRA – HOW WINES CHANGE – …

… Bearing this experience in my mind, I happened to be present at the office of a prominent wine merchant in the city, having been invited there, in order to taste some very wonderful Madeira. I bowed with awe to the wine Solon, who, though he received me graciously, listened half abstractedly to what I had to say, and who cut me quite short by presenting me with half a dozen straw-stem glasses all at the same time. I handled the glasses between my fingers like chop-sticks, and succeeded at last in putting them all down safely on the table before me. I was in search of information, and as tasting was my object and not talking, I thought I was likely to get all I wanted. The wine man opened a cabinet, in which were stored innumerable bottles, and, after pondering for a while, drew out a decanter. If the glass recipient had been full of the fulminate of mercury, likely to explode with the merest vibration, he could not have been more careful. Next he took with equal precaution an old-fashioned quart bottle and stood it beside the decanter. "This is the wine in its original bottle, and this is the same decanted yesterday," was what he said. He poured a little into a glass, threw it out, probably as a libation to the gods, then filled my glass, the glasses of two other gentlemen, and his own. The silence became oppressive. I was conscious that I was present on a solemn occasion, and was on my guard. I knew I was in the august presence of a sage, and felt all the awe of a humble pupil. At last, before putting his glass to his mouth, the great wine man talked, and this is how he commenced: "This wine is Madeira. Its date is authenticated. It came to Charleston in 1810. In 1812 it went to Savannah. Here is an invoice of the wine, for it was bottled in 1814. It remained in Savannah until the war, when it was shipped here. Originally it was twenty-five dozen; now about ten dozen are left. It is undoubtedly sixty years old." …

1335 *The Evening Post*, December 7, 1874. (New York City, NY); *Newport Daily News*, December 9, 1874. (Newport, RI); *The Argus*, December 10, 1874. (Albany, NY); *The Indianapolis Sentinel*, December 14, 1874. (Indianapolis, IN); *The Columbian Weekly Register*, December 19, 1874. (New Haven, CT).

1336 Henry R. Mygatt (1810-1875), a distinguished lawyer from New York.

1337 Robert Morris (1734-1806), a native of Liverpool, England, who emigrated to Philadelphia, where he became a successful merchant. He is known in American History as "the Financier of the Revolution" for his role in raising money to support George Washington's army. He was also a signer of the Declaration of Independence, the Articles of Confederation and the United States Constitution.

1338 A different version of this (untitled) text was published in several sources: «A New York man expects to exhibit at the Centennial a bottle of Madeira wine which was put up and hermetically sealed by Robert Morris in 1774.» *The Logansport Daily Star*, February 2, 1875. (Logansport, IN); *Rockfort Weekly Gazette*, February 25, 1875. (Rockford, IL); *The Hamilton Guidon*, March 4, 1875. (Hamilton, OH. Published in the section "Paragraphs of all Sorts").

1339 *The New York Times*, October 17, 1875. (New York City, NY); *The Burlington Daily Hawk-Eye*, October 31, 1875. (Burlington, IA).

[Untitled][1340]

At a sale of wines belonging to the late John P. Healey,[1341] of Boston, some Madeira was brought out that had passed around the world in the frigate Constitution nearly forty years ago. Captain John Percival, her commander, while at Madeira,[1342] ordered a cask of the best wine to be obtained on the island. This was carried through the rest of the voyage, and afterward bottled.

Old Madeira Wine.[1343]

The finest of old Madeira wine is to be found on the tables of several of the Justices of the Supreme Court at Washington, and the way it was procured is interesting. Before the Revolution a few old mercantile houses in Alexandria imported a large supply of Madeira, and some of this is still in private cellars in Washington city. The Honorable Josiah Lee, of Baltimore, had a large supply from these Alexandria importations, and at his death in 1852 it sold at prices ranging from $24 to $77,50 per gallon. It would be hard to fix a price upon the few bottles of this wine that still remain in the hands of *connoisseurs*.

[Untitled][1344]

At a silver wedding to be celebrated in New York soon there will be served Madeira wine bottled in 1800. We shall, with some interest, await the account of the wedding to see what the effect is of putting such rare old wine in comparatively new human bottles.

[Untitled][1345]

At a reception given by one of the Cabinet officers the other night gentlemen who were shown to the cloakrooms were much surprised to see on the mantels rows of dust-covered bottles, enticingly labeled "Madeira, 1839," "Oporto, 1852," "Sherry, 1847," and so on. The guests examined them with interest and there was a discussion as to whether the bottles were intended as ornaments or for use. As there were neither corkscrews nor glasses handy, the first theory was accepted with some regret, for even the exterior was sufficient to awaken an appetite that was not satiated by the champagne and punch in the dining hall below. One Senator who is distinguished for his devotion to the doctrines enunciated in the celebrated message of the Governor of North Carolina to the Governor of South Carolina, suggested that the bottles must have been intended as favors such as are given

---

1340 *The Atlanta Constitution*, May 11, 1883. (Atlanta, GA).
1341 John P. Healey (1810-1883?), a native of New Hampshire, was a Dartmouth graduate, studied law at the office of Daniel Webster, in Boston, of whom he became an associate later on. He was also both a senator and representative at various times.
1342 Where he arrived on June 24, 1844. See section 6.1.1.14. of this anthology.
1343 *Juniata Sentinel and Republican*, January 21, 1885. (Mifflintown, Juniata County, PA).
1344 *The Cincinnati Commercial Gazette*, February 6, 1886. (Cincinnati, OH. Published at the section "NOTES OF THE DAY.").
1345 *New York Daily Tribune*, February 17, 1886. (New York City, NY).

at a german, or like bouquets laid beside the plates of ladies at fashionable dinner parties to take away. The suggestion was popular, but it was not carried into effect.

FORTUNES IN WINES.[1346]
Some Well-Filled in New York City.
Men Who Will Offer a Fabulous Price for a Famous Wine – New Yorkers Who Take Pride in Their Private Cellars – Old Wine in New Bottles.

Every reader of fiction has dwelt with delight upon those passages in his favorite works where the jolly host orders up from his dungeon cellar a dusty, cobweb-covered bottle, which he clasps lovingly before he carefully draws the cork, and his mouth is sure to feel dry and a longing thrill his frame when the limpid liquid gurgles melodiously into the delicate glass, while the host descants upon its virtues and relates how that identical wine was laid away by that grim-looking warrior ancestor whose portrait adorns the east side of the picture gallery. Every one has felt a sad regret that not one of his friends has such a cellar or such a story to tell.

But the fact is that one need not go to the shores of "Merry England" nor glide gently down the beautiful Rhine in order to find hosts who are the possessors of rich wines, which they dispense with prodigal hospitality.

Right here in our own great city they can be found, and in plenty, too. I learned this one day last week when Mr. John Jacob Astor[1347] walked into the warerooms of a wholesale wine merchant down town, who also happens to be a friend of mine.

"Mr. – ," said Mr. Astor, "I understand that some of the Bloodgood Madeiras are on the market. If any can be obtained, I would like them. I am willing to pay a good price for any that are authentic."

"I doubt that they can be had at any price," returned the merchant. "Jim Husted or some of those other collectors would grab at them as quick as a wink if they had the opportunity."

"Well, see what you can do," returned the millionaire, "and remember that the price is no object so long as I get the genuine article."

With that Mr. Astor went away.

"He will never in the world get them," said my friend, turning to me.

"Why? what are they?" I inquired, never having heard of those evidently famous wines.

"What! never heard of the Bloodgood Maderias?"[1348] cried my friend in astonishment, "and you pretend to know something about New Yorkers!"

[1346] *Cleveland Plain Dealer*, May 22, 1887. (Cleveland, OH). This text was published, without the illustrations, in some other sources: *The Sunday Oregonian*, May 22, 1887. (Portland, OR. Published under a slight different title: "FORTUNES IN RARE WINES. Some Well-Filled Cellars in New York City. Men who will Offer a Fabulous Price for a Famous Wine – Sketches of New Yorkers who Take Pride in their Cellars."). *Fort Worth Daily Gazette*, June 20, 1887. (Forth Worth, TX. Published under the titles "MONEY IN RARE WINES – Some Cellars in New York City – Men Who Will Offer a Fabulous Price for a Famous Wine.", referring that the text had been transcribed from the *New York Mail and Express*).

[1347] John Jacob Astor (1763-1848), a native of Waldorf, Germany, who emigrated to the United States after the American Revolutionary War, becoming a business magnate, merchant, investor and the first prominent member of the Astor family. Due to the success of his businesses he became the first multimillionaire in America.

[1348] The right spelling is Madeiras.

I humbly admitted my ignorance, and he sunk back in his easy chair as he related what follows:

"The Bloodgood Maderias[1349] are so called because they come from the stock of a wine dealer who was famous as an importer of Maderia[1350] wines half a century ago. He had a very large business and catered to the best families. Business was done in an old-fashioned way then, and every family of any standing imported its own Madeira. If Mr. John Jacob Astor or Mr. Geolet[1351] or any of the other big men of that day wanted any Medeira[1352] he would go to Bloodgood and say:

"'Order one cask of old Madeira for me.'

"Then Bloodgood would send out an order something like this:

Figure 89. "Mine Host His Own Butler." Article illustration. Author unknown.

"'Messrs. – : Send to John Jacob Astor, in my care, one cask Madeira vintage.'

"In that way Mr. Astor would be sure to get his wine direct from the grower or exporter in Madeira, and the wine would come to New York marked with his name. I was clerk in a wine house of a similar kind fifty years ago, and I remember very well when some of the rich people would come down and order their pipes or quarters. Those were the names they usually called the casks, which indicated their size. Think of a dealer going to the trouble of ordering a quarter of a cask of wine from Madeira for a customer! But, of course, he always had a lot of such orders ready when the vessel sailed, besides what he needed himself.

"When old Bloodgood died he left a large quantity of fine Madera,[1353] which was bought up by his old customers. Occasionally some small quantity of this will get on the market, and then there is a mighty big scramble for it, I can tell you. Money is no object to some of our men, and Jim Husted or Herman[n] Oelrichs[1354] or half a dozen other prominent men that I can name would raise each other blind for a long time before anyone would call. If you have never tasted a Bloodgood Madeira, then you don't know what a good Madeira wine is."

"Madeira was evidently the favorite wine some years ago," I remarked. "It is not now, certainly."

"No, it is not," he continued. "Claret and champagne are all the go now; and the quantity of stuff that is drunk in the name of champagne is enough to poison a colony of goats."

"Fifty years ago this was not so. Then every family of consequence had a supply of Madeira and a decanter of that wine could always be found upon the sideboard. As good

---

1349 The right spelling is Madeiras.
1350 The right spelling is Madeira.
1351 Robert Goelet (1841-1899), a native of New York, was a real estate developer in New York City and a director of the Chemical National Bank. He lived at 591, 5th Avenue, Manhattan, and owned a mansion in Newport, RI.
1352 The right spelling is Madeira, although we presume that the author intended to phonetically transcribe the English pronunciation of this word.
1353 The right spelling is Madeira.
1354 Hermann Oelrichs (1850-1906), was born aboard the *SS Kaiser Wilhelm der Grosse*, in the Atlantic Ocean, during his mother's trip to America, where he became a multimillionaire businessman, and owned the Norddeutsche Lloyd shipping company. He also built the Rosecliff mansion, in Newport, RI.

Figure 90. "Old Wine in New Bottles."
Article illustration. Author unknown.

Madeira came to this country as went to any other in the world. The American sailing vessels took out boards and staves to Madeira and brought back the wine in return.

"But one year a peculiar pestilence swept over the island of Madeira and killed all the vines.[1355] After that it became impossible to do more than supply the wealthy buyers in Europe and the American trade ceased. Every one who could afford it laid in a quantity, but it took a long time for the news of the pestilence to reach here, and a long time for the orders to get back to Madeira, so no one was enabled to secure a very large amount.

"An attempt was made to substitute sherry for Madeira, but the people who had been drinking the best old Madeira were not going to put up with new sherry, and the trial was unsuccessful."

"Is there much of that old wine hanging around those diggings?" I inquired.

"Yes, there is considerable of it in the wine cellars of some of our old families. I can mention the names of a number of prominent people who have inherited and carefully added to this old stock. In fact, I may say that this old Madeira has given origin to many well- stocked wine cellars in New York. People who would never have thought of buying more than enough wine to suffice for their present needs have been tempted, through having this old wine as a nucleus, to buy whenever a good opportunity presents itself.

"It is wonderful how jealous these people are of this old wine. They hoard it as misers do gold. You cannot buy it for its weight in bullion, I verily believe, and the only chance we dealers have is when some family dies out and the estate has to be divided. Then the wine usually has to be sold in order to settle up the estate, but even then it is rarely that we can get very much of it. Either some of the heirs bid it in or some private collector, glad of the opportunity to increase his stock, runs up the price beyond all competition on our part.

"I remember one instance of my attempts to secure a stock of this wine. A young man of good family, but whose name I cannot reveal, came to me some time ago and said that he had inherited some fine old wines which he would like to sell. I knew him by reputation. He was married and lived in Fifth avenue. He had recently come into a large fortune by the death of his father and was joint heir with his mother and sister. I went up and looked at the collection, or rather at his share of it, and I will never forget the appearance of grief and indignation with which the two ladies met his announcement of his intention to sell. They not only absolutely refused to part with their portions, but would not even listen to my suggestion to have it examined for the purpose of seeing whether it needed rebottling."

"Do you mean to say that you rebottle old wine? I thought it was considered sacrilege to disturb it in any way, even in pouring it into the glass before it is disposed of."

"So it is," he replied, "but we don't disturb it. We handle it as carefully as a young mother does her first born. We would not shake the contents of a bottle of good wine for anything you can name. But it is frequently necessary to look after wine that has been put away in the American fashion and allowed to remain undisturbed for a long time. If it is not done, when the owners want to use the wine they will find it unfit to drink.

[1355] In 1852, when the vines were destroyed by the oidium, as we have already seen, on section 9.7. of this anthology.

"Americans do not lay away their wines as the English and nearly all other nationalities do. The latter place the bottles on their sides. Of course, the longer they remain in that position the heavier the sediment that forms on the side near the ground. That makes it necessary to handle it very carefully, and if it should be shaken the sediment would become stirred in the wine and spoil it.

"To avoid this danger some enterprising American suggested that the bottles be stood up, and that has ever since been the custom here.

"But now an unforeseen danger has arisen. The average cork will last about twelve years. Then it begins to rot. Portions of the cork fall into the wine from the upright position of the bottle, and in a short time the wine is spoiled. This has brought into being a branch of our business which is peculiar.

Figure 91. "A Corner in Mrs. Carew's Cellar." *Article illustration. Author unknown.*

"When the corks in the bottles begin to rot new corks must be put in. This is a delicate matter, because if any of the cork falls in then the whole of the wine has to be filtered through paper of French manufacture; or, if any of the sediment at the bottom is disturbed, so that it gets into the wine proper, the same process has to be gone through.

"We frequently have to rebottle wine that has lain very long. We carefully draw off the top, leaving only the sediment. This is generally put in with some new wine and allowed to remain until all its good proportions have been absorbed.

"Many old American families would rather let the wine they have received through inheritance rot than use or sell it. In many instances they will not even allow it to be attended to. They look upon it as a sacred heirloom, and each bottle possesses, in their eyes, the same inviolable nature with which they would view the bones of their ancestors. I think I can say without exaggeration that thousands of bottles of wine are spoiling between Wall street and Central park at the present moment because of the prejudice of the owners against having them disturbed. They seem to regard these inherited wines as a proof of their good lineage, somewhat as a European might look upon the family plate which was made somewhere in the Fifteenth century.

"Some time ago I received a letter from Mrs. Charles Carew, the wife of an old-time New York shipping merchant. Her husband was well known here when I was a clerk fifty years ago. He had travelled a great deal himself and was acquainted with every captain who came into his port. This acquaintance enabled him to gratify his passion for collecting fine wines, and a more select lot of wines than Mrs. Carew now has is not to be found in this country. Since her husband's death, some years ago, she has lived very much retired in West Forty-sixth street, and her wines have hardly been touched. Her letter requested me to examine them, and I tell you what, I just gloated over that job. I went down into the cellar with my assistants and let in what light I could. Then I carefully picked up each bottle and held it up to the light, and feasted my eyes on the soft shades of ruby and yellow. Some of the corks were decayed and the wine had to be rebottled. It was an awful temptation to see that beautiful liquid poured out like so much oil! There were only about 2000 bottles in her collection, but each bottle has a history. Mrs.

Carew knows them all, but she is an old lady now, and I don't know whether she would say very much about them.

"James Husted,[1356] the speaker of the assembly, has the finest collection of wines of any man along the Hudson, and probably in the country. He doesn't drink much himself, but he entertains royally at his home in Peekskill.

"A. T. Stewart[1357] was one of my best customers. I don't believe he ever drank a drop, but he bought a large stock of all kinds and always tried to get the choicest. I don't believe he was himself a judge of wine, but he was shrewd enough not to buy from any one he was not positive he could trust. He served his best wines freely to his friends at all events. One of the last transactions I had with him was to sell him ninety cases of choice French claret. He paid me $2400 in gold for them, which was not high for the quality of wine he obtained. I do not know why, but he sent part of it to his hotel at Saratoga, the Grand Union.[1358] I know it was not sold at the table. The last went up to his marble palace on Fifth avenue. Instead of putting it in the cellar, he put it at the top of the house.

"All the Astors have choice wine cellars. They go more extensively into the rare wines than most Americans. They have the choice Rhine wines, tokays, chiantis and so forth. The ordinary American's wine cellar has few wine outside of Madeira, champagne and claret.

"When I say the Astors I include the branches also. Mrs. Colford Jones[1359] is an Astor and so was Woodbury G. Langdon.[1360] The latter is dead now, but his wine cellar had a very good reputation and included some of the choicest Madeira in New York. Mrs. Jones' cellar also has a good reputation, and is well stocked with rich old wines. The Astors are continually on the lookout for choice wines and never grumble at the price so long as they are assured of the genuineness of the wine. Now I know Mr. Astor would willingly pay me a good margin if I could secure him some of this Bloodgood Madeira.

"Among the other men who will not shrink from paying a high price for what they want is William B. Dinsmore,[1361] the president of the Adams express company. He is one of the most liberal buyers in the country. I don't believe I ever saw him drink a glass of wine, even at dinner, although I believe he occasionally drinks a glass of champagne. Like nearly all the prominent wine collectors he buys with the idea of handsomely entertaining his friends rather than tickling his own palate. A great many who are almost total abstainers build big wine cellars and stock them with fine wines. Those men never lack for guests at their dinners and entertainments. A short time ago President Dinsmore offered me $150 a dozen for some rare Hock wines.

"Speaking of big wine cellars, it is getting to be more and more the thing for big collectors to have their particular notions. A number of collectors who have choice wines have the best put in separate bins and never allow the keys to go out of their own keeping.

1356 James W. Husted (1833-1892), an American lawyer and politician, who was elected six times as Speaker of the New York State Assembly during his 22 years of service there. During his political career he became known as the "Bald Eagle of Westchester".

1357 Alexander Turner Stewart (1803-1876), a native of Ireland, who emigrated to New York in the summer of 1823. Being a business genius, he opened the largest retail store in the world, at Broadway. He also owned several mills and factories. In a short time he became a multimillionaire by selling dry goods.

1358 Hotel located at Saratoga Springs, NY, which was managed by A. T. Stewart from 1872 to 1876. In 1876 it claimed to be the world's largest hotel.

1359 Rebecca Jones who, just as her sister Mary Mason, were wealthy widowers who owned and developed real estate in New York City.

1360 A multimillionaire owner of real estate in New York City.

1361 A native of New Hampshire and successful entrepreneur, who died in New York City in 1886.

"I called with some friends on one of these gentlemen, and old acquaintance of mine, several weeks ago, and in the course of conversation he told us that he had secured a very fine Moselle wine.

"I'll let you try some, he said, and left the room.

"He returned in about five minutes. His hands were covered with dust where he had been groping in the cellar, and he had several bottles of wine carefully laid in a basket which he carried. As I knew that he had a very good butler I inquired why he had gone to the bother of getting the wine himself.

"'James is a very good servant and knows a thing or two about handling wines,' he replied. 'He's honest, too, but I'd rather trust him with my pocketbook than my choice wines. I make it a rule never to let any one touch the keys to the best wines, although it discommodes me at times.'

"Herman[n] Oelrichs,[1362] the ex-president of the New York athletic club,[1363] is another big buyer. He bought a very large lot of choice wines recently in Baltimore. He paid a fancy price for them, too, I understand. Mayor Hewitt[1364] has only enough wine to provide for his present needs. He entertains frequently and therefore has to have a certain amount on hand, but neither he nor his wife inherited any. Peter Cooper, his father-in-law, didn't care a rap for wine and did not bother to create a wine cellar for his children's use. I understand, however, that the mayor is thinking of fixing up a first-class wine cellar now.

"A very large collection of fine Madeira wines is owned by James G. King's[1365] sons, the Wall street brokers and bankers. Their father was a connoisseur and imported largely in casks about sixty years ago. He ran it off into bottles, every one of which bears his private seal. The young men are very chary about using it.

"Every branch of the Remsen family has a share of the wines laid away by the ancestral stock somewhere about the beginning of the present century. You couldn't buy a drop of it though you came provided with nuggets of gold. Frederick Schuchardt,[1366] one of the Remsens, and a society leader, left a very choice collection when he died several years ago. Not a bottle was sold or got into the hands of strangers, however, but was amicably divided among his heirs. The Remsens have been carefully adding to their stock in a quiet manner and bid fair soon to have one of the most select collections in the city.

"Among the other prominent collectors and owners of choice wines are J. W. Girard, Mrs. W. W. Peck, A. A. Low and Judge Hilton.[1367] Charles A. Dana[1368] is an excellent judge

---

1362 See Note 1354.
1363 A private social and athletic club in New York City, established in 1863, which still exists today.
1364 Abraham Hewitt (1822-1903), a native of New York, was a teacher, lawyer, iron manufacturer, chairman of the Democratic National Committee, U.S. Congressman, and Mayor of New York City, from 1887 to 1888.
1365 James Gore King (1791-1853), a native of New York and a Harvard graduate, was a businessman and politician, notorious for his banking activities, owning the banking firm James G. King & Sons.
1366 Frederick Schuchardt (1805-1885), a native of Germany, was for many years a prominent New York merchant and banker.
1367 Henry Hilton (1824-1899), a native of New York, was a judge of the Court of Common Pleas from 1853 to 1863, and a park commissioner for many years. He was also the executor of the estates of some wealthy New York families, such as of Alexander Turney Stewart. Judge Hilton is also associated with anti-Semitism in post-Civil War America for, while managing the Grand Union Hotel, he refused entry of the Jewish Joseph Seligman and his family. This fact was widely advertised on the press of the time and created a nationwide controversy.
1368 Charles Anderson Dana (1819-1897), a native of New Hampshire, was an American journalist (linked to the *New York Tribune*), author and government official, best known for his association with Ulysses S. Grant during the American Civil War and his aggressive political advocacy after the war.

of wines, and serves some of the rarest and finest at his elegant entertainments. George Washington Childs[1369] has a large wine cellar at his home in Philadelphia.

"There are many other prominent people whose collections compare favorably with those of Europeans, and, if American gold continues to flow as liberally as it has, no doubt many European collections will be transferred bodily to this country."

My friend poured out a glass of rich Burgundy as he concluded, and after letting it gently glide down my parched throat, I went away more than ever impressed with the growth of this nation and the advance in munificence of its first citizens.

CHARLES J. ROSEBAULT.[1370]

RARE OLD LIQUORS.[1371]
HIGH PRICED MADEIRA AND BRANDY AND OLD CHERRY BOUNCE.

Lancaster, Sept. 25. – It is doubtful whether there is another town in this country that has an establishment keeping in stock Madeira wine at $25 a bottle and brandy held at $50 a gallon, or one that has cherry bounce which is known to have been in the bottles over 60 years. Lancaster has such a store in the century-old Reigart wine shop on East King-street. On the shelves of this old shop, now the property of the present Postmaster of Lancaster, Major H. A. Slaymaker,[1372] are long rows of dust-covered bottles containing Madeira of the vintage of 1793, 1800, and succeeding vintages up to 1840. These wines were imported directly by the founder of the store, Adam Reigart and his successors. The early vintages were obtained in exchange for Lancaster County corn and other products.

When the 1798 Madeira was first sold here $2 a gallon was charged for it. Madeira was then the popular drink among the farmers and others. To-day $2 would hardly buy a wine-glassful of this rare beverage. There are on the shelves of this store a number of dozen of Madeira of the vintage of 1827, which Mr. Slaymaker says is the finest Madeira in existence, the vintage of that year never having been equaled. Two or three years ago Sam Randall, W. U. Hensel, and B. J. McGrann of Lancaster took a Southern trip. At Atlanta they were royally entertained by Henry A. Grady of the Atlanta *Constitution*. On his return to Lancaster Mr. McGrann ordered two cases of the famous and rare 1827 Madeira sent to Mr. Grady in recognition of the hospitality he had extended to the party.

At $25 a bottle there is not much of a demand for the 1793 Madina.[1373] Out of the dusty rows of bottles containing it only three vacant spaces are visible. Two of these were made vacant by an oil millionaire of Pittsburg, who took home with him two bottles of the precious stuff. The other space was made vacant by B. J. McGrann, who purchased the bottle and cracked it in honor of Judge Thurman,[1374] who was in Lancaster two years ago visit-

---

1369 Editor of the *Philadelphia Ledger* and a philanthropist of worldwide renown.
1370 Author of several books, among which the one entitled *When Dana was the Sun: A Story of Personal Journalism*, published in New York, in 1931, on which there is a brief reference to Madeira Wine.
1371 *The New York Times*, September 27, 1888. (New York City, NY).
1372 Henry Edwin Slaymaker (1828-1905), a native of Pennsylvania, was well known in his community on account of his connections with Reigarts Old Wine Store, then a leading business house, located on East King Street, that had been established by Adam Reigart, his grandfather.
1373 We assume the author meant to say Madeira.
1374 Allen Granberry Thurman (1813-1895), a native of Virginia, was a Democratic Representative, Ohio Supreme Court Justice and Senator for Ohio.

ing his sister. The bottles containing this rare wine are of the last century pattern, when bottles were blown and shaped without the aid of molds. They are irregular in outline and very heavy.

The particular quality of brandy that Major Slaymaker will not sell for less than $50 a gallon he imported himself 30 years ago, and it was then well along in years. Simon Cameron,[1375] Col. James Duffy, B. J. McGrann, and other wealthy connoisseurs have frequently offered $45 a gallon for this brandy, but its owner will not sell a drop of it at less than the fifty-dollar rate.[1376]

SOCIETY TOPICS OF THE WEEK.[1377]

If ever there was "too much of a good thing," it may be said that the past week brought too many weddings. The society table, which appears to be well spread this year, is having a little too much, however, of the first course, and is beginning to feel that even brides, their belongings, their presents, and their gowns have become monotonous. On Wednesday there were no less than nine marriages of fashionable interest and importance, and the other days of the week favored by Hymen[1378] have not been far behind. ...

An enthusiastic maiden who was present at the wedding ceremony of Mr. Hillhouse[1379] and Miss Remsen[1380] on Wednesday stated last night in her parlor that there were almost as many people there as at the football game yesterday afternoon. ... But if the ceremony which made Miss Remsen Mrs. Hillhouse was an unusually notable one, what shall be said of the following reception, and who can adequately describe its enjoyments and its

---

1375 Simon Cameron (1799-1889), a native of Pennsylvania, was the politician who served as U.S. Secretary of the War for Abraham Lincoln, at the start of the American Civil War. He made his fortune in railways, canals and banking, having founded the Bank of Middletown.

1376 A brief summary of this text was published in other sources, under the title of "Rare Old Wines.", in these words: «In the quaint century old Reigart wine shop at Lancaster, Pa., there is a priceless stock of old Madeira wines, including the vintages of 1798, 1800 and every succeeding year to 1840. There is quite a lot of the famous 1827 wines, the best ever made. The 1798 Madeira is held at $25 a bottle.» *Lebanon Daily News*, November 19, 1888. (Lebanon, PA); *The Dunkirk Observer-Journal*, October 24, 1888. (Dunkirk, Chaut Co., NY. Published in the "Relics and Rarities" section); *The Syracuse Standard*, October 28, 1888. (Syracuse, NY. Published in the same section as in the previous source). Another shorter version of this text was published in other newspapers, under the title "Maj. Slaymaker's Aged Wines.", adding that it had been transcribed from the *Philadelphia Press*, in these words: «Maj. Slaymaker, Postmaster at Lancaster, has a cask of brandy for which Simon Cameron has offered him $45 a gallon, an offer that was refused. The brandy was imported by the present owner's grandfather. The pipe in which it came from France bears the custom house marks of 1808. Maj. Slaymaker has also Madeira of the vintages of 1793, 1800, 1808, 1812, 1827 and 1840. The vintage of 1827 was one of the best in the history of Madeira and there is but little of it in existence to-day. The Madeira of 1793 was bottled in 1798 by Philip and Adam Reigart, who imported the wine, received in exchange for corn. When they received it they sold it as a common drink to the farmers, who drank it as beer is drank nowadays. The wine is in the original bottles and can not be purchased for less than $25 a bottle to-day. When James Buchanan went to England as minister from this country he took with him several cases of old Madeira, as there was none to be had in that country. The newest wine in Maj. Slaymaker's cellar was bottled in 1844. When Samuel J. Randall, Col. K. Jamison, W. U. Hensol, and Barney McGrann went on their southern trip, two or three years ago, they were treated so royally by Henry W. Grady, at Atlanta, that when they returned they sent two cases of Maj. Slaymaker's '93 Madeira to him as a recognition of his hospitality. Maj. Slaymaker has also cherry-bounce in his cellar that was bottled in 1828.» *The San Antonio Daily Express*, May 16, 1889. (San Antonio, TX); *Sundance Gazette*, October 18, 1889. (Sundance, WY. Published under the titles "OLD LIQUOR – Brandy That Was Imported in 1808 and Madeira of 1793.").

1377 *The New York Times*, November 25, 1888. (New York City, NY).
1378 The Greek and Roman goddess of marriage.
1379 Charles Betts Hillhouse (1856-1937), a native of New Haven, CT.
1380 Georgiana Delprat Remsen (1862-1933), a native of New York.

attractions? In the large parlors of Mr. Remsen's Fifth-avenue residence[1381] there met one of the most jovial and genial throngs ever assembled on a like occasion. The front room, where the bridal party stood, was crowded; but the supper room was impassable. It seemed as if all the clubmen in New-York were present, and the head of the household, Mr. Robert G. Remsen,[1382] dispensed his 100-year-old Madeira in a truly patriarchal way. Judicial mingling of the rare old wine and the more modern but popular champagne produced a babel of tongues, a flashing of eyes, and flushing of cheeks that gave the scene unwonted animation. It will be a long while before the echoes of the handsome entertainment, particularly the reminiscences of the old Madeira, will have been forgotten. …

WINES A CENTURY OLD.[1383]
Savannah Claims to Have the Oldest Wines in America.
From the Savannah News.

Savannah is believed to have the oldest wines in America. A well-known Savannahian, who is a connoisseur in wines, said a few days ago that he had a lot of Madeira of the vintage of 1833 – over half a century ago. There are wines in Savannah, though, much older than that. Some of the oldest families here have Madeira nearly a century old. One gentleman has several lots of the famous All Saint's Madeira, imported in 1791 and 1793, the year of the great fire in Savannah. Two pipes were imported that year one for the great grand-father of the late William Gibbons and one for the father of Nat Heyward, a prominent South Carolina planter. The night of the fire one pipe was left under the bluff by mistake and the other was burned up on the bay. The pipe under the bluff was divided between Gibbons and Heyward, as the only fair way of settling their loss. The gentlemen who now has several lots of the wine bought it in from Gibbons and Heyward's descendants eighty years after the division.

1381 Located at 87, 5th Avenue.
1382 Robert George Remsen (1821?-1896), a native of New York, was one of the best-known men in the social world of New York City and also known to the fashionable people of Boston, Washington, Philadelphia and Baltimore. He was also a member of the St. Nicholas Club, the New York Yacht Club, the Century Club, and the South Side Club.
1383 *San Antonio Daily Light*, December 6, 1888. (San Antonio, TX); *The Evening Post*, December 11, 1888. (Washington, D.C.); *The Sun*, December 2, 1888. (New York City, NY. Published under the same title but a different subtitle: "Madeira for Which $100 a Bottle Has Been Refused", reporting also that the article had been transcribed from *The Savannah News*); *The Knoxville Journal*, December 19, 1888. (Knoxville, TN); *New York Herald Tribune*, February 13, 1889. (New York City, NY. Published under the titles "SOME OLD MADEIRA WINE IN SAVANNAH. From the Savannah News.", but incomplete, ending at "Savannah was a large wine importing port a century ago." This text was also published, in a shorter version – starting from "Some of the oldest families here…" and ending at "Savannah was a large wine importing port a century ago.", also adding that it had been transcribed from the Georgia's *Savannah News* – under the title "Old Wines in Savannah", in different sources: *Oelwein Register*, March 22, 1889. (Oelwein, IA); *The Daily Yellowstone Journal*, March 27, 1889. (Miles City, MT); *Waco Evening News*, April 3, 1889. (Waco, TX). Two other abbreviated and untitled versions of this text were also found in the American press: «SAVANNAH claims the oldest wine in America. Some of the oldest families there have Madeira nearly a century old. One gentleman has several lots of the famous All Saints' Madeira, imported in 1791 and 1793.» *Jackson Sentinel*, February 28, 1889. (Maquoketa, IA); *La Porte City Review*, February 28, 1889. (La Porte City, IA); *The Eau Claire News*, March 1, 1889. (Eau Claire, WI). *The Ackley Enterprise*, March 1, 1889. (Ackley, IA); *The Waterloo Courier*, March 6, 1889. (Waterloo, IA). «SAVANNAH, Ga., claims the oldest wine in America. Some of the oldest families have Madeira nearly a century old. One gentleman has several lots of the famous All Saints Madeira, imported in 1791 and 1793, the year of the great fire in Savannah. Then there is the famous Hunter wine, imported about the same time. Some of it is still in the hands of the family. The late Mr. DeRenne, who inherited some of this wine, was offered $100 a bottle for it.» *The Boston Daily Globe*, February 18, 1889. (Boston, MA. Published in the section "Odd items from Everywhere"); *The Athens Messenger*, February 28, 1889. (Athens, OH); *Fort Worth Daily Gazette*, February 28, 1889. (Fort Worth, TX. Published under the "News and Notes" section, but incomplete).

Then there was the famous Hunter wine, imported about the same time. Some of it is still in the hands of the friends of the family. The late Dr. DeRenne, who inherited some of this wine, often offered $100 a bottle for it.

One gentleman has over twenty lots imported from the old Madeira house of Newton and Gordon from 1802 to 1830. Savannah was a large wine importing port a century ago. The following is a fac-simile of an old bill of landing for an old shipment of wine in 1780, the completion of a single order for 300 pipes or 1,000 hogsheads.

"Shipped, by the grace of God, in good order and well-conditioned, by Newton, Gordon & Co. in and upon good ship called the Two Sisters whereof is Master, under God, for this present voyage, William Smith, and now riding at anchor in the Road of Funchal, and by God's grace bound for Savannah or Charleston, to say, one hundred and fifty pipes, fifty hogsheads, and forty quarter casks, equal to two hundred pipes of Madeira wine – also twelve boxes lemons and some onions, all for account and risk of John Shoolbred, Esq., being marked and numbered as in the Magin, and are to be delivered in the like Good Order and well-conditioned, at the foresaid Port of Savannah or Charleston (the danger of Seas only excepted) unto Wm. Smith, and in his absence to Mr. J. Shoolbred and Moodie, or to Affigins, he or they paying Freight for the said Goods with Primage and Average accustomed. In witness whereof the Master or Purser of the said Ship hath affirmed to five Bills of Landing, all of their Tenor and Date, the one of which five Bills being accomplished, and others stand void. And so God send the good Ship to her designed Port in safety. Amen. Dated in Madeira this June 20, 1780. Wm. Smith."

A part of this wine is in Savannah yet. There are many lots here over half a century old.

IT WILL TICKLE THE PALATE.[1384]
The Will of the Late William Paine Contains a Curious Legacy.

SALEM, Mass., Sept. 21. – A curious legacy is contained in the will of the late William Paine of North Beverly. It is nothing less than a bequest of a quantity of mellow Madeira and sherry that our grandfathers drank.

He leaves to his oldest son two bottles of Haymaker Madeira, two bottles of Serceal[1385] Madeira, two bottles of Teneriffe Madeira,[1386] two bottles of Tinta Madeira, one bottle of Essex Madeira, one bottle of R. G. sherry, and one bottle of B. T. sherry, all of which came to Mr. Paine by will from his grandfather, and, besides all these, there is a bottle of Kier's Madeira, which was taken round the world in 1776, and was originally the property of Gen. Sumner of Brookline.

Mr. Paine's property goes to his wife and son.

1384 *The Boston Daily Globe*, September 21, 1889. (Boston, MA).
1385 The right spelling is Sercial.
1386 Wine made in Teneriffe.

OLD FRIENDS, OLD WINE.[1387]
Cheery Rounding Out of Judge Woodbury's Three Score and Ten.

Yesterday was Hon. Charles Levi Woodbury's[1388] 70th birthday.

The veteran of veteran Democrats never appeared in better cheer than he did last evening, seated at a table at the Parker House, where he was royally entertained by a few personal friends.

Those present were Ex-Mayor Frederick O. Prince,[1389] Judge Colt[1390] of the United States Court, Woodbury Blair of Washington, D.C., Gen. Samuel C. Lawrence, Hon. Leopold Morse, Hon. Benjamin Dean, Col. G. H. Campbell of the Governor's staff, Col. Hugh Cochrane, E. H. Muzzey, G. H. Merriam and George F. Babbitt.

There were no speeches. Story telling and reminiscences were the order of the evening.

Judge Woodbury has dined at the Parker House uninterruptedly for the past 45 years.

One of the pleasing events of the evening was the breaking of a bottle of Madeira of Gov. Brook's[1391] bottling in 1837, by the judge's friends, and the drinking of his health.

Judge Woodbury, however, outdid his friends, when he produced a bottle of the same, bottled in 1813, presented to him by Harrison Gray Otis.[1392]

GOSSIP GOING ROUND.[1393]

Two wine experts discussing the Manhattan cellar yesterday and the private stock of Madeira used by Herman[n] Oelrichs[1394] in his famous terrapin had this to say about the sherrys and Madeiras of New York. The first said: "I have $30,000 worth of wines and liquors in my cellar and while I am not boastful of it I believe it is to be a fact that few, if any, other experts in this city have now a cellar that represents more solid wealth as well as solid worth. I have Madeiras that cost $200 a bottle, and of which I know the history for 150 years. I have any number of dozen of sherrys which cost me from $20 to $30 a quart, and while you and I can tell at a glance and by a sniff of their bouquet the respective ages of the $200 and $20 wines, you would be surprised to know how many men of excellent taste and judgement in such things decidedly prefer the $20 to the $200 bottles. I do not know why it is, but the older a man gets the drier he likes his wines and the less flavor there seems to be in his favorite brands, and as for this 'aniressed' taste in Madeira, I don't believe there are two dozen men in New York who really like it or know why they like it."

1387 *The Boston Daily Globe*, May 23, 1890. (Boston, MA).
1388 Charles Levi Woodbury (1820-1898), a native of New Hampshire, was a lawyer and politician, and the U.S. District Attorney for Massachusetts and a member of the Massachusetts state legislature.
1389 Frederick Octavius Prince (1818-1899), a native of Boston, MA, was a lawyer, politician and Mayor of Boston, serving in this office from 1879 to 1881.
1390 James D. Colt, of Pittsfield, Justice of the Supreme Judicial Court.
1391 John Brooks (1752-1825), a native of Massachusetts, was a doctor, military officer and politician who served as the 11th Governor of Massachusetts, from 1826 to 1823.
1392 Harrison Gray Otis (1765-1848), a native of Boston, MA, was a businessman, lawyer and politician, having become one of the most important leaders of the United States' first political party, the Federalists.
1393 *The World*, February 20, 1891. (New York, NY); *Galveston Daily News*, May 7, 1891. (Galveston, TX. Published under the title "Rare Old Wines." and referring that it had been transcribed from the previous source).
1394 See Note 1354.

PRICELESS OLD MADEIRA.[1395]
Rare Vintages at Lancaster – How American Vines Restored Madeira Vineyards.

"The largest and most complete collection of rare old Madeira wines in this or, probably, any country is owned by Major Slaymaker of Lancaster, Pa.," said a wine merchant and connoisseur. "The oldest Madeira he has is of the vintage of 1793. There are in the cellars of two or three old Savannah families a few bottles of Madeira, which are of the famous All Saints vintage of 1791, of which two pipes were imported to that city in 1793. What is left of this wine is now in the cellars of the Gordons and De Rennes, I think, it having come into the possession of those families some 60 years ago by purchase.

"Besides the wine of 1793, the vintages of 1800, 1808, 1812, 1818, 1827 and 1840 are largely represented in Major Slaymaker's stock. The 1793 wine was bottled in 1798 by Phillip and Adam Reigart, who imported it in that year, having exported corn in exchange for it. The original bill of landing for this importation is in the possession of Major Slaymaker. One bottle of any of these old vintages is worth almost as much now as a pipe of it when the wine was imported. The Reigarts and Major Slaymaker's grandfather and great-grandfather imported all these wines. Their great value becomes apparent when it is known that the oldest Madeira in the possession of any dealer on the very island where the wine is made does not date back further than 1815. Some of the vintage of Madeira in the Slaymaker collection – notably the 1818, 1827, and 1840 – are especially rare and valuable. The rarest of all is the '27 vintage, the Madeira of that year being the finest in the history of the island. It is doubtful whether there is a bottle of it in any cellar in this country.

"In 1855 only 20 pipes of genuine Madeira wine were made, against 16,000 in 1891, and there was absolutely no Madeira made for six years after that. But for the introduction into Madeira of vines from the United States the chances are that there would never have been any more of this delicate vintage at all. This ruinous lapse in the production of Madeira wine was caused by a tiny insect known as the ordium,[1396] and so terrible were its ravages that in four years it had almost annihilated every vineyard on the island. Nothing could be found to stay its ravages until the vines of two American grapes were introduced upon the island – the Catawba and the Isabella. These were used as stock upon which to graft the native vines, it having been found that the former were entirely resistant to the disease. These hardy American vines restored the native vineyards, and to this day the Portuguese Government supplies them to the wine-growers of Madeira free of charge.

"In the making of Madeira wine, from the picking of the grape to the final stage of the vintage, the methods are the same as those of the first winemakers on the island, who began more than 400 years ago. The grapes are all white and grow on trellises. At least one-half the crop is allowed to hang on the vines until the grapes become raisined, or half dry. These raisined grapes are used in making the choicest wines. The juice is pressed from

---

[1395] *The Sun*, June 19, 1892. (New York City, NY); *Cleveland Plain Dealer*, June 26, 1892. (Cleveland, OH); *The Morning Call*, July 10, 1892. (San Francisco, CA. Published under the same title but different subtitle "The Largest and Finest Collection in the United States.", reporting that it had been transcribed from the *New York Sun*). The contents of the first part of this article had already been presented in a previous source, but we present it as well since it contains an interesting section regarding the fact that American vines were used to restore the Madeira vineyards.

[1396] The right spelling is oidium. Its scientific name is *oïdium tuckeri*.

the grapes in some places by the feet of the peasants, and elsewhere in rude presses. The juice is stored in casks at the vineyards until the crop is pressed, and then is carried to the dealers, or perfectors, at Funchal, in goatskins, holding each about 10 gallons.

"Often a company of from 25 to 40 men, with a leader who sings cheerily some quaint and ancient folk song, may be seen coming along the narrow mountain roads, each man with a goatskin of new wine on his shoulders, going to Funchal.

"The wine is perfected in the storehouses of the merchant at Funchal. The new grape juice is turned from the goatskins into casks to ferment and from year to year older wine is added to take the place of that which has evaporated. This method constantly improves the quality of the wine in each cask, and adds to its market value.

"Besides this rare vintage of Madeira, Major Slaymaker has a cask of brandy that his father imported in 1808. It is not known how old it was then. The owner of this old brandy once refused an offer of $45 a gallon for it, made by the late Simon Cameron.[1397] He has also in his cellar a quantity of that favorite tipple of a past generation, cherry bounce, which was bottled in 1828."'

Some Old Madeira.[1398]

TO THE EDITOR OF THE SUN – *Sir:* I read with great interest in your issue of last Sunday the article entitled "Priceless Old Madeira," and particularly that part wherein it is stated that Major Slaymaker of Lancaster, Pa., has in his possession "some of the rarest of all Madeira wines – the vintage of 1827, the finest in the history of the island." You add that it "is doubtful if there is a bottle of it in any other cellar in the country."

It may be interesting to wine connoisseurs to learn that there is a small quantity of this '27 vintage in New York city, the history of which is as follows: It was imported in the year 1837 by the well-known Philadelphia wine merchants, Cochrane & Sons, at which time it was guaranteed ten years old. James T. Sanford, Esq., owner of the Sanford line of steamers, running between New York and Philadelphia before the civil war, purchased all the wine of that vintage imported by Cochrane & Sons, 100 gallons, and stored it in the cellars of his palatial residence on Flashing Bay, where it remained until eighteen years ago, when he sold his residence and grounds to Wm. Steinway, Esq., the millionaire piano manufacturer. Mr. Sanford and his family then removed to California, after storing the wine in the cellars of Bluxome & Co.'s ponded wharehouses in West street, where it has remained ever since. Mr. Jas T. Sanford died eight years ago, the surviving member of the family being his sister and administratrix of the estate, Miss Josephine Sanford, residing in California.

The late John Tucker, the well-known President of the Philadelphia and Reading Railroad, was a great connoisseur of wines, and upon one occasion, when dining with Mr. Sanford, was so much taken with his old Madeira that he begged his host to let him have five gallons, for which he paid $300. John Tucker knew a good thing when he found it. And you are right in saying the vintage of '27 is the richest and rarest of all Madeira wines.

New York, June 22.
FREDERIC PERKINS.

1397 See Note 1375.
1398 *The Sun*, June 23, 1892. (New York City, NY).

SOME EXPENSIVE DRINKS.[1399]
Five Hundred Dollars a Bottle Is What One of the Rothschilds[1400] Once Paid.

A lady high up in the prohibitionary circles of New Jersey has a bottle of wine in her cellar over fifty years old, for which a Union League club man offered $50 for a chance to test it only, and then to buy it at the lady's own price. Although she does not desire to drink the wine herself, she says the wealthy clubman has not money enough to persuade her to part with it.

Wines do occasionally fetch extraordinary prices, says the New York Advertiser. At a recent auction in London some Madeira, supposed to have been presented by Napoleon III., was sold at £3 3s. a bottle. Imperial Tokay has been sold at £3 a bottle. A few years ago two bottles of old Burgundy were sold at £80 each. There are a dozen cases of holy wine at the Hotel de Ville, or town hall, Bremen, which have been valued, considering the original price and cellerage and interest for 250 years, at £400,000 a bottle, £54,476 a glass, and £60 a drop. The Rothschilds are in possession of some 1778 Madeira wine, which went down in a ship which was wrecked at the mouth of the Scheldt.[1401] It was not recovered until 1814. Forty-four bottles were sold to Rothschild at £114 per bottle.

An Expensive Wine.[1402]

The "1814 pipe" of Madeira was probably the most expensive ever offered for sale at public auction. Connoisseurs regarded it as the rarest and choicest wine ever put upon the market. It was sold in Paris as part of the effects of the late Duchesse de Raguse, and the sale caused the greatest excitement. The pipe was picked up near Antwerp, in 1814. It had lain under water pinned down in the wreck of a ship that had been lost at the mouth of the river Scheldt in 1778, and the discovery of the treasure was at once made known to Louis XVII, of France, who immediately sent off an agent to secure the wine. The French consul who had helped to recover it was awarded a share of the precious contents of the derelict pipe, and in this way it found its way into the cellars of the Duc de Raguse. Of all that was thus picked up there remained but forty-four bottles, each one of which was sold, literally, for its weight in gold to a member of the Rothschild family. – Kentucky Punch.[1403]

1399 *Evening Democrat*, December 21, 1894. (Warren, PA); *The Daily Journal*, January 2, 1895. (Logansport, IN); *Hopkinsville Kentuckian*, January 11, 1895. (Hopkinsville, KY); *The Arizona Republican*, January 16, 1895. (Phoenix, AZ).
1400 A family of German Jewish origin that established a European banking dinasty in Europe since the late 18th century.
1401 A 350-km long river in northern France, west Belgium and the southwestern part of the Netherlands.
1402 *The San Antonio Day Light*, September 30, 1895. (San Antonio, TX)
1403 There were also some other shorter versions of this text, which were widely diffused by the American press, the first one being published under the title "Costly Wines": «At a sale in 1858 of the effects of the deceased Duchesse de Raguse the late Baron Rothschild paid its weight in gold for forty-four bottles of Madeira. This wine, it appears, was fished up in 1814 from a ship wrecked at the mouth of the Scheldt in 1778, where it had lain during that interval. Louis XVIII bought it at that time, and part of it was presented to the French consul, and thus came into the hands of the Duc de Raguse. The weight of a bottle of wine, including bottle, is about two pounds, avoirdupois, so that at this calculation each bottle would have cost about $570. ...» *The Leader*, February 28, 1895. (Davenport, IA. Reports that it had been transcribed from the *Brooklyn Eagle*); *The Daily Bulletin*, March 14, 1895. (Honolulu, HI. Published under the title of "Wine Worth Its Weight in Gold."); *Daily Kennebec Journal*, March 29, 1895. (Augusta, ME); *The Cedar Rapids Evening Gazette*, April 4, 1895. (Cedar Rapids, IA); *Indiana County Gazette*, April 17, 1895. (Indiana, PA. Adds that it had been transcribed from the *Brooklyn Eagle*); *Oshkosh Daily Northwestern*, June 8, 1895. (Oshkosh, WI. Adds that it had been transcribed from the same source). Two other shorter and untitled versions were also published in several sources: «The

ABOUT $3 A TEASPOONFUL.[1404]
Costly Wine Used at Banquet of Maryland Honest Money League.

BALTIMORE, Md, Nov 28 – In tiny glasses of real Jeffersonian Madeira wine of the vintage of 1800 the honest money democratic league of Maryland, at a banquet given in honor of Harry Parr, its popular president, tonight toasted Pres-elect McKinley, Pres Cleveland and the memory of Thomas Jefferson. The actual value of the wine is about $3 a teaspoonful.

Douglas H. Thomas,[1405] who donated it for this occasion of rejoicing over the triumph of sound money, is a great connoisseur in Madeiras, and has one of the best private cellars in Baltimore.

The wine reposed in the famous cellars of Thomas Jefferson at Monticello until 1834, when it was purchased at the sale of the effects of the founder of the democratic party by Phillip Evan Thomas, the first president of the Baltimore & Ohio railroad.

From Mr. Thomas it descended to his daughter, Mrs. John Wethered, and the remainder of the original purchase, about six gallons, was bought by Douglas H. Thomas, after Mrs. Wethered's death in 1886. Congressman John K. Gowen was the principal speaker at the banquet.[1406] …

---

most famous Madeira ever known was the "1814 pipe," which was fished up in that year from the timbers of a wrecked vessel in the Scheldt, where it had lain thirty-six years. The greater portion was purchased at an auction at Antwerp by Louis XVIII. The King presented his Consul at Antwerp with several dozen, which he sold to the Duke of Raguse. In 1858, after the death of his Duchess, four dozen remained in her cellar, which were sold for over their weight in gold to Baron Rothschild.» *Los Angeles Herald*, May 31, 1879. (Los Angeles, CA); «In 1858 there was a sale of Madeira wine in Paris, when forty-four bottles were bought by Rothschild for their weight in gold. The wine was from the famous 1814 pipe of Madeira, which had lain at the bottom of the sea for thirty-six years.» *The Boston Daily Globe*, June 23, 1891. (Boston, MA); *Jackson Daily Citizen*, June 24 and 30, 1891. (Jackson, MI. Published under the title "Worth Their Weight in Gold."); *Wheeling Register*, June 26, 1891. (Wheeling, WV. Published untitled in the section "Odd Items From Everywhere."); *Evening Daily Bulletin*, July 11, 1891. (San Francisco, CA. Published under the title "Worth Their Weight in Gold."); *The Cape Girardeau Democrat*, August 8, 1891. (Cape Girardeau, MO); *The Hazel Green Herald*, August 28, 1891. (Hazel Green, KY).

1404 *The Boston Daily Globe*, November 29, 1896. (Boston, MA).

1405 Douglas H. Thomas (1847-1919), President of the Merchants-Mechanics' First National Bank, of Baltimore.

1406 This costly wine was also mentioned in three other articles, published in other sources. The first one was entitled "DINNER TO MR. PARR. – It was of the Kind that Have Given Maryland a Worldwide Fame. – SOME RARE OLD MADEIRA – From the Cellar of Thomas Jefferson, the Father of Democracry.": «[…] A notable feature of the dinner was a toast to Jeffersonian democracry, which was drunk with rare old Madeira of the vintage of 1800, which at one time reposed in the wine cellar of Thomas Jefferson. This wine was presented by Mr. Douglas H. Thomas, one of the diners. It was part of a supply of about twenty bottles bought by Mr. Thomas in 1890 at a sale of the Wethered effects, near Catonsville. It came into possession of Mrs. John Wethered through her father, Philip Evans Thomas, who bought the wine at the sale of Thomas Jefferson's effects./ Mr. Thomas was the first president of the Baltimore and Ohio Railroad. […]/ The wine, which has a rich, fruity flavour, cost originally $3 a gallon. It would now represent, according to the usual method of compounding an accumulated investment, over $1,500 a gallon. Further calculation shows that each teaspoonful of this old Madeira would represent a valuation of $3 50. Mr. Douglas H. Thomas is an ardent connoisseur of old wines and still retains a few bottles of the Jefferson article.» *The Sun*, November 30, 1896. (Baltimore, MD). The second article, under the title "Personal and Pertinent.", presented the following contents: «Madeira wine as old as that in which the Jeffersonian democrats of Baltimore drank their president's health is probably rare in the land, for it was of the vintage of 1800 and had remained in the Monticello cellars till 1834. But it is not impossible that a bottle or two as old could be found in Charleston, S. C., or in Philadelphia. The madeira that was imported in the early days of the republic was as much a household furnishing as the mahogany, and, though more perishable it was more carefully treasured.» *The World*, December 2, 1896. (New York City, NY); *The Omaha Daily Bee*, December 7, 1896. (Omaha, NE. Published at the section "Personal and otherwise"); *The Sunday News Tribune*, December 13, 1896. (Duluth, MN. Published untitled in the section "On Various Topics."). Last but not least, the third text, entitled "Wine Worth a Dollar a Drop.", contained the following notes: «BALTIMORE, NOV. 28. – One of the features of the dinner that was given to-night to Harry A. Parr, President of the Honest-Money Democratic League of Maryland, was some Jeffersonian Madeira wine for the Jeffersonians who were present. The wine is of the vintage of 1800, and its authenticity is beyond any question./ It reposed in the famous wine cellars of Thomas Jefferson at Monticello until 1834, when it was purchased at the sale of the effects of the founder

VERY RARE OLD MADEIRA.[1407]
FAMOUS VINTAGES HELD BY SOUTH CAROLINA FAMILIES.
Earthquake Wine 150 Years Old – The Limit of Excellence Reached Generally in Half a Century – Art of Maturing Madeira – The Charleston Jockey Club Wines.

CHARLESTON, S. C., Jan. 27. – The following extract from the wine list of a New York restaurant stirs general memories in the hearts of the old Charleston people, and the more question of its accuracy has evoked numberless anecdotes from those who remember the good old days of mahogany and Madeira and the life of leisure of which these things may be in a way regarded as the fine and typical flower:

MADEIRA – 257, CHARLESTON JOCKEY CLUB MADEIRA, $15 PER BOTTLE.

This Madeira was buried[1408] by the above-named club at the time of Gen. Sherman's march to the sea[1409] and bought after the war by one of the Barings of London, who sold it to Messrs. Sam Ward and Kesne. These gentlemen presented it to President Chester A. Arthur[1410] in 1881. Mr. – bought it from the executor of the Arthur estate in 1887 and sold it the next day to a relative of President Arthur, from whom he has now purchased it back again. Sam Ward's[1411] letter to the President is in Mr. –'s possession. The wine is over sixty years old.

Several Charleston gentlemen to whom this statement was shown believe it to contain inaccuracies, but before entering upon these doubtful points it is of interest to know why Charleston Jockey Club Madeira should be thus used as a name to conjure with. The South Carolina Jockey Club was an association formed in the last century by gentlemen who owned fine horses and raced them annually for a cap or a whip or a piece of plate, or even for such prizes as a finely embroidered jacket. There was a great racecourse here more than a hundred years ago, and the Jockey Club had charge of all the meetings. Until 1792 the Jockey Club races took place at the Newmarket course. After that they were held at the Washington course. The period about the year 1786 was considered the golden time

---

of the democratic party by Philip Evan Thomas, the first President of the Baltimore and Ohio railroad. From Mr. Thomas it descended to his daughter, Mrs. John Wetherd, and the remainder of the original purchase, about six gallons, was bought by Douglas H. Thomas after Mrs. Wetherd's death in 1886, from the cellar of her country place at Catonsville. It was served with dessert./ This is one of the wines that is often described as being worth a dollar a drop. If the money that was originally invested in it had instead been placed in a savings bank and kept there the amount which it originally took to purchase a gallon of this wine would now have grown to about $1,500. Douglas H. Thomas, the donor of the wine, is a connoisseur in Madeira, and has one of the best cellars in Baltimore. He has samples of all the greatest vintages, including many even older, it is said, than the one served at to-night's banquet.» *The Sun*, December 6, 1896. (New York, NY. Quotes the *Chicago Times Herald*). Under this title and "Maryland Democrats Drink Madeira from Thomas Jefferson's Cellars." as a subtitle, this text, with slight changes, was published in the following sources: *The Dubuque Daily Herald*, December 11, 1896. (Dubuque, IA); *The Morning Star*, December 17, 1896. (Rockford, IL. Published with a different subtitle – "Maryland Democrats Drink Madeira from Thomas Jefferson's Cellars" – and not mentioning its source); *The Wichita Daily Eagle*, January 1, 1897. (Wichita, KS); *The Weimar Mercury*, January 9, 1897. (Published in Weimar, TX); *The Daily Iowa Capital*, March 1, 1897. (Des Moines, IA). This article was also published, untitled, but starting as "A dinner was given the other night...", in *The Xenia Gazette*, December 2, 1896. (Xenia, OH).

1407 *The Sun*, January 29, 1899. (New York City, NY).
1408 We found other references to Madeira Wine being buried in the South in order to escape seizure or destruction by the Union Army. When it was dug out, after the end of the conflict, this wine would be named Resurrection Madeira.
1409 See Note 106.
1410 See Note 105.
1411 See Note 104.

of racing in South Carolina. Race week in Charleston began then to be a sort of festival for the whole State. The men attended the races in clothes of latest London style and make, and the women were richly dressed. Courts adjourned, schools gave holidays and the leading business houses were closed, while clergymen and Judges and all the dignitaries of the town hastened to lend their countenance to the animated scene. On Friday of race week the Jockey Club ball was given and the cream of the society of the State was present in all its splendor. Thus it was that the club began to have its rich living and its wines, and in time the things to drink at the club grew famous.

As far back as 1763 it was recorded of Charleston that "Madeira wine and punch are the common drink of the inhabitants," but it was not until the present century that the descendants of the early inhabitants began to realize that the pipes of Madeira purchased by their ancestors had gained a bouquet and flavor quite remarkable, and that their wine, once the "common drink" of the province, had become a rare and constantly augmenting treasure. In the middle of the eighteenth century Madeira wine became fashionable in England, owing to the recommendation of officers who served in the West Indies and America. It became customary to ship the wine from Madeira to the West Indies, or even to India, and thence back to England, with the idea of improving its taste, indeed, many Madeira merchants sent their wines either to the East of West Indies and back often more than once, as the voyage was held to mature the wine, while the intense heat of the ship's hold and the constant motion gave it a peculiar flavor much prized; and this journey took the place, in great measure, of the former custom of submitting the wine to a high temperature in stone buildings heated by flues. In 1852 the wines of the island of Madeira were attacked by the dread *oidium* disease and totally destroyed. The vineyards were at once replanted, but later the phylloxera affected every vineyard in Madeira, and reduced the production of these wines. Of late years they have gone out of fashion in England, being largely replaced by light wines of Germany and France. The exportations of Madeira wine have never since been so great as before these visitations, although it is said that there has been recently a revival in the taste for Madeira.

No doubt the drinking of Madeira in the Carolinas began because it was the fashion in the mother country. Then it happened, too, that Madeira was among the non-enumerated articles in which England permitted the colonies to trade with the Canary and Madeira Islands. The ships which carried goods from Charleston were glad enough to bring back pipes of Madeira and to sell them cheap. In fact, the best Madeira at that time did not cost the consumer more than $3 or $4 a gallon, although some Charleston Madeira since the war has sold for $65 a dozen. It was found that the climate of Carolinas and Georgia was especially adapted to mellowing the wine and imparting to it that peculiar bouquet and flavor so prized by connoisseurs.

Old drinkers used to say that twenty years in a garret in Charleston, with but little light, was enough to ripen Madeira, and that afterward it should be placed in a cellar or a room with northern exposure, where it should be occasionally inspected, and the corks removed about every twenty years. Another gentleman of the old school in Charleston, however, tells of Madeira owned by his uncle, which, as a boy, he was bidden to decant. Upon testing it the old gentleman shook his head.

"Put it back, my boy," he said: "it has been in the garret thirty years, but it must go back again. It is not yet ripe."

Tastes, however, differed in this respect. Mr. Pettigru liked his Madeira so strong that a special bottle was always set apart for him in this same hospitable home, and it was always spoken of as "Mr. Pettigru's wine."

Dr. Gabriel Manigault[1412] of Charleston has in his possession to-day a few dozen bottles of wine purchased in the island of Madeira in the year 1816. It is, therefore, eighty-three years of age. A few dozen bottles of the celebrated Belvidera wine, so called from the name of the vessel which brought it from Madeira in 1838, are also in Dr. Manigault's possession. This wine, which is of the very best vintage, has now, in its owner's opinion, reached, at the age of sixty years, the limit of its excellence. Being of a very rare and delicate flavor, it is not one of those Madeiras which continue to improve, or, at least, refrain from deteriorating, for a period of one hundred years. The Poinsette wine, brought from Madeira in 1816, was never of so delicate a flavor as the Belvidera, which probably accounts for its more lasting qualities. This wine, Dr. Manigault believes, is the oldest in Charleston, though it is said that there is some Madeira in this city more than one hundred years old.

"The Blake family of South Carolina," says Dr. Manigault, "have in their possession a wine which they call the 'earthquake wine,' in consequence of their having bought it in the year of the Lisbon earthquake, 1755. In 1855 it was still considered in good preservation. The descendants of Ralph Izard,[1413] of the Revolutionary period, have had some of his wine with was bottled in 1774. It can scarcely, however, be considered good now, which is doubtless due to its having been neglected and air having been admitted to the bottles."

A well-known gentleman of Charleston, who knows all about Madeira, says that a good deal of the Jockey Club Madeira was imported between 1855 and 1860, and that, in his opinion, this wine would now, at the age of from forty to forty-five years, be at the height of its excellence. Indeed, while it is now conceded that Madeira has preserved its flavor under favorable conditions for one hundred years, the general opinion of connoisseurs seems to fix from forty to fifty years as the best age for the wine. Some of the Jockey Club Madeira was sent to Columbia during the war and placed for safekeeping in the cellar at the lunatic asylum. This was spared on account of the awe with which the Union army regarded the building and its inmates.

After the war the Jockey Club decided to sell its Madeira. Part of it was bought by an agent of Baring Brothers of London. It was generally understood at the time that it was not bought for the firm, but for one of the members. The agent who purchased the wine is under the impression that the Madeira described in the wine list quoted is not sixty years old, if it is the Jockey Club Madeira. The members of this famous club were convivially rather than commercially inclined, and they were not likely to have left much of their old wine to furnish wonder for succeeding generations and to enrich the pockets of their descendants. Nevertheless he does not say positively that this is not sixty years old, and other members of the Jockey Club say that to the best of their recollection there was some 1838 Madeira in the possession of the club and that this was the wine probably sold to Baring Brothers. On the other hand, some of the famous 1838 Belvidera wine was actually sold soon after the sale of the Jockey Club wine and was bought by Baring

---

[1412] Gabriel Edward Manigault (1833-1899), a physician and osteologist, educator, amateur architect and curator of the Charleston Museum.

[1413] Ralph Izard (1741/2-1804), a native of South Carolina, was an American politician, having served as President *pro tempore* of the United States Senate in 1794. Before that, during the American Revolutionary War, he pledged his large estate in South Carolina for the payment of war ships to be used in the conflict against the British.

Brothers. In all points of the story, with the exception of the name given to it, the Belvidera Madeira would seem to fit the description given to the wine list.

When a bottle of old Madeira was opened it had to be drunk at once. The lees were never disturbed. The custom was to draw off a bottle of Madeira with a siplion so as not to disturb this deposit. All the lees were put together in one bottle, and when the bottle was filled it was set aside to clear. Years after a connoisseur would say: "This is fine. This must have come from the lees." Good wine was known here in those days. Owners of Madeira would send it from all parts of the United States to ripen in Charleston garrets. When Ogilvie[1414] was British Consul here it was desired to purchase fine wines for the Queen's[1415] table. Consul Ogilvie was asked to get some Madeira, and the old Charleston gentlemen supplied some fine wine for the Queen.

A connoisseur was asked the other day if the men in Charleston were ever the worse for drinking old Madeira.

"Well," he said, "in those days it was not considered that a gentleman was any the worse because he drank large quantities of good old wine and was a trifle hazy when he went to bed. No gentleman ever drank a drop before dinner. Charleston was then the summer resort for the planters, and it was in the summer that most of the drinking was done. There were dinners and wine parties constantly, and I believe it was the general opinion, and I believe it was the general opinion that wholesome wine would not harm any one. Two of these drinkers of good wines, however, came to a tragic end. They were great friends, and when they drank together, two quart decanters of old Madeira was the usual allowance of each. They were not dissipated men in any sense of the word, but they could drink a good deal at a sitting. One of the gentlemen, in crossing the river to take his carriage to his plantation, stepped overboard and was drowned. The other took his bath, dressed himself in a summer suit of white, went to his garret and fell upon his sword. Well, I don't know that you would say they were any the worse for the wine. They remained gentlemen to the last. But it was generally believed that there was no harm in old Madeira."

SIMPLY PRICELESS WINES.[1416]
JUSTICE TRUAX TELLS OF SOME NEW YORK CELLARS.
Old Madeiras Owned Here Which Cannot Be Bought – The Costliest Rhine Wines –
A Chance Missed by Hermann Oelrichs[1417] in Chicago – Proper Serving of Wine.

Justice Charles H. Truax[1418] of the Supreme Court is a connoisseur of rare old wines. His judgment on them is frequently sought by his friends and at the clubs of which he is a member, notably the Manhattan, with its famous cellars. Justice Truax is himself a collector of wines. His cellar is among the finest so far as quality goes, in this city. It is by no means a small cellar. In his study of wines he has reached some decided convictions as to

---

1414 William Ogilby, Her Britanic Majesty's Consul for North and South Carolina. He remained in office since his appointment, in 1830, to the mid 1840's.
1415 Queen Victoria (1819-1901), who was the monarch of the United Kingdom from 1837 until her death.
1416 *The Sun*, July 2, 1899. (New York City, NY).
1417 See Note 1354.
1418 Charles H. Truax (1846-1910), an Hamilton College graduate, was elected Judge of the Supreme Court in 1880, serving for fifteen years. In 1895 he was elected to the Supreme Court bench.

the way in which they should be kept and served. To collect and study wines is a recreation for him and he likes to talk on the subject. A question as to what was the oldest and most costly wine in New York drew from him the other night a discussion of a few of the rare wines in New York of which he knew and some of those in his own cellar.

"It would be impossible for me to say," he began, "what is the oldest and most costly wine in this city to-day. Speaking generally, I should say that it was an old Madeira. There are some very old Madeiras in the cellar of Hermann Oelrichs. He has one of the best cellars in New York. George W. De Witt has some very old Madeiras. Perhaps no one has any better than John Hone, who has Madeira that was in the cellars of his uncle, Philip Hone,[1419] Mayor of New York in 1825. It was a good wine even then. James Lenox[1420] had some very fine 1804 Madeira. Some of it was sold to the Manhattan Club for $8 a bottle. None of it is on the club's wine list now. I have myself some Madeira that was sold in 1873 for $12 a bottle. I was fortunate enough to get it in 1880 for less. Some of the very fine Madeiras of S. I. M. Barlow[1421] were bought by me for the Manhattan Club at $12 and $15 a bottle.

"But to say anything as to the value in money of the wines I have mentioned in private cellars – and there are doubtless many others as good of which I have not knowledge – is quite impossible. Those wines are priceless. They were not bought to be sold again. There is no fixing a price upon them. The prices which they would bring at auction would show little or nothing. They would vary so much with the number of men who were in need of such wines and the quantity of such wines available."

Without putting it in so many words, Justice Truax spoke as if the arbitrary limit of price for such wines was $25 a bottle. If they could be bought at all, it would be at some such price as that. ...

WINES MORE THAN HUNDRED YEARS OLD[1422]
Old Habersham Mansion Has a Priceless Stock Within It.
LAST OF MANY COLLECTIONS
Family Cellars Have Been Noted Since Colonial Days.
MADEIRAS AND SHERRIES WITHIN AGE
Fame of the Collection Has Been Scattered Far and Wide by Those
Who Have Been Favored.

Savannah, Ga., November 13. – (Special.) Stored in two upper rooms of the old Habersham mansion on the corner of Harris and Barnard streets, in this city, are casks and kegs and carboys ad flasks and bottles of wine of almost priceless kind. The entire

---

[1419] Philip Hone (1780-1851), the son of a German immigrant carpenter, who became wealthy in the auction business, was elected Mayor of New York in 1826, serving only one term, from that year until 1827.

[1420] James Lenox (1800-1880), a native of New York, was an American bibliophile and philanthropist. In 1855 he was the third richest man in this city.

[1421] Samuel Latham Mitchell Barlow (1826-1889), a well-known New York lawyer and book collector.

[1422] *The Atlanta Constitution*, November 14, 1899. (Atlanta, GA). Also quoting this newspaper, this article was divulged in the following sources, under different titles: *The Kansas City Star*, November 29, 1899. (Kansas City, MO. Published under the title "WINES THAT ARE PRICELESS. – A Savannah Collection That Has Flasks From the R. E. Lee Cellars."); *The Sunday News Tribune*, March 11, 1900. (Duluth, MN. Published under the title "WINE 100 YEARS OLD. A Fine Stock in a Cellar Down in Savannah.").

store will aggregate possibly three thousand quarts and contains old Madeiras and sherries that for half a century have been the delight of epicures in every part of the country.

The collection is the property of the estate of the late William Neyle Habersham,[1423] who died about six weeks ago, at a very advanced age. Mr. Habersham inherited a part of the present collection and had added to it throughout all his long life. The cellars of the family had been noted among the "bon vivants" of Savannah since the days of the colony's foundation, and each successive generation had added to the collection of old and almost priceless vintages. The family, among the wealthiest existent in the early history of Georgia, had abundant means to gratify what was at once a passionate fad for the gathering together of wines that had become renowned and of regaling their many and frequent guests with the garnered and fermented sunshine of the isle of Madeira and old Spain.

A Foretaste of Beatitude.

To wander through the room in which these wines are stored is in itself a treat. To partake of an occasional sip of the old Madeira is a foretaste of beatitude. The rooms are constructed as for a conservatory and in the early days of the old mansion it is possible that they served this purpose. There is no floor division between them, other than an open framework, across which boards are laid and through which the sunlight filters freely. On every side and on the roof is glass, admitting the rays of the sun without hindrance. Mr. Habersham was accustomed to transfer his rare vintage from one part of the two rooms to another, to the end that they might imbibe from the sunlight some of its warmth and strength. His wines were the pride of his life and he could not gain his own consent to immure them in the darkness of some underground cellar. He liked to spend his time in their company, inhaling their delicate aroma and gloating over the matchless color.

Crowing Glory of the Collection.

The Madeiras are the crowning glory of the collection. The old Sercial Madeira has a reputation throughout the country and there are other rare vintages of no less value. There is a store of the old wine known as Malmsey, in a butt of which nectar the ill-fated Clarence is said to have ended his life. They tell a tale of a connoisseur who was once dining with the Habershams, to whom some of the Malmsey came in the course of the meal. This gentleman raised his glass to his lips and sipped the wine with appreciative deliberation. A glow of perfect content spread over his face as he said:

"Well, Mr. Habersham, if the wine in which Clarence drowned himself was anything like this, I don't know that I have it in my heart to blame him."

Some of the Madeiras came to this country direct from the island of that name. Some of them came via London, where for years before their importation they had held positions and places of honor in the cellars of the wine merchants of that city. The oldest of the collection is of the vintage of 1827, and there is much that wears the antique honors of an age almost as great.

Wines from Lee's Arlington.

Among the most prized stock in the collection is a number of flasks from the cellars

---

[1423] William Neyle Habersham (1817-1899), a native of Savannah, GA, and a Madeira Wine collector, as can be seen through this article.

of General R. E. Lee,[1424] at Arlington, of which Mr. Habersham obtained possession after the war. There are a number of casks of the Newton Gordon Madeira, of numerous special brands and marks.

The sherries in the Habersham collection are about as fine as the Madeiras; some of them older, one of the wines bearing the vintage of 1823. ...

The New York reputation of the Habersham collection of wines was brought about by Ward McAllister,[1425] who was a personal friend of William Neyle Habersham and had personal acquaintance with the qualities of the vintage in the Habersham cellars. There were many receptions of the four hundred that found inspiration for wit and gallantry in the wines that came from Savannah.

New York Clubs Have It.

There are many clubs in New York and other northern cities that count the possession of a case or two of the Madeira or sherry from the Habersham collection as among their rarest treasures.

There was a time when the wine cellars of the old Savannahians were noted throughout the country. Ships reached the port from every clime and brought to Savannah merchants the choicest vintages of their hills and valleys. In those old days there was ample means to satisfy every whim and such wide culture as added to the enjoyment of the best things in life. Those old collections have vanished one by one, and none remains but that of the Habershams. Soon this will be gone also and Savannah's wine cellars will be either things of the past or else filled with the products of a newer age.

SOUTHERN JOCKEY CLUB[1426]
THE FAMOUS OLD SOUTH CAROLINA ORGANIZATION PASSES INTO HISTORY HAS IMMORTALIZED ITSELF

Features of the Great Race Week – Some Noted Southerners Who Followed the Manly Sport.

... The races were usually held at the height of the social season, which was also the off-season for the planters, about the end of January or the first of February. One of the famous "Saint Cecilia balls" was always given during the week, to which, however, only guests of the very highest social standing were ever invited. Splendid private entertainments were given on the other nights, and there was always some special attraction at the very good theater – for Charleston was also the first city to have a theater – either a fine concert or one of Shakespeare's plays. But the horses were the main subject of conversation, at night as well as by day. Many were the wonderful tales told of fine racers as the men sat over their fine wines, for by this time the Jockey club had become famous also for its Madeira wine, which was imported directly for its own use.

This Madeira of the South Carolina Jockey club was, by the way, the most famous wine ever brought to this country, and, the lovers and rare old-wine tasters in Charleston used

---

1424 Robert Edward Lee (1807-1870), a native of Virginia, was an American career military officer who is best known for having commanded the Confederate Army of Northern Virginia during the American Civil War.

1425 See (2nd part of) Note 1310.

1426 *The St. Paul Globe*, April 1, 1900. (St. Paul, MN). This article can be considered a complement to the previous one dealing with this famous Southern club, therefore we present it as well.

to say, the finest in the world. It was brought over in the holds of ships especially prepared for it, the casks lying between boards, which allowed the casks to be gently rocked by the motion of the boat, and gave it, according to the experts of Charleston, its peculiar fine flavor, which was still further improved after it had laid for years in the damp cellars of Charleston. None of this wine was ever in President Arthur's possession, as it was claimed, nor can it be purchased anywhere now. One of the oldest members of the club said not long ago that the Madeira that was still in the possession of the Jockey club until after the war, was distributed among the officers of the club when it was decided to abandon racing. These few devoted members, prizing it more than any gold, slowly drank it up on rare and great occasions. There may be a few bottles of it still in Charleston, but it never has been and never will be for sale.

Races were held every year with unvarying success on the Washington race course in Charleston until the Civil war. Mr. James Rose, judge of wine as well as of thorough-bred horses in the state, was a most successful president of the South Carolina Jockey club for a great number of years. …

Some Happenings in Good Society.[1427]

… Yesterday brought another fashionable wedding, that of Miss Elizabeth Bradhurst, daughter of Mr. Charles Cornell Bradhurst[1428] of Newark, N. J., and Thomas Henry Randall. This took place at 4 o'clock in the Church of the Transfiguration. This wedding had been set for May of 1899, but Miss Bradhurst was taken with typhoid fever, and for weeks lay seriously ill, so that it had to be postponed. A dinner for the bridal party was given at Sherry's Friday evening. … At the reception and collation at Sherry's which followed the wedding the health of the bride was drunk in some century-old Madeira, bottled by the bride's greatgrandfather, Thomas Cornell Pearsall,[1429] who married[1430] Miss Fanny Buchanan,[1431] daughter of Thomas Buchanan,[1432] one of the founders of the Chamber of Commerce,[1433] and sister of Mrs. Peter Goelet.

9.13. Madeira Wine Auctions across the United States

Since the terrible failure of the grape crop in Madeira, in 1852, and consequent supply shortage of its wine in America, the best way to buy excellent Madeira Wine was through the auctions that were made everywhere, with a special focus on the big cities such as New York and Philadelphia, once flooded with this fine wine. Those events presented an excellent opportunity for Madeira Wine *connoisseurs* to complete their

---

1427 *The New York Times*, May 6, 1900. (New York City, NY).
1428 Charles Cornell Bradhurst (1840-1905), who married Catherine Ten Broek Rodwell, and had two children, Elizabeth Bradhurst, mentioned in this article, and Henry Maunsell Bradhurst.
1429 Thomas Cornell Pearsall (1768-1820), was a wealthy New York merchant and ship owner.
1430 On June 17, 1791.
1431 Frances Buchanan (c.1770-?). From this marriage she had a son, Thomas Pearsall.
1432 He had a company in partnership with his cousin Walter. They dealt in dry good imports from Great Britain, and were also large ship owners.
1433 Established in 1768.

collections by bidding on rare vintages, which usually were sold at very high prices, depending on the age of the wine. The following twenty-nine texts describe summarily those auctions, published in different sources from 1828 to 1900.

Old Wine.[1434] – A demijohn, containing five gallons of old Madeira wine, imported in 1815, was yesterday sold by Mr. L. N. Mitchell, at auction, for $70; and another of like size, having about one gallon out, for $50! – *Savannah Georgian.*

Hard Times.[1435] – Nine demijohns of old Madeira wine were sold the other day, at twenty dollars a gallon, or one hundred dollars a demijohn, and ten more, not so old, at ten dollars a gallon. The nine were taken by one individual for family use. – *Jour. Com.*

GREAT DISTRESS.[1436] – At the sale of wines yesterday, by the Messrs. Pell, Cole's Madeira brought $117 per dozen, being $9 75 per bottle! On the same day, Indiana State stock sold as low as $19 50 per $100, Illinois as low as $19, and Harlaem Rail Road as low as $10 a share. It would take but a very few bottles of wines, at this rate, to buy up some pretty large concerns. One bottle would buy 2 1-2 shares U.S. Bank stock, being at the rate of 14,000 bottles for the whole $35,000,000. – [*N. Y. Jour. Of Com.*]

Paying dear for the Whistle.[1437]

At Baltimore, on Thursday the 11th inst., a part of the private stock of wines and liquors of the late JOSIAH LEE, Esq.,[1438] were sold at auction, and brought extraordinary prices. Fifty demijohns of various brands of Madeira were struck off at prices ranging from twenty-four dollars to forty-nine dollars per gallon; and one lot of twenty-two bottles commanded the extreme price of fifteen dollars and fifty cents per bottle – which, at five bottles to the gallon, is at the rate of seventy-seven dollars and fifty cents per gallon! The following are the particulars of several lots, as reported in the Baltimore American:

1 demijohn of Pine Apple Butler Madeira Wine, $24 per gallon.
I do of old Charleston Madeira, $26.50 per gallon.
I do of old Madeira, "Patterson," $24 per gallon.
I do from the stock of James Cox, "Holmes" Madeira, from $41 to $49 per gallon.
7 do of the same, $31 per gallon.
30 do of J. Cox, Madeira Wines of various kinds, at prices varying from $12 to $24 per gallon.
22 bottles of celebrated J. Cox, "Sheffield" Madeira Wines, at $15½ per bottle.

1434 *The Republican Compiler*, June 25, 1828. (Gettysburg, PA).
1435 *The Charleston Courier*, March 4, 1841. (Charleston, SC). *The Pittsfield Sun*, March 11, 1841. (Pittsfield, MA. Also quotes the *Journal of Commerce*).
1436 *Albany Argus*, December 28, 1841. (Albany, NY).
1437 *Jeffersonian Republican*, November 25, 1852. (Stroudsburg, PA).
1438 Josiah Lee (?-1852), a native of Maryland, was engaged in extensive banking, ownig the firm Lee & Co. By the time of his death, on May 11, 1852, he was worth half a million dollars.

[Untitled]¹⁴³⁹

A QUANTITY of old Madeira wine, belonging to the estate of R. Bulord, deceased, was sold at auction in New York on Wednesday, for $31 75 per gallon. This is equal to about fifty cents per wine glass.

HENRY H. LEEDS, Auctioneer.¹⁴⁴⁰

BY H. H. LEEDS & CO. – TUESDAY, June 13, at 10½ o'clock, at the residence No. 3 Gramorey-park, west side, between 20th and 21st-sts – …

… Also, a choice assortment of wine, all expressly selected for the owner's own use, of the highest order, viz, choice south side Madeira, Hement, Houghton & Co., 1840, do Howard, March & Co., 1839, Blackburn, 1841, old Brahaun, 1822 old Reserve, imported by John Vaugham, of Philadelphia, 1821 and 1833, with other very superior Madeiras. Also a large stock of choice sherry, hock, &c. Every bottle purchase expressly for the use of the owner.

MADEIRA WINE.¹⁴⁴¹

The attention of the trade and consumers is respectfully called to the sale of a choice lot of Madeira wine, to be sold this day at W. B. Griffin's Auction rooms, commencing at 10 o'clock, A. M. It is imported, and can be relied on as an excellent wine.

SALE OF CHOICE MADEIRA WINES.¹⁴⁴² – The finest lot of Madeira wine ever in Boston was sold this week. It was selected by the late Edward Codman, Esq., and comprised 145 demijohns in seven lots. The first lot of 55 gallons, imported in 1837 and demijoned in 1842, marked "Capt. Bragg," not the Captain Bragg upon whom Gen. Taylor¹⁴⁴³ called for "a little more grape,"¹⁴⁴⁴ sold for $13,50 per gallon. The second lot, of 88 gallons, imported at the same time, marked "J. C. J." brought $12 per gallon. The third, imported in 1841,

---

1439 *Daily Evening Transcript*, March 5, 1853. (Boston, MA). This fact made news in other American newspapers: «In New York, a day or two ago, some Madeira wine was sold as high as $31 75c, per gallon.» *Pennsylvania Inquirer*, March 7, 1853. (Philadelphia, PA); «A lot of old Madeira sold in New York for $31,75 per gallon, last week.» *The Pittsfield Sun*, March 10, 1853. (Pittsfield, MA. Published in the section "VARIOUS ITEMS"); «SALE OF MADEIRA WINE. – A quantity of old Madeira wine, belonging to the estate of R. Buloid, deceased, was sold at auction by Mr. Pelt, yesterday, for $31 75 per gallon. – This is equal to about fifty cents per wine glass. Rather an expensive beverage. *N. Y. Com. Adv.*, 3d.» *State Gazette*, March 10, 1853. (Trenton, NJ).
1440 *The New York Daily Times*, June 12 and 13, 1854. (New York City, NY).
1441 *Daily Constitutionalist*, June 11, 1862. (Augusta, GA).
1442 *Daily Milwaukee News*, December 25, 1864. (Milwaukee, WI).
1443 See Note 798.
1444 "Give them a little more grape, Captain Bragg" is the misquote of General Taylor's order to Braxton Bragg (1817-1876), a United States Army officer, at the Battle of Buena Vista, during the Mexican War. Originally the General given him the following order: "double-shot your guns and give them hell, Bragg". The expression "A little more grape, Captain Bragg" was used afterwards by General Taylor as the campaign slogan that carried him into the White House. "A little more grape, Captain Bragg" is also the name of a National Song, dedicated to General Zachary Taylor, by William J. Lemon, and the title of a painting depicting the triumph of this General at the Battle of Buena Vista, during the afore mentioned conflict.

and marked "Carvalhal," brought the highest price of any, $25,50 per gallon. The other prices were: Meteor "Monteiro," imported in 1834, $25 per gallon; "Cama de Lobos,"[1445] imported in 1837, $18 per gallon; "Ornellos,"[1446] imported same year, $12,50 per gallon. These prices sound rather high, but are no doubt justified by the difficulty of obtaining pure wines, which are really unknown to the majority of drinkers here.[1447]

MORRIS WILKINS, AUCTIONEER.[1448]
Sale by order of Isaac H. Knoz, administrator of estate of Henry J. Burden,[1449] deceased.
A very rare collection of choice Wines, being part of the stock of J. Howard March & Co., of Madeira

E. H. LUDLOW & CO. will sell at auction on THURSDAY, MAY 26, 1870, at 12 o'clock, in the basement No. 5½ Pine street, next door but one is their office, removed for convenience of sale.

Madeiras, vintage of 1834, 1836, 1838, 1840, 1844, 1846, of following brands: – Bual, Imperial Sercial, Verdelho, Reserve, Blandy, H. J. Bover, G. J. Malmsey, &c., Grape Juice, &c., also Johannisberger, choice Sherries, old Port, Brandy, Rhine &c., all being part of the private stock of the late owner. The wines will be sampled by Mr. Owen Byrne, and sold in lots to suit purchasers. The sale of these choice wines will give those wishing to increase their stock and those not so fortunate in having this variety of the prince of wines to add some of it to their collection. An opportunity is seldom offered to secure undoubted reliable old wines direct from the original importer's stock. No gentleman entertaining should be without some of this choice old Madeira, which seldom is to be obtained except through sales of old stock like the above.

No other wines will be admitted.

Catalogues will be sent on application by mail.

1445 See Note 381.

1446 The right spelling is Ornelas.

1447 This article was also published, untitled, in another source, in these words: «– A Boston contemporary has the following in regard to the sale of choice wine in that city: – "Samuel Hatch, the Water street auctioneer, sold at auction yesterday probably the finest lot of Madeira wine that has been bought in this city for years. It was selected by the late Edward Codman, Esq., and comprised one hundred and forty-five demijohns in seven lots. The first lot of fifty-five gallons, imported in 1837 and demijohned in 1842, marked 'Captain Bragg' – not the captain upon whom General Taylor called for 'a little more grape' – sold for thirteen dollars and fifty cents per gallon. The second lot of eighty-eight gallons, imported at the same time, marked J. C. J., brought twelve dollars per gallon. The third, imported in 1841, and marked 'Carvalhal,' brought the highest price of any, twenty-five dollars and fifty cents per gallon. The other prices were: – Meteor 'Monteiro,' imported in 1834, fifteen dollars per gallon; 'Cama de Lobos,' imported in 1837, eighteen dollars per gallon; 'Ornellos,' imported same year, twelve dollars and fifty cents per gallon. These prices sound rather high, but are no doubt justified by the difficulty of obtaining pure wines, which are really unknown to the majority of drinkers here."» *The Philadelphia Inquirer*, January 5, 1865. (Philadelphia, PA, at the section "Summary of News.").

1448 *The New York Herald*, May 21, 1870. (New York City, NY).

1449 Henry John Burden, a former wine merchant in Madeira who had moved to New York after the grape blight of 1852, and was very instrumental there in securing relief for the distressed Madeirans, as we have already seen. He died in Paris, on November 23, 1868, at the age of 60.

[Untitled][1450]

The stock of choice wines belonging to the estate of the historian Prescott,[1451] forty-two cases in all, was sold at auction in Boston on the 16th. The entire amount realized was $1,300. A case of "Tilden Juno" Madeira brought the highest figure, being knocked down at $5 50 per bottle.

Sale of Rare Old Wines.[1452]

A rare lot of fine old Madeira and other wines and brandy was sold at auction, by Messrs. Samuel Hatch & Co., at their rooms, No. 156 Tremont street, yesterday noon. As the following schedule of prices will show, capital bargains were made by some of the purchasers: 150 bottles Madeira, bottled in 1820, $3 a bottle; seventy-nine bottles of 1823, $2 50 a bottle; twenty-five bottles, 1818, $2 37½; thirty-four do., $2 75; 104 do., $2 25; 125 bottles, imported in 1817, $3 75; sixty-one bottles, imported in 1816, $2 12½; fifteen bottles, same price; forty-six bottles, imported in 1820, $3 50; eighty bottles, imported in 1816, $2 87; six bottles, $2 37; twenty-eight bottles Madeira, 1826, $3 12½; nineteen bottles Pico Madeira,[1453] 1826, $3; fourteen bottles Monteiro Madeira, 1830, $3 12; five bottles Madeira, 1823, $3; eleven bottles Madeira, $2 75; eighteen bottles Madeira, 1822, $1 75; nine bottles Malmsey, $2 12½; ten bottles port, Charming, 1827, $3; nine bottles old port, $2 87½; twenty bottles Lisbon wine, 1843, 2 12½; eleven bottles old Vidonia, $2; nine bottles brandy, 1835, $3 50; five bottles Caracoa Duddwites, $3.

OLD WINES.[1454]

Attention is called to the sale of very old Madeira and Sherry to take place on Friday, May 21, at Ludlow's Auction Rooms, No. 3 Pine-st. These wines belonged to the late Thomas P. Barton,[1455] son-in-law of Edward Livingston,[1456] and at one time Chargé d'Affaires of the United States in France. Mr. Barton was a connoisseur in old wine, and the age and pedigree of his wines are both remarkable. Their perfect condition is no less so. Mr. Barton always attended to them himself, and they were kept in a room built expressly for this purpose, to which no one but himself had access. Really pure old Madeira is exceedingly valuable and hardly to be bought at all. This is therefore an opportunity unique in its way, by which all true connoisseurs should profit. The Governor Wine is of 1796, the Gracie Madeira of

---

1450 *The Democratic Pharos*, January 11, 1871. (Logansport, IN).
1451 William Hickling Prescott (1796-1859), a native of Massachusetts, was an American historian and Hispanist, who is widely recognized by his peers as the first American scientific historian. He was one of the most eminent historians of 19th century America.
1452 *The Boston Daily Globe*, October 22, 1873. (Boston, MA).
1453 Wine made at the island of Pico, Azores, often termed in America as "Fayal Madeira" or "Pico Madeira".
1454 *New York Daily Tribune*, May 20, 1875. (New York City, New York).
1455 Thomas P. Barton (1805-1870), who once was the secretary of the American Legation, in Paris, accompanying his father-in-law.
1456 Edward Livingston (1764-1836), a native of Louisiana, was an American jurist and statesman. He was the Envoy Extraordinary and Minister Plenipotentiary at Paris, France, from 1833 to 1835.

the vintage of 1823, McLeod's Laycock[1457] Madeira, imported in 1837; old Seton Wine of 1841, and real Amontillado Sherry, imported in 1825. All of them were corked, drawn off, and labeled by Mr. Barton. Nothing could be more authentic.

SALE OF WINES IN GEORGIA.[1458]

The Augusta (Ga.) *Constitutionalist* of the 9th inst. says: "Yesterday, Alexander Philip, Executor of the estate of James Hope, deceased, sold the remnants of the stock of wine belonging to the estate of Mr. Hope. This lot was perhaps the oldest wine in the South, if not among the oldest in America. Mr. Hope was always noted for the choice brands of his wines, and at this death his cellars contained many brands now extinct. The first lot sold for $85; there were just one dozen bottles of different brands of sherry and Madeira. The second lot of 12 bottles brought $40; two of these were bottled in 1816 and five in 1833; two bottles were of the celebrated Leacock Madeira. The third lot brought $35; fourth, $35, and the fifth, $40; each contained 12 bottles of Madeira. The sixth and seventh lots brought each $40. The eighth lot, consisting of eight bottles of Lucas Madeira and four of London Particular, brought $85 per dozen, or a little over $7 per bottle. The ninth and tenth lots brought each $35. Some of the brands bore date of 1836 and 1844. Six bottles of Medora Madeira, very rare; four bottles of Hopley Madeira, two of Lucas' Madeira, two of Leacock, two of Belvidere, one of Medora, and one of Tuckerman Madeira brought $40; 10 bottles of Gov. Schlev Madeira brought $40; six bottles of Orbit brought $30, and one dozen of Hopley brought $35; six boxes of Lucas' Madeira, of 12 bottles each, brought $100. This same wine was sold in 1860 to Mr. Hope, by a gentleman now of this city, for $105 in gold. Two other boxes of Blandy Madeira, bottles in 1834, in India, brought $80."

PERSONAL.[1459]

M. Outrey,[1460] the former French Minister, left in his wine-cellar at Washington, to be sold at auction, about fifty dozen bottles of Madeira of the vintage of 1791.

IMPORTANT PUBLIC SALE[1461]
of Madeira, in bottle, on Thursday, June 19, without reserve.

MESSRS. SOUTHARD & Co., Sworn Brokers, of 2 St. Dunstan's Hill, have received instructions from Messrs. Cossart, Gordon & Co., the oldest and by far the largest shippers of Madeira wines, and who have been established in that particular branch of the

---

1457 The right spelling is Leacock.
1458 *The New York Times*, February 12, 1877. (New York City, NY); *The Perry Chief*, April 12, 1877. (Perry, IA. Published under the title "Sale of a Georgia Planter's Wines.").
1459 *New York Daily Tribune*, May 25, 1882. (New York City, New York).
1460 Georges Maxime Outrey (1822-1888), Envoy Extraordinary and Minister Plenipotentiary of France at Washington, from 1877 to 1882.
1461 *New York Daily Tribune*, May 17 and 31, 1884. (New York City, NY). This article is very interesting since it advertises, in New York, an important sale of Madeira Wine that would take place in London.

wine trade since 1745, to sell by public auction, at the London Commercial Sale Rooms, Mincing-lane, on Thursday, June 19, their entire stock of bottled Maderias,[1462] consisting of over 7,500 dozen (duty paid) and lying in their cellars, at 75 Mark-lane; and over 1,500 dozen (in bond), bottled in Madeira, and which have been shipped over, and are lying in the London Docks – total 9,000 dozen; also about 200 demijohns (in bond), holding between four to five gallons each of very old wines, and of great scarcity, the whole being of the very best quality. The reason of this unique sale is on account of Messrs. Cossart, Gordon & Co.'s immensely increasing trade for Madeira in bulk, as is seen by following ratios, viz: Sales in bulk, 1881, 1,005 2-3 pipes; 1882 1,232 ½ pipes; 1882, 1,445 ½ pipes; and (in first quarter) 1884, 599 ¼ pipes. Messrs. Cossart, Gordon & Co. also find that there is now no need to keep a stock of Madeiras in bottle (for convenience of the trade), as the qualities of their wines are so well known that their numerous friends prefer to bottle themselves. It is to be noted that the whole of this stock (which, as before mentioned, was bottled for the convenience of the trade) is only dipped in plain black wax, with no seal or name.

THOMAS DOWLING, Auctioneer.[1463]
SPECIAL CONSIGNMENT OF FINE OLD MADEIRA WINE DIRECT FROM WELSH BROS., MADEIRA, PER BRITISH BRIGANTINE POTOMAC, AT AUCTION.

On MONDAY MORNING, JULY TWELFTH, 1886, at ELEVEN O'CLOCK, at my auction rooms, I shall sell the above consignment, consisting of twenty-four cases of fine old Madeira wine, vintages of 1825 and 1835.

The reputation of this house for genuine wines is well known to connoisseurs, and I would advise consumers of this wine to secure a portion of the consignment. It is put up in cases of one dozen quart bottles each.

TOPICS OF THE DAY.[1464]

An auction sale of about 400 bottles of rare old wines from the cellars of Mrs. Harrison Gray Otis[1465] takes place in Boston to-day, of which the Boston Post makes this tantalizing mention: More than half of the stock is the famous Boardman Madeira of 1820, and suggests by its name that Mrs. Otis' family knew what was delicious in wines, while the little lot of Madeira bearing the name of Governor Brooks[1466] has a politico-social flavor which

---

1462 The right spelling is Madeiras.
1463 *The Evening Star*, July 8, 1886. (Washington, DC). At the eve of the publication of this auction announcement, the same source published the following note: «FINE OLD WELSH MADEIRA AT AUCTION. – Mr. Dowling has just received per British brigantine Potomac, from Welsh Bros., Madeira, to be sold at auction, a consignment of fine old Madeira wine, vintages of 1825 to 1835. Connoisseurs and consumers of these wines should not fail to attend the sale. See advertisement for date of sale.» On the edition of December 9, 1886 of the same newspaper, this Auctioneer announced another auction sale, for December 10th, «of twenty- four cases of fine old Madeira wine, vintage of 1825 and 1835.»
1464 *The Washington Critic*, November 1, 1886. (Washington, DC).
1465 Sally Foster Otis, wife of Harrison Gray Otis (1765-1848), a native of Boston, MA. He was a businessman, lawyer, politician, and one of the wealthiest men of his city during this time. He also served as the 3rd Mayor of Boston, a Senator from Massachusetts, President of the Massachusetts Senate, member of the House of Representatives, and U.S. Attorney for the District of Massachusetts.
1466 See Note 1391.

it is good to taste amid the asperities of the present gubernatorial campaign. I fear that if a man were to sample these bottles freely he would not care whether Andrew or Ames[1467] was elected. The catalogue shows one case containing fifteen bottles of the famous Juno Madeira, which goes back to 1829 – a famous vintage which Dr. Holmes has celebrated in the bankers' dinner when he makes his epicurean connoisseur.

> Remark that "Whitetop" was considered fine,
> But swear the "Juno" is the better wine.[1468]

Besides these Madeira, the famous Duff Gordon, dating back to 1820, is represented in the sale by a trifle of nine bottles, just enough to open at birthdays and weddings in a small family. Under date of 1827 is a lot of ten bottles of Madeira which belonged to Isaac P. Davis, the typical diner out of Boston of fifty years ago, and to whom, if I am not mistaken, Daniel Webster[1469] dedicated a volume of his speeches.[1470] Other little lots of Madeira in the sale are "John Tyler," 1845, and the Otis "Platamore" brand 1854. Port, which Dr. Johnson[1471] said was the liquor for men, but which of late years seems to be reserved for invalids, is represented by the Johnson, Bordeaux, brand of 1840.

Figure 92. "Mrs. Harrison Gray Otis". After her death her husband's choicest Madeiras were sold at auction, in order to settle the estate, the usual procedure. *19th century engraving published in the 2nd edition of the book* The Republican Court, or, American Society in the Days of Washington *(New York, 1856).*

SALE OF OLD WINES.[1472] – At a sale on Monday in Boston of the fine old wines belonging to the estate of Mrs. Harrison Gray Otis, fourteen cases of Madeira of 1820 was knocked down in little lots at 85 cents a bottle. The "Gov. Brooks" Madeira of 1820, of which there were only thirteen bottles, went for 94 cents a bottle. … the Madiera[1473]-Otis, "P. Catamore," 1851, at $1,10, and the rest of the Sherry and Claret were lumped at 95 cents. One case of "Duff Gordon" Madeira of 1820, in excellent condition, brought 90 cents a bottle.[1474]

1467 Oliver Ames (1831-1895), a native of Massachusetts, was a politician and financier, and also the 35th Governor of this state.
1468 Lines from the poem "The Banker's Dinner", by the American poet Oliver Wendell Holmes.
1469 See Note 72.
1470 This dedication consisted on the following words: «TO ISAAC P. DAVIS, Esq./ My Dear Sir:/ A warm private friendship has subsisted between us for half our lives, interrupted by no untoward occurrence, and never from a moment cooling into indifference. Of this friendship, the source of so much happiness to me, I wish to leave, if not an enduring memorial, at least an affectionate and grateful acknowledgement./ I inscribe this volume of speeches to you./ DANIEL WEBSTER.» [WEBSTER, Daniel], *The Works of Daniel Webster*, Volume II, Charles C. Little and James Brown, Boston, 1851.
1471 Alexander Johnson, the author of an article entitled "The History of Ancient and Modern Wines", published in 1825.
1472 *Gettysburg Compiler*, November 9, 1886. (Gettysburg, PA).
1473 The right spelling is Madeira.
1474 As can be seen, when compared to other similar auction-related articles, these choicest wines were sold at unusual low prices.

[Untitled][1475]

Figure 93. Samuel J. Tilden, a former Governor of New York, possessed 70 bottles of old Madeira when he passed away, which were auctioned for $3.50 apiece. *19th century photograph c. 1880-86. Author unknown.*

The Tilden[1476] collection of wine sold at auction in New York footed up $6,000. When the Steinberger Cabinet Imperial (1868) was reached, A. Wolff, jr., of No. 40 East Thirty-eight street, bid $9 a quart for two dozen bottles. E. C. Sampson got two dozen at $7.50. H. L. Leach took three dozen at $5.50. Peter Marie was satisfied with one dozen bottles at $4.50 apiece. The last dozen went to Samuel S. Barger, of No. 111 Broadway, who bought them, it was reported, from Chauncey M. Depew. Mr. Gurnee snapped up the seventy bottles of Old Madeira at $3.50 apiece, when Mr. Draper sung out: "Why don't you bid on this wine? You know what it is. You go to Delmoncio's[1477] and pay $3.50 or $4 for a bottle of champagne and drink it up in a minute. A bottle of this good old Madeira at the same price will last you all the evening."

So it proved that the average wine bibber of to-day does not know what old Madeira is.

INTERESTING GOSSIP OF THE DAY.[1478]

One of the largest buyers at the auction sale of the late Samuel J. Tilden's wines on Tuesday was a dealer whose name is little known to the general public, but is very familiar in the most exclusive set in New York society. He paid no attention to the champagnes or clarets, but bid on the high-priced Steinberger cabinet Rhine wine, and gathered in the best of the Madeiras. This man has supplied the wealthiest people of New York with fine wines for half a century. His specialty is the old-time American favorite, Madeira. He is probably the only dealer in New York who possesses some of the famous Bloodgood Madeira. He is acquainted with the history of every good wine cellar in this country. He went into business as an apprentice to a big wine firm when John Jacob Astor, the elder, used to import his Madeira in casks direct from the grower, and still maintains, as far as possible, the old style of conducting business.[1479]

1475 *The Daily Times*, November 16, 1888. (Richmond, VA).
1476 Samuel Jones Tilden (1814-1886), a native of New York, famous for being the Democratic candidate to the U.S. Presidency in the disputed election of 1876. He also served as the 25th Governor of New York, serving from 1875 to 1876.
1477 The right spelling is Delmonico's, New York's first (French) restaurant, established in 1837, by the Delmonico brothers, located at the intersection of Beaver, William and South William Streets, which still exists today and claims to be America's first restaurant.
1478 *The Sun*, November 18, 1888. (New York City, NY).
1479 In this article it is interesting to underline that the best buyer of the Madeiras was a New York wine dealer, with the obvious intention of reselling it to his regular customers.

TREASURES FOR AN ART GALLERY.[1480]
Brisk Competition at Leavitt's for the Contents of a Newporter's Wine Cellar.

Auctioneer Merry sold about 2,225 bottles of wines and spirits for about $4,750 at the Leavitt art rooms, 787 and 789 Broadway, yesterday morning. The stock was consigned by Thomas Burlingham of Newport, to close an estate of which he is executor. The reason the sale did not take place in Rhode Island was because of the prohibitory laws of that model commonwealth. Previous to the sale a temporary bar was opened in the auction room, and the stock was extensively sampled by prospective purchasers, and still more extensively sampled by persons who only pretended to be purchasers. There was no license needed for this extemporized bar, because the liquor was given away. The auction opened promisingly with the sale of five dozen 1795 Cognac, of Judah Touro[1481] and Webster stock, at $6 the bottle. Eight dozen Seacock[1482] Madeira, 1828, of equally good lineage, which sold at the Winthrop sale in Newport in 1873 for $8 a bottle, brought but $3.25 for the first two cases and $2 a bottle for the rest. The wine was said to be spoiled. The highest price of the sale was brought by five cases of Juno Madeira of the vintage of 1817. Their leading the list was due to the annoyance of a bidder known as J. S. on discovering that, in place of all five cases being knocked down to him at $4 a bottle, one case belonged to a Mr. Jones, whose bid was simultaneous. He insisted on the wine being put up again, but Mr. Jones got his one case all the same. He had to pay $6.75 a bottle, to be sure, but the had the satisfaction of seeing J. S. pay $6 a bottle for his four cases.

OLD LIQUORS SOLD.[1483]

The old liquors belonging to the estate of Oliver Byrne were sold at auction Wednesday. The first lot, 12,000 gallons of cider, sold at about 3 cents a gallon. About 1,650 gallons of whisky, from good to choice, sold at from $2 25 to $6 60 a gallon. About 125 gallons of brandy brought from $5 50 to $9. Some Amontillado sherry brought $8 per gallon. A magnum of cognac, 40 years old, brought $13, and a gallon of Otard cognac, 1850, brought $11. Madeira of 1831, 1834, 1839, and 1846 brought by the bottle from $4 25 to $5 50. All the best goods sold without sample.

1480 *The Sun*, December 28, 1888. (New York City, NY).
1481 Judah Touro (1775-1854), a native of Newport, RI, was an American businessman and philanthropist, whose father, Isaac Touro, a Portuguese Sephardic Jew who had exiled himself in Holland prior to going to America, had been chosen as the *hazzan* (chief singer) at the Touro Synagogue, a Portuguese Sephardic congregation in Newport. The Touro Sinagogue, dedicated in 1763, still exists today, being the oldest synagogue building of the Colonial era still standing. Its cornerstone had been laid by Aaron Lopez, another Portuguese Sephardic Jew, who became a prominent Newport merchant, involved in whaling and spermaceti candlemaking.
1482 The right spelling is Leacock.
1483 *The New York Times*, March 23, 1889. (New York City, NY).

A. T. STEWART'S WINES AT AUCTION.[1484]
Fair Prices for Rare Old Vintages From the Dead Merchant's Cellars.

Figure 94. Alexander Turney Stewart, New York's "merchant prince" had a collection of excellent Madeiras, which were auctioneed after his death. *19th century engraving c. 1860. Author unknown.*

The entire contents of the wine cellars of the late A. T. Stewart[1485] were sold under hammer yesterday afternoon by Auctioneer John H. Draper at 240 Fifth avenue. The sale was ordered by the executors of Mr. Stewart's will, Henry Hilton[1486] and Charles J. Clinch. The wines have been packed away in the big white mansion in Fifth avenue ever since Mr. Stewart's death.

The biggest part of the collection consisted of Madeiras, all of which were regarded as excellent, and some of them of considerable value. Although the total sum realized yesterday was large, low prices prevailed. Many of the wines were sold far below what they cost Mr. Stewart. For instance, thirteen dozen of 1844 Johannisberg went yesterday at $4 and $4.50 a bottle. Mr. Stewart paid $6 for it. Again, Judge Hilton bought in two dozen March & Benson "Bual" at $2.25 a bottle, for which Mr. Stewart had paid $4 in 1865.

Judge Hilton, Prescott Hall Butler,[1487] and Judge Horace Russell[1488] sat on a front seat throughout the sale, and were free buyers. Judge Hilton bought more than any other man. Brayton Ives, Ed Glimore, Mr. Starbuck, George De Witt, and A. J. Quinian, also bought considerable. Manager Gilmore showed a preference for rare old Madeiras. Eugene Higgins[1489] bought some good red wines, and Alfred F. Walcott was a steady bidder on all sorts of wines, and secured a number of lots.

It was generally supposed that the Manhattan Club meant to buy a good assortment of the wines. Only one lot, of thirty-six bottles of choice Madeira, was bought under the club's name, however. …[1490]

1484 *The Sun*, March 6, 1890. (New York City, NY).
1485 See Note 1357.
1486 See Note 1367.
1487 A prominent New York lawyer.
1488 Horace Russell (1843-1913), a native of New York, who graduated at Dartmouth College and continued his studies at the Harvard Law School. He was Assistant District Attorney, in New York, from 1873 to 1880, and a member of the Superior Court from 1880 to 1883. Besides this, he was also the general counsel to the estate of the late A. T. Stewart, who was known as the "merchant prince".
1489 Eugene Higgins (1860-1948), a multimillionaire bachelor, and *bon vivant* whose name is associated to Madeira because of the fact that, on November 16, 1909, the *Varuna*, his luxurious yacht, went ashore at Achadas da Cruz, on the southwestern coast of the island, and was considered lost, being dashed to pieces by the furious waves, in the following weeks. This sad occurrence was widely revealed in the American press of the time.
1490 The article continued with an in-depth list of the wine sold and its buyers.

LIGHT BIDDING FOR OLD MADEIRAS.[1491]
A RARE COLLECTION OF WINES BELONGING TO THE STEWART ESTATE AUCTIONED OFF.

The wines in the wine cellar of the late A. T. Stewart were sold at auction yesterday in the Fifth Avenue Auction Rooms at prices that were a serious disappointment to the executors.

Among the list of wines were some of the finest Madeiras sold in this country for many years, and it was expected that the sale would realize a very large figure. But for some reason the bidding was very light, and the rarest vintages in the collection went at prices far below what Mr. Stewart had paid for them twenty or twenty-five years ago. He had undoubtedly the greatest assortment of Madeira in the country, having been the principal buyer at the time March & Benson's cellars were cleared out nearly a quarter of a century ago.

This firm, both members of which have been dead for years, is still famous among old time New Yorkers. March and Benson[1492] were great swells and occupied high positions in the four hundred of their day.[1493] March was a personal friend of Daniel Webster[1494] and Benson was one of the richest men of the period. His brother[1495] owned one of the principal Madeira vineyards, of which the firm was the agent in this country. It was on this account that they were so heavily stocked with these wines when they closed their cellars.

About $8,000 was realized from the sale yesterday, despite the lack of willing buyers. Most of the lots were bought in by Judge Hilton, his son-in-law, Judge Horace Russell, and Prescott Hall Butler,[1496] one of the heirs. There were a number of representatives present from the different clubs that pride themselves on their wine cellars, but the offerings were evidently not to their taste, as the only club that bought anything at all, as far as could be ascertained, was the Manhattan, on whose account three cases of choice "South Side Madeira" were bid in at $24 a dozen. Next to Judge Hilton and his friends the heaviest buyer was Brayton Ives. Edward Gilmore, of Niblo's Garden, had the distinction of paying the highest price that was realized for any of the wine, three bottles of "Lynch, 1817," being knocked down to him at $7 25 apiece. Mr. J. Murphy, who said he was buying for a gentleman who did not desire to have his name made public, secured some of the choicest lots offered. …[1497]

1491 *The New York Herald*, March 6, 1890. (New York City, NY). This article is a complement to the previous one, with the same contents, but as it sheds new light about the origin of the Madeiras owned by A. T. Stewart, we chose to present it as well.

1492 In the early 1800's this wine-trading company was located at different Manhattan addresses: 34 South Street; 71 Washington Street; 47 South Street; and 14 Broad Street.

1493 Phrase coined by Ward McAllister. See (2nd part of) Note 1310.

1494 See Note 72.

1495 Clement March's brother, John Howard March, the U.S. Consul at and wine merchant at Funchal for many years. He was a partner of this New York company for many years but around the 1820's he established his own company, John Howard March Co.

1496 Prescott Hall Butler (1848-1901), a resident in Long Island, NY.

1497 The article continued with an in-depth list of the wine sold and its buyers. Among the choicest Madeiras sold at auction were the following: One case Madeira, bottled 1807; Nine cases Madeira, "Camara de Lobos," 1830; Nineteen cases "Bual," 1846; Seven cases "Verdalho," [Verdelho] 1846; Four cases "Sercial" Madeira, 1815; Two demijohns, five gallons, Cama de Lobos, Madeira, imported 1837; Three demijohns, March & Benson Madeira, Brahmin via India, May, 1826; and one bottle "Sercial," 1836, Madeira.

Old Wines.[1498]
Court Journal.

The rage for buying old wines is raising the price to an enormous figure, as was seen at two sales by auction last month. Now, if there be one law of nature which knows no exception it is that all things organic are subject to decay, and wine is an organic product, and when its ripest stage is reached and passed the process of decomposition begins. You may stave off the decay, for a short time only, by alcohol and other devices, but it goes on. Yet when an "old cellar" is auctioned fabulous prices are paid for undrinkable wine.[1499] In 1858 there was a Madeira sale in Paris, when forty-four bottles were bought by Rothschild for their weight in gold. The wine was from the famous 1814 pipe of Madeira which had lain at the bottom of the sea for thirty-six years. Now, the antiquity of the wines of the ancients is attributable to their artificial composition. Spices and fragrant roots and sea water were added to the pure vintage. The best authenticated stories of fine old wines that retained their quality tend to the belief that they were strongly fortified.

RARE OLD WINES AT AUCTION.[1500]
Ward McAllister Buys Madeira that Has Travelled to China and Back.

They sold rare old wines at Wetmore's, 240 Fifth avenue, yesterday afternoon. One woman, three young men, a dozen men of middle age, and a score of more old men were there to watch and buy. There was not an idler in the crowd. Ward McAllister was there to buy a little Madeira for his cellars. He sat back in a corner and bid mildly, and, although he got some pretty good things, he did not pay a high price for them. W. C. Castler and Louis Delmonice were chief among the bidders and buyers. The woman came out strong toward the end and got some fine Madeira at a low figure. She was a comfortable, middle-aged woman, and evidently know what she was about. First they sold some wines and liquors of the estate of Edward Brandon, then other wines and liquors of a superior quality from the cellar of William Fletcher, and then they came to the event of the day.

Southerners have been particularly fond of Madeira. They import it and then let it lie in wood and glass for decades. Sometimes they have sent great casks of it around the Cape to China seas and back, for the long voyage shakes up the wine, clears it of impurity, and deepens its color. Often the same casks would go on two, three, and even four of those long trips.

It was such madeira that was sold yesterday. There was sherry, too, to delight the eye with its clear yellow or rich amber, and such port as is seldom seen. The sherry brought fairly good prices – from $1.50 to $3.50 the bottle. There were two bottles which sold better. One was a gem – a great, portly, stately bottle with dust and cobwebs on it. It took seven bottles to make this one. First seven separate bottles are allowed to settle. Then, as one evaporated, the contents of the others were gradually poured in until, when the wine was formed from the sediment, there remained but one bottle – and this was it. It brought $5, and the auctioneer looked sad. But the bidders were looking for port and Madeira.

1498 *Daily Alta California*, November 23, 1890. (San Francisco, CA); *The Mountain Democrat*, October 17, 1891. (Placerville, CA. Published without mentioning its source).

1499 It was not the case with Madeira Wine, which improves with age.

1500 *The Sun*, March 19, 1891. (New York City, NY).

The first sold at high prices. It dated back to 1847, 1820, 1878, and the bidders paid $3.25 to $6.25 the bottle. Of the port the centre of attraction was five bottles of old white port, than which there is none finer. It is of a delicate straw color and reflects the sunbeams like a diamond. Its bouquet is delicious, that odor of gentle and luxurious fermentation which comes from the oldest port only.

The Madeiras sold well, and toward the end the bidding was more spirited. Some fine Francis Amory Madeira, imported in 1800 and 1811, brought the best prices - $5,50 to $6.50. All of this wine antedated 1840, and some of it dated back to 1796. It came from the cellar of the De Renne estate, in Savannah. It was a great opportunity to get rare wines for the cellar without paying fancy prices for it, and those who bought were evidently well satisfied.[1501]

PERSONAL AND PERTINENT.[1502]

The sale of the Kennedy wines in Baltimore at auction was an event of great interest. Most of the wine was madeira of a very venerable age. John Pendleton Kennedy,[1503] the Maryland novelist and statesman, was Secretary of the Navy in Fillmore's Administration. It was in his time that Commodore Perry took his fleet to Japan to negotiate the first treaty with that country, and on his outward voyage, stopping at the island of Madeira, he purchased a cask of wine on commission for the Secretary. Some of this wine was included in the sale. Nearly all of it was in the nature of treasure-trove, for it was found unexpectedly by the executors of the estate in the cellar of the old homestead.

AUCTION PRICES OF OLD WINES[1504]
Connoisseurs and Dealers Bid for Keteltas Estate Madeiras.

A few white-haired old New Yorkers mingled with a score of wine dealers in sampling the old sherries and Madeiras belonging to the estate of Eugene Keteltas[1505] as a preliminary to an auction sale of the entire stock yesterday forenoon. A large proportion of these wines were bought by Mr. Keteltas for his private cellars in 1839 and some of them were declared to be more than one hundred years old. The sale was conducted by Du Vivier & Co. in Townsend & Montant's salesrooms, 87 and 89 Leonard street. Representatives of the Keteltas estate said that the prices were ridiculously low.

Thirty-two bottles of Ferdinand sherry, said to be the very last of a celebrated Montillo wine brought $5 a bottle and were taken in small lots by three different persons. The other old sherries commanded from $1.25 to $2.75 the bottle. There was more spirited bidding for the Madeiras. One lot of eleven bottles of the vintage of 1828, said to have been

---

1501 A summary of this text was revealed in *The Boston Daily Globe*, March 20, 1891, (Boston, MA), under the title "The Uncrowned Buys Cautiously.": «NEW YORK, March 19. – At a sale of rare old wines Wednesday Ward McAllister bought cautiously and moderately of old Madeira for his cellars. He did not pay any more than the wine was worth, and most of the antique fluid went to W. C. Oastler and Louis Delmonico and an unknown woman who knew perfectly well what she was about.»

1502 *The World*, December 25, 1896. (New York City, NY). See the last article of section 9.5. of this anthology.

1503 See Notes 993 and 992.

1504 *The Sun*, April 18, 1900. (New York City, NY).

1505 Eugene Keteltas (1804-1876), a native of New York, a lawyer and a member of one oldest families of this city.

purchased from John Hone, Jr., in 1836, was bid in by James A. Montant at $5 a bottle. Mr. Montant bought several small lots of other wines for different friends. From $2.50 to $5 a bottle was paid for 116 bottles of "South Side Wedding Wine. Very old Madeira," by four or five bidders. Judge Charles H. Truax[1506] got thirty-two bottles at the lowest price mentioned. J. R. Brown bought seventeen bottles of "Old Gordon" Madeira at $3 a bottle.

Ten bottles of old whiskey, presented by the famous "Falstaff" Hackett to Mr. Keteltas in 1850, were bought by J. J. Wysong at $3 a bottle. The most eager bidding of the sale was over eleven bottles of old Blue Seal "Rain Water" Madeira. This wine was described as "of the old style of the last century, having been made probably in 1740 or 1750." It was bought by James A. Montant for $8.50 a bottle. Some peach brandy of 1800, of which there were but thirteen bottles of old Gibbs brandy brought $6.50 a bottle. About two-thirds of the wine were purchased by dealers.[1507]

Some Things That Are Said and Done in NEW YORK[1508]
Old Wine: Old Bottles.

Figure 95. "Of the vintage of 1740."
Article illustration. Author unknown.

At an auction sale of wines the other day, $8,50 per bottle was successfully bid for 11 bottles of old blue seal "Rain Water" Madeira. This wine was said to have been made "probably in 1740 or 1750." and the bidding was lively.

From the viewpoint of the old-fashioned wine expert, the price was absurdly high. Dr. Weir Mitchell,[1509] who is as great an authority upon Madeira as upon nervous diseases or revolutionary history, makes one of his characters say: "I have never drank a wine over 70 years old which had not something to regret."[1510]

Besides, this wine was bottled; and this practice, Dr. Mitchell says, "is simply fatal." It is likely that the buyer of this extremely old Madeira was a rich amateur with little knowledge of the subject. At the same sale, 11 bottles of the vintage of 1828, which should be at its zenith of mellow excellence, went for but five dollars per bottle, a price that the ordinary vintage may bring.

The truth is that the days of careful appreciation of the flower and flavor of wine are passing. The stiff-chokered

---

1506 See Note 1418.

1507 A shorter version of this article was published, untitled, in another source, in these terms: «At an auction sale of old wines belonging to the estate of Eugene Keteltas, yesterday, thirty-two bottles of Ferdinand sherry, said to be the last of a celebrated Montillo wine, brought $5 a bottle. Eleven bottles of Madeira of the vintage of 1828 went for $5 a bottle. More than 100 bottles of "South Side Wedding Wine" were sold at from $2.50 to $5 a bottle. The liveliest bidding was done for eleven bottles of old blue seal "Rain-Water" Madeira. This wine was described as "of the old style of the last century, having been made probably in 1740 or 1750." It was sold for $8.50 a bottle. – New York Post.» *The Banner Democrat*, October 20, 1900. (Lake Providence, LA).

1508 *Logansport Daily Reporter*, May 10, 1900. (Logansport, IN). This text focus on the subject of the previous one, but complements it, therefore we decided to present it as well.

1509 Silas Weir Mitchell. See section 6.2.14. of this anthology.

1510 Quote from Mitchell's text "A Madeira Party." Idem.

old gentleman who could tell within a mile of the place where any wine was grown simply by tasting it, are dead. The rich man of today has different, and, I believe, nobler tastes. So long as a wine assuages his thirst or suits his taste, he cares little about its date or birthplace. He is more interested in golf and yachting.

Of all the famous millionaires whose money and whose lavish expenditure of it so interest the public, there is hardly one whose wine cellar shows the expert's knowledge. And there is a far larger proportion than would be the case in any other land who never have much to do with wine, upon principle.

9.14. Amusing episodes involving Madeira Wine

The last section of this chapter contains a selection of twenty-eight articles, showing the same number of amusing Madeira Wine-related episodes, some of them more hilarious than others, involving sometimes several well-known names in the American political, judicial, social and economical arena, which were published in different sources, between 1801 and 1907, that will certainly amuse the reader.

[Untitled][1511]

An Indian chief, being asked his opinion of a cask of Madeira wine, presented to him by an officer, said, he thought it a juice extracted from women's tongues and lion's hearts; for after he had drank a bottle of it, he [said he] could talk forever, and fight like the devil.[1512]

[1511] *Philadelphia Repository*, June 13, 1801. (Philadelphia, PA); *The Sun*, April 23, 1803. (Dover, NH); *The Fredonian*, March 6, 1810. (Boston, MA. As a curiosity we add that the last word of the text – "devil" – was spelled like this: "d–l"); *The American*, August 14, 1816. (Hanover, NH. Presents the same spelling of the last word); *Columbian Register*, December 19, 1820. (New Haven, CT); *Hillsboro Telegraph*, January 6, 1821. (Amherst, NH); *The Schenectady Cabinet*, November 12, 1834. (Schenectady, NY). Under the title "A GOOD ONE." and preceded by the following remark: «The following is about the best thing in the anecdote line, we have seen lately:», this text was published in the following sources: *Macon Weekly Telegraph*, January 19, 1847. (Macon, GA); *Daily Chronicle & Sentinel*, January 23, 1847. (Augusta, GA). Changing the expression "a cask of wine" for "a case of wine", this text was published in the following sources: *Gettysburg Centinel*, April 9, 1806. (Gettysburg, PA); *Geneva Gazette*, January 10, 1816. (Rochester, NY); *The State's Advocate*, November 27, 1828. (Milton, PA); WOODWORTH, S., *The Ladies' Literary Cabinet, being a Repository of Miscellaneous Literary Productions, in Prose and Verse*, New Series, Vol. I., Samuel Huesties, New York, 1820, page 30.

[1512] This story also had five other similar versions, published in different sources: «An Indian Chief being asked his opinion of a cask of Madeira Wine, presented to him by an officer of the East India Company's service, said he thought it was a juice extracted from women's tongues and lion's hearts; for after he had drank a bottle of it, he said, *he could talk forever, and fight the devil.*» *The National Advocate*, July 31, 1821. (New York, NY); *The Salem Gazette*, August 7, 1821. (Salem, MA); *New-York Advertiser*, August 15, 1821. (New York, NY); *Village Register and Norfolk County Advertiser*, August 17, 1821. (Dedham, MA); *The Miscellany*, August 18 and 25, 1821. (Litchfield, CT). «WOMAN'S TONGUE. – An Indian chief being asked his opinion of a cask of Madeira wine, presented to him by an officer, said "he thought it was like the juice extracted from woman's tongue and lion's heart, for when he drank a bottle of it he could talk forever and fight like a tiger."» *The Republican Compiler*, November 27, 1843. (Gettysburg, PA); «A Strong Inference. – An Indian chief who had been presented sometime previous with a keg of Madeira wine, was asked what he supposed it was made of? To which he replied that he thought the juice was extracted from women's tongues and lions' hearts, for when he drank a bottle of it he could talk forever and fight the devil.» *Wisconsin Free Democrat*, March 3, 1847. (Milwaukee, WI); «That was not a bad idea of the Indian, who being asked his opinion of Madeira wine, said he thought it a juice extracted from women's tongues and lion's hearts; for after he had drank a bottle of it he could talk forever and fight like the duce.» *Californian*, November 17, 1847. (San Francisco, CA). «GOOD INDIAN. – An Indian Chief, being asked his opinion of a cask of Madeira wine which had been presented to him, said that he thought it was juice extracted from woman's tongue and lion's heart, for after he had drunk it he could talk forever, and fight anybody.» *Janesville Morning Gazette*,

[Untitled]¹⁵¹³

Mr. Caleb Whiteford¹⁵¹⁴ was at an entertainment, in which Madeira of a fine flavor was plentifully served during dinner. After dinner a bottle of Cape wine was introduced. It was so excellent that the company gave several hints that another bottle would be very gratifying. The hint was not taken: on which Mr. W. said, "Well, if we cannot *double the Cape*, we must return to *Madeira*."

YANKEE HORSE RACE¹⁵¹⁵

Two yankees lately lodged at an inn for about ten days – they called for the best the house afforded, and drank two or three bottles of Madeira per day. During the ten days they frequently made bets, and generally referred the decision to the landlord. At length a *dispute* arose on the swiftness of their horses. The argument was conducted with apparent warmth, and they agreed to decide it by a race – the landlord was judge – the yankees were mounted – the landlord gave the word – *one – two – three* – and GO. – Off they went, and have neither been seen nor heard of since; leaving the landlord to remunerate himself for their broad and lodging, by the honor of being judge of a *Yankee horse race*.

WONDERFUL AGILITY IN OLD AGE.¹⁵¹⁶

Youth may boast of health and vigour,
Young men of a graceful figure;
Whilst sportsman on a distant shore,
But here *old men* can boast of more.

On Wednesday evening last a large party of the inhabitants of this township were invited by Mr. Nicholas Wyckoff to partake of a sumptuous entertainment, after raising a frame house on his farm. – The guests were seated at a table which groaned beneath a weight of luxuries, placed beneath the spreading bows of a weeping willow, where hospitality reigned in state. During the convivial moments of the bottle, two ancient sons of Columbia, cherished a fond recollection for past times, introduced many subjects embracing feats of their valour through the Revolutionary war, which terminated in a friendly dispute between them. One of them boasting of his superior agility above the other, was challenged immediately to leap for a dozen of Madeira, which was accepted. The parties

---

March 8, 1858. (Janesville, WI); *The Compiler*, March 22, 1858. (Gettysburg, PA. Published untitled and ending the text as "and fight everybody"); *Prairie Du Chien Courier*, March 25, 1858. (Prairie du Chien, WI. Published under the title "GOOD INDIAN"); *Racine Daily News*, March 30, 1858. (Racine, WI. Published under the title "GOOD INDIAN" and ending as "and fight everybody"); *Mariettian*, June 19, 1858. (Marietta, PA. Published untitled).

[1513] *Commercial Advertiser*, July 7, 1808. (New York, NY); *New Bedford Mercury*, August 5, 1808. (New Bedford, MA).
[1514] Caleb Whiteford (1734-1810), was a Scottish merchant, diplomat and political satirist. In 1872 he served as Lord Shelburne's envoy to Benjamin Franklin on the Peacce Commission at Paris, where, on September 3, 1783, was signed the Treaty of Paris, that put an end to the American Revolutionary War between Great Britain and the United States of America.
[1515] *The Independent American*, August 13, 1811. (Ballston Spa, NY); *Political Barometer*, August 14, 1811. (Poughkeepsie, NY. Published untitled).
[1516] *Nantucket Inquirer*, July 16, 1822. (Nantucket, MA).

were a Mr. Waley, aged seventy six years, and a Mr. Bogart, aged sixty five, (both of this township.) They covered eight yards and a half in three standing leaps! Mr. B. having gained over his antagonist only three inches in the last leaps, won the wager!!!

Long Island Star.

[Untitled][1517]

Take no credit to yourself for making virtuous resolutions, and keeping them, when your high resolves were not subject to temptation. We once heard a ragged rascal, hatless and shoeless, declare that he was so well convinced of the injurious tendency of eating oysters and drinking Madeira for supper, that he was resolved neither to touch one or the other. If he did not keep this resolution, the probabilities are that his poverty did.

[Untitled][1518]

A letter from Saratoga, published in a New York paper, states that at a dinner at Congress Hall, where Mr. De Figaniere, the Portuguese Minister,[1519] was present, all the gentlemen ordered *Madeira* wine, in Compliment to the Minister for his exertions in procuring the reduction of the duty on that peculiar brand.[1520] He enjoyed the compliment, and ordered a bottle of Newark cider in return!!

[Untitled][1521]

"Ward Nicholas B[1522] – ," he said, "was a man of fortune, of dignified manners, and of a hospitable character. He had two weaknesses – his Madeira wine and his relationship to John Quincy Adams.[1523] While that gentleman was President, Mr. B – was fortunate enough to entertain him at his country-seat, and invited the most presentable people

---

1517 *Adams Sentinel*, March 4, 1844. (Gettysburg, PA).

1518 *Alexandria Gazette*, August 10, 1844. (Alexandria, VA); *The Sun*, August 16, 1844. (Baltimore, MD. Published under the title "RETURNING THE COMPLIMENT"); *Tioga Eagle*, August 21, 1844. (Wellsboro, PA. Published under the title "NATIONAL COURTESY", adding that its source had been a letter from Saratoga published in a New York paper).

1519 Cesar Henrique Stuart de la Figanière, Portuguese Minister Plenipotentiary in Washington.

1520 In fact, on the previous month, the duties levied on Madeira Wine imports to the U.S. were dropped significantly as we can read on another newspaper article: «*Important to Importers of Wine*. A decision of the Treasury Department has just been made on the subject of the duties paid on Madeira wine. Instead of paying sixty cents per gallon, as heretofore, the rates hereafter will be only seven and a half cents in casks, and fifteen cents in bottles. The tariff act of 1842, has been found to be an infringement of our treaty with Portugal. It exacted sixty cents per gallon on Madeira wines, while the white wines of other nations were put at the low rates above mentioned. Our treaty with Portugal, stipulates that the wines of that country shall be received on the terms of the most favored nations. The treaty of course prevails over the act. The amount to be refunded to importers, will not fall short of four hundred thousand dollars, and may reach half a million. [New York Express.]» *Boston Courier*, July 25, 1844. (Boston, MA).

1521 "Harper's New Monthly Magazine", Volume XIII, June to November, 1856., Harper & Brother, Publishers, New York, 1856, pages 221-222; CLEMENT, J., "The Western Literary Messenger, A Family Magazine of Literature, Science, Art, Morality, and General Intelligence", Thomas & Lathrops, Publishers, Buffalo, [New York], 1856, pages 245-246.

1522 Ward Nicholas Boylston (1747-1828), a native of Boston, MA, was a man of wealth and refinement, merchant, philanthropist, and a great benefactor of Harvard University.

1523 See Note 70.

Figure 96. Ward Nicholas Boylston, a wealthy Boston merchant, once had a unique Madeira that had travelled the world, and was highly prized by him. *Painting by John Singleton Copley, 1767.*

of the vicinage to meet him – among whom was the parson, the Rev. Mr. – a man of no little er-u-di-tion (as Dominie Sampson[1524] would call it), and much simplicity of character. He invited, also, distinguished persons from Boston to meet, as his note expressed it, 'my cousin, John Quincy Adams, President of the United States.' In his cellar, while he had many a butt of most delicious wine, there was one particular kind of Madeira he prized above all the rest. 'It had been,' he had often told the parson, 'all the way from Madeira to the Cape of Good Hope – from the Cape of Good Hope to Calcutta – from Calcutta to Canton, in the East Indies – from Canton it had been brought back to Calcutta – from Calcutta, by the land-route, to Egypt – and from Egypt to the United States.' A bottle of this wine he was to produce on this occasion, and to make what we would call in New Hampshire 'a great spread.'

"Well, the guests came, and among others, 'his cousin, John Quincy Adams, the President of the United States.' The viands were good, the conversation entertaining, and the host gratified. After the meats were removed, and the bottles on the table had made their circuits a number of times, our host says, 'Gentlemen, I am about to offer you a glass of wine that I can particularly commend to your kind appreciation. It has been all the way from Madeira to the Cape of Good Hope, from the Cape of Good Hope to Calcutta, from Calcutta to Canton, in the East Indies, from Canton it has been brought back to Calcutta, from Calcutta by the land-route to Egypt, and from Egypt to the United States. I think you will like it.' The guests sipped and tasted, tasted and sipped, sipped and tasted again; and, as in duty bound, pronounced it superb. When the bottle had made its first revolution and reached the host, he was gratified to find that it had not suffered material diminution, no guest, of course, having taken a full glass. But what was his horror, at seeing, on its second course, our friend the Parson pouring the inestimable liquid into a tumbler, and *drinking* it with absolute *nonchalance!* In vain he essayed quietly to attract his attention – no hint or pantomimic action could reach the absorbed Parson, who had, indeed, got into a theological controversy with one of his neighbors, and, of course, was totally indifferent to every thing else. Again the bottle made its rounds and again reached the Parson, who, at this unfortunate moment being deep into original sin, poured, in the excitement of the moment, the whole contents into his fatal tumbler. The cousin of John Quincy Adams, President of the United States, sat aghast, the perspiration ran from his features – but he was a gentleman, and stifled his emotion.

"A day or two afterward he met the clergyman. 'Reverend and dear Sir,' said he, 'how could you be guilty of such an outrage at my table the other day?'

"'Outrage! my dear Sir? What *can* you mean? Did I show too much heat in my controversy with that latitudinarian I so easily demolished?'

"'I know nothing of your controversy. I did not hear a word of it. It is not that I was speaking of.'

"'What then, my dear Sir? Was I guilty of some solecism in manners, for you know I am country-bred? Did I violate some etiquette?'

[1524] A schoolmaster in Sir Walter Scott's novel *Guy Mannering, or the Astrologer.*

"'D – n etiquette! I beg your pardon, reverend and dear Sir; but I was not thinking of your manners. But I produced a bottle of wine for my cousin, John Quincy Adams, President of the United States, which had been all the way from Madeira to the Cape of Good Hope, from the Cape of Good Hope to Calcutta, from Calcutta to Canton, in the East Indies, from Canton back to Calcutta by the land-route to Egypt, and from Egypt to the United States. It was the best wine I had in my cellar – the best in the country – and more than a half century old. My cousin, John Quincy Adams, President of the United States, pronounced it superb! and you –'

"'Go on, my excellent friend.'

"'Why you, reverend and dear Sir, when it reached you the second time, poured it out like water IN YOUR TUMBLER!'

"'Law!' said the parson, 'is this all? I did not notice the wine particularly; *but not seeing any cider on the table, poured this out instead;* for my argument had made me very thirsty.'"

ANECDOTE.[1525] – "Friend Franklin,"[1526] said Elijah Tate, a celebrated Quaker lawyer of Philadelphia, one day, "thee knows, almost every thing; can thee tell me how I am to preserve my small beer in the back yard? my neighbors are often tapping it of nights." "Put a barrel of old Madeira, by the side of it," replied the Doctor, "let them get but a taste of the Maderia,[1527] and I'll engage they never will trouble thy small beer any more."

[Untitled][1528]

… Accompanying Thayendanegea to the "Moor School" were several other Mohawk youths, and two Delawares had entered the school before him. The name of one of Thayendanegea's companion was William, a half-breed, who was supposed to be the son of his patron. Only two of the number remained to receive the honours of the future college. The others, impacient of the restraints of a school, and delighting more in the chase of game than of literary honours, returned to their hunter state in about two years. Thayendanegea probably left school at the same time. He used, when speaking of the school, to relate with much pleasantry an anecdote of "William," who, as he affirmed, was one day ordered by Mr. Wheelock's son to saddle his horse. The lad refused, alleging that, as he was a gentleman's son, the performance of such a menial office would be out of character. "Do you know," inquired the younger Wheelock, "what a gentleman is?" "I do," replied William: "a gentleman is a person who keeps racehorses and drinks Madeira wine, and that is what neither you nor your father do – therefore, saddle the horse yourself!" …

1525 *Weekly Standard*, November 23, 1864. (Raleigh, NC); *The Barnstable Patriot*, September 11, 1833. (Barnstable, MA). Published under the title "Anecdote of Dr. Franklin", with slight changes, namely referring that the question had been asked by Mayers Fisher and adding another paragraph at the end: «This same great philosopher used often to say too, 'that if parents would but give their sons an early taste for the Medeira [Madeira] of learning, they would hardly ever take to the detestable small beer of vice'.»).

1526 Benjamin Franklin.

1527 The right spelling is Madeira.

1528 STONE, William L., *Border Wars of the American Revolution*, In Two Volumes, Vol. I., Harper & Brothers, Publishers, New York, 1857, pages 28-29.

JOHN JACOB ASTOR.[1529]

... Thus the great merchant recompensed great services. He was not more just in rewarding small ones. On one occasion a ship of his arrived from China, which he found necessary to dispatch at once to Amsterdam, the market in New York being depressed by an over-supply of China merchandise. But on board this ship, under a mountain of tea chests, the owner had two pipes of precious Madeira wine which had been sent on a voyage for the improvement of its constitution.

"Can you get out that wine," asked the owner, "without discharging the tea?"

The captain thought he could.

"Well, then," said Mr. Astor, "you get it out, and I'll give you a demijohn of it. You'll say it's the best wine you ever tasted."

It required the labor of the whole ship's crew for two days to get out those two pipes of wine. They were sent to the house of Mr. Astor. A year passed. The captain had been to Amsterdam and back, but he had received no tidings of his demijohn of Madeira. One day, when Mr. Astor was on board the ship, the captain ventured to remind the great man, in a jocular manner, that he had not received the wine.

"Ah," said Astor, "don't you know the reason? It isn't fine yet. Wait till it is fine, and you'll say you never tasted such Madeira." The captain never heard of that wine again.

These traits show the moral weakness of the man. It is only when we regard his mercantile exploits that we can admire him. He was, unquestionably, one of the ablest, boldest, and most successful operators that ever lived. He seldom made a mistake in the conduct of business. Having formed his plan, he carried it out with a nerve and steadiness, with such a firm and easy grasp of all the details, that he seemed rather to be playing an interesting game than transacting business. "He could command an army of five hundred thousand men!" exclaimed one of his admirers. That was an erroneous remark. He could have commanded an army of five hundred thousand tea chests, with a heavy auxiliary force of otter skins and beaver skins. But a commander of men must be superior morally as well as intellectually. He must be able to win the love and excite the enthusiasm of his followers. Astor would have made a splendid commissary-general to the army of Xerxes,[1530] but he could no more have conquered Greece than Xerxes himself. ...

[Untitled][1531]

"Doctor, said a nervous patient, I had such a disagreeable dream last night. I dreamt that my grandfather stood by my bed for hours shaking his cane at me. "What did you drink before you went to bed? "Oh nothing but half a bottle of Madeira. "Well, if you had drank the other half you would doubtless have also seen your grandmother standing by your bed, threatening you with the broomstick."

1529 "Harper's New Monthly Magazine, Volume XXX., December, 1864, to May, 1865., Harper & Brothers, Publishers, New York, 1865, page 816. See Note 1347.

1530 Reference to the Second Invasion of Greece, that took place on 480-479BC, during the Greco-Persian Wars, when King Xerxes I of Persia sought to conquer all of Greece.

1531 *The Atlanta Constitution*, August 31, 1871. (Atlanta, GA).

[Untitled]¹⁵³²

A physician, calling one day on a gentleman who had been severely afflicted with gout, found, to his surprise, the disease gone, and the gentleman rejoicing in his recovery over a bottle of wine. 'Come along, doctor,' exclaimed the valetudinarian, 'you are just in time to taste this bottle of Madeira. It is the first of a pipe that has just been broached.' 'Ah!' replied the doctor, 'these pipes of Madeira will never do. They are the cause of all your suffering.' 'Well, then,' rejoined the gay incurable, 'fill your glass, for now that we have found out the cause the sooner we get rid of it the better.'

PERSONAL.[1533]

JAY GOULD[1534] thinks he would have carried his Pacific Railroad bill through the Senate had Sam Ward been in Washington. Sam's dinners, and especially that ham boiled in Madeira wine, used to carry the stomachs and votes of Congressmen by storm. – *Augusta Chronicle*.

[Untitled][1535]

… There is an old Boston story of a hard-headed parson who, being lucky enough to own a cellar of good Madeira and frank enough to own that he liked it, once pressed a glass on a brother of the cloth dining with him who was a prominent leader in the temperance movement. The abstainer, a miracle of health and vigor, after several coy refusals, finally observed that, as he was far from well and had been advised by his physician to try a restorative now and then, he thought he would try a single glass, "the first I have tasted for months!" "Brother –," replied the honest old bibber, looking him straight in the eye as he filled the glass – "Brother –, if we like wine let us drink wine, and let us thank God for the chance of getting it, but – let us not lie about it!"

Tom Reid's Wine.[1536]

Last night there arrived in this city by express three boxes of Madeira wine from Tom Reid, Consul at the Madeira Islands,[1537] as a remembrance to his friends here. The boxes

---

1532 *The Adams Sentinel*, November 22, 1831. (Gettysburg, PA); *The Sandusky Clarion*, July 24, 1848. (Sandusky, OH. Published under the title "WITTY APOLOGY"); *The Anderson Intelligencer*, November 19, 1874. (Anderson Court House, SC. Published untitled); *The Orangeburg News*, November 28, 1874. (Orangeburg, SC).
1533 *The National Republican*, May 7, 1878. (Washington, D.C.).
1534 Jason "Jay" Gould (1836-1892), a native of New York, was a leading American railroad develloper and speculator.
1535 *The World*, February 6, 1879. (New York City, NY).
1536 *Oshkosh Daily Northwestern*, March 20, 1879. (Oshkosh, WI). This article was transcribed in another Wisconsin newspaper, under a different title – "WINE FROM TOM REID." – and preceded by the following paragraph: «A number of gentlemen in this city have at various times been promised gifts of Madeira wine from TOM REID, late of the Menasha Press and now U.S. Consul at Madeira. It will doubtless interest them to learn, from the following notice in the Oshkosh Northwestern, that TOM is commencing to redeem a few of his several hundred pledges to Wisconsin friends:» *Wisconsin State Journal*, March 24, 1879. (Madison, WI).
1537 Thomas B. Reid, a native of Wisconsin, was the U.S. Consul at Funchal, Madeira, from 1877 to 1882.

were directed to Geo. W. Burnell, with instructions to distribute the bottles according to the labels on them. The labels were apparently printed especially for the occasion and read:

> MADEIRA WINE.
> COMPLIMENTS OF THOMAS B. REID.
> TO _____
> Oshkosh, Wis.

The blank was filled out with the name of the friend to whom the bottle was consigned. As soon as it got noised around that the wine had been received, there was a general rush of Tom's old friends to Burnell's office, each expecting to find his name on some bottle. Some, of course, were disappointed, as it would be impossible to remember all his old acquaintances, but those who were not disappointed shouldered their bottle and marched off.

JUDGE MILLER'S[1538] MADEIRA STORY.[1539]
An Old Dodge Which a Member of the Supreme Court Broke Up.
[Washington Letter.]

Speaking of wines and dinners, I am reminded of what I shall have to call the "Old Madeira Dodge." There is no reason Philadelphians should know anything about it, for there is no pretense in Philadelphia. The Veneerings do not live there. You must know that the judges of the supreme court are the highest of the high in social life. There are only nine of them. They are in life and get $10,000 a year apiece. They, of course, are invited everywhere – generally in a body, a practice which they hate like a famine. You can easily see the reason. Each has his stock of jokes and stories, his illustrations, his history, his recollections, and his big cases. Each one has told these over and over again, and they individually have heard the same thing from their brothers of the bench for so many years that the things affects them like their thirtieth quail. But this is a Madeira story. I remember hearing Mr. Justice Miller recount his experience with the old Maderia[1540] fiend. He said that one of the first things he noticed in social life in Washington was the existence of a large amount of fine, rich old Maderia[1541] in this city. He would go with his associates to the house of a leading lawyer. Before the dinner would be over the host would say that he had some Maderia he would like to have his friends taste – nothing like it in the country

---

1538 See Note 1307.
1539 *Lancaster Daily Intelligencer*, February 6, 1883. (Lancaster, PA. Published under the title "THAT "OLD MADEIRA." Justice Miller Preferred a Little Bourbon Whisky." adding that it was a Ramedell's Letter to the Press but published without some of the sentences of the first paragraph); *Springfield Republican*, February 11, 1883. (Springfield, MA. Published under the title "JUSTICE MILLER AND THE "OLD MADEIRA" adding that it had originated in a Washington Letter. This text present some slight changes when compared to the one in former source); *The Omaha Daily Bee*, February 26, 1883. (Omaha, NE. Published under the title "Judge Miller on Madeira"); *Marble Rock Weekly*, March 8, 1883. (Marble Rock, IA. Published under the title "Judge Miller's Story."); *The Brooklyn Daily Eagle*, March 11, 1883. (Brooklyn, NY); *The St. Paul Daily Globe*, March 16, 1883. (St. Paul, MN); *New Ulm Review*, March 21, 1883. (New Ulm, MN. Published under the title "Judge Miller's Story"); *Freeport Daily Bulletin*, March 31, 1883. (Freeport, IL. Published under the title "Judge Miller's Story."); *Journal & Republican*, July 26, 1883. (Lowville, NY).
1540 The right spelling is Madeira.
1541 The right spelling is Madeira.

– only a few bottles left, the present a great occasion, and one bottle quite enough to go round. Next the court would dine with a cabinet officer – same old story – gentlemen, let me beg of you to try this old Maderia – nothing like it in the world – an old invoice of my grandfather's – never get a glassful like it in your life, wonderful, gentlemen, wonderful – I beg you to try it. The court goes next to a senator's house. The dinner, gentlemen, has not been worthy the occasion, but I have something that will make you feel glad you came. It is a glass of old Maderia[1542] 400,000 years old.[1543] I'll tell you how I got hold of it. Some years ago I obtained for a young man an appointment in the navy. He felt very grateful, and wanted to know what he would do for me. I told him, just as he was going to sail, to get some good Maderia.[1544] Gentlemen, he was ten years getting this wine. He had to pay $200 a bottle for it, and even at this price was only able to find a few bottles. You'll find it worth drinking, gentlemen. This sort of thing lasted for a year or two. Every house into which the judge went had some celebrated old Madeira. I don't know how it was with the other judges, but Miller, who never pretends to anything, and is noted for his level-headed common sense, and is as great a hater of shams as I ever saw, became very tired of the old Madeira.

Andy Johnson[1545] was president, and O. H. Browning,[1546] of Illinois, was secretary of the interior. Browning was a fussy old fellow with ruffled shirts and dignified manners. He lived very nicely and very quietly on Georgetown heights. He asked the judges to dinner. They came. Good dinner. At the proper time old Browning demanded the attention of his guests. He said that he did not often comment on the things he set before his guests. He thought it vulgar, but he had something so rare that he thought he might be excused. (Then Miller knew that Madeira was coming.) In fact, he wanted to call the attention of his friends to some rare old Madeira he had – smooth as oil and fit for the gods. He had obtained it from some bankrupt king or prince, and there was nothing like it in the world. Gentlemen, said he, let us taste it. As I have said, nobody in the world hates a sham more than Miller, and ne could not stand the Madeira business any longer, so he said: "Now, Browning, look here. We have had too much of this d– Madeira business. We have not been in a house in Washington for the last three years that the finest glass of finest old Madeira in the world has not been set before us, and the thing is getting a little tiresome. Now, Browning, you are from Quincy, Ill., and I am from Keokuk, Iowa. Neither of us know a d– thing about Madeira, and both of us had rather have poor whisky without comment than the finest of Madeira with such fulsome commendation. Put your Madeira aside; let's have a glass of whisky." That little speech was noised abroad, and strange to say it, it very properly stopped hosts from reminding guests what great attention was being shown them, especially as to Madeira.[1547]

1542 The right spelling is Madeira.
1543 This age is clearly exaggerated since Madeira Island has not been inhabited for that long, neither its wines date back to all those years. Maybe the author meant to say 400 years old, which would be the truth, in the 19th century.
1544 The right spelling is Madeira.
1545 See Note 129.
1546 Orville Hickman Browning (1806-1881), a native of Kentucky, and a Republican Senator from Illinois. President Andrew Johnson appointed him Secretary of the Interior, a position he held from 1866 to 1869.
1547 A different version of this text was published in *The Alden Times*, March 2, 1883, (Alden, IA). Published under the title "Fine Old Madeira.": «The Judges of the United States Supreme Court got tired of being invited out to dinner, and hearing all about the "fine old Madeira." So one day when Secretary Browning, of Andrew Johnson's Cabinet, who was giving a dinner, wanted to call the attention of his friends to some rare old Madeira; he had – smooth as oil and fit for the gods – obtained it from some bankrupt King or Prince, and there was nothing like it in the world, Justice Miller

JUICE OF THE GRAPE. ...[1548]

... The Association of epicures known as the Terrapin club are constantly on the lookout for choice Madeira, which they use in cooking their feasts[1549] of diamond backs. Recently a member found five bottles of it at an old wine shop in a cheap quarter of the city. The place had changed hands and the new proprietor was asked what he would take for the liquor. He was getting $1.50 a bottle for his Madeira and he gladly sold the epicure the five bottles at that price. When he discovered that it was some choice old wine, worth at least five dollars a bottle, he tried in vain to a annul the bargain.

A. J. CUMMINGS.

DANIEL WEBSTER[1550] AND A "CUB."[1551]
They Both Drink From the Same Jug.
But It's a Long Time Between Drinks.

New York, Aug. 6. – The celebrated Colton mansion at Paterson, N. J., was burglarized by four young hoodlums, of which Paul Clews was the leader, and the rare old vintages from the wine cellar were carried away. They stole three demijohns, containing in all about fifteen gallons. All were captured, but not without a struggle. Richard Rossiter, secretary of the Colt interests appeared before the recorder and testified that the fifteen gallons of wine were worth $600. The wine was Madeira, of the rare vintage of 1815. Offers of $50 dollars had been refused for it. One of the demijohns had been only partly used. It was served when Daniel Webster last visited the Colt mansion. The great orator was most enthusiastic in his appreciations of it, and praised it so highly that the demijohn was sealed up and ever since remained untouched in honor of the occasion. Daniel Webster took the last glass then, and the next drink was taken by this barefooted hoodlum, Paul Clews. All youths have been held for prosecution.

---

could not stand it any longer and said: "Now, Browning, look here. We've had too much of this Madeira business. We have not been in a house in Washington for the last three years that the finest glass of finest old Madeira in the world has not been set before us. You are from Quincy, Ill., and I am from Keokuk, Iowa. Neither of us know a thing about Madeira, and both of us had rather have poor whisky without comment than the finest of Madeira with such fulsome commendation. Put your Madeira aside and let's have a glass of whisky."»

[1548] *The Syracuse Herald*, November 6, 1887. (Syracuse, NY).

[1549] In the late 1700's and throughout most of the 1800's, one of the favorite dishes of the American cuisine was the terrapin, a turtle living in fresh or brackish water, prepared with good Madeira Wine, hence the epicure's endless search for this precious nectar.

[1550] See Note 72.

[1551] *Mitchell Daily Republican*, August 6, 1888. (Mitchell, SD). A shorter version of this article was published, untitled, in another source: «Four hoodlums ransacked a Paterson, N. J., wine cellar in the historic Colt mansion and drank and wasted fifteen gallons of Madeira, worth $600. It was of the rare vintage of 1815. One demijohn had been sealed in honor of the verdict of Daniel Webster, who had once extolled the wine's exquisite bouquet.» *The San Antonio Daily Light*, August 10, 1888. (San Antonio, TX).

Likely.[1552]
Epoch.

Clara – Poor, dear little Charlie Smith called last night, and although only seventeen, he mustered up enough courage to propose. Then the darling fainted.

Ada – What did you do?

Clara – I brought him back to consciousness by giving him three glasses of papa's old Madeira.

Ada – He probably fainted on purpose to get it.

... "CRISIS" MADEIRA FOR JELLY.[1553]
Quaint Anecdote of Col. Thomas Scott[1554] – ...
CORRESPONDENCE TRIBUNE.

Boston, July 30, 1889.

... A DISGUSTED HOUSEHOLDER.

The most disgusted householder in the modern Athens[1555] just at present is a Beacon street gentleman, whose family in the summer time resides at Nahant – that "slice of cold-roast Boston," as the exclusive watering-place in question has been appropriately called. The other day, upon returning to his seashore villa from his daily avocation in the city, he remarked to his wife with some alarm that, having had occasion to visit his town-house for the purpose of assuring himself that everything was safe, he had sought in vain for six bottles of priceless old Madeira which were stowed away in a small cupboard by themselves, for safekeeping.

"The cupboard in the corner near the bookshelf?" inquired the lady.

"Yes, indeed; that was the place,"

"I'm sorry, my dear," said she, "but the fact is that I used those six bottles to make jelly with just before we came away. It was uncommonly good jelly too, though I regret it very much if I have taken any wine that you desired particularly to keep. But, indeed, there was none other handy?"

"Could you not find some for your jelly that was worth less than $1000 a bottle? asked the husband, with a groan.

"A thousand dollars a bottle! Why, what can you mean?"

"Simply that I cannot replace those six bottles at that or any other price. They were my especial treasure, never intended to be drank, save possibly as events in a lifetime. It was a brag of mine to say that I had that quantity of real old Madeira in my house; now it is gone, and for jelly. Ye gods!"

"It was remarkably good jelly," was all the poor woman could think of saying, by way of apology.

And it is no wonder that the gentleman of Beacon street was distressed. How many bottles of old Madeira do you suppose there are at present in these United States? About 100

1552 *Daily Alta California*, May 5, 1889. (San Francisco, CA).
1553 *The Salt Lake Daily Tribune*, August 4, 1889. (Salt Lake City, UT).
1554 Thomas Alexander Scott (1821-1881), a native of Pennsylvania, was an American businessman, and the 4th President of the Pennsylvania Railroad, the largest world corporation during the 1800's.
1555 Nickname for Boston. This city is also known as the Athens of America.

perhaps, and connoisseurs in wine can tell you who owns pretty nearly every quart of it. Years ago a dreadful bug attacked the vines and exterminated them. The insect was subdued at length, and slips of the same varieties were planted; but alas! the new grape produced a different juice. The Madeira of to-day comes from the same island and the same vegetable, but it is no more like the original than chalk is like cheese. Hence the enormous value possessed by the small remnant of the ancient product. It cannot be said that there is any quotation in the market for it. Simply, it is not for sale. The few bottles of it that still exist are owned by persons in well-to-do circumstances who do not care to sell it at any price.

A generation ago, there was an old gentleman in Philadelphia who had the good fortune to possess half-a-pipe of this precious wine – probably the largest amount owned at that time by any individual living; for even then its value had grown to be fabulous. He figured it up that the supply would last him, if he used one pint at dinner daily, precisely so many years, months and days. So, like a mariner in distress for water, he placed himself on an allowance of that much per diem, never on any account to be exceeded. Life was not worth living, he said, without Madeira at dinner, and when his little stock should come to an end, it was his intention to die with as little delay as possible. And so, curiously enough, he did, within 24 hours of the time when the last small bottle of the "crisis" vintage was wiped out.

The late Thomas Scott, of Pennsylvania railway fame, rose to almost fabulous wealth from a position of the humblest obscurity. It is not surprising that he should have lacked that delicate perceptive faculty, ordinarily acquired through generations of refinement and gentle training, which renders discrimination in questions of taste a matter of instinct. Accordingly, it was with no notion of offending in any manner that he bought it, at a price no one else could afford to pay, the stock of old Madeira which had been the special pride and joy of a distinguished Philadelphian at that time recently deceased. Nor, so far, was Colonel Scott guilty of any breach of the proprieties. But it seems that, having occasion to give a huge ball at his house soon afterward, he thought it would be the swell thing to open the precious nectar from bug-destroyed vines by wholesale on the festive occasion, in order that everyone might have as much of it as he wanted to drink.

It was in the midst of the festivities, while supper was in progress and a crowd of young men in claw-hammer coats was crowding with eager appetite around the tables in the salle-a-manger, struggling for fried oysters and salad, and gulping down the wine as fast as the waiters could supply it in bottles, that Col. Scott, who had remained conversing with two or three other railway magnates in the half-deserted ball-room, saw approaching him a gentleman well known to him as a person of social distinction. The Colonel hastened to address him, saying: "My dear Mr. B., you look warm."

"Sir," exclaimed the new-comer, whose family name is to this day an aristocratic pedigree in itself, "I consider that I have been insulted in your house and I shall leave it at once."

"Insulted in my house?" echoed the Colonel, astonished.

"Grossly insulted, sir," reiterated Mr. B. angrily. "I found a crowd of young men about the supper tables just now, swilling Madeira. I ventured to take a glass and tasted it, sir – tasted it!"

"Well, wasn't it good, asked Colonel Scott, mystified.

"Good!" fairly shouted the angry man. "It was Crisis Madeira, poured out by the gallon for swigging in goblets by a crowd of boobies who don't know the difference between sherry and port. "You are perfectly well aware, Colonel Scott, that I and many other gentlemen here tonight, who possess cultivated tastes instead of vulgar millions, would regard it as the utmost luxury to have a single wine-glass of that Madeira once a month, if he could afford to buy it. But we cannot as you know; and so you take advantage of this opportunity to outrage our feelings by serving it in tubs, as one might say, for a lot of young pigs. Good-night, sir!"

And with this the righteously wroth bon vivant strode out of the room, picked up his hat and coat outside, and left the house with indignation and disgust in his heart for all newly-acquired wealth and gastronomic philistinism.

REMARKABLE WINE-TASTER.[1556]
A Charlestononian Has a Palate for Wines That Can't Be Deceived.

It was at the club, says the N. Y. *Evening Sun.* they had been talking of wine connoisseurs. Old Ante Bellum has heard them out patiently. When they had all finished he raised his hand in his well-known way. This meant that he was going to add his experience to the others, and as usual they gathered around him.

"Well, gentlemen," he said slowly, "those are good stories and do show remarkable ability in detecting various vintages of wine. I once knew a man who possessed the power himself in a most remarkable way. The story I shall tell you occurred in Charleston, way back in the 50's. You know that Charleston was famous then for its Madeiras. There is not much of that wine drunk nowadays, but even then every gourmet prided himself on his collection of fine old Madeira vintages.

"Old Mr. Ashley had not only a fine cellar, but he used to say that he could make no mistake in the matter of vintage, importation, or owner, even.

"Some of the young men determined to test the old gentleman's ability in this direction.

"So one day, when the conversation drifted to this subject, one of the young fellows offered to wager a large sum, $5,000 I think it was, that Mr. Ashley could not sit at the table and pass on as many Madeiras as he could bring up.

"Mr. Ashley promptly accepted the wager, and the test was appointed for the next afternoon at 4 o'clock.

"At that time Ashley walked in and seated himself at a table along which stood eight or ten glasses of Madeira, each from the cellar of a different owner.

"He started at the glass at the left. 'That,' said he, 'is the vintage of '37, and is from the cellar of Mr. Cooper. The next is of the date of '28, and comes from my own collection.'

"And so he passed down the row till only one glass was left.

"The gentleman who had made the bet was perfectly unconcerned, and smiled grimly when old Ashley took up the last glass.

"The old gentleman lifted it to his lips and instead of merely tasting it as he had done with the others, he emptied the glass and put it down with a sigh of regret.

"'That sherry,' he exclaimed, 'is the best yet, and there is none finer. It was imported before we began to take records, I should say about 1795, or thereabouts. It is from the cellar of old Mr. Butler.'

"The gentlemen present gave a roar of laughter at this, and young Lane, who had made

---

[1556] *The Mountain Democrat*, May 30, 1891. (Placerville, El Dorado County, CA); *Indiana Democrat*, August 6, 1891. (Indiana, Indiana Co., PA).

the bet, said, 'Why, Ashley, we sent down to the corner grocery for that, and it cost 50 cents a bottle. You've lost, old man.'

"'Not so fast,' answered Ashley. 'I will double the bet, if you wish, that I am right. Where was it bought?'"

"They got the name of the storekeeper and appointed several gentlemen a committee to look the matter up. The grocer admitted to these gentlemen that he had bought the wine from a sailor, and further inquiry developed the fact that Mr. Butler's cellar had been robbed some time before, the wine was compared with his, and acknowledged by all to be the same.

"Young Lane acknowledged his defeat and paid the bet.

"No more attempts were made to trip the old gentleman up, either."

A silence fell on the group when Ante Bellum finished this story, and was unbroken till some one suggested an adjournment to the cafe to test some new whisky the club had received.

The motion was carried.

Geographical item.[1557]

Teacher – Do any of you know where Madeira is?

Tommy – Yes, I know. There is some in a bottle in pa's desk. – Texas Siftings.

THREE CHRISTMAS STORIES.[1558]
George B. McClellan[1559] Presents Some Reminiscences of Christmas.

… I remember very distinctly a story that my father once told me about an incident of his own boyhood. I had climbed upon his knee one Christmas eve and asked for it. "What is the first Christmas that you remember?" was my question.

"Oh, it is a very long time ago," answered my father. "Your grandfather gave a dinner to his old friend, Daniel Webster.[1560] Although I was scarcely out of dresses, I had been intrusted by the butler with the very responsible function of decanting the Madeira. The manner in which I performed the task was revealed later on, when the great statesman, after sipping his wine in evident dismay, suddenly said, 'McClellan, you were always noted for the excellence of your Madeira, but this is the most extraordinary wine I ever tasted.' I hope the spirit of Don Webster has forgiven me. In my zeal I had mixed the sherry with his best Madeira." …

GLANCES HERE AND THERE.[1561]

1557 *The Bradford Era*, March 24, 1892. (Bradford, M'Kean County, PA); *Logansport Daily Reporter*, April 25, 1892. (Logansport, IN).

1558 *The Salt Lake Tribune*, December 24, 1892. (Salt Lake City, UT); *The Pittsburg Dispatch*, December 25, 1892. (Pittsburg, PA. Published under the titles "THREE CHRISTMAS TALES – ... Spoiling the Wine for Daniel Webster – ..."); *The Evening Capital Journal*, March 7, 1893. (Salem, OR. Published under the title "A Youngster's Mistake."and adding that it had been written by George B. McClellan and published at the *New York Herald*.).

1559 George Brinton McClellan (1826-1885), a native of Philadelphia, was a major general during the American Civil War and the Democratic Party Candidate for President in 1864. He was also the 24th Governor of New Jersey.

1560 See Note 72.

1561 *New York Daily Tribune*, December 18, 1893. (New York City, NY); *The Evening Herald*, December 21, 1893. (Shenandoah, PA. Published on the "OBSERVATIONS" section).

There is one good thing in a hotel in this city, of which the public is not aware (and the writer is going to disclose only half the secret). When the hotel was built, several years ago, the proprietor placed in the cellar a stock of extremely good Madeira wine. The demand for this beverage is extremely light and little attention was paid to this "good thing." It lay in the cellar for a long time, and a man who is fond of good living changed in a whim is glass of sherry before dinner to a glass of Madeira. He was joyfully surprised to discover the merit of the wine; he was astonished to find that the price was only 15 cents a glass. That, he afterward learned, was a mistake on somebody's part. It should originally have been listed on the card at 25 cents, but had gone on year after year, no one taking the trouble or caring enough to make the change. So the lucky discoverer has continued since that day to get an excellent glass of Madeira – better, he thinks, than anywhere else in town – for a moderate price, saying nothing to his friends, except a favored few, about it, for he does not want the patrons of that hotel to "start a run" on the treasure and exhaust it. Meanwhile the head barkeeper, who should know something about wines, must be "winking the other eye." And the hotel – that is what the reader now wants to know about. Well, that is the other half of the secret.

A COFFIN FOR A SIDEBOARD.[1562]
Ghastly Revels in the Cobweb Hall of an Old New York Saloon.
LIKE THE PARIS "CAFÉ OF DEATH."
The Musty Cellar Where "Gnomes" and "Chickens" Make Merry Among the Skeletons and Skulls.

A Score of rollicking, noisy fellows, young and old, gathered about a musty, worm-eaten bier deep down in a mustier old cellar, eating bread and beefsteaks; a coffin for a sideboard, holding foaming flagons and tobies of ale; a great jar of tobacco and dozens of long-stemmed churchwarden pipes; all this walled in with tuns and hogsheads of wine casks and barrels of brandy and whiskey, flasks of rare old cordials, and over all the dust of decades and gleaming skulls peering down from odd places through the dusk, which the flickering candle light only served to make more ghastly.

Figure 97. "In the Club Rooms of the Strangest Club in New York." *Article illustration. Author unknown.*

This is not a scene from degenerate Paris, but an actual scene in old New York. It is one of the monthly meetings of the Gnomes – a drinking club of old Ninth warders, and held in the sub-cellar of a famous-time drinking place at the corner of Fourth and Charles streets.

It is not a new institution – this gathering of sub-surface revelers, with their ghoulish tastes. For upward of fifty years the Ahrens, father and son, have kept a drinking place in the little old Dutch red brick building, and during that time it has been a favorite resort for the politicians and men-about-town of the old Ninth Ward and old Greenwich village. …

1562 *The World*, January 26, 1896. (New York City, NY). Without the illustration, and under the title "A COFFIN FOR A SIDEBOARD", this text was published in these other sources: *The Rockford Republic*, February 29, 1896. (Rockford, IL); *The Narka News*, March 6, 1896. (Narka, Republic Co., KS); *The Broad Ax*, March 14, 1896. (Salt Lake City, UT).

The chief interest in the place, however, lies in the old cobwebby cellar, or rather in the banquet-room of the cellar. This is a little room, not more than fourteen feet square, walled in with barrels and casks grimy with dust and cobwebs. Thick, black webs hang from the weather-stained rafters and where the spiders have failed to string their nots artificial webs have been made of pack thread to which paper-mache spiders as big and as ugly as horned toads cling and wink their glass bead eyes with looks of devilish ferocity. Two bats live in the cellar and occasionally stir up the dust with their skinny wings, and skulls grin everywhere.

One thing that is always pointed out to the visitor is a cask of Madeira wine which it is claimed is forty years old. It is so old, or rather the cask is, that the hoops look as if they were falling off. The cask is never tapped except on the occasion of a marriage or birth in the family, and upon the occasion of the five-year reunions which the old Roosters hold. Another old cask of liquor is Otard Dupuy brandy, which has been in stock since 1860. This is never touched except for medicinal purposes, and upon a physician's prescription.

An enormous coffin, in which is a paper-mache skeleton, and the worm-eaten bier are the principal articles of furniture. The coffin is the sideboard of the club. …

[Untitled][1563]

A host of Daniel Webster[1564] in handing him a glass of Madeira out of a dusty and cobwebbed bottle said that he had made a little calculation that the wine had cost him $2 a glass, counting the interest from the time he bought the wine. Webster reached for the bottle and helped himself to a second glass, saying: "I really must stop that confounded interest."

HAD THE TIME OF HIS LIFE[1565]
Man Spent Days Curled Up Beside a Cask of Old Madeira Wine
Special to The Herald.

PHILADELPHIA, Pa., Oct. 26. – John Slater was found yesterday morning asleep in a room at 221 North Twelfth street. Nobody knows how long he had been there – he doesn't know himself. The man lay curled up beside a cask of old Madeira wine, and the police believe he had been there since last Monday.

He had broken into the house just to get a place to sleep. Joy came into his heart when he saw the cask of wine, and he drank from the spigot. He thinks he awoke some time the next day and again filled himself with wine and repeated the act daily.

Dr. J. D. Albright, who has an office in the house and who owned the wine, found the man and notified the police, who dragged Slater away to a station house cell.

"I had the time of my life," he said to Magistrate Gallagher. "Give me three months. It was worth it." The prisoner was sent to jail for ten days.[1566]

1563 *The Railroad Telegrapher*, March 1, 1900. (St. Louis, MO).
1564 See Note 72.
1565 *Los Angeles Herald*, October 27, 1905. (Los Angeles, CA).
1566 This text also had a shorter and untitled version published in another source: «A Philadelphia tramp crawled into a deserted room for a nap and found in it a cask of Madeira. He drank copiously and slept till the next day. He then

JOHN MARSHALL'S[1567] MADEIRA.[1568]

Associate Justice Story[1569] relates many an anecdote about Chief Justice John Marshall. His favorite one was that while he and Judge Marshall were boarding together in Washington, during their term in the Supreme Court, they had come to the conclusion that Madeira wine was apt to be more of a habit than a necessity with them, so concluded not to take it excepting when it was raining; then it was excusable on the ground that it would either prevent or cure a cold. They stuck to their pledge pretty firmly, though secretly both chafed under it, for in those days a man could take wine without feeling that he was a sinful being, and, indeed, it was customary to have it at meals. Marshall was the first to evidence his impatience with the pledge, as Washington was laboring under a long, dry spell just then.

Figure 98. Chief Justice John Marshall loved to drink Madeira Wine and was once the protagonist of an amusing episode involving it. *Portrait by Henry Inman, 1832.*

"Oh, Story," he said one day, from the depths of his chair, "won't you please go to the window and see if it is raining?"

Story opened the window, screwed his head in all directions, then sadly gave the bulletin: "No rain in sight – not a cloud."

"Umph" said the Chief Justice," "that's in Washington. Well, our jurisdiction extends over a vast territory. It surely must be raining somewhere in it. Say, Story, let's have some Madeira."[1570] – Our Country for July.

---

drank again, and slept until the following day. He kept this up for four days, and then was arrested and sent to jail for ten days. He said it was worth a month. A tramp is notoriously of an optimistic nature.» *Wellsboro Gazette*, November 23, 1905. (Wellsboro, PA).

1567 See Note 88. Later in life John Marshall used to often drink Madeira after his meals, as a guest once noticed when visiting him: «Judge Marshall – A correspondent of the New York Commercial Advertiser, who is at Richmond, thus writes of the venerable Chief Justice of the United States./ "I must tell you something concerning my progress with the bust of Judge Marshall. I have taken two sittings; one more, and I have him immortal. The venerable Chief Justice received me with every expression of kindness. His health is good, and he looks extremely well for one so advanced in years. He is drawing nigh to eighty. Yesterday he bade me come and dine with him. He has no family about him except his domestics. – His wife, he tells me, was taken to a better world, two years ago. […]/ […] He has a fine constitution, and eats with a hearty appetite. When the cloth is removed, he takes two or three glasses of old Madeira wine. He gave me some that he told me was thirty years old./ So you see that cheerfulness and vivacity contribute to longevity. Franklin was so, – Jefferson was so, and so was the elder Adams; – and all lived to a good old age; – and Judge Marshall seems likely to live to be as old as any one of them."» *The Southern Patriot*, June 14, 1834. (Charleston, SC).

1568 *The Frankfort Roundabout*, July 6, 1907. (Frankfort, KY).

1569 See Note 949.

1570 This story was told, in other words, in another U.S. newspaper, namely the *Newark Daily Advocate*, January 16, 1884, (Newark, OH), under the title "Judge Marshall and the Wine", reporting that it had been transcribed from the *Louisville Courier-Journal*: «The following incident is related by Josiah Quincy as having been told him by Justice Story, of that court, the father of the sculptor. It was mentioned in speaking of the rule prevailing in 1826 among the justices of the supreme court in regard to the acceptance of social invitations and the use of wine. Judge Story said of himself and the other members of the supreme court:/ "We judges take no part in Washington society. We dine once a year with the president, and that is all. On other days we take our dinner together and discuss at table the questions which are argued before us. We are great ascetics, and even deny ourselves wine, except in wet weather."/ Here the judge paused as if thinking that the act of mortification he had mentioned placed too severe a tax on human credulity, and presently added:/ "What I say about the wine, sir, gives you our rule; but it does sometimes happen that the chief justice will say to me, when the cloth is removed, 'Brother Story, step to the window and see if it does not look like rain.' And, I tell him that the sun is shining brightly, Judge Marshall will sometimes reply, 'All the better, for our jurisdiction extends over so large a territory that the doctrine of chances makes it certain that it must be raining somewhere.'/ "You know that the chief was brought up upon Federalism and Madeira, and he is not the man to outgrow his early prejudices."»

10. Madeira Wine in America through British Eyes

The British are known for drinking Port since the 17th century, and some scholars state that they acquired a taste for Madeira after the British Army had gone to America to fight the rebels who had seceded from England, during the American Revolutionary War and, upon returning home, the "Red Coats" took with them the habit of drinking Madeira, which they spread in the United Kingdom. Having this in mind we researched several books written by British authors, throughout the 19th century, containing their personal impressions about the United States, in order to find out how they portrayed this special wine.

In this section, in chronological order, are several excerpts of texts written by seventeen authors and published in the United Kingdom, (with a single exception), where they express their views about the Madeira Wine they found in the United States and the ways in which it was kept, consumed, and admired by the American wine bibbers.

10.1. John Davis

In 1803, John Davis published in London a book entitled *Travels of Four Years and a Half in the United States of America; During 1798, 1799, 1800, 1801, and 1802*,[1571] depicting his impressions of America, gathered during his wanderings in this country at the turn of the 19th century. In six chapters of his book he mentions Madeira Wine, which he drank in New York, South Carolina and Virginia. In the latter state, he found in a tavern, for sale, some Madeira that "has been thrice across the ocean".

CHAP. I.

… About this period, my friend the Doctor[1572] relinquished his house, and rented a little medicinal shop of a Major Howe, who was agreeably situated in Cherry-street. As the Major took boarders, I accompanied the Doctor to his house, determined to eat, drink, and be merry over my two hundred dollars. With some of the well-stamped coin I purchased a few dozen of Madeira, and when the noontide heat had abated, I quaffed the delicious liquor with the Major and the Doctor under a tree in the garden.

Major Howe, after carrying arms through the revolutionary war, instead of reposing upon the laurels he had acquired, was compelled to open a boarding-house in New-York, for the maintenance of his wife and children. …[1573]

1571 DAVIS, Thomas, *Travels of Four Years and a Half in the United States of America; During 1798, 1799, 1800, 1801, and 1802. Dedicated by Permission to Thomas Jefferson, Esq., President of the United States.*, R. Edwards, London, 1803.
1572 According to his book he was Doctor De Bow, who was established at Ferry Street, in New York.
1573 DAVIS 1803, pages 21-22.

CHAP. II.
… – A Journey on foot from Charleston to Coosobatchie.

… A dinner of venison, and a pint of Madeira, made me forget I had walked thirty miles; and it being little more than four o'clock, I proceeded forward on my journey. The vapours of a *Spanish* segar promoted cogitation, and I was lamenting the inequality of conditions in the world, when night overtook me.[1574] …

CHAP. III.
MEMOIR OF MY LIFE
IN THE WOODS OF SOUTH CAROLINA.
… – Deer-Hunting – …

… After killing half a dozen deer, we assembled by appointment at some planter's house, whither the mothers, and wives, and daughters of the hunters had got before us in their carriages. A dinner of venison, killed the preceeding hunt, smoked before us; the richest Madeira sparkled in the glass, and we forgot, in our hilarity, there was any another habitation for man but that of the woods. …

CHAP. V.
… – A visit to Long Island – …

… Farmer *Moore*, brother to Bishop Moore,[1575] of New-York, (I love to give their names, and kindred), always entertained me with a hearty welcome. Every one acknowledged his daughter was charming

> *A maiden never bold;*
> *Of spirit so still and quiet, that her motions*
> *Blush'd at itself.*[1576]

Indeed the manners of the whole family were worthy of the Golden Age.

Mr. *Remsen*, who lived with more magnificence on the river-side, opposite *Flushing*,[1577] gave me sumptuous dinners, and Madeira after each repast. His lady was not without elegance; but his two daughters were lovely.[1578] …

CHAP. VIII.
MEMOIR OF MY LIFE

[1574] DAVIS 1803, page 61.
[1575] Right Reverend Benjamin Moore (1748-1816), a native of New York, Bishop of the Protestant Episcopal Church, in that city, who had been consecrated in St. Michael's Church, in Trenton, NJ, on September 11, 1801.
[1576] Quote from Scene VIII of the play "Othello, the Moor of Venice", by William Shakespeare.
[1577] Flushing, founded in 1645, was one of the first Dutch settlements on Long Island.
[1578] DAVIS 1803, page 156.

ON THE BANKS OF THE OCCOQUAN.[1579]

... Art is here pouring fast into the lap of nature the luxuries of exotic refinement. After clambering over mountains, almost inaccessible to human toil, you come to the junction of the *Occoquan* with the noble river of the *Potomac*,[1580] and behold a bridge, whose semi-elliptical arches are scarcely inferior to those of princely *London*. And on the side of this bridge stands a tavern, where every luxury that money can purchase is to be obtained at a first summons; where the richest viands cover the table, and where ice cools the Madeira that has been thrice across the ocean.[1581]...

CHAP. IX.
... – Visit to Mr. George on Long Island – ...

... I did not fail to visit my old friends on *Long Island*. Parson *Vandyke* was afflicted with the jaundice, but his wife was still as notable and narrative as ever. Farmer *Titus* had lost none of his accustomed hospitality; nor was Farmer *Moore* less kind to the stranger within his gates. Mr. *Remsen* continued to regale his guests with Madeira, and his sons were increasing their ideas under the tuition of my literary friend. Nor were the daughters of these worthy people less lovely, or less amiable. Joy be to *Newtown*; Joy to its rosy damsels; and may Heaven preserve their charms from decay![1582] ...

10.2. Henry Bradshaw Fearon

Henry Bradshaw Fearon (c.1770-18 ?), a London surgeon, published at his hometown, in 1818, a book entitled *Sketches of America*,[1583] where he describes a dinner he had with former U.S. President John Adams,[1584] on September 20, 1817, at which Madeira Wine was served.

THIRD REPORT.
... – VISIT TO THE LATE PRESIDENT ADAMS. – ...

Albany, the River Hudson, &c. Sept. 1817.

... On the 20th of September I walked to *Bunker's Hill*: it is about two miles from the centre of Boston. ... In the afternoon of this day, young Mr. Adams came from Quincy to conduct me to his grandfather's (the late President) at that place. ...[1585]

1579 Occoquan River, a tributary of the Potomac River, in Northern Virginia.
1580 Potomac River, a 405-miles long river that flows into the Chesapeake Bay.
1581 DAVIS 1803, page 244.
1582 DAVIS 1803, page 319.
1583 FEARON, Henry Bradshaw, *Sketches of America. A Narrative of a Journey of five thousand miles through The Eastern and Western States of America; contained in eight reports addressed to the Thirty-nine English Families by whom the author was deputed, in June 1817, to ascertain whether any, and what part of the United States would be suitable for their residence. With Remarks on MR. Birkbeck's "Notes" and "Letters".*, Printed for Longman, Hurst, Rees, Orme, and Brown, London, 1818.
1584 See Note 53.
1585 FEARON 1818, page 110.

The ex-president is a handsome old gentleman of eighty-four; – his lady is seventy-six: – she has the reputation of superior talents, and great literary acquirements. I was not perfectly a stranger here, as a few days previous to this I had received the honour of an hospitable reception at their mansion. Upon the present occasion the minister (the day being Sunday) was of the dinner party. As the table of a "*late king*" may be amusing, take the following particulars: – first course, a pudding made of Indian corn, molasses, and butter; – second, veal, bacon, neck of mutton, potatoes, cabbages, carrots, and Indian beans; Madeira wine, of which each drank two glasses. We sat down to dinner at one o'clock; at two, nearly all went a second time to church. …[1586]

10.3. Isaac Candler

In 1824, this Englishman published a book in London and Edinburgh entitled *A Summary View of America; comprising a Description of the Face of the Country, and of Several of the Principal Cities; and Remarks on the Social, Moral and Political Character of the People: being the result of Observations and Enquiries during A Journey in the United States*.[1587] In this book there are two references to Madeira Wine, in two different chapters, namely in Chapter VI, during a description of American dinners, in which the author compares the customs of both sides of the Atlantic concerning them, and in Chapter XXIX, in the allusion to America's lack of wine production.

CHAPTER VI.
DOMESTIC LIFE.

… Dinner takes place at two, or seldom later than three o'clock, and nearly corresponds with ours. Soups are in much use. In Virginia and Carolina, solid joints of meat are less frequently seen, than fowls with ham and greens. Turkies are very common. I cannot say much in praise of their cookery. When I first landed, I fancied that every article on table was inferior to what I had been accustomed to at home; further experience convinced me, that the difference was mainly occasioned by the cookery. The Americans should take a few lessons from the French on this valuable science. They are particularly unskillful in making pastry. The pie is baked in a shallow dish so that it has no syrup. I did not taste a single fruit pie of prime quality. The wines commonly taken, are Claret in summer, and Madeira in winter. Dr. Johnson said that he could abstain from wine, but that when he took it, he liked a copious draught. The Americans are more rational. The decanters are frequently removed with the cloth; if not, seldom above two or three glasses are drank after, as they are not, like the English, in the habit of sitting for an hour or two passing the bottle around; and it is earnestly to be desired that they never may. It is expensive, injurious to health, and deprives us of the company of "the sex whose

---

[1586] FEARON 1818, pages 111-112.
[1587] [CANDLER, Isaac], *A Summary View of America: A Summary View of America; comprising a Description of the Face of the Country, and of Several of the Principal Cities; and Remarks on the Social, Moral and Political Character of the People: being the result of Observations and Enquiries during A Journey in the United States*, By an Englishman, T. Cadell, London; W. Blackwood, Edinburgh, 1824.

presence civilizes ours." They never urge their guests to take more than is agreeable. O! that the Scotch, many of whom in the middle rank of life are prone to jollity, would generally imitate them in this. True politeness seems to dictate, that each should be left to his own free inclination. Though in this particular I approve the Americans, I think they might make their dinners more comfortable than they do. Where is the necessity of eating so rapidly, as to distance an Englishman to a degree quite perplexing? ...[1588]

CHAPTER XXIX.
MANUFACTURES AND COMMERCE.

... It is very remarkable, that a people so active and enterprising as the Americans, should not attempt to cultivate and bring to perfection many of those productions for which they are now indebted to foreign countries. The vine indeed has been tried in Pennsylvania by Germans competent to its proper culture, but without success. But surely many parts of the southern States must be adapted to it both as it respects soil and climate: yet France and Madeira supply the whole country with wine. ...[1589]

10.4. Basil Hall

A Scottish-born officer of the Royal Navy, traveller, and author, Basil Hall (1788-1844) visited the United States in the late 1820's and upon his return to the United Kingdom published a book, in three volumes, entitled *Travels in North America, in the Years 1827 and 1828*,[1590] depicting what he had seen in the New World. In the first one we can see Madeira Wine mentioned as being liberally supplied in a New York reception.

Figure 99. Basil Hall mentions in his travel book the rich old Madeira he saw in a New York reception. *19th century engraving. Author unknown.*

CHAPTER I.

... Be all this, however, as it may, we were greatly flattered by the kindness of our reception at New York; and I only regretted that my abstemious habits did so little justice, in return, to the goodly suppers of oyster-soup, ham, salads, lobsters, ices, and jellies, to say nothing of the champagne, rich old Madeira, fruits, and sweetmeats, and various other good things, which were handed round at all the parties with little intermission, in a style truly hospitable and liberal.[1591] ...

1588 [CANDLER] 1824, pages 79-80.
1589 [CANDLER] 1824, page 443.
1590 HALL, Basil, *Travels in North America, in the Years 1827 and 1828.*, In Three Volumes, Vol. I., Third Edition, Robert Cadell, Edinburgh; Simpkin and Marshall, London, [1830],
1591 HALL [1830], page 17.

10.5. James Boardman

James Boardman, a self-designated "citizen of the world", visited the United States for the first time in May 1829, having departed from Liverpool aboard an American packet. Four years later he published, in London, the book entitled *America, and the Americans*,[1592] with his impressions of this country. In this work there are three references to Madeira Wine, in three different chapters. The first one is made during a description of a meal at The Eagle Hotel, in Buffalo, NY; we find the second one in the description of the festivities of the New Year's Day; and the third one is made during the narrative of a funny episode involving a certain Temperance Society and its quest to deny all brandy whatsoever, even the Madeira used in Church ceremonies until then.

CHAP. IX.

... Nearly one hundred persons of both sexes sat down to meals, most of whom were storekeepers and their assistants.

The females were first shown to their usual station, the upper end of the long table, and then came the eager rush of hungry "business men," summoned from all parts of the village by the great alarm bell fixed on the summit of the building. We invariably noticed, that the American females had delicate appetites, and ate very little, although they permitted their plates to be loaded unmercifully, seldom refusing any thing, however opposite in taste. We often saw half a dozen different meats and vegetables upon the same plate, the chief of which was sent away untouched; and children appeared to be excessively indulged in regard to food, nothing being denied them. The charge for wine at the hotels is extravagant, when it is recollected that the duty is so trifling. The consequence is, very little, if any, is called for. We were charged at Buffalo nine shillings for a bottle of Madeira, although half that sum would have afforded the proprietor of the hotel an ample retail profit.

The charge for board and lodging, in fact, for every thing of the best and in great abundance, except wine, was about five shillings per day each person for transient visitors; ...[1593]

CHAP. XVII.

... If, however, the "business men" of New York have, in their wisdom, abolished some of the usages of the good old times, they have made ample amends by the establishment of a custom at once rational and agreeable, and which, on the western continent, is peculiar to themselves.

This substitute for the jollity of Christmas in the "old country" is the gay observance of New Year's Day, when the ladies hold their annual levees, and receive the congratulatory visits of the other sex. Every house is opened on the occasion; and the tables spread with all the variety which the confectioner and the vineyards of France or Madeira can supply.

1592 [BOARDMAN, James], *America, and the Americans*, By a Citizen of the World, Longman, Rees, Orme, Brown, Green, & Longman, London, 1833.
1593 [BOARDMAN] 1833, pages 156-157.

The visiters, whose female acquaintance are numerous, can afford but a short time to each; and such proceed from house to house in topographical order, an omission of this customary act of politeness without a substantial reason being looked upon as unpardonable neglect. ...[1594]

CHAP. XVIII.

... As all institutions, however valuable, are liable to suffer from the indiscreet zeal of their friends, so the Temperance Societies have not escaped ridicule. Forgetting that it is the abuse, and not the use, which constitutes the crime, some enthusiastic persons have denied themselves even those liquors, which, taken, as all things should be, in moderation, contribute to nourish the body and exhilarate the spirits; in short, to innocent gratification, mental as well as bodily: and we witnessed, in several instances, the tables of these "righteous overmuch" groaning under every eatable luxury, but on which no liquid but that of the crystal fountain was allowed to be seen.

A ridiculous instance of scrupulosity as to the use of ardent spirits occurred a few months previous to our leaving New York. The circumstances are as follows: – As port wine is little drunk by Americans, that people, from custom, have recourse to the wine of Madeira in the ordinance of the Sacrament. Now, the Madeira, being adulterated for the American as for the English market with a considerable portion of brandy, was denounced by the more rigid members of the Temperance fraternity as an abomination, and a substitute was immediately thought upon. Such was opportunely found in the wines of fine France, which are not subjected to any admixture; and an advertisement soon after appeared from an eminently zealous individual, recommending the use of Burgundy, of which some friend had received a good supply. What rendered the matter still more ridiculous, the advertisement was accompanied by a chemical certificate of the total absence of brandy in its composition. The effect of this solemn farce was the immediate re-stocking of the vestry wine bins, and of course the easing of many tender consciences, who had periodically polluted their lips with wine in which there might have been a portion of brandy. ...[1595]

10.6. Thomas Hamilton

In 1833, Thomas Hamilton (1789-1842), a Scottish philosopher and author, published in London the book *Men and Manners in America*,[1596] in which he alludes to Madeira Wine in two chapters of his work, the most important of which is a description of a dinner party, where this noble liquid was served.

1594 [BOARDMAN] 1833, pages 331-332.
1595 [BOARDMAN] 1833, pages 359-361.
1596 [HAMILTON, Thomas], *Men and Manners in America*, In Two Volumes, Vol. I., William Blackwood, Edinburgh; T. Cadell, London, 1833.

CHAPTER III.[1597]
NEW YORK – HUDSON RIVER

... The 25th of November, being the anniversary of the evacuation of the city by the British army, is always a grand gala-day at New York. To perpetuate the memory of this glorious event, there is generally a parade of the militia, some firing of canon and small arms, a procession of the different trades, and the day then terminates as it ought, in profuse patriotic jollification.[1598] But on the present occasion it was determined, in addition to the ordinary cause of rejoicing, to get up a pageant of unusual splendour, in honour of the late Revolution in France. This resolution, I was informed, originated exclusively in the operative class, or *workies*, as they call themselves, in contradistinction to those who live in better houses, eat better dinners, read novels and poetry, and drink old Madeira instead of Yankee rum. The latter and more enviable class, however, having been taught caution by the results of the former French Revolution, were generally disposed to consider the present congratulatory celebration as somewhat premature, but finding it could not be prevented, prudently gave in, and determined to take part in the pageant. ...

CHAPTER V.[1599]
NEW YORK.

... At length the first course is removed, and is succeeded by a whole wilderness of sweets. This, too, passes, for it is impossible, alas! to eat for ever. Then come cheese and the dessert; then the departure of the ladies; and Claret and Madeira for an hour or twain are unquestioned lords of the ascendant.

The latter is almost uniformly excellent. I have never drunk any Madeira in Europe at alle-qualling what I have frequently met in the United States. *Gourmets* attribute this superiority partly to climate, but in a great measure to management. Madeira, in this country, is never kept as with us, in a subterranean vault, where the temperature throughout the year is nearly equal.[1600] It is placed in the attics, where it is exposed to the whole fervour of the summer's heat, and the severity of the winter's cold. The effect on the flavour of the wine is certainly remarkable.

The Claret is generally good, but not better than in England; ...

1597 [HAMILTON], pages 59-60.
1598 "Evacuation Day" was a former celebration of the evacuation of British troops from New York City, on November 25, 1783, after which General George Washington triumphantly led the Continental Army throughout the city. At the present-day this ephemeris is almost forgotten, but was yearly celebrated until World War I.
1599 [HAMILTON] 1833, pages 120-121. As a matter of curiosity we also add what the American writer Asa Green wrote about Madeira Wine in New York, quoting Thomas Hamilton, on page 193 of his book *A glance at New York: Embracing the City Government, Theatres, Hotels, Churches, Mobs, Monopolies, Learned Professions, Newspapers, Rogues, Dandies, Fires and Firemen, Water and Other Liquids, &c. &c.*, A. Greene, New-York, 1837: ".../ Wine in New York is better; and, if we except that compound called Port, is the best liquor in the city. The Madeira is very fine; as even those most grumbling and fastidious of guests – the British journalists – acknowledge. The author of "Men and Manners" ascribes this to the wine being placed "in the attics, where it is exposed to the whole fervor of the summer's heat and severity of the winter's cold," instead of being kept, as in England, "in a subterraneous vault."/ The Claret in New York is also good. So are the Sherry and the Champagne. Of the latter and of Madeira large quantities are drunk. The sound-headed old wine-drinkers prefer the Madeira; the dashing young blades choose Champagne. ..."
1600 Contrary to what this author states, in America it was a tradition to keep Madeira Wine in cellars, and there are not many references to it as being stored in attics, except in the South.

The gentlemen in America pique themselves on their discrimination in wine, in a degree which is not common in England. The ladies have no sooner risen from the table, then the business of winebibbing commences in good earnest. The servants still remain in the apartment, and supply fresh glasses to the guests as the successive bottles make their appearance. To each of these a history is attached, and the vintage, the date of importation, &c., are all duly detailed; then come the criticisms of the company, and as each bottle produced contains wine of a different quality from its predecessor, there is no chance of the topic being exhausted. At length, having made the complete tour of the cellar, proceeding progressively from the commoner wines to those of finest flavour, the party adjourns to the drawing-room, and, after coffee, each guest takes his departure without ceremony of any kind. …

10.7. Sir Charles Augustus Murray

A British author and diplomat, Sir Charles Murray (1806-1895) spent some time in the United States in the 1830's, and even lived among the Pawnee in 1835. Four years later, he published in London and New York, a book in two volumes, entitled *Travels in North America during The Years 1834, 1835, & 1836*,[1601] which achieved some popularity at the time. In both volumes of this work there are some references to Madeira Wine. In the former it is referred as a compound of a famous drink at the time and is also associated with Southern hospitality, besides being used in a 4th of July celebration, whereas, in the latter his remarks about this wine are among the best impressions about Madeira Wine consumed in America written by an English author.[1602]

Figure 100. Sir Charles Augustus Murray wrote some of the most complimentary remarks about the Madeiras he found in Charleston and Philadelphia. *19th century engraving by George Tobel.*

CHAPTER III.
… – Pico Wine. – …

… There is little or no society in Pico,[1603] as it belongs chiefly to proprietors who reside in Fayal,[1604] and who visit their property only at those seasons when their presence is necessary. Wine is the sole produce worth mentioning. The quantity made in

---

[1601] MURRAY, Charles Augustus, *Travels in North America during The Years 1834, 1835, & 1836. Including A Summer Residence With the Pawnee Tribe Of Indians, in the Remote Prairies of the Missouri, and A Visit to Cuba and The Azore Islands.*, In Two Volumes., Richard Bentley, London, 1839.
[1602] While Charles Murray remained in the United States he tried to secure the position of Secretary of the British Legation, but failed this purpose, and upon his return to England he wrote about this affair in a thinly-disguised novel, in three volumes, entitled The Prairie-Bird, published in London, in 1844. In this book there are six references to Madeira Wine. We also add, as a curiosity, that this work achieved some success since it was republished several times both in England and in the United States, having also been translated into German and Polish and published, in several editions, in Germany and Poland, some of which on the 20th century.
[1603] See Note 683.
[1604] See Note 682.

this island, and sold in London as Madera,[1605] is much greater than is generally known, or than the English merchants would be content to acknowledge. On the island it may be very cheaply purchased: it is always mixed with a considerable portion of brandy, and the best that I have tasted is certainly equal to Madera[1606] of second quality. ...[1607]

CHAPTER IV.
... – Mint Julep. – The celebrated Compounder of this Nectar.

... I spent two or three days here[1608] very agreeably, being at once introduced to many members of the best society from all parts of the Union. During the morning we strolled on the shore, bathed, rode, or drove about in light carriages, which the active horses of this country draw at a speed truly surpassing: the evenings were passed in music or dancing; and after the ladies had retired, I joined some of the younger men of the party, in smoking a cigar under the verandah, fanned by the cool night breeze from the sea, and making my first acquaintance with a beverage approaching more nearly to nectar than any that I had ever tasted or imagined. The American reader will at once know how to apply this panegyric; but how shall I attempt to convey to English senses all thy fragrant merits? divine mint julep! This delicious compound (which is sometimes in the southern and western states denominated "hail-storm") is usually made with wine, (madera[1609] or claret,) mingled in a tumbler with a soupçon of French brandy, lime, or lemon, ice pulverized by attrition, and a small portion of sugar, the whole being crowned with a bunch of fresh mint, through which the liquor percolates before it reaches the drinker's lips and "laps him in Elysium." This beverage is supposed to be of southern origin, and the methods of preparing it vary in the different states; some Carolinians will assert that it can only be found in perfection at Charleston; but I believe, that, by common consent, the immortal Willard (who kept the bar of the city hotel in New York for many years) was allowed to be the first master of this art in the known world. ...[1610]

CHAPTER IX.
... – House of Judge Coalter – hospitable Reception by that Gentleman. – ...
– Judge Marshall – his House. – ...

... A wooden bridge is thrown across the river, on the opposite bank on which stands Chatham,[1611] the house of Judge Coalter.[1612] It is beautifully situated on an eminence,

---

[1605] The right spelling is Madeira. On the New York's edition of this book this name is always spelled correctly.
[1606] The right spelling is Madeira.
[1607] MURRAY 1839, Vol. I., page 41.
[1608] At (the) Rockaway (Peninsula), in the New York City borough of Queens, as the author referred previously on his text.
[1609] The right spelling is Madeira.
[1610] MURRAY 1839, Vol. I., pages 67-68.
[1611] Chatham Manor, the Georgian-style home completed in 1771 by William Fitzhugh, on the Rappahannock River in Stafford County, VA, opposite Fredericksburg. This mansion still stands today as the National Park Service Headquarters for the Fredericksburg and Spotsylvania National Military Park.
[1612] John Coalter (1771-1838), a native of Virginia, who was a tutor in the family of Judge St. George Tucker and studied law at the College of William and Mary. After practicing law for a few years, in Staunton, VA, and being

commanding a view of the town, and of the bold sweeping course of the Rapahanoc,[1613] whose wanderings the eye may trace up to Falmouth, a pretty village, where they are made to lend their aid to some extensive flour-mills, established by Mr. Gordon, a Scottish proprietor, and one of the richest (as I am informed) in Virginia.

The first glance at Mr. Coalter's house impressed me with the idea that it was of anti-revolutionary date: the old brown-coloured bricks, the strait green walks in the terraced garden, and the formal grenadier row of stately poplars, all betoken the old dominion. The family not being at home I asked, and obtained, permission to view the river and valley from the garden, which I enjoyed with much pleasure for some time. As I was on the point of retiring the judge returned, and politely interrupted my apologies for intrusion by an invitation to go in and take a glass of Madera.[1614] Agreeably to this hospitable arrangement, I entered a small entrance-hall, floored with polished pine boards; the wainscotting of the parlour attracted my notice, when the Judge informed me, that the house was of the date which I supposed, and had been built by a Mr. Fitzhugh,[1615] well known at the time. …[1616]

His House[1617] is small, and more humble in appearance than those of the average of successful lawyers or merchants. I called three times upon him; there is no bell to the door: once I turned the handle of it, and walked in unannounced; on the other two occasions he had seen me at the door, although he was at the time suffering from some very severe contusions received in the stage while travelling on that road from Fredericsburgh to Richmond, which I have before described. I verily believe there is not a particle of vanity in his composition, unless it be of that venial and hospitable nature which induces him to pride himself on giving to his friends the best glass of Madera[1618] in Virginia. In short, blending, as he does, the simplicity of a child and the plainness of a republican with the learning and ability of a lawyer, the venerable dignity of his appearance would not suffer in comparison with that of the most respected and distinguished-looking peer in the British House of Lords. …[1619]

CHAPTER XIII.
… – Commemoration of the 4th of July. – Pawnee Visiters. – …

… On the 4th of July, the usual commemoration took place, of firing twenty-four guns; after which ceremony we adjourned to an excellent dinner; and madera[1620] and champagne were the order of the day. We had spent an hour or two in the festivities of the table, when

---

Commonwealth's Attorney for some time, he was appointed to the General District court for Staunton in 1809, and two years later was appointed to the Supreme Court of Appeals of Virginia. Around 1821 he moved to Richmond, VA, where he lived until his death.

1613 Rappahannock River, a 195-mile long river in eastern Virginia which traverses the entire northern part of the state, from the Blue Ridge Mountains in the west, across the Piedmont, to the Chesapeake Bay, at the south of the Potomac River.

1614 The right spelling is Madeira.

1615 William Fitzhugh (1741-1809), was an American planter and statesman who served as a delegate to the Continental Congress for Virginia in 1779, and the builder of Chatham Manor, as mentioned before.

1616 MURRAY 1839, Vol. I., pages 153-154.

1617 Judge Marshall's. See Note 88.

1618 The right spelling is Madeira.

1619 MURRAY 1839, Vol. I., pages 159-160.

1620 The right spelling is Madeira.

news was brought in that a hundred and fifty Pawnees had arrived, under the guidance of Mr. Dogherty, one of the principal Indian agents; and, upon an invitation from the officers, twelve or fourteen of their chief warriors came into the mess-room. I had already seen many Indians, but none so wild and unsophisticated as these genuine children of the wilderness. They entered the room with considerable ease and dignity, shook hands with us all, and sat down comfortably to cigars and madera.[1621] I was quite astonished at the tact and self-possession of these Indians, two-thirds of whom had never been in a settlement of white men before, nor had ever seen a fork, or table, or chair in their lives; yet, without asking questions, or appearing to observe what was passing, they caught it with intuitive readiness, and during the whole dinner were not guilty of a single absurdity or breach of decorum. …[1622]

CHAPTER XV.
CHARLESTON – HOSPITALITY OF THE INHABITANTS – … – PHILADELPHIA; ITS SOCIETY AND HOSPITALITY – …

… There is one subject connected with Charleston on which I am afraid to venture, lest I be suspected of being a confirmed *gourmand* – I mean the madera;[1623] which is so soft, so delicate, so fragrant, that one fancies it fit only for the fairy banquet of a Calypso,[1624] or an Armida,[1625] and to be poured forth by Hebe,[1626] and not by the good-humoured, grinning, black Ganymede,[1627] in whose hands, methinks, I now see it before me. …[1628]

From hence I went on to Philadelphia, which has always been my favourite of all the American cities: there is here more quiet and leisure, more symptoms of comfort, than elsewhere. It contained many of my friends, and, in the beauty of its women, it yields to no place that it has yet been my lot to visit. With this I feasted my eye. My ear was entranced by the very sweetest and most powerful harpist whose fingers ever swept the chords. Madera[1629] poured forth for me her thousand choicest vintages, and every culinary temptation, from the rich Pennsylvania butter to the luscious terrapin, wooed my stay. …[1630]

10.8. Frederick Marryat

In 1839, the renowned Royal Navy officer and novelist Frederick Marryat (1792-1848) published in London a book entitled *A Diary in America: with remarks on its*

1621 The right spelling is Madeira.
1622 MURRAY 1839, Vol. I., page 253. We had already presented this excerpt in section 5.2. of this anthology.
1623 The right spelling is Madeira.
1624 A sea nymph in Greek mythology, who lived on the island of Ogygia, where she detained Odysseus for several years, so that she could make him her immortal husband.
1625 A Saracen sorceress created by the Italian poet Torquato Tasso, a character in his epic poem "Gerusalemme liberata", on which she is sent to stop Rinaldo, a soldier in the First Crusade, while he was sleeping. But instead of murdering him, she fell in love with the crusader, attracted by his good looks. Then she creates an enchanted garden where she holds him as a lovesick prisoner.
1626 The goddess of youth in Greek mythology.
1627 A divine hero of Greek mythology whose homeland was Troy, who is described by Homer as the most beautiful of mortals.
1628 MURRAY 1839, Vol. II., pages 281-282.
1629 The right spelling is Madeira.
1630 MURRAY 1839, Vol. II., pages 290-291.

institutions,[1631] where some references to Madeira Wine in the United States can be found. Among other things he states that it was in America that he ever found the best Madeira. It is also interesting to note that he also presents the wine list of the Astor House, a famous New York hotel,[1632] where different Madeiras can be seen, the best ones commending high prices, and also describes how to make mint julep, a drink that could be made using this wine as one of its ingredients, referred to by the previous author.

Figure 101. Frederick Marryat also praised the Madeira Wine he found in America, presenting in his book the wine list of the Astor House, where a wide variety of Madeiras available for sale to the guests of this famous New York hotel could be seen. *19th century engraving. Author unknown.*

CHAPTER IV.
TRAVELLING.

… Claret, and the other French wines, do very well in America, but where the Americans beat us out of the field is in their Madeira, which certainly is of a quality which we cannot procure in England. This is owing to the extreme heat and cold of the climate, which ripens this wine; indeed, I may almost say, that I never tasted good Madeira, until I arrived in the United States. The price of wines, generally speaking, is very high, considering what a trifling duty is paid, but the price of good Madeira is surprising. There are certain brands, which if exposed to public auction, will be certain to fetch from twelve to twenty, and I have been told even forty dollars a bottle. I insert a list of the wines at Astor House, to prove that there is no exaggeration in what I have asserted. Even in this list of a taverm, the reader will find that the best Madeira is as high as twelve dollars a bottle, and the list is curious from the variety it offers.

MADEIRA.

	D.[1633]	C.[1634]
Sea Bird	2	00
Halaway	2	00
Bobby Lennox	2	50
Howard, March and Co's Madeira, imported for the Astor House, F.	2	00
Dunn & Co., imported 1833, E.	2	00
" " O.	2	50
Newton, Gordon, and Murdock's (NGM)	2	50
Phelps, Phelps, and Laurie, vintage 1811, via East Indies	2	50
Yellow Seal, old, bottled, East India	3	00
Vaughan, two voyages to East Indies, vintage 1811, (yellow seal)	3	00

1631 MARRYATT, Frederick, *A diary in America: with remarks on its institutions*, Part Second, In three volumes, Vol. I., London, 1839.
1632 See Note 955.
1633 Dollars.
1634 Cents.

Monterio, 1825, MT.	3	00
Old West India, WI.	3	00
Murdock, Yuille & Woodrope, MYW.	3	00
Nabob	3	00
Brahmim, A.	3	50
Mary Elizabeth, Jr.	3	50
Red Seal, old, bottled, East India	4	00
Monteiro, 6 years in East Indies, Metior.	4	00
Old racked East India Leacock Madeira, EIL, (black seal).	4	00
Boston (Dr. Robbins)	4	00
Davis' Sercial	4	00
Old Calcutta, bottled in Calcutta, 1814, imported 1824	4	50
Rapid, imported 1818.	4	50
Stark's Madeira, bottled in Calcutta, imported 1825.	5	00
Edward Tuckerman, Esq., Boston, Madeira March's Wine – went to East Indies in 1818, bottled 1820, E. I. M.	5	00
Edward Tuckerman, Esq., Scott, Laughnan, Penfold, and Co's., imported 1820, P. M.	5	00
Gov. Phillips, Page, Phelps, and Co's. Sercial, imported 1820.	5	00
Gratz, (yellow seal), 1806.	5	00
Do. (green seal), "	5	00
Do. (black seal), "	5	00
Do. (red seal), bottled 1806	5	00
Robert Oliver's 25 years in bottle.	5	00
Oliver Baltimore, (Oliver's own).	5	00
Wanton, (exceedingly delicate), 30 years in wood, W.	5	00
Sercial, 20 years in bottle, saved from the great conflagration	5	00
John A. Gordon's Madeira, imported into Philadelphia 1798	5	00
Everett, 25 years in bottle.	5	00
Gordon, Duff, Ingliss, Co's. imported by H. G. Otis and Edward Tuckerman, Esqrs., 1811, G.	6	00
Essex, Jr., imported 1819.	6	00
Smith and Huggins, (Dyker's white top,) bottled 1800, in St. Eustatia.	7	00
Wedding Wine	8	00
Gov. Phillips'.	9	00
Gov. Kirby's original bottles, OO.	12	00

But the Americans do not confine themselves to foreign wines or liqueurs; they have every variety at home, in the shape of compounds, such as mint-julep and its varieties; slings in all their varieties; cock-tails, – but I really cannot remember, or if I could, it would occupy too much time to mention the whole battle array against one's brains. I must, however, descant a little upon the mint-julep, as it is, with the thermometer at 100º, one of the most delightful and insinuating potations that ever was invented, and may be drank with equal satisfaction when the thermometer is as low as 70º. There are many varieties such as those of Claret, Madeira, &c.; but the ingredients of the real mint-julep are as follows. I learnt how to make them, and succeeded pretty well. Put into a tumbler about a dozen sprigs of the tender shoots of mint, upon them put a spoonful of white sugar, and equal proportions of peach and common brandy, so as to fill up one-third, or perhaps a little less. Then take rasped or pounded ice, and fill up the tumbler. Epicures rub the lips of the tumbler with a piece of fresh pine-apple, and the tumbler itself is very often incrusted outside with stalactites of ice. As the ice melts, you drink. I once overheard two ladies talking in the next room to me, and one of them said, "Well, if I have a weakness for any one thing, it is for a mint-julep –" a very amiable weakness, and proving her good sense and good taste. They are, in fact, like the American ladies, irresistible.

The Virginians claim the merit of having invented this superb compound, but I must dispute it for my own country, although it has been forgotten of late. ...[1635]

10.9. Archibald Montgomery Maxwell

Archibald Montgomery Maxwell (?-1845) was an English Lieutenant-Colonel of the 36th Regiment, stationed in New Brunswick in the late 1830's, who was involved in the 1838/39 Aroostook War, a non-confrontational conflict between the United States and the United Kingdom over the international boundary between the British North America and the state of Maine, that ended up being solved diplomatically. On August 1840 he got a leave from his Regiment and traveled to the United States, a country he was eager to get to know better, starting his rambles in Yankee territory in Boston. During his stay in America he wrote a few letters to a friend in England. A year later these were gathered and published in a two-volumes' book, entitled *A Run through the United States, During the Autumn of 1840*.[1636] In a letter written on October 6, 1840, at the Union Hotel, in Philadelphia, and included in Volume II of his work, there are some interesting references to old Madeira Wine served at a party held in a mansion

Figure 102. Archibald Montgomery Maxwell briefly mentions in this book the old Madeiras he saw being served at a dinner held at a Philadelphia mansion. *Engraving from the frontispiece of Vol. I. of his work* My Adventures, *published in London, in 1845. Author unknown.*

of that city, although the author's favorite wine was the Château Margaux, a French wine produced in Bordeaux.

LETTER XLVII.

... – PHILADELPHIA – Party at Mr. Cadwallader's – Luxurious Table – ...

... When we arrived at the Union Hotel, we found a pressing note of invitation from our kind friend Mr. Cadwallader; and dressing as speedily as might be, we drove to his mansion, where a party was assembled to meet us, and where our reception was most kind. If his splendid residence, well-appointed household, elegant dinner arrangements, admirably

---

[1635] MARRYATT 1839, pages 112-118.
[1636] MAXWELL, A.[rchibald] M.[ontgomery], *A Run through the United States, During the Autumn of 1840*, In Two Volumes, Henry Colburn, Publisher, London, 1841.

cooked viands, and choice wines may be taken as a sample of the internal economy of an American private gentleman's establishment, I can only say that the New World is not a jot behind the Old. Fifty years' old Madeira, which was absolute nectar – old East India Sherry – Champagne, Mousseaux, and still – sparkling Hock and Hermitage – with delicious Château Margaux were on the table from the commencement of the feast, and within the reach of all the guests, and not paraded round the table at half-hour time, as you and I have sometimes seen it in very pompous places. The first course was excellent; the second superexcellent, consisting of pheasants, quail, partdriges, rail, and teal, dressed in a variety of ways, and followed by souflets, and all sorts of correct things. The whole was would up by a profusion of ices of various kinds. The cloth removed, still older and still more nectar-like Madeira was produced; but the real business of the evening was transacted in glorious Château Margaux, twenty years old. …[1637]

10.10. James Silk Buckingham, Esq.

James Silk Buckingham (1786-1855), a native of Cornwall, author, journalist and traveler, published in 1842 a book, in three volumes, with his impressions of the United States, under the title *The Eastern and Western States of America*.[1638] In Chapter I of Volume II he describes the way of doing business by the merchants of Philadelphia, recurring to very expensive sherry and Madeira Wine, in order to secure orders from their Western peers.

AMERICA,
HISTORICAL – STATISTIC – AND DESCRIPTIVE.
EASTERN AND WESTERN STATES.

CHAP. I.
… – Arts of decoy practised to obtain business – …

… The Americans are not a penurious people, and their passion for money is not avarice. They strive for its possession more eagerly than any other people known, and concentrate all their energies of body and mind towards the one great end of all their efforts, to acquire wealth; but it does not appear to be for the purpose of heaping it up, so much as of scattering it, as fast as it is acquired. It is spent freely, in the purchase of present gratification; and as a large house, fine furniture, and costly dresses for the female portion of the family, seem the first objects of every man's ambition, these are often procured on the speculative probability of being able to pay for them out of profits to be made, rather than out of gains actually *realized*. To accomplish this, a "great stroke of business," as it is called, must be done; and those who keep stores here, to supply the Western merchants as they come from the interior in the spring and fall, employ a set of clerks, who are qualified

---

1637 MAXWELL 1841, Vol. II, pages 231-232.
1638 BUCKINGHAM, Esq., J.[ames] S.[ilk], *The Eastern and Western States of America.*, In Three Volumes, Fisher, Son, & Co., London and Paris, 1842.

for the duty, to visit the hotels, inspect the register or list of arrivals, make the acquaintance of new-comers at the dinner-table, invite them to take wine, and always of the most expensive kind, (10 and 15 dollars a bottle, prices unheard of in Europe being sometimes paid for old sherry and madeira here,) treat them to the theatre, pay all their expenses, and then invite them to the warehouse or store on the next morning, to select the goods they require. In this eagerness to obtain customers, they often give credit to persons of whom they have no knowledge, beyond that acquired in a few hours of such acquaintance as this; and, as might be expected, they are often deceived, and make bad debts that absorb all their profits; when they break up, and "clear out," as the expression is here, "for the Far West," from thence to carry on, upon some new adventurers in business, in other towns, the same practices as those by which they were themselves defrauded and made bankrupt by others. ...[1639]

Figure 103. James Silk Buckingham states in his travel book that expensive Madeira was normally used in Philadelphia while conducting business. *Portrait by Clara S. Lane.*

10.11. John Robert Godley

John Robert Godley (1814-1861), an Irish statesman, traveled extensively over the United States after graduating from Oxford. He gathered his views of this country in a book, published in two volumes, in 1844, under the title *Letters from America*.[1640] In Letter III, written at Saratoga, NY, the author refers to the drinking habits of New Yorkers, in which Madeira wine was always present, although not drunk in large quantities, which was due, in part, to the spread of temperance societies.

Figure 104. John Robert Godley alludes to the drinking habits of New Yorkers and mentions that little wine was drunk, and when they did it, it was Madeira. *19th century photograph. Author unknown.*

LETTER III.

SARATOGA.
HOTELS. – ...

... For the comfort which an Englishman finds in the privacy and solitude of his box in the coffee-room, his muffin and his newspaper, the American cares not. His idea of a luxurious breakfast is the greatest possible variety of eatables, discussed in the shortest possible space of time; and this national taste he certainly has the means here of gratifying to any extent. Wines are dear (I know not why, for the duty is low), and very few

---

1639 BUCKINGHAM 1842, Vol. II, pages 3-4.
1640 GODLEY, John Robert, *Letters from America.*, In Two Volumes, John Murray, London, 1844.

people, comparatively speaking, drink them. Those that do, drink madeira and champagne. Peninsular and German wines are hardly ever called for. I have been much surprised at the small quantity that is drunk at dinner. Very often at a table, at which fifty people are sitting, you see only one or two bottles of wine, and no beer. The Americans have not inherited our taste for malt, and water is the universal beverage. Those who drink, do so after dinner at the bar, where there is a perpetual concoction of every kind of euphonious compound, such as mint julep, sherry-cobler, egg-nog, &c.; on the whole, however, in those hotels which I have seen, the temperance in using spirituous liquors is very remarkable; I am told that it is of recent date, and owing partly to the spread of temperance societies, partly to the pecuniary embarrassment which prevails, and which necessitates economy. ...[1641]

10.12. Lauchlan Bellingham Mackinnon

Lauchlan Bellingham Mackinnon (1815-1877), a Captain of the Royal Navy, published in 1852, in New York, a book containing the impressions of his extensive travels, under the title *Atlantic and Transatlantic: Sketches Afloat and Ashore*.[1642] In Chapter I the author describes, among other topics, the magnificent dinners of New York, in which Madeira Wine was usually served.

TOUR IN AMERICA.

CHAPTER I.
NEW YORK.
... – Dinners and Balls in private Houses – ...

... The grand dinners in private houses are truly magnificent, and are generally supplied by contract. No doubt this system saves trouble and annoyance in the household, but it is extremely expensive. As a general rule, the hospitality of the table is less practiced than in England; none but the wealthy being able to entertain their guests in what is considered the proper style. Moreover, they do not understand the art of making a dinner-party pleasant, chatty, and agreeable. The lady of the house generally goes in after her husband, leaving the company to follow as they best can. This certainly is not as attentive as if the lady came in last, according to English custom. After the cloth is removed, cigars are lighted, and the wine is passed round, as in England.

Nothing can exceed the delicacy of the wine and viands Madeira, of enormous value, that has been ten, twenty, and even fifty years in bottle, is introduced; but this wine, although keenly relished in America, rarely suits the palate of a newly-arrived Britisher. When a dinner-party is given, no pains or expense is spared to make it perfect; and it is no more than justice to the entertainments of New York to assert, that they are superior in wines, viands, lighting, and general splendor, to those either of Paris or London. ...[1643]

1641 GODLEY, 1844, Vol. I, pages 33-34.
1642 MACKINNON, Lauchlan Bellingham, *Atlantic and Transatlantic: Sketches Afloat and Ashore*, Harper & Brothers, Publishers, New York, 1852.
1643 MACKINNON 1852, pages 25-26.

10.13. Alfred Bunn

In 1853, Alfred Bunn (1796-1860), an English theatrical manager, poet and lecturer, published in London a book, in two volumes, entitled *Old England and New England, In a Series of Views Taken on the Spot*,[1644] depicting his views of America, which he had visited for the first time in September of the previous year, spending a few months in this country, where he remained until June 1853. In two chapters of Volume II there are large references to the impressive U.S. relief to Madeira island, of which he was an eye-witness, praising the American philanthropic generosity, and also portraying the way in which Americans saw and cherished Madeira Wine in the United States, not forgetting to allude to its adulteration and other reproachable actions concerning the sale of this product, in an amusing episode.

CHAPTER VI.
… – MADEIRA WRETCHEDNESS AND MADEIRA WINE – EXTRAORDINARY VALUE
OF A GLASS OF IT – …

… If it be true that the first thing a man has to do in this world is to make as much money as he possibly can (and we have certainly pointed out the way by which a vast quantity *has* been made), there can be no doubt that the next thing he should do, is to dispense it properly; and we are bound to say, that in many cases America's sons set a noble example to the world at large. During the early part of our recent visit to the States, advices were received of the probable annihilation of the Island of Madeira, owing to the total failure of her vineyards. Few people require telling that the very existence of this small speck in the ocean, depends upon two things alone – the cultivation of its vines, and the salubrity of its climate, which attracts such numbers of invalids from all quarters of the globe; and if the one should fail, it must, or it is supposed to, arise from some impurity of the atmosphere, which naturally affects the other, and her ruin thereby becomes complete. You might just as well expect a person in his senses to take up his residence in a neighbourhood where cholera or any other fearful epidemic was raging, as to find a consumptive sufferer sailing to Madeira, when the place is eaten up with blight, and contagion is spreading in every direction. It is infinitely better to remain at home in the hope of living, than to go abroad in the certainty of dying; and while it may be that, at the very height of blasting and desolation, Madeira is as healthy as ever, you cannot make people believe so, and the consequences we have reason to apprehend have been most disastrous. In an emergency so dreadful as this, Boston did a noble action well worthy of imitation by New York, or New York did it for Boston to copy, as it may be – (we should be sorry, by any want of respect or preference, to set these two rival cities to loggersheads) – which was to equip a vessel, and freight her, to the extent of her capacity, with every commodity necessary for the salvation of human life.

Clothing and bedding for the naked, food for the hungry, medicine for the sick, and money for the needy, were contributed on all sides; and no ship ever sailed the seas with a

---

[1644] BUNN, Alfred, *Old England and New England, In a Series of Views Taken on the Spot*, In Two Volumes, Vol. II, Richard Bentley, Publisher in Ordinary to Her Majesty, London, 1853.

more laudable object. Actions such as these elevate the moral character of a country, and give it an enviable station in the estimated of the wide world; they depict the proper use of money in its true colours, and establish the desirability of riches. There has, however, rarely been done a good deed, without some detractive motive being ascribed to it, on the principle, perchance, that they who cannot lay claim to the possession of any excellence of nature themselves, are apt to deny its existence in others. The wags, therefore, will tell you that this sublime act was based altogether upon selfishness, and that America would never have dreamed of doing a deed of such seeming magnificence, if it had not been to serve herself. "As how?" the ready will naturally inquire. Madeira wine is the grand beverage of the United States, whenever it can be got – in perfection if possible, but in any condition rather than not at all. An American thinks of his finest Madeira, what an Englishman and a Frenchman think of their port and claret, or what a dweller by the Rhine thinks of his hock; and he will pay a far greater price for it, than all these together will disburse for the beverage they prefer. We had more than one opportunity of tasting, at the table of an American millionaire, white Madeira wine, for which the enormous price of sixteen dollars (£3 6s. 8d. in English currency) per bottle had been given – something very much like 5s. 6d. per glass; and the princely donor remarked that if he knew where it was possible to procure more, he would willingly give the same sum for any quantity of it.

While it is impossible to conceive any liquid of a finer flavour, it is equally so to get rid of the idea that you are swallowing molten gold. Men who have the wealth, and who are in love with the wine, would despatch a steamer at their individual cost, with material enough to keep the whole island in luxury for a year, for the bare prospect of being enabled to poke out some hole or corner there, where any portion of such Madeira as this could be impounded. The philanthropic citizens of America stand, therefore, charged by some of their own kith, with having done a charitable action, the charity of which, like too many others, began at home. We are never inclined to this way of thinking – we prefer looking at the bright side of the question, without inquiring into the cause of its brightness; to feel satisfied with what is good, without seeking to ascertain the cause of its goodness; and if we become happy by the generosity of our fellow-man, not to trouble ourselves much about the motive which led to his generosity. We thought at the time we made these remarks, and we think so now at the moment of making them public, that the timely aid rendered to Madeira in her hour of suffering, by America in her hour of prosperity, is an act worthy of being chronicled in the fairest annals of men and empires. There are two ways of doing a thing, and proceeding upon that of *bis dat qui cito dat*,[1645] the offering of the modern Samaritan was doubly acceptable. In putting upon record, from time to time and from place to place, the various traits of American character that have presented themselves to our observation, we necessarily labour under the impression of having to contend with a double difficulty – the one, of giving dissatisfaction by faint praise, and the other, of incurring displeasure by dealing out censure.

The prejudice (if there be any left) in the mind of a British blockhead would probably object to the bestowal of any praise at all on America, her people, and her institutions; while the vanity of an American is not always to be satisfied, unless everything the stranger beholds in his country is laid out in *couleur de rose*. The one is just as absurd as the other; and say what you will, there is but a steady path to pursue after all – let truth be your motto,

---

1645 Latin expression meaning "he gives twice who gives promptly".

and justice be your guide. Amongst the many excellencies in the system, in the character, in the pursuits, and consequent progress of the American, on which we have thus far had the pleasure of commenting, we cannot trace one which reflects higher honour on him than this spontaneous aid to the sufferers of "his own beloved island of sorrow." ...[1646]

CHAPTER VII.
... – HOW TO CHOOSE AMERICAN WINES, OR RATHER WINES IN AMERICA – ...

... AMERICAN WINES. – There can be no question of there being, as we have previously stated, some splendid wine in the United States; at the same time, it is equally true that it is principally confined in the cellars of private individuals. It would strike an Englishman with astonishment to find those cellars (at least for the preservation of white wines) always arranged at the top of the house, the underground ones being devoted to the reception of red wines, malt liquors, &c.; and the observation of your host saying, he will go *up* into his cellar for a bottle of his best madeira, sounds oddly in the ear of one who always goes *down* into his, for any beverage he may want. While we admit that nothing can be finer than some of the wines we have drank at private tables, it is an undoubted fact that some of the vilest rubbish, called wine, is vended at nearly all the hotels throughout the Union, and that the Americans, as well as the visitors to their country, pay a most exorbitant price for the villainous compounds they imbibe. As respects the price demanded at *tables-d'hôte*, we may observe that you can get Sauterne from 6*s*. to 8*s*. a bottle; claret, from 4*s*. to 12*s*.; port, from 8*s*. to 20*s*.; moselle, from 8*s*. to 10*s*.; hock, from 8*s*. to 16*s*.; burgundy, from 8*s*. to 12*s*.; and champagne, from 8*s*. to 10*s*. (wines, be it understood, to which they do not attach any very great importance); but madeira runs from 6*s*. to 48*s*. a bottle; and sherry, from 6*s*. to 40*s*. per bottle. You may make up your mind to stand 12*s*. for a bottle of "Judge Story's judicial wine," presuming he must be "a good judge" of *that*, if of nothing else; but as you are sipping the legal liquor, it may perhaps turn out to be Monteiros, at 6*s*.; and when you have screwed up your courage to disburse 48*s*. for a bottle of Amory's (be sure it has got the letter M marked on it!) or a similar sum for a magnum bonum of the Old City Hotel, you have no guarantee that you are not imbibing a bottle of common "sercial," or "London particular," forgetting that the said letter can be marked on any bottle.

We were discussing this subject with a highly intelligent friend, who gave us a graphic illustration of our remarks – so good and so true, that we cannot do better than relate the anecdote embodied in his acute description. He was told by the landlord of a very respectable house, in Philadelphia, that the greater portion of wine in his cellar cost him from 75 to 80 cents a gallon (a trifle more than 6*d*. British, per bottle), which wine he supplied at his public table at, from two dollars (about 8*s*. 4*d*.) to three, four and five dollars, according to the wine the gentlemen ordered from the wine list. If they call for pale Sherry, two dollars! Eclipse, three dollars! very old East India Madeira, K. B. C. H. L. X., black seal, thirty-two years in bottle, five dollars! It was, however, all the same wine; but as none of his customers knew the difference, he made up his mind that there was no difference, and he also made no secret of it. "If," said he, "I was only to charge 50 cents a bottle for my wine,

---

1646 BUNN 1853, pages 203-208.

nobody would drink it. Why, it was but yesterday," continued he, "that that gentleman as sot (sat) at the upper *eend* (end) of the table, called for a bottle of madaree (madeira). He drank a glass, and turning to me, for I was jist (just) behind, carving the wild ducks: 'Landlord,' ses he, 'this is damned bad wine.' Well now, he said it so kind o' natural like, that at first I thought he really did know something about it. 'I am very sorry, Sir,' ses I, 'you don't like it; its ginerly (generally) approved on.' 'Well,' ses he, 'I think its damn bad; I can't drink it. What's the price of this wine?' 'T*ew* (two) dollars a bottle,' ses I. 'Oh,' ses he, 'that akeounts (accounts) for it. Landlord, I've been used to drink good wine, and I can't drink bad wine. Send me a bottle of your five dollar wine.' Well, as soon as he said that, I knowed the chap I had to deal with; so I takes away the decanter, and goes to the bar, and puts the very same wine into another decanter, and brings it back again at five dollars a bottle instead of t*ew* (two). 'Now, Sir,' ses I, 'here's some wine,' ses I, 'I rather guess you'll like; Gineral Harrison dined here one day, and he wouldn't drink no other.' Well, he poured out a glass and smelt it; held it up; looked at it mighty knowin'; put it to his lips and smacked 'em. 'Ah!' ses he, 'this is something like wine! This is wine fit for a gentleman to drink!' 'Ah, Sir!' ses I, 'I see you know what good wine is, and it taint no use tryin' to make *you* drink bad wine, nohow.' 'Why no, landlord,' ses he, 'lookin' as knowin' as Julus Seezur (Julius Caesar), I rather guess I git up a l*ee*tle too early for that; so don't you try it on; and whenever I call for wine, send me this.' 'I will Sir,' ses I – ' five dollars instead of t*ew* (two)!'" …[1647]

10.14. Reginald Fowler, Esq.

In 1854, this English author published in London the book *Hither and Thither; or Sketches of Travels on both sides of the Atlantic*.[1648] As a matter of curiosity we add that the first chapter of this work is entirely dedicated to Madeira Island, where its wine is among the variety of topics tackled by him. But the focus of our attention should be directed to Chapter VII, where, when describing his wanderings in mid 19th century New York, he mentions Madeira Wine and also the prevalence of the Temperance movement.

CHAPTER VII.
FROM NEW YORK TO CANADA. – …

… The trains stop frequently for refreshments, which consist chiefly of pastry and other kindred eatables. Amazing cups of tea are swallowed in an almost scalding state. The hotels in this part of the State of New York are chiefly conducted on the temperance principle. The feeling against drinking is general. Active measures are taken to suppress it, and, it appeared to me, with success. The newspapers are full of articles against this vice, and the walls of the hotels covered with highly-coloured prints, professing to show the state of the internal economy of those who drink spirits to any extent – from the mere occasional sipper of a glass, to the confirmed sot. The gradations of inflammatory action were too

---

1647 BUNN 1853, pages 251-255.
1648 FOWLER, Esq., Reginald, *Hither and Thither; or Sketches of Travels on both sides of the Atlantic*, Frederick R. Dalby, London, 1854.

carefully regulated to be strictly true to nature. Where the worst stage was depicted, the eye could scarcely rest on the subject for a moment, so horribly disgusting did it appear! As a warning, these prints, doubtless, do good. At Bagg's Hotel, in Utica (where I dined and slept), about forty people were at table, and not one drank anything but tea and water. Very few afterwards went to the bar to drink, which, in the more Southern States, is the usual practice. Wines are exceedingly dear throughout the Union. No decent Madeira, which is the favourite wine, is anywhere to be had for less than one-and-a-half or two dollars the bottle: other wines are about the same price. There is a Madeira (Governor Kirby's) in the Astor House wine list at fifteen dollars a bottle. I wonder who drinks it. …[1649]

10.15. Thomas Colley Grattan

In the summer of 1839, Thomas Colley Grattan (1792-1864), the Irish-born lawyer and author, was appointed British Consul to the State of Massachusetts, and lived in Boston during the time he held that position. Twenty years later he published a book, in London, entitled *Civilized America*,[1650] in which he strongly criticizes the Boston society. Among his opinions can be also found his impressions of Madeira Wine consumed by the upper classes of that city.

CHAPTER VII.
THE SOCIAL SYSTEM IN NEW ENGLAND
… – Dinners, Clubs, Parties – …

… Taking Boston, for instance, I will give a sketch of the manner in which social intercourse is carried on.

The visiting circle of what is considered in that city "fashionable society," embraces, I should say, at a rough guess, from two hundred to three hundred families; though the *élite*, the *crème*, as I have already intimated is confined to a much smaller number. In this large body, reinforced by numerous stragglers from the country round, by the young men students at Harvard University, officers in the army and navy, and travelling strangers, native and foreign, it may well be supposed that almost all the elements for a good social circle are to be found. And so it is, in fact. Everything essential to the most agreeable society exists among them, with one exception – and that one is the spirit of sociability. It is actually unknown. Entertainments in abundance are given, in every form of dinners, suppers, balls, *soirées*. The whole outward appearance of hospitality is there, but the soul is wanting. There is a strong mixture of ostentation and bad taste in the way they manage those things. The weight of the dinners – the sixteen or twenty elderly men, and the one solitary lady, forming a heavier portion than even the aliments that load the table – is oppressive beyond description. The quantity of wine that is drunk is very great, chiefly, almost entirely indeed, Madeira, but of such exquisite quality that it carries in some degrees its excuse with it. A

1649 FOWLER 1854, pages 185-186.
1650 GRATTAN, Thomas Colley, *Civilized America*, In Two Volumes, Vol. I., Second Edition, Bradbury and Evans, London, 1859.

great variety is produced; and I observed that this favourite wine is generally distinguished by the name of some individual or some event, which has made each particular sort remarkable. These great dinners, with a very few exceptions, were disappointing to me during my earlier sojourn in Boston. Taking but little wine, unable to enter entirely into the spirit of the conversation, disliking mere eating and drinking parties, where there was no mixture of female animation or of youthful vivacity, it required an effort to preserve an appearance of satisfaction at these repasts. There were certainly exceptions. I have dined occasionally – but the occasions were *very* few and far between – with mixed parties of ladies and gentlemen in Boston, which made a delightful contrast to the general rule of entertainment.

There are several friendly associations among the gentlemen, such as "The Agricultural Society," "The Humane Society," which entail on each member the necessity of giving a dinner in his turn to the others, and to which a few strangers are invited. Besides these, there are those minor and more restricted associations before mentioned, called clubs, such as the Wednesday and Friday clubs, being merely meetings of a certain number of acquaintances at each other's houses, on those evenings, to chat, eat supper, and smoke cigars. These latter reunions I could not stand at all. The heavy meal at nine o'clock, the quantity of Madeira, the nuisance of the tobacco smoke, and the accompaniment of spitting on mats laid down for the occasion, were too much for me. I very soon renounced them on one excuse or another; and I sincerely regretted that those favourite forms of social intercourse in Boston were such as I could not become naturalized with, for I found it impossible to improve the several pleasant acquaintanceships I formed at first without falling into the habits of my neighbours. ...[1651]

10.16. Sir William Howard Russell

Figure 105. William Howard Russell drank unique Madeiras at a South Carolina plantation shortly after the beginning of the American Civil War. 19th century photograph c. 1854. Author unknown.

Sir William Howard Russell (1821-1907), the Irish journalist considered to be the first war correspondent in Press History, also visited the United States, in 1861, and wrote extensively about the reality he found in this country in the two volumes' book *My Diary North and South*,[1652] published in London, two years later. In his work can be found his brief encounters with Madeira Wine, in America, on three different occasions. From these, we have selected the most significant one, presented in Volume I, during the author's visit to a South Carolina plantation, that took place on April 22, 1861, just a few days after the beginning of the American Civil War, (whose hostilities had started on April 12, when Confederate forces attacked Fort Sumter, in South Carolina).

1651 GRATTAN 1859, pages 128-130.
1652 RUSSELL, William Howard, *My Diary North and South*, In Two Volumes, Bradbury and Evans, London, 1863.

CHAPTER XVII.
Visit to a plantation; hospitable reception – …

… It was five o'clock before we reached our planter's house – White House Plantation.[1653] My small luggage was carried into my room by an old negro in livery, who took great pains to assure me of my perfect welcome, and who turned out to be a most excellent valet. A low room hung with coloured mezzotints, windows covered with creepers, and an old-fashioned bedstead and quaint chairs, lodged me sumptuously; and after such toilette as was considered necessary by our host for a bachelor's party, we sat down to an excellent dinner, cooked by negroes and served by negroes, and aided by claret mellowed in Carolinian suns, and by Madeira brought down stairs cautiously, as in the days of Horace[1654] and Maecenas,[1655] from the cellar between the attic and the thatched roof.

Our party was increased by a neighbouring planter, and after dinner the conversation returned to the old channel – all the frogs praying for a king – anyhow a prince – to rule over them. Our good host is anxious to get away to Europe, where his wife and children are, and all he fears is being mobbed at New York, where Southerners are exposed to insult, though they may get better in that respect than Black Republicans would down South. Some of our guests talked of the duello, and of famous hands with the pistol in these parts. The conversation had altogether very much the tone which would have probably characterized the talk of a group of Tory Irish gentlemen over their wine some sixty years ago, and very pleasant it was. Not a man – no, not one – will ever join the Union again! "Thank God!" they say, "we are freed from that tyranny at last." And yet Mr. Seward calls it the most beneficent government in the world, which never hurt a human being yet!

But alas! all the good things which the house affords, can be enjoyed but for a brief season. Just as nature has expanded every charm, developed every grace, and clothed the scene with all the beauty of opened flower, of ripening grain, and of mature vegetation, on the wings of the wind the poisoned breath comes borne to the home of the white man, and he must fly before it or perish. The books lie unopened on the shelves, the flower blooms and dies unheeded, and, pity 'tis, 'tis true, the old Madeira garnered 'neath the roof, settles down for a fresh lease of life, and sets about its solitary task of acquiring a finer flavor for the infrequent lips of its banished master and his welcome visitors. This is the story, at least, that we hear on all sides, and such is the tale repeated to us beneath the porch, when the moon while softening enhances the loveliness of the scene, and the rich melody of mocking-birds fills the grove.

Within these hospitable doors Horace might banquet better than he did with Nasidienus,[1656] and drink such wine as can be only found among the descendants of the ancestry who, improvident enough in all else, learnt the wisdom of bottling up choice old Bual and Sercial, ere the demon of oidium had dried up their generous sources for ever. To these must be added

---

[1653] Located at Pee Dee River, Prince George Winyah Parish, Georgetown County, SC, which still exists today and is privately owned.
[1654] Quintus Horatius Flaccus (65BC-8BC), known in the English-speaking world as Horace, was the leading Roman lyric poet during the time of Augustus, the founder of the Roman Empire and its first Emperor. He became a friend of Maecenas and became a spokesman for the new regime.
[1655] Gaius Cilnius Maecenas (70BC-8BC), was an ally, friend and political adviser to Octavian, who later on became the first Emperor of Rome as Caesar Augustus. The name Maecenas became a byword for a wealthy, generous and enlightened patron of the arts.
[1656] Nasidienus, a character in Horace's *Satires* that served Chian wine at an excessively sumptuous dinner party. By then Chien wine was rare and expensive in Rome, and drinking it was considered an extreme luxury.

excellent bread, ingenious varieties of the *galette*, compounded now of rice and now of Indian meal, delicious butter and fruits, all good of their kind. …[1657]

10.17. John Walter

John Walter (1818-1894) arrived in New York on September 21, 1866, from Liverpool, aboard a *Cunard* steamer, for a three months' tour in the United States. When in this country he wrote a few letters, depicting his views about it, which were sent home. In the following year they were gathered in a book, entitled *First Impressions of America*,[1658] which were "printed at the request of some very dear friends, who wished to possess a record of the author's travels." At the end of Letter II he expresses his best impressions of New York and also his astonishment for the expensive prices charged for some beverages, including Madeira Wine, which was among the most exorbitant to be found in that city.

LETTER II.

NEW YORK, Sept. 26, 1866.

… On the whole, my week's sojourn in New York has impressed me very much with the astonishing vigour and energy of the people. There is an *intensity* in the expression of their countenances which I have never observed in those of other people. It is almost impossible to believe that the vast accumulation of wealth and prosperity which you see around you is the growth of little more than half a century. Should they go on improving at the same rate, I am afraid they will beat us in most things by the end of the century. They are becoming every year more cultivated, and are improving in taste and the love of art. Everything at present is enormously dear. It costs less to have a suit of clothes made in London, and sent across the Atlantic, paying an exorbitant duty into the bargain, than to be fitted out by a New York tailor; so at least several of my friends, who have tried it, assure me. Wine is almost a forbidden luxury. Champagne costs about 15s. a bottle; sherry, with any pretensions to quality, from 15s. to 30s.; Madeira, from 20s. to 45s. The wonder is that any one can be found to pay such prices; but a Yankee will have what he wants, if he spends his last shilling in getting it. Fortunes are soon made, and soon spent; and a Yankee speculator has as many lives as a cat. …[1659]

Next, we present a brief excerpt from the text "An Englishman's Reflections on Our Manners", taken from the late 1810's American press,[1660] where can be found the views of a Mr. Hale, an Englishman living in Boston, regarding the profusion of Madeira Wine provided by the American hosts to their guests.

1657 RUSSELL 1863, Vol. I, pages 188-189.
1658 [WALTER, John], *First Impressions of America*, Printed for Private Circulation, London, MDCCCLXVII [1867].
1659 [WALTER 1867], pages 23-24.
1660 *The American*, August 28, 1819. (New York City, NY. Quotes the *Boston Daily Advertiser*); *The Weekly Visitor, and Ladies' Museum*, September 11, 1819. (New York City, NY).

... I saw gentlemen introducing eight or ten different qualities of the same wine, the favorite of your country, the Madeira, all of them most accurately labelled, and the cost of each bottle and its age, as well as its quality, were the subjects of perpetual discussion. I have seen wine introduced and drank freely the cost of which was announced to be 12s. sterling a bottle. This would rather remind us of the earlier and lower ages of the Roman empire – we should fancy ourselves at the tables of Macaenas,[1661] and Lucullus,[1662] and Apicius,[1663] rather than of a republic, yet in its infancy, and boasting to be one of the most enlightened that the world has ever produced. ...

Last but not least we add a newspaper article transcribed from the English press that describes the Americans' Madeira wine taste, in which are present some interesting facts.

DRINKERS OF MADEIRA WINES.[1664]
AMERICANS LIKE THEM THIN, ACID, AND SLIGHTLY LEATHERY.
From the London Daily Telegraph.

The taste of American wine drinkers differs wholly from that of English bons vivants. The Americans like a Madeira which is really potent, but which, when their familiar acquaintance is made with it seems to be somewhat thin, slightly acid, and slightly leathery in taste; while the favorite Madeiras at London tables are full, round wines, which "catch on" so soon as the first glass is swallowed.

Some years ago an American gentleman from Baltimore came to England and called upon a friend to whom he had shown princely hospitality while the latter was traveling in the States, and the recipient of his favors hastened to invite him to dinner at a Pall Mall club renowned for the excellence of its wines. On the morning of the festival he wired to the steward telling him to put two bottles of the very finest Madeira in the club cellars on the table after dinner. The dinner took place, and the American guest had his fair share of the Madeira produced. At the conclusion of the repast, on being pressed for his candid opinion on the vintage, he frankly replied "that it was a very fair specimen of a young wine."

Nettled at this disparaging criticism, the host took the steward severely to task for sending a juvenile vintage to table. "Well, Sir," expostulated the servitor, "I did the best I could; it's seventy years old." No, here was a case in which the age of the wine had, to the thinking of the English consumer, considerably improved its quality; still, had that particular vintage been a hundred years old, it would yet have failed to please the American.

1661 See Note 1655.
1662 See Note 1311.
1663 Marcus Gavius Apicius, was a Roman gourmet and lover of refined luxury, who lived sometime in the 1st century AD, during the reign of Tiberius.
1664 *The New York Times*, July 17, 1892. (New York City, NY).

11. Madeira Wine in American Cuisine

Madeira Wine was widely used in 19th century American gastronomy as one of the main ingredients in the preparation of several dishes and desserts. In order to provide an insight into the flavor of the cuisine of the past, we have selected a few recipes published back then, gathered from either cookbooks or the press. By presenting them, organized by their source and in chronological order, we give the opportunity to present-day readers to try them anew, although some of them might have gone out of fashion.

11.1. Recipes from Cookbooks

11.1.1. Soups

VENISON SOUP.[1665]

TAKE four pounds of freshly killed venison cut off from the bones, and one pound of ham in small slices. Add an onion minced, and black pepper to your taste. Put only as much water as will cover it, and stew it gently for an hour, keeping the pot closely covered. Then skim it well, and pour in a quart of boiling water. Add a head of celery cut into small pieces, and half a dozen blades of mace. Boil it gently two hours and a half. Then put in a quarter of a pound of butter, divided into small pieces and rolled in flour, and half a pint of port or Madeira wine. Let it boil a quarter of an hour longer, and then send it to table with the meat in it.

No. 26. GIBLET SOUP.[1666]

Scald and clean three or four sets of goose or duck giblets; cut the gizzards into four pieces; put the giblets into a pot with one or two pounds of beef, a scrag of mutton, three onions, a large bunch of sweet herbs, a tea-spoonful of white pepper, a table-spoonful of salt, and five pints of water, and simmer the whole until the gizzards are quite tender; then skim the soup, add a quarter of a pint of boiled cream, or two glasses of Madeira; let it boil a few minutes, and serve with the giblets; when in the tureen add a little salt, and a little Cayenne.

1665 LESLIE, [Eliza], *Directions For Cookery, in Its Various Branches*, Eleventh Edition, with Improvements and Supplementary Receipts, Carey & Hart, Philadelphia, 1840, page 28. This book contained several recipes having Madeira Wine as one of its ingredients but we have selected just a few.

1666 BLISS, Mrs., *The Practical Cook Book, containing upwards of One Thousand Receipts; consisting of Directions for Selecting, Preparing and Cooking all kinds of Meats, Fish, Poultry and Game, Soups, Broths, Vegetables, and Salads; also, for making all kinds of Plain and Fancy Breads, Pastries, Puddings, Cakes, Creams, Ices, Jellies, Preserves, Marmalades, Etc., Etc., Etc., Together With Various Miscellaneous Receipts, and Numerous Preparations for Invalids.*, Lippincott, Grambo & Co., Philadelphia, 1850, page 30. This book contained several recipes having Madeira Wine as one of its ingredients but we have selected just a few.

MOCK TURTLE SOUP.[1667] – Boil together a knuckle of veal (cut up) and a set of calves' feet, split. Also the hock of a cold boiled ham. Season it with cayenne pepper; but the ham will render it salt enough. You may add a smoked tongue. Allow, to each pound of meat, a small quart of water. After the meat has come to a boil and been well skimmed, add half a dozen sliced parsnips, three sliced onions, and a head of celery cut small, with a large bunch of sweet marjoram; and two large carrots sliced. Boil all together till the vegetables are nearly dissolved and the meat falls from the bone. Then strain the whole through a cullender, and transfer the liquid to a clean pot. Have ready some fine large sweetbreads that have been soaked in warm water for an hour till all the blood was disgorged; then transferred to boiling water for ten minutes, and then taken out and laid in very cold water. This will blanch them, and all sweetbreads should look white. Take them out; and remove carefully all the pipe or gristle. Cut the sweetbreads in pieces or mouthfuls, and put them into the pot of strained soup. Have ready about two or three dozen (or more) of force-meat balls, made of cold minced veal and ham seasoned with nutmeg and mace, enriched with butter, and mixed with grated lemon-peel, bread-crumbs, chopped marjoram and beaten eggs, to make the whole into smooth balls about the size of a hickory nut. Throw the balls into the soup, and add a fresh lemon, sliced thin, and a pint of Madeira wine. Give it one more boil up; then put it into a tureen and send it to table.

This ought to be a rich soup, and is seldom made except for dinner company.

If the above method is *exactly* followed, there will be found no necessity for taking the trouble and enduring the disgust and tediousness of cleaning and preparing a calf's head for mock turtle soup – a very unpleasant process, which too much resembles the horrors of a dissecting room. And when all is done a calf's head is a very insipid article.

It will be found that the above is superior to any mock turtle. Made of shin beef, with all these ingredients, it is very rich and fine.

Mock Turtle Soup.[1668] – Cut the meat clean from the bones of a fine calf's head. Then boil the bones in a quart of water until the liquor is reduced to a pint; season it with cayenne, nutmeg, and mace; pour into it a pint of Madeira wine, and a little parsley and thyme.

11.1.2. Meats

NECK OF VEAL A-LA-BRAISE.[1669]

LARD the best end with bacon rolled in parsley chopped fine, salt, pepper, and nutmeg;

1667 LESLIE, Eliza, *Mrs. Leslie's New Cookery Book*, T. B. Peterson and Brothers, Philadelphia, [1857], pages 69-70. This book contained several recipes that used Madeira Wine but we have selected just a few.
1668 SHINN, Esq., Isaac, *The Ready Adviser and Family Guide. A New Compilation of Valuable Recipes and Guide to Health; with directions what to do in cases of emergency; comprising over One Thousand Valuable Rules and Recipes Useful to Every Body, and divided into Four Parts. With a Full Index for Each Part.*, Church & Goodman, Chicago, 1866, page 184.
1669 [BARNUM, H. L.], *Family Receipts, or Practical Guide for the Husbandman and Housewife, containing a Great Variety of Valuable Recipes, relating to Agriculture, Gardening, Brewery, Cookery, Dairy, Confectionary, Diseases, Farriery, Ingrafting, and the Various Branches of Rural and Domestic Economy. To which is added a Plain, Concise, Method of Keeping Farmer's Accounts, with Forms of Notes of Hand, Bills, Receipts, &c. &c.*, Lincoln & Co. Printers, Cincinnati, 1831, page 195. This book contained four recipes having Madeira Wine as one of its ingredients but we have selected just two of them.

put it into a tosser, and cover it with water. Put to it the scrag-end, a little lean bacon or ham, an onion, two carrots, two heads of celery, and about a glass of Madeira wine. Stew it quick two hours, or till it is tender, but not too much. Strain off the liquor: mix a little flour and butter in a stew-pan till brown, and lay the veal in this, the upper side to the bottom of the pan. Let it be over the fire till it gets coloured; then lay it into the dish, stir some of the liquor in and boil it up, skim it nicely, and squeeze orange or lemon-juice into it.

BEEF FILLET IN MADEIRA.[1670] Lard a good fillet of beef, the same as for roasting, join the ends together, and place it in this manner in a stewpan, with some onions, carrots, and a *bouquet garni*, some *consomme* and Madeira, cover it with a buttered paper; let it boil for a moment, and afterwards let it boil slowly. Put fire upon the top of your stewpan. When it is done strain the broth through a silk sieve, reduce it, and serve it as a sauce to your meat.

HAM ROASTED WITH MADEIRA.[1671] Take a fine Westphalia or Bayonne ham, pare and trim it of as round a form as possible, take off the end bone, and remove the rind from the knuckle; then lay the ham on a gridiron over the fire, till you can take it up with ease; soak it, if necessary, and put it in a pan, with slices of carrots and onions, thyme, bay-leaf, and coriander; pour a bottle of Madeira upon it, cover it with a clean cloth, and close the pan as tight as possible, and let it remain twenty-four hours; then wrap the ham in very thick paper, fasten it with paste, so that it may be completely enclosed, tie it on a spit, and put it to roast for three hours; then make a small hole in the paper, and pour in, by means of a funnel, the Madeira wine, paste paper over the hole, and let it roast another hour. When done, take off the paper carefully, so that none of the gravy may escape, mix it with some reduced *espagnole*, glaze the ham, and serve it.

PIG, BARBICUED.[1672] Scald, &c., a pig, of about nine or ten weeks old, the same as for roasting; make a stuffing with a few sage-leaves, the liver of the pig, and two anchovies boned, washed, and cut extremely small; put them into a mortar, with some bread-crumbs, a quarter of a pound of butter, a very little cayenne pepper, and half a pint of Madeira wine; beat them to a paste, and sew it up in the pig; lay it at a good distance before a large brisk fire; singe it well; put two bottles of Madeira wine into the driping-pan, and keep basting it all the time it is roasting; when half done, put two French rolls into the dripping pan; and if there is not wine enough in the dripping pan, add more; when the pig is nearly done, take the rolls and sauce, and put them into a saucepan, with an anchovy cut small, a bunch of sweet herbs, and the juice of a lemon; take up the pig, send it to table with an apple in its mouth, and a roll on each side; then strain the sauce over it.

[1670] *The Cook's Own Book: being a complete Culinary Encyclopedia: comprehending all valuable receipts for Cooking Meat, Fish, and Fowl, and composing every kind of Soup, Gravy, Pastry, Preserves, Essences, &c. that have been published or invented During the Last Twenty Years, particularly the very best of those in the Cook's Oracle, Cook's Dictionary, and Other Systems of Domestic Economy, with Numerous Original Receipts, and a complete system of Confectionery, by a Boston Housekeeper,* Boston, New York and Philadelphia, 1832, page 13. This book contains several recipes that used Madeira Wine as an ingredient but we have selected just a few.
[1671] *The Cook's Own Book [...]* 1832, page 93.
[1672] *The Cook's Own Book [...]* 1832, page 144.

Some barbicue a pig of six or seven weeks old, and stick it all over with blanched almonds, and baste it in the same manner with Madeira wine.

TERRAPINS.[1673]

Have ready a pot of boiling water. When it is boiling very hard put in the terrapins, and let them remain in till quite dead. Then take them out, pull off the outer skin and the toe-nails, wash the terrapins in warm water and boil them again, allowing a tea-spoonful of salt to each terrapin. When the flesh becomes quite tender so that you can pinch it off, take them out of the shell, remove the sand-bag, and the gall, which you must be careful not to break, as it will make the terrapin so bitter as to be uneatable. Cut up all the other parts of the inside with the meat, and season it to your taste with black and cayenne pepper, and salt. Put all into a stew-pan with the juice or liquor that it has given out in cutting up, but not any water. To every two terrapins allow a quarter of a pound of butter divided into pieces and rolled in flour, two glasses of Madeira, and the yolks of two eggs. The eggs must be beaten, and not stirred in till a moment before it goes to the table. Keep it closely covered. Stew it gently till every thing is tender, and serve it up hot in a deep dish.

Terrapins, after being boiled by the cook, may be brought to table plain, with all the condiments separate, that the company may dress them according to taste.

For this purpose heaters or chafing-dishes must be provided for each plate.

LARDED SWEET-BREADS.[1674]

PARBOIL three or four of the largest sweet-breads you can get. This should be done as soon as they are brought in, as few things spoil more rapidly if not cooked at once. When half boiled, lay them in cold water. Prepare a force-meat of grated bread, lemon-peel, butter, salt, pepper, and nutmeg mixed with beaten yolk of egg. Cut open the sweet-breads and stuff them with it, fastening them afterwards with a skewer, or tying them round with packthread. Have ready some slips of bacon-fat, and some slips of lemon-peel cut about the thickness of very small straws. Lard the sweet-breads with them in alternate rows of bacon and lemon-peel, drawing them through with a larding-needle. Do it regularly and handsomely. Then put the sweet-breads into a Dutch oven, and bake them brown. Serve them up with veal gravy flavoured with a glass of Madeira, and enriched with beaten yolk of egg stirred in at the last.

TERRAPIN VEAL.[1675] – Take some cold roast veal (the fillet or the loin) and cut it into *very small* mouthfuls. Put into a skillet or stew-pan. Have already a dressing made of six or

---

1673 LESLIE 1840, pages 66-67.
1674 LESLIE 1840, pages 104-105.
1675 LESLIE, [Eliza], *The Lady's Receipt-Book; A Useful Companion for Large or Small Families. Being a Sequel to her Former Work on Domestic Cookery; comprising New and Approved Directions for preparing Soups, Fish, Meats, Vegetables, Poultry, Game, Pies, Puddings, Cakes, Confectionary, Sweetmeats, Jellies, &c., also A List of Dishes for Breakfast, Dinner, and Supper Tables.*, Carey and Hart, Philadelphia, 1847, pages 63-64. This book contained several recipes having Madeira Wine as one of its ingredients but we have selected just a few.

seven hard-boiled eggs minced fine; a small tea-spoonful of made mustard; a salt-spoonful of salt; and the same of cayenne pepper; a large tea-cupful (half a pint) of cream, and two glasses of sherry or Madeira wine. The dressing must be thoroughly mixed. Put it over the veal, and then give the whole a hard stir. Cover it, and let it stew over the fire for ten minutes. Then transfer it to a deep dish, and send it to table hot.

Cold roast duck or fowl may be drest as above. Also venison.

WHITE FRICASSEE.[1676] – Cut a pair of chickens into pieces, as for carving; and wash them through two or three waters. Then lay them in a large pan, sprinkle them slightly with salt, and fill up the pan with boiling water. Cover it, and let the chickens stand for half and hour. Then put them immediately into a stew-pan; adding a few blades of mace, and a few whole pepper-corns, and a handful of celery, split thin and chopped finely; also, a small white onion sliced. Pour on cold milk and water (mixed in equal portions) sufficient to cover the chickens well. Cover the stew-pan, set it over the fire, and let it stew till the chickens are thoroughly done, and quite tender. While the chickens are stewing, prepare, in a smaller sauce-pan, a gravy or sauce made as follows: – Mix two tea-spoonfuls of flour with as much cold water as will make it like a batter, and stir it till quite smooth and free from lumps. Then add to it, gradually, half a pint of boiling milk. Next put in a quarter of a pound of fresh butter, cut into small pieces. Set it over hot coals, and stir it till it comes to a boil, and the butter is well melted and mixed throughout. Then take it off the fire, and, while it is hot, stir in a glass of madeira or sherry, and four table-spoonfuls of rich cream, and some grated nutmeg. Lastly, take the chickens out of the stew-pan, and pour off all the liquor, &c. Return the chicken to the stew-pan, and pour over it, hot, the above-mentioned gravy. Cover the pan closely, and let it stand in a hot place, or in a kettle of boiling water for ten minutes. Then send it to table in a covered dish.

To the taste of many persons, this fricassee will be improved by adding to the chicken, while stewing, some small, thin slices of cold boiled ham.

Rabbits or veal may be fricasseed in the above manner.

MINCED MEAT.[1677]

376. Four pounds of tongue or tender beef; Three pounds of suet; Eight pounds of chopped apples; Three pounds of currants (washed, dried and picked); Three pounds of seeded raisins; Six pounds of white sugar, or brown if preferred; Two pounds of citron cut into small, thin pieces; The grating of one orange; One ounce of cinnamon; A quarter of an ounce of cloves; A quarter of an ounce of mace; A quarter of an ounce of allspice; The grating of four nutmegs; One quart of Madeira wine; One pint of brandy.

[1676] LESLIE 1847, pages 93-94.
[1677] WIDDIFIELD, Hannah, *Widdifield's New Cook Book; or, Practical Receipts for the Housewife. Comprising all the Popular and Approved Methods for Cooking and Preparing All Kinds of Poultry, Omelets, Jellies, Meats, Soups, Pies, Vegetables, Terrapins, Pastries, Pickles, Syrups, Rolls, Preserves, Puddings, Desserts, Sauces, Cakes, Fish, &c.*, T. B. Peterson, Philadelphia, [1856], pages 311-312. This book contained several recipes having Madeira Wine as one of its ingredients but we have selected just a few.

Boil the meat in salted water until tender; when cold, chop it very fine. After removing every particle of membrane from the suet and chopping it fine, mix it through the meat, with salt just sufficient to remove the fresh taste; to this add the apples, after which, the sugar, fruit, spice and other ingredients.

Mix all well together, and cover close. If too dry (before using), the quantity required may be moistened with a little sweet cider.

TRIPE DRESSED AS TERRAPINS.[1678]

464. Scrape and wash three pounds of tripe, which boil in salted water until very tender; when done, cut it into small pieces, and put it in a stew pan with one gill of boiling water; then mix one dessert-spoonful of flour with one three ounces of butter until very smooth, and stir in half at a time, then season with salt, black and red pepper, to taste. After letting it simmer a few minutes, flavor with Madeira wine, and send to table hot.

VENISON STEAKS, No. 2.[1679]

497. Wash two steaks, season with salt, black and red pepper mixed, and fry a light brown on both sides. When done, place them on a dish, and dredge into the pan one dessert-spoonful of browned flour, to which add gradually one cupful of boiling water; stir well, and season to taste. As soon as it comes to a boil, flavor nicely with either sherry of Madeira wine; then pour it over the steaks while hot. Garnish the top of each with currant jelly, and send to table on a well heated dish.

MADEIRA HAM.[1680] – This is a dish only seen at dinner parties. No one can believe, for a moment, that hams really cooked in Madeira wine are served up every week at hotels, particularly at those houses where there is no other superfluity, and where most of the great dishes exist only in the bill of fare. A genuine Madeira ham is cooked as follows: – Take a ham of the very finest sort; should be a Westphalia one. Lay it in hot water, and soak it all day and all night, changing the water several times, and every time washing out the pan. Early in the morning of the second day, put the ham into a large pot of cold water, and boil it slowly during four hours, skimming it well. Then take it out, remove the skin entirely, and put the ham into a clean boiler, with sufficient Madeira wine to cover it well. Boil, or rather stew it, an hour longer, keeping the pot covered except when you remove the lid to turn the ham. When well stewed take it up, drain it, and strain the liquor into a porcelain-lined saucepan, Have ready a sufficiency of powdered white sugar. Cover the ham all over with a thick coating of the sugar, and set it into a hot oven to bake for an hour.

Mix some orange or lemon-juice with the liquor adding plenty of sugar and nutmeg. Give it one boil up over the fire, and serve it up in a tureen, as sauce to the ham.

1678 WIDDIFIELD [1856], pages 364-365.
1679 WIDDIFIELD [1856], pages 393-394.
1680 LESLIE [1857], pages 240-241.

What is left of the ham may be cut next day into small pieces, put into a stew-pan, with the remains of the liquor or sauce poured over it, and stewed for a quarter of an hour or more. Serve it up all together in the same dish. While it is on the fire, add a little butter to the stew.

WELSH RABBIT.[1681] – Cut one pound of cheese into small slips, if soft – if hard, grate it down. Put it into a tin dish, with an ounce of butter, and set the dish over a spirit-lamp, or a gentle fire. Have ready the yolk of an egg, whipped with half a glass of Madeira wine, or as much ale or beer. Stir your cheese, when melted, until thoroughly mixed with the butter; then add gradually the egg and wine. Keep stirring it till it forms a smooth mass. Season with cayenne pepper and grated nutmeg. To be eaten with a thin, hot toast.

11.1.3. Fowls

STEWED WILD DUCKS.[1682] – Having rubbed them slightly with salt, and parboiled them for about twenty minutes with a large carrot (cut to pieces) in each, to take off the sedgy or fishy taste, remove the carrots, cut up the ducks, and put them into a stew-pan with just sufficient water to cover them, and some bits of butter rolled slightly in flour. Cover the pan closely; and let the ducks stew for a quarter of an hour or more. Have ready a mixture in the proportion of a wine-glass of sherry or madeira; the grated yellow rind and the juice of a large lemon or orange, and one large table-spoonful of powdered loaf-sugar. Pour this over the ducks, and let them stew in it about five minutes longer. Then serve them up in a deep dish with the gravy about them. Eat the stewed duck on hot plates with heaters under them.

Cold roast duck that has been under-done is very fine stewed as above. Venison also, and wild geese.

5281. **Salmi of Pheasants.**[1683] – For this dish roast the pheasant only half an hour. When cold, cut it up as if for eating. Put the parings into *sauce à salmi*. If two pheasants are thus prepared, do not use the legs, except for flavouring. Cut each side of the breast into three slices, and fry the same number of slices of bread of equal size; the meat put into a covered stew-pan to prevent it drying. Now prepare the sauce by frying together a small bit of lean ham, four eschalots cut small, some parsley roots, a carrot cut in dice, some thyme, a bay leaf, six cloves, mace, ten grains of allspice. Add either brown sauce or a spoonful of flour, two glasses of Madeira, and a ladleful of veal gravy. Season with salt and pepper, put in the trimmings, and boil all together; skim off all the fat, and, if it taste bitter, add some sugar. Keep the sauce thick enough to cover the meat, over which pour it through a tamis, and warm both together without boiling them. This dish may be made with truffle sauce by adding to the sauce the trimmings of truffles, and by boiling some truffles cut neatly in sauce by themselves. Put the truffles in the middle of the dish when it is served.

1681 SHINN 1866, page 184.
1682 LESLIE 1847, pages 94-95.
1683 WEBSTER 1856, page 905.

WILD DUCK SOUP.[1684] – This is a company soup. If you live where wild ducks are abundant, it will afford an agreeable variety occasionally to make soup of some of them. If you suspect them to be sedgy or fishy, (you can ascertain by the smell when drawing or cleaning them,) parboil each duck, with a carrot put into his body. Then take out the carrot and throw it away. You will find that the unpleasant flavor has left the ducks, and been entirely absorbed by the carrots. To make the soup – cut up the ducks, season the pieces with a little salt and pepper, and lay them in a soup-pot. For a good pot of soup you should have four wild ducks. Add two or three sliced onions, and a table-spoonful of minced sage. Also a quarter of a pound of butter divided into four, and each piece rolled in flour. Pour in water enough to make a rich soup, and let it boil slowly till all the flesh has left the bones, – skim it well. Thicken it with boiled or roasted chestnuts, peeled, and then mashed with a potato beetle. A glass of Madeira or sherry will be found an improvement, stirred in at the last, or the juice and grated peel of a lemon. In taking it up for the tureen, be careful to leave all the bones and bits of meat in the bottom of the pot.

11.1.4. Sauces

WINE (MADEIRA) SAUCE.[1685] Take a tea-spoonful of flour, and a preserved green lemon, cut into dice, mix them with a glass of Madeira wine, and a little *consomme*, add an ounce of butter, some salt and nutmeg; set these on a very hot stove to boil for a quarter of an hour; then take it off, put in a quarter of a pound of butter, set it again on fire, stirring constantly till the butter is melted.

GENERAL SAUCE.[1686] – Chop six shallots or small onions, a clove of garlic, two peach leaves, a few sprigs of lemon-thyme and of sweet basil, and a few bits of fresh orange-peel. Bruise in a mortar a quarter of an ounce of cloves, a quarter of an ounce of mace, and half an ounce of long pepper. Mix two ounces of salt, a jill of vinegar, the juice of two lemons, and a pint of Madeira. Put the whole of these ingredients together in a stone jar, very closely covered. Let it stand all night over embers by the side of the fire. In the morning pour off the liquid quickly and carefully from the lees or settlings, strain it and put it into small bottles, dipping the corks in melted rosin.

This sauce is intended to flavor melted butter or gravy, for every sort of fish and meat.

HASLET SAUCE FOR ROAST PIG[1687]

145. This sauce is made of the feet, tongue, liver, and heart of the pig.

Scald the tongue, and take off the skin. Clean the feet, liver, and heart; put them in a sauce-pan, with a pint of water, and, and a little salt. Let them boil until they are tender; then take them up, chop them very fine, and return them to the sauce-pan, with the water

---

1684 LESLIE [1857], pages 66-67.
1685 *The Cook's Own Book [...]* 1832, page 245.
1686 LESLIE 1840, page 173.
1687 WIDDIFIELD [1856], pages 133-134.

they were boiled in. Pare and mince one onion, a little sweet marjoram and parsley, and add to it. Place the sauce-pan over the fire. Mix one tea-spoonful of flour into one ounce of butter, and stir it into the sauce, then season with cayenne pepper and salt, if more is necessary. Boil all well together. Before it is removed from the fire, add one gill of madeira wine. Serve hot.

This sauce requires to be very highly seasoned.

WINE SAUCE.[1688]

154. Two ounces of butter; Two teaspoonsful of flour; Half a pint of boiling water; One gill of Madeira wine; A quarter of a pound sugar; Half a grated nutmeg.

Mix the flour and butter together, pour in the boiling water, let it boil a few minutes; then add the sugar and wine. Just before going to table add the nutmeg. Serve hot.

Madeira.[1689] – Mix cold in a saucepan two ounces of butter with a tablespoonful of flour, set on the fire and stir till it turns rather brown; when add nearly a pint of gravy, stir till it is becoming thick; then add half a pint of Madeira wine, little by little, stirring the while, give one boil only, salt to taste, and then strain and use.

Soubise.[1690] – Put about half a pint of good meat gravy in a saucepan; set it on the fire, and when boiling add half a gill of Madeira wine; when well mixed, add also two or three tablespoonfuls of *purée* of white onions, salt, and pepper; boil five minutes, stirring now and then, and it is made.

MADEIRA SAUCE.[1691] – Two cups of white sugar, three-quarters of a cup of butter; beat to a cream, and add by the teaspoonful, a cup of Madeira wine. Mix well, place the bowl containing the mixture in a vessel of boiling water, and stir to a cream. Serve hot.

1688 WIDDIFIELD [1856], page 138.
1689 BLOT, Pierre, *Hand-Book of Practical Cookery, for Ladies and Professional Cooks. Containing The Whole Science and Art of Preparing Human Food.*, D. Appleton and Company, New York, 1867, page 105. Pierre Blot was a Professor of Gastronomy and the Founder of the New York Cooking Academy. This book contained several recipes having Madeira Wine as one of its ingredients but we have selected just a few.
1690 BLOT 1867, page 109.
1691 FROST, S.[arah] Annie, *The Godey's Lady's Book Recipes and Household Hints., Carefully Selected and Arranged*, Evans, Stoddart & Co., Philadelphia, 1870, page 59. This book contained several recipes having Madeira Wine as one of its ingredients but we have selected just two of them.

11.1.5. Preserves

STRAWBERRIES IN WINE.[1692]

248. Stem the finest and largest strawberries; put them into wide-mouthed pint bottles. Put into each bottle four large table-spoonsful of pulverized loaf sugar; fill up the bottles with Madeira or Sherry wine. Cork them closely, and keep them in a cool place.

11.1.6. Desserts

STRAWBERRY TART.[1693] Pick, and put into a basin two quarts of the best scarlet strawberries, then add to them half a pint of cold thick clarified sugar, and half a pint of Madeira, with the juice of two or three lemons; mix these well together, without breaking the strawberries, and put them into a puff paste, previously baked; be careful to keep them very cool.

FAMILY MINCE PIES.[1694]

Boil three pounds of lean beef till tender and when cold chop it fine. Chop three pounds of clear beef suet and mix the meat, sprinkling in a table-spoonful of salt.

Pare, core and chop fine six pounds of good apples; stone four pounds of raisins and chop them; wash and dry two pounds of currants; and mix them all well with the meat. Season with powdered cinnamon one spoonful, a powdered nutmeg, a little mace and a few cloves pounded and one pound of brown sugar – add a quart of Madeira wine and half a pound of citron cut into small bits. This mixture, put down in a stone jar and closely covered will keep several weeks. It makes a rich pie for Thanksgiving and Christmas.

WINE WHEY.[1695] – Boil a pint of milk; and when it rises to the top of the sauce-pan, pour in a large glass of sherry or Madeira. It will be the better for adding a glass of currant wine also. Let it again boil up, and then take the sauce-pan off the fire, and set it aside to stand for a few minutes, but do not stir it. Then remove the curd, (if it has completely formed,) and pour the clear whey into a bowl and sweeten it.

When wine is considered too heating, the whey may be made by turning the milk with lemon juice.

1692 WIDDIFIELD [1856], page 210.
1693 *The Cook's Own Book [...]* 1832, page 216.
1694 HALE, S.[arah] J.[osepha], *The Good Housekeeper, or The Way to Live Well and To Be Well While We Live. Containing Directions for Choosing and Preparing Food, in regard to Health, Economy and Taste.*, Weeks, Jordan and Company, Boston, 1839, page 73. This book contained two recipes having Madeira Wine as one of its ingredients but we have selected just this one.
1695 LESLIE 1840, page 415.

Trifle.[1696] – Place several alternate layers of Savoy biscuit and bitter almond macaroons in a handsome glass bowl, or dish, and saturate them with the best Madeira wine; cover the surface of the top layer with any kind of jelly, jam, or marmalade (red currant jelly is generally preferred); then take the whites of four eggs, half a pound of pulverized loaf sugar, the juice of one sound lemon, a little rose-water, and one pint of cream; whisk all to a froth, and put lightly into the bowl, in the shape of a cone; and ornament according to fancy, with coloured sugars.

SPANISH BLANC-MANGE.[1697] – Weigh half a pound of broken-up loaf-sugar of the best quality. On one of the pieces rub off the yellow rind of a large lemon. Then powder all the sugar, and mix with it a pint of rich cream, the juice of the lemon, and half a pint (not less) of madeira or sherry. Stir the mixture very hard, till all the articles are thoroughly amalgamated. Then stir in, gradually, a second pint of cream.

Put into a small sauce-pan an ounce of the best isinglass, with one jill (or two common-sized wine-glass-fulls) of cold water. Set the pan over hot coals, and boil it till the isinglass is completely dissolved, and not the smallest lump remaining. Frequently, while boiling, stir it down to the bottom; taking care not to let it scorch. When the melted isinglass has become lukewarm, stir it, gradually, into the mixture of other ingredients; and then give the whole a hard stirring. Have ready two or three white-ware moulds, that have just been dipped and rinsed in cold water. Fill them with the mixture, and set them immediately on ice, and in about two hours (or perhaps more) the blanc-mange will be congealed. Do not remove it from the ice till *perfectly* firm. Dip the moulds for a moment in lukewarm water; then turn out the cream on glass dishes.

This will be found a delicious article for a dessert, or an evening party, provided the receipt is exactly followed. We highly recommend it, and know that if fairly tried, precisely according to the above directions, there can be no failure. It is superior to any of the usual preparations of blanc-mange. The wine (which must be of excellent quality) gives it a delicate beautiful colour, and a fine flavour.

GENEVA CAKES.[1698]

Beat, to a cream, half a pound of butter and half a pound of white sugar; then add four well beaten eggs, a glass of Madeira, and a little salt; beat well, then stir in lightly half a pound of sifted flour; pour it into buttered tins to the depth of a quarter of an inch, and bake to a light brown; when done, sift sugar over it, cut it into smaller cakes of fanciful forms, put drops of jelly on each, a ring of icing around the jelly, and serve.

1696 PARKINSON, [Eleanor], *The Complete Confectioner, Pastry-Cook, and Baker. Plain and Practical Directions for Making Confectionary and Pastry, and for Baking; With Upwards of Five Hundred Receipts; consisting of Directions for Making all Sorts of Preserves, Sugar-Boiling, Comfits, Lozenges, Ornamental Cakes, Ices, Liqueurs, Waters, Gum-Paste Ornaments, Syrups, Jellies, Marmalades, Compotes, Bread-Baking, Artificial Yeasts, Fancy Biscuits, Cakes, Rolls, Muffins, Tarts, Pies, &c. &c.*, Lea and Blanchard, Philadelphia, 1844, page 118.
1697 LESLIE 1847, pages 147-148.
1698 BLISS 1850, page 175.

WINE CAKE.[1699]

Rub one pound of butter into two and a half pounds of sifted flour; add eight eggs without beating, half a pint of yeast, and three quarters of a pint of Madeira wine; mix this, and let it stand until perfectly light; then add one pound of stoned raisins soaked in one glass of brandy, one glass of rose-water, one pound and a half of fine white sugar, one quarter of an ounce of mace, and one tea-spoonful of cinnamon; mix it well, put the mixture into deep baking-pans buttered, let it rise again, and then bake it.

STRAWBERRY ICE CREAM WITH EGGS.[1700]

Into the yolks of twelve eggs, mix gradually one and a half quarts of milk; stir it over the fire until it adheres to the spoon, then pass it through a sieve, and add to it the juice of two pounds of fresh ripe strawberries, in which is dissolved a pound and a half of fine white sugar; stir in three glasses of Madeira, mix well, and freeze as directed for Apricot Ice Cream; when half frozen, add a pint of whipped cream, and a little prepared cochineal to give it a color.

CHARLOTTE RUSSE.[1701] – Split, cut up, and boil a large vanilla bean in half a pint of rich milk, till it is highly flavored, and reduced to one-half. Then strain out the vanilla through a strainer so fine as to avoid all the seeds. Mix the strained milk with half a pint of rich cream. Beat five eggs till very smooth and thick. Strain them, and add them gradually to the cream when it is entirely cold, to make a rich custard. Set this custard over the fire (stirring it all the time) till it simmers; but take it off before it comes to a boil, or it will curdle. Set it on ice. Have ready in another sauce-pan an ounce of the best Russia isinglass, boiled in half a pint of water, till it is all dissolved into a thick jelly. When both are cold, (but not hard) mix the custard and the isinglass together, and add four table-spoonfuls of powdered loaf sugar. Then take a large lump of loaf sugar, and rub off on it the yellow rind of two large lemons. Scrape off the lemon grate with a tea-spoon, and add it to the mixture, with the lump of sugar powdered and crushed fine. Mix together the strained juice of the lemons, and two glasses of madeira; dissolve in them the lemon-flavored sugar, and mix it with a pint of rich cream that has been whipped with a whisk to a strong froth. Add the whipped cream gradually to the custard, stirring very hard at the time, and also after the whole is mixed. Then set it on ice.

Cover the bottom of a flat oval dish with a slice of almond sponge cake, cut to fit. Prepare a sufficient number of oblong slices of the cake, (all of the same size and shape) to go all round; with one extra slice, in case they should not quite hold out. Dip every one in a plate of beaten white of egg to make them adhere. Stand each of them up on one end, round the large oval slice that lies at the bottom. Make them follow each other evenly and neatly, (every one lapping a little way over its predecessor) till you have a handsome wall

---

1699 BLISS 1850, page 198.
1700 BLISS 1850, page 215.
1701 LESLIE [1857], pages 507-509.

of slices, cemented all round by the white of egg. Fill it quite full with the custard mixture. Cover the top with another oval slice of cake, cemented with a little white of egg to the upper edge of the wall. Make a nice icing in the usual way, of powdered sugar beaten into frothed white of egg, and flavored with lemon, orange, or rose. Spread this icing thickly and smoothly over the cake that covers the top of the charlotte, and ornament it with a handsome pattern of sugar flowers. There is no charlotte russe superior to this.

PLUM CAKE.[1702] – In making very fine plum cake first prepare the fruit and spice, and sift the flour (which must be the very best superfine,) into a large flat dish, and dry it before the fire. Use none but the very best fresh butter; if of inferior quality, the butter will taste through every thing, and spoil the cake. In fact, all the ingredients should be excellent, and liberally allowed. Take the best bloom or muscatel raisins, seeded and cut in half. Pick and wash the currants or plums through two waters, and dry them well. Powder the spice, and let it infuse over night in the wine and brandy. Cut the citron into slips, mix it with the raisins and currants, and dredge all the fruit very thickly, on both sides, with flour. This will prevent its sinking or clodding in the cake, while baking. Eggs should always be beaten till the frothing is over, and till they become thick and smooth, as thick as a good boiled custard, and quite smooth on the surface. If you can obtain hickory-rods as egg-beaters, there is nothing so good; but if you cannot get *them*, use the common egg-beaters, of thin fine wire. For stirring butter and sugar you should have a spaddle, which resembles a short mush-stick flattened at one end. Stir the butter and sugar in a deep earthen pan, and continue till it is light, thick, and creamy. Beat eggs always in a broad shallow earthen pan, and with a short quick stroke, keeping your right elbow close to your side, and moving only your wrist. In this way you may beat for an hour without fatigue. But to stir butter and sugar is the hardest part of cake making. Have this done by a roan servant. His strength will accomplish it in a short time – also let him give the final stirring to the cake. If the ingredients are prepared as far as practicable on the preceding day, the cake may be in the oven by ten or eleven o'clock in the forenoon.

For a large plum cake allow one pound, (or a quart) of sifted flour; one pound of fresh butter cut up in a pound of powdered loaf sugar, in a deep pan; twelve eggs; two pounds of bloom raisins; two pounds of Zante currants; half a pound of citron, either cut into slips or chopped small; a table-spoonful of powdered mace and cinnamon, mixed; two grated nutmegs; a large wine-glass of madeira (or more), a wine-glass of French brandy, mixed together, and the spice steeped in it.

First stir the butter and sugar to a light cream, and add to them the spice and liquor. Then beat the eggs in a shallow pan till very thick and smooth, breaking them one at a time into a saucer to ascertain if there is a bad one among them. One stale egg will spoil the whole cake. When the eggs are very light, stir them gradually into the large pan of butter and sugar in turn with the flour, that being the mixing pan. Lastly, add the fruit and citron, a little at a time of each, and give the whole a hard stirring. If the fruit is well floured it will not sink, but it will be seen evenly dispersed all over the cake when baked. Take a large straight-sided block tin pan, grease it inside with the same butter used for the cake, and put the mixture carefully into it. Set it immediately into a well-heated oven,

---

1702 LESLIE [1857], pages 516-517.

and keep up a steady heat while it is baking. When nearly done, the cake will shrink a little from the sides of the pan; and on probing it to the bottom with a sprig from a corn broom, or a splinter-skewer, the probe will come out clean. Otherwise, keep the cake in the oven a little longer. If it cracks on the top, it is a proof of its being very light. When quite done, take it out. It will become hard if left to grow cold with the oven. Set it to cool on an inverted sieve.

SAUCES FOR PUDDINGS.

Madeira.[1703] – Set a saucepan on the fire with one ounce of butter in it; as soon as melted, add half a tablespoonful of flour, stir till it turns rather yellow, and add also one pint of water, four ounces of sugar, and a few drops of burnt sugar; boil gently, about twenty-five minutes; add nearly a gill of Madeira wine, boil again ten minutes, and serve in a boat.

FROZEN PUDDING[1704]

Take a stale plum and sponge cake; slightly butter a tin pudding-mould, of a melon shape; put a layer of cake at the bottom, then a layer of either strawberry or raspberry jam, then cake, them jam; and so on, until the mould is nearly full; turn on a teacup of good strong Madeira wine or brandy. Make and boil a soft custard; fill the mould; let it stand until the cake is soft. Place it in ice and salt; cover it all over; let it stand six or eight hours; dip the mould into boiling water quickly, and then turn it on to the dish.

ANOTHER PUDDING SAUCE[1705]

Two cups of fine white sugar, one cup of butter, a wineglass of Madeira wine, and two eggs; beat all this together for half an hour, then let it scald, not boil. If you wish it to look very yellow add one more egg.

CALF'S FOOT JELLY.[1706]

Soak in cold water two hours four large feet; put them into six quarts of water, and boil them six hours, when it will be reduced to three quarts, or a little less. Then strain it through a sieve into a stone jar; the next day take off the fat, take the jelly out of the jar, and take off the sediment from the bottom. Put the jelly into a preserving-kettle; add a pound of loaf sugar, one pint and a half of good old Madeira wine, a teacupful

---

1703 BLOT 1867, pages 111-112.
1704 PUTNAM, E.[lizabeth H.], *Mrs. Putnam's Receipt Book, and Young Housekeeper's Assistant.*, New and Enlarged Edition, Sheldon and Company, New York, 1869, pages 146-147.
1705 PUTNAM 1869, page 148.
1706 PUTNAM 1869, pages 149-150.

of brandy, three lemons cut up and the seeds taken out, the whites of six or seven eggs beat to a froth, a very little saffron, and a few cloves. Stir this all up together, and set it on the fire; throw in the egg-shells, stir it frequently, and boil it twenty minutes. Then take it off the fire, and set it where it will keep hot without boiling; turn in a cup of cold water, and let it stand fifteen minutes. Have ready the jelly-stand and flannel bag. Put over the top a thin towel, dip the jelly into it; it will strain through and be as clear as amber, unless it is too thick. If so, turn it all into the kettle, add a little more water and the whites of two eggs, and strain it as before stated. This may be put into moulds hot, or in glasses when it is cold.

In the winter, when calves' feet are very costly, use the shins of veal. Two shins, well soaked in cold water two or three hours, will make the same quantity as above. When this is done, it will make two quarts of jelly.

Pigs' feet, well cleansed, make quite as handsome a jelly as calves' feet, and it looks more glassy. Four feet will make at least three pints when it is done. Make it the same as calf's foot jelly.

WINE JELLY[1707]

Dissolve an ounce of Russia isinglass in a cup of water; sweeten and flavor a quart of good old Madeira wine, and add the isinglass. Heat it very hot, strain it through a hair sieve into a mould, and let it stand six or eight hours.

MADEIRA CREAM.[1708] – Take seven sponge cakes, split them in halves, line a glass dish with the pieces, mix together two wineglassfuls of Madeira wine or sherry, and one wine-glassfull of brandy. With a teaspoon pour a little of this mixture over the layer of pieces, on this again put a layer of raspberry jelly, which can readily be made by putting a pot of raspberry jam in the oven; in a few minutes it will be warm, when the liquid, which is the jelly, can be strained from it and poured over the pieces. Now put the other layer of pieces, soak this with wine, as before, but omit the raspberry; make a custard as directed for boiled custard. When cold, and just as the dish is going to table, pour the cold custard over, and sprinkle some ratafias on the top.

11.1.7. Drinks

TO MAKE NECTAR.[1709]

Put half a pound of loaf sugar into a large porcelain jug; add one pint of cold water; bruise and stir the sugar till it is completely dissolved; pour over it half a bottle of hock and

---

1707 PUTNAM 1869, page 151.
1708 FROST 1870, pages 247-248.
1709 [BARNUM] 1831, page 147.

one bottle of madeira. Mix them well together, and grate in half a nutmeg, with a drop or two of the essence of lemon. Set the jug in a bucket of ice for one hour.

BITTERS.[1710] – Take two ounces of gentian root, an ounce of Virginia snake root, an ounce of the yellow paring of orange peel, and half a drachm of cochineal. Steep these ingredients, for a week or more, in a quart of Madeira or sherry wine, or brandy. When they are thoroughly infused, strain and filter the liquor, and bottle it for use. This is considered a good tonic, taken in a small cordial glass about noon.

11.2. Recipes from the Press

11.2.1. Soup

Turtle Soup a la Creole.[1711]

Here is the ancient Creole receipt for turtle soup: Cut the turtle in small pieces, let it brown in a pot with a little lard; cut up several onions, a slice of ham and a little garlic, and stir and mix well with the pieces of turtle. Then let the mixture brown well. Put in some flour, and mix. Pour a quantity of soup stock or water into the pot. Let it boil, and add a knee-joint of veal. Let this simmer for a full hour, after adding half a bottle of white wine. Then put in some thyme, laurel leaf, parsley and shallots, and when everything is cooked add a slice of lemon, chopped boiled eggs and a little more parsley. Just before dishing add a wineglassful of Madeira, and you will have a turtle soup fit for a king's table.

11.2.2. Meats

FILLET OF BEEF, MADEIRA SAUCE.[1712] – The Fillet of beef, weighing one pound and ten ounces, was larded with salt pork; then put into a pan with a few slices of onion, the same of carrot, and a little less of turnip (the Professor thinks it is not possible to make a good gravy or sauce without carrot and onion – the sugar they contain, he says, is indispensable;) about an ounce of salt pork, cut fine, and the same of suet, was added to the contents of the pan, and the beef placed on top of all; a pint of broth was next added, and seasoning to taste. The fillet so prepared should be placed on the range just for a moment or so before being set in the oven, where it remains until cooked – rare or well done, according to preference. The Madeira sauce is made with one tablespoonful of flour, the same of butter, and the juice of the beef, together with a few drops of burnt sugar. It should boil for one moment, and then be strained over half a gill of wine – almost any kind will do,

---

1710 LESLIE 1840, page 419.
1711 *The Postville Review*, June 3, 1898. (Postville, IA).
1712 *Daily National Republican*, March 17, 1866. (Washington, D.C.).

but Madeira is the best. The gravy can be poured over the meat or sent to the table in a separate dish. – *Prof. Blot*.

Roast Ham.[1713]

Scrape, soak, and wipe the ham. Put it in a dish; pour a bottle of Madeira wine all over; cut a carrot and two onions in slices, which put over also, with two bay leaves, two cloves, and six stalks of parsley. Baste now and then, and leave thus for twenty-four hours; then remove the bone at the larger end; trix off fat and lean, and put it in a bake-pan; turn the seasonings over it, put in the open, baste now and then until cooked, which you ascertain with a skewer. Dish it, strain the gravy over it, and serve with a Madeira or Champagne sauce. Proceed in the same way as if cooked on the spit. A ham, either baked, boiled, or roasted, may be served warm with mashed spinash or mashed potatoes, or any other vegetables. It is also served with apple sauce, or currant jelly, or tomato sauce.

ROGNON DE BOEUF SUPERBE.[1714] – Take a nice beef kidney, remove all the fat and skin, and cut it in rather thin slices. Season with salt, nutmeg, cayenne, and chopped parsley, and, if you can get it, eschalot. Fry the slices brown over a quick fire. Then make a nice brown gravy, add a glass of Madeira, and pour it into the pan with the meat. Let it boil up, throw in a spoonful of lemon juice, and a small piece of butter. Pour the whole into a dish and arrange about it *croutons* of fried bread.

SWEETBREADS LARDED.[1715] – Parboil five of the largest sweetbreads you can get. When half boiled lay them in cold water; prepare forcemeat of grated bread crumbs, lemon peel, butter, cayenne pepper and nutmeg; mix together with the beaten yolk of egg. Cut open the sweetbreads and stuff them with it, tying them round with pack thread. Have ready some slips of fat bacon and lemon peel, cut in very thin and narrow strips. Lard the sweetbread with them in alternate rows of bacon and lemon peel, drawing them through it with a larding needle. Do this regularly and handsomely. Then put them in the oven and let them brown. Serve with a sauce made of melted butter, a dessert-spoonful of browned flour and gill of water, stirring all the time. Add salt, pepper, the beaten yolk of egg, and a glass of Madeira wine at the last.

THANKSGIVING DISHES[1716]
New Recipes by Famous Women, Prepared Especially for The National Tribune.

... Mrs. Crosby is famous for her terrapin, and she gives me her recipe, as follows:
After boiling the terrapin quite tender and taking them from the shell, to three terrapin take a small tablespoonful of flour; dredge over and season with cayenne pepper and salt;

[1713] *Pomeroy's Democrat*, February 28, 1874. (Chicago, IL).
[1714] *New York Daily Tribune*, August 22, 1880. (New York City, NY. Published at the "Household Notes" section).
[1715] *Sacramento Daily Record-Union*, June 18, 1881. (Sacramento, CA. Published at "The Household" section).
[1716] *The National Tribune*, November 20, 1890. (Washington D.C.).

one-half pound of butter; one-half tumbler of Madeira wine, with as much water (oyster juice is better), and let them come to a boil. Take the yolks of three eggs and beat them in two tablespoonfuls of wine; after taking them off the fire pour in the egg slowly, till it thickens like a cream; put them near the fire to keep hot, but do not suffer them to boil.

L. A. CROSBY.

BOILED HAM, MADEIRA SAUCE.[1717] – Select a ham of about twenty pounds, not too fat nor too lean; steep in cold water over night, and boil slowly for three hours; drain on a dish, take off the rind, sprinkle with granulated sugar, put in the oven with two glasses of Madeira wine, and glaze to a nice color, basting occasionally with the wine; trim the hock bone, ornament it with a fancifully made paper ruttle, place on a dish; pour Madeira sauce round the ham, and serve with more sauce in a sauce-bowl. Madeira sauce – Put a quart of Spanish sauce in a saucepan with a pinch of red pepper, a ladleful of tomato sauce, and a gill of Madeira wine; stir steadily, and briskly for ten minutes; then press through a napkin. – German Culinary Art.

11.2.3. Fish

BAKED RED-SNAPPER.[1718] – Dress the fish as for boiling, score it on one side, season it with salt and pepper, place small strips of fat salt pork in the cuts, and lay it in a baking-pan on a bed of the following vegetables pared and sliced: one onion, one turnip, half a carrot, a bay leaf, a sprig each of parsley and some sweet herb, and six cloves; add half a pint of water, put the pan in the oven and bake the fish fifteen minutes to a pound. To make the sauce for the fish take it up on a hot dish without breaking, pour the contents of the pan into a stout sieve and rub them through it with a potato-masher, season it with salt and pepper to taste and add a glass of Madeira wine to it; serve it in a gravy dish with the fish, which looks well garnished with some fresh parsley or slices of lemon.

1717 *The McKean Democrat*, March 3, 1893. (Published in Smethport, M'Kean County, PA). A similar receipt was published in another source: «Boiled Ham, Sauce Madere – Take one ten-pound ham, soak in cold water during the night, then boil it slowly for about three hours; drain it well, take the rind off, sprinkle it with granulated sugar, pour a cup of Madeira wine on the baking pan and bake it in a moderate oven till of a nice brown color, basting frequently with the wine. Serve with a Madeira sauce made as follows: Madeira Sauce – Take a pint of thick brown gravy, add a cupful of tomato sauce, a pinch of red pepper and a glass of Madeira wine; let come to a boil, press through a very fine sieve and serve. A good way of improving the ham is to boil it in the evening, and let it stay in its own water over night.» *The Salt Lake Tribune*, September 22, 1900. (Salt Lake City, UT).

1718 *Dodge City Times*, February 28, 1880. (Dodge City, KS); *The Red Cloud Chief*, April 1, 1880. (Red Cloud, Webster Co., NE).

11.2.4. Seafood

MADEIRA WINE GOES IN.[1719]

Split two good-sized, fine, freshly boiled lobsters. Pick all the meat from out the shells, then cut it into one-inch length equal pieces. Place it in a sauce pan on the hot range with one ounce of very good fresh butter. Season with one pinch of salt and half a saltspoonful of red pepper, adding two medium-sized, sound truffles cut into small disk-shaped pieces. Cook for five minutes, then add a wineglassful of good Madeira wine. Reduce to one-half, which will take three minutes. Have three eggs yolks in a bowl with half a pint of sweet cream, beat well together and add it to the lobster. Gently shuffle for two minutes longer, or until it thickens well. Pour it into a hot tureen and serve hot.

MRS. JOHN WANAMAKER.

TO CREAM LOBSTER.[1720]

PREPARE the lobster on Saturday and keep in a cool place until needed on Sunday. Have placed on the table with your chafing dish a daintily-prepared tray, containing a small bowl, in which you have already creamed one tablespoonful of flour with one tablespoonful of butter, one half teaspoonful of salt, with a dash of pepper. After all are seated place in your clusfing dish one pint of cream. When this comes to the boiling point stir in the butter and flour, etc. Stir constantly until it becomes creamy; then add one tablespoonful of Madeira wine, then the squares of lobster. Cook until well heated, then add one tablespoon of Madeira and serve.

How to Make Lobster a la Newburg.[1721]

This is the dish that has taken New York by storm. It originated years ago with a gentleman who lived at Newburg, N. Y., on the Hudson, and Delmonico[1722] used to make it for him.[1723] It has recently been revived. Take the meat of a well boiled lobster and put it into a chafing dish, with a tablespoonful of butter and start the fire in the alcohol lamp. Stir for a few moments, then pour in a heaping wineglass of Madeira. Cook and stir for three or four minutes, and then pour over all the substance of two well beaten eggs. Blow out the lamp and your lobster a la Newburg is ready.

1719 *The Pittsburg Dispatch*, February 23, 1890. (Pittsburgh, PA).
1720 *The Morning Times*, April 21, 1896. (Washington D.C.).
1721 *The Salem Daily News*, May 21, 1891. (Salem, OH).
1722 See Note 1477.
1723 Another recipe, entitled "Lobster à la Newberg, or Delmonico", can be found on page 220 of the book *Delmonico's – A Century of Splendor*, published by Lately Thomas, in Boston, in 1967.

Scalloped oysters.[1724] – Put a layer of oysters in an oval dish, and dredge in a little salt, pepper and butter; then a layer of rolled crackers, and another of oysters; dredge the oysters as before, and cover with crackers; over the crackers grate a little nutmeg, and lay on small pieces of butter. Bake twenty minutes in a quick oven; add a glass of Madeira wine if you choose. Allow four crackers, two spoonsful of butter and one teaspoonful of pepper to one quart of oysters. Fill the dish to within an inch of the top.

11.2.5. Fowls

CHICKEN DRESSED AS TERRAPINS.[1725] – Boil a fine, large, tender chicken; when done and while warm, cut it from the bones into small pieces, as for chicken salad; put it into a stewpan with one gill of boiling water; then stir together until perfectly smooth one quarter of a pound of butter, one teaspoonful of flour, and the yolk of one egg, which add to the chicken, stirring all well together; then season with salt and pepper. After letting it simmer about ten minutes, add half a gill of Maderia[1726] wine and send to table hot.

How to Terrapin-Chicken.[1727]

Take three pounds of boneless boiled chicken, chopped fine, add to it a pint of broth, one-half pint cream, four hard boiled eggs, five heaping teaspoonfuls richly browned flour, one teaspoon salt, one cup butter. Rub the eggs through sieve, add the browned flour, broth, eggs and cream to chicken, with two pieces of chopped celery. Cook slowly 15 minutes, season with mace and pepper to suit taste. Just before serving on golden browned toast add two wineglasses madeira wine.

THE THANKSGIVING TURKEY.[1728]
How it Should be Cooked – The Recipe of an Expert.

Ingredients: Roast turkey extra; one turkey, one pound of veal, one pound of sausage-meat, parsley, cold chicken, pepper and salt, twenty-five large chestnuts, two stalks of celery, three-quarters of a pound of butter, one wineglass of Madeira wine.

After cleaning the fowl, prepare the dressing of veal, chopped fine, chicken, sausage meat, pepper and salt. While this is being prepared, boil in very salt water the chestnuts with the green heads of the celery stalks. When the chestnuts are sufficiently done, reduce

---

1724 *The Indiana Progress*, September 11, 1879. (Indiana, PA).
1725 *The Red Cloud Chief*, March 29, 1877. (Red Cloud, NE. Published at the "Useful Recipes" section); *The Wellsboro Agitator*, July 4, 1882. (Wellsboro, Tioga County, PA. Published at the section "Household Knowledge").
1726 The right spelling is Madeira.
1727 *The Fort Wayne Sentinel*, May 22, 1899. (Fort Wayne, IN); *Mendocino Dispatch Democrat*, July 7, 1899. (Ukiah, Mendocino County, CA).
1728 *The Washington Critic*, November 23, 1886. (Washington, D.C.).

them to a pulp and mix them with the dressing with a quarter of a pound of butter. When this has been inserted in the fowl, put it on the spit and baste freely with butter which has been salted and peppered, and dissolved before being put in the wine. When perfectly done, little jets of smoke will issue like miniature volcanoes from the turkey. Meanwhile the remainder of the two heads of celery having been carefully washed, trimmed and cut into pieces about five inches long, place in the dripping-pan when the turkey is half done, where it will become thoroughly impregnated with the savory juices from the bird. It will then form a pleasant accompaniment to a delicious dish, the cooking of which should last from two hours to two hours and a quarter, according to the size of the fowl.

11.2.6. Pasta

STEWED MACARONI.[1729] – Break the macaroni into pieces an inch long, throw them into boiling water. Boil half and hour and drain. Put into a stew-pan a pint of cream, an ounce of butter, one well-beaten egg, pepper and salt. Stir over a clear fire till it thickens, but do not boil. Add the macaroni, boil five minutes, toss in wineglassful of Madeira, and serve hot.

11.2.7. Desserts

A TRIFLE.[1730] – One quart of milk, six eggs, reserving the whites of two, which beat to a stiff froth, and when the milk boils drop in spoonfuls; in a minute or two remove carefully to a plate; after beating the eggs light pour the boiling milk slowly into the egg, stirring the egg quickly the while; sweeten it and place over the fire, stirring all the time until it simmers – it must not boil. If it should curdle, pour it immediately into another pan and stir until cool. Place sponge cake, moistened with Madeira wine, (and on which preserved strawberries or other fruit has been spread,) in the bottom and sides of a glass or china bowl, and when the custard is cool flavor with vanilla, and pour into the bowl, placing the white balls carefully on top; then surround the bowl with ice or stand it in cold water until required.

PLUM-PUDDING GLACE.[1731] – Make a custard as for vanilla or lemon ice-cream and freeze it. Then take ¼ pound each of raisins, currants, and citron, mince the citron and raisins, add ¼ pound of chocolate, and boil all together in a pint of Madeira wine. When it is quite cold, stir it in with the cream in the freezer, and give a few more turns to freeze all together. It should be remembered that this kind of fruit is only enough for about a quart and a half of the cream.

1729 *The Alden Times*, March 7, 1879. (Alden, IA).
1730 *M'Kean Miner*, August 11, 1863. (Smethport, M'Kean Co., PA).
1731 *Fair Play*, August 3, 1876. (St. Genevieve, MO); *The Andrew County Republican*, August 3, 1876. (Savannah, MO).

SAUCE FOR PUDDING.[1732] – One cupful white powdered sugar, one-half cupful butter; beat to a cream; add a wineglass Madeira; flavoring to suit the taste; stir well together; put in the sauce tureen; pour in boiling water slowly. The sauce will look like cream and foam.

EGG-NOGG.[1733] – Take the yolks of sixteen eggs and sixteen table-spoonfuls of pulverized loaf-sugar and beat them to the consistency of cream. To this add nearly a whole nutmeg grated, half a pint of good brandy or rum, and two glasses of Madeira wine. Beat the whites to a stiff froth, mix them in, and finish by adding six pints of milk. No heating is necessary in this formula, and the quantity should suffice for a party of twenty.

PLUM PUDDING GLACE.[1734] – Slice two ounces of fresh citron very thin, add two ounces of stoned raisins and the same of currants, which have been carefully washed and dried; mix them with a quarter of a pound of grated chocolate and cover all with Madeira wine and stew fifteen minutes. When quite cold stir this mixture into three quarts of vanilla ice-cream and freeze it in a mold.

RICE CAKES.[1735] – Rice cakes are a nice side dish for dinner, or may be used in place of pastry. Boil some rice until it is soft, then roll it in your hands in cakes; dip them in beaten egg, and then in Indian meal; see that they are covered in the meal. Then fry them in a little very hot lard. If to be served with meat lay them around the edge of the platter; if for dessert, make a sauce with the butter, sugar and flour, and flavor it with Madeira wine and a very little grated nutmeg. Serve warm.

ELECTION CAKE.[1736] – Five pounds flour, one and three-quarter pounds butter, two pounds sugar, two pounds stoned raisins, one nutmeg, half pint brandy, one gill sherry or Madeira wine, one pint yeast, one quart new milk. Rub part of the butter into the flour, as it would not rise so well with the whole, or melt it in the milk, as it rises better to be warm. Add the milk and yeast at night. If well risen in the morning, add the other ingredients; if not, let it stand till well risen. Flour, butter, milk and yeast to be put together at night.

SQUASH PIE.[1737] – One quart of stewed and strained squash, a scant quart of boiling milk, two-thirds of a nutmeg, one and one-half teaspoonfuls of salt, two cupfuls of sugar. Mix slowly and well; when cold add four well-beaten eggs, and, if one chooses, two

---

1732 *Jackson Sentinel*, October 18, 1877. (Maquoketa, IA. Published in the section "Domestic Economy").
1733 *The Algona Republican*, October 8, 1879. (Algona, Kossuth County, IA).
1734 *The National Tribune*, February 4, 1882. (Washington, D.C. Published at the section "Things to Make a Note Of").
1735 *The County Paper*, January 12, 1883. (Oregon, MO. Published at the "Domestic Recipes" section).
1736 *New York Tribune*, May 27, 1883. (New York, NY. Published at the "Household Notes" section); *Evening Bulletin*, June 9, 1883. (San Francisco, CA. Published at the "HOUSEHOLD HINTS" section.
1737 *Western Kansas World*, May 20, 1893. (Wakeneeney, KS. Published at the "For the Cook" section).

tablespoonfuls of Maderia.[1738] Line deep plates with a plain paste, and after filling with the mixture bake in a modern oven for forty minutes.

A Dainty Dessert[1739]

Put into a saucepan six egg yolks, three ounces of sugar and half a pint of Madeira wine. Beat on the fire with an egg beater until thick and frothy and serve immediately.

[1738] The right spelling is Madeira.
[1739] *The Hocking Sentinel*, January 16, 1896. (Logan, OH).

12. Conclusion

Madeira Wine is deeply associated with America's history and culture since the Colonial days. Different generations of Americans drank it, from U.S. Presidents to wealthy aristocrats in the main cities of the Northern and Southern states, and they were all very proud of their Madeiras, whose history they knew by heart and shared with their friends, when tippling it with them, usually after the removing of the cloth from the table. This taste for Madeira led them to becoming wine collectors, and in some American cellars some rare vintages were stored for decades, eventually passing on to their descendants.

Being a noble wine, it was termed in America as the king of wines, and was used in the most solemn occasions, to make toasts, either in political ones, such as toasting the promulgation of the Declaration of Independence, the Louisiana Purchase, several Fourth of July cerimonies, or in common life events, such as marriages, births, funerals, or even at the gathering of old friends, in the once so famous Madeira Parties.

Everybody loved Madeira in the America of the past, so much so, that it was reflected in American Literature, on one hand, where dozens of references to it can be found, expressing its qualities such as its unique bouquet, flavor, and sweetness. On the other hand, the 19th century American press is flooded with a wide variety of topics related to Madeira Wine, some of which we disclosed. From the latter source we learned that until the mid 19th century Madeira Wine trade in America went on as usual but then, when the *oïdium* destroyed the island's vineyards, it became scarce and true hunts for it occurred in several auctions across the country, and in the midst of that scarcity the New Yorkers and Bostonians, large appreciators of Madeira, were surprised to find out that there were still large stocks of old Madeiras kept in the South, some of which were over a hundred years old, and purchased part of it through wine auctions. The supply shortage led somehow to a shortage in the demand, and little by little, Madeira Wine went out of fashion, in the last decades of the 19th century, being replaced by sherry, champagne and other foreign wines, in a time when the domestic wine production, especially in California, started to present reasonable wines as well.

Americans developed a special taste for Madeira Wine and treated it kindly across the country. A thousand and one cares were put upon its preservation so that it did not spoil. The kindness shown towards the Madeiras in America is also shown through the familiar names attributed to it. In the island they were know by its type – like Malmsey, Bual, Sercial or Verdelho – but in the United States they were usually named after the ship in which they had been imported in, by a special event that had occurred during its arrival to America, or even after the name of the family that owned it, and different names arose like the Juno Madeira, the Comet Madeira, or sometimes it was just commonly termed "south side Madeira", a synonym for the best wine the island produced. Surprisingly enough, some American *connoisseurs*, aware of the fact that a long sea voyage improved their Madeiras, used to send them on long sea voyages to the West Indies (or even to the far-off India) and back, sometimes more than once, in order to have a unique wine.

For over two centuries, Madeira Wine reached the United States in casks, quarter-casks and demijohns, depending on the quantity or type of wine imported, transported by sailing vessels, bound for the main cities along the eastern seaboard, such as Charleston, Savannah, New York or Boston. By then, the appreciators of Madeiras made their order with the importers, who, in turn would send for them to the island. But from the 1870's onwards, a time when Madeira Wine trade in America was slow, due to the two blights that affected the island's vineyards, the trend changed with the "democratization of the sea", after the end of the Civil War, with the growth of American tourism bound to Mediterranean seaports. Until then, Madeira was only familiar to merchant and U.S. Navy ship crews, due to the frequent stops at the island during their Atlantic cruises, and to a few American civilians that sought the island, most of whom for health reasons since Madeira was, for a long time, a famous resort for consumptives. After the inaugural Mediterranean tour of the *Quaker City*, in 1867, in which traveled Mark Twain, who later on published the book *The Innocents Abroad* depicting this experience, it became fashionable, to upper and middle class Americans, to visit Europe, and Madeira Island was usually the first port of call after leaving New York. This way, thousands of Americans had the chance to see before their eyes "the land of the wine" – which most of them had only heard about in travel books or newspaper articles – and also wandered through Funchal, sightseeing, visiting different wine-stores and purchasing their own wine, in bottles, to take home as a precious souvenir of their visit to Madeira.

For several decades into the 20th century, Madeira Wine was produced just as it had been in the past, by stomping the grapes thrown into the wine presses, and then carrying the newly-made wine in goatskins to the wine stores in Funchal. But this is all history now, since in the last decades the entire process was modernized and mechanized, by the wine-producing companies, thus diminishing the human touch. However, the old-fashioned way of making wine is still used all over the island by the farmers, in order to make their own wine, for their own consumption.

Throughout the 20th century, Madeira Wine trade to America continued, with some ups and downs, and in the last decades, its exports to America have been increasing.

These days the wine is shipped in sealed bottles, packed in cardboard boxes, to some American cities that once were famous importers of this appreciated wine, such as Charleston, New York and Boston. But just as in everything in life, there is an exception worth mentioning. With a special permit from the island's authorities, Madeira Wine is also shipped to America in large steel containers, once a year, to be consumed in New Bedford, MA, at the famous Feast of the Blessed Sacrament – which started back in 1915, organized by the local Madeiran community, and presently ran by the Club Madeirense S. S. Sacramento, Inc. – an event that occurs yearly, in the first weekend of August, and gathers tens of thousands of people, being the largest Portuguese Feast in America.

As this anthology fully demonstrates, Madeira Wine was, for many centuries past, fully entrenched in the American Culture and drinking Madeira was a sign of wealth and social status. Our hope is that Madeira would regain the prestige it once had in the United States, for several generations, in the years to come. And we suggest, why not use Madeira Wine once again, to celebrate the Fourth of July, as it was done in the early years of the nation?

13. Attachments

13.1. Report of the Madeira Relief Fund Committee

This first attachment provides part of the report about the 1853's international relief effort towards Madeira, in response to an appeal made from the island on the previous year, due to the unprecedented failure of the grape. From this document, published anonymously, in London, in 1854, will be shown the most significant excerpts, namely those related to the United States, which was, by far, the country that contributed the most to this noble cause, and also how the relief was distributed among the distressed islanders.

REPORT[1740]

Having been solicited and appointed by the civil governor of this island, under date the 22nd day of November, 1852, to act as a committee, to receive and distribute amongst its distressed classes such contributions as might reach us from foreigners, and foreign countries, in mitigation of their suffering; and having so far discharged the trust thus reposed in, and undertaken by us, to the best of our ability, we think it our duty to submit, for the information and satisfaction of His Most Faithful Majesty's government, and that of the numerous generous and benevolent contributors to the relief funds which have been under our control, as well as that of all persons interested, a brief statement to the close of the past year of our mode of action, and how the charitable succours have been appropriated.

On assuming the responsibility of the trust we undertook, we printed an appeal for aid, under date 25th November, 1852, (of which we subjoin a copy,) and took measures to have it extensively circulated in Europe, America, and other parts of the world; and as that appeal was liberally responded to, we issued another public address on the 29th March, 1853, (of which a copy is also annexed,) for the double object of explaining our plan of affording relief, and in the hope of adding to our means of dispensing it, by endeavouring to enlist sympathy and philanthropy, in a still greater degree, on behalf of those oppressed by an unprecedented calamity, whose unhappy and disastrous consequences, we felt, could hardly be exaggerated.

These steps, with our individual pressing private appeals for assistance, and the effects previously produced by the circular letter which the civil governor addressed to the merchants of Madeira, on the 24th of August, 1852, aroused the most friendly feeling, genuine sympathy, and zealous co-operation in foreign countries in support of the cause in which we have been engaged; and we estimate the relief which we have received in food and money, in consequence thereof, to be, as follows, viz: –

1740 *Report of the Madeira Relief Fund Committee; Established In The Year 1853.*, [London, 1854], pages 1-31.

	In Food.	In Money.	Total value of food and money.
	RS.	RS.	RS.
From Hamburgh	...	556,520	556,520
„ Russia	...	873,600	873,600
„ the United States of America	19,660,780	3,215,190	22,875,970
„ Great Britain and Ireland	48,000	10,073,080	10,121,080
The amount of a collection made at British chapel here, after a charity sermon by the Rev. T. K. Brown	...	464,000	464,000
The amount of collections made by us here, from British, American, and German merchants, and other British subjects, including our own contributions	...	2,536,600	2,536,600
Premium obtained on sovereigns imported	...	54,554	54,554
	19,708,780	17,773,544	37,482,324

and to enable a more correct opinion to be formed on the subject, we annex a detailed list of the names, as far as they are known to us, of the contributors and the amount of their respective contributions.

Before entering upon further details, the very gratifying duty devolves upon us, in name and on behalf of His Most Faithful Majesty's government and His Majesty's suffering subjects in this afflicted portion of His dominions, to offer to these generous benefactors our grateful thanks and cordial acknowledgements for a manifestation of sympathy and liberality in sending such munificent supplies, to an extent, indeed, which has excited feelings of thankfulness and admiration amongst all classes here, and of which no terms we can employ can express an adequate sense. We take the opportunity also of recording our grateful appreciation of the confidence placed in our fidelity and discretion by the numerous benevolent donors.

The food from America was sent in three vessels; – the *Nautilus*, from Boston, – the *Tally Ho*, from New York, – and the *Aaron J. Harvey*, from Philadelphia, We are ignorant of the names of subscribers to the funds for defraying the expense of these cargoes, with the exception of the contributors in Philadelphia to the latter, amounting, by the invoice, to Rs.[1741] 3,515.180. The arrangements made for dispatching the *Nautilus*, and the subscriptions raised for that charitable enterprize, were promoted and carried into effect by two estimable philanthropists, in Boston, who placed it entirely at Mr. March's individual disposal, to appropriate in any way he might judge fit, as a "Gift from the city of Boston to the poor of Madeira." The means were raised for forwarding the cargo of the *Tally Ho* from New York by the personal exertions of many influential and charitable parties there connected with this island, as well commercially as socially; and who formed a committee to superintend the realization of their humane intensions, and it was consigned by the mayor, or chief magistrate of New York, to Mr. March, for the relief of our destitute

---

1741 See Note 1191.

population. The cargo by the *Aaron J. Harvey*, from Philadelphia, may be divided into three portions: one to the value of Rs. 699.330, was provided for by the merchants and citizens of Providence, R.I., and also addressed to Mr. March's consignment; the second, to the amount of Rs. 1,699.340, was purchased with funds supplied by the committee in New York, and was consigned, as well as the third portion, valued at Rs. 3,515.180, as already stated, to us. The sum required for dispatching this third portion, was obtained in Philadelphia by the benevolent zeal and laudable exertions of parties in that city, who have evinced, by their good deeds, the warm interest they take in the welfare of this island, and the names of all the subscribers thereto appear in the contribution list.

Although a great part of the food, as has just been explained, was placed exclusively under Mr. March's individual orders, he at once transferred it to our collective control; and all donations influenced or received by the other individual members of our committee, were likewise held applicable to our appropriation collectively, so that our actions, in this cause of charity, were in every respect unfettered and without restriction, beyond that of exercising our own unbiassed discretion in endeavouring to do the greatest possible amount of good with the means so magnanimously placed at our disposal.

We felt however that the distribution of these charitable succours involved serious responsibility, and it therefore caused us unwearied anxiety and much painful reflection; but in discharging so sacred a trust, although we have not accomplished all the good which we earnestly could have wished, and may have overlooked many deserving objects who might have expected relief, still we do indulge the hope that we have administered it fairly and justly, under all the difficult and onerous circumstances which pressed upon our attention, and that the immediate as well as the prospective results were satisfactory.

We have carried out as closely as possible, the plan of appropriation promulgated in our address of 29th March, already referred to, and we annex tables or statements explaining in an abridged form how this has been effected.

I. This shews an expenditure of upwards of Rs. 9,000,000 on the new road leading from Funchal to Camara de Lobos, and although we are disappointed that the whole road has not been completed, as we had anticipated, from so large an outlay, and which may be partly, if not wholly, attributed to difficulties over which we had no control, and could not remove; still enough has been done to encourage its being continued when funds are available, and the pleasing reflection remains that a large number of necessitous work-people, averaging from 200 to 300 daily, got employment for a period of six months, and many of whose families, but for such timely assistance, must have been reduced to great misery, if not to actual want.

II. The other numerous works undertaken, with the concurrence of the local authorities in most districts of the Island, for the relief of the able unemployed classes; such as repairing, cleaning, and opening roads and water courses, and others of public utility, were entrusted to the selection and direction of sub-committees, composed of respectable parties known in their respective localities as possessing zeal, local information, and practical knowledge. Their names are given in the statement, with the particulars of the funds put at their disposal; the amount of the whole being, as exhibited therein, estimated at Rs. 9,081,000.

The reports which we have received, satisfy us that the gentlemen forming the sub-committees have generally been indefatigable to do the greatest possible extent of good in their different districts, with the means to which we considered them fairly entitled, and that their efforts to aid us in this work of charity have been satisfactory and successful. These reports and the voluminous accounts and documents which have accompanied them, are in our possession, for the inspection of all parties interested, when occasion may require; and we would take this occasion of acknowledging our sense of, and grateful thanks for, the valuable services which have been so willingly and obligingly rendered us.

III. The sub-committee of ladies have, we have every reason to believe, most usefully employed the funds put at their disposal, in providing suitable work for numerous females who would otherwise have been in a state of extreme destitution, and they, with the kind assistance of two other ladies, have at a vast amount of time and trouble, and at comparatively small expense, enabled us to convert upwards of 5,000 sacks which came from America with food for the poor, into more than 2,000 useful and substantial articles of clothing and bedding for the same helpless class. These ladies also gave us the advantage of their humane services in assisting us to distribute ... a considerable portion of this clothing and bedding; and we cannot too strongly express our sense of their valuable co-operation in the execution of our trust, for which they have our unfeigned acknowledgments; but their own inward consciousness and satisfaction of giving their important aid in carrying out a work of charity, for the benefit of their suffering fellow-creatures, will be to these excellent and philanthropic ladies, a far better reward than any expression of thanks which can emanate from us; which however we cannot now deny ourselves the gratification of recording.

IV. A considerable quantity of potatoes and corn meal, with some Indian corn, biscuit, rice, beans, clothes, and bedding, as well as a little money, (partly to provide salt and suitable food for the sick in certain localities, where such relief seemed to be especially required) have been distributed, as explained in this statement; in all parts of the island and Porto Santo, to those who are altogether without the means of subsistence, whether from disease, age, infirmity, or any other cause. The distribution of the potatoes in Funchal, was made under our own direction, chiefly to coopers, who, as a class, were said to be suffering more than any other; and their appropriation with that of the other articles of food and clothing in the rural districts, were placed under the control of the respective intelligent sub-committees on the spot; the ladies, who were so zealous in superintending the making up of the clothes and bedding, having also, as already stated, aided in judiciously distributing a due portion of them, and a small sum in money, in Funchal and the adjoining parishes.

V. An amount of money to the extent of Rs. 2,000,000 was also applied to the relief of the same helpless indigent classes, by the parochial clergy all over the island, in proportion to the population and supposed existing poverty of their respective parishes, but only after we had been furnished with voluminous statistical information on the subject; and subsequent returns from each, after the distribution, were exacted for our satisfaction, and are in our possession, distinctly specifying the *name, age, residence, number of persons in the family, and sum given to each person, or head of the family relieved.* A copy of the returns in question, from each parish, was also directed to be affixed at the doors of the respective churches, to shew the just application of the charity to all interested in the various localities. We have, no doubt, but that the clergy generally were sincerely desirous, and took much trouble to realize our earnest wish, that this charity should reach those in most urgent want. The clergy in all countries are looked upon as, and certainly are, the best channels of acquiring knowledge as to the extent of sickness, wretchedness, and poverty, within their respective parishes; and as they ought, therefore, to be the best medium of administering relief and consolation to those in that unhappy state, we sought their assistance, and we feel assured that their readiness to give it, which has been justly appreciated by us, will be acknowledged by the prayers of their helpless parishioners, whose distress they were thereby enabled to mitigate.

VI. We have, from time to time, voted small quantities of flour and other articles of food, and also small sums of money to numerous helpless, indigent, and reduced persons of both sexes, many of whom have been in better circumstances and held more respectable positions in society, but who from misfortune, and the calamity under which the inhabitants of this island in general, and they in particular, are now oppressed, are reluctantly compelled, however painful to their feelings, to seek means of subsistence, to avoid positive starvation, from any available source. A little relief has also been awarded, in limited sums, to a few of the smaller proprietors whose solicitations made, we are assured, from the most urgent necessity, we did not feel ourselves at liberty to disregard, and the names of, and amounts given to all such recipients, are registered in the archives of our committee for reference to on all necessary occasions. Applications for aid from this latter numerous and respectable class of the population (the proprietors), have, however, been so rare, that we deem it only an act of justice on our part, to bear our testimony to their extreme patience under the severe and trying circumstances to which they have been, and continue to be exposed, owing to the unparalleled calamity with which it has pleased Providence to visit this formerly productive and prosperous island.

VII. The members of the committee have, individually, dispensed, in both food and money, alms from the Public Relief Fund under their management, since they entered upon their duties, to the extent exhibited in this statement, in small quantities to each of a great many really miserable and indigent persons, whose state of extreme destitution has appeared undeniable; and they have kept records of the names and condition of such persons as they thus thought it their duty to relieve; that their anxious solicitude to discharge faithfully the arduous and delicate trust committed to their discretion, may be made patent when needful to all interested parties.

VIII. This statement will shew, that in proportion to the means under our direction, the charitable, useful, and pious establishments have been properly attended to; and it is a source of much satisfaction to us to know, from the commissioners administering the affairs of the hospital and poor-house, and from parties in charge of the other establishments so sadly impaired in resources from the unfortunate visitation which caused the formation of our committee, that the aid which we have felt it our duty to afford them, has enabled them, if not entirely, at all events, partially, to remove such pressing difficulties as hazarded the very existence of the most important and useful, and the utility of others being seriously deteriorated.

IX. The Relief Fund has had to defray a variety of unavoidable expenses, such as those incurred in landing, storing, and meting out the food from the United States of America, &c., and the charges attending its transport to numerous localities, in all parts of the island, where its distribution was to be made; likewise those incurred in printing and circulating here and in Great Britain, appeals to the public for support, and numerous other incidental ones, which we deemed it expedient to sanction, amounting altogether, as this statement shews, to a considerable sum; but in authorizing these disbursements we derived comfort in the reflection, that we were relieving many boatmen, labourers, and others, who, without such relief, would have probably been unemployed, with their families exposed to great privation; and that we were thus dispensing charity without pauperising the people by the hurtful tendency of gratuitous relief.

X. A summary of our proceedings, as comprehended under the foregoing heads, will shew at a glance how the distribution of the food and money has been effected. The cash balance of Rs. 4,142021, remaining in the treasurers' hands on the 31st of December last, is held applicable to certain defined charitable objects. So soon as it has been distributed in conformity therewith, a statement, detailing the manner of its appropriation, will be published.

To make the annexed statements of the distribution of the food intelligible, perhaps it may be well here to mention, that it has been valued therein, both in return for labour and in gratuitous relief, at about 6 p cent. under its invoice cost, including freight, which exceeded to that extent its fair average value here.

We think it due to the Civil Governor of the island to express the just sense we entertain of His Excellency's promptitude in assuming the responsibility of exempting the provisions sent here, as charitable contributions, from import duty and imposts of all kinds, and which enabled us to take measures for their immediate distribution on arrival. The legislature of Lisbon subsequently, as was naturally to be expected, released His Excellency from this responsibility, which, however, does not make us less desirous of acknowledging his readiness to remove such a serious obstacle to instant action on our part.

We cannot close this report without expressing a fear that we may have but imperfectly performed the sacred and anxious duties which have devolved upon us; and our regret, therefore, that they were not confided to other and abler hands. We take credit only for an earnest desire to act fairly, justly, and impartially, and we throw ourselves, with much confidence, on the indulgence of all who have taken an interest in and watched our proceedings, should any of our decisions appear to have been questionable. Errors of judgment may have been committed, and wrong impressions may have been entertained, (few, if any, however, we hope and believe,) which may have resulted unintentionally on our part in advantage to the unscrupulous, and disappointment to the deserving; but we do flatter ourselves that any such act, whether real or apparent, may not be attributed to design, or any other feeling or motive than that of an earnest desire to act equitably and righteously; and we shall esteem it a rich reward if, at the close of our labours, we shall be really found to have been instrumental in promoting the welfare of the land we live in.

When we felt ourselves justified in acceding to appeals made to us for relief, we had satisfaction in acknowledging our willingness to do so; and in not replying to many of the numerous Communications which reached us, we trust that it may not be imputed to any want of courtesy to the parties from whom they came, but to our painful conviction of not feeling warranted in granting their requests, and finding it impracticable to undertake, satisfactorily, any correspondence beyond what became imperative, in consequence of the accumulation of labour which the execution of this service entailed upon us, occupying time which was not infrequently abstracted from (to ourselves) important private avocations.

George Stoddart, British Consul, Chairman.
George Hasche, Prussian Pro-Consul.
Richard Davies, British Merchant, Treasurer.

Funchal, Madeira,
20th February, 1854.

Our colleague, Mr. J. H. March, United States' consul, although he has taken part in all our more important deliberations, and concurred in our decisions is not, at present, in the island to sign this report, but Mr. Stoddart has full power from him, in writing, to act for him during his absence; Mr. Nuno A. Carvalho, the other member of our committee, has been in Portugal during a considerable portion of the time it has been in action, and being now permanently settled there, is also unable to attach his name to this report of its proceedings.

G. S.
G. H.
R. D.

DISTRESS IN THE ISLAND OF MADEIRA.

A calamity has fallen on Madeira unparalleled in its history; the vintage, the revenue of which furnished the chief means for providing subsistence for its inhabitants, has been *a total failure;* and the potato crop, formerly another important article of their food, is still extensively diseased. All classes, therefore, are suffering; and as there are few sources in the island to which they can look for food, clothing, and other necessaries of life, their distress must increase during the winter, and the future is contemplated with painful anxiety and apprehension. Under such appalling prospects, the zealous and excellent Civil Governor, Snr. José Silvestre Ribeiro, addressed a circular letter to the merchants of Madeira, on the 24th of August last, for the purpose of bringing the unfortunate and critical position of the population under his government to the notice of the benevolent and charitable classes in foreign countries, and in the hope of exciting their sympathy with, and assistance to, so many of their fellow-creatures threatened with famine. His Excellency's appeal having been responded to by various parties to a limited extent, and expectations having been raised, that with a systematic organization, and management, very considerable succours would be forthcoming, he has named us, in an alvará of the 22nd instant, as a committee to receive and superintend the distribution of all such money and other articles as may be placed at our disposal, towards the alleviation of the suffering and indigent classes in the island.

We willingly accept the trust with which His Excellency has charged us, with an earnest desire to promote the laudable work of charity which he has so much at heart, and although we do so with a fervent determination to use all the means in our power to discharge it to the advantage of the distressed, and to the satisfaction of the philanthropic contributors towards their relief, we undertake the duty with a full knowledge of its difficulty; in the hope that we can calculate upon the counsel and co-operation, when applied for, of the numerous persons in the island possessing intelligence and local knowledge, and in the full reliance of experiencing, in all our actions, every necessary indulgence.

The under-named parties have kindly undertaken to receive subscriptions, and to transmit them to the island.

IN GREAT BRITAIN.
Messrs. A. E. Campbell and Co., 56, Moorgate Street, London.
 Cossart, Gordon, and Co., 6, New Broad Street, do.
London and Westminster Bank, 1, St. James's Square, do.
Messrs. Priestley, Griffith, and Cox, Bankers, Liverpool.
Sir Benjamin Heywood, Bart., and Co. Bankers, Manchester.
Messrs. Wm. Terrell and Sons, Bristol.

IN AMERICA.
Messrs. Boorman, Johnston, and Co., New York.
 March and Benson, ... do.
George M. Lewis, Esq. .... do.
William Depeu,[1742] Esq. .... do.
Messrs. Robert Adams and Co., Philadelphia.

IN FRANCE.
Messrs. Ad. Marcuard and Co., Paris.

IN RUSSIA.
Messrs. Thomson, Bonar, and Co., St. Petersburgh.
 William Pertheau and Co., ... do.

IN PRUSSIA.
Dr. A. Rucker, &c., &c, &c., Berlin.

IN GERMANY.
Messrs. John Gabe and Son, Hamburgh.
Joachim David Hinsch, Esq.

GEORGE STODDART, British Consul, Chairman.
J. HOWARD MARCH, United States' Consul.

1742 The right spelling is Depew, as we have seen before.

13.1. REPORT OF THE MADEIRA RELIEF FUND COMMITTEE

GEORGE HASCHE, Prussian Pro-Consul.
RICHARD DAVIES, British Merchant, Treasurer.
NUNO A. CARVALHO, Secretary.

Madeira,
25th November, 1852.

DISTRESS IN THE ISLAND OF MADEIRA.

The committee formed in Madeira for the management and distribution of contributions from foreign countries towards the relief of the destitute population of the island, having put forth a public appeal in their behalf, on the 25th of November last, and that appeal having been liberally responded to by many benevolent persons in America, Great Britain, Russia, and Hamburgh; they deem it due to those who have so generously placed confidence in their appropriation of such timely, although they fear inadequate, succours; and in the hope of encouraging other charitable individuals to follow their example, briefly to explain their plan of applying these succours for the advantage of the distressed working classes who are unable to find employment; and of the sick, aged, infirm, and helpless who cannot work, and are without any means of subsistence.

1. Conceiving it to be of the utmost importance to make charity useful without encouraging mendicity, labour has, with the concurrence and co-operation of the local authorities, been provided for those who are able and willing to work on a new road, which is being made between the town of Funchal and the village of Camara de Lobos, and which the committee hope to be able to complete. It will be the first carriage road opened in Madeira, and afford the means of easy and agreeable exercise to the numerous invalids who annually resort to the island for the alleviation of sickness and suffering, and the want of which has been much felt by many visitors who have hitherto sought its congenial clime in search of the blessing of health, including Her late Majesty the Queen Dowager, Adelaide, of Great Britain,[1743] and others of rank and distinction. Other useful works will be afterwards undertaken in various localities where the destitution is greatest, and to such an extent as may be warranted by the means at the disposal of the committee.

2. As there are many females in all parts of the island, but particularly in Funchal, who could earn a livelihood for themselves, and assist in supporting their families, by needlework, and other work suited to their habits and abilities, could they procure labour of such a description; the committee have fortunately succeeded in securing the services of five ladies of the highest respectability, possessing intelligence, local knowledge, and much benevolent zeal, to act as a sub-committtee, to provide the required employment, and have placed funds at their disposal for that purpose, with the express understanding that the product of such female labour is to be converted into money as the means of continuing a reproduction of similar labour, and ultimately applied to strictly charitable purposes.

1743 Adelaide Amelia Louise Theresa Caroline of Saxe-Meiningen (1792-1849), was the queen consort of King William IV of England. She became a widower in 1837. Due to health issues, she spent the Winter of 1847 in Madeira, where she arrived on November 2, and lived at Quinta Vigia for five months, returning to England, with her health improved, on April 11, 1848. As a matter of curiosity we add that Adelaide, the capital city of South Australia, is named after her.

3. The committee think it their imperative duty, as far as their means will permit, not to neglect the wants of those who cannot work, and who are entirely without the means of subsistence, whether from disease, age, infirmity, or any other cause; and they have adopted measures to obtain from each parish in the island the most exact statistical returns on the subject, comprehending specification of ages, causes of poverty, and such other detailed information, as will enable them to arrive at just decisions as to the real and deserving objects of charity; and to whom a fair proportion of the funds at their disposal, has been, and will continue to be distributed, by competent delegates, under their own instructions.

4. The committee feel that the state of the public hospitals, poor-house, infant school, and other useful charitable establishments, requires their anxious attention; as their sources of income and support are sadly reduced, indeed nearly annihilated, in consequence of the unprecedented calamity to which this island has been a victim, occasioning almost universal suffering; and that, therefore, these establishments have a just claim upon a share of their funds, so as to avert their usefulness being impaired, or probably the still more painful alternative – of their being altogether closed.

The following parties will continue to receive contributions, namely: –

… In America.
Messrs. Boorman, Johnston, and Co., New York.
      March and Benson, ... do.
George M. Lewis, Esq. .... do.
William Depeu,[1744] Esq. .... do,
Messrs. Robert Adams and Co., Philadelphia. …

George Stoddart, British Consul, Chairman.

J. H. March, United States' Consul.

George Hasche, Prussian Pro-Consul.

Richard Davies, Treasurer.

Nuno A. Carvalho, Secretary.

1744 See Note 1742.

13.1. REPORT OF THE MADEIRA RELIEF FUND COMMITTEE

Madeira, 29th March, 1853.

SUBSCRIBERS NAMES TO THE MADEIRA RELIEF FUND.

LIST OF SUBSCRIPTIONS FOR THE RELIEF OF THE SUFFERING CLASSES IN THE ISLAND OF MADEIRA …

From Mr. JOHN M. LEWIS, *New York.*

	$	
Messrs. John A. F. Rachan, by hands of Mr. H. J. Burden	100	
George M. Lewis, ditto ditto	100	200·000
Blackburn and Brooking	100	
John Caswell and Co.	100	
Ebenezer Stevens' Sons	100	
Henry H. Leverich	100	
Stephen Whitney	100	
S. F. Nicoll and Co.	50	
Barclay and Livingston	50	
Renauld and Francois	25	
Robert E. Kelly and Co.	25	
Davis and Henriques	25	
George Douglas	25	
Charles E. Quincy	25	
M. Lienau	25	
J. A. Machado	25	
William Findlay	25	
H. and F. W. Meyer	20	
John N. Wyckoff	20	
Continued	840	200·000

		Madeira Currency.
Continued	840	200·000
Messrs. C. Moran	20	
James W. Hayward	20	
W. G and Co.	20	
Allen and Paxson	10	
Chas. M. Fry and Co.	10	
Nesmith and Sons	10	
Conklin and Smith	10	
W. and J. Scrymser	10	
John B. Surdy	10	
J. Hunter	10	
H. G. Eilshemurs	10	
A. B. Belknap	10	
F. Karck	10	
V. Barsalaw	10	
A. McAndrew	10	
E. H. E.	10	
Cash	20 50c.	
Messrs. Wyckoff and Hazon	5	
Scrymser, Brazier, and Co.	5	
A. Lowerg	5	
Cornelius Oakley	5	
R. Tucker	5	
John Goldschmidt	5	
Udolpho Wolfe	5	
T. C. J.	5	
W. Humerkock	2 50c.	
V. J. P.	1	
B. E.	1	
Charles H. Meyers and Brothers, Baltimore	5	
	$1,100	1,085·000
		Rs.1,285·000

	$
Mrs. Rackan and family	50
The Rev. Joseph Andrade	25
The Rev. Jerome P. Nobriga	25
Messrs. F. and A. Wiggins	20
C. Strucker	20
Thos. Dixon	15
Cassidy and Cleever	15
Robert Ayres	12
Lorenzo Delmonico	10
N. L. McCready and Co.	10
H. Durght	10
G. C. M.	10
Charles Bellows	5
Thomas McMullen	5
D. A. Scrymser	5
Owen Byrne	5
Continued	242

26

	$
Continued	650
Messrs. S. N. Waln and Co.	50
J. A. Brown	50
Browns and Bowen	50
William P. Hinds	50
Adams and Co's. Express	50
C. H. Fisher	25
Robert F. Walsh	25
S. and W. Welsh	25
McKean, Borie, and Co.	25
Furness, Brinley, and Co.	25
P. L. Laguerenne	25
H. and A. Cope and Co.	25
Joseph C. Harris	25
Stuart and Brother	25
James Dundas	25
John Wagner	25
J. S. Lovering and Co.	25
Horace Binney	25
Emlen Physic	25
John B. Meyers	20
Joseph R. Evans and Co.	20
John Tucker	20
John N. Neumann	20
American Mutual Insurance Company	20
Messrs. M. Echivaria	15
H. Bridport	10
James P. Perot and Brothers	10
Wm. S. Smith and Co.	10
Bucknor, Mc'Cammon, and Co.	10
Clock and Miller	10
McLean and Lentz	10
Bailey and Co.	10
James L. Claghorn	10
Wm. Chancellor	10
Joseph Gratz	10
Warton Chancellor	10
H. Kuhn, Jun.	10
Mrs. Lehman	10
Messrs. Jacob M. Thomas	10
Richard S. Smith	10
Penrose and Burton	10
C. J. Lewis	10
Jacob Sinder, Jun.	10
Thomas Biddle and Co.	25
Th. Cuyler	10
Eli K. Price	10
C. Fallon	10
Jno. Ashurst	10
George A. Tatham	10
M. Newkirk	10
George G. Presbury, Jun.	10
Continued	1,640

13. ATTACHMENTS

	$
Continued	1,640
Messrs. Henry Bohlen	10
H. Kuhn	10
N. A. Smith	10
Rosengarten	10
Dennis McCauley	10
Richard Price	10
E. U. Clark and Co.	10
C. McAllister	10
Dallett, Brothers	10
John Devereux	10
John Boulton	10
Tingley, Caldwell, and Co.	10
David S. Brown	10
Richard D. Wood	10
Cabb, Cope, and Co.	10
Dr. Jayne	10
Messrs. John Mason and Co.	10
Still, Arnold, and Co.	10
John Guy, Jun.	5
Madame Borie	5
Messrs. N. G. Howard	5
John Elliott	5
B. M. B.	5
Paul J. Jones	5
Hance Hamilton	5
Anson Grey	5
L. Baker	5
Ramon Palanca	5
Messenger	5
Wm. Baker	5
Crouch and Fitzgerald	5
Three benevolent Friends	3
Messrs. Roberts and Co.	5
Drexel and Co.	5
J. B. Budd	5
Waterman and Osborne	5
J. L. Laffitte	5
P. Langstroth	5
Mrs. P. Langstroth	5
Messrs. H. Langstroth	5
Frederick Brown	5
L. Austin Allebone	5
Com. Reed	5
J. Richardson	5
G. Leppencott	5
F. Plait and Co.	5
Dr. Page	5
Messrs. Samuel C. Morton	5
Geo. A. Wood	5
E. Simpson and Co.	5
Caspar Heft	5
Continued	1,983

	$
Continued	735·000
Messrs. William Reynolds	25
P. and W. Elling	10
James H. and T. Hart	10
Via "Blood's Dispatch"	5
Messrs. Robert Creighton	5
Geo. Rundle	5
Moore and Son	10
A Widow	1
Mrs. A. S. Willing	5
Messrs. C. E. H. Jones, Reading	5
Shober, Bunting, and Co.	20
Via "Blood's Dispatch"	10
Messrs. Butcher and Brother (5 barrels Pork, value 95 dollars)	
McCutchen and Collins	50
Charles Norris (per E. S. Sayers)	5
William B. Potts and Co.	10
Watson and Co. (20 barrels Bread, value 60 dollars)	
Horace B.	15·200
St. Peter's Protestant Episcopal Church, in Philadelphia, by the Rev. W. H. Odenheimer	234·520
Messrs. J. B. Mitchin (1 barrel Flour, value 5·250)	
Thomas H. Jacob and Co.	10
William V. A. Anderson	5
John R. Rue	5
D. S. Smith, Jun.	5
W. S. Boyd	5
John J. Thompson	5
J. P. Morris	5
Washington Keith	5
J. R. and J. C. Vogdes	5
Robert Neilson	5
E. and L. Moss	5
C. L. Bovie	5
B. M. Mahony	5
Joseph Pleasants	5
Horatio C. Wood	10
Via "Blood's Dispatch"	5
Messrs. E. C. Knight (1 barrel Rice, value 10·500)	
Isaac Barton	30
Hacker, Lea, and Co.	50
Samuel Volans	5
Martin Thomas	5
John D. Thomas	2·500
Merino and Yeaston	5
Unknown	10·440
	1,357·660

	Madeira Currency.
Messrs. R. Adams and Co. collected, in Philadelphia, provisions in the value of Rs.183·500, and the sum of Rs.1,357·660 in cash, amounting together to	1,541·160

From Mr. H. Selby Hayward, *New York.*

Messrs. H. and T. W. Meyer, (second subscription)	20	
J. Mathews	10	
Schieffelen, Haines, and Co.	5	
		35·000

Messrs. H. E. Pierrpont, New York, by the hands of Messrs. Blackburn, Temple, and Co.	25	
Edwd. F. Sanderson, by the same	25	
		50·000

Mr. Philip N. Searle, New York, by the hands of Mr. Wm. Higgins	20·000

From Messrs. Figueira, Stoever, and Langstroth, *Philadelphia.*

Messrs. Figueira, Stoever, and Langstroth	100
Insurance Company of North America	100
Union Mutual Insurance Company	100
Delaware Mutual Insurance Company	100
Philadelphia and Reading Railroad Company	100
Mr. William H. Stuart	100
Washington Mutual Insurance Company	50
Continued	650

	$	Madeira Currency.
Continued	728	
Messrs. A. Belmount	50	
R. S. Howland	25	
Schlesinger	10	
D. Loyd	5	
G. G. Sampson	25	
J. H. Baldwin	5	
Colgate	5	
H. H. Smythe	25	
Gilbert, Coe, and Johnson	50	
A friend to the free reading of the Bible	15	
Messrs. J. P. G. Foster	10	
E. H. G.	10	
Henry Porter, Medford	20	
Francis E. Butler	10	
Richard Irom	20	
St. Andrew's Church, Berlin, N.Y.	6	
	1,019	1,003·800

13.1. REPORT OF THE MADEIRA RELIEF FUND COMMITTEE

		$
Continued	...	1,983
Messrs. Joseph Ripka	...	5
Clement C. Biddle	...	5
M. F. Miller	...	5
A. Benson and Co.	...	5
Wm. Goodrich	...	5
B. M. Jones	...	5
Rowley Ashbourne and Co.	...	5
Charles M. Brancker	...	5
Paul Pohl	...	5
A. E. Outerbridge	...	5
De Coursey, L., and Co.	...	5
Bingham and Dock	...	5
Hoskins, Heisken, and Co.	...	5
Mitchell and Allen	...	5
C. Kulm	...	5
St. Joseph's College	...	5
Messrs. G. M. Troutman	...	5
Lems	...	5
Rev. — Surm	...	10
Messrs. Green and Brother	...	25
C. Herdt	...	4
Joseph Howell and Co.	...	10
E. and C. Yarnall and Co.	...	10
W. H. Gray	...	5
Thompson, Carlze, and Young	...	5
Field and Kechwile	...	5
Evans 5, Kraft 3, Newbold and Morgan 2	...	10
James Montgomery	...	5
Rev. O'Conner	...	5
Messrs. John Mutland	...	5
S. L. Witmer	...	5
A. R. F.	...	5
E. P. Ikwin	...	5
Siter, James, and Co.	...	10
Malonie and Co.	...	3
E. A. Souder and Co.	...	5
Leslie and Co.	...	5
Powers and Waithman	...	10
Js. Still and Co.	...	5
A. G. Cattell and Co.	...	10
Gladding and Christian	...	5
J. Cassedy and Son	...	5
Freak Stoever	...	10
Unknown	...	15

This amount of Rs.2,270 was appropriated in purchasing part of the provisions which came to this island by the barque "*Aaron J. Harvey*," less Rs.4·400 expenses.

From Messrs. R. ADAMS & Co., *Philadelphia*.

		$
Messrs. Robert Adams and Co.	...	50
W. H. Hart	...	20
Francis A. Depau	...	10
Wm. G. Cochran and Co.	...	10
Jos. Swift (£12 remitted to Mr. March,) and 40 dollars paid to Messrs. R. A. and Co.	...	40
George McHenry and Co.	...	10
S. Baldwin and Co.	...	10
Odenheimer and Cook	...	25
Jauretchi and Carstam	...	10
Lewis, James, and Co.	...	50
Edw. S. Sayers	...	25
Lewison and Newborn	...	10
Wm. Platt and Sons	...	25
Robert Taylor and Co.	...	10
George Blight	...	9
John Gibson, sen., and Co.	...	25
Wm. Cummings	...	10
J. D. S.	...	10
Geo. and James Benners	...	10
H. Catherwood and Son	...	10
J. Garrison and Co.	...	10
White and Vausyckels	...	10
J. P. H.	...	10
Evans Rogers	...	10
Richard Willing	...	25
C. F.	...	10
Richards and Miller	...	20
M. and A.	...	10
Andrew C. Craig	...	5
W. Woodnutt	...	10
Jas. S. Smith	...	5
J. Francis Usher	...	20
Mrs. A. C. Sheaff, Whitemarsh	...	10
Messrs. Evan Syckel	...	10
Losobel and Wilmer	...	10
J. H. Stevenson and Co.	...	5
Thaddeus, Norris, and Co.	...	10
T. Cadwaladers	...	10
J. R. Barton	...	10
Robert M. Ball	...	10
Nathan, Trotter, and Co.	...	10
William Harmar	...	10
Tatham and Brothers	...	10
P. S.	...	50
P.	...	30
E. Ganstron	...	10
Jno. Brocklam and Co.	...	10
H. Messch	...	5
Continued	...	735·000

From Messrs. BOORMAN, JOHNSTON, & Co., *New York*.

Messrs. Boorman, Johnston, and Co.	...	100
Joseph Sampson	...	100
Andrew Notteboken	...	20
Anonymous	...	5
Messrs. G. R. Lewis, New London	...	10
J. H. Wells, Hartford	...	20
Dennistoun, Wood, and Co.	...	50
B. H. Field	...	5
H. M. Schieffelin	...	10
Cash through the Post Office	...	3
Messrs. J. J. H. and F. H. C.	...	10
P.	...	5
Duncan, Sherman, and Co.	...	100
J. T. Johnston	...	25
Maitland, Phelps, and Co.	...	100
A Friend	...	50
Messrs. Martyn	...	20
W.	...	5
De Launcy, J. and Co.	...	50
Helorticus	...	10
A. Cockind	...	5
F. Clarke, Northampton	...	25
Continued	...	728

		$	Madeira Currency.
Continued	...	242	
H. M.	...	5	
Cash	...	5	
Ditto	...	5	
Ditto	...	5	
Mr. John Rouch	...	1	
Cash	...	0 75c.	
Mr. Jas. Van Beuschoten ... 1 tierce and 1 barrel Rice			
Messrs. Wheeler and Co. ... ditto			
S. Freeman and Co. ... 1 barrel Flour			

This amount $263 75c. Was delivered to the New York Committee for account of the purchase of provisions transmitted to this island.

Balance of subscriptions collected by the New York Committee, and remitted by Messrs. H. J. Burden, G. M. Lewis, and Wm. Depeu, at the request of the said Committee ... $530 80 519·410

Subscribed through the *New York Herald*, and handed over by Messrs. Burden and Coleman ... 6·000

569

13.2. Madeira Wine-Related Iconography

As we have seen so far, in the 19th century American sources we have researched for this anthology, the iconography related to Madeira Wine is very scarce, therefore we were compelled to look elsewhere for a set of images depicting several aspects of its culture and production, in order to illustrate this final chapter. On the next pages will be displayed a series of watercolors, plates, engravings, and late 19th/early 20th century postcards and photos, illustrating some aspects of the Madeira Wine production cycle.

13.2.1. Watercolors

19th century Madeira was widely depicted in watercolors painted by British artists, most of them amateurs, during their sojourns on the island. In this section will be presented some of them, related to the transportation of Madeira Wine from the countryside to Funchal's wine stores.

13.2.2. Plates

Figure 106. *Borracheiros* (wine carriers). *Author unknown. Courtesy of Casa-Museu Frederico de Freitas – Funchal.*

Figure 107. Two different perspectives of a *borracheiro* using a *borracho* (goatskin) to carry wine. *Author unknown. Courtesy of Casa-Museu Frederico de Freitas – Funchal.*

Figure 108. Carrying wine on an ox sledge in Madeira. *Author unknown. Courtesy of Casa-Museu Frederico de Freitas – Funchal.*

Figure 109. Another way of carrying wine, in a barrel, at the back of a horse. *Author unknown. Courtesy of Casa-Museu Frederico de Freitas – Funchal.*

13. ATTACHMENTS

Some colored Madeira-related scenes illustrate a few books published in England throughout the 19th century. Here we show some of those plates, whose main theme is Madeira Wine.

Figure 110. "Wine press on Madeira." by Thomas Picken. SPRINGETT, W. S. Pitt, *Recollections of Madeira* (London, 1843). *Courtesy of Casa-Museu Frederico de Freitas – Funchal.*

Figure 111. "Madeira Sledge". *Machire & Macdonald, Lith. rs Glasyore. (R. Innes, Funchal). Courtesy of Casa-Museu Frederico de Freitas – Funchal.*

13.2. MADEIRA WINE-RELATED ICONOGRAPHY

Figure 112. "Manner of Bringing Wine to Town When Clear." COMBE, William, A *History of Madeira*, (London, 1821).

This plate was accompanied by a text and a poem.[1745] *Author's collection.*

Figure 113. "Manner of drawing Pipes &c. by means of the Sledge." COMBE, William, *A History of Madeira*, (London, 1821).

This plate was accompanied by a text.[1746]

Part of this plate was duplicated in an engraving present in Charles W. March's book. See Figure 29. *Courtesy of Biblioteca Municipal do Funchal.*

1745 «After the wine is pressed from the grape, it is allowed to remain for a certain time in a state of fermentation, and when clear, is transported to town in barrels, carried by small ponies, a race of horses peculiar to the island of Madeira. In the same manner they carry bags of rice, flour, baggage, of all descriptions, from the town into the country. .../ .../ To Madeira./ How oft thy juice, benignant isle,/ Has made the Briton's heart to smile!/ How oft the flowing of thy vine/ Has proved a cordial medicine!/ And, having wandered o'er the seas,/ Will give the failing stomach ease./ And shall we not, with pleasure, see/ The course of art and industry,/ Which does such beverage prepare/ For British luxury to share?// With all that Britain's isle can boast,/ Bacchus' inspiring boon she lost;/ Who gives her nought to make her merry,/ But apple juice and sparkling perry;/ Or on those mixtures to regale,/ Those dulling fluids, beer and ale,/ The Goths' invention, and ne'er known/ By those who live near Helicon./ How oft thy juice, benignant isle,/ Has made a Briton's heart to smile;/ For 'tis to thee, and climes like thine,/ That Britain's sons must look for wine!» [COMBE, William], *A History of Madeira. With a Series of Twenty-seven coloured Engravings, illustrative of the Costumes, Manners, and Occupations of the Inhabitants of that Island.*, R. Ackerman, London, 1821, pages 85-86.

1746 «This is the usual way of transporting wine from one part of the town to the other. The coopers of Funchal are known to be excellent workmen, and the pipes made are very much admired for their perfect construction. The oxen employed on the occasion, which are natives of the island, are a very beautiful race of animals, and highly useful, both for their strength and tractable character.» [COMBE] 1821, page 87.

13. ATTACHMENTS

Figure 114. "An Accident upon the Road." COMBE, William, *A History of Madeira*, (London, 1821).
This plate was accompanied by a text and a poem.[1747]
An engraving made from this plate was also used in Charles W. March's work. See Figure 28.
Courtesy of Biblioteca Municipal do Funchal.

13.2.3. Henry Vizetelly's Book Engravings

Henry Richard Vizetelly (1820-1894) was an English publisher, a skilled wood engraver and also a wine *connoisseur* who wrote extensively about different European wines. In one of his books, *Facts about Port and Madeira*,[1748] published in London and New York, in 1880, there are five chapters dedicated to Madeira Wine,[1749] illustrated with several sketches made chiefly by his son, Ernest Alfred Vizetelly. We will present this set of fourteen engravings – the best of their kind, according to us – not by the order in which the author arranged them, but following the Madeira Wine production cycle.

1747 «As the characteristic circumstance displayed in the plate admits of an humorous idea, an humorous title has been given to it, but altogether consistent with the natural habits of the peasants employed in the office of Wine-carriers. When the grapes have been duly pressed, the wine is carried by peasants, as represented in the plate, in goatskins, to a store, where it is emptied into suitable vats, or vessels, for the process of fermentation. Such is the fatigue occasioned by the inequalities of the road, and the usual heat of the season, that these carriers are sometimes tempted to refresh and sustain themselves, by taking certain liberties with their loads, which extreme thirst suggests, and favourable opportunities encourage. Sometimes a goat's skin may burst from unavoidable accidents, which give a right to the overflowing juice; but, under very pressing circumstances of thirst and weariness, it may so happen, that an artificial accident is contrived to relieve them. The wine in this state acts as an enlivener and restorative without any subsequent stupor. [...] Whether it were a forward thrust/ That compels the skin to burst,/ Urg'd by the bearer's daring thirst –/ Or whether he his throat is filling/ To save the precious juice from spilling,/ And that this native spring of mirth,/ Should not be cast on barren earth –/ Can, 'tis presum'd, be only known/ To that same pleasant thought alone,/ Which, tender of the flowing wine,/ Display'd the humorous design./ But, whatsoe'er the truth may be,/ A gen'rous, kind philosophy/ Will not the welcome bev'rage grudge/ To the poor, thirsty, swelt'ring drudge,/ Who, as his weary way he saunters,/ The goat's-skin in his lips decanters,/ To give him spirits on his way,/ And make his future journey gay./ While we view the bleeding skin,/ And see him suck the juice within./ 'Tis a hard heart who here would blame:/ Nine out of ten would do the same.» [COMBE] 1821, pages 89-90.

1748 VIZETELLY, Henry, *Facts about Port and Madeira, with Notices of the Wines Vintaged Around Lisbon, and the Wines of Teneriffe*, Ward, Lock, and Co., London; Scribner and Welford, New York, 1880.

1749 One of them had been published in an American newspaper, as we have seen before, at the section 9.1. of this anthology.

13.2. MADEIRA WINE-RELATED ICONOGRAPHY

Figure 115. Untitled. Whenever foreigners arrived at Madeira Island they went on horseriding tours to get to know the outskirts of Funchal. During those rides they always found high walls protecting the *quintas*, as referred on many travel accounts. Their passage always excited the curiosity of the natives, as can be seen in this illustration. On both sides of the streets one can see vine trellisses with clusters of grapes. *Courtesy of Biblioteca Municipal do Funchal.*

Figure 116. "Gathering grapes at Santa Cruz." *Courtesy of Biblioteca Municipal do Funchal.*

Figure 117. "The vintage at Mr. Leacock's Quinta at São João, near Funchal, Madeira." *Courtesy of Biblioteca Municipal do Funchal.*

575

13. ATTACHMENTS

Figure 118. "Treading grapes in the lagar of Messrs. Krohn Brothers at Santa Cruz, Madeira." *Courtesy of Biblioteca Municipal do Funchal.*

Figure 119. Untitled. Sketch of a Madeiran lady, possibly one of many that were engaged in the picking of the grapes, seen at her right hand side. *Courtesy of Biblioteca Municipal do Funchal.*

Figure 120. Untitled. *Borracheiros* carrying wine in goat skins, alongside Ribeira dos Socorridos, to Funchal's wine stores. Below the road, on the left, and above it, on the right, are also seen vine trelisses. *Courtesy of Biblioteca Municipal do Funchal.*

13.2. MADEIRA WINE-RELATED ICONOGRAPHY

Figure 121. "Landing casks of wine from the north side of the Island." The best Madeira was the "south side" but sometimes some merchants used to mix a part of it with wine from the northern side and exporting it as good Madeira. This practice raised some criticism in the United States for it was seen as wine adulteration. The loading of Madeira Wine aboard the vessels that would take it to America was also done this way, by floating the casks on the sea, due to the absence of a pier in Funchal harbor. *Courtesy of Biblioteca Municipal do Funchal.*

Figure 122. "The Armazens and Cooperage of Messrs. Cossart, Gordon, & Co. at Funchal." *Courtesy of Biblioteca Municipal do Funchal.*

Figure 123. "Interior of the Armazem of Messrs. Krohn Brothers at Funchal, Madeira." *Courtesy of Biblioteca Municipal do Funchal.*

13. ATTACHMENTS

Figure 124. "Interior of the Armazens of Messrs. Blandy Brothers at Funchal, Madeira." *Courtesy of Biblioteca Municipal do Funchal.*

Figure 125. "Interior of the Armazem of Mr. H. Dru Drury at Funchal, Madeira." *Courtesy of Biblioteca Municipal do Funchal.*

Figure 126. "The Armazem and Cooperage of Messrs. Henriques, Lawton, & Co. at Funchal." The imposing building at the background still exists today, at the corner of Rua do Castanheiro and Rua de São Pedro. *Courtesy of Biblioteca Municipal do Funchal.*

Figure 127. "Messrs. Cossart, Gordon, & Co.'s Estufas." The heathouses were adopted by Madeira's wine merchants in the 19th century, in order to age wine through intense heat, instead of sending it in long and expensive voyages to the East Indies and back. *Courtesy of Biblioteca Municipal do Funchal.*

Figure 128. "The Armazem dos Vinhos Velhissimos of Messrs. Cossart, Gordon, & Co. at Funchal." In this wine store were kept the old vintages, that were laid for decades in casks, and received high prices. The long stone-arches are a feature of Madeira's architecture which can still be seen on many old buildings of downtown Funchal. In the past, as can be seen by this sketch, they facilitated the moving of wine casks. *Courtesy of Biblioteca Municipal do Funchal.*

13.2.4. Late 19th / Early 20th Century Postcards

From the late 19th century onwards postcards played an important role in the disclosure of some sights and scenes of Madeira island. Among them we found the following ones, which once traveled the world, showing some aspects of the Madeira Wine production cycle.

Figure 129. "Madeira, View of the [Funchal] town from the sea." On these verdant hills was once produced the famous "south side Madeira," so dear to American taste. *Author's collection.*

Figures 130 and 131. Two postcards portraying the same vine trellice in Madeira. *Author's collection.*

13.2. MADEIRA WINE-RELATED ICONOGRAPHY

Figures 132 and 133. Old wooden wine presses in operation. *Author's collection.*

Figures 134, 135 and 136. Parties of *borracheiros* carrying wine to the Funchal's stores. The last picture seems to have been taken at a photo studio. *Author's collection.*

Figures 137 and 138. Photo postcards of large parties of *borracheiros* heading to Funchal's wine stores. *Author's collection.*

13.2. MADEIRA WINE-RELATED ICONOGRAPHY

Figure 139. "Landing wine from the Country". Due to the absence of roads and cars in 19th century Madeira, wine had to be taken from remote parts of the island to Funchal by boat. *Author's collection.*

Figure 140. "View of Cooperage" of Cossart Gordon & Co., established in 1745. *Author's collection.*

Figure 141. "Steam Pump at Work. Pumping wine from Lofting Tank." *Author's collection.*

Figure 142. "Entrance to the Serrado Stores", belonging to the firm Cossart Gordon & Co. *Author's collection.*

Figure 143. "Madeira. Corça de Bois." Oxen sledges were used for a long time in Madeira for carrying wine casks. *Author's collection.*

Figure 144. Photo postcard of Largo do Chafariz, one of the busiest squares in Funchal, where one can see a wine cask being carried in a sledge. *Author's collection.*

13.2.5. Late 19th/ Early 20th Century Photographs

Another pictorial source where we can find old scenes related to Madeira Wine production cycle are the old Black and White photos that depict, with vivid detail, some aspects of this culture.

Figure 145. After the picking of the grapes they sit in willow-made baskets waiting for their time to be stomped in the wine press. *Author's collection.*

Figure 146. After the stomping of the grapes they are gathered in a bee-hive like circle and surrounded by a rope before the pressure of the lever in order to extract all the juice from them. *Author's collection.*

Figure 147. A party of *borracheiros* heading for the warehouse. *Author's collection.*

13.2. MADEIRA WINE-RELATED ICONOGRAPHY

Figure 148. *Borracheiros* unloading wine from the goatskins into wine casks. *Author's collection.*

Figure 149. Detail of the process of unloading the content of a goatskin into a wine cask through a wooden-made funnel. *Author's collection.*

Figure 150. Casks of wine ready for exportation. *Author's collection.*

Figure 151. The transportation of the casks from the wine stores to the beach, prior to its loading on the ships was sometimes made on horse-drawn sledges. In the background, next to the palm tree, stands the back of Funchal's cathedral, which is also portrayed in Figure 30. *Author's collection.*

585

14. Bibliography

14.1. Books

- ADAMS, William T., (Oliver Optic, pseud.), *Isles of the Sea; or, Young America Homeward Bound. A Story of Travel and Adventure*, Lee and Shepard, Publishers, Boston; Charles T. Dillingham, New York, 1877.
- ADLUM, John, *A Memoir of the Cultivation of the Vine in America, and the Best Mode of Making Wine*, Davis and Force, Washington, 1823.
- BAKER, Charlotte Alice, *A Summer in the Azores, with a glimpse of Madeira*, Lee and Shepard, Boston, 1882.
- [BARNUM, H. L.], *Family Receipts, or Practical Guide for the Husbandman and Housewife, containing a Great Variety of Valuable Recipes, relating to Agriculture, Gardening, Brewery, Cookery, Dairy, Confectionary, Diseases, Farriery, Ingrafting, and the Various Branches of Rural and Domestic Economy. To which is added a Plain, Concise, Method of Keeping Farmer's Accounts, with Forms of Notes of Hand, Bills, Receipts, &c. &c.*, Lincoln & Co. Printers, Cincinnati, 1831.
- [BELCHER, John Henshaw], *Around the World: A Narrative of a Voyage in The East India Squadron, under Commodore George C. Read., By an officer of the U.S. Navy.*, Vol. I., Charles S. Francis, New York, Joseph H. Francis, Boston, 1840.
- BENAULY [pseud.], *Cone Cut Corners: The Experiences of a Conservative Family in Fanatical Times; involving some account of a Connecticut village, the people who lived in it, and those who came there from the city*, Mason Brothers, New York, [1855].
- BENJAMIN, Samuel Greene Wheeler, *The Atlantic Islands as Resorts of Health and Pleasure*, Harper & Brothers, Publishers, New York, 1878.
- BIDDLE, Anthony J. Drexel, *The Madeira Islands*, First Edition, Drexel Biddle & Bradley Publishing Company, Philadelphia, 1896.
- BIDDLE, Anthony J. Drexel, *The Madeira Islands*, Volume I and II, Drexel Biddle, Philadelphia, 1899.
- BLACKBURN, Rev. William Maxwell, *The Exiles of Madeira*, Presbyterian Board of Publication, Philadelphia, [1860].
- BLAKE, Rev. John L.[auris] Blake, *A Family-Text Book for the Country; or The Farmer at Home: being a Cyclopaedia of the More Important Topics in Modern Agriculture, and in Natural History and Domestic Economy, adapted to Rural Life*, C. M. Saxton, Agricultural Book Publisher, New York, 1853.
- BLAKE, Rev. J.[ohn] L.[auris], *The Family Encyclopedia of Useful Knowledge and General Literature*, Peter Hill, New York, 1834.
- BLAKE, Rev. John Lauris, *The Parlor Book; or, Family Encyclopedia of Useful Knowledge and General Literature. [...]*, Fourth, New and Improved Edition, John L. Piper, New-York, 1837.
- BLISS, Mrs., *The Practical Cook Book, containing upwards of One Thousand Receipts; consisting of Directions for Selecting, Preparing and Cooking all kinds of Meats, Fish, Poultry and Game, Soups, Broths, Vegetables, and Salads; also, for making all kinds of Plain and Fancy Breads, Pastries, Puddings, Cakes, Creams, Ices, Jellies, Preserves, Marmalades, Etc., Etc., Etc., Together With Various Miscellaneous Receipts, and Numerous Preparations for Invalids.*, Lippincott, Grambo & Co., Philadelphia, 1850.
- BLOT, Pierre, *Hand-Book of Practical Cookery, for Ladies and Professional Cooks. Containing The Whole Science and Art of Preparing Human Food.*, D. Appleton and Company, New York, 1867.
- [BOARDMAN, James], *America, and the Americans*, By a Citizen of the World, Longman, Rees, Orme, Brown, Green, & Longman, London, 1833.
- [BRIDGE, Horatio], *The Journal of an African Cruiser; Comprising Sketches of the Canaries, The Cape de Verds, Madeira, Sierra Leone, and other places of interest on the West Coast of Africa*, Wiley and Putnam, New York and London, 1845.
- BROOKS, Noah, *The Mediterranean Trip, A Short Guide to the Principal Points on the Shores of the Mediterranean and the Levant*, Charles Scribner's Sons, New York, 1895.
- BUCKINGHAM, Esq., J.[ames] S.[ilk], *The Eastern and Western States of America.*, In Three Volumes, Fisher, Son, & Co., London and Paris, 1842.
- BUNN, Alfred, *Old England and New England, In a Series of Views Taken on the Spot*, In Two Volumes, Vol. II, Richard Bentley, Publisher in Ordinary to Her Majesty, London, 1853.

14. BIBLIOGRAPHY

- [CANDLER, Isaac], *A Summary View of America: A Summary View of America; comprising a Description of the Face of the Country, and of Several of the Principal Cities; and Remarks on the Social, Moral and Political Character of the People: being the result of Observations and Enquiries during A Journey in the United States*, By an Englishman, T. Cadell, London; W. Blackwood, Edinburgh, 1824.
- CHOULES, Rev. John Overton, *The Cruise of the Steam Yacht North Star; a narrative of the Excursion of Mr. Vanderbilt's Party to England, Russia, Denmark, France, Spain, Italy, Malta, Turkey, Madeira, etc.*, Gould and Lincoln, Boston, Evans and Dickerson, New York, 1854.
- CLARK, Joseph G., *Lights and Shadows of Sailor Life, as exemplified in fifteen year's experience, including the More Thrilling Events of the U.S. Exploring Expedition, and Reminiscences of an Eventful Life on the "Mountain Wave."*, John Putnam, Boston, 1847.
- COLVOCORESSES, George Mulasas, *Four Years in a Government Exploring Expedition; To the Island of Madeira – Cape Verd Islands – Brazil – Coast of Patagonia – Chili – Peru – Paumato Group – Society Islands – Navigator group – Australia – Antarctic Continent – New Zealand – Friendly Islands – Fejee Group – Sandwich Islands – Northwest Coast of America – Oregon - California – East Indies – St. Helena, &c., &c., In one volume.*, Cornish, Lamport & Co., Publishers, New York, 1852.
- [COLTON, Rev. Walton], *Ship and Shore: or Leaves from the Journal of a Cruise to the Levant*, Leavitt, Lord & Co., New York, 1835.
- [COMBE, William], *A History of Madeira. With a Series of Twenty-seven coloured Engravings, illustrative of the Costumes, Manners, and Occupations of the Inhabitants of that Island.*, R. Ackerman, London, 1821.
- COOPER, James Fenimore, *Redskins; or, Indian and Injin: being the conclusion of the Littlepage Manuscripts*, In Two Volumes, Vol. I., Burgess & Stringer, New York, 1846.
- COOPER, James Fenimore, *Satanstoe; or, The Littlepage Manuscripts. A Tale of the Colony.*, In Two Volumes, Vol. I., Burgess, Stringer & Co., New York, 1845.
- COOPER, J.[ames] Fenimore, *The Pilot: A Tale of the Sea*, W. A. Townsend and Company, New York, 1859.
- COOPER, James Fenimore, *The Spy: A Tale of the Neutral Ground*, In Two Volumes, Vol. I., Fourth Edition, Charles Wiley, New-York, 1824.
- CURTIS, Newton M.[allory], *The Patrol of the Mountain. A Tale of the Revolution*, Williams Brothers, New York, 1847.
- DAVIS, Thomas, *Travels of Four Years and a Half in the United States of America; During 1798, 1799, 1800, 1801, and 1802. Dedicated by Permission to Thomas Jefferson, Esq., President of the United States.*, R. Edwards, London, 1803.
- DELAVAN, Edward C., *Letter to the Bishops of the Episcopal Church on the Adulteration of Liquors, &c.*, C. Van Benthuysen, Albany [New York], 1859.
- De PUY, Henry W.[alter], *The Mountain Hero and His Associates*, Dayton & Wentworth, Boston, 1855.
- [DIX, John Adams], *A Winter in Madeira. And a Summer in Spain and Florence*, William Holdredge, New York, 1850.
- DUNN, Rev. James B., *The Adulteration of Liquors, with A Description of the Poisons Used in their Manufacture*, National Temperance Society and Publication House, New York, 1869.
- DUYCKINCK, Evert A.[ugustus]; DUYCKINCK, George L.[ong], *Cyclopaedia of American Literature; embracing Personal and Critical Notices of Authors, and selections from their writings. From the Earliest Period to the Present Day; with Portraits, Autographs, and Other Illustrations*, In Two Volumes, Vol. I., Charles Scribner, New York, 1866.
- DWIGHT, William T., *The Work and the Workmen. A Discourse in behalf of the American Home Missionary Society, preached in the city of New York, May 8, 1859.*, American Home Missionary Society, New York, 1859.
- *Executive Documents printed by order of The House of Representatives, during the Third Session of the Thirty-Seventh Congress, 1862-'63*, In Twelve Volumes, Government Printing Office, Washington, 1863.
- FEARON, Henry Bradshaw, *Sketches of America. A Narrative of a Journey of five thousand miles through The Eastern and Western States of America; contained in eight reports addressed to the Thirty-nine English Families by whom the author was deputed, in June 1817, to ascertain whether any, and what part of the United States would be suitable for their residence. With Remarks on MR. Birkbeck's "Notes" and "Letters."*, Printed for Longman, Hurst, Rees, Orme, and Brown, London, 1818.
- FLAGG, Edmund, *Report on the Commercial Relations of the United States with All Foreign Nations*, (Prepared and Printed under the Direction of the Secretary of State, in Accordance with Resolutions

of the House of Representatives.), Volume III, Cornelius Wendell, Printer, Washington, 1857.
- FOWLER, Esq., Reginald, *Hither and Thither; or Sketches of Travels on both sides of the Atlantic*, Frederick R. Dalby, London, 1854.
- [FRANKLIN, Benjamin], *Memoirs of Benjamin Franklin. Written by Himself, and Continued by his Grandson and Others, with his Social Epistolary Correspondence, Philosophical, Political, and Moral Letters and Essays, and his Diplomatic Transactions as Agent at London and Minister Plenipotentiary at Versailles, Augmented by much matter not contained in any former edition with a Postliminious Preface*, In Two Volumes, Vol. II, M'Carty & Davis, Philadelphia, 1840
- [FRANKLIN, Benjamin], *The Essays, Humourous, Moral and Literary, of the late Dr. Benjamin Franklin*, John West and Co., Boston, 1811.
- FRANKLIN, Samuel Rhoades, *Memories of A Rear-Admiral Who has Served for More than Half a Century in the Navy of the United States*, Harper & Brothers Publishers, New York and London, 1898.
- FRENEAU, Philip, *A Collection of Poems, on American Affairs, and a variety of other subjects, chiefly moral and political; Written between the year 1797 and the Present Time*, Vol. I., New York, 1815.
- FROST, John, *The Battle Grounds of America, Illustrated by Stories of the Revolution; with Fourteen Engravings*, J. C. Derby & Co., Auburn, NY, 1846.
- FROST, S.[arah] Annie, *The Godey's Lady's Book Recipes and Household Hints., Carefully Selected and Arranged*, Evans, Stoddart & Co., Philadelphia, 1870.
- FUESS, Claude Moore; STEARNS, Harold Crawford, *The Little Book of Society Verse*, Houghton Mifflin Company, Boston and New York, 1922.
- GOODRICH, Charles A., *A New Family Encyclopedia; or Compendium of Universal Knowledge: comprehending a plain and practical view of those subjects most interesting to persons, in the ordinary professions of life*, Second Improved Edition, Philadelphia, 1831.
- GOODRICH, Samuel Griswold, *Peter Parley's Illustrations of Commerce*, H. H. Hawley & Co., Hartford [CT] and Hawley, Fuller & Co Utica [NY], 1849.
- GRAGG, William F., *A Cruise in the U.S. Steam Frigate Mississippi, Wm. C. Nicholson Captain, to China and Japan, From July, 1857, to February, 1860.*, Damrell & Moore, Printers, Boston, 1860.
- GRATTAN, Thomas Colley, *Civilized America*, In Two Volumes, Vol. I., Second Edition, Bradbury and Evans, London, 1859.
- [GRAYDON, Alexander], *Memoirs of a Life, Chiefly passed in Pennsylvania, within the last Sixty Years; With occasional remarks upon the General Occurrences, Character and Spirit of that Eventful Period*, Printed by John Wyeth, Harrisburg [PA], 1811.
- GREEN, Asa, *A glance at New York: Embracing the City Government, Theatres, Hotels, Churches, Mobs, Monopolies, Learned Professions, Newspapers, Rogues, Dandies, Fires and Firemen, Water and Other Liquids, &c. &c.*, A. Greene, New-York, 1837.
- HALE, S.[arah] J.[osepha], *The Good Housekeeper, or The Way to Live Well and To Be Well While We Live. Containing Directions for Choosing and Preparing Food, in regard to Health, Economy and Taste.*, Weeks, Jordan and Company, Boston, 1839.
- HALL, Basil, *Travels in North America, in the Years 1827 and 1828.*, In Three Volumes, Vol. I., Third Edition, Robert Cadell, Edinburgh; Simpkin and Marshall, London, [1830].
- [HAMILTON, Thomas], *Men and Manners in America*, In Two Volumes, Vol. I., William Blackwood, Edinburgh; T. Cadell, London, 1833.
- [HARE, Robert], *Standish the Puritan: A Tale of the American Revolution*, Volume III, Harper & Brothers, Publishers, New York, 1850.
- HARASZTHY, Agoston, *Grape Culture, Wines, and Wine-Making, with notes upon Agriculture and Horticulture*, Harper & Brothers, Publishers, New York, 1862.
- HAWKS, Francis Lister, *Narrative of the Expedition of an American Squadron to the China Seas and Japan, performed in the years 1852, 1853, and 1854, under the command of Commodore M. C. Perry, United States Navy, by order of the Government of the United States. Compiled from the original notes and journals of Commodore Perry and his officers, at his request and under his supervision.*, Beverley Tucker (Senate Printer), Washington, 1856.
- HAWTHORNE, Nathaniel, *The House of the Seven Gables, A Romance*, Tickner, Reed, and Fields, Boston, 1851.
- HAWTHORNE, Nathaniel, *Twice-Told Tales*, In Two Volumes, Vol. II. A New Edition, Ticknor, Reed, and Fields, Boston, 1851.

14. BIBLIOGRAPHY

- HAZEN, Jacob A., *Five Years Before The Mast; or, Life in the Forecastle, aboard of A Whaler and Man-of-War*, Willis P. Hazard, Philadelphia, 1854.
- HILLIARD, Henry W.[ashington], *Politics and Pen Pictures at Home and Abroad*, G. P. Putnam's Sons, New York and London, 1892.
- HOLLEY, O.[rville] L.[uther], *The Life of Benjamin Franklin*, George F. Cooledge & Brother, New York, [1848].
- HOLMES, Oliver Wendell, *Elsie Venner: A Romance of Destiny.*, In Two Volumes, Volume I, Ticknor and Fields, Boston, MDCCCLXI [1861].
- HOMANS, I.[saac] Smith; Homans, Jr., I.[saac] Smith, *A Cyclopedia of Commerce and Commercial Navigation, with Maps and Engravings*, Second Edition with recent statistics, Harper & Brothers, Publishers, New York, 1860.
- HUBBARD, Frederick; SHECUT II, Linnaeus C., *Notes of Travel in Europe and the East in the years 1855-1856, and 1857: A Yankee Engineer Abroad*, Part I, "Europe", AuthorHouse, Indiana.
- INGERSOLL, Charles Jared, *A View of the Rights and Wrongs, Power and Policy, of the United States of America*, Philadelphia, 1808.
- JENKINS, John S., *United States Exploring Expeditions: Voyage of the U.S. Exploring Squadron, commanded by Captain Charles Wilkes, of the United States Navy, In 1838, 1839, 1840, 1841, and 1842: together with Explorations and Discoveries Made by Admiral D'Urville, Captain Ross, and other navigators and travellers; and an Account of the Expedition to the Dead Sea, under Lieutenant Lynch*, Alden & Beardsley, Auburn and Rochester, New York, 1855.
- JENNINGS, Paul, *A Colored Man's Reminiscences of James Madison*, George C. Beadle, Brooklyn, 1865.
- JOHNSTON, James D., *China and Japan: Being a Narrative of the Cruise of the U.S. Steam-Frigate Powhatan, in the years 1857, '58, '59, and '60. Including an Account of the Japanese Embassy to the United States. Illustrated with Life Portraits of the Embassadors and Their Principal Officials.*, Charles Desilver, Philadelphia, Cushings & Bailey, Baltimore, 1860.
- JOHNSON, Joseph, *Traditions and Reminiscences chiefly of the American Revolution in the South: including Biographical Sketches, Incidents and Anecdotes, few of which have been published, Particularly of Residents in the Upper Country*, South Carolina, Walker & James, Charleston, S.C., 1851.
- JONES, J.[ohn] Richter, *The Quaker Soldier; or, The British in Philadelphia. A Romance of the Revolution*, T. B. Peterson & Brothers, Philadelphia, 1866.
- LACOUR, Pierre (of Bordeaux), *The Manufacture of Liquors, Wines, and Cordials, Without the Aid of Distillation. Also the Manufacture of Effervescing Beverages and Syrups, Vinegar, and Bitters. Prepared and Arranged Expressly for the Trade*, Dick & Fitzgerald, Publishers, New York, 1868.
- *Letter of the Secretary of State, Transmitting a Report on the Commercial Relations of the United States with Foreign Nations, for the year ended September 30, 1866*, Washington, Government Printing Office, 1867.
- LIEBER, Francis; Wigglesworth, Edward; Bradford, Thomas Gamaliel, *Encyclopaedia Americana. A Popular Dictionary of Arts, Sciences, Literature, History, Politics and Biography, brought down to the present time; including A Copious Collection of Original Articles in American Biography; on the basis of the seventh edition of the German Conversations-Lexicon*, Vol. XIII., Carel, Lea, & Blanchard, Philadelphia, 1833.
- LIPPARD, George, *Washington and his Generals: or, Legends of the Revolution.*, G. B. Zieber and Co., Philadelphia, 1847.
- LITTLE, Capt. Geo.[rge], *The American Cruiser's Own Book*, Richard Marsh, New York, [1846].
- LOSSING, Benson J., *The Pictorial Field-Book of The Revolution; or, Illustrations, by Pen and Pencil, of the History, Biography, Scenery, Relics, and Traditions of the War for Independence*, In Two Volumes, Vol. I., Harper & Brothers, Publishers, New York, 1855.
- LYNCH, William Francis, *Naval Life; or, Observations Afloat and On Shore. The Midshipman.*, Charles Scribner, New York, 1851.
- MACKINNON, Lauchlan Bellingham, *Atlantic and Transatlantic: Sketches Afloat and Ashore*, Harper & Brothers, Publishers, New York, 1852.
- MALTE-BRUN, M., *Universal Geography, or A Description of All the Parts of the World, On a New Plan, According to the Great Natural Divisions of the Globe; Accompanied with Analytical, Synoptical, and Elementary Tables, Improved by the addition of the most recent information, derived from various sources*, Volume IV, Containing the Description of Africa and Adjacent Islands, likewise additional

- matter, not contained in the European Edition, and Corrections, Wells and Lilly, Boston; E. Bliss and E. White, New York, 1825.
- [MARCH, Charles Wainwright], *Sketches and Adventures in Madeira, Portugal, and the Andalusias of Spain*, Harper & Brothers, New York, 1856.
- MARQUART, John, *600 Miscellaneous Valuable Receipts, Worth Their Weight in Gold. A Thirty Years Collection, to which is added Two Simple Gauging Tables, to enable merchants to take inventory of their stock.*, Christian Henry, Lebanon, PA, 1860.
- McALLISTER, Ward, *Society as I Have Found It*, Cassell Publishing Company, New York, 1890.
- McMULLEN, Thomas, *Hand-Book of Wines, Practical, Theoretical, and Historical; with a description of Foreign Spirits and Liqueurs*, New York, 1852.
- M'CULLOCH, J. R., *M'Culloch's Universal Gazetteer, A Dictionary, Geographical, Statistical, and Historical, of the Various Countries, Places, and Principal Natural Objects in the World*, New York, 1855.
- MARRYATT, Frederick, *A diary in America: with remarks on its institutions*, Part Second, In three volumes, Vol. I., London, 1839.
- MAXWELL, A.[rchibald] M.[ontgomery], *A Run through the United States, During the Autumn of 1840*, In Two Volumes, Henry Colburn, Publisher, London, 1841.
- MELISH, John, *Travels in the United States of America, in the years 1806 & 1807, and 1809, 1810, & 1811; including An Account of Passages Betwixt America and Britain, and Travels through Various Parts of Great Britain, Ireland, and Upper Canada.*, Illustrated with Eight Maps., In Two Volumes, Vol. I., Thomas & George Palmer, Philadelphia, 1812.
- MELVILLE, Herman, *White Jacket; or, The World in a Man-of-War*, Vol. I., Richard Bentley, London, 1850.
- [MERCIER, Henry James; GALLOP, William], *Life in a Man-of-War, or Scenes in "Old Ironsides" during her cruise in the Pacific. By a Fore-Top-Man.*, Lydia R. Bailey, Printer, Philadelphia, 1841.
- MITCHELL, Silas Weir, *A Madeira Party*, The Century Co., New York, 1895.
- MITCHELL, S.[ilas] Weir, *A Masque and Other Poems*, Houghton, Mifflin and Company, Boston and New York, 1887.
- MITCHELL, Silas Weir, *Dr. North and His Friends*, The Century Co., New York, 1900.
- MITCHELL, S.[ilas] Weir, *In War Time*, The Century Co., New York, 1900.
- MOORE, Frank, *Diary of the American Revolution. From Newspapers and Original Documents*, Volume I, Charles Scribner, New York, Sampson Low, Son & Company, London, 1860.
- MORSE, Jedidiah; Parish, Elijah, *A New Gazetteer of the Eastern Continent; or, A Geographical Dictionary: containing, in alphabetical order, a description of all the Countries, Kingdoms, States, Cities, Towns, Principal Rivers, Lakes, Harbors, Mountains, &c. &c. in Europe, Asia, and Africa, with their adjacent islands, carefully compiled from the best authorities*, Second Edition, Thomas & Andrews, Boston, 1808.
- MORSE, Jedidiah; Morse, Sidney Edwards, *A New System of Geography, Ancient and Modern, for the Use of Schools, accompanied with an Atlas, Adapted to the Work*, Twenty-Fourth Edition, Richardson & Lord, Boston, 1824.
- MURRAY, Charles Augustus, *Travels in North America during The Years 1834, 1835, & 1836. Including A Summer Residence With The Pawnee Tribe Of Indians, in the Remote Prairies of the Missouri, and A Visit to Cuba and the Azore Islands*, in Two Volumes, Vols. I. and II., Richard Bentley, London, 1839.
- MURRELL, William Meacham, *Cruise of the Frigate Columbia around the world, under the command of Commodore George C. Read, in 1838, 1839 and 1840*, Benjamin B. Mussey, Boston, 1840.
- NEAL, John, *Authorship: A Tale*, Gray and Bowen, Boston, 1830.
- NOTT, Eliphalet, *Lectures on Temperance*, Sheldon, Blakeman & Co., New York; Gould & Lincoln, Boston; S. C. Griggs & Company, Chicago; Trubner & Co., London, 1857.
- [Old Distiller, By an], *The Complete Grocer: being a Series of Very Valuable Receipts, For Distilling and Mixing Cordials of All Kinds, Brandy, Rum and Gin, with a Variety of Information Respecting the Making and Treatment of Both Foreign and Home Made Wines, and Other Things too Numerous to Mention., Particularly Dedicated to Merchants, Wine Dealers and Others Engaged in the Business*, Published for the Author, John H. Turner, Printer, New York, 1832.
- PARKINSON, [Eleanor], *The Complete Confectioner, Pastry-Cook, and Baker. Plain and Practical Directions for Making Confectionary and Pastry, and for Baking; With Upwards of Five Hundred Receipts; consisting of Directions for Making all Sorts of Preserves, Sugar-Boiling, Comfits, Lozenges, Ornamental Cakes, Ices, Liqueurs, Waters, Gum-Paste Ornaments, Syrups, Jellies, Marmalades, Compotes, Bread-

- *Baking, Artificial Yeasts, Fancy Biscuits, Cakes, Rolls, Muffins, Tarts, Pies, &c. &c.*, Lea and Blanchard, Philadelphia, 1844.
- PARTON, James, *Life of Thomas Jefferson, Third President of the United States*, Seventh Edition, Houghton, Mifflin and Company, Boston, 1883.
- [PAULDING, James Kirke], *The New Mirror for Travellers; and Guide to the Springs.*, By an Amateur., G. & C. Carvill, New York, 1828.
- PAULDING, James Kirke, *Westward ho!: A Tale.*, In Two Volumes, Vol. I., J. & J. Harper, New York, 1832.
- PERCIVAL, James G.[ates], *Poems*, Published for the Author, New Haven, 1821.
- [Perry, Matthew Calbraith], *Narrative of the Expedition of an American Squadron to the China Seas and Japan, performed in the years 1852, 1853, and 1854, under the command of Commodore M. C. Perry, United States Navy, by Order of the Government of the United States.*, Volume II, A. O. P. Nicholson, Washington, 1856.
- [POE, Edgar Allan], *The Narrative of Arthur Gordon Pym. Of Nantucket. Comprising the Details of a Mutiny and Atrocious Butchery on Board the American Brig Grampus, on her Way to the South Seas, in the month of June, 1827. With an Account of the Recapture of the Vessel by the Survivers; Their Shipwreck and Subsequent Horrible Sufferings from Famine; Their Deliverance by Means of the British Schooner Jane Guy; The Brief Cruise of this Latter Vessel in the Antarctic Ocean; Her Capture, and the Massacre of her Crew Among a Group of Islands in the Eighty-Fourth Parallel of Southern Latitude; Together with the Incredible Adventures and Discoveries Still Farther South to Which that Distressing Calamity Gave Rise.*, Harper & Brothers, New-York, 1838.
- POORE, Ben Perley, *Perley's Reminiscences of Sixty Years in the National Metropolis*, Vol. I., A. W. Mills, Publishers, Michigan, [1886].
- PUTNAM, E.[lizabeth H.], *Mrs. Putnam's Receipt Book, and Young Housekeeper's Assistant.*, New and Enlarged Edition, Sheldon and Company, New York, 1869.
- QUINCY, Junior, Josiah, *Reports of Cases argued and adjudged in the Superior Court of Judicature of the Province of Massachusetts Bay, between 1761 and 1772*, Little, Brown, and Company, Boston, 1865.
- RAGUET, Condy, *The Principles of Free Trade, illustrated in a series of Short and Familiar Essays. Originally published in the Banner of the Constitution*, Second Edition, Philadelphia, 1840.
- RANDOLPH, Thomas Jefferson (editor), *Memoir, Correspondence, and Miscellanies, from the papers of Thomas Jefferson*, Volume IV, Letter CXLVI, Charlottesville, 1829.
- READING, Joseph Hankinson, *The Ogowe Band – A Narrative of African Travel*, Reading & Company, Publishers, Philadelphia, 1890.
- *Report of the Commissioner of Agriculture for the Year 1865*, Government Printing Office, Washington, 1866.
- *Report of the Commissioner of Patents for the year 1860. Agriculture.*, Government Printing Office, Washington, 1861.
- *Report of the Madeira Relief Fund Committee; Established In The Year 1853.*, [London, 1854].
- RIPLEY, George; DANA, Charles A., *The New American Cyclopaedia, A Popular Dictionary of General Knowledge.*, Vol. XI., Macgillivray-Moxa., D. Appleton and Company, New York and London, 1861.
- RIXFORD, E. H., *The Wine Press and the Cellar. A Manual for the Wine-Maker and the Cellar-Man*, Payot, Upham & Co., San Francisco; D. Van Nostrand, New York, 1883.
- RUSSELL, William Howard, *My Diary North and South*, In Two Volumes, Bradbury and Evans, London, 1863.
- S., P. S. T., *Astounding Disclosures and Frauds in the Liquor Traffic.*, Tract Society, Philadelphia, 1860.
- *Selections from The Poems of S. Weir Mitchell*, Macmillan and Co., London, 1901.
- SHELTON, Rev. F.[rederick] W.[illiam], *Peeps from a Belfry*, Dana and Company, New York; Sampson Low, Son and Company, London, 1856.
- SIMMS, William Gilmore, *Eutaw - A sequel to The Forayers; Or, The Raid of the Dog-Days. A tale of the Revolution*, W. J. Widdleton, Publisher, New York, [1856].
- SIMMS, William Gilmore, *The Partisan - A Romance of the Revolution*, New and Revised Edition, W. J. Widdleton, Publisher, New York, [1852].
- SIMMS, William Gilmore, *The Sword and the Distaff: or, "Fair, Fat, and Forty." – A Story of the South, At the Close of the Revolution*, Lippincott, Grambo, & Co., Philadelphia, 1853.

- SIMS, J.[ames] Marion, *The Story of My Life*, Edited by his son, H. Marion-Sims, D. Appleton and Company, New York, 1884.
- SLEEPER, John Sherburne, *Jack in the Forecastle: or, Incidents in the Early life of Hawser Martingale*, Crosby, Nichols, Lee and Company, Boston, 1860.
- SPALDING, J. Willet, *The Japan Expedition - Japan and around the world - An account of three visits to the Japanese Empire with sketches of Madeira, St. Helena, Cape of Good Hope, Mauritius, Ceylon, Singapore, China, and Loo-Choo*, J. S. Redfield, New York, 1855.
- SPARKS, Jared, *The Life of Benjamin Franklin*, Tappan & Dennet, Boston, 1844.
- SPRINGETT, W.S.Pitt, *Recollections of Madeira*, Published for the author, London, 1843.
- STEVENS, Benjamin F., *A Cruise of the Constitution. Around the World on Old Ironsides – 1844 to 1847*, New York, 1904.
- STONE, William L., *Border Wars of the American Revolution*, In Two Volumes, Vol. I., Harper & Brothers, Publishers, New York, 1857.
- *Stories of the American Revolution; comprising a complete Anecdotic History of that Great National Event*, Grigg & Elliot, Philadelphia, 1847.
- TAYLOR, Rev. Fitch Waterman, *The Flag Ship: or A Voyage Around the World, in the United States Frigate Columbia; attended by her consort The Sloop of War John Adams, and bearing the broad pennant of Commodore George C. Read*, Vol. I., D. Appleton & Co., New York, 1840.
- THOMAS, Rev. Charles W., *Adventures and Observations on the West Coast of Africa, and its islands. Historical and Descriptive Sketches of Madeira, Canary, Biafra and Cape Verd Islands; Their climates, inhabitants and productions. Accounts of places, peoples, customs, trade, missionary operations, etc., etc., On that part of African coast lying between Tangier, Morocco and Benguela.*, Derby & Jackson, New York, 1860.
- TOMES, Robert, *The Americans in Japan: An Abridgment of the Government Narrative of the U.S. Expedition to Japan, under Commodore Perry*, D. Appleton & Co., New York and London, 1857.
- *The Book of Commerce by Sea and Land, exhibiting its connexion with Agriculture, the Arts, and Manufactures, to which are added A History of Commerce, and a Chronological Table; designed for the use of schools*, Boston, 1834.
- *The Book of Commerce by Sea and Land, exhibiting its connection with Agriculture, The Arts, and Manufactures, to which are added A History of Commerce, and a Chronological Table.*, Uriah Hunt, No. 101 Market Street, Philadelphia, 1837.
- *The Book of Commerce by Sea and Land, exhibiting its connection with Agriculture, The Arts, and Manufactures, to which are added A History of Commerce, and a Chronological Table.*, Uriah Hunt & Son, 44 N. Fourth Street, Philadelphia, Applegate & Co., Cincinnati, 1857.
- *The Collected Poems of S. Weir Mitchell*, The Century Co., New York, 1896.
- *The Complete Poems of S. Weir Mitchell*, The Century Co., New York, 1914.
- *The Emporium of Arts and Sciences*, New Series Conducted by Thomas Cooper, Esq., Volume I, Kimber and Richardson, Philadelphia, 1813.
- *The Poetical Works of James Gates Percival. With a Biographical Sketch.*, In Two Volumes, Vol. II., Ticknor and Fields, Boston, 1863.
- *The Treasury of Knowledge, and Library of Reference: containing an English Grammar, English Dictionary, Universal Gazetteer, Chronology and History, Classical Dictionary, Law Dictionary, with Various Other Useful Information*, Parts I, II & III, Fifth Edition, Enlarged and Corrected, Conner & Cooke, New York, 1834.
- *The World in a Pocket Book, or Universal Popular Statistics; Embracing the Commerce, Agriculture, Revenue, Government, Manufactures, Population, Army, Navy, Religions, Press, Geography, History, Remarkable Features and Events, Navigation, Inventions, Discoveries and Genius of every nation on the Globe. ....*, Third Edition, Greatly Enlarged and Improved; with a Copious Appendix of changes and events, down to the present time, George S. Appleton, Philadelphia, D. Appleton & Co., New York, 1845.
- TORREY, F.[ranklin] P., *Journal of a Cruise of the United States Ship Ohio, Commodore Isaac Hull, Commander, in the Mediterranean, In the Years 1839, '40, '41.*, Samuel N. Dickinson, Boston, 1841.
- *Treasury of Knowledge and Library of Reference. Vol. I. Containing a New Universal Gazetteer or Geographical Dictionary, describing the various countries, states, provinces, cities, towns, villages, seas, harbors, rivers, lakes, mountains, capes, and islands, of the Known World, with Population and Other*

> Statistical Tables, and an Appendix, containing numerous additions, bringing geographical and historical information down to the present time, to which is added an Epitome of Chronology and History, and a compendious Classical Dictionary, New and Revised Edition, J. W. Bell, New York, 1855.
> Thrilling Incidents of the Wars of the United States: comprising the most Striking and Remarkable Events of The Revolution, The French War, The Tripolitan War, The Indian War, The Second War with Great Britain, and the Mexican War., with three hundred engravings., By the Author of "The Army and Navy of the United States", Carey & Hart, Philadelphia, 1848.
> Transactions of the American Institute of the City of New York, for the year 1852, Charles Van Benthuyen, Albany, 1853.
> TURNER, R., The Parlour Letter-Writer, and Secretary's Assistant: consisting of Original Letters on Every Occurrence in Life, Written in a Concise and Familiar Style, and Adapted to Both Sexes, to which are added Complimentary Cards, Wills, Bonds, &c., Thomas, Cowperthwait, & Co., Philadelphia, 1845.
> VIZETELLY, Henry, Facts about Port and Madeira, with Notices of the Wines Vintaged Around Lisbon, and the Wines of Teneriffe, Ward, Lock, and Co., London; Scribner and Welford, New York, 1880.
> [WALTER, John], First Impressions of America, Printed for Private Circulation, London, MDCCCLXVII [1867].
> WATSON, Winslow C., Men and Times of the Revolution; or, Memoirs of Elkanah Watson, including Journals of Travels in Europe and America, From 1777 to 1842, with his correspondence with public men and reminescences and incidents of the Revolution, edited by his son, Winslow C. Watson, Dana and Company, Publishers, New-York, 1856.
> [WEBSTER, Daniel], The Works of Daniel Webster, Volume II, Charles C. Little and James Brown, Boston, 1851.
> WEBSTER, Fletcher, The Private Correspondence of Daniel Webster, In Two Volumes, Volume II, Little, Brown and Company, Boston, 1857.
> WELD, Rev. H. Hastings, Benjamin Franklin: his Autobiography; with a narrative of His Public Life and Services., with numerous designs by J. G. Chapman, Harper & Brothers, Publishers, New York, Sampson Low, London, 1849.
> WELLS, David Ames, Things Not Generally Known: A Popular Hand-Book of Facts Not Readily Accessible in Literature, History, and Science, D. Appleton and Company, New York, 1863.
> WILKES, Charles, Narrative of the United States Exploring Expedition. During the years 1838, 1839, 1840, 1841, 1842., In Five Volumes, and an Atlas, Vol. I., Lea & Blanchard, Philadelphia, 1845.
> WILSON, James Grant, The Memorial History of the City of New-York: From its first settlement to the year 1892, Volume II, New-York History Company, 1892.
> WOOD, M.D., George Bacon; BACHE, M.D., Franklin, The Dispensatory of the United States of America, Eighth edition, Grigg, Elliot, and Co., Philadelphia, 1849.
> WOOD, William Maxwell, Fankwei; or, The San Jacinto in the Seas of India, China and Japan, Harper & Brothers, New York, 1859.
> WOODWORTH, S., The Ladies' Literary Cabinet, being a Repository of Miscellaneous Literary Productions, in Prose and Verse, New Series, Vol. I., Samuel Huesties, New York, 1820.
> WOODWORTH, Samuel, Melodies, Duets, Trios, Songs, and Ballads, Pastoral, Amatory, Sentimental, Patriotic, Religious, and Miscellaneous. Together with Metrical Epistles, Tales and Recitations, James M. Campbell, New York, 1826.

14.2. Magazines

> ADAMS, R. E. W., (et allii), "The North American Journal of Homeopathy", Volume XIII, William Radde, New York, 1865.
> "Ballou's Monthly Magazine", Volume XXXI, From January to June, 1870, Office American Union, Flag of Our Union, and Novelette, Boston, [1870].
> BROWN, Simon; HOLBROOK, Frederick; FRENCH, Henry F., "The New England farmer; A Monthly Journal, devoted to Agriculture, Horticulture, and their kindred Arts and Sciences; and Illustrated with Numerous Beautiful Engravings.", Volume XI., Nourse, Eaton & Tolman, Boston, 1859

14.2. MAGAZINES

- BURTON, William E., "The Gentleman's Magazine.", Volume I., From July to December., Charles Alexander, Philadelphia, 1837.
- CLEMENT, J., "The Western Literary Messenger, A Family Magazine of Literature, Science, Art, Morality, and General Intelligence", Thomas & Lathrops, Publishers, Buffalo, [New York], 1856.
- De BOW, J. D. B., "De Bow's Review, Industrial Resources, Etc.", New Series, Vol. VII, Nos. I & II, January & February 1862, New Orleans.
- "Every Saturday: A Journal of Choice Reading selected from Foreign Current Literature", Vol. I., January to June, 1866, Ticknor and Fields, Boston, 1866.
- "Every Saturday: A Journal of Choice Reading selected from Foreign Current Literature", Vol. VI., July to December, Fields, Osgood, & Co., Boston, 1868.
- "Frank Leslie's Popular Monthly", January 1879, New York, 1879.
- GUNN, Moses; ROBINSON, L. G., "The Medical Independent: a Monthly Review of Medicine and Surgery", Volume 3, Detroit, 1857, pages 307 and 313-314.
- "Harper's New Monthly Magazine", Volume 12, Issue 71, New York, April 1856.
- "Harper's New Monthly Magazine", Volume XIII, June to November, 1856., Harper & Brother, Publishers, New York, 1856.
- "Harper's New Monthly Magazine, Volume XXX., December, 1864, to May, 1865., Harper & Brothers, Publishers, New York, 1865.
- "Harper's New Monthly Magazine," Volume XXXVII, June to November, 1868, Harper & Brothers, Publishers, New York, 1868.
- "Harper's New Monthly Magazine", Volume 54, Issue 323, New York, April 1877.
- IRVING, Washington, "The Analectic Magazine", Vol. 10, From July to December, 1817, M. Thomas, Philadelphia, 1817.
- JACQUES, D. H., "The Rural Carolinian; An Illustrated Magazine, of Agriculture, Horticulture and the Arts", Walker, Evans & Cogswell and D. Wyatt Aiken, Charleston, S. C., 1871.
- "Scribner's Monthly, an illustrated magazine for the people", Volume 9, Issue 2, December 1874.
- LEWIS, Enoch, "Friend's Review; A Religious, Literary, and Miscellaneous Journal", Volume III., Published by Josiah Tatum, Philadelphia, 1850.
- LITTELL, E., "Littell's Living Age", Second Series, Volume IV, (From the beginning, Volume XL), January, February, March, 1854, Massachusetts.
- "Merchant's Magazine and Commercial Review", Volume Thirty-Eight, From January to June, Inclusive, 1858, New York, 1858.
- PRATT, Luther, "The American Masonic Register, and Ladies' and gentlemen's magazine", Benedict Bolmore, New York, 1821.
- SILLIMAN, Benjamin, "The American Journal of Science and Arts", Vol. XXIV, July 1833, New Haven.
- SKINNER, John S., "American Farmer, containing Original Essays and Selections on Rural Economy and Internal Improvements, with Illustrative Engravings and the Prices Current of Country Produce", Vol. IV, J. Robinson, Baltimore, 1823.
- SKINNER, John S., *The American Farmer, containing Original Essays and Selections on Rural Economy and Internal Improvements, with Illustrative Engravings and the Prices Current of Country Produce*, Vol. III., J. Robinson, Baltimore, 1822.
- "The American Agriculturist; Designed to Improve the Planter, the Farmer, the Stock-breeder, and the Horticulturist", Vol. I., New York, 1843.
- "The Atlantic Monthly", Volume 111, 1913.
- "The Army and Navy Chronicle," Volume VI, New Series, From January 1, to June 30, 1838, B. Homans, Washington City, 1838.
- "The Evergreen: A Monthly Magazine of New and Popular Tales and Poetry.", Volume I., January to December, 1840, J. Winchester, Publisher, New York, 1840.
- "The Friend. A Religious and Literary Journal", Volume XLIII, William H. Pile, Philadelphia, 1870.
- "The New-York Farmer and Horticultural Repository. Devoted to Practical Husbandry and Gardening, and embracing the most important information in the sciences, intimately connected with rural pursuits. Under the Patronage of the New-York Horticultural Society," Volume I, New-York, 1828.
- "The North American Magazine", Vol. III, Philadelphia, 1834.

14. BIBLIOGRAPHY

- "The Port Folio", Vol. 2 for 1816, Harrison Hall, Philadelphia, 1816
- "The Southern Literary Messenger: devoted to Every Department of Literature and the Fine Arts", Vol. VII, Richmond, 1841.
- "United Service Journal: Devoted to the Army, Navy and Militia of the United States", October 2, 1852.

14.3. Newspapers (Listed by State)

Alabama (AL)
- Daily Alabama Journal

Arizona (AZ)
- The Arizona Republican

California (CA)
- California Farmer and Journal of Useful Sciences
- Californian
- Daily Alta California
- Evening Daily Bulletin
- Evening Bulletin
- Los Angeles Herald
- Mendocino Dispatch Democrat
- Sacramento Daily Record-Union
- Sacramento Daily Union
- San Jose Mercury Herald
- The Fresno Republican
- The Morning Call
- The Mountain Democrat

Connecticut (CT)
- American Mercury
- American Sentinel
- Columbian Register
- Connecticut Herald and General Advertiser
- Connecticut Journal
- New-London Daily Chronicle
- Republican Farmer
- The Columbian Weekly Register
- The Connecticut Courant
- The Courier
- The Miscellany
- Windham Herald

Delaware (DE)
- American Watchman
- Mirror of the Times & General Advertiser

Georgia (GA)
- Albany Patriot
- Columbus Enquirer-Sun
- Daily Chronicle & Sentinel
- Daily Constitutionalist
- Macon Weekly Telegraph
- The Atlanta Constitution
- The Georgia Telegraph
- The Georgian
- The Macon Telegraph
- The Weekly Georgia Telegraph

Hawaii (HI)
- Hawaiian Gazette
- The Daily Bulletin
- The Hawaiian Star

Illinois (IL)
- Edwardsville Spectator
- Freeport Daily Bulletin
- Illinois Daily Journal
- Illinois State Register
- Oak Park Reporter
- Pomeroy's Democrat
- Rockfort Weekly Gazette
- Sangamo Journal
- Sycamore True Republican
- The Alton Weekly Courier
- The Daily Alton Telegraph
- The Decatur Daily Review
- The Dixon Telegraph
- The Morning Star
- The Rockford Republic

Indiana (IN)
- Logansport Daily Reporter
- The Critic
- The Daily Gazette
- The Daily Journal
- The Democratic Pharos
- The Fort Wayne Sentinel
- The Indianapolis Sentinel
- The Logansport Daily Star

Iowa (IA)
- Burlington Hawk-Eye
- Daily Hawk-Eagle & Telegraph
- Davenport Morning Tribune
- Democratic Banner
- Jackson Sentinel
- La Porte City Review
- Marble Rock Weekly
- Oelwein Register
- Palo Alto Reporter
- The Ackley Enterprise
- The Alden Times
- The Algona Republican
- The Atlantic Telegraph
- The Burlington Daily Hawk-Eye
- The Cedar Rapids Evening Gazette
- The Daily Iowa Capital
- The Dubuque Daily Herald
- The Evening Sentinel
- The Independent
- The Leader
- The Malvern Leader
- The Perry Chief
- The Postville Review
- The Waterloo Courier

Kansas (KS)
- Belleville Telescope
- Dodge City Times
- The Narka News
- The Weekly Kansas Chief
- The Wichita Daily Eagle
- Western Kansas World
- Wichita Eagle

Kentucky (KY)
- Hopkinsville Kentuckian
- The Frankfort Roundabout
- The Hazel Green Herald
- The Western American

Louisiana (LA)
- Gazette and Sentinel
- The Banner Democrat
- The Daily Picayune
- The Morning Star and Catholic Messenger

Maine (ME)
- American Advocate and Kennebec Advertiser
- Bangor Daily Whig and Courier
- Biddeford Daily Journal
- Daily Eastern Argus
- Daily Kennebec Journal
- Lewinston Evening Journal
- The Bath Independent

Maryland (MD)
- Baltimore Patriot
- Eastern Shore Herald and Intelligencer
- Federal Gazette & Baltimore Daily Advertiser
- Federal Republican & Commercial Gazette
- Hornet
- Republican Advocate
- The Maryland Herald, and Elizabeth-Town Weekly Advertiser
- The Mechanic's Gazette; and Merchant's Daily Advertiser
- The North American, and Mercantile Daily Advertiser
- The Sun

Massachusetts (MA)
- Berkshire County Eagle
- Boston Commercial Gazette
- Boston Courier
- Boston Daily Advertiser
- Boston Evening Transcript
- Boston Gazette
- Boston Semi-Weekly Courier
- Columbian Courier, or Weekly Miscellany
- Columbian Minerva

- Daily Evening Transcript
- Franklin Monitor And Charlestown General Advertiser
- Gazetteer
- Gloucester Telegraph
- Independent Chronicle
- Lowell Daily Citizen & News
- Massachusetts Spy
- Massachusetts Weekly Spy
- Nantucket Inquirer
- National Aegis
- New Bedford Gazette and Courier
- New Bedford Mercury
- New Bedford Register
- Newburyport Herald
- Salem Gazette
- Salem Register
- Springfield Daily Republican
- Springfield Republican
- The Barre Patriot
- The Daily Republican
- The Barnstable Patriot
- The Boston Daily Atlas
- The Boston Daily Globe
- The Boston Herald
- The Boston Recorder
- The Federal Spy
- The Fredonian
- The Hive
- The Independent Ledger, and The American Advertiser
- The Massachusetts Gazette
- The Norfolk Democrat
- The Pittsfield Sun
- The Salem Gazette
- Village Register and Norfolk County Advertiser

Michigan (MI)

- Jackson Daily Citizen
- Muskegon Daily Chronicle
- The Marshall Statesman
- The Sunday Advocate

Minnesota (MN)

- New Ulm Review
- The Princeton Union
- The Saint Paul Daily Globe
- The St. Paul Globe
- The Sunday News Tribune

Missouri (MO)

- Daily Missouri Republican
- Fair Play
- The Andrew County Republican
- The Cape Girardeau Democrat
- The County Paper
- The Kansas City Journal
- The Kansas City Star
- The Railroad Telegrapher

Montana (MT)

- The Daily Yellowstone Journal

Nebraska (NE)

- The McCook Tribune
- The Omaha Daily Bee
- The Red Cloud Chief

New Hampshire (NH)

- Courier of New Hampshire
- Dartmouth Gazette
- Hillsboro Telegraph
- New-Hampshire Patriot
- Oracle Post
- The American
- The Farmer's Cabinet
- The New Hampshire Gazette
- The Portsmouth Journal of Litterature & Politics
- The Sun

New Jersey (NJ)

- Daily State Gazette
- Newark Daily Advertiser
- New-Jersey Journal
- State Gazette
- Trenton State Gazette
- Watertown Daily Times

New York (NY)

- Albany Argus
- Albany Evening Journal

14.3. NEWSPAPERS (LISTED BY STATE)

- American Citizen
- Banner of Liberty
- Commercial Advertiser
- Farmer's Register
- Gazette of the United States
- Geneva Gazette
- Hornellsville Weekly Tribune
- Hudson Gazette
- Journal & Republican
- Lewis County Banner
- Middletown Daily Press
- New-York Advertiser
- New York Commercial Advertiser
- New York Daily Tribune
- New-York Gazette & General Advertiser
- New York Herald Tribune
- New-York Spectator
- New York Tribune
- Otsego Herald; or, Western Advertiser
- Political Barometer
- Republican Watch-Tower
- Semi-Weekly Courier and New York Enquirer
- St. Lawrence Republican
- The Albany Centinel
- The Albany Gazette
- The Albany Register
- The American
- The Argus
- The Balance, and Columbian Repository
- The Brooklyn Daily Eagle
- The Daily Advertiser
- The Diary; or, London's Register
- The Dunkirk Observer-Journal
- The Enquirer
- The Evening Gazette
- The Evening Post
- The Independent American
- The Mercury
- The National Advocate
- The New York Daily Times
- The New-York Journal; or, The General Advertiser
- The New York Times
- The Olean Democrat
- The Patriot
- The Schenectady Cabinet
- The Spectator
- The Syracuse Herald
- The Syracuse Standard
- The Sun
- The Weekly Herald
- The Weekly Visitor, and Ladies' Museum
- The World
- Watertown Daily Times
- Weekly Museum

North Carolina (NC)

- The North Carolina Journal
- Weekly Standard
- North Dakota (ND)
- Bismark Daily Tribune

Ohio (OH)

- Anti-Slavery Bugle
- Cincinnati Daily Gazette
- Cleveland Daily Plain Dealer
- Cleveland Morning Leader
- Cleveland Plain Dealer
- Daily Commercial Register
- Daily Ohio Statesman
- Daily Zanesville Courier
- Fremont Journal
- Hamilton Daily Democrat
- Lima Times Democrat
- Newark Daily Advocate
- Plain Dealer
- Springfield Globe-Republic
- Steubenville Herald
- The Athens Messenger
- The Cincinnati Commercial Gazette
- The Cincinnati Daily Enquirer
- The Democratic Standard
- The Hamilton Guidon
- The Hocking Sentinel
- The News Herald
- The Salem Daily News
- The Sandusky Clarion
- The Xenia Gazette
- Zanesville Daily Courier

14. BIBLIOGRAPHY

Oklahoma (OK)
- *Muskogee Phoenix*

Oregon (OR)
- *Evening Capital Journal*
- *The Oregonian*
- *The Sunday Oregonian*

Pennsylvania (PA)
- *Adams Sentinel*
- *Aurora General Advertiser*
- *Daily Gazette and Bulletin*
- *Evening Democrat*
- *Examiner and Democratic Herald*
- *Gazette of the United States*
- *Gazette of the United States, and Philadelphia Daily Advertiser*
- *Gettysburg Centinel*
- *Gettysburg Compiler*
- *Indiana County Gazette*
- *Indiana Democrat*
- *Jeffersonian Republican*
- *Juniata Sentinel and Republican*
- *Kline Carlisle Weekly Gazette*
- *Lancaster Daily Intelligencer*
- *Lancaster Examiner and Herald*
- *Lebanon Daily News*
- *Mariettian*
- *M'Kean Miner*
- *North American*
- *North American and United States Gazette*
- *Pennsylvania Inquirer*
- *Pennsylvania Inquirer and National Gazette*
- *Philadelphia Repository*
- *Public Ledger*
- *The Adams Sentinel*
- *The Adams Sentinel and General Advertiser*
- *The Bradford Era*
- *The Compiler*
- *The Daily Morning Post*
- *The Evening Herald*
- *The Harrisburg Daily Patriot*
- *The Huntingdon Journal*
- *The Indiana Democrat*
- *The Indiana Progress*
- *The Mail; or, Claypoole's Daily Advertiser*
- *The McKean Democrat*
- *The North American and Daily Advertiser*
- *The Oracle of Dauphin, and Harrisburg Advertiser*
- *The Pennsylvania Ledger: Or the Virginia, Maryland, Pennsylvania, and New-Jersey Weekly Advertiser*
- *The Philadelphia Inquirer*
- *The Pittsburg Dispatch*
- *The Pittsburgh Press*
- *The Republican Compiler*
- *The Star and Banner*
- *The State's Advocate*
- *The Washington Reporter*
- *The Wellsboro Agitator*
- *Tioga Eagle*
- *Titusville Morning Herald*
- *Warren Ledger*
- *Wellsboro Gazette*

Rhode Island (RI)
- *Newport Daily News*
- *Newport Mercury*
- *Providence Patriot and Columbian Phenix*
- *Providence Phoenix*
- *Rhode Island American, and General Advertiser*
- *Rhode Island Republican*

South Carolina (SC)
- *Charleston Daily Courier*
- *City Gazette and Commercial Daily Advertiser*
- *The Anderson Intelligencer*
- *The Charleston Courier*
- *The Charleston Daily News*
- *The Charleston Mercury*
- *The Daily Phoenix*
- *The Georgetown Gazette*
- *The Orangeburg News*
- *The Southern Patriot*

South Dakota (SD)
- *Mitchell Daily Republican*

Tennessee (TN)
- *Memphis Daily Appeal*

- Nashville Union and American
- The Knoxville Journal
- The Memphis Daily Avalanche

Texas (TX)
- Fort Worth Daily Gazette
- Galveston Daily News
- Galveston Weekly News
- San Antonio Daily Light
- The Eastern Texian
- The San Antonio Day Light
- The San Antonio Daily Express
- The Texan Mercury
- The Weekly Independent
- The Weimar Mercury
- Waco Evening News

Utah (UT)
- Deseret Evening News
- Salt Lake Daily Herald
- The Broad Ax
- The Salt Lake Daily Tribune
- The Salt Lake Tribune

Vermont (VT)
- Columbian Patriot
- Rutland Herald
- The Green Mountain Patriot
- Vermont Gazette
- Vermont Journal
- Vermont Mercury
- Vermont Republican
- Weekly Wanderer

Virginia (VA)
- Alexandria Daily Advertiser
- Alexandria Expositor
- Alexandria Gazette
- Harrisonburg Rockingham Register
- Phenix Gazette
- Richmond Enquirer
- The Daily State Journal
- The Daily Times
- The Reporter
- The Richmond Whig & Public Advertiser
- The Roanoke Times
- Virginia Herald

West Virginia (WV)
- Wheeling Register

Wisconsin (WI)
- Daily Free Democrat
- Daily Milwaukee News
- Democratic Standard
- Democratic State Register
- Eau Claire Daily Free Press
- Grand County Herald
- Green Bay Advocate
- Green Bay Spectator
- Janesville Morning Gazette
- Jeffersonian Democrat
- Madison Express
- Manitouwoc County Herald
- Milwaukee Daily Sentinel
- Oconto Pioneer
- Oshkosh Daily Northwestern
- Oshkosh Weekly Courier
- Prairie Du Chien Courier
- Racine Daily Argus
- Racine Daily Journal
- Racine Daily News
- Richland County Observer
- Superior Chronicle
- The Daily Wisconsin Patriot
- The Eau Claire News
- The Evening Times
- Weekly Wisconsin
- Wisconsin Free Democrat
- Wisconsin State Journal
- Wisconsin Weekly Free Democrat
- Wisconsin Enquirer

Wyoming (WY)
- Sundance Gazette

15. Brief notes about the Author

Born in Funchal, Madeira Island, Duarte Miguel Barcelos Mendonça is a University of Madeira graduate and holds a Degree in Modern Languages and Literatures and a Master's Degree in Anglo-American Culture and Literature.

He is the author of five books, namely the biography *João de Lemos Gomes (1906-1996) – Médico Cirurgião* (Funchal 500 Anos, 2006); his Master's thesis *Da Madeira a New Bedford – Um capítulo ignorado da emigração portuguesa nos Estados Unidos da América* (Drac, 2007); the anthology *Impressões de uma viagem* à América – Pe. Alfredo Vieira de Freitas (CMSC, 2009); the translation *Memórias da Minha Vida – Um Inverno na Madeira*, containing Archduke Maximilian of Hapsburg and Charlotte of Belgium's texts regarding Madeira Island; and last but not least, the anthology *Carlos e Zita de Habsburgo - Crónica de um Exílio Imperial na Cidade do Funchal* (CMF, 2013).

He is a lecturer, having presented many lectures about historical subjects at symposiums held in Madeira, Lisbon, Azores, Paris and in the United States, and has hundreds of articles published both in Madeiran and Portuguese-American press.

Presently he is a librarian at Biblioteca Municipal do Funchal, in Madeira Island.

www.ingramcontent.com/pod-product-compliance
Lightning Source LLC
Chambersburg PA
CBHW080537230426
43663CB00015B/2622